Hard Neighbors

Hard Neighbors

*The Scotch-Irish Invasion of Native America
and the Making of an American Identity*

COLIN G. CALLOWAY

OXFORD
UNIVERSITY PRESS

OXFORD
UNIVERSITY PRESS

Oxford University Press is a department of the University of Oxford. It furthers
the University's objective of excellence in research, scholarship, and education
by publishing worldwide. Oxford is a registered trade mark of Oxford University
Press in the UK and certain other countries.

Published in the United States of America by Oxford University Press
198 Madison Avenue, New York, NY 10016, United States of America.

© Oxford University Press 2024

All rights reserved. No part of this publication may be reproduced, stored in
a retrieval system, or transmitted, in any form or by any means, without the
prior permission in writing of Oxford University Press, or as expressly permitted
by law, by license, or under terms agreed with the appropriate reproduction
rights organization. Inquiries concerning reproduction outside the scope of the
above should be sent to the Rights Department, Oxford University Press, at the
address above.

You must not circulate this work in any other form
and you must impose this same condition on any acquirer.

Library of Congress Control Number: 2024919434

ISBN 978–0–19–761839–4

DOI: 10.1093/oso/9780197618394.001.0001

Printed by Sheridan Books, Inc., United States of America

To Marcia,
To Graeme and Meg,
And in memory of my parents

Contents

List of Figures — ix
List of Maps — xi
Acknowledgments — xiii
List of Abbreviations — xv
Terminology — xvii

Introduction — 1

PART I. BORDERLAND PEOPLE

1. Origin Stories and Atlantic Migrations — 25
2. Valley Paths to Native Lands — 48
3. A Devil's Bargain — 85
4. Hard Neighbors — 110

PART II. FIGHTING FOR AMERICA

5. We Are Now the Frontier — 135
6. Indian-Killers — 169
7. Scotch-Irish Captives and Scotch-Irish Indians — 194
8. Black Boys and White Savages — 217
9. Indian-Killers to Patriots — 251

PART III. SCOTCH-IRISH AMERICANS AND AN EXPANDING NATION

10. Fighting Landlords, Indians, and Taxes — 289
11. Andrew Jackson and the Triumph of Scotch-Irish Indian Policy — 324

12. Across the Mississippi	352
13. To Texas and Beyond	376
14. How the Scotch-Irish Became Americans and Americans Became Scotch-Irish	404
Notes	415
Index	489

Figures

2.1. James Logan.	61
5.1. The Province of Pensilvania by T. Kitchin, 1756.	142
5.2. Map of Carlisle to Fort Granville, 1756.	156
6.1. Lithograph depicting the Paxton massacre of the Indians at Lancaster, by Thomas Sinclair.	178
6.2. Political cartoon by James Claypoole.	188
6.3. Cartoon attributed to David James Dove.	189
7.1. Mary Jemison in her old age.	205
7.2. Col. James Smith.	213
8.1. James Robertson.	233
9.1. John Vanderlyn, *The Murder of Jane McCrea*, 1804.	262
9.2. Andrew Pickens.	272
9.3. Brigadier General William Irvine.	276
10.1. General Benjamin Logan.	301
11.1. Major General Andrew Jackson.	325
11.2. David Crockett.	345
12.1. Sam Houston.	368
13.1. Kit Carson.	393
13.2. Black Beaver.	397
13.3. James Kirker.	398

Maps

1.1. Borderlands to borderland: Migrations to Ulster.	34
2.1. Scotch-Irish migrations in America.	50
2.2. Distribution of Scotch-Irish settlements, ca. 1780.	83
3.1. Scotch-Irish settlements, Indian villages, and tribal migrations in Pennsylvania and the Susquehanna Valley, 1720s–1740s.	93
5.1. The French and Indian War in the Scotch-Irish backcountry.	136
8.1. Scotch-Irish settlement areas in the Upland South and Cherokee country.	234
11.1. Andrew Jackson's campaigns in the Creek War, 1813–1814, and Indian treaties, 1814–1820.	338
12.1. Scotch-Irish and immigrant Indians in the Ozarks.	356
13.1. Indigenous Nations, immigrant Indians, and immigrant colonists in the Texas borderlands.	382
13.2. Delaware and Scotch-Irish migrations from Pennsylvania to Texas.	395

Acknowledgments

In researching this book, I have delved into areas of history where I have little experience or expertise. I am grateful to the many fine scholars of Irish history in general and Irish diasporic studies in particular whose work I have relied upon, whose controversies I have tried to navigate, and whose writings convey the depths and complexities of Irish historical experiences in America.

At Dartmouth College, several former students—Sarah Sim, Marc Novicoff, Jonah Hirsh, and Julia Berman—assisted me in the early stages of the project, and Hatley Post helped me to compile an archive of relevant articles from early American newspapers. I am, as always, grateful to my colleagues in Native American and Indigenous Studies, the History Department, and the Baker-Berry Library, who have made Dartmouth a wonderful place to do the work I do, and to my students who have made it a pleasure and a privilege to teach there.

Much of the research and writing for this book was carried out during a pandemic. For assistance, support, suggestions, answers to inquiries, and pointing out directions along the way, I am grateful to many individuals and institutions: my longtime friend and colleague N. Bruce Duthu; Melissah Pawlikowski; Mary Offenback, Researcher at the Historical Society of Pennsylvania; Warren Hofstra, Debbie Spero, Patrick Griffin; Todd Hoppock at the South Caroliniana Library at the University of South Carolina; and the Tennessee State Archives and Library. In securing illustrations and permissions, I received prompt, efficient, and helpful assistance from Lexy Nilles at the Historical Society of Pennsylvania; Stacey Stachow at the Wadsworth Atheneum; Amy Frey at the Pennsylvania Historical and Museum Commission; Vicki Cooper at the W. Frank Steely Library, Northern Kentucky University; Katherine Gould at the Cincinnati Museum Center; Debbie Shaw at the Tennessee State Museum; the Tennessee State Library and Archives; and the Library Company of Philadelphia.

I am grateful to master cartographer Jeffrey Ward for his skill, care, and patience in transforming my multiple sketches and composite drafts into the maps that are integral to the story I'm trying to tell.

I have had the very good fortune to work with Timothy Bent as editor on my last four books. Tim supported this project from the first, even when he did not have a good idea of what it would look like because I did not. I am grateful for his encouragement and guidance and for his careful, thoughtful, and insightful editing of the manuscript that helped me to bring out more clearly the story I wanted to tell. Although I have written many books, and had made many revisions myself to this one, Tim's queries, comments, and suggestions showed me that I still have plenty to learn about writing a good book. I expect and hope that that will always be the case.

The copy editing, proof review, and indexing were done while I was learning to live with cancer, and many people helped me with that. At Dartmouth Hitchcock Medical Center, I am grateful for the care and expertise of Dr. Lou Kazal, Dr. Rodwell Maebera, Dr. Sivan Rotenberg, Dr. Bassem Zaki, and their teams; in my extended family, I am grateful for the kindness and support of Dr. Hejung Kim, Dr. Robert Press, and my sister-in-law Sue Calloway, who has seen it all before.

And Marcia, of course, has been with me every step of the way and helped me through some dark days. My wife and parents shared the dedication of my first book. Nearly forty years on, it seems fitting that, along with my grown children, they should do so again. My parents are long gone but I continue to appreciate how fortunate I was to have had them in my life and how fortunate I have been to have Marcia in my life.

Abbreviations

ASPIA	*American State Papers: Documents, Legislative and Executive, of the Congress of the United States. Class II: Indian Affairs*, ed. Walter Lowrie and Matthew St. Clair Clarke. 2 vols. Washington, DC: Gales and Seaton, 1832–1834.
Calendar of Virginia State Papers	*Calendar of Virginia State Papers*, ed. William P. Palmer. 11 vols. Richmond: Virginia State Library, 1875–1893.
C.O. 5	Colonial Office Records, Series 5, National Archives (formerly Public Record Office), Kew, England.
Col. Recs. Penn.	*Colonial Records of Pennsylvania*, ed. Samuel Hazard. 16 vols. Harrisburg and Philadelphia: T. Fenn, 1838–1853 (vols. 1–10: *Minutes of the Provincial Council of Pennsylvania*; vols. 11–16: *Minutes of the Supreme Executive Council of Pennsylvania*).
DAR	*Documents of the American Revolution*, ed. K. G. Davies. 21 vols. Shannon: Irish University Press, 1972–1981.
Digital Paxton	Digital Paxton: A Digital Archive and Critical Edition of the Paxton Pamphlet War; http://digitalpaxton.org/works/digital-paxton/manuscripts?path=archive.
Draper	Lyman Draper Manuscripts, Wisconsin State Historical Society, microfilm.
EAID	*Early American Indian Documents: Treaties and Laws, 1607–1789*, gen. ed. Alden T. Vaughan. 20 vols. Bethesda, MD: University Publications of America, 1979–2004.
HSP	Historical Society of Pennsylvania, Philadelphia.
IILC	*Irish Immigrants in the Land of Canaan: Letters and Memoirs from Colonial and Revolutionary America, 1675–1815*, ed. Kerby A. Miller, Arnold Schrier, Bruce D. Boling, and David N. Doyle. New York: Oxford University Press, 2003.
NCCR	*The Colonial and State Records of North Carolina*, ed. William Saunders and Walter Clark. 30 vols. Raleigh: Secretary of State, 1886–1914. Vols. 1–9.
NCSR	*The Colonial and State Records of North Carolina*, ed. William Saunders and Walter Clark. 30 vols. Raleigh: Secretary of State, 1886–1914. Vols. 10–30.

PAJ	*The Papers of Andrew Jackson Digital Edition*, ed. Daniel Feller and Michael E. Woods. Charlottesville: University of Virginia Press, Rotunda, 2015–. Main series. 10 vols.
Penn. Archives	*Pennsylvania Archives.* 9 series. 138 volumes. Philadelphia and Harrisburg, 1852–1949.
Penn Mss.	Penn Family Manuscripts, HSP.
PMHB	*Pennsylvania Magazine of History and Biography.*
Territorial Papers	*The Territorial Papers of the United States*, ed. Clarence Edwin Carter. 28 vols. Washington, DC: Government Printing Office, 1934–1975.
WJP	*The Papers of Sir William Johnson*, ed. James Sullivan et al. 14 vols. Albany: State University of New York, 1921–1965.

Terminology

Throughout this book, I use *Scotch-Irish* and *Indian*, two terms that are out of fashion and which some people find offensive. Both were words that had meaning in other times, even if they carried negative connotations, as both often did. Growing up in a family where most of my relatives were Highland Scots, I learned early in life that Scotch is a drink; people are *Scots*. However, people in the eighteenth century did not necessarily subscribe to, or care about, the distinction. The term *Scotch* was commonly used, and in the United States *Scotch-Irish* was widely applied, especially in the nineteenth century. When historian Kerby Miller was deciding which term to use, he preferred *Scots Irish*, "largely a scholars' invention," because of "the term's relative modernity and specificity," although it appears less often than Scotch-Irish in the historical record. He avoided using Scotch-Irish because of its "inclusivity and vagueness."[1] With respect to those on different sides of the debate, who all have a point, I have opted to use Scotch-Irish as a term with historic roots precisely because of its inclusivity and vagueness, and I follow the *Journal of Scotch-Irish Studies* in embracing in that term both Ulster immigrants to America and subsequent generations of American Scotch-Irish descendant communities.[2]

Scotch-Irish people in the backcountry and on the frontiers were regularly referred to as *settlers*, and I have followed the same practice. The term should not be interpreted as implying they were the first or only settlers, rather, that they were settler colonists, *re*settling lands already occupied and shaped by Native settlers.

Collective terms are necessary in writing about Indigenous peoples, although none is entirely satisfactory. The term *Indian* is a European conception, or rather misconception, about the first Americans. Although it is now commonly regarded as outdated and even disrespectful, it is the term that appears most often in historical documents and is still used today by some organizations (National Congress of American Indians, American Indian Movement), institutions (National Museum of the American Indian), and many Native people, and the term *Indian Country* has a variety of geographic, social, political, and legal usages. Many people prefer *Native*

American, although that term can also cause confusion if used in references to American *Indian* policy or applied to anyone born in America, and, as we will see, is also a term claimed by some descendants of settler colonists. *Indigenous* is commonly used and often preferred today, although it has multiple definitions and applications internationally. I use all three terms somewhat interchangeably in the absence of more suitable designations that do not require explanation or create confusion. In the same way, rather than inaccurately lumping Germanic, Celtic, and other peoples together as "Anglo," I occasionally use *white*, for lack of a better collective term, when referring to peoples of multiple European ancestries.

Although Northern Ireland technically refers to the modern country rather than the historic region of the north of Ireland, I have retained the capitalization throughout in the interests of consistency.

Introduction

On December 14, 1763, a group of vigilantes calling themselves the Paxton Boys killed and scalped six "friendly" Indian people at a tract of land known as Conestoga Manor in Pennsylvania. The Conestoga Indians, survivors of the once-powerful Susquehannocks, resided at the Manor under the protection of the colonial government. They had English names, wore English clothes, lived in log cabins, and peddled baskets and brooms among their colonial neighbors. Two weeks later, and two days after Christmas, the Paxton Boys rode to Lancaster and killed fourteen more Conestoga people—the entirety of the population—who had been given refuge in the town workhouse. In each case, they murdered and mutilated men, women, and children. In early February, more than two hundred Paxton Boys and their supporters marched roughly one hundred miles to Philadelphia, threatening to kill more Indian people who had sought safety there, venting their outrage against the Quaker-dominated Pennsylvania Assembly which had repeatedly failed to protect *them* against Indian attacks, and demanding increased representation in government.

In this climate of fear and resentment against their government's perceived pandering to other groups, people distant from the centers of power and privilege struck out in violence and race hatred, justifying their actions as a defense of freedom and democracy. It is a story we know well.[1]

The "Paxton Massacre" was only one of many such atrocities attributed to a population of white frontiersmen who cut a bloody swath through Indian country and were often the cutting edge of the colonial dispossession of Native people. They were Scotch-Irish. Descended primarily from Presbyterian Scots who had been transplanted to Ulster in the early seventeenth century to act as a buffer against the "wild" Catholic Irish, Scotch-Irish people who emigrated to North America in the eighteenth century brought with them a long history of borderland violence. Disembarking at Philadelphia and neighboring ports, they moved to the western frontiers of Pennsylvania in search of land, where they once again acted as a buffer, this time against the "wild" Indians. James Logan, provincial secretary of

Pennsylvania who helped place them in that position, described them as "troublesome settlers to the government and hard neighbors to the Indians."[2]

In one historian's estimation, the Scotch-Irish were, "if not the first, certainly the most conspicuous squatters in American history."[3] They trespassed on Indian lands in the Susquehanna Valley and elsewhere, necessitating purchases by the Pennsylvania government to avoid or end conflict; Scotch-Irish families bore the brunt of Indian raids when wars erupted, and Scotch-Irish vigilantes like the Paxton Boys turned William Penn's "peaceable kingdom" into a nightmare of racial violence.[4] From Pennsylvania, Scotch-Irish colonists pushed down the Shenandoah Valley, following the Great Wagon Road to Virginia and the Carolinas, and headed west through the Cumberland Valley to Kentucky and Tennessee, where they clashed with Shawnees and Cherokees. Scotch-Irish, generally, were zealous in the Patriot cause during the Revolution, and traded atrocities with Native Americans on the frontiers where both groups fought as proxies in parallel wars.

Although some historians have assumed that after independence Scotch-Irish people immediately became "Americans," assimilating into the social fabric of the new nation, many retained a separate identity, bonded by their shared religion, kinship, and experiences. Indeed, "Scotch-Irish" is essentially an American term that came into common usage in the century after independence. They maintained a distinct presence in Indian country, squatting on land and defending their claims against both Native inhabitants and eastern elites. Second- and third-generation migrants from core areas of Scotch-Irish settlement and culture spread across the upland South and beyond the Mississippi, establishing what we might call descendant communities. Scotch-Irish people, attitudes, and practices dominated frontier societies in these areas, and featured prominently in Andrew Jackson's brutal campaigns in Indian country and his Indian removal policies during his presidency. Scotch-Irish immigrants in the Ozarks region of Missouri and Arkansas coexisted with Delaware, Shawnee, and Cherokee immigrants they had previously helped to drive west, and they edged into Spain's northern province of Texas. When the newly independent Mexican state invited American emigrants to settle there as a buffer against the Comanches and other Indigenous nations on the southern plains, Americans of Scotch-Irish ancestry—Samuel Houston, David Crockett, and others—did so, continuing patterns of migration, settlement, and conflict that were long established in Scotch-Irish history. They joined other American migrants, as well as, again, migrant Delawares, Shawnees, and Cherokees, and took up positions protecting the provinces of northern Mexico against the Plains tribes. When the new Republic of Texas implemented policies of ethnic cleansing, Scotch-Irish Texans once again proved "hard neighbors to the Indians." Ulster Scots were the foot soldiers of empire, and their descendants were the shock troops of westward expansion, writes activist, historian, and writer Roxanne Dunbar-Ortiz, tracing the Scotch-Irish ancestry and migrations of her own Okie family in her memoir, *Red Dirt*. They "spilled blood for independence and spilled rivers of blood to acquire Indian land," and they "won the land by 'bloodright,' leaving bloody footprints across the continent." Overwhelmingly frontier settlers and constantly on the move, "they cleared forests, built log cabins, and killed Indians."[5]

In some areas European colonists managed, at least for a time, to construct "middle grounds" of coexistence with Native people.[6] Not the Scotch-Irish, apparently. They were recurrent colonizers and they perpetually opened new killing grounds. They inhabited so many frontier regions and in such large numbers that they were involved—"implicated," says historian Patrick Griffin—in all the major developments. Yet their behavior was hardly distinctive. The massacre of 1763 was not the only moment when frontier lines hardened around race and cautious accommodation turned into horrific violence.[7] Nor was it the only time when white people lacking political power struck out in violence against their government's policies toward non-white people. Those of us who work in Native American history insist on recognizing diversity within Indian country, yet we do not always acknowledge diversity among "whites" and "settler colonists." Indiscriminate application of the term "English" or "Anglo" as synonymous with "white" homogenizes and smooths over the complexities of British, American, and Native American history, and limits opportunities for more nuanced explorations and interpretations of "settler colonialism," a term that is also loosely applied.[8] Scotch-Irish people were no more monolithic or unanimous in their opinions and actions than, say, Delaware Indians or members of the United States Congress. Like Indian country, the colonial backcountry they inhabited was multiethnic and multilingual. Scotch-Irish attitudes and actions often merged with, mirrored, and were indistinguishable from those of other peoples. They have often disappeared into the broader story of settler colonists in America and tracking diverse strands within larger groups is challenging. Yet it is no more appropriate to ignore Scotch-Irish experiences because they were similar to those of other settler colonists than it is to ignore

Delaware, Cherokee, or Comanche experiences because they resembled those of other Indigenous peoples.

For all that relations between the Scotch-Irish and Indigenous peoples were hard-edged, the story of those relations is, as it were, fuzzy. It is not always clear just where it begins and ends, or whom exactly it involves. It is clear that there is a story there, though, and it adds depth and diversity to the story of America's beginnings.

Who Are These People?

Thomas Cresap, an expatriate Yorkshireman and a notorious figure on the contested borderland between Pennsylvania and Maryland, was in no doubt about the identity of the sheriff's posse of Pennsylvanians who came to arrest him for murder in 1736; they were, he yelled, "Damn'd Scotch Irish Sons of Bitches."[9] Yet, historians often have more difficulty distinguishing Scotch-Irish people from other groups of colonists, and tracing their origins in historic documents. They seem to be everywhere and nowhere in the records of the frontier. People who migrated from place to place generated fewer records than people who stayed put and whose presence is marked in birth and death dates, land purchases, public service, court appearances, wills, and estate inventories.[10] Surnames offer a guide to Scottish and Irish identity but no guarantee. Many Scottish and Ulster names are also common English names. Many emigrants to America modified their names, transforming the Irish into the Scottish form by changing, for example, O'Donnell to MacDonald or O'Neill to MacNeill, and some dropped the prefix altogether to produce a more "English" name. The classification of Scotch-Irish has never figured in official computations of American population.[11]

Identities are not static and it was not unusual for identities to be forged, submerged, lost, and confused in the jumble of migrations that constituted the European invasion of America in the eighteenth century.[12] Irish roots mattered, but the process of determining who they were as a group in America depended on how people defined themselves and how they understood their shared history, experiences, and destiny. Ultimately, writes one Irish historian, "the question of ethnicity is not one of ancestral birthplace or religious affiliation but one of individual and collective identification which in turn is subjective and variable, shaped by a multitude of shifting social, cultural, political and psychological circumstances."[13] Time and again in borderland regions of competing and uncertain authorities, individuals modified their identities and shifted their loyalties.[14] The lines distinguishing Scotch-Irish from other settler colonists were as fluid as those distinguishing members of different Indian nations who intermixed and intermarried.

Patrick Griffin calls the Scotch-Irish "a people with no name." In fact, they were given several names, none of them entirely appropriate or accurate in conveying their identities and experiences. Contemporaries rarely drew clear distinctions among emigrants from Scotland, Ireland, or other parts of the British Isles, or between Scotch-Irish, Anglo-Irish, and native Irish, and they often called people from Ulster simply *Irish* or *Presbyterians*. People leaving Ulster did not call themselves "Scotch-Irish"; they thought of themselves as Irish, Anglo-Irish, and Scots. Although it was used in the eighteenth century, it did not come into common usage until the nineteenth century, when second- or third-generation Protestant Irish Americans employed it to differentiate themselves from newly arrived Catholic Irish immigrants. In other words, immigrants from Ulster became Scotch-Irish in America rather than Ireland, and, like many other American immigrants, discovered, constructed, or invented their ethnicity in the new country, rather than importing it fully formed from the old.[15] Scotch-Irish identity had roots in Northern Ireland but was largely made in America.

Many cultural norms, practices, and preconceptions that were forged during the seventeenth century in Northern Ireland were perpetuated in subsequent generations in Pennsylvania, North Carolina, and other core areas of the North American backcountry.[16] Pushing through the Cumberland Gap into southern Appalachia and on to the Ozarks, Scotch-Irish people carried their music, culture, politics, Calvinist religion, and Presbyterian church government into what became the Bible Belt, and as they went they left an indelible imprint on American society, culture, character, and identity.[17] Across large swaths of the country, becoming more "American" for the Scotch-Irish meant becoming more "southern." Their contributions to politics, religion, attitudes, music, and values have long been recognized. In addition, they developed a reputation for fierce independence, clannishness, a touchy sense of honor, eye-for-an-eye standards of justice, defiance of authority, dislike of elitism, a populist version of democracy, a strong military tradition, and general combativeness.[18] Writers created a myth of Scotch-Irish essentialism, attributing such distinctive traits of individualism, militarism, and anti-elitism to history and inheritance: emigrants from Ulster transmitted their cultural characteristics undiluted across the Atlantic and across the generations, and descendants exhibited the same characteristics as their Ulster ancestors, even a single Ulster ancestor.

But Scotch-Irish identity was not wholly dependent on Ulster origins. People's old-country origins often played little part in their daily lives in a new country.[19] Many of the people in this story were born in Ulster or had parents who were. Others had more distant geographical or genealogical connections. What was true for first-generation migrants—the "Irish born"— may not have been true for subsequent generations.[20] The Scotch-Irish who pushed west were often a generation or more removed from their forebears who had crossed the Atlantic and often included a mixture of people.[21] At the same time, ethnic characteristics survived, often in muted and subtle form, beyond the generation that stepped off the boat.[22] Living in the backcountry, it has been argued, reinforced rather than diminished Scotch-Irish traits. It also introduced some new ones. In this view, the true Scotch-Irish might be American-born descendants who pushed west across the mountains, leaving behind earlier immigrants who were content to stay put and sink roots.[23]

Going back deeper into history, the people who became the Scotch-Irish were of mixed identity, reflecting varying degrees of Celtic, Roman, Scandinavian, German, French, English, Irish, and Highland and Lowland Scottish ancestry. They had mixed and intermingled for several generations before they migrated from Ulster, and their identity and culture there, like everyone else's identity and culture, were products of change and in the process of changing. By the beginning of the eighteenth century, dissenting Protestants in Ulster—the core of the Scotch-Irish—included small groups of Quakers, English, Welsh, German Baptists, and French Huguenots, as well as Scots Presbyterians. So, when they came to America, they did not bring with them a pristine traditional culture, but one that was evolving and derivative—much like the one they encountered and entered in America.[24]

As they had in Ulster, Scotch-Irish people in America adapted to changing cultural and political contexts and redefined their understandings of themselves over time. They interacted with English, Germans, African Americans, and Native Americans, and they remade their music.[25] Archaeology at Appalachian Scotch-Irish settlements reveals as much about adaptation and change as about the transference and preservation of unchanging material culture.[26] Like those of many other people in motion, Scotch-Irish identities were shaped by exile and migration, grievance and dispute.[27] Identities in diasporic circumstances are fluid and contingent and always evolving. People may inherit core aspects of their identity from the past, but they rework them in the present and through relationships of conflict and exclusion with other peoples, and there can be differences within identities as well as between them.[28]

Whatever the complexities of identity and origin, Scotch-Irish settler colonists came to think of themselves as frontier people.[29] Remote from centers of political power and markets, they relied on kinship networks as the basis of borderland society. Their loyalties and economic interdependence were local, centered on community rather than national interests; they had little time for or trust in laws and policies generated by distant governments that seemed to contribute little to their lives.[30] At the same time, English, Scots, Welsh, Irish, and other people who found themselves living in predominantly Scotch-Irish settlements in backcountry areas of Pennsylvania, Virginia, and North Carolina—what one historical geographer termed "hearth areas"—sometimes took on the identity of, or at least identified with, the larger community.[31] For example, John Harris, an Indian trader who gave his name to the ferry across the Susquehanna and to the town that was later built there, was born in Yorkshire. His son, John Jr., became a magistrate and merchant and a Presbyterian, and through marriage and business ties the Harris family became, as one historian has called them, "foster children of the Ulster Scots" who settled around them.[32] This story will include numerous individuals who, like Harris, were not Scotch-Irish themselves but lived in or had connections to Scotch-Irish communities.

Ethnic identity was an evolving concept in the eighteenth century. This was particularly true among emigrants to North America, but it was also the case with those who stayed home, where a new British identity developed as English, Scots, Welsh, and Irish inhabitants of the British Isles came to see themselves as one people, largely in response to perpetual national wars against the French. In that sense, Britons too were—as James Webb described the Scotch-Irish—"born fighting." Yet as historian Linda Colley notes, "identities are not like hats"; people can wear several at once.[33] The Scotch-Irish not only were trying on a new British identity; after the Revolution they also took on a new American identity. That did not mean they gave up identifying as Scotch-Irish. Wearing multiple hats of identity, they became and remained Scotch-Irish Americans, even as the arrival of other groups reduced their dominance in frontier regions and newcomers claimed for themselves characteristics formerly attributed to Scotch-Irish pioneer folk. Colonists who severed political ties with Britain to create a new nation found that severing commercial and cultural ties took much longer.

They struggled to unbecome British without a coherent sense of what they would become afterward, an uncertainty that fueled their need to establish their "whiteness" as a social construct to distinguish themselves from racialized others inhabiting the American continent. Changing identity to become Americans—whether by English colonists, Scotch-Irish immigrants, or occupants of the Texas borderlands—was more often a process than a simple choice.[34]

Although employing ethnic cultural traits to understand American history can obscure more than it reveals,[35] cultural traits and identities do persist, even as they change. Folkways and kinship systems with roots in Northern Ireland have endured across generations and space in substantial areas of America.[36] Some still attribute Scotch-Irish contributions to state-building to immigrants from Ulster after several generations.[37] People's identity does not necessarily diminish because they have left their homeland. At Scottish festivals in the United States, I have met people who identify more strongly with a place, culture, or history the farther removed they are from those things. Place that is remembered or imagined can be as powerful as place that is inhabited in defining identity. Identity is often concentric and negotiated, without distinct criteria to distinguish it from other identities, and "expiration dates" on identity are unclear and vary. Describing second- or third-generation descendants of Scotch-Irish immigrants as Scotch-Irish may stretch the flexible bounds of identity, yet it is not unlike referring to French-speaking colonists in North America as French, which historians regularly do, even though most of them had never set foot in France.

Settler colonists who invaded Indian country in the eighteenth century may have shared similar experiences, yet they were divided by ethnic and religious differences, and those divisions were sometimes rancorous. European emigrants brought ethnic enmities with them to America, animosities re-emerged when groups came into contact, and intergroup prejudices, stereotypes, and even hostilities persisted across generations because children and grandchildren were taught about their ancestors' ethnic pasts. No self-respecting MacDonald or MacLean would forgive or forget that the Campbells had allied with the English and perpetrated the Glencoe massacre back in the Highlands in 1692. English, Germans, Scots, Scotch-Irish, Welsh, and other groups looked down on one another; Anglicans, Quakers, Presbyterians, Lutherans, and others disparaged one another. Many of the characteristics attributed to Scotch-Irish (or to Germans, frontier people, poor people, Indian people, enslaved people, women) came from the pens of writers whose observations were clouded by prejudice and couched in stereotypes. Only over time did Scotch-Irish and other groups subsume their ethnic differences and develop a shared identity as white Americans. How that happened is part of the story of their invasions of Indian country.[38]

Even as they met and mixed with other peoples, they also identified themselves, and were identified, in comparison to those peoples. Like the Scotch-Irish, German immigrants had to learn how to live on a new land and encountered Indigenous people. However, Germans and Scotch-Irish seem to have kept their distance and engaged in limited social intercourse. Germans had a reputation as orderly, industrious, and frugal people who rarely had trouble with Indians. The Scotch-Irish, by contrast, were regarded as quick-tempered, impetuous, irregular in their work habits, too fond of drinking, and prone to violence against Indians. Traveling to Carlisle, Pennsylvania, in 1784, the Philadelphia physician Benjamin Rush, one of the most distinguished figures in early America, passed riverside farms that were owned mainly by Germans, and bore "all the marks of the industry of those people." A few miles from the river, in contrast, "we traced the marks of the Irish Settlers—Houses without windows—Water wasting itself in public roads instead of being drawn over fields so as to make meadow—dead timber standing in forests in fields of grain—low or broken fences, & lean Cattle." Even worse, for a temperance crusader like Rush, "near many of the houses in the Irish Settlements we saw Still Houses." Whereas Germans tended to make permanent settlements and built homes constructed of "squared timbers," Scotch-Irish made homes by felling trees, stacking them into walls, and filling gaps with clay or mud. Unlike their German neighbors, it seemed, Scotch-Irish people were never satisfied with their residences for long and were restless and always ready to move.[39] Writing in 1769, the Lutheran pastor Henry Melchior Muhlenberg said that the frontier regions formerly "were inhabited almost exclusively by Irish settlers," but wherever German people settled down, worked hard, and managed to make ends meet, the Irish gradually withdrew, sold their farms to the Germans, and moved farther west.[40]

Different people faced with the same events experienced them in different ways and responded with different adaptations. A culture is not just a collection of shared traits; it also derives and develops from fundamental shared experiences. Scotch-Irish identity and culture did not just arrive from Ulster and then disappear as Scotch-Irish people merged into American society. Especially in the backcountry, it grew and developed. Thousands of second- and third-generation Scotch-Irish preserved and perpetuated a distinctive identity that incorporated their experiences on the American frontier. For many people of Scotch-Irish descent, a new Appalachian identity emerged.[41] Scotch-Irish culture and identity developed regional variations. People who settled in core or hearth areas in Pennsylvania, North Carolina, or Tennessee and then moved on carried with them the culture that had developed in the hearth area, not a collection of ethnic traits imported from Ulster and preserved without change.[42] Identities are often rooted in place, but they also emerged from shared experiences of movement across contested landscapes as people made sense of new places and reworked memories of places left behind. In America as in Ireland, "settler mobility" could generate more fluid senses of identity than settler stability.[43]

For all the reasons above, *Hard Neighbors* will not apply rigid criteria as to who was or was not Scotch-Irish, nor will it attribute attitudes and actions on the basis of ethnicity. The people broadly and variously identified as Scotch-Irish were predominantly but not exclusively Presbyterian; their ancestors in Ulster came prominently but not exclusively from Scotland, and they predominantly but not exclusively settled in Ireland before emigrating to America. *Hard Neighbors* recovers the experiences of Scotch-Irish immigrants, their children, and grandchildren and places their presence and participation in broader patterns of British colonialism and American expansion.

What defined them most was conflict. Common to their experiences in each region and generation was their invasion of Indian country and conflict with outside governments over relations with Indian peoples. Shared histories of Indian fighting and government neglect did more than Ulster memories in forging social cohesion and group identity in Scotch-Irish frontier communities. As on colonial frontiers in other parts of the world, most people's minds and lives were dominated by war, the threat of war, and recovery from war, even in times of relative peace.[44] Exposure, vulnerability, and sufferings in war were defining experiences for Scotch-Irish colonists. Memories and stories drawn from years of Indian fighting became part of their regional identity and backcountry folk culture. They saw themselves as self-reliant borderland people, fighting for their lands and lives against Indian enemies with no help from eastern governments; simultaneously heroes and victims, they were bound together by ties of kinship, community, and church, with a distrust of outsiders and a siege mentality.[45] In the same way, some Protestants in borderland landscapes in modern Northern

Ireland see themselves as an embattled community, and draw on histories of violence and atrocity to define themselves and their relationships to others. Borderlands and frontiers may be zones of flux where identities become blurred, but they can also be places where identities form and harden.[46] And yet, reflecting on Irish identities at home and in America, journalist and author Fintan O'Toole suggests that perhaps "the only fixed Irish identity and the only useful Irish tradition is the Irish tradition of not having a fixed identity."[47]

In the end, Scotch-Irish is an imprecise description for people whose identity was imprecise and changeable. As descendant communities of Scotch-Irish people pushed deeper into Indian country and eventually across the continent, their attitudes and actions were shaped less by memories of ancestral experiences in Northern Ireland than by their own, their parents,' and their grandparents' experiences in North America, which they invoked in their sense of themselves. Although ethnicity, religion, occupation, and class mattered, what really mattered was resistance to power exerted from outside the local community, whether by Native Americans or East Coast governments. This was a building block of their identity.[48] They saw themselves as a beleaguered people left to fight for themselves by a distant government. Although Scotch-Irish borderland identity diminished as it was absorbed into a larger American mythology of how the West was won, people who identified and were identified as Scotch-Irish featured repeatedly on the contested borderlands of early America. They added a volatile ingredient to the kaleidoscopic competitions between imperial and colonial governments, federal and state governments, land companies and settlers, colonists and Indigenous peoples, and they gave expression to an ideology of settler colonialism that tracked west with American expansion.

Frontier Myths

The story of Scotch-Irish encounters with Native Americans is shrouded in the myth of the Scotch-Irish as quintessential pioneers who built frontier societies demonstrating typically American characteristics.[49] It is subsumed in well-worn narratives of American expansion and Native American resistance that force Scotch-Irish as well as Indian peoples into one-dimensional roles. Depending on one's view of the American frontier—which, in a country that sees its frontier past as foundational to its democracy and national character, often means depending on one's view of America—the Scotch-Irish were either heroic pioneers or vicious Indian-killers. Neither leaves much room for considering their experiences as people living alongside, even if it was hard up against, Native people in the borderland regions they both occupied.

"True myths are generated on a subliterary level by the historical experiences of a people," cultural historian Richard Slotkin wrote in his seminal work on the mythology of the American frontier. In American mythogenesis, the real founding fathers were not the bewigged gentlemen who created a nation with their words and pens at Philadelphia; they were the ordinary men and women who forged a nation out of the wilderness with their guns and plows. Their hopes, fears, violence, and self-justifications, as expressed in literature, laid "the foundation stones of the mythology that informs our history." A myth, said Slotkin, is "a narrative which concentrates in a single, dramatized experience the whole history of a people in their land."[50] The carrier of that myth could be an individual, like Daniel Boone or Davy Crockett, or a group of people, like the Scotch-Irish.

The Scotch-Irish pioneer of popular myth fits perfectly Frederick Jackson Turner's famous model of frontier development. Soon after the Census Bureau in 1890 declared that population density in the United States had reached a point where the frontier could no longer be said to exist, Turner wrote "The Significance of the Frontier in American History." In passages that have been quoted and re-quoted by generations of historians, Turner argued that "the existence of an area of free land, its continuous recession, and the advance of American settlement westward, explain American development." In Turner's mind, that development involved returning to "primitive conditions" and perennial rebirth on successive frontiers as European colonists adopted Indian modes of dress, travel, hunting, farming, and thinking in order to survive but gradually built civilization where none had existed. They re-emerged, not as Europeans, but as Americans. Turner envisioned a cavalcade of colonizers advancing across the continent—traders, pioneers, farmers, miners, town builders—each bringing a different stage of development. The pioneer farmer who occupied the land for a time, cutting down trees, clearing fields, and building a spartan cabin, even if he never became the owner of the soil, and who then moved on to take up new land as others pressed in behind, was key to the process. "The Scotch Irish and the Palatine Germans, or 'Pennsylvania Dutch,' furnished the dominant element in the stock of the colonial frontier," Turner stated. Western expansion promoted nationalism, and the individualism and self-reliance that frontier life demanded promoted the growth of democracy, although, Turner acknowledged, "the democracy born of free land, strong in selfishness and individualism, intolerant of administrative experience and education, and pressing individual liberty beyond its proper bounds, has its dangers as well as it benefits."[51]

Turner's thesis has long since been debunked. Almost one hundred years ago, historian Thomas Perkins Abernethy concluded: "The frontier is most aptly characterized not by the cry of the frontiersman for more freedom, but by the cry of the speculator for more land."[52] Subsequent generations of historians have exposed Turner's inattention to issues of race, class, gender, and genocide. Nevertheless, Turner's vision of the American frontier endures in America's sense of itself, and the Scotch-Irish endure in America's myth of its pioneers. Like Turner's first colonists, the Scotch-Irish on the frontier at first succumbed to the "wilderness"—contemporary travelers and eastern elites routinely described them as "more savage than the Indians." Then, as Patrick Griffin describes, they demonstrated the Turnerian transformative process at work. The trappings of civil society emerged, a frontier elite took shape, Presbyterian meetinghouses were established, and the Scotch-Irish "tamed a frontier as they tamed themselves." By the time Turner presented his frontier thesis, the Scotch-Irish had come to represent everything he lauded as American. Violence on a "fighting frontier" separating "civilization and savagery" shaped the culture of the West and by implication the larger nation, and competition molded the character of a people schooled in self-sufficiency and individualism. These frontier communities had turned their backs on the Atlantic Ocean and created a new society free from the old forms of dominance. As we will see, descendants of eighteenth-century Scotch-Irish pioneers championed their ancestors' role in forging America at the very moment Turner published his essay announcing the importance of the frontier.[53]

The experiences of Scotch-Irish settler colonists who battled aggressive neighbors, first on the frontiers of Northern Ireland and then on successive frontiers in North America, while at the same time building and preserving strong familial and community networks, became a part of the national narrative. Writing more than one hundred years ago, Henry Jones Ford asserted that Scotch-Irish character was so deeply rooted and durable "that its fibre is singularly hard and strong and it retains this nature wherever it is planted." When the majority of Scotch-Irish immigrants moved to the frontier, "they constituted the border garrisons; they were the explorers, the vanguard of settlement in the interior. Their Ulster training had inured them to hostile surroundings."[54]

Popular histories portray the Scotch-Irish as tough, take-no-guff-from-anyone pioneers who won the Old West with guts and guns, built new societies on independence and self-reliance, democratized American politics, and furnished the nation with essential and enduring values based on the family farm and the family Bible. Celebratory accounts of their achievements, such as the series of short and somewhat repetitive books which Armagh County author and journalist Billy Kennedy calls *The Scotch-Irish Chronicles*, first published thirty years ago, continue to have significant appeal. Kennedy credits the Scotch-Irish with contributing "more than any other race [sic] of white people," to the ultimate defeat of the tribes on the Appalachian frontier.[55] James Webb, a decorated Vietnam War combat veteran, senator from Virginia, and secretary of the Navy under President Ronald Reagan, portrayed his Scotch-Irish ancestors as "born fighting." They were individualists who hated established authority and were driven by "a values based combativeness, an insistent egalitarianism, and a refusal to be dominated from above." They showed no hesitation in pushing into Indian country and settling on Indian land, and rather than curtail uprisings by their defensive presence, they helped "light the torch of Indian resentment."[56] In *Red Dirt*, Roxanne Dunbar-Ortiz depicts her Ulster Scots ancestors as seasoned colonialists before they set foot in America, people who "had perfected scalping for bounty on the indigenous Irish" before they ever met Native Americans.[57]

In such portrayals, emigrants from the British borderlands were uniquely qualified by history and temperament to colonize North American borderland zones that required fluidity, adaptation, and resilience. In Northern Ireland they occupied and defended lands taken from the native Irish population; they did the same to the Indigenous population in America. Assessing the influence of British regional folkways on different regions of America, historian David Hackett Fischer argued that the endemic violence of the North British borderlands shaped a culture where blood relationships were vital in world of danger and treachery. Scotch-Irish immigrants brought their belligerence with them, as well as "an indelible memory of oppression which shaped their political attitudes for decades to come."[58] In a region marked by social tensions, power struggles, and the inherent brutality of slavery, some writers have attributed historic codes and patterns of violence in the American South to a Celtic heritage of borderland violence.[59]

Some historians dismiss the myth that the Scotch-Irish were natural frontiersmen as nonsense.[60] Others are not so sure. The idea that Ireland served as a blueprint for America may be exaggerated, yet, they argue, the colonization of Ireland produced a tough subculture prone to resettlement and, with by far the highest rates of overseas migration in the British Isles in the eighteenth century, the Scotch-Irish constituted the shock troops of European settlement in distant lands.[61] The image of the Scotch-Irish as rough, tough, ruthless, and violent persists. Of course, though, as one writer found in researching her own family history, thousands of Scotch-Irish families "have never been like that."[62]

Troublesome Settlers and Hard Neighbors

What is beyond dispute is that time and again, Scotch-Irish people placed themselves, or found themselves placed, in borderland spaces, where they grated against Indian country and Indian communities. Yet though they were agents of colonialism, they saw themselves as victims. Their relations with Native people did not develop and then disintegrate into violence in isolation. They were part of a triangular relationship. As inhabitants of frontier regions, they faced Indian people to the west who were neighbors and enemies, and they looked east to the colonial, state, or federal government that positioned them on the frontier, encouraged their incursions on Indian land, then denounced them and failed to defend the frontiers when contestation turned to conflict.[63] Such triangular relationships are not unusual. As evidenced by the situation in modern Northern Ireland where many Protestants continued to see themselves, and to be seen, as settler colonists confronting both a hostile Native population and an unsympathetic and unsupportive government in London, ambivalence toward the metropolis is often a central feature of settler societies.[64]

Intended to bring security and order to vulnerable and dangerous frontiers, Scotch-Irish colonists repeatedly generated instability and *created* dangerous frontiers for Indian peoples. They perpetrated and experienced violence. Occupying regions where the boundaries of colonial, federal, state, and territorial authority were contested,[65] they demanded that government support them in acquiring land and fighting Indians, at the same time that they insisted that government not interfere in their lives—part of an enduring American political tradition.[66]

Whereas other forms of colonialism targeted Native labor and resources, settler-colonialism centered on expropriating Native land.[67] Patrick Wolfe explained that it operated on the "logic of elimination," removing or destroying Indigenous people to make their land available.[68] Land hunger for speculators meant amassing acreage for oneself. It involved something more for farming families. They had to secure a livelihood from the land, produce a surplus for trade, and provide for the next generation. Growing populations quickly exceeded the supply of land. Children and grandchildren had to move on and find land of their own or become tenant farmers or wage laborers. To perpetuate their way of life and sustain their dreams of economic independence, each generation needed more and more land, propelling expansion into Indian country. American families achieved landed autonomy by destroying the autonomy of Native American families who stood in their way.[69]

Scotch-Irish settlers moved early and often onto Indian land and carried out the logic of elimination inherent in settler colonialism. The case against the Scotch-Irish as quintessential Indian-killers looks solid. They served as shock troops on the violent edge of empire. Colonial governments and the federal government frequently outsourced Indian fighting to Scotch-Irish frontier militia and vigilantes, who sometimes perpetrated horrific massacres of Native people. Even members of their own colonial and national governments condemned them and blamed them. No group of colonists surpassed them in their assaults on Indian lands or people. The Scotch-Irish were Indian fighters, or at least Indian-killers.

As this book will show, that is only part of the story. Not all Scotch-Irish people lived in the backcountry, and some ascended the political hierarchy like anybody else.[70] Some Scotch-Irish were members of the colonial elite, although Anglo-Irish Anglicans from Ulster tended to secure higher positions than Scotch-Irish Presbyterians. Some Scotch-Irish on the frontiers also attained positions as local elites. For the majority of Scotch-Irish people living in backcountry regions, however, the frontier experience was defined by the neglect or interference of government, as well as by the presence and threat of Indian people. Contrary to what many commentators at the time and many writers since have assumed or asserted, the so-called savagery of Scotch-Irish people had less to do with their ethnic heritage than with their position as buffers. Indian-hating, Henry Jones Ford noted more than a century ago, "was not a Scotch-Irish characteristic but a frontier characteristic."[71]

People killed Indians for various reasons, but not usually because they were naturally or ethnically predisposed. Attributing murders and massacres to Indian-hating and explaining perpetrators' actions as a function of harsh frontier experiences in Northern Ireland ignore the broader contexts and workings of colonialism. Scotch-Irish people, initially at least, did not kill Indians out of blind racial hatred. The racial violence with which eastern elites associated them stemmed in part from colonial agendas that generated Indian resistance, and from fearmongering by those who advanced those agendas. The members of distant governments who denounced the Scotch-Irish were often the same people whose policies pushed Scotch-Irish settlers hard up against the Indigenous inhabitants of contested lands in the first place, who outsourced the dirty work of empire-building to them. Scotch-Irish people and Indian people managed to coexist, uneasily it must be said, for long periods; they killed each other most often when state policies demanded Indian dispossession, encouraged rapid colonization, and mobilized men and resources for war. Indian warriors protected their own families and lands by attacking the settler families who invaded their lands. The terrors of Indian raids, recounted countless times, turned Scotch-Irish backcountry settlers into Indian-killers and turned them against government. Indian-hating was more often a product of war than the cause of it and was fueled by resentment toward governments that seemed to do more for "others" than for them.[72]

A French traveler in 1765 summarized the experience of the Scotch-Irish and their neighbors during the French and Indian War and Pontiac's War, calling them "poor wretches" who were sent to distant frontiers "to serve as a barrière betwixt the lower settlers and the Indians" and left "to be butcher'd." They were forced by circumstances to "be industrious in riseing all their necessaries within themselves" and create their own defenses.[73] Like the Native peoples they encountered and dispossessed, the Scotch-Irish were a "betwixt" people, inhabiting contested spaces and buffeted by forces unleashed by those who viewed them as barbarous and expendable. Indian peoples, too, were placed between competing powers, and Indigenous powers sometimes placed other Indian groups between themselves and colonial powers.

The Scotch-Irish in America's backcountry occupied a peripheral intermediate zone between a so-called civilized core and an outside region viewed as wild, savage, and barbarous. In such situations, the metropole typically regards the peripheral zone and its inhabitants as essentially unstable and violent, and then encourages them to take out this violence on others. Manipulated into carrying out a genocidal agenda, they are encouraged to see themselves as the representatives of "civilization" against "savagery," while the elites in fact look on them as little better than savages themselves.[74] As we will see, those who used the Scotch-Irish and their neighbors to advance their own agendas complained that they lived like Indians.

Settler colonialism was not monolithic. Some acts were carried out by agents of the state (colonial administrators, land agents, militia); others by independent agents who employed the resources of the state.[75] Although colonial powers used Scotch-Irish people as instruments of colonialism, Scotch-Irish people were sometimes willing instruments, taking advantage of opportunities and resources. Sometimes, they were in conflict with colonialism's agendas, policies, and restraints. At once instruments and victims of colonialism, they were distrustful of distant governments who put them out there to destabilize Indian country and contain Indian resistance and then left them to bear the brunt of conflict. Sir William Johnson, the British superintendent of Indian affairs north of the Ohio, reported to the Lords of Trade in 1765, a year of mounting defiance of imperial authority, that frontier settlers had "a confirmed hatred for all Indians" and at the same time displayed "their Disregard of the Peace and Contempt of the Governments they live under."[76] Similar complaints emanated from officials in Philadelphia, Virginia, the Carolinas, Georgia, and, later, Washington, D.C.

Contrary to portrayals of Scotch-Irish frontiersmen, colonial authorities that hoped to create a cordon of fighting farmers or soldier settlers were often sadly disappointed. Time and again—in the French and Indian War, Pontiac's War, the Revolution—buffers collapsed as frontier inhabitants abandoned their homes and fled eastward for safety. Poorly armed, poorly organized, and reluctant to leave their families unprotected while they campaigned elsewhere, frontier militia earned a reputation as unreliable. Scotch-Irish backcountry inhabitants desperate for assistance from the colonial governments that had placed them in harm's way generated more petitions and pleas for help than acts of armed resistance.

Although dispossession was the essence of colonialism and invasion, it was not the whole story. They were processes that involved multiple encounters and relationships, established and sustained structures of oppression, and exposed all participants to change. On the ground in contested areas, spatial distinctions and clear boundaries between colonizers and colonized peoples often tended to break down.[77] Although the Scotch-Irish committed atrocities and massacres, they and their Indian neighbors, like marginalized people in other frontier regions, developed local networks of cooperation and exchange that involved sharing space, resources, and knowledge, and, for a time, maintained relationships and patterns of coexistence that were based on mutual benefit and mutual dependence.[78] That relationships devolved into bloodshed had less to do with an inherent Scotch-Irish predilection for violence than with outside pressures and the workings of colonial powers. Murders and atrocities perpetrated between neighbors who knew each other by name ruptured rather than typified relationships.

Of all the books I have written, this is the only one for which I remember the moment I decided to write it. It was mid-morning, two days after the presidential election of 2016. I was traveling on a flight from Washington, D.C., to Nashville, Tennessee, on a day that was as clear and bright as my mood was black. During the week or so before my flight, at the George Washington Presidential Library at Mount Vernon, I had been reading petitions from desperate backcountry colonists, many if not most of them Scotch-Irish, who were caught by Indian raids on their scattered and isolated mountain valley settlements at the outbreak of the French and Indian War. This was a familiar story to me. However, looking down on those mountain valleys that morning, I appreciated for the first time just how vulnerable and exposed those people had been, and realized that I needed to understand them better in order to better understand settler colonialism, Indian-white relations, and racial violence in early America.

In an earlier book, *White People, Indians, and Highlanders* (2008), I had explored the parallel and connected experiences of tribal peoples with colonialism in Scotland and America. Displaced Highland Scots coexisted and cohabited with Indigenous peoples in many periods and places, and many of their descendants were and are members of tribal nations. I have family ties and feel an affinity with Highland Scots. I have none with the Scotch-Irish. They are not "my people." Not only did the Scotch-Irish and their descendants have a reputation for unrelenting violence in their sustained assault on Native America, but many of the traits attributed to the Scotch-Irish in the eighteenth century resemble those attributed to Trump's base in the twenty-first century.

The purpose of history is to understand the past, not to feel good or guilty about it. *Hard Neighbors* doesn't involve ethnic chauvinism or ethnic condemnation and won't add to the extensive literature and debates over

Scotch-Irish identity, trace the lineages of presidents and performers, or show how the Scotch-Irish contributed to regional or national American culture. It also won't establish clear criteria for who was or was not Scotch-Irish. Instead, it seeks to deepen understanding of the so-called white frontier that is too often described in monolithic terms. It highlights stories that have been subsumed under the mantra of "American expansion" or "settler colonialism," shows that overlapping buffers of Native and non-Native "peoples in between" were a recurrent feature of colonialism, and traces shifting relationships involving Scotch-Irish people on the frontier, neighboring Indian peoples, and more distant governments.

Hard Neighbors follows the people who came to be known as Scotch-Irish from their genesis on a colonial borderland on one side of the Atlantic to their role in the borderlands of Indian country on the other. It traces their relations with Native Americans over time and across the continent, examines their experiences as marginalized and expendable people living between colonial powers and Indigenous peoples, and demonstrates their roles as protective and disruptive forces on the hard edge of colonialism. Although the Scotch-Irish fought Indian wars and shaped the frontier, they themselves were shaped by their experiences living near and fighting against Indians. They exerted influence on national attitudes and policies, and they transformed Indian people into racial others as they transformed themselves into Americans.

The three-part division of the book reflects shifts in approach and emphasis in telling key parts of the story. Part I establishes the historical experiences of the Scotch-Irish, and many of their Indian neighbors, as mobile borderland people. Part II adopts a more chronological approach in reconstructing Scotch-Irish experiences in the wars for America waged between Indigenous people and colonists, and between rival colonial powers, during which Scotch-Irish people fought for their own place in America. Part III considers the role of Scotch-Irish and their descendants, now increasingly identifying and identified as Americans, in U.S. expansion across Native America.

In short, the story this book tells is less about the Scotch-Irish as a distinct ethnic group than as a people in motion who, in collusion and conflict with colonial authorities, repeatedly inserted themselves on Native land. Instead of a tale of unified westward expansion, it recovers the experiences, encounters, and humanity of groups of people enmeshed in the violence of colonialism and reconstructs the roles of multiple peoples placed as buffers between competing powers on the frontiers of North America. Expansion, and the accompanying expulsion and killing of Indian people, helped to create American unity and identity and, ultimately, made the Scotch-Irish Americans. Never identified by name or brought to justice, the Paxton Boys who had murdered the Conestoga Indians resumed their lives and took their places in society. Subsequent generations of Scotch-Irish, once marginalized as little better than Indians, reaffirmed their reputation as Indian-killers and made a place for themselves in America, as Americans.

PART I
BORDERLAND PEOPLE

1
Origin Stories and Atlantic Migrations

According to John Heckewelder, a Moravian missionary who spent much of his life among them and published a book about his experiences, the Delaware people believed their ancestors emerged into this world from under a dark lake. Some accounts tell of a great flood after which the creator, *Gicelamu'kaong* or *Kishelemukong*, brought dirt from the submerged earth and created a new world on the back of a giant turtle. Other traditions say that the people moved from a great body of water in the west to the mid-Atlantic coast. The Delawares were a coalition of Algonquian-speaking groups known collectively in their own language as Lenape, meaning "common" or "original people." By the seventeenth century, three main language groups inhabited the Delaware River valley—the Munsees (or Minisinks) around the Delaware Water Gap, the Unalachtigos (or north Unamis) on the eastern bank in New Jersey, and the Unamis (or Lenni Lenapes) on the west shore of the lower Delaware River, near the future site of Philadelphia. They met the Dutch at Manhattan, accommodated Swedish colonists in the Delaware Valley, and welcomed William Penn as he founded his new colony in 1680.

As more and more Europeans migrated into the region, they pushed the Indigenous inhabitants out, initiating two centuries of movement, in which Delaware unity and identity were forged in dealings with other peoples and powers. Colonial governments and the Haudenosaunee, or Iroquois, who constituted the dominant Native power in northeastern North America, treated the several Delaware groups as one nation. Some of the groups migrated west to escape Iroquois domination, English colonialism, and then American expansion, and they recreated homelands in Pennsylvania, Ohio, Indiana, Ontario, Kansas, Missouri, Texas, and Oklahoma. By the late eighteenth century, the majority were located in Ohio and identified themselves as one people and a nation. Migration and relocation were deeply rooted in the history and identity of the Delaware people.[1]

Foremost among the people who pressured, pushed, and pursued the Delawares in their westward diaspora were the Scotch-Irish. They, too, were a people in motion and they forged their identity and culture in a history of migrations on multiple frontiers. Those migrations were part of a series of population movements within the British Isles and part of the massive movement of peoples from Europe, across the Atlantic, and into the interior of North America. At first, migration to America was simply an additional outlet for people already on the move, a spillover of patterns in Europe, which sent people from the German states east as well as west, and which drew a constant flood of humanity from throughout the British Isles to London. In time, however, the American magnet began to shape European movements. Propelled by political, religious, and economic forces on one side of the Atlantic and drawn by the pull of land and opportunity on the other, hundreds of thousands of largely anonymous individuals made personal choices and small-scale exoduses. These produced local streams of migration in the momentous transfer to the Western Hemisphere of people from Africa, the European mainland, and the Anglo-Celtic offshore islands of Europe.[2] The Scotch-Irish emerged as one stream in the flood—one stream, and yet of disproportionate importance. "There is nothing more remarkable in all history than this vast swarming from a few little counties in a tiny corner of a small island, unless it be the Greeks spreading over Persia and the Orient," declared Henry Noble McCracken, the president of Vassar College, in an address to the Ulster-Irish Society of New York in 1939. "But the Greeks were an army of conquest, the Irish of Ulster poor farmers."[3]

Planting Protestants

English monarchs had tried to extend their dominion over Ireland since the Middle Ages. In the twelfth century, King Henry II invaded Ireland and distributed lands to Anglo-Norman followers in four Irish kingdoms—Connaught, Leinster, Munster, and Ulster. For the next five hundred years, English monarchs tried to subdue the island by sending military campaigns and giving land to Anglo-Norman families whose influence, it was hoped, would help "domesticate" the Irish. However, many Norman barons embraced Gaelic values, customs, and language, married Irish women, and began to live like Irish clan chiefs. They occupied a middle space on the frontier. The Irish saw them as English invaders, but the English saw them as having "degenerated" and having become "more Irish than the Irish." Although they adopted some Irish ways, they still regarded themselves as Englishmen, and deserving of better treatment than they received from the royal government.[4] As the Gaelic Irish reasserted themselves and absorbed the invaders, the descendants of the Normans maintained a foothold in Dublin and the surrounding region known as the Pale, derived from *palus*, the Latin word for a stake or pailing in a picket or fence. They regarded the lands and people "beyond the Pale" as wild and unruly. At the same time, passage between Scotland and Ireland was common; at its narrowest, the sea channel between northeastern Ireland and southwestern Scotland is only thirteen miles and people crossed it easily and often. Mercenaries—called "gallowglass" from the Irish *gallóglaigh*, meaning "foreign warriors"—crossed over from the Western Isles of Scotland as early as the thirteenth century, receiving land for their services from Irish chiefs who recruited them to bolster their military strength.[5]

The English Crown's drive to conquer and control Ireland intensified with the injection of an enduring religious division. In 1534 the Tudor King Henry VIII, desperate to satisfy his personal and dynastic goals by divorcing his first wife Katherine of Aragon and marrying Anne Boleyn, broke with Rome and established England as a Protestant kingdom. At odds with the Catholic powers of Europe, the English now viewed Catholic Ireland as a breeding ground for religious enemies and a potential back door to invasion by France and Spain. They also regarded Irish peasants as the epitome of backwardness and savagery, citing characteristics and criteria they would also apply to Native people in America.

The so-called Irish problem drained the Crown of money and manpower. No region offered more resistance to English colonization schemes than Ulster, described by an English soldier in the Irish wars as "very large and withal mountainous, full of great loughs of fresh water," with few towns but many castles scattered throughout the province where the inhabitants took refuge "in times of war and troubles." Henry VIII and Anne Boleyn's daughter, Protestant Queen Elizabeth I (1558–1603), waged a nine-year war (1594–1603) against an alliance of Catholic lords led by Hugh O'Neill of Tyrone. After the Earl of Essex with a large English army failed to defeat O'Neill and colonize County Antrim in the northeast, Elizabeth in 1601 created a new military establishment in Ireland. The commander, Charles Blount, Lord Mountjoy, launched scorched-earth campaigns, cutting down corn and depopulating the country.[6] The Elizabethan government now viewed the Pale as a colonial frontier that should be pushed outward.[7]

It was, however, a Scottish king who extended his new united kingdom of "Great Britain" and sought to subdue and "civilize" the Gaelic regions of both the Scottish Highlands and Ireland. When Elizabeth the Virgin Queen died without an heir in 1603, the Crown passed to James VI of Scotland, who then became James I of England. King James tried to extend "civilization" to Ireland by colonizing the region with Protestant settlements. He also tried to rid his newly united kingdom of the unruly elements that had made endemic conflicts a feature of life on the Anglo-Scottish border for centuries.

From the late Middle Ages until the end of Elizabeth's reign, the Anglo-Scottish borders were a turbulent and bloody buffer zone between the two nations. Stretching some seventy miles from Berwick on Tweed on the North Sea southwest to the Solway Firth, the border region encompassed the historic English counties of Cumberland and Westmoreland (now incorporated into Cumbria) and Northumberland, as well as parts of what are now Dumfries and Galloway and the Scottish Borders. Government officials known as wardens policed six Marches (derived from the word for "edge" or "boundary")—three on either side of the border between England and Scotland—but they sometimes turned a blind eye to depredations they could do nothing to curtail. Efforts to assert Crown control in areas distant from London and Edinburgh where powerful families dominated, competed, and pursued their own agendas proved futile. Armstrongs, Bells, Charltons, Elliotts, Grahams, Kerrs, Irvines, Johnstons, Maxwells, Rutherfords, Scotts, and other clans and families defied outside authority and perpetuated an economy and culture of raiding, rustling, and blood feuds. Some, like the Armstrongs and Grahams, lived on both sides of the border—although Armstrongs in Scotland felt little kinship with Armstrongs in Cumberland. Using or ignoring the frontier as and when it suited them, border families fought and plundered with seeming indifference to national interests and loyalties. Scots pillaged Scots and Englishmen robbed other Englishmen; feuds were as deadly between families on the same side as they were across the border, and borderland people frequently aided and abetted raiders and invaders from across the line. At the same time, alliances, marriages, and kinship ties spanned the frontier. Half-English and half-Scottish, the border region became a separate entity between the two countries, what one novelist and historian born and raised in the area called "a thing in itself."[8]

Following his accession to the throne of England, King James and his officers embarked on a systematic program to pacify the region which now lay in the middle of his kingdom and purged the outlaw clans. The Grahams, who had been a thorn in the side of both kingdoms, were hunted down, evicted from their lands, and banished. Many went to the Low Countries.

Many were deported to Ireland, where the Lord Deputy of Ireland, Sir Arthur Chichester, observed, "They are now dispersed, and when they shall be placed upon any land together, the next country will find them ill neighbours, for they are a fractious and naughty people."[9]

Many other people followed them across the Irish Sea. When immigrants from both sides of the Anglo-Scottish border transplanted to Northern Ireland in the early seventeenth century, they entered another environment of endemic violence, where they lived on the edge of subsistence, endured frequent famine, and suffered political, economic, and religious oppression. Their Scotch-Irish descendants who migrated to America in the eighteenth century, in historian David Hackett Fischer's words, "thus included a double-distilled selection of some of the most disorderly inhabitants of a deeply disordered land."[10] Meanwhile, the border region between England and Scotland, dotted with the remains of peel towers (fortified keeps) and gaunt castles (there are seventy in the county of Northumberland alone), retains to this day a distinct character and still, to some degree, its own identity.[11]

Simply put, as one genealogical society put it in 1926, "the Scotch-Irish were Scotch-English people who had gone to Ireland to take up the estates of Irish rebels confiscated under Queen Elizabeth and James I."[12] In 1607 Hugh O'Neill and Rory O'Donnell, the Earl of Tyrconnell, fled to the mainland of Europe with about ninety followers, hoping to generate support for a new war. King James took advantage of this "Flight of the Earls" and confiscated nearly four million acres of land in six of Ulster's nine counties. (In addition to the present-day counties of Fermanagh, Armagh, Antrim, Down, Tyrone, and Londonderry, Ulster then also included Monaghan, Donegal, and Cavan, which are now part of the Republic of Ireland.) The Crown then redistributed the lands to English and Lowland Scottish "undertakers," as they were known—men of substance who were charged with securing and arming tenants for their lands. Native and Catholic Irish were reassigned to poorer and more remote areas. "Planting" Protestants in the soil of Ulster and binding their loyalty to the Crown was designed to spread the true religion and to strengthen the security of the new British kingdom.[13]

Under the colonization scheme, these "undertakers" were given allotments of between 1,000 and 3,000 acres. They were expected to live on the land for at least five years and to populate their estates with settlers according to the size of the grant. The settlers were to include no Irish; the estates were intended to be British outposts. Chief undertakers were to be allowed 3,000 acres, on condition that they resided on the land, settled English or

Scottish families, and undertook to bear arms and build defenses.[14] Much of Coleraine County was set aside for twelve London companies who established the "Irish Society" in 1613 to manage their new asset, and renamed it Londonderry. King James considered importing Dutch or even German settlers to displace Irish Catholics, but Sir Francis Bacon recommended Lowland Scots. The Reverend Andrew Stuart, a Scottish minister who settled in the port town of Donaghadee in County Down, left a famous description of the impoverished and displaced people for whom migration to the Ulster plantation offered an outlet and an opportunity:

> From Scotland came many, and from England not a few, yet all of them generally the scum of both nations, who, for debts, or breaking and fleeing from justice, or seeking shelter, came hither, hoping to be without fear of man's justice in a land where there was nothing or but little, as yet, of the fear of God.... Going for Ireland was looked upon as the miserable mark of a deplorable person.[15]

There is little evidence to suggest that many of the new tenants shared the civilizing mission of the plantation promoters. Many were disbanded soldiers, and, as one historian has put it, "from what is known of the disposition of English soldiers in Ireland during the late sixteenth century, it must be considered extremely doubtful whether they proved successful agents of English civility."[16]

Most of the migrants were Scots. They were used as a bulwark against dispossessed Irish chiefs and their tribes, especially in areas where English tenants could not be induced to settle. An English planter in Armagh who proposed a scheme for settling land in Monaghan in 1622 said it would be good to settle Scots there first, "for the English then wilt gladly sitt down upon the other when the Scots shall be as a walt [wall] betwixt them & the Ireish."[17] In return, the immigrants received land, and, although always second-class citizens, status. Most of the Scottish immigrants were Lowlanders. Drawn from counties adjacent to the English border and up the west coast to Argyllshire, they were linguistically distinct from the English (although they spoke Scotch, an English dialect, rather than the Gaelic spoken in the Highlands) and most were Presbyterians hostile to the Church of Ireland. The majority settled in dispersed farmsteads; many were dispossessed smallholders, refugees from the increasing commercialization and enclosure of lowland agriculture.[18]

The settlement of Scots in Ireland was another episode in a long history of mobility and "domestic migration" across the Irish Sea. Scots had been moving back and forth across the narrow straits for centuries and the northeastern counties of Antrim and Down contained substantial Scottish populations.[19] Trade with Ireland became important to Scotland's western ports by end of the sixteenth century.[20] And from the late sixteenth through the mid-seventeenth century, "Scotch-Irish" was a pejorative term that Irish Anglicans and Lowland Scots Presbyterians applied to Gaelic-speaking Catholic Highlanders who migrated back and forth between Argyll and the Western Isles and north Antrim.[21]

Implemented in 1609, the Irish colonization scheme came just two years after founding of Jamestown in Virginia. It was, said Sir Arthur Chichester, King James's Lord Deputy for Ireland, "as if His Majesty were to begin a new plantation in America, from which it does not greatly differ."[22] Scholars have long seen the Elizabethan and Jacobean colonization of Ireland as a test run or "apprenticeship" for the colonization of North America. It established perceptions, policies, and practices for dealing with Native peoples and generated an ethic of conquest that justified conquest and colonization. In English eyes, the wild Irish were savages, living in tribes beyond the pale of civilization; herders who had no concept of property, did not plant or improve their lands, and did not settle in towns. When the English began colonizing Virginia and New England, they carried with them a fully developed mythology about Native peoples, compared Indians to the Irish, and projected the definitions of savagery they had developed in dealing with the Irish onto Native Americans. The ethic of conquest was transferable to North America: depicting "savage Indians," like "wild Irish," as heathens who did not use, or underused, the land necessitated and legitimated imposing Christianity and civilization and taking over the land.[23]

Out of the Plantation of Ulster, Northern Ireland emerged as British and Protestant, and the Scotch-Irish emerged as a colonizing people. However, it was not a foregone conclusion and it involved years of problems, setbacks, and bloodshed.[24] Although the government intended that the colonists would dispossess the native Irish and stand as a wall against them, the reality on the ground was often rather different. The Irish population in many areas remained in place and increased. Rather than expelling the local population, undertakers sometimes relied on it. The existence of an "English Street," an "Irish Street," and a "Scotch Street" to this day in towns such as Downpatrick and Dungannon reflects the proximity of natives and newcomers four centuries ago. Catholics were not permitted to settle inside Derry, but they were allowed into Belfast, and towns like Armagh and Cavan retained significant native populations.[25]

Migrations to Ireland were much larger than migrations to America in the seventeenth century. As many as 200,000 English and 130,000 Scots went there by 1700, making the colonization of Ireland the largest migration of the century.[26] Migration occurred in streams and chains linked by family, congregation, region, and commercial connections. Estimates of the numbers involved vary, and the periods on which scholars base their estimates sometimes overlap, but a sampling conveys a sense of the magnitude and the ebb and flow of the population movements. By 1630, maybe 4,000 British families had settled in Ulster, mainly in the two eastern counties closest to Scotland.[27] In one two-year period in the 1630s at least 10,000 Scots migrated to Ireland.[28] The northern part of Ulster became increasingly Scottish during the course of the century.

By 1640, an estimated 100,000 Scots and 20,000 English had settled in Ulster. Migration stalled during the English Civil War, 1640–1646, when the armies of King Charles I and Oliver Cromwell marched through Ireland, as did a Scottish army. In 1641, after several decades of relative calm, the native Irish rose against the Ulster Scots in a bloody rebellion that killed or expelled thousands of Protestant settlers and sparked a civil war that lasted eleven years. Inflated and recycled tales of rebel atrocities—mass hangings and drownings, torture, sexual violence, pregnant women disemboweled, children impaled—reinforced Protestant views of the Catholic Irish as treacherous savages. A Scottish army under General George Monroe landed at Carrickfergus, ravaged Antrim, Down, and Cavan, and contained the rebellion. Following the defeat of the Royalists in England, Cromwell invaded Ireland in 1649, stamped out the rebellion in a series of brutal campaigns, and earned lasting infamy for the siege and massacre of Drogheda, in which as many as 800 civilians were killed. He then imposed a harshly repressive regime on the defeated Catholic Irish, executing or expelling priests, dispossessing Catholic landowners in three of Ireland's four provinces and relocating them to Connacht, and replacing them with more Protestant farmers. Memories of the atrocities and sufferings of the Irish rebellion and civil war endured for generations.[29]

Thousands more Scots fled to Ireland during the reigns of Charles II and James II. When James II became king of England in 1685, he intended to reimpose Catholicism and bring Ulster Scots to heel but was ousted in the so-called Glorious Revolution in 1688, which brought William of Orange to the throne as King William III. James fled to France and then brought a French army to Ireland in a bid to regain his throne. Ulster Scots took refuge in fortified towns, and Londonderry endured a 100-day siege before it was relieved in mid-1690. William's Dutch, English, German, and Irish-Protestant army defeated James's French and Irish-Catholic forces at the Battle of the Boyne in July. Escaping bad weather and bad harvests and attracted by Protestant landlords who wanted Protestant tenants as bulwarks against future Catholic rebellion, Scots continued to take up cheap Ulster lands that were left tenantless after campaigns of 1688–1689. Some 50,000–80,000 new immigrants arrived between 1690 and 1715, not only Lowland Scots and English but also Welsh and French Huguenots.[30] In 1600, less than 2 percent of the population of Ireland was of Scots or English descent; by the early 1700s, it was 27 percent[31] (Map 1.1).

By 1715, Scotland was no longer the feeder for Ulster settlement. The accession of William III to the throne restored the Presbyterian Church as the Kirk of Scotland. The days of cheap land in Ulster came to an end; the Act of Union with England in 1707 generated improved economic conditions in the Scottish Lowlands, and growing American trade offered more attractive opportunities for Scottish dissidents.[32] Of a total Irish population of about 2,100,000, Ulster's population in 1715 was about 600,000, of whom about one-third were Presbyterians. Yet the Protestants owned 95 percent of the country's property and monopolized political power. Outnumbered by impoverished Catholics and haunted by memories of 1641, Protestants in Ireland lived in fear of another revolt that might cost them their property and their lives. They developed a biblical sense of themselves as a chosen people, embattled and ever vigilant in a world of danger.[33]

Dissenting Protestantism became an important element in the identity, character, and worldviews of an Ulster-Scots community and culture that embraced both shores of the North Channel, an area that might be called "Ulster-Scots Land."[34] The Presbyterian Church had developed in Scotland in opposition to the Anglican Church, based on reformer and minister John Knox's system of presbyteries, councils of ministers and elders, which were organized into synods. Although there were multiple differences and denominations within Presbyterianism, they shared the distinctive commonalities of a Calvinist creed and church governance from the bottom up. Representatives or elders within the congregation elected a minister and assisted him in daily responsibilities; issues involving neighboring congregations were addressed at regular presbytery meetings; matters

Map 1.1 Borderlands to borderland: Migrations to Ulster.

pertaining to the entire church were discussed annually by the synod, a group of ministers; and theological, financial, and other matters were typically discussed by the assembly as a whole. Needless to say, Presbyterians regarded the established church with distrust.

As colonizing Protestants, Ulster Presbyterians stood above the native Irish Catholics, although their position depended upon English power. They were comparatively affluent and occupied the best lands. They did not suffer the restrictions under the Penal Laws, enacted by the Irish Parliament from the 1690s onward, which prohibited Catholics from holding a commission in the army, entering a profession, possessing weapons, and studying law or medicine. Nevertheless, the so-called Test Act imposed during Queen Anne's reign required anyone who wished to hold public office to first take communion within the Anglican Church of Ireland, effectively preventing dissenters as well as Catholics from holding public office.[35] Ulster Presbyterians had freedom of worship but not equality. They had to pay tithes to the Anglican Church; they retained land rather than owning it, and they were largely excluded from political office. Sent to Ireland by the British government to occupy space between the English and the native Irish, they now occupied a middle rung between a landowning Anglican elite and a dispossessed Catholic majority.[36]

The experience of being a Presbyterian minority in Catholic Ireland had an enduring and defining impact on the colonizers, and Presbyterianism became a defining characteristic and enduring core of Scotch-Irish identity in America.[37] Protestants constituted only a quarter to a third of the Irish population, but 75 percent of the transatlantic emigrant population between 1700 and 1776. About 70 percent of those were Ulster Presbyterians, with some Anglo-Irish Episcopalians and others mixed in. The Presbyterian migrations of the eighteenth century were small compared to the mass migrations of Catholic Irish in the nineteenth century, although between 150,000 and 200,000 people departed, constituting a significant loss of population from a country of 2–3 million and from a Presbyterian community of 400,000–600,000. While the main motives for migration were economic rather than religious, many emigrants, or their descendants, claimed they left to escape religious and political oppression, and they cited tithes as a major factor. In their view, history was a morality play in which they were Old Testament Israelites escaping Anglican pharaoh landlords.[38]

Coming to America

Ulster Scots who migrated to America, then, were already a people in motion. Some of the people who set out in the first waves of emigration to America may well have been part of the last great immigration of Scots to Ulster in the 1690s. For these people, leaving Ulster was not abandoning their identity; it was an expression and continuation of their identity of a people in search of a promised land.[39]

The first British colonies in North America were established overwhelmingly by English people,[40] and many came from the nobility, the gentry, and the yeoman classes. By the end of the seventeenth century, however, the populations of the colonies were becoming less English, as other groups crossed the Atlantic and enslaved Africans began to satisfy American demands for labor. Most immigrants in the eighteenth century were non-English and came from the poorer classes in Germany, Switzerland, Scotland, and Ireland.

An estimated 110,000 German-speaking immigrants, fleeing famine, war, and disease in Europe, arrived in the American colonies by the time of the American Revolution.[41] They came from many different regions—the Palatine, Alsace, Baden, Bavaria, Hesse, and Switzerland—and their migrations were part of larger population movements within German lands. They tended to migrate together and settle together. William Penn invited German Quakers, Moravians, and Mennonites to settle in Pennsylvania, and several thousand did so in the late 1600s. In the early 1700s, thousands of German Lutherans and Reformed settlers arrived, attracted by the promise of cheap land and religious toleration. Since they spoke Deutsch, they became known as Pennsylvania Dutch, although some people of that name actually were Dutch, from the border regions of Holland and Germany. Germans in the Delaware Valley mingled with French, Dutch, Swedes, Danes, Finns, Scots, Irish, English, Delawares, and other Algonquian-speaking people. People of German descent also settled throughout the colonies—in Maine, New York, New Jersey, Maryland, Virginia, Georgia, and the Carolinas. The path of eighteenth-century German settlement can be seen in place names like Herkimer, Mannheim, and New Berlin in New York; Germantown, Bethlehem, Hanover, and Gettysburg, in Pennsylvania; Fredericksburg, Virginia; and New Bern, South Carolina. German place names, languages, and customs became prevalent in the mid-Atlantic region. Benjamin Franklin, seeing German population growth in Pennsylvania by mid-century, feared that they would "swarm into our settlements, and by herding together, establish their language and manners, to the exclusion of ours."[42]

Irish immigrants also troubled Franklin. He was concerned that the situation in Ireland, where absentee Anglo-Irish landlords controlled most of the land, should not be replicated in Pennsylvania, and he looked toward including Irish immigrants as part of a multiethnic community in Pennsylvania. However, he also worried that the influx of Irish laborers would drive down wages and pose a threat to social and economic stability.[43]

The Scotch-Irish migration that concerned Franklin and other Pennsylvania officials came as part of the last of four great migrations identified by David Hackett Fischer from the British Isles to North America before the American Revolution. From 1629, when the Great Migration began with the settlement of Boston, until 1640, the mainstream comprised English Puritans from the eastern areas of England, such as East Anglia, to Massachusetts. Puritans eventually dominated the colonies of Massachusetts, Rhode Island, Connecticut, and New Hampshire. In the mid-seventeenth century there was substantial migration from Kent, Devon, Warwickshire, and Northamptonshire to Virginia. Between 1675 and 1715, Quakers from the North Midlands fueled a steady migration to the Delaware Valley. For most of the eighteenth century, however, emigrants from the northern counties and Celtic borderlands—Ulster, Scotland, Northumberland, Yorkshire, and Lancashire—dominated British migration to America and spearheaded the European invasion of Indian country.[44]

Estimates of the numbers of emigrants from Ireland are often guesstimates because early immigration records are incomplete. Between 50,000 and 100,000 people left Ireland for America in the seventeenth century; most of them were Catholics from the south, and many went to the West Indies.[45] In 1707, William Penn's provincial secretary James Logan, himself a Quaker from Lurgen in Ulster, informed Penn that two emigrants had just arrived in Philadelphia from the north of Ireland via Maryland; one of them, "a most extraordinary young man" named Patrick Henderson, he thought was Scotch by birth. "Of such as these, the more always the better," he added.[46] Many more followed, although the first substantial emigration from Northern Ireland to North America did not occur until after 1714. Perhaps 3,000 people emigrated from Ulster to North America between 1680 and 1716; between 4,500 and 7,000 from 1717 to 1719; and about 20,000 in the 1720s. Fifty thousand may have made the journey from 1730 to the start of the French and Indian War, although some figures may be inflated; the historian Bernard Bailyn found "no realistic figure" for Scotch-Irish migration before 1760.[47] An estimated 28,000 Scotch-Irish emigrated to America between 1771 and 1775. A commonly accepted estimate suggests that 200,000 to 250,000 Scotch-Irish people emigrated to America before 1775, although many scholars consider that number too high. One historian estimates "more than 100,000." Another concludes that "a reliable minimum" of 150,000 Scotch-Irish came to America between the 1680s and 1810, "possibly more, arguably many more." According to some historians, Irish immigrants outnumbered any other white immigrant group in colonial America.[48]

The French American writer Hector St. John de Crèvecoeur observed in *Letters from an American Farmer*, published in 1782, that "the rich stay in Europe, it is only the middling and poor that emigrate."[49] As in all migrations, however, push-and-pull factors motivated people to move. Irish migration in the eighteenth century was facilitated by transportation systems that had already developed in bringing German immigrants to America and by trade networks between Ireland and Philadelphia in particular. Close ties between Scotland and Ireland and growing ties between Ireland and Pennsylvania meant that migration from the north of Ireland fluctuated in response to conditions at home and opportunities in the colonies as the British state expanded its reach over the Atlantic world.[50]

Linen was the most significant Irish export. In 1696, England allowed Irish linens duty-free entry to the English market. By 1715, Ireland was forbidden to export into England any livestock or livestock products except wool, and was forbidden to export raw wool or woolen products to any foreign country except England, but was free to export linen goods and provisions to the colonies. As a result, Northern Ireland became dependent on the linen trade. Throughout the eighteenth century, linen exports comprised about half of Ireland's total exports, and flaxseed for the manufacture of linen became a major import from the American colonies. Linen cloth exports rose from half a million yards in 1698 to more than 40 million yards per year a century later. Life in Ulster's many market towns revolved around the yarn and cloth trade, and by the late eighteenth century almost every rural household was involved in spinning or weaving linen. A skilled weaver could earn 1 shilling (12 pence) a day, while his wife earned 3 or 4 pence spinning linen, often as side income to supplement farming. (Wages in Ulster were higher than other areas, but rural wages were typically lower than in metropolitan Dublin.[51]) The manufacturers exploited this rural proletariat, who became increasingly dependent on fluctuating linen prices as their numbers grew and rents rose steadily while the size of their holdings shrank through subdivision. Philadelphia supplied Ireland with grain and flour, lumber, and, especially, flaxseed. The ships usually departed in the fall and sailed to Belfast and Londonderry. They returned in the spring and summer to New

Castle in Delaware and Philadelphia, their holds filled with paying cargos of emigrants whenever hard times struck and whenever the linen industry tanked. The emigrants helped fulfill the demand for labor in the colonies. Flaxseed and emigrants established a new commercial relationship and determined the rhythm of transatlantic trade between northern Irish ports and the American colonies. This "trade in strangers" was a lucrative business for merchants, agents, and ship captains, offering passengers a regular means of crossing the ocean.[52]

Migrations from the north of Ireland came in waves, driven by rising rents, low wages, high food costs, famines, and poor crops, with major influxes in 1717–1720, 1725–1729, 1740–1741, 1754–1755, and 1771–1775.[53] The first substantial emigrations to North America, the 1717–1720 influx, took place because the generous leases that had been offered to attract newcomers to Ulster in the seventeenth century began to expire. When the Ulster Plantation was established, undertakers were prohibited from raising rents for one hundred years as an incentive to encourage and sustain settlement. When the ban expired, landlords consolidated farms, doubled or even tripled rents, and adopted a policy of "rack renting," giving leases to the highest bidder instead of simply renewing the leases of old tenants. A series of natural disasters added to the misery. Drought started in 1714 and the dry seasons persisted through the next six years. There were severe frosts, crop failures, sheep "rot"—a form of hoof infection—in 1716, smallpox in 1718, and soaring food prices. Religious issues had of course been a source of discontent for years, but economic hardship pushed thousands of distressed people for the first time to consider exchanging the poverty of a life they knew for the hope of an unknown way of life.[54] Jonathan Dickinson, a minister and central figure of the Great Awakening, wrote from Philadelphia in October 1717 that "many hundreds" had arrived from the north of Ireland in about four months. In October 1719 he reported that twelve or thirteen ships from the north of Ireland had arrived during the summer, bringing "a swarm of people."[55]

The second wave, 1725–1729, was so large that the English Parliament became concerned and appointed a commission to investigate the causes of emigration.[56] About 5,000 people from Ireland, including 3,500 from Ulster, were said to have landed in America in two years.[57] In July 1728, seventeen ships in Northern Ireland ports were taking on emigrants for Pennsylvania and New England. Irish migration to America that year reached 3,000 for the first time. Hugh Boulter, the primate of Ireland, informed the Duke of

Newcastle in July, "we have hundreds of families (all protestants) moving out of the north to *America*." He complained that agents from the American colonies "deluded the people with stories of great plenty" while those who left complained of high food prices and "the oppressions they suffer here." What Boulter called "the infatuation" for going to the West Indies was still spreading at the end of the year, and what he described to the Archbishop of Canterbury as a "frenzy" persisted into the next: "the humour of going to America still continues, and the scarcity of provisions certainly makes many quit us," he wrote Newcastle in March. The "strange humors" that drove these people to America stemmed from a succession of bad harvests—1729 was a year of famine following years of famine—and the effects of a century of imperial policy. Between high food costs, high rents, and high tithes, people were "sorely distressed." Seven vessels left Belfast carrying 1,000 people in March 1729; by July 25, more had left Londonderry for America with 3,500 passengers. Estimates indicate more than 4,000, and perhaps as many as 6,000 Irish emigrants disembarked at the Delaware River ports of Philadelphia and Newcastle that year.[58] In May, Pennsylvania, which had recurrent concerns about the influx of Germans, passed an "Act for laying a Duty on Foreigners & Irish Servants, &c. imported into the Province."[59]

The winter of 1739–1740 in the north of Ireland, the beginning of the third influx, was known as "the time of the black frost." Cattle and sheep died, crops failed, and an estimated 400,000 people died in Ireland in the famine of 1740–1741, producing another surge in emigration.[60] Crop failures again in 1755 caused food shortages, reduced employment, and another surge in emigration—the fourth influx.[61] People in Northern Ireland enjoyed greater prosperity than the rest of the country. "No sooner did we enter Ulster than we noticed the difference," wrote the itinerant Methodist preacher John Wesley in 1756. "The ground was cultivated just as in England, and the cottages not only neat, but with doors, chimneys, and windows."[62] Nevertheless, the linen-dependent economy was fragile and emigration recurrent.

In the twenty-five years between 1750 and the outbreak of the Revolution, 442 ships sailed directly to America from Ulster ports, carrying linen and immigrants and most having carried flax across the Atlantic to Ireland.[63] The flow of emigrants rose steadily from 1763 to 1773. Newspapers advertised 194 vessels leaving northern Irish ports with emigrants to America in the 1760s, the peak years being 1766 and 1767; 165 of them were engaged in the linen trade and more than 90 percent sailed to Philadelphia and New York.[64] There was a sharp increase in emigration when rack renting reached new heights in the north of Ireland in the late 1760s and early 1770s, the fifth influx, and then a slump in the linen trade in 1771–1772, with food scarcities and high bread prices. More than 55,000 Protestant Irish emigrated to America between 1760 and 1775, some 30,000 between 1770 and 1775.[65] The numbers caused concerns in Ireland about depopulation and in London, where the Board of Trade reported in 1772 that emigration from Great Britain and Ireland had "increased to a very alarming degree."[66]

Touring Ireland in the late 1770s, English agriculturalist Arthur Young was eager to discover the causes of the emigrations "which made so much noise in the north of Ireland." Although he was assured that those who left were principally "idle people," the poor and unemployed who would not be missed, many weavers and spinners and their families emigrated. At Belfast, where the emigrations were greatest, he was told that about 2,000 people had departed every year for many years. Emigration had peaked in 1772 and 1773 with a decline in the linen trade. People stopped going when the American Revolution broke out in 1775, but at Lurgen he was told that "if the war ends in favor of the Americans, they will go off in shoals." Young noted that the usual recourse of factory hands thrown out of employment was to enlist, but in the north of Ireland linen manufacturers who were made idle would rather sell their property and cattle to pay for passage to America than join the military. "The spirit of emigrating in Ireland appeared to be confined to two circumstances, the Presbyterian religion and the linen manufacture," Young concluded; "when the linen trade was low, the passenger trade was high."[67]

While crop failures, downturns in the linen industry, and rent racking at home and the attraction of landownership in the colonies motivated migration from Ulster to America, it was spurred on by letters, sermons, and newspaper advertisements.[68] Emigrants wrote letters home that prompted more emigration. Positive reports from friends, neighbors, and family members who had gone before convinced many people that the voyage to America was a risk worth taking. Land agents and shipping agents promoted emigration in person, in the press, and through contacts on both sides of the Atlantic. Many of the most effective promoters were immigrants themselves.[69] Hugh McCulloch (from Ulster) in North Carolina, William Johnson (from County Meath) in New York, and James Patton (from Ulster) in Virginia all planted settlements of immigrants.[70]

Most Ulster emigrants left from one of five ports: Newry in County Down, Belfast, Londonderry, and Larne and Portrush in County Antrim.[71] Voyages of eight to ten weeks across the Atlantic were standard during the eighteenth century. Under normal conditions, it took about fifty days to reach Philadelphia and Newcastle on the Delaware, if departure was between July and September, the most popular time to leave (longer if the departure was earlier). After Philadelphia, Charleston became the second most attractive American port for vessels from Ulster during the 1760s, many of them coming from Larne. The longer journey to Charleston was usually made in the fall and took eight or nine weeks.[72] During the crossing, emigrants endured disease, a lack of sanitation, poor food, hunger, seasickness, and storms. Although generally lower than on ships carrying German emigrants, convicts, British soldiers to the West Indies, or Africans crammed aboard slave ships in chains, mortality rates among Ulster emigrants on transatlantic voyages were sometimes appalling.[73] Portholes and other forms of ventilations were virtually unknown before the American Revolution; smallpox, dysentery, and typhus thrived in cramped and damp conditions, and shortages of food and water were common.

For example, the sloop *Seaflower* sailed from Belfast on July 10, 1741, with 108 passengers. By the time it reached Philadelphia on October 31, it had lost its captain and 40 passengers "through hunger and want of provisions." Some of the survivors had resorted to cannibalism.[74] John Smilie of County Down sailed from Belfast in the spring of 1762. Delayed by calms and contrary winds, the voyage lasted nearly fifteen weeks, creating severe shortages of food and water. Sixty-four crew members died, and the cries of distressed children and mothers unable to relieve them turned the ship into, as Smilie put it, "a real Spectacle of Horror." Smilie survived, however, and described the voyage in a letter to his parents from his new home on the Susquehanna in Lancaster County, Pennsylvania, in November.[75] In 1767, an epidemic broke out on the *Nancy* sailing from Belfast to South Carolina. The owners, Samuel Jackson of Philadelphia and Robert Well of Belfast, had crammed 300 people in its hold to claim the bounties offered by South Carolina. Thirty or so people died at sea; more died after docking in Charleston. The conditions were so bad that South Carolina authorities refused to pay the *Nancy*'s owners the bounty money. Henry Laurens, who was serving in the Assembly, said he had seen nothing during ten or twelve years in the African slave trade to equal "the Cruelty exercised upon these poor Irish." Slavers took some care of their wretched cargo to sell them at the slave markets, "but no other care was taken of those poor Protestant Christians from Ireland but to deliver as many as possible alive on Shoar upon the cheapest terms, no matter how they fared upon their Voyage nor in what condition they were landed." The *Britannia*, carrying 250 families from Belfast to Georgia, suffered an outbreak of smallpox and measles that killed 29 children and had to be quarantined upon arrival.[76] Twenty-five children died of smallpox on the ship *James and Henry* sailing from Larne to New York in 1773. Almost 140 emigrants were reported to have died from sickness on another voyage the following year. In 1785, the ship *Faithful Steward* that had crossed from Derry with 249 passengers ran aground off Cape Henlopen; only 68 people were saved.[77]

John O'Raw, a schoolmaster and an emigrant from north Antrim, experienced a particularly disastrous voyage to Charleston in 1806–1807. After his ship departed Belfast, it was nearly wrecked on the coast of Donegal. Three weeks of storms and headwinds drove it into the Bay of Biscay off the French coast. Many of the passengers fell ill with dysentery and a child died. The weather continued to be dreadful for six weeks, with thunderstorms and lightning, and O'Raw was deathly sick for four weeks. After nearly two months being blown about on the Atlantic, the ship was wrecked on the coast of Bermuda. The passengers were saved but lost most of their possessions. When they went to the island's capital, most of O'Raw's friends were forcibly conscripted into the British Navy. O'Raw and his remaining companions hid out in remote areas of the island until they were able to chart a small vessel to carry them to Charleston. More violent storms nearly sank that ship as well. O'Raw finally made it to Charleston, after a voyage of more than five months. Immigrants arriving in Charleston's notoriously unhealthy climate had to survive a "seasoning" period of about six months, and even though O'Raw left Charleston for the healthier South Carolina upcountry, he was ill with fever for four months and almost died before he could resume his occupation as a schoolmaster. Like many immigrants, he was able to rely on a network of kin and friends who had gone before. He attained a degree of prosperity, became an American citizen, and served his adopted country in the War of 1812. In the 1820s, though, he returned home to County Antrim, where he died in in 1841.[78]

Between 1720 and 1770, passage across the Atlantic, including provisions, cost between £3.5s and £9. Emigrants who intended to farm needed an additional £10 for inland transportation, fees for land grants, tools and seeds, and so on, amounting to more than a year's wages for most weavers and laborers.

Most emigrants could not afford such costs and secured free passage in exchange for indenting their service, bound to labor for four to seven years in return for passage, food, clothing, lodging, and the promise of freedom and some material reward when their term of service was over. Some were bound to the shipmaster, who sold his indenture on arrival in America; some paid back the cost of passage after arriving and indenting on the best terms they could find. Before the Revolution, more than half and perhaps as many as two-thirds of Irish immigrants came to America as indentured servants, bound by contract to work for colonial masters for a period of years to pay off their passage. According to one estimate, 100,000 Scotch-Irish came to America as indentured servants in the eighteenth century. Whereas only 12 percent of Pennsylvania's indentured servants were Irish-born in the 1680s, nearly 94 percent were Irish in the 1740s.[79]

During 1745 and 1746, 529 Irish immigrants were bound to masters in Philadelphia. Among them, in October 1745, Robert Black, the seven-year-old son of widow Elizabeth Black "(who was likewise present and expressed her consent)" bound himself as a servant to Adam Hodge, a baker in Philadelphia County, for thirteen years and five months "in consideration of his being educated and maintained, and his being taught to read and write." At the expiration of his term, Robert was "to have one suit of new apparel besides his old ones." In the spring of 1746, William Rankin assigned a steady stream of servants newly arrived from Ireland to various people. And in September of that year, as recorded, "Daniel McKendry on consideration of £14: paid [to] Robert Blair for his passage from Ireland indents himself servant to Thomas McMollin of Chester County, weaver, for five years and a half from this date, to be taught the trade of a weaver, and to have customary dues." A good number of servants, perhaps as many as one-fifth, were bound to Irish or Scotch-Irish masters.[80] There tended to be fewer indentured servants and more tradesmen in the new wave of migration from Ulster after the American Revolution, allowing them greater freedom of movement on arrival.[81]

In all, approximately 400,000 emigrants from Ireland settled in North America between the late 1600s and the end of the Napoleonic wars in 1815. Perhaps two-thirds of them were Presbyterians, and the vast majority of the Presbyterians and perhaps half of the Catholics and many of the Anglicans and other Protestants came from Ulster. Many of the others came from counties bordering on Ulster.[82] Ulster Scots stood out from Catholic Irish emigrants, from whom they kept their distance. But distinctive Scotch-Irish communities also evolved because Ulster women emigrated as well, something not replicated elsewhere in Ireland, except Dublin, until the nineteenth century.[83]

By the time of the first United States census in 1790, Irish-born Americans and their descendants constituted one-eighth of the white population in New York, a quarter in Pennsylvania, more than a quarter in Georgia and South Carolina, between a quarter and a third in Kentucky and Tennessee, and one-sixth in Maryland and Virginia.[84] The numbers of immigrants were relatively small compared with the mass migrations of Irish people in the nineteenth century, perhaps, but were enormous in proportion to contemporary population levels in Ulster, Ireland, and America. In the late 1750s, there were probably fewer than half a million Presbyterians in Ulster, and only about 2.4 million people in the whole of Ireland; the population of Britain's North American mainland colonies was about 1.5 million, white and Black. As late as 1790, Ireland's population was only about 4 million, and the United States had 3.23 million white inhabitants. In other words, migration from Ulster had dramatic consequences in Ireland and America. Early Irish migrants and their offspring became a significant presence in many seaports and inland towns, and those who moved on dominated frontier settlement. All played important roles in the social conflicts, economic developments, religious revivals, and political upheavals that created and shaped the new American nation.[85]

Ulster emigration did not end with the America Revolution; in fact, it continued at high or higher levels in the three decades after the Revolution.[86] More Ulster Presbyterians (and other Irish immigrants) migrated to the United States in the half century or so after the Revolution than had left Ireland for Britain's North American colonies in the one hundred years before 1776.[87] Between the end of the Napoleonic Wars in 1815 and the onset of the Great Famine thirty years later, Irish emigration to America numbered between 800,000 and 1,000,000, about twice the total for the preceding two hundred years.

However, the character and composition of the emigration was changing significantly. In the prolonged postwar economic crisis, the emigration impulse spread far beyond Ulster to all parts of Ireland, and the emigrants became increasingly Catholic and poor. Ulster Protestants were still the majority in the mid-1820s and comprised about 50 percent from 1827 to 1835, but by the early 1840s most emigrants were poor Catholics from southern Ireland.[88] The Great Famine, generally set between 1845 and 1852, sent emigration soaring. Between 1845 and 1870, more than 3 million people left Ireland, most for the United States. By 1911, Ireland's population was only 4.4 million, almost half what it had been before the famines (8.2 million).[89]

The migration of the people who became the Scotch-Irish in North America was part of broader Irish historical experience of migration and diaspora, and of a momentous shift of human population that changed the world on both sides of the Atlantic.[90] Writing at a time (in the 1830s) when "the ultimate results of American migration to the west are still hidden in the future," Alexis de Tocqueville foresaw that it would spread across the continent from the Atlantic to the Pacific:

> So the European quits his hovel to go and dwell on the transatlantic coast, while the American who was born there moves off in turn into the central solitudes of America. This double movement of immigration never halts; it starts from the depths of Europe, continues across the great ocean, and then goes on through the solitudes of the New World.... Nothing in history is comparable to this continuous movement of mankind except perhaps that which followed the fall of the Roman Empire.

Tocqueville attributed the driving force of this movement to the energy and industry of "the English race" who became Anglo-Americans.[91] The people and the process he described, however, were largely Scotch-Irish.

Like their Delaware neighbors who had built a new world on the back of the giant turtle after journeying out of darkness, the people who became the Scotch-Irish built their new world and their sense of themselves through migration and mobility. Propelled across the Irish Sea and then the Atlantic Ocean, they pushed on into the interior of America, adding new migration experiences to their foundational myths. Like many Indian peoples, they believed the Creator had found the best place for his people. And if, as their history suggested they would, they had to fight for their place in the promised land, their stern Calvinist Old Testament religion armed them with a theology for dealing with the heathens they found there: "When the Lord your God brings you into the land which you are entering to take possession of it, and clears away many nations before you . . . then you must utterly destroy them; you shall make no covenant with them, and show no mercy to them" (Deuteronomy 7:1–2). Dispossessing the Indigenous inhabitants, they would, eventually, claim for themselves the role of original people in the land they occupied.

2
Valley Paths to Native Lands

Simple overviews of American expansion suggest that settler colonialism spread across the continent, engulfing Indian country like a tidal wave. The flood seems natural, inevitable, and irresistible, and perhaps it was. However, the Scotch-Irish invasion of Native America did not surge from east to west in a single tide. Rather, it seeped along river valleys, some of which ran north and south. It grew into an arc of Scotch-Irish settlement running the length of the colonies, as immigrants first pushed west from coastal ports and then they and their children tracked southwest, following the valleys that served as migration highways. It was made up of streams of people in motion who entered Indian worlds that were also in motion, as tribal peoples relocated and jostled for position, and it pooled and sometimes reversed course when it came up against Indigenous resistance. Indian peoples often defined their homelands by river valleys and waterways governed Indigenous conceptions of space.[1] Unlike mountain chains that separated people, valleys served as pathways, bringing people into contact. When Scotch-Irish and other settler colonists arrived, however, they brought people into conflict as they competed for fertile valley lands.

In the early eighteenth century, when Scotch-Irish immigration to North America began to gather momentum, the British colonies constituted a narrow strip of territory along the Atlantic seaboard. In the seventeenth century, Europeans had established a series of footholds—the French on the St. Lawrence River and the Great Lakes; the Dutch on the Hudson; Swedes and Finns along the Delaware River; Spaniards in New Mexico and Florida; and the English in the Chesapeake and New England, along with some Germans and Scots—and began the creation of their New World societies, sometimes using imported African slave labor, and usually with devastating effects for Indigenous peoples. In 1650, perhaps fifty thousand Europeans lived on the eastern shores of North America. New France had a mere two thousand colonists; New Netherland, a little over three thousand; and New England already outstripped its rivals with more than twenty-two thousand. In 1680, the European population edged toward one hundred fifty thousand. By 1750, that number had jumped over one million, and settler colonists pushed into the interior in growing numbers.

Internal population growth in the eighteenth century occurred less by natural causes than by massive immigration. Immigrants from Europe, often victims themselves of wrenching economic changes, land enclosures, community destruction, and population dislocation, resettled large areas of North America. They came from dozens of countries, hundreds of regions, and thousands of communities, leaving a continent where land was scarce, heavily populated, and beyond most people's reach, for a world where land was plentiful, supposedly unoccupied, and "free." Unlike nineteenth-century immigration, pre-industrial immigration was not primarily an urban phenomenon, in which Old World peasants were transformed into city dwellers; the newcomers gravitated to the frontier and settled on American land rather than in American cities.[2]

Directed by the geography of the country they invaded, as well as by the resources it offered, Scotch-Irish colonists trekked south and west but also, in some cases, north and east, in waves of migration and settlement (see Map 2.1). They migrated in groups and settled in clusters of families, friends, or religious communities as they moved down or crossed through the Appalachians.[3] Once the earliest and wealthiest families began to create settled societies in one area, newer arrivals, poorer emigrants, and younger people—sometimes the children or grandchildren of the original colonists—would push farther into new backcountry areas and start the process over again.[4] Often, as Scotch-Irish departed from locations they had colonized, other peoples arrived to take their places, in larger numbers, so that the distinctive Scotch-Irish character of a particular community diminished or disappeared in one area to resurface in another. By the time of the American Revolution, the Scotch-Irish had created communities in Indian country from Maine to Georgia. In the process they rubbed shoulders and exchanged blows with Native Americans. Having displaced the native Irish in Ulster, they repeatedly displaced the Indigenous inhabitants in America.

North from Boston

On a Sunday morning in June 1718 in the thatched Presbyterian meetinghouse at Aghadowey in County Londonderry, a minister named James McGregor addressed his congregation of poor tenant farmers, weavers,

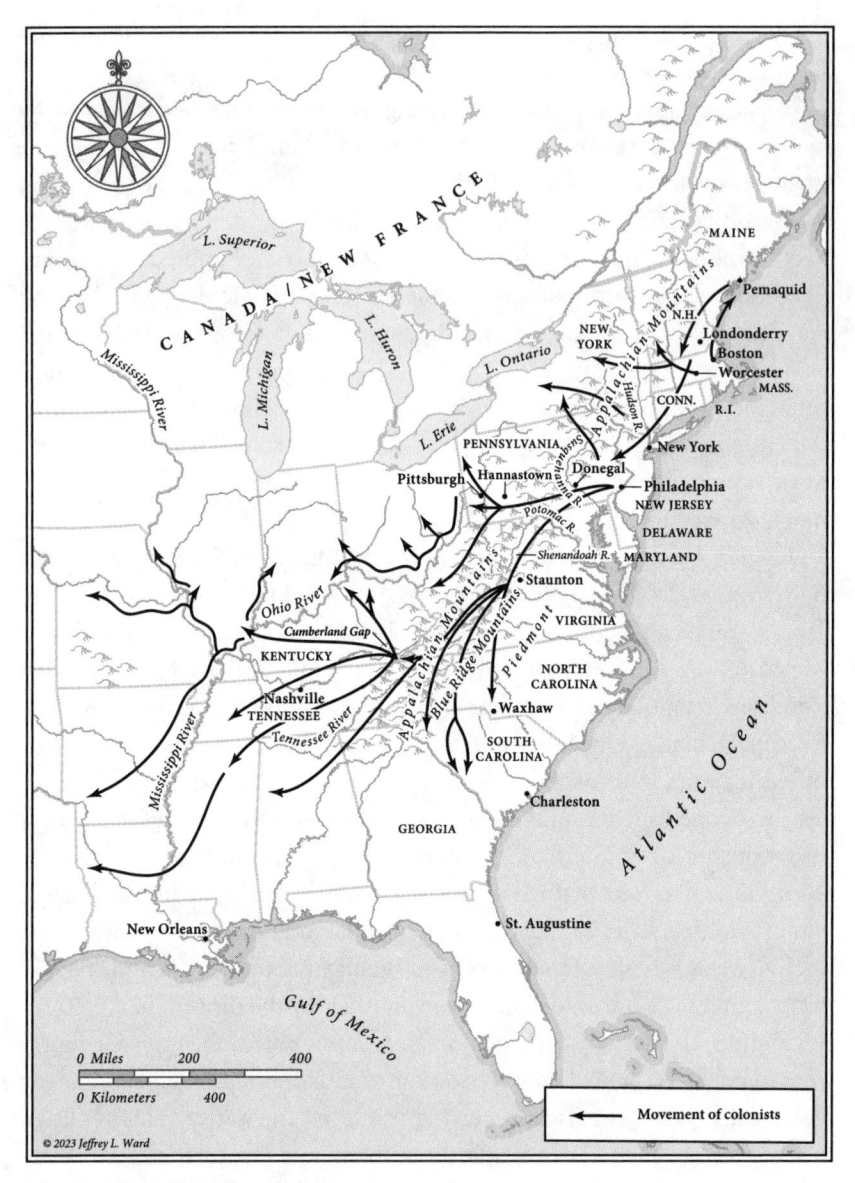

Map 2.1 Scotch-Irish migrations in America.

landless laborers, and their families. "Brethren, let us depart for God has appointed a new country for us to dwell in," he told them. "It is called New England. Let us be free of these Pharaohs, these rackers of rents and screwers of tithes and let us go into the land of Canaan. We are the Lord's own people and he shall divide the ocean before us." In the seventeenth century there had been a trickle of emigration from Ulster to Maryland (the first distinctively Scotch-Irish settlement in America was established on the eastern shore of Maryland between 1649 and 1669) and some Irish emigration to Massachusetts, but McGregor's group marked the start of mass migration. McGregor organized five ships to carry members of his and neighboring congregations from Londonderry to Boston.[5]

Boston newspapers reported fifteen vessels arriving from Ireland in 1718, bringing about 1,000 people. Between 1718 and 1720 about forty vessels from Northern Ireland disembarked perhaps 2,600 emigrants at Boston, most of them in families.[6] The first arrivals endured a hard winter. In December 1718, the Massachusetts House of Representatives directed that 150 bushels of Indian corn should be provided at public expense "to the Poor *Irish* People." The next year, the House had to take measures to quarantine passengers who arrived in Boston aboard a ship from Ireland carrying smallpox. The governor of Massachusetts directed the Boston selectmen "to take the proper care, to prevent the heavy charge, likely to arise to this Town, by the coming in of poor People from Abroad, especially those that come from *Ireland*."[7]

Needy Scotch-Irish Presbyterians met a cold reception from New England Puritans, although the Reverend Cotton Mather and other leaders saw the potential for redirecting them to the frontiers, where few English had settled, as buffers against Indians. As ships from Ireland docked in Boston harbor in the summer of 1718, Thomas Lechmere, surveyor-general of Customs in the city, wrote to his brother-in-law John Winthrop in Connecticut (the son of Governor John Winthrop of Massachusetts) expressing his fears that "all the North of Ireland will be over here in a little time" and that "these confounded Irish will eat us all up, provisions being most extravagantly dear, & scarce of all sorts." Contrary to what Winthrop might have heard, said Lechmere, most Irish immigrants were not servants. "They are generally men of estates, & are come hither for no other reason but upon encouragement sent from hence upon notice given that they should have so many acres of land given them gratis to settle our frontiers as a barrier against the Indians."[8]

After a quarter century of conflict with the French that ended, temporarily it turned out, with the close of Queen Anne's War in 1713, New England expanded its frontiers to the west and northeast. The governments of Massachusetts Bay and New Hampshire made grants of land, set off as townships, to proprietors, who in turn needed to attract colonists to settle the lands.[9] Scotch-Irish immigrants moved away from Boston in search of farmland. They settled at Pelham, Coleraine, and Worcester in western Massachusetts. Although only fifty miles from Boston, Worcester was still a frontier outpost with some two hundred inhabitants living in log cabins. It had been abandoned in King Philip's War in 1675 and again in 1702 during Queen Anne's War. Although the Scotch-Irish provided additional protection and contributed to the town's defensive measures when an Indian war broke out in 1722, there were conflicts with Congregationalists and a mob tore down the immigrants' meeting house and drove them north and west. Worcester became a feeder for Scotch-Irish settlements throughout western New England. From western Massachusetts, some colonists moved north into what is now Vermont, settling on the west bank of the Connecticut River in what became Orange and Caledonia counties. Others settled in southern New Hampshire, and along the Kennebec and Casco Bay in Maine. In almost every place in New England where Scotch-Irish people arrived, they were encouraged or compelled to move to the frontiers where they could provide protection for older communities against Indians and the French.[10]

At the end of October 1718, James McGregor submitted a petition to the Massachusetts General Court for a grant of land for twenty-eight Ulster families then in Boston and forty others still in Ireland. Two weeks later, one John Armstrong and thirty-four other Irish immigrants petitioned the House of Representatives for a grant of land at Casco Bay. About three hundred people sailed north from Boston to search out places for settlement on the coast of Maine. Most of them selected the Casco Bay–Falmouth area, although some moved on to Kennebec. But after a miserable winter, most sailed back south. Some went to Pennsylvania. Others—sixteen or twenty families depending on the source—entered the Merrimack River and followed it upstream until they found an unoccupied tract on West Running Creek, where they settled at Nutfield, the future Londonderry, in the spring of 1719.[11]

The area was disputed between Massachusetts and New Hampshire, and various individuals based competing land claims on different Indian deeds. To counter charges that the Scotch-Irish had occupied the land illegally and violently, and to strengthen their claim by having acquired aboriginal title, McGregor sent Governor Samuel Shute a petition from Nutfield in February 1720. The site was not disputed by the original inhabitants nor wrested from them by force, he wrote, "Seeing no body in the Least offered to hinder us to Settle down in a desolate Wilderness." After settling there, they found that two or three different parties claimed Nutfield "by virtue of Indian deeds, and we were Given to understand, that it was Necessary for us to *hold the Soil by Some Right purchased from the Natives.*" Accordingly, they applied to Colonel Wheelwright of Wells and obtained "his Deed being of Ninety Years Standing, and Conveyed from the Chiefe Sagamores between the Rivers of Merrimack and Piscattaqua, wth the Consent of the whole Tribe of the Indian Nation."[12] Many Pennacook, Amoskeag, and other Indigenous inhabitants of the region had migrated north to villages such as Odanak (St. Francis) on the St. Lawrence River, but the region was hardly as unoccupied as the newcomers claimed or imagined.[13]

By April 1721, the settlement had grown to 360 people. The government of New Hampshire gave it full incorporation in 1722, and the residents renamed it Londonderry the next year. Reverend David McClure, whose grandfather emigrated from Northern Ireland to Boston in 1729, said that Londonderry then was a frontier outpost, "exposed to the depredations of Indians." It was basically a settlement of log cabins with two stone garrison houses as places of refuge. The inhabitants distributed land, built sawmills and gristmills, laid out highways, and erected and funded a meetinghouse. During all the French and Indian wars, Londonderry was never attacked; local legend attributed it to the story that James McGregor and the Marquis de Vaudreuil, governor of Quebec in the 1720s, had been schoolmates in the Netherlands.[14]

Londonderry was the most successful Scotch-Irish settlement in New England. The Reverend James MacSparran, an Irish clergyman in Rhode Island, described it in 1752 as "all *Irish*, and famed for Industry, and Riches."[15] It attracted emigrants from Ulster and, as Scotch-Irish settlers spread out across the countryside, it also served as a feeder community for a second generation of satellite Scotch-Irish communities in the Merrimack Valley and beyond, although those towns were more ethnically mixed, sometimes with an English majority and the Scotch-Irish minority living in one section. Matthew Patten, who was born in Ireland in 1719 and emigrated with his father in 1728, became one of the first settlers of the neighboring township of Bedford in 1738. He was also one of the most successful and kept a diary that provides detailed accounts of the workings of a New Hampshire Scotch-Irish farm. Others established towns, such as Goffstown, Derryfield, Antrim, Peterborough, and Hillsborough in New Hampshire, and crossed the Connecticut River to Vermont, joining the Scotch-Irish colonists moving northward from Worcester.[16]

Scotch-Irish people in Londonderry and the Merrimack Valley turned much of their acreage over to cultivating flax and developed a thriving linen-manufacturing industry. They also brought the potato—introduced to Europe and Ireland from South America—to New England, and, like their English neighbors, blended European and Native American foods in their diets.[17] In the mid-1700s, Samuel and John Dunlap and their extended family and apprentices, in workshops in Amherst, Henniker, Antrim, Chester, Salisbury, and Goffstown, began making furniture that reflected the cultural heritage and traditions of the region's early Scotch-Irish settlers.[18] Still, New Hampshire Governor Jonathan Belcher noted, "the people of this country seem to have an aversion to them." It was an aversion Belcher shared.[19] As their countrymen would on other frontiers, Scotch-Irish colonists on the New Hampshire frontier felt mistreated and unsupported by the government they saw themselves defending.

The Scotch-Irish dominated early colonial settlements along the eastern shore in Maine, where Boston land speculators recruited immigrants to meet the terms of their land grants.[20] By 1720 about one hundred families lived on the east side of the Kennebec River. Nevertheless, efforts to colonize Maine were pegged back by Indian resistance. In July 1720, Wabanakis threatened the inhabitants of Cork that they would "be knocked on the head if they continued there any longer," which prompted the colonists to beat a hasty retreat downriver. Wabanaki attacks at the start of the conflict generally known as Dummer's War, 1722–1725, sent settlers scurrying from the area around Merrymeeting Bay. Some went to Londonderry, many to Pennsylvania. Others turned up as refugees in Boston, where their names were recorded on the lists of people warned out of town. Nearly all of them were Scotch-Irish. Daniel Hunter and his wife and James Savage and his wife and five children were specifically identified as "Irish people from Small Point." Most of the colonists left the Kennebec region by the end of the decade.[21]

Irish emigrants "suffered the loss of all we had in the world excepting our lives" in Dummer's War, Reverend James McGregor wrote to the Duke of Newcastle and Robert Walpole in January 1727. They were ready and willing to return to their plantations, he said. Many others had recently arrived and petitioned the General Assembly for unappropriated lands to the eastward where, settling together in large numbers, they would have been able to defend themselves against the Indians "and been a strong Frontier to all the Eastern Parts." But the Assembly had rejected the petition. Instead, it passed an act prohibiting further settlements to the north and eastward and withdrew all soldiers from the eastern frontier. As a result, "your Garrison is left entirely to the mercy of the Indians" and many families were "forced to lease their lands and dwellings within his Maj[est]y's cultivated land to the Indians." New England's antipathy against all Presbyterians, the Reverend added, was "very great."[22]

Nevertheless, colonization efforts in the Northeast rebounded after the war. Multiple groups jostled for position in contested areas, angling for boundaries that facilitated their own expansion and trying to limit the expansion of others.[23] Governor Richard Philipps of Nova Scotia claimed that the land between Nova Scotia and New England belonged to his province; Lieutenant Governor of Massachusetts Bay William Dummer (in office until 1730) and Jonathan Belcher, as governor of Massachusetts and New Hampshire from 1730 to 1741, claimed that all the land as far as Nova Scotia was under the government of Massachusetts. New England colonists were eager to expand into lands between the Kennebec and St. Croix rivers, an area the Penobscots had fought to defend in Dummer's War.

In 1729, Colonel David Dunbar, a Scotch-Irish officer and recently appointed surveyor-general of the King's Woods (his job was to stop colonists from poaching the tall white pines reserved for masts for the Royal Navy), arrived in Maine with instructions from the Board of Trade to settle Irish and Palatine Germans between the Kennebec and St. Croix. Dunbar offered generous grants of 50–100 acres of land to each head of family to recruit migrants to his new province, which he called Georgia. Within a few weeks of his arrival, he reported to the Board of Trade, "a great many hundred men of those who came lately from Ireland as well as some English & Irish familys many Years settled here" applied for lands east of the Kennebec. He established six towns in the area, and repaired the old fort at Pemaquid, which the French and Indians had destroyed thirty-three years before, as a defense against Indian attacks, naming it Fort Frederick. He intended to build a colony of Scotch-Irish settlers and hold the region in defiance of Massachusetts's claim to the region. The combative and quick-tempered Dunbar feuded with Massachusetts officials, aggressively enforced laws against cutting trees that might be used for masts for the Royal Navy, and clashed with others who claimed land under old royal grants or Indian deeds.[24]

In a region of overlapping and competing claims, other settlers resented the intrusions of Dunbar's colonists. Some complained of rough treatment at the hands of the Scotch-Irish. Josiah Grover, for example, owned lands at New Harbor which his ancestor had bought from an Indian sachem in 1625. A group of armed Scotch-Irish captured Grover and his crew and seized his schooner and its cargo. Grover managed to escape and made a formal complaint to Governor Belcher and the Council in Boston "of the Evil treatment they had received at the Eastward from the Irish People, which might be enlarged with many more Instances of the like nature too tedious to be inserted."[25]

Looking up the coast from Portsmouth, New Hampshire's Lieutenant Governor Benning Wentworth saw the Scotch-Irish and the fort at Pemaquid as first steps in colonization. There was fine country all the way to Mount Desert Island, he told the Lords of Trade. If Dunbar could "Settle Strong on that Coast" the Indians in a few years "will be obliged to quit that Country, or come into their Living as the English do, for the Settlements will drive all the Hunting far from them, and I don't know but a just Treatment of them in all our Trade will bring them to be our friends."[26]

At first, Dunbar seemed to get along with the Penobscots. He was confident that giving them presents and treating them well would keep them at peace and friendly.[27] Employing John Gyles, a former captive and trader, as his messenger, he informed the Penobscot chiefs of his plans to settle at Pemaquid. They were already aware of what he was doing. Since he was resettling an old site they gave their approval, but warned him not to go beyond the boundaries they had agreed to in their treaty with Massachusetts at the end of Dummer's War. "If you Pass St. Georges River we shall be Vnasy," they said, signing the letter with their totems.[28]

Penobscot leaders visited Dunbar many times at Pemaquid that fall. One delegation stayed for a week in November, meeting with Dunbar during the day and retiring each evening to their encampment nearby. They expressed their desire to live in peace with the colonists; they wanted only to hunt and fish without molestation and to trade their furs at a post where they were not cheated, they said. Masking his ethnocentric and condescending attitudes, Dunbar gave them assurances and presents, and they parted on good terms.[29] Nevertheless, the Penobscots remained concerned that the colonists would encroach beyond the treaty line. They sent Dunbar a message in May 1730 that they would "by no means consent to any Settlements near Penobscot." In his circumstances, Dunbar could hardly force them, "so that I am perplexed which way to behave upon this occasion." He alleged that "Endeavours had been used to set the Indians against him."[30]

In truth, Dunbar appears to have needed little help in alienating people. The king and Privy Council finally decided he had overstepped his authority and he was removed from his position in 1731. The colony of Georgia was officially terminated. Left to fend for themselves, most of the Scotch-Irish families who had settled in the area moved away to other locations.

Some relocated to land on St. George's River offered by the wealthy Boston merchant and land speculator Samuel Waldo, who held a grant between the St. George and Penobscot rivers. Penobscots complained to Belcher that Waldo's title to the land was based on a controversial deed which they had never acknowledged and the settlements were unauthorized. Belcher disliked both Waldo and the Scotch-Irish, and the General Court sided with the Penobscots, who quietly evicted the colonists in 1736.[31] In conference with Belcher in the Council Chamber in Boston that June, the Penobscot delegates Arexis and Espequent reported that Waldo had asked them whether they would prefer to have English or Irish as neighbors. "We said English for tho sometimes we fell out as boys do at play, yet afterwards we were reconciled and got friends again. But as to foreign men we were not acquainted with their manners and did not know their customs." Once again, the Scotch-Irish colonists were left to fend for themselves.[32]

Samuel McCobb, who emigrated in 1728 from County Tyrone, at the age of twenty-one, with his brother and a number of Scotch-Irish families, accepted Dunbar's inducements to settle in the Pemaquid region. He took up 100 acres and built a log cabin at Lobster Cove in Townshend at Boothbay. He recalled many years later that they "lived from the first exposed to the utmost Extremities of Indigence and Distress, and at the same Time in almost continual Alarms from the Savages all around." In 1745 Indians attacked the settlements on the St. George's River and the inhabitants abandoned their homes and fled west. They returned around 1749 after peace was restored but "the Indians, tho' in a Time of Peace fell on their Neighborhood, burnt Barns, killed many Cattle, attacked the little Garrisons kept by the People and carried away a Number of Men, Women & Children into Captivity." The survivors took refuge in little forts, where they lived in constant fear of the Indians, until peace was made. Then other colonists claimed their lands, some by Indian deeds that had never been approved by law and others by right of occupation. McCobb and the Scotch-Irish at Boothbay hung on, but it was a precarious hold.[33] Describing the situation in Maine and Massachusetts to a correspondent back home in Ulster in 1752, Reverend James MacSparran wrote, "In these two Eastern Provinces many *Irish* are settled, and many have been ruined by the *French Indians*, and drove from their homes." He expected the next generation to have an easier time than their fathers.[34]

In New York, great estates along the Hudson limited the land market, and the colony made little effort to attract immigrants from Northern Ireland with generous land grants. Scotch-Irish communities in New England sent shoots out to New York, but nothing on the scale that developed in Pennsylvania. In 1741 the Reverend Samuel Dunlop prevailed on several Scotch-Irish families to settle on a large patent at the head of Cherry Valley, and in the next thirty years more Scotch-Irish families planted settlements at other points on the Susquehanna.[35] In 1741 William Johnson brought in sixty Scotch-Irish families to settle at Warrenbush, who were joined shortly after by about thirty immigrants from the Scotch-Irish community at Londonderry. Other communities developed around 1750 near Goshen in Orange County and Wallkill in Ulster County. Migrants from New England formed another settlement near Salem and Stillwater, close to the Vermont border.[36]

Sir William Johnson came from County Meath and he seems to have wanted to recreate something of an Irish world on his estate at Johnson Hall. However, he perhaps more accurately wanted to recreate a Gaelic world. He attracted and made homes for expatriate Scottish Highlanders, but toward the end of his life grew lukewarm at the prospect of encouraging immigrants from Northern Ireland. "I know not how far a Settlement on my Lands might contribute to their Service or answer their Desires," he wrote in 1772; "I have no longer occasion to be at any trouble or Expence for their Settlement."[37]

Emigrants from Londonderry, New Hampshire, and Maine, as well as families brought directly from Ulster, settled in Mi'kmaw country in the early 1760s. Alexander McNutt, an ambitious promoter of American lands in Ireland, turned his sights on Nova Scotia. Born in Londonderry in Ulster in 1725 or 1726, McNutt emigrated to America as a young man. After settling at Staunton in the Valley of Virginia by 1753 and serving as a militia officer under Major Andrew Lewis in an expedition against the Shawnee Indians in 1756, he relocated to Londonderry in New Hampshire, where he became a leader of the Ulster Scots community, served as a Massachusetts provincial captain, and attempted to raise troops for the conquest of Canada. In 1761, on the recommendation of Nova Scotia Governor Jonathan Belcher (the younger), the Board of Trade endorsed McNutt as an official agent for the recolonization of Nova Scotia. McNutt's plan involved recruiting Scotch-Irish settlers from New England and Ireland to replace the more than 15,000 Acadians who had been dispersed throughout the British Atlantic during the French and Indian War. In October of that year, McNutt returned with 300 Irish settlers under the promise of 200 acres of land per colonist. However, the British government did not support his plans, and privately funded ventures also fell through. McNutt moved to Nova Scotia in the late 1760s, and when the Revolutionary War began, he appears to have tried to play both sides, earning the distrust of both. He traveled to Boston and Philadelphia in 1778–1779 to obtain compensation for damage to his property in Nova Scotia by American raiders and in hopes of persuading Congress to invade the province, but the delegates provided only monetary assistance. By the end of the war, he was back in Nova Scotia, developing plans to turn the province and adjoining lands in Massachusetts into an independent nation called New Ireland. Frustrated on every front, McNutt returned to Virginia in 1796 and died in obscurity around 1811.[38]

Meanwhile, some Scotch-Irish pushed into northern Vermont and Maine, where families sometimes moved back and forth across the border with Canada, with branches on both sides.[39]

West from Philadelphia

Pennsylvania quickly became a magnet for Scotch-Irish emigrants and the center for Scotch-Irish settlement and growth in America. They were welcomed, offered good land at good rates, and enjoyed religious toleration in the colony William Penn had built on Quaker principles and on Indian land. Unlike many colonial leaders, Penn insisted on purchasing the land from Indians to establish clear title for subsequent sales to colonial settlers. "By this cheap act of justice at the beginning," wrote the Irish statesman and politician Edmund Burke, Penn earned a reputation for fair and honest dealings with Native people, which made his subsequent transactions easier when he sought to populate the country after he had taken possession of it.[40] In reality, Penn often sold lands to settlers or speculators before the Indigenous inhabitants had agreed to sell, and the intruders increased the pressure on them to evacuate or sell the land. He also reserved land for resident and migrant Indians, which allowed him to control the pace and pattern of white settlement.[41] Scotch-Irish immigrants to Pennsylvania benefited from the policies Penn established, although they had little interest in perpetuating a policy of purchasing Indian land before settling it.[42]

The first large-scale Scotch-Irish migration to Pennsylvania began in 1718, the year that William Penn's death started a fourteen-year contest for control of the province between his second wife, Hannah, and his various children.

Penn's three sons, John, Thomas, and Richard, became joint proprietors but spent little time in the colony and delegated administration to a succession of deputy governors. Thousands of Scotch-Irish immigrants arrived in Pennsylvania looking for land during a time when no one had clear legal authority to purchase, survey, or sell land.[43]

An Ulster-born Quaker official helped fill the void and played a major role in determining the pattern of Scotch-Irish settlement on the frontiers. James Logan (Figure 2.1) was born in 1674 in Armagh near Belfast, the son of an Anglican clergyman who became a Quaker. He was apprenticed to a linen merchant in Dublin at age thirteen and then fled with his family to England during the troubles in 1688. William Penn recruited him and in 1699 appointed him provincial secretary, and he served mainly as Penn's agent, administering land sales and Indian relations. Moving into the power vacuum after Penn left the province in 1701 and suffered a stroke in 1712, Logan used his position to build his personal fortune. He served successively, among other offices, as provincial secretary, commissioner of property, president of the council, and de facto superintendent of Indian affairs. He seemed to have his finger in every pie, especially in Indian trade and Indian land. He was the most successful fur trader in early eighteenth-century Pennsylvania, operating a lucrative scheme that earned him profits in three ways: on furs purchased from Indians, on manufactured goods sold to his network of traders, and on land he seized from Indians as well as from traders who fell into debt. He regularly hosted large numbers of Indian guests at his home at Stenton, sometimes for weeks at a time. In a council at Philadelphia in 1742, by which time Logan was old and in ill health, the Onondaga speaker Canasatego publicly expressed satisfaction for his services, calling him "a wise Man & a fast friend to the Indians." Canasatego hoped that when Logan died the governor would appoint in his place "another Person of the same Prudence and Ability in Counselling, and of the same tender disposition and Affection for the Indians." Whatever connections he had made in Indian country, and with the Iroquois in particular, Logan made a fortune trafficking in Indian lands and furs. He was ideally placed to take advantage of the influx of Scotch-Irish immigrants into Pennsylvania.[44]

Logan encouraged the settlement of his "brave fellow countrymen"—as he called them—on the frontier west of Philadelphia. Years later, he recalled that around 1720 "a considerable Number of good Sober People came in from Ireland, who wanted to be Settled" at a time when "we were under some apprehensions from northern Indians of whose Claims to the Lands on Sasquahannah I was not then sensible." Assuming that Ulster immigrants

Figure 2.1 James Logan. Oil on canvas. Thomas Sully, 1831. The Ulster-born politician, land speculator, and trader was a key figure in placing his countrymen on the frontiers of Indian country.

After an original by Gustavus Hesselius. Commissioned to replace a portrait lost by fire. Library Company of Philadelphia

who had lived as a Protestant minority amid a hostile Catholic majority were well suited to establish a foothold in Indian country, he "therefore thought it might be prudent to plant a Settlem^t of fresh men as those who formerly had so bravely defended Derry and Inniskillen [*sic*] as a frontier in case of any

Disturbance. Accordingly the Town Ship of Donegal was Settled." He had expected that if the Irish settlers were well treated, they would be "orderly as they have hitherto been and easily dealt with," and would also be an example to others.[45]

Almost from the start, the Scotch-Irish proved not "easily dealt with." Writing to the provincial government in 1724, Logan reported, "They have generally taken up the western lands; and as they rarely approach me to propose to purchase, I look upon them as bold and indigent strangers, giving as their excuse, when challenged for titles, that we had solicited for colonists, and they had come accordingly."[46] Colonial governments enticed emigrants to their frontiers with the promise of land that was free for the taking, and emigrants expected it. In practice, the emigrants often found that they had to purchase or rent land from land companies, wealthy landlords, and speculators who had been granted huge tracts of territory. Even when land was made available to them at generous rates or rent-free for an initial period, families who had expended what little they had on the cost of moving could ill afford to pay the expenses of surveying, patenting, and securing title to land. Instead, they assumed squatters' rights. As Logan explained to the Penns in 1725, nearly 100,000 acres were occupied by people "who resolutely sitt down and improve, without any manner of Right or Pretence to it." Most of them were so poor they had nothing to pay with and expected to be allowed to stay there as renters. Lacking secure title and unable to accumulate enough money to purchase the land, or to pay quitrents and taxes, poor squatter families usually stayed a few years and then moved on in search of better opportunities elsewhere. The Penns sold land on the Pennsylvania frontier for relatively low prices—1.4 shillings per acre between 1719 and 1731, and 1.9 shillings from 1732 to 1764—yet only 12 of the first 65 men to arrive in Paxton Township on the Susquehanna in the late 1720s bought land there.[47]

Two years later, in 1727, Logan complained to John Penn about the thousands of foreigners, mostly Palatines, already in the country—"many of them are a surley people"—and the hundreds more pouring in. "We have from the North of Ireland, great Numbers yearly, 8 or 9 Ships this last fall discharged at Newcastle. Both these sorts sitt frequently down on any spott of vacant Land they can find, without asking questions." Just the week before, one Scotch-Irish leader had applied to Logan in the name of four hundred immigrants who, he said, "all depended on me, for directions where they should settle. They say the Proprietor invited People to come & settle his Country; they came for that end, & must live; both they and the Palatines pretend they would buy, but not one in twenty has anything to pay with." The Irish generally settled near Maryland in an area where overlapping colonial charters gave rise to a long-running legal conflict between the Penns and Lord Baltimore over the border between their two colonies, and no lands could be honestly sold until the dispute was decided.[48]

Supposing the immigrants to be Irish Catholics, the Penns told Logan they should not be allowed to settle until they had sworn oaths of loyalty to the king and the laws of the country. And they should settle "Backwards to Sasquehannah or north in ye Country beyond the other settlements" like the Palatines, and not along Pennsylvania's disputed southern border with Maryland.[49] Logan, however, did settle Scotch-Irish colonists in the disputed area, as a buffer against Maryland. Lord Baltimore also offered 200 acres to families and 100 acres to individuals rent-free for three years to attract buffers against Indians and Pennsylvanian settlers, and Scotch-Irish colonists took up the offer. In other words, Pennsylvania and Maryland each recruited Scotch-Irish people to hold the disputed territory against the other. Pennsylvania's disputed southern borderland with Maryland was the first area of extensive Scotch-Irish squatting. (It was in this contested area that Baltimore's agent Thomas Cresap, who used force and intimidation to evict Pennsylvania settlers, met the Lancaster County sheriff and posse "with Oaths & Imprecations," calling them "Damn'd Scotch Irish Sons of Bitches, and the Proprietor & people of Pensilvania Damn'd Quaking Dogs & Rogues." The posse burned Cresap's house in the course of making the arrest.)[50]

Many Scotch-Irish immigrants squatted on Indian lands in the chaotic environment of land affairs after William Penn's death in 1718. By the 1720s they were settling the Forks of the Delaware, even though the Native inhabitants had not relinquished title to the lands. Between 1728 and 1730, they built a cluster of dwellings in the Forks known as Hunter Settlement, just north of the Delaware town of Clistowackin. Another group under the patronage of William Allen established a settlement below the Delaware town of Hockendauqua on the Lehigh River. John Boyd, who was born near Edinburgh in 1699, moved with his family to Antrim in 1700, and then migrated to America in 1714, where he married Jane Craig, who had also been born in Scotland. The couple joined her brother Colonel Thomas Craig of Philadelphia and other families from Philadelphia and settled on Catasauqua Creek. The area became known as the Irish Settlement or Craig's

Settlement, and later Allentown. Although, according to Scotch-Irish tradition in Northampton County, a Delaware woman brought spring water to the first settlers, relations with the Delawares would be marked by acrimony rather than harmony.[51]

Scotch-Irish immigrants moved west of Philadelphia into Chester County and north along the east bank of the Susquehanna River, where Pennsylvania officials encouraged them to settle. They took up lands that Logan had set aside for them in what became the townships of Donegal and Paxton, and established a Presbyterian church at Donegal. With Indian villages to the north and on the west bank of the Susquehanna, Donegal and Paxton were Pennsylvania's farthest frontier in the 1720s. Paxton was the northernmost township in Lancaster County when it was established in 1729.

The Susquehanna Valley was a busy and complicated place. Described as the longest non-navigable waterway in the world, the Susquehanna is a river of rocks, islands, and shoals. Native people paddling canoes traveled the watercourse, but European explorers foundered.[52] For years, the valley had been a warpath of nations where Iroquois raiders traveled south to strike Cherokees and Catawbas, and Cherokees and Catawbas reciprocated with raids to the north. By the time the Scotch-Irish arrived, the valley's original Susquehannock inhabitants had been driven out by war and disease. New peoples—Delawares, Nanticokes, Tutelos, and Shawnees, already dislodged by colonial pressures to the south and east—had taken up residence there, encouraged by the Iroquois in New York, the League of the Six Nations, who used them as a buffer to protect their own interests and homelands. Both the Indigenous inhabitants and the Six Nations who looked from farther afield watched with concern as settler colonists advanced up the Susquehanna. At a council meeting at Philadelphia in July 1727, the Indian delegates requested that no new settlements be permitted higher up the Susquehanna than Paxton. In reply, the governor said that no settlements had been allowed yet and although they would spread as young people grew up, it would "not be very speedily."[53] In August, the Conestoga chief Civility asked James Logan to forbid "Christians or white People" from settling west of the river. Logan replied that the government did not want people settling there "& therefore we shall be very pleased, if ye Indians will hinder all, Christians or white people, whatsoever English, Dutch & all other nations, from making any settlem[en]ts on ye farther or West side of the Sasquehanna." The government also expected the Indians to keep Marylanders from "coming hither."[54]

In other words, Logan wanted the Indians to police the borders. Indian people began to withdraw from the Paxton region.

The Scotch-Irish kept coming. Edmund Burke, in his *Account of the European Settlements in America* (published in 1757), said 6,208 people migrated to Pennsylvania in 1729, "four fifths of whom at least were from Ireland."[55] Hundreds of immigrants disembarked at Newcastle and Philadelphia in the late spring and summer of 1729, Logan reported to John Penn: "It looks as if Ireland is to send all its inhabitant hither." He feared they would take over the province if they continued to come in such numbers. "It is strange that they crowd in where they are not wanted," he said. After they landed, most of them headed for the backcountry and squatted on whatever land they could find without any regard for the claims of the Indians or anyone else. Alarmed by "the swarms of strangers" invading their lands, the Indians had "an Aversion to the Irish" who were "generally rough to them." As a result, warned Logan, "we can expect no less than a breach with them."[56] When colonists murdered some Iroquois people in the spring of 1730, Civility was "of opinion that ye Irish have done it," and Logan thought it "but too probable."[57]

By 1729 there were at least six Scotch-Irish settlements along the Susquehanna River.[58] By 1730 at least one hundred Ulster-born families had moved north of Derry and settled in Paxton. Most of them were squatters, and conflicts with Logan's and Penn's surveyors in the early 1730s prompted many of them to move across the Susquehanna. Pennsylvania west of the Susquehanna was soon Scotch-Irish country, but not until 1736 did the Penn family make a treaty with the Six Nations extinguishing Indian claims to the west bank of the river.[59]

By 1730, Logan had changed his tune about the benefits of settling his countrymen on Pennsylvania's frontiers. "A settlement of five families from the North of Ireland gives me more trouble than fifty of any other people," he wrote. "Before we were broke in upon, ancient Friends and first settlers lived happily; but now the case is quite altered." By the fall of 1731 "great Numbers of wilful people from the North of Ireland [had] over-run all the back parts of the Province as far as Susquehannah and are now to the further disaffection of the Indians, passing over it." They were, Logan concluded, "troublesome to the government and hard neighbors to the Indians."[60] Never shy about acquiring Indian land himself, James Logan spilled a lot of ink complaining about his countrymen who squatted on Indian land.[61]

Frequently ignoring laws that restricted where they could settle, Scotch-Irish people proceeded to settle in all directions, often on the property of absentee landlords, refused to pay quit rents to the proprietors, and defied government officers sent to remove them. Powerless to enforce civil authority over "ye Irish, who declare themselves determined to keep possession," Logan suggested to the Proprietor in 1743 that it might not be a bad idea to give them a taste of their own medicine and let them "feel ye Inconvenience of Lawless force a little longer, for they begin to practice it upon one another." Some of the first settlers had complained to Logan that the newcomers crowded in on them "& knowing that ye former settlers had no better right than themselves, & that they were equally Trespassers, ... sate down where they pleased, every man according to his forces, by himself or friends, thereby occasioned great Quarling & disorders."[62] The tendency to squat on land that was not legally theirs added to the antipathy of colonial Pennsylvanians around Philadelphia who regarded the backcountry as a different world, inhabited by "foreigners," namely Germans and disorderly "Irish." In many ways, colonial elites like provincial secretary Richard Peters would have preferred their frontier to be inhabited by Indians under the control of the Iroquois, rather than by "the lower sort of People who are exceedingly loose and ungovernable." They also worried that those people might develop close ties with Indians.[63]

Squatters were perpetually on the move. Paxton was founded in 1715 as a predominantly Scotch-Irish settlement. By mid-century, however, it was becoming increasingly German. Comparing the names on tax and assessments lists in Paxton from year to year after 1750 reveals a highly transient population, sometimes with changes of 40–50 percent in the population from one year to the next. People who intended to move on preferred to squat on land rather than go through the legal process and expenses of surveying, patenting, and purchasing it. And those who bought a small amount of land at low cost and made improvements could make a profit when they sold it and moved on. Turnover was so common that one scholar calls Paxton a "community of strangers." Although Paxton grew in size, it lacked community stability, cohesion, and infrastructure, which meant that community-wide responses to crises like Indian attacks tended to be ad hoc and temporary. Many inhabitants evidently joined the migration stream down the Great Wagon Road that passed through Paxton and led through the Shenandoah Valley of Virginia and on into the Carolina Piedmont.[64]

As they moved, immigrants created new towns with old names taken from Britain's borderlands, like Carlisle, Cumberland, Derry, Donegal, and Lancaster. "The settlers adjoining this river were some Irish families in the name of Patton," wrote Rhoda Barber in her journal of the settlement at Wright's Ferry on the Susquehanna. "The Township above was called Donegal, settled by the Irish, Andersons, Cook, Tate, Hays."[65] In doing so, settler colonists reinscribed the landscape. Indigenous place names tended to convey the ecological characteristics of an area or how it was used; Europeans often named places after localities in Europe or after the new "owner." Replacing Indigenous with European names, imposing new boundaries on existing human geographies, arbitrarily including, excluding, or dissecting Indian country, calling it wilderness, vacant land, or "terra incognita" on maps, was all part of the process of dispossessing Native peoples and excluding them from the new world that colonists conjured up on parchment and paper.

The main flow of Scotch-Irish migration moved northwest up the Susquehanna to the junction with the Cumberland, then headed southwest along the mountain ranges.[66] The Scotch-Irish began to enter the Cumberland Valley before 1730 and poured in after 1734, encouraged by authorities who made land available at low prices to attract them as a barrier against the Indians and a buffer against the intrusion of Marylanders from the south. Francis Campble and his older brother emigrated from County Derry in 1734 to Philadelphia, where they worked in trade for a couple of years. Taking advantage of the patronage of Philadelphia merchant and land speculator Edward Shippen, Francis moved to the Middle Spring settlement of what became the town of Shippensburg, where he worked as Shippen's agent, while his brother in Philadelphia supplied him with goods to trade to the local settlers. He found himself among his own kind. New settlers were arriving every week, spreading along the streams and through the woodlands. They were hardy people, well fitted to endure the privations that were inevitable in forming a new settlement, Campble noted in his journal in 1737. "The entire people of this settlement is of Irish origin and Presbyterian in faith. I have been told by some of the first settlers that there is not a single family here who are not natives of the Province of Ulster." They built the Middle Spring Presbyterian Church near Shippensburg in 1738 and by 1745 had formed ten Presbyterian congregations in what became Cumberland County. More than 5,000 people lived in the Cumberland Valley by mid-century, "all but a handful of Ulster origin."[67]

Scotch-Irish squatter families moving up the Susquehanna headed west along the Juniata Valley. The Juniata River itself is only 100 miles long, but its many tributaries drain about 3,400 square miles and the valley provides a natural corridor between the Susquehanna and Delaware valleys and the Ohio Valley. Scotch-Irish squatters used it as a pathway to move beyond the reach of colonial authorities.[68] Local histories in the nineteenth century portrayed them as Scotch-Irish pioneers. The "bold and daring men" who pushed into the Juniata Valley around 1741 were "nearly all Scotch-Irish."[69] The first to settle the neighborhood of Fort Granville in present-day Lewiston were Arthur Buchanan and his two sons, and three other families, "all Scotch-Irish." Buchanan asked Shawnees at Ohesson for permission to settle on the Juniata, and evidently developed ties with Shawnee chief Kishacoquillas.[70] In the spring of 1749, Pennsylvania provincial secretary Richard Peters informed the proprietors that the Scotch-Irish were "going over the Hills to Settle in the Lands at Juniata." Moving inland along the many streams—the Codorus, Great Conewago, Yellow Breeches, Conodoguinet, Shermans Creek, Juniata—they then fanned out across the region.[71] In 1751 Captain James Patterson, remembered as "an adventurous Scotch-Irishman" in local history, and five or six others traveled across the country from Cumberland County and made the first settlement in what became Juniata County, near the present-day town of Mexico. The first to settle at the mouth of Licking Creek, around 1750, was Hugh Hardy, "a Scotch-Irishman," who "was followed by families named Castner, Wilson, Law, Scott, Grimes, and Sterrit, all Scotch-Irish." The first settlers in Tuscarora, about the same time, came from Cumberland County and were "all Scotch." The earliest settlement of the Cove area (Great Cove, Little Cove, and Canolloways) "was effected by Scotch-Irish" as early as 1749. Many of the first squatters were expelled by Richard Peters after the Six Nations appealed to the government of Pennsylvania to remove squatters from lands they had not yet sold.[72]

The pressure of Scotch-Irish colonists who settled first and asked later, if at all, about surveys, titles, and purchases fueled resentment in Indian country and concern in Philadelphia. Indian leaders complained about trespassers, and colonial officials responded with orders to remove them, and sometimes enforced the orders by burning squatters' cabins. At a treaty conference with Lieutenant Governor George Thomas in 1742, Delawares and Shawnees complained that white people were encroaching on their side of the Kittanning Mountains (also called the Kittochtinny Hills, and the Blue or Endless Mountain). Thomas issued a proclamation against settling Indian lands in Lancaster County west of the mountains.[73] People evidently ignored it. Deputy Governor James Hamilton gave the Métis interpreter Andrew Montour permission to settle over the Kittochtinny Hills so that he could use his influence to dissuade the people from settling there on lands not purchased from the Indians, report on their movements, and "open the Eyes of these unthinking People."[74]

The extent and magnitude of squatting and the difficulties of preventing or punishing it in the backcountry, where settlement preceded survey and settlers marked out their own land before or without applying for survey warrants,[75] eventually forced the proprietors to accept "settlement rights." After all, proprietary land policy had encouraged the occupation of unsettled land by people who had no legal claim to it in the first place. Recognizing those who occupied and cleared land as having priority when it came to purchase meant that squatting became an accepted method of settlement.[76] Like the colonial government of Pennsylvania, the federal government of the United States would struggle to curtail squatting, even as it recognized its role in destabilizing the frontier and opening the way for expansion into Indian country.

Like Indian people, Scotch-Irish colonists seemed to be kept on the move ahead of increasing European population. The population of Pennsylvania grew from 20,000 in 1700 to 100,000 in 1740, to 150,000 in 1750, and 220,000 by 1760.[77] Counties, the basic unit of government in colonial Pennsylvania, with the township as a subdivision, developed as population seeped west. Originally, in 1682, three counties were established: Bucks, Chester, and Philadelphia. By time of the Revolution, eight more had been added: Lancaster in 1729, York in 1749, Cumberland in 1750, Berks in 1752, Northampton in 1752, Bedford in 1771, and Northumberland and Westmoreland in 1772.[78] As greater numbers of settlers moved in, many Scotch-Irish moved on. Pennsylvania became the source from which Scotch-Irish people spread across large swaths of America. One Pennsylvania historian likened the out-migration of Scotch-Irish from towns like Paxton and Derry to bees swarming out from the parent hive to find other locations.[79] Another described the Cumberland Valley as the headquarters of the Scotch-Irish, not only in Pennsylvania but in America; the "seed plot and nursery" which, once filled, sent out streams of emigrants to the north, south, and west.[80] The streams pushed deeper into Indian country.

South to Virginia and the Carolinas

Moving ahead of advancing settlement and rising land prices, migrants followed the Great Valley of Pennsylvania (also known as the Great Appalachian Valley) as they tracked westward for a hundred miles or more through the Cumberland Valley. Then they hit the Allegheny Mountains, and the orientation of the terrain deflected their migratory thrust southwestward through the broad valleys stretching along the eastern side of the mountains and into the Virginia and Carolina backcountry. They followed the valley as it turned southwestward across the Potomac to become the Shenandoah Valley, and they pushed through mountain passes into what became Kentucky and Tennessee. This was all Indian country when Scotch-Irish migrants pushed up against it and through it. The Scotch-Irish led the way in repeopling the southern highlands, but the first migration into the old Southwest was not truly "Southern"; most of it came originally from Pennsylvania.[81]

As early as 1701, with a looming threat from French and Indians in the west, the Virginia House of Burgesses passed an act "for the better strengthening of the frontiers." It allowed the Virginia Council to issue grants of between 10,000 and 30,000 acres of land to companies and societies that would settle one "Christian warlike man" for every 500 acres granted. The act had little immediate effect, but it set the precent and policy for building a frontier buffer of Protestant farmers in decades to come.[82]

A few Ulster families settled on the northern reaches of the lower Shenandoah Valley in 1719, but large-scale migration into western Virginia did not begin until the late 1720s and 1730s, when Lord Fairfax and Lieutenant Governor William Gooch granted huge plots of land to speculators.[83] In 1730–1732 Gooch and the Virginia Council issued nine grants amounting to 385,000 acres west of the Blue Ridge Mountains, on condition that the grantees recruit one settler family per 1,000 acres within two years. Between 1730 and 1734, Scotch-Irish migrants led by the Kerr and Lewis families began moving south from the Cumberland and upper Potomac valleys into the Shenandoah.[84] By 1735 some 160 families, many of them attracted from Pennsylvania, had settled in the region; by the early 1740s, almost 10,000 people settled in the Shenandoah Valley. As London had planted Scottish and English Protestants in Northern Ireland in the seventeenth century to guard against Catholicism and the barbaric Irish, now imperial authorities encouraged settlement by Scotch-Irish, Germans, and other foreign Protestants to shield Chesapeake settlements against Catholic French, barbarous Indians, and potential slave rebellions.[85]

In 1731 or 1732 a German immigrant named Jost Hite and sixteen German and Scotch-Irish families, more than one hundred people with their wagons, belongings, and livestock, carved out what came to be known as the Philadelphia Wagon Road or the Great Wagon Road. It became the major highway for Scotch-Irish migration. The road, which roughly follows what is now Interstate 81, then roughly followed the Great Warriors' Path that the Iroquois and southern Indians traveled in their raids against one another. Leading from Philadelphia to Lancaster and York, across the Potomac into the Shenandoah Valley, and then south to Winchester, Stephensburg, Strasburg, and Staunton, it crossed the James River and ran south to Roanoke. At Roanoke one branch turned east through the Blue Ridge Mountains and ran south along the edge of the mountains to Wachovia in North Carolina. From there, Scotch-Irish and other emigrants by the 1750s spread out into South Carolina between the Yadkin and Catawba rivers. The southwestern branch became the Wilderness Road, which followed the trail discovered by Thomas Walker of Virginia and blazed by Daniel Boone from the Great Valley through the Cumberland Gap into Kentucky and extended through the Cumberland Basin to Tennessee. South of Catawba country, the Great Wagon Road merged with the Cherokee Path that led from Charleston to the mountains. It shaped the direction of American expansion into the interior and the nature of settlement. Connecting with other branch roads along its length, it became an artery for commerce as well as travel, carrying western produce to eastern markets, and stimulated the development of towns along its route. Over the years, a slow, southward-moving exodus of thousands of men, women, and children, riding in or walking alongside covered wagons pulled by oxen or horses and loaded with family possessions, leading trains of pack animals, and driving livestock along the rocky, tree-strewn, and deeply rutted road, spread Pennsylvania family farm culture—small-farm mixed-grain-livestock agriculture, ethnic diversity, and religious diversity, rather than the slave-tobacco plantations, Anglo-American patriarchy, and Anglican conformity of Old Virginia—to the Carolinas by mid-century, and west to Ohio, Kentucky, and Tennessee in the Revolutionary era.[86]

The Iroquois at the northern end of the valley road and the Cherokees at the southern end pushed colonial expansion into the region's center. The English negotiated use of the path in a series of treaties with the Iroquois and, at the Treaty of Lancaster in 1744, they acquired the land itself. (The road to the Susquehanna backcountry ran through Lancaster's main street, noted the secretary to the Maryland treaty commissioners.[87]) However, control of the entire length of the Valley did not come until Iroquois and Cherokee power was broken in the Revolution.[88]

Hite had a grant from the government of Virginia for 40,000 acres in the Shenandoah Valley, contingent on recruiting 140 settlers to help secure the frontier. In 1732 he founded a settlement on the banks of Opequon Creek, a few miles from present-day Winchester. According to the *Annals of Augusta County*, "the settlers were almost exclusively of the Scotch-Irish race, natives of the north of Ireland, but of Scottish ancestry." One of the earliest was John Lewis, who was reputed to have emigrated from Donegal after a violent affray with an oppressive landlord.[89] His sons, Thomas, Andrew, Charles, and William, figured prominently in Virginia's expansion into Indian country. Samuel Glass emigrated from County Down and settled on Opequon Creek in 1735, and the eleven families who constituted the first generation at Opequon were all recent immigrants from Ulster. They established farms, producing grain and livestock, over an area roughly six miles long and four miles wide. They intermixed spatially and did business with Germans, English, and native Virginia colonists, but they married and conveyed land to their own kind and they worshipped in a single Presbyterian congregation. The Opequon settlement was not an ethnic town or village, but a dispersed community of Scotch-Irish farmers tied by threads of family, kinship, ethnicity, land, and congregation. Opequon retained its social cohesion and identity until people began moving west to Kentucky—again in kin groups—after the American Revolution.[90]

Two land grants stimulated Scotch-Irish movement into the Valley. William Beverley, a wealthy planter-merchant from Essex County, Virginia, saw the opportunity. He was convinced that if he could get a grant of land in the Shenandoah Valley, he would be able to get people from Pennsylvania to settle there.[91] In 1736 Governor Gooch granted Beverley, John Robinson, and John and Richard Randolph 118,000 acres in northern Augusta County. Taken over by Beverley, it became known as the "Beverley Grant." Gooch made a second grant, 500,000 acres comprising most of Rockbridge County and the southern part of Augusta County, to Benjamin Borden of New Jersey. Beverley and Borden worked hard to attract colonists. They employed relatively well-to-do immigrants from Ulster to help them, as speculators, agents, and surveyors. James Patton went into partnership with them, importing settlers to the Shenandoah Valley. Born in Londonderry in 1692 to a family that originally were landed gentry in Fife and had emigrated to Ulster during the King James Plantation, Patton served in Royal Navy and then became a merchant ship captain, carrying cargoes of pelts and tobacco to Britain and returning with emigrants from Ulster. He was said to have crossed the Atlantic more than twenty times.[92]

The first settlers on Borden's tract were reputedly Ephraim McDowell and his family. McDowell, by then an old man, was born in 1673 and had been at the siege of Londonderry. After migrating to America, he moved in 1737 with his adult children John and Mary, at least two other sons, and Mary's husband James Greenlee to the Shenandoah Valley to purchase land in Beverley Manor. The family settled there themselves, and John McDowell and James Greenlee also surveyed and allocated tracts of land for new settlers on Borden's behalf. Negotiating with their kinsmen and former neighbors from Pennsylvania and Ulster, they attracted McClungs, McCues, McCowns, McElroys, McKees, McCambells, Campbells, Stuarts, Paxtons, Lyles, Irvines, Caldwell, Calhouns, Alexanders, and others. The majority of Scotch-Irish families, whether recently arrived from Ireland or American-born, came from Pennsylvania via the Cumberland Valley. So many people with names like McClure, Houston, Colter, and McKee settled in the Beverley/Borden grant between the Blue Ridge and Appalachian Mountains that within ten years it became known simply as the "Irish Tract." The tract made the southern end of the Valley of Virginia the second major center for Scotch-Irish settlement after southeastern Pennsylvania and acted as a spur to the southward migration of the Scotch-Irish.[93] Augusta and Rockbridge counties were heavily Scotch-Irish, and Rockingham County was predominantly Scotch-Irish until 1750, by which time Germans became the majority. By 1775, the population of the valley had reached 35,000, of whom almost two-thirds were in the lower valley, and roughly two-thirds of that population were Scotch-Irish. Based on data compiled from county order books, deed books, will books, and land tax records, although German emigrants predominated in the northern region of the Shenandoah Valley and were more numerous in Shenandoah and Rockingham counties, Scotch-Irish people dominated the central and southern portions. They constituted 58 percent of the population of Augusta County; 73 percent of Rockridge County.[94]

A "Pennsylvania road" and an "Irish Path" in Augusta and Rockingham counties indicated the direction and composition of the migration. The Reverend John Craig, who was born in County Antrim in 1709 and educated at Edinburgh University, landed in New Castle on the Delaware in August 1734, and migrated to Lancaster, Pennsylvania, two years later. Licensed to preach in 1737, he was sent nearly three hundred miles "to a new settlement in Virginia of our own people." He arrived in Augusta in August 1740, the first permanent Presbyterian clergyman west of the Blue Ridge Mountains, and remained there for the rest of his life. He founded the Augusta church in 1740 and organized the Tinkling Spring congregation in 1741, and preached at the two churches on alternate Sundays. Craig baptized numerous children who later figured prominently in the Scotch-Irish invasion of Native America, including Benjamin Logan, Arthur and William Campbell, and Joshua and William Renix or Renick.[95]

Shenandoah Valley society was not particularly egalitarian or democratic. Families who arrived early and enjoyed connections with tidewater gentry and the original patentees constituted a frontier elite that controlled land distribution and political offices. By 1745 nearly 78 percent of the land patented in Augusta County had been granted, in tracts of one thousand acres or more, to just thirteen families. Scotch-Irish and predominantly Presbyterian, the upper valley gentry—men like James Patton, John McDowell, John Lewis and his sons, William Preston, William Fleming, William Christian, Arthur Campbell, and their extended families—relied on kinship connections to acquire, maintain, and distribute wealth and power. Like Virginia's eastern gentry, they supported the colony's defensive measures and Indian policies, but they also knew that most Scotch-Irish settlers had different attitudes and priorities and, as leaders of the local militia, they sometimes had to cater to the demands of their followers.[96]

The Shenandoah Valley was a site of through migration as well as settlement. William Byrd, who acquired a large tract of land on the Virginia/North Carolina border which he opened to Scotch-Irish settlers from Pennsylvania, compared their coming to the barbarian invasions of Rome: they "flock over thither in such numbers, that there is not elbow room for them. They swarm like the Goths and Vandals of old & will over-spread our Continent soon," he wrote.[97] Waves of emigrants fleeing famine in Ulster in 1740–1741 swelled the numbers of settlers in the Valley.[98] Edmund Burke, in his *Account of the European Settlements in America*, wrote that the number of white people in Virginia was growing every day "by the migration of the Irish, who, not succeeding so well in Pennsylvania as the more frugal and industrious Germans, sell their lands in that province to the latter, and take up new ground in the remote counties in Virginia, Maryland, and North Carolina. These are chiefly Presbyterians from the northern part of Ireland, who in America are generally called Scotch Irish."[99]

Before 1750, Scotch-Irish migration into Virginia was largely confined to the Great Valley, but by mid-century people were pushing west and south. The Reverend James MacSparran, who had himself emigrated from County Londonderry, describing America to a correspondent back in Ireland in 1752, spoke of "the Swarms that, for many Years past, have winged their Way Westward out of the *Hibernian* Hive" and reported that "[t[here has lately been made, upon and behind the Mountains of *Virginia*, a new *Irish* Settlement, by a Transmigration of sundry of those that, within these thirty Years past, went from the North of *Ireland* to *Pennsylvania*."[100] By the time Burke wrote in 1757, the Shenandoah was filling up and thousands of Scotch-Irish and Germans, having crossed the Great Valley and the Shenandoah, traveled eastward through the Staunton River and Maggoty Creek gaps in the Blue Ridge Mountains, swung south close to the Blue Ridge and passed through the hilly country of southern Virginia, and went on beyond the Dan River into the open spaces of the Carolina Piedmont.[101]

A couple of examples illustrate the pattern of migration, settlement, mobility, and resettlement. John Caldwell led a large group of Presbyterians from Ulster to Pennsylvania in 1726. In 1739 he led a couple of hundred Presbyterians south into Virginia, settling in the Cub Creek area near present-day Charlotte County. When Lunenburg was formally organized as a county, John and William Caldwell were appointed members of the first county court, but after the Caldwells died in 1751, many of their community moved on, first to South Carolina and later some to Kentucky. The Cub Creek community ceased to be exclusively Scotch-Irish as other people moved in to replace those who left.[102]

Andrew Pickens's ancestors had left Scotland for France, returned after the Revocation of the Edict of Nantes in 1685 removed legal protections for Protestant groups like the Huguenots, and then migrated to Ireland. Andrew's parents emigrated from Ulster before 1720 and moved west to Paxton, where Andrew was born in 1739. When he was an infant, the family joined the stream of Scotch-Irish emigration heading down the Great Wagon Road to Augusta County, where they joined Reverend John Craig's congregation at Tinkling Spring. In 1752 or 1753, they moved again to the Waxhaws country to take up land grants offered by the government of North Carolina and secure economic security for the sons.[103] The Waxhaws took its name from a creek that flowed from North Carolina into the Catawba River in

South Carolina, which in turn took its name from the Waxhaw people who had merged into the Catawbas.

Scotch-Irish migration into the Carolina Piedmont constituted a third wave, after Pennsylvania and Virginia, and comprised predominantly second-generation families. Like the governments of Pennsylvania and Virginia, the governments of North and South Carolina sought Protestants to build settler communities as a line of defense against Indians in the mountains and the west.[104] They were to serve as protection against growing numbers of enslaved Africans as well. Scotch-Irish Presbyterians began settling along the Eno and Haw rivers in the late 1730s and along the Catawba around 1740.[105] They often interspersed with German settlements in the Catawba, Yadkin, and Waxhaw valleys, but they were the largest group among the early settlers of western North Carolina. Land speculator Henry McCulloch in the 1730s petitioned for some 50,000 acres of land on branches of the Cape Fear River and at the head of the New River, undertaking to settle three hundred people there in the first ten years. He persuaded a colony from Ulster to settle on his expected land grant in what became Duplin County, North Carolina.[106] Although the Scotch-Irish lived near settlements of Scots Highlanders and other groups, they populated the area between Catawba and Pee Dee rivers so heavily that it became known as "Scotch Irish Mesopotamia."[107]

Over thirty years, three successive governors of North Carolina actively promoted Scotch-Irish immigration to the province. Gabriel Johnston, a lowland Scot from Dumfriesshire, was governor from 1734 to 1751; Matthew Rowan, president of the Council in 1753–1754, was from Antrim; and Arthur Dobbs, governor from 1754 to 1765, was from Carrickfergus. They used their relatives, friends, connections, and acquaintances in the north of Ireland and south of Scotland.[108]

Attracted by stories of rich land in western North Carolina and by the cheapness and ease with which land could be acquired, and driven by fears of Indian raids in Pennsylvania and Virginia in the 1750s, migrants arrived in droves. The population of North Carolina doubled between 1730 and 1750, and then almost tripled between 1750 and 1770.[109] When Johnston took office in 1734, the population was about 50,000; when he retired seventeen years later, it was 90,000. Writing to the Board of Trade in London in 1751, Johnston reported, "Great numbers of Families keep daily crowding into the Back Parts of this Country." They came overland in wagons from Pennsylvania and other parts of America that were "overstocked with people and some directly from Europe." A "hardy and laborious Race of Men," they "commonly seat themselves towards the west and have got near the mountains."[110] After the failure of the Jacobite Rebellion in 1746, Johnston was accused of turning Palatines off their lands "to make room for Scotch rebels."[111] Matthew Rowan told the Board of Trade in 1753 that whereas Anson and Rowan counties in the Piedmont region had not been able to raise more than one hundred fighting men or militia seven years earlier, they could now raise at least three thousand, "for the most part Irish Protestants and Germans," and their numbers were increasing daily.[112]

As a Member of Parliament for Carrickfergus, Arthur Dobbs in 1729 had introduced a bill in the Irish House of Commons to restrict emigration. He also published *An Essay on the Trade and Improvement of Ireland* (Dublin, 1730), identifying the causes of emigration and advocating the development of manufacturing to help retain population. A quarter century later, now as governor of North Carolina where he had bought himself a large estate in 1745, Dobbs encouraged Presbyterian farmers, including tenants from his own estates in Antrim, to emigrate to his American lands and build up his own Ulster colony in America.[113] Through his association with Hugh McCulloh, Lord Granville's agent, three colonies of Ulster men came to North Carolina in 1751, 1754, and 1755.[114]

Dobbs's lengthy reports to the Board of Trade offer glimpses of the Scotch-Irish people who migrated from Pennsylvania down the Great Wagon Road and built communities of extended families in the North Carolina backcountry. Coming in hundreds of wagons from the north to take up land in the back settlements, they either sent "some of their own people to come before them to look out for Lands, or some of their friends already settled here," and they sought tracts of 500 or 600 acres "to accommodate 2 or 3 families together in the same grant," Dobbs wrote in November 1754.[115] Since North Carolina's trade with Ireland was limited, he explained in 1755, most of the "Servants and Irish Protestants who choose to come to reside in this Climate" took ship to Philadelphia. From there, "at a great Expense they come by Land in Waggons to the Province, but their Wealth being expended they are incapable of improving or cultivating the Lands they take up for sometime."[116] In June 1755, Dobbs undertook a tour of his lands, the western frontier, and the Catawba nation. Of the 75 Scotch-Irish families on his lands,

> I viewed betwixt 30 and 40 of them, and except two there was not less than from 5 or 6 to 10 children in each family, each going barefooted in their shifts in the warm weather, no woman wearing more than a shift

and one thin petticoat; They are a Colony from Ireland removed from Pensylvania, of what we call Scotch Irish Presbyterians who with others in the neighbouring Tracts have settled together in order to have a teacher of their own opinion and choice.

Dobbs also had twenty-two families of industrious Germans or Swiss.[117] There was drought in Ulster. Dobbs declared that as many as ten thousand emigrants had landed in Philadelphia in a single season and that many of them were "obliged to remove to the Southward for want of Lands to take up and as that Colony has of late extended far to the Westward of Susquehana."[118] According to Bishop Spangenburg, many emigrants settled in North Carolina "on account of poverty as they wished to own land & were too poor to buy in Pennsylvania or New Jersey." Many Irish did so under the misapprehension that they did not need to feed stock in winter; they would find they were badly mistaken, the bishop warned.[119]

The Scotch-Irish population in the Yadkin Valley in North Carolina grew steadily. Anson County was formed in 1749 and settlers submitted eighty petitions for land, mostly Scotch-Irish heads of large families. The rich bottom lands of the Yadkin and Catawba Valley were advertised to the Scotch-Irish much as the Shenandoah was years before, and the region became one of the largest predominantly Scotch-Irish settlements in America. There were at least fourteen families in the "Irish Settlement" between the Yadkin and Catawba rivers by 1749. Between 1752 and 1762, more than one hundred families, mostly Scotch-Irish and mainly from Pennsylvania and Maryland, obtained title to lands there. They moved into areas inhabited by Saponi and Tutelo people between the Yadkin and Catawba rivers, and by the Catawbas and Waxhaws south of the Catawba River.[120]

In 1763 Benjamin Franklin estimated that 10,000 families had migrated from Pennsylvania to North Carolina in the previous three years.[121] "All the Settlers in the back Country came by Land from Pensylvania," Governor Tryon of North Carolina told the Board of Trade in 1764; "they knowing no Boundary Line constantly took out their Claims from this Province."[122] Two years later, he reported that his colony was "settling faster than any on the continent." The previous fall and winter nearly one thousand wagons from the north had passed through Salisbury with families to settle in his province.[123]

Although German migrants also settled in the North Carolina backcountry, the two groups evidently maintained separate communities and identities, a situation that was not entirely the result of Scotch-Irish "clannishness." A German minister in western North Carolina advised his young people not to marry with either the English or the Irish. The latter, he said, "are lazy, dissipated and poor, live in the most wretched huts and enjoy the same food as their animals."[124]

Scotch-Irish migrants arrived in numbers in the Waxhaws in the Piedmont region along the North Carolina and South Carolina border in the 1750s. Some came from Maryland, Pennsylvania, and Virginia, especially from Augusta County; others moved there from the Irish Settlement in North Carolina.[125] At first, people settled close to one another for mutual protection, but then adopted their preferred dispersed settlement patterns.[126] Scotch-Irish settlement in regions such as the Waxhaws was shaped by the push and pull of land and kinship. Land drove migration and settlement, and kinship ordered it. The search for rich, well-watered farmland, preferably old Indian fields that had been abandoned, pushed people apart, but the need to settle near friends and family who provided companionship, protection, trust, and shared resources pulled them together.[127]

As American-born Scotch-Irish pushed south into the Carolina backcountry, they mixed with smaller streams of emigrants who came directly from Ulster, landed in Charleston, and made their way up the river valleys into the interior. South Carolina officials who feared that an Indian war could trigger a slave revolt initiated an immigration assistance program and implemented a township plan for the specific purpose of placing "free poor Protestants" at strategic locations along the frontier, creating a buffer between Indian country and low country plantations. The first Scotch-Irish came to South Carolina under Governor Robert Johnson's township scheme of 1730. South Carolina laid out eleven new townships sixty or more miles inland and issued cheap land grants to Swiss, Germans, and Scotch-Irish in the 1730s. Swiss immigrants were sent to the frontier southwest of the Santee River. Scotch-Irish immigrants arriving from Belfast went north of the river, settling Williamsburg, Kings Town, Queensborough, and Fredericksburg in the middle country, and then pushed on to join emigrants from Pennsylvania and Virginia in backcountry Piedmont regions on the northwest frontier. In 1732 Scotch-Irish from Virginia, along with a group of Quakers, established Pine Tree Hill (later Camden), South Carolina's oldest inland city, along the Catawba trading path.[128]

South Carolina's inducements were widely advertised in Ulster. In County Down, six-year-old Robert Witherspoon's family responded to the promise of free passage, land grants of fifty acres per person, tools, and a year's provisions. In 1734 his extended family, including his grandparents who had migrated from Scotland to Ulster a generation earlier, sailed to Charleston. His grandmother died at sea and his sister Sarah died in Charleston, where she became the first person buried in the graveyard of the "Scotch Meeting House." The rest of the Witherspoon clan carried on, traveling more than one hundred miles by sea and river, and settled along the Black River on the coastal plain near Williamsburg. Writing about the experience more than four decades later, Witherspoon remembered they were alarmed by the Indians; "when they came to hunt in the Spring they were in great numbers and in all places like the Egyptian locast [sic] but they were not hurtful."[129]

The South Carolina House of Assembly struggled to deal with the influx of "Poor Protestant People of Ireland" like the Witherspoons who "transport themselves and their Families into this Province with a Desire to cultivate Lands as they had been accustomed to do." The newcomers strained South Carolina's resources. In the winter of 1737–1738, citizens submitted multiple complaints to the Assembly that because no provision had been made for the poor Protestants who had recently arrived, Charleston was "filled with People begging from Door to Door" who would become "a perfect Nuisance" if relief was not provided soon.[130] Concerned by "the great Danger this Province is exposed to for Want of a sufficient Number of white People therein," a House committee recommended additional measures to encourage poor Protestant immigrants and to supplement the tax on imported African slaves as the source of funding for the program.[131] The committee found that settling the immigrants on the frontiers was often hindered by the fact that many of the best lands designated for them by the king were "held by private Persons who neither inhabit nor settle the same." In addition, large numbers of enslaved workers were being brought into the area and doing jobs normally performed by white people. To help reduce the threat of slave insurrection, the committee recommended prohibiting taking African slaves into the area. To encourage poor Protestants to settle in communities, a salary of £50 per year was allowed for the maintenance of ministers in townships; the term of service for indentured Protestants was limited to three years (except for minors), and land near the Wateree Township was to be reserved for the use of North Britons.[132] In 1744–1745, the committee recommended that commissioners be appointed in every military district between the Savannah River and Santee River to purchase twenty-acre tracts of land and "convey the same to Poor Protestants and their Heirs as shall come to settle in this

Province on the Encouragement hereby proposed."[133] Nevertheless, funding from "the Negro Duty" remained inadequate and the government had to resort to relief measures for distressed Protestants stranded in Charleston.[134]

After the earliest settlements at the Waxhaws, Scotch-Irish migrants from Pennsylvania by way of Virginia created settlements at Long Canes in South Carolina near modern-day Abbeville and other locations in the mid-1700s, including on western side of the Catawba on Fishing Creek, and on a tributary of the Tyger River in the present districts of Spartansburg and Union.[135] The first white settler in present Greenville County, South Carolina, was reputedly Richard Pearis, who was born in Ireland, moved south from Virginia as a trader, married a Cherokee woman, and through her acquired large tracts of land in what is today the town of Greenville.[136] Robert Colquhoun had emigrated from Scotland to Ireland in the seventeenth century, where the spelling of the surname became Colhoun. In 1733 his great-grandson James Patrick Colhoun and his family emigrated from County Donegal to Pennsylvania, where the spelling became Calhoun. After James Patrick died, his widow and children moved with other families of Scotch-Irish emigrants to Augusta County, Virginia. When the defeat of General Edward Braddock's British army in 1755 unleashed a storm of Indian raids on the Virginia frontier, four Calhoun brothers and their families joined a steady stream of Scotch-Irish settlers heading south through the foothills of the Appalachians. Patrick Calhoun, who was born in County Donegal in 1727 and had migrated with his parents as a boy, together with his brothers John, William, and Ezekial, and their mother Catherine Calhoun were said to be the first to settle at Long Canes. Other Scotch-Irish families followed. Patrick became a surveyor, Indian fighter, and a prominent South Carolina politician. His son, John C. Calhoun, was born near Abbeville in 1782.[137]

In 1761 the South Carolina Assembly passed legislation, renewed in 1765, to encourage the immigration of poor Protestants and their settlement in the upcountry to bolster its frontier defenses against slave revolts, Creeks, and Cherokees. The government advertised for hard-working settlers to take up their own lands and offered extra incentives, including defraying the expense of their Atlantic passage, granting headrights, and giving temporary tax exemption. In order to qualify for the cash bounty and land grants, the immigrants on landing had to formally petition the governor's council and present documentation showing they were Protestants of good standing at home. Except for a small number of Germans, all the individuals applying for South Carolina's land bounty appear to have come from Northern

Ireland. After disembarking, most of them pushed into the interior of South Carolina and Georgia, where they put their cultural stamp on the region. The new emigrants tended to be much poorer than those who arrived from Pennsylvania and Virginia.[138]

Northern Irish merchants John Torrans, John Greg, and John Paug extended their business to carrying foreign Protestants—French as well as Scotch-Irish—to Charleston. Largely responsible for beginning emigration from Ulster to South Carolina, they lobbied and obtained the bounty to encourage Protestant settlers to migrate to South Carolina and petitioned for land grants to accommodate them. They used their connections back home to recruit emigrants and then directed the flow of immigration to specific settlements in the Carolina backcountry.[139]

The white population of western North Carolina grew by 229 percent between 1755 and 1767. Scotch-Irish emigrants from Ireland and from Virginia and North Carolina (along with German immigrants) were largely responsible for doubling South Carolina's white population to 70,000 between 1763 and 1775.[140] The drift southward continued, and Scotch-Irish people were penetrating Indian lands in Georgia by the eve of the Revolution. Acting governor James Habersham received a written application for land in 1772 "from two Presbyterian Congregations in North Carolina, and signed by 360 Men, principally Heads of Families." More worrying, he told Scotch-Irish trader George Galphin, "a percel of stragling northward People" were squatting on Indian lands and some had "built Hutts." Many of these "idle People from the Northward" were reputed to be "great Villians, Horse Stealers &c." They had no settled habitation, and lived by hunting and plundering industrious settlers. These "Crackers," as Habersham called them, were "by no means the sort of People that should settle those lands." The governor issued proclamations ordering them to remove but he expected their numbers to increase.[141]

By the eve of the American Revolution, Scotch-Irish colonists had established communities in New England, New York, Pennsylvania, and Maryland, and along the 700-mile arc of the Great Wagon Road through Virginia and the Carolinas (see Map 2.2). More than 500 settlements spread over almost all the American colonies and dominated a 1,500-mile frontier along the spine of the Appalachians from northern New England to Georgia. Ninety percent of the population of the Cumberland Valley (present-day Cumberland and Franklin Counties) in Pennsylvania was Scotch-Irish; there were more Scotch-Irish in the Carolina Piedmont than all other groups

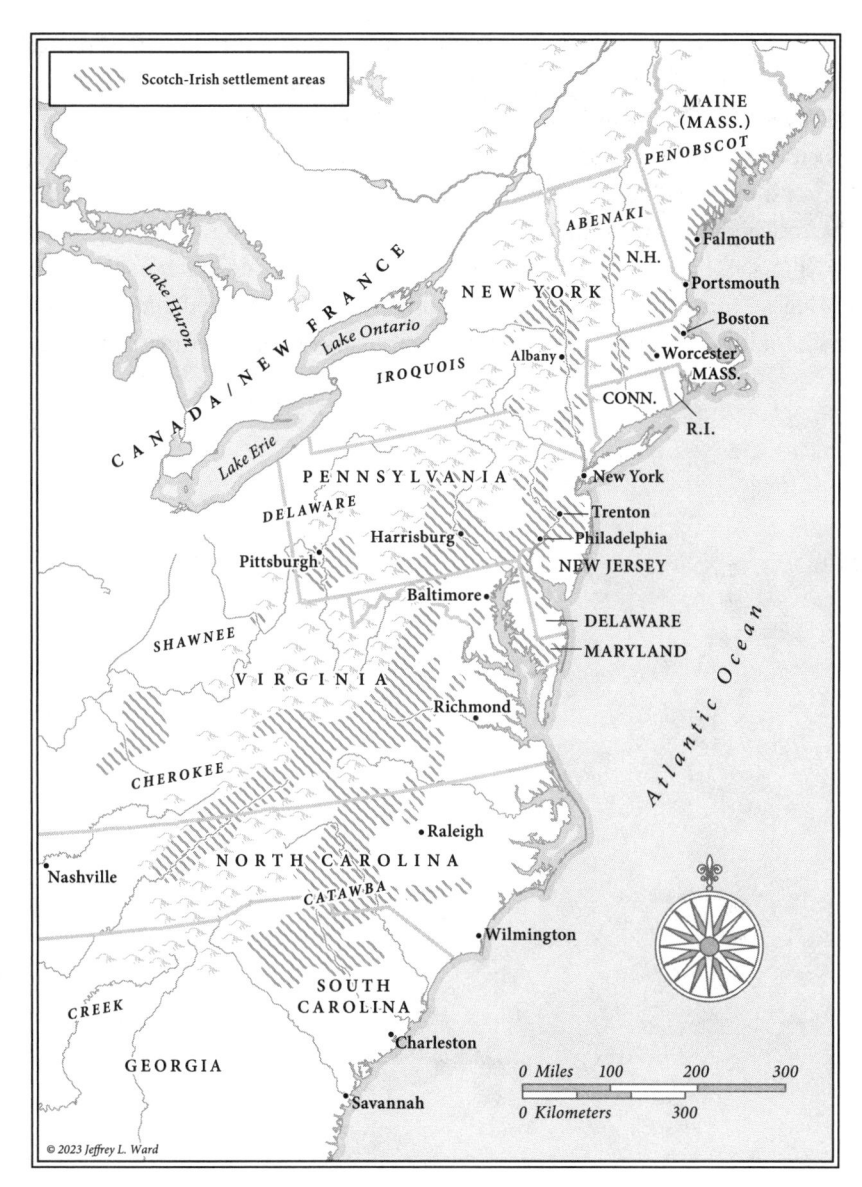

Map 2.2 Distribution of Scotch-Irish settlements, ca. 1780.

together, and they were also moving into the upper valley of the Savannah River in Georgia. "A map of their settlements is almost a map of the pre-Revolutionary frontier," wrote historian Bernard Bailyn.[142] Some were looking beyond the mountains into Kentucky and Tennessee. Long hunters who went for months on extended hunting expeditions often identified routes for subsequent family migrations through mountain passes and destinations for eventual settlement.[143] Often recruited by colonial authorities to take up positions on the edges of Indian country and often squatting on Indian lands beyond where colonial authorities wanted them to be, Scotch-Irish families had pushed their way into the homelands and hunting grounds of Wabanaki, Iroquois, Delaware, Shawnee, Catawba, Cherokee, and other nations. In doing so, they created borderland worlds where they clashed and coexisted with multiple Indian peoples, many of whom, like them, were on the move.

3

A Devil's Bargain

In an essay dated December 1728, the Anglo-Irish satirist Jonathan Swift—of *Gulliver's Travels* fame—asked why so many families were migrating from Ireland and why "our *Northern* People" were so eager to undertake a long and dangerous ocean voyage and settle in America. One reason was clear. Like the Romans who had filled their ranks with barbarous people "for no other service than to blunt their Enemies Swords," the English in America needed men "to inhabit that Tract of Ground, which lyes between them, and the *Wild Indians*." Consequently, "our People who Transport themselves, are settled in those interjacent Tracts, as a screen against the Insults of the *Savages* and may have as much Land, as they can clear from the Woods, at a very reasonable Rate, if they can afford to pay about a *hundred* years Purchase by their Labour."[1] People who had been placed on a borderland in Ulster as buffers against the "wild Irish" were now being placed on borderlands in America as buffers against the "wild Indians." Time and again in the decades that followed, Scotch-Irish colonists encroached on Indigenous lands, created a hard edge of settler colonialism that grated against Indian country, and protected fellow colonists against Indian attacks. At the same time, the British government recruited Highland Scots as well as Irishmen to serve the Empire on its frontiers and in its regiments.[2]

As Swift well knew, his countrymen were not the first people in history to have been used as expendable defensive barriers. Nor, in North America, were they the only ones. Almost everywhere they settled, Scotch-Irish people encountered Indian peoples who were also living between contending powers, both Native and non-Native. Like colonial powers, some tribal peoples constructed layered buffer zones to protect themselves and their interests by putting other peoples in harm's way.

In the more than 130 years since Frederick Jackson Turner presented his famous thesis, scholars have questioned, qualified, and complicated the notion of a "frontier"—with good reason. North American frontiers were porous zones of interaction, a series of shifting and overlapping borderlands that existed between and merged with other worlds. Empires, nation-states, and colonies drew sharp lines on maps as they aspired to establish hard borders that clearly defined the extent of their territorial reach and authority. Yet as colonial power seeped into Indian country, borderland regions were fuzzy, fluid, and temporary. Indians, wrote the colonial cartographer Lewis Evans, "do not generally bound their Countries by Lines, but by considerable Extents of Land," and they "fix their Towns commonly on the Edges of great Rivers for the Sake of the rich Lawns to sow their Corn in. The intermediate Ground they reserve for their Hunting, which equally serves for that purpose and a Frontier."[3]

It was not unusual for Native nations to share zones in which they hunted but did not permanently inhabit with other Native nations. Similarly, when Europeans arrived, sovereignties sometimes overlapped, and Natives and newcomers shared and contested spaces that no one controlled. Settler colonists had to work out their own relations with Indian peoples who wielded local power, possessed local knowledge, and provided access to local resources and extensive trade networks. For people on the ground, borderlands were "lived spaces" where they came and went and interacted in personal ways with little or no regard for lines on maps in distant capitals. They forged patterns of coexistence and even collaboration, and they found strength in interdependency and building alliances. At the same time, inhabiting the borderlands sometimes meant fighting for survival, sometimes seeking refuge with more powerful neighbors.[4]

Rather than confronting an undifferentiated mass of "white" invaders, multiple Indian peoples contended with multiple groups of colonists, first from different regions of Europe and then from the different geographic cultural regions the immigrants created within America. And rather than invading a monolithic Indian world, the Scotch-Irish intruded into a kaleidoscopic geopolitical landscape created by competing colonial and Indigenous powers. Some Native people moved into borderland areas to take advantage of the opportunities they offered for trade and took up intermediary roles with colonial and Indigenous neighbors. Smaller groups sought security and shelter under the protection of more powerful neighbors, whether Native or non-Native. Some groups strengthened their positions by building alliances and extending kinship ties; some absorbed refugees and built new communities. All sought protection, and protection came at a cost as Native and non-Native powers sought to control their respective backcountry populations.[5] Indigenous nations watched their Indigenous neighbors as closely as they did European invaders, induced or coerced other Indigenous people into occupying strategic regions, and sometimes even allowed colonists to settle on the edges of tribal territory.

Moving allies or dependent peoples to particular locations also allowed competing powers to assert their claims or reaffirm their sovereignty over contested lands and corridors by populating them with their own subordinate groups. Like the fingers of European settlement reaching into Indian country, the buffer zones they constructed often ran along river valleys—the Susquehanna, the Shenandoah, and the Tennessee.[6] Placed in these regions to advance colonial agendas, Scotch-Irish people found their lives were often shaped, and sometimes upended, by Indigenous agendas.

Indian Peoples in Motion

Borderland peoples were perpetually on the move and often jostled for position. By the time the Scotch-Irish pushed their way into Indian country, Indian country itself was in motion. Multiple Native peoples migrated to escape war or disease and sought safer or more advantageous locations as the repercussions of colonialism played out across their homelands and balances of power shifted. Many of the Indigenous groups the Scotch-Irish encountered were, like them, diasporic people.

Scotch-Irish colonists on New England's northern frontiers—those, as mentioned in the previous chapter, who went to Maine and New Hampshire—found themselves in a precarious situation. Establishing settlements as a buffer against the French and Indians meant intruding into the homelands of Abenakis, Penobscots, and other Wabanaki peoples, which had been transformed into borderlands between the English to the south and the French to the north. King Philip's War, a multi-tribal war of resistance against English colonialism led by the Wampanoag chief Metacomet in 1675–1676, devastated Native communities in southern and central New England and sent reverberations and some of the survivors northward into Abenaki country. As English colonists pressed up the Connecticut and Merrimack Valleys, many Abenaki bands began retreating northward themselves, ahead of the expanding English frontier. They eventually built new communities around French mission villages at Odanak and Bécancouer on the St. Lawrence River. The French also sent Jesuit missionaries south into Wabanaki communities and cultivated alliances with Indian peoples who shared their commitment to stemming the northward flow of English settlement. During times of peace, Wabanakis maintained networks of coexistence and cooperation and moved back and forth across the borderland, praying at French mission villages in the north yet trading with the English at posts on the Connecticut and Merrimack rivers and on the coast. When wars broke out, however, they aligned with French. The French used Wabanakis as a buffer against the English, but Wabanakis were not pawns; the French were valuable allies in their resistance to English expansion.[7]

Scotch-Irish people who were encouraged by colonial authorities to settle areas north and west of Philadelphia encountered Indian peoples in the Susquehanna Valley who had been displaced by wars and diseases. Flowing more than four hundred miles from Iroquois country in the north to the Chesapeake Bay in the south, the Susquehanna River facilitated the passage of traders, warriors, emissaries, and migrants and brought diverse peoples into convergence and competition. It was a key corridor of movement and settlement, and the Iroquois were key players shaping that movement and settlement.

Stretching across what is now upstate New York, the five nations that comprised the League of the Iroquois—the Mohawks, Oneidas, Onondagas, Cayugas, and Senecas—called themselves Haudenosaunee, meaning "People of the Longhouse," and they envisioned their League as a longhouse that could be extended to include other people. They encouraged displaced tribes to take up residence in the Susquehanna, Wyoming, Shamokin, and other valleys and extended their protection over smaller groups who served as "props"—proxies of a sort—to the Longhouse. The arrangements allowed the League to extend its influence and commercial connections southward with a network of satellite groups, while controlling the diplomatic paths from Philadelphia and Shamokin to Onondaga. In return, the props, who submitted to generally light-handed control from Onondaga, agreed to aid the Iroquois when wars broke out, deferred to them in matters of diplomacy, and provided a bulwark against raids by southern Indian enemies and colonial encroachment. The League of the Five Nations became known as the Six Nations in the early 1720s when it took in between 1,500 and 2,000 Tuscaroras who had migrated northward after the so-called Tuscarora war with North Carolina in 1711–1713 and positioned them along the southern border of Oneida country. In a world of Indigenous mobility, with an "Abudance of Indians ... moving up and down," said the Mohawk chief Hendrick, the Iroquois reserved the lands at Shamokin and Wyoming on the North branch of the Susquehanna for allied nations. "We shall invite all such to come and live here, that so We may strengthen ourselves." On the edges of Iroquoia itself, the Iroquois homeland, they created borderlands where European and Native communities coexisted, and colonial and Indian settlers met and mingled.[8]

At the time of first contacts with Europeans, the original inhabitants of the Susquehanna were the Iroquoian-speaking Susquehannocks, who occupied the valley from the West Branch of the river in Pennsylvania southward to Maryland and Virginia and dominated large stretches of the Chesapeake and Delaware Bay regions. The core of the Susquehannocks' homeland on the lower Susquehanna Valley, which they called Gandastogue, was a center of trade and a hub of communication networks that reached from the Great Lakes to the Atlantic coast. In the seventeenth century the Susquehannocks extended their trade to include the Dutch, English, French, and Swedish colonies. Although Susquehannock appears to have been an Algonquian name meaning the "people of the Muddy River," the French usually called them "Andastes," derived from their Huron name Andastoerrhonon, while the Dutch and Swedes referred to them as "Minquas," a term given to them by their Delaware neighbors. The English adventurer and settler of Jamestown Captain John Smith met them when he traveled upriver in 1608 and described them as "great and well proportioned men" who "seemed like giants to the English," an observation supported by archaeological and other evidence which indicates that, while perhaps not tall by modern standards, Susquehannock men likely towered over seventeenth-century Europeans.[9]

At the peak of their power in the mid-1600s, the Susquehannocks may have numbered 1,300 warriors, with a total population of more than 6,000. Epidemic disease and intertribal conflicts scythed their numbers and, according to one account, they had dwindled to 300 by 1675. Pressured by the Iroquois who extended their power and their raids southward, Susquehannocks relocated south to the Piscataway. They had traded with the English inhabitants of Maryland and many now sought refuge there. The Maryland government encouraged their migration, hoping they would provide "a Bulwarke and Security of the Northern parts of this Province" against anticipated Iroquois aggression. Instead, in the conflicts spawned during Bacon's Rebellion—a revolt by English settlers against the policies of the colonial government— in 1675–1676, militia from Virginia and Maryland drove the Susquehannocks back north. In an assault on one Susquehannock village, when the inhabitants sent out five emissaries to sue for peace, they were, in William Penn's words, "betrayed out of their lives"; "against all reason and the Law and Custome of all nations," the colonists beat their heads in. One of the murderers was the great-grandfather of George Washington. Many of the surviving Susquehannocks were adopted into various Iroquois nations. Some took refuge with the Delawares. A small number settled with Shawnees and Senecas at the site of an ancient village and trading center at the junction of Conestoga Creek and the Susquehanna River in Pennsylvania. They became generally known as the Conestoga Indians.[10]

As Indian refugees moved up the Susquehanna and settled in valley locations, they had to sort out relationships and issues of space and sovereignty with one another, as well as with the Iroquois and Pennsylvania, both of whom laid claim to the important transportation corridor and its fertile lands. Remnants of fractured Susquehannock communities rebuilt ties of alliance with Native and non-Native powers.[11]

In 1700 two Susquehannock chiefs from Conestoga granted William Penn "all the said River Susquehannagh, and all the islands therein, and all the Lands Situate lying, and being upon both sides of said River" which formerly belonged to "the People or Nation called the Susquehannagh Indians." In return, Pennsylvania undertook to keep immoral individuals out of the Indians' lands. Struggling themselves to stave off encroaching colonists, the Susquehannocks agreed to let the colonial government police the boundary.

Indian peoples resettling in the valley did not necessarily view the increasing presence of the Pennsylvania government as a bad thing: Pennsylvania could serve as a counterweight to the Iroquois, who also sought to assert dominance over the valley and its peoples. When Penn sailed home to England in 1701, several chiefs sent the king a letter expressing their appreciation of Penn's just dealings with them, and their confidence "that we and our children and people will be well used and be encouraged to continue to live among the Christians according to the agreement that he and we have solemnly made for us and our posterity as long as the sun and moon shall endure, one head one mouth and one heart."[12] Sixty-two years later, the Paxton Boys murdered and mutilated the last Susquehannocks when they destroyed the small community at Conestoga.

When they first encountered Europeans, the Piscataway people inhabited numerous settlements north of the Potomac in the Chesapeake Bay region. Reduced by war, disease, and colonization in the seventeenth century, many Piscataways migrated northwest in the eighteenth century. One group in the border area between Maryland and Pennsylvania, where they were known as Ganawese, migrated up the Susquehanna and moved into the orbit of the Iroquois, who called them Conoys and allowed them to establish a town at Conoy Creek near Conestoga in Pennsylvania. A Conoy chief told the governor of Pennsylvania in 1743 that the Iroquois had "told 'em there was Land enough, they might chuse their place of Settlement any where about Sasquehannah" and "accordingly they thought fit to remove higher up Sasquehannah to the Conoy Town, where they now live."[13]

The most powerful tribe inhabiting Pennsylvania when the Scotch-Irish arrived were the Delawares. The Iroquois used the Delawares as a buffer against the colony, much as the colony used the Scotch-Irish as a buffer against the Delawares. Scotch-Irish and Delaware people had both been displaced and relocated "in between" on the respective frontiers of English and Iroquois hegemony.

Like the Scotch-Irish, Delaware people oriented their lives around clusters of small communities and kin groups. Most lived along the tributaries of the Lenapewihittuck, which the Dutch and Swedes called the South River and the English named the Delaware.[14] During the seventeenth century, prior to William Penn's arrival, Delawares coexisted and traded with the Dutch, Swedes, and Finns. Despite recurrent losses to imported epidemic diseases, they retained control of their territory and supplemented their traditional lifeways with new goods and technology, such as metal tools and weapons and woolen blankets.[15] The English seized the Delaware region, along with the rest of New Netherland—the Dutch colony that stretched from Albany in New York down to Delaware Bay—in 1664. The influx of immigrants into William Penn's colony in the 1680s disrupted Delaware life far more than the Dutch and Swedes had done. By 1690 more than 8,800 English, Welsh, Scots, Irish, German, and French Huguenots inhabited the Delaware Valley, along with remaining Finns, Swedes, and Dutch. The population of Pennsylvania reached 21,000 in 1700; 37,000 in 1720.[16]

Diseases continued to thin the population. At least three smallpox epidemics had struck the Delawares by 1677 and worse followed. A German minister who lived in Pennsylvania during the smallpox epidemic of 1688–1691 said so many died "that there are hardly more than a fourth part of the number existing that were to be seen when I came to the country ten years ago." In a letter written in 1698, a Welsh colonist estimated the population collapse at more than 90 percent. Another colonist heard "the Indians themselves say, that two of them die for every one Christian that comes in here."[17]

William Penn established a reputation for fair dealings with the Indigenous inhabitants, but his land policies left little room for Native conceptions of land use, which involved seasonal occupation of sites and sharing resources among different groups. He sold more than 800,000 acres in his first decade. Although some Delawares attempted to coexist with the colonists, most began to withdraw from southeastern Pennsylvania as the newcomers took over the land and transformed the landscape into a world of farms, fields, and fences. Some retreated north to the Forks of the Delaware, where the Lehigh and Delaware rivers meet, and some settled in the Tulpehocken and Brandywine valleys. Others began to move west to the Susquehanna. In the first decade of the eighteenth century, displaced Delawares and Shawnees founded a new town on the Susquehanna at a shallow point ideal for river crossings and named it "Peshtank," meaning "place where the waters stand still," in Delaware. Sometime before 1709, the Delaware chief Sassoonan took his people there from Tulpehocken to avoid conflict with encroaching settlers. Shortly after, another Delaware band led by Chocochinican left the Brandywine area for the same reason. A Shawnee band joined them in 1711. The Scotch-Irish were not far behind them. In less than a decade, emigrants from Ulster were beginning to push the Native people out of the area. Peshtank became Paxtang or Paxton in English.[18] Squeezed between expanding European settlement, the migration of Susquehannocks and Conoys into the Susquehanna Valley, and the powerful Iroquois confederation to the north, some Delawares moved farther up the Susquehanna. Others joined Shawnees in a growing movement west to other valleys: the Allegheny and the Ohio (see Map 3.1).[19]

The Shawnees originated in the Ohio Valley.[20] When the Jesuit missionary Jacques Marquette traveled down the Mississippi in 1673, his Indian guides told him there were large numbers of Shawnee villages clustered along the banks of the Wabash-Ohio. French maps in the late seventeenth century located the Shawnees on the Ohio and Cumberland rivers, and some labeled the latter the "rivière des Chaouanons."[21] By then, Shawnee people were on the move, to escape the violence brought by Iroquois war parties raiding the Ohio country and to pursue new trading opportunities. Some fled to the Great Lakes. Many migrated to the southeast, where South Carolina welcomed them to help protect its settlements against other Indians, notably the Westos. The Westos themselves had been displaced from the shores of Lake Erie by Iroquois attacks and migrated south, where they raided other Native people for slaves and traded them to Virginia and South Carolina. Now the Shawnees raided the Westos for captives and sold *them* as slaves in Carolina in exchange for guns. Shawnees also fought against the Catawbas

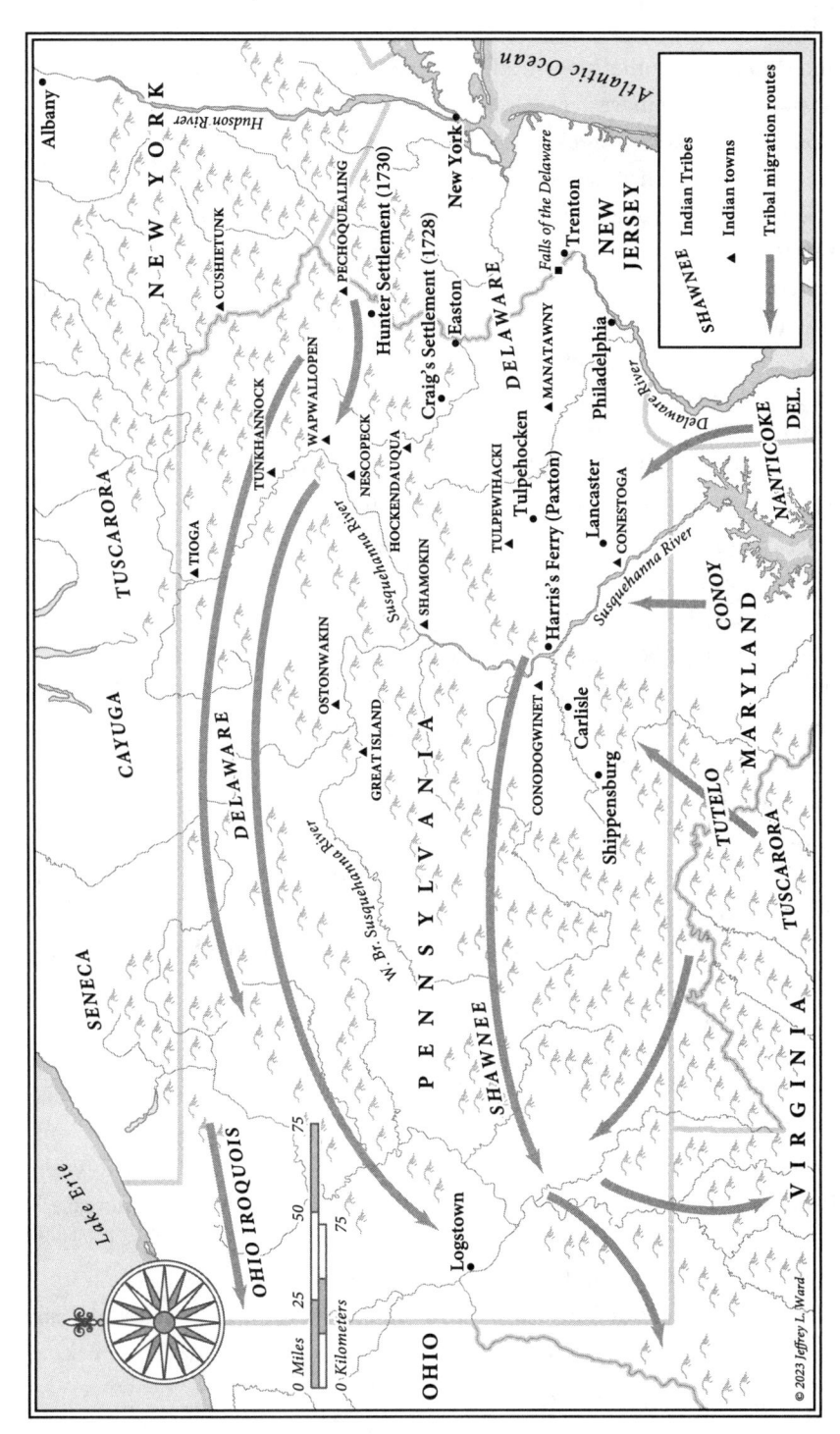

Map 3.1 Scotch-Irish settlements, Indian villages, and tribal migrations in Pennsylvania and the Susquehanna Valley, 1720s–1740s.

and clashed with other slave-trading nations such as the Chickasaws.[22] Other Shawnees settled in western Virginia, on the Savannah River in Georgia, and alongside Muskogee Creeks on the Tallapoosa River in Alabama.

In the 1690s, Shawnees established a large village on the Delaware River and built other villages along the Susquehanna, where, according to one Pennsylvania official, they "had two or three towns of their own but they scattered into divers places . . . living promiscuously & intermarrying" with neighboring tribes. James Logan, secretary of the province of Pennsylvania, reminded Shawnee chiefs visiting Philadelphia in 1739 that forty years earlier "a considerable number of families of your nation . . . applied to the Indians of Susquehanna to settle among them." Logan reported in 1705 that Shawnees who had recently fled from Maryland had settled near Conestoga. More moved from the Savannah River to Pennsylvania in 1707, to escape increasing hostilities with Carolina; another band followed after relations between English colonists and their major Native trade partners broke down in the Yamasee War in 1715–1717. By the time the Scotch-Irish began arriving in numbers a decade or so later, Shawnee towns were scattered through the middle Atlantic region. Joining other peoples displaced by war and disease, they positioned themselves between the English and "foreign Indians"—as the colonizers referred to those not allied with them—and between the Iroquois and their southern enemies like the Catawbas, who also used the Susquehanna corridor to raid northward. These Shawnees traded and built alliances with other communities, but they found little respite in the Susquehanna Valley.[23]

Both Pennsylvania and the Iroquois tried to control the Shawnees, who seemed to be everywhere. According to James Logan, "the 5 nations who claim Susquehannah and Account themselves Masters of all the Indians of Pennsylvania kept a Jealous Eye over them." In 1728 the Grand Council at Onondaga, which met each year and oversaw the interests of the Iroquois League, appointed the Oneida chief Shikellamy as its ambassador or "half king" to keep that eye on the Shawnees and speak for them in councils with Pennsylvania. Meanwhile, Pennsylvania's booming population increased the pressure on Indian lands. As German and Scotch-Irish settlers pushed into the Susquehanna Valley, Shawnee people began to move again. In the 1720s and 1730s, communities in the lower valley relocated upriver and then from the West Branch of the Susquehannah west to Conemaugh Creek, a tributary of the Allegheny River in western Pennsylvania. Shawnees at the village of Chillisquaque, on the West Branch just north of present-day

Northumberland, left for Ohio around 1728. Other Shawnees followed and then began to filter across the Appalachians through the valleys of the West Branch, Juniata, Youghiogheny, and Monongahela, settling in the Allegheny and Ohio valleys. Moving west and returning home, the Shawnees distanced themselves from the British and the Iroquois. They rebuilt ties with other Native groups in the Ohio country and repositioned themselves between the British and the French in the Europeans' growing competition in the region, trading and dealing diplomatically with both. That worried Logan, who tried to entice them back to the Susquehanna with the promise of a large reservation of land on the west bank.[24]

In addition to Conoys, Delawares, and Shawnees on the move, and Tuscaroras who stopped at various locations along the way as they traveled north to join the Iroquois, the Susquehanna Valley became home for Mahicans displaced from the Hudson River, Nanticokes from Maryland, and Tutelos from the border of Virginia and North Carolina. Refugee peoples established towns along creeks up and down its length. There were almost fifty Indian towns in the valley in the eighteenth century.[25] Many of them were multiethnic communities. Shamokin, the largest, at the junction of North and West Branch of the Susquehanna River (later Fort Augusta, present-day Sunbury), was inhabited by Delawares, Mahicans, Shawnees, Conoys, Nanticokes, Tutelos, and Iroquois people. It had more than fifty houses and three hundred inhabitants when missionary David Brainerd visited it in 1745. With major water routes running in three directions and a dozen trails radiating from it, Shamokin was a congregation point for tribal peoples, a rendezvous for travelers, and "the veritable Indian capital of Pennsylvania."[26]

By the time Scotch-Irish people entered the upper Susquehanna and its tributaries in 1720s and 1730s, many of the Native peoples they met had diasporic histories much like their own.

Iroquois Props and Pennsylvanian Buffers

Weakened by a cycle of wars, the Iroquois pursued a formal policy of neutrality after 1700 to avoid entanglement in conflicts between Britain and France. Restoring their strength and sustaining their influence by diplomacy rather than war, they adroitly played off each imperial power against the other. The British courted them as allies against the French because, as the Lords of Trade and Plantations explained to James Stanhope, George I's

Secretary of State for the South, in 1715, "the Five Nations of Indians lying on the back of New York, between the French of Canada and our settlements, are the only barrier between the said French and their Indians, and His Majesty's Plantations as far as Virginia and Maryland."[27]

For their part, the Iroquois also strengthened their hand in dealing with Pennsylvania. Seeing that Pennsylvania was pushing north and west into the Susquehanna Valley, the Iroquois acted as intermediaries between Pennsylvania and the smaller tribes inhabiting the province, thereby increasing their influence with both. The Onondagas, the central council fire of the Longhouse, and the Senecas, the largest tribe and the keepers of the western door, took the lead in building these arrangements; the Susquehanna River led into Onondaga country and many Senecas had kin living among the Indian peoples in the valley. The Mohawks, the keepers of the eastern door, primarily focused their diplomatic relations on Albany and Montreal.[28] The refugee, remnant, and relocated peoples who clustered in villages along the length of the Susquehanna protected Iroquois country against Catawba and Cherokee raiders who were likely to strike Iroquois "props" as they headed north before, or instead of, reaching the Iroquois themselves. Pennsylvanians even suspected the Iroquois were trying to use *them* as a buffer. Governor William Keith complained to his council in 1720 that Iroquois war parties were insolent and threatening; they robbed traders and threw their weight around. Having raided their southern enemies, they retreated to the vicinity of Pennsylvania's settlements to escape retaliation, "So that it seems as if they intended to make us a Barrier by drawing their provok'd Enemies first upon us before they can come at them."[29]

Scotch-Irish colonists who pushed into the Susquehanna Valley, then, not only displaced Indian people; they also, often, threatened or disrupted existing intertribal relationships. It was an issue that Governor Patrick Gordon of Pennsylvania invoked in April 1732 when complaining to Governor Ogle of Maryland about the activities of his agent Michael Cresap and his settlement of colonists in the disputed borderlands between their two colonies. The Six Nations had long claimed the Susquehanna River and its tributaries as theirs, other Indians acknowledged their claim, and treaties had been made with them about those lands, Gordon said; "what may be the issue of it when they see such great Numbers settled as they will now find of those distressed people of Ireland, who have generally without any permission from this Governm^t sat down on those Lands, is very uncertain."[30]

It suited Pennsylvania to recognize Iroquois claims to the Susquehanna Valley. James Logan energetically pursued an alliance to bring the Iroquois tribes and Pennsylvania together "as one people & one Body" and implement a new policy that, in Thomas Penn's words, would "strengthen the hands of the Six Nations, and enable them to be the better answerable for their Tributaries." Logan floated the idea in the summer of 1732 when a delegation of Seneca, Cayuga, and Oneida chiefs, including Shikellamy, Onondaga's half king in the Susquehanna Valley, arrived in Philadelphia to discuss the terms of an alignment with the Pennsylvania proprietors. The alliance was solidified four years later when the Iroquois formally aligned themselves with Pennsylvania. Operating on the assumption that the Iroquois "have an absolute Authority over all our Indians, and may command them as they please," as Governor Gordon put it, the Pennsylvania government gave the Iroquois its backing to exert that authority over the other tribes. It encouraged refugee tribes—such as the Conestogas, Conoys, and Shawnees—to settle in the province in the hope of bringing security to its frontiers and acquiring more Indian allies against the French. The Six Nations received material and political support from Pennsylvania in return for exerting their clout in Pennsylvania's interests, which often meant conveying title to Indian lands.[31]

The Pennsylvania proprietors and Six Nations chiefs disagreed on specific issues, but they cooperated to oversee the disposition of other peoples' lands and direct the settlement of frontier communities whose presence in their respective areas of control gave them protection and broader claims to territory.[32] Six Nations delegates in Philadelphia in 1736 asserted that only they, and not the Conestoga chief Civility, had authority to speak for Indian peoples on the Susquehanna and sell land. If Civility should try to sell any lands, colonial officials must let the Iroquois know because "he hath no Power to do so & if he does anything of the kind, they, the Indians will utterly disown him." Moving Civility out of the equation, the Iroquois put themselves forward, in other words, rather than the people who actually lived there, as the legitimate authority to sell lands on the Susquehanna.[33]

Delawares, who had come to regard the traditions of fair treatment established by William Penn as integral to the conduct of diplomacy, now faced an Iroquois-Penn pact that rode roughshod over those traditions.[34]

Penn's sons took advantage of the Six Nations' assertions of dominance over the Delawares who had removed to Pennsylvania and settled on lands the Iroquois claimed. The Iroquois ritually expressed that dominance by making the Delawares metaphorical "women," denying them the authority to make war—a male activity—without Iroquois approval. The Delawares for their part acquiesced, acknowledging themselves under Iroquois protection, and agreed not to wage war without their approval, focusing instead on making and maintaining peace, a role which they had traditionally exercised among eastern tribes and for which women held great responsibility in Iroquois society. Calling the Delawares "women" defined the symbolic relationship. But the meaning attached to the Delawares' metaphorical womanhood shifted. Europeans misread it as demeaning. In time, as Iroquois sold Delaware lands without consulting them, Delawares found it demeaning as well.[35]

Logan's cynical policy was put into effect in the infamous "Walking Purchase." Eager to extinguish Delaware claims to lands not yet purchased in the upper Delaware and Lehigh valleys, Thomas Penn and his associates in 1734 claimed to have found a copy of a deed made in 1686 in which certain Delaware chiefs granted William Penn and his heirs land "as far as a man can go in a day and a half" and from there to the Delaware River and down its course. The deed had ostensibly transferred land on the west bank of the Delaware north of Tohickon Creek, including lands in the Forks where Delawares lived. In May 1735, acting on behalf of Penn's sons, Logan presented a copy of the old deed to several Delaware chiefs. The original was allegedly missing. Strongarmed into agreeing, the chiefs confirmed the deed in Philadelphia a year later. When it came to measuring out the lands, instead of dispatching a single individual to walk the woods, the Pennsylvanians cleared a path and sent a relay team of three runners racing along it. The runners—Edward Marshall, James Yeates, and Solomon Jennings—were paid £5 each and promised 500 acres of land within the purchase. By noon on the second day, they had covered about sixty-five miles and reached the farthest possible point to the northwest; a line was then drawn from the end of the walk to the Delaware River. This "Walking Purchase" gobbled up 1,100 square miles and deprived the Delawares of their last lands in the upper Delaware and Lehigh valleys. According to a late-nineteenth-century history of the region, the course of the walk went "directly through the Irish Settlement that had been formed nine years before," namely Craig's Settlement or Allentown. It wrested from the Delawares their lands there and finally brought the Irish Settlement under the control of the proprietary government.[36] Logan set aside ten square miles at the Forks as a reservation for the Indians while Thomas Penn released patents to new buyers. One hundred families settled in the area by 1740.[37]

The Delawares protested that they were "Very much Wronged & Abused of having Our Lands taken & Settled & We know not how," but Logan's Indian policy was intended to deal with such problems.[38] Summoning Delaware and Six Nations delegates to Philadelphia in July 1742, Thomas Penn turned to the Onondaga spokesman Canasatego and the Six Nations to silence the complaints. "As you on all Occasions apply to Us to remove all White people that are settled on Lands before they are purchased from You, and we do our Endeavours to turn such People Off," he said, "We now expect from You that you will cause these Indians to remove from the Lands in the fforks [sic] of the Delaware, and not give any further Disturbance to the Persons who are now in Possession." Canasatego duly browbeat the Delawares into acquiescing in the Pennsylvanian land thefts. "You ought to be taken by the Hair of the Head and shak'd till you recover your Senses," he told them. He had seen the deed with his own eyes and it was just, he said. The Delawares had acted foolishly and were threatening to break the chain of friendship with Pennsylvania. "We conquer'd You, we made Women of you, you know you are Women, and can no more sell Land than Women." The Delawares must leave the ceded lands at once and go to Wyoming or Shamokin, where "we shall have you more under our eye, and Shall see how You behave."[39] Reasserting their dominance over the Delawares and moving them into the upper Susquehanna Valley, the Iroquois reaffirmed their own importance in the minds of the colonial ally, whose interests they promoted at the same time as they strengthened the buffer zone between themselves and Pennsylvania.

Caught between a Pennsylvania rock and an Iroquois hard place, most of the Delawares living at the Forks moved to the refugee towns on the upper Susquehanna. Almost twenty years later, the eastern Delaware chief Teedyuscung was still fuming over what had been an outright land grab. "This very Ground that is under me (striking it with his Foot) was my Land and Inheritance and is taken from me by Fraud," he declared at a treaty council in Easton.[40] Governor William Denny responded that in Indian society, memory of land sales sometimes died with those who made the sale, "and as you do not understand Writings and Records, it may be hard for me to satisfy you of the Truth, though my Predecessors dealt ever so uprigthly."[41]

Holding the Alliance and Controlling the Buffers

While Canasatego was rebuking the Delawares in Philadelphia, events in the Shenandoah Valley to the south were testing the bonds of Pennsylvania's alliance with the Six Nations. Before it became the Great Wagon Road that carried Scotch-Irish migrants from Pennsylvania to Virginia and the Carolinas, the Shenandoah Valley was a major route of the Great Warriors' Path. Iroquois warriors traveled south to raid the Cherokees and Catawbas, and Cherokees and Catawbas traveled north to raid the Iroquois, conflicts that both sides maintained had been going on "since we were created."[42] Although colonial settlements in the area were few and slight in the early years, war parties traveling the path as they had done for years clashed with the newcomers to the Shenandoah Valley. The governors of New York, Pennsylvania, and Virginia met with the Iroquois at the Treaty of Albany in 1722 to resolve this and other problems, and the Iroquois agreed to keep their war parties west of the Blue Ridge, though conflicts increased as more colonists spilled over the mountains and took up lands along the path.

As the threat of war with France loomed, Pennsylvania's Iroquois alliance was more important than ever, and neither the colonies of Virginia, Pennsylvania, and Maryland nor the Six Nations wanted bloodletting on their frontiers. In June 1744, some 250 Iroquois people assembled at Lancaster to meet with the governors of those colonies. (One of the colonial secretaries described Lancaster as a filthy place whose German and Scotch-Irish inhabitants were "not as yet in the least troubled" by "the spirit of cleanliness."[43]) Governor George Thomas of Pennsylvania opened the conference by reminding his fellow colonial officials that, positioned as they were on the frontiers of the colonies, the Iroquois could defend the settlements if they were friends; ravage them if they were enemies; or deny the French passage if they were neutral. It was therefore vital to cultivate "a good Understanding with them" and avoid any rupture. "Every advantage you gain over them in War will be a Weakening of the Barrier of these Colonies, and Consequently will be in Effect Victories over your selves and your Fellow Subjects," he warned.[44] Rather than have the empire defend the frontiers, Thomas saw the Iroquois as the most expedient means of protecting the colonies from attack, much as Logan had viewed the Scotch-Irish in the 1720s.[45]

Canasatego reasserted Iroquois ownership of other peoples' lands in Maryland with an oratorical flourish and a dubious claim to aboriginal occupancy. He also assented unknowingly to a massive cession of lands beyond the Appalachian Mountains. To avoid conflicts in the Shenandoah Valley, the Iroquois delegates allowed colonists to cross the Valley of Virginia and ceded their claims to land on Virginia's western border. They were not aware that Virginia's original royal charter granted the colony land "from sea to sea"— in other words, from the Atlantic to the Pacific! As the Treaty of Lancaster was written, the Iroquois ceded an enormous swath of territory belonging to other tribes and opened the Ohio country to British colonial expansion, setting the stage for a collision with France in the area and a global war that would enmesh Native nations and colonists alike.[46]

There were no guarantees that either the individual colonies or the Six Nations would act as one. As long as the Six Nations remained neutral, Pennsylvania would remain shielded. However, if colonial rulers in New York or New England induced the Mohawks to go to war against the French, Cayugas and Senecas farther west and closer to the French might side with France and threaten Pennsylvania.[47] But the alliance held. "You are sensible that we are a frontier Country between your Enemy & You, so that we have been your Guard, & things have been manag'd so well as to keep the War from your Doors," Canasatego reminded Deputy Governor James Hamilton of Pennsylvania in Philadelphia in August 1749.[48]

Nevertheless, the relentless expansion of colonial settlers put repeated pressure on borderland regions. In time, many of the displaced Indian peoples living in the Susquehanna Valley were displaced again as Germans, English, and Scotch-Irish intruders disrupted their fur-hunting economy and cleared lands for settlement.[49] Conoys left the lands reserved for them by the proprietors and moved to the Juniata Valley because "the Setling of the White people all around them had made Deer Scarce." They found little respite there and had abandoned their towns at the mouth of the Juniata by 1750.[50] Iroquois deputies in Philadelphia complained about the growing settlements on the branches of the Juniata "on hunting grounds of our Nanticoke cousins" and other nations, pointing out that "white people are no more obedient to you than our young Indians are to us." The Iroquois offered to cede the uplands on the east side of the Susquehanna from the Blue Hills or Chambers Mill to where the Scotch-Irish trader Thomas McKee lived and leave it up to Pennsylvania to assign the value to them, but they urged the government to remove the squatters so that the country was left "entirely vacant."[51]

Squatters on lands still unpurchased along the Tuscarora, Sherman's Creek, and other streams caused consternation among the Native people living in the area, the Onondaga council of the Six Nations, who claimed to control the lands, and the government in Philadelphia, which wanted orderly and peaceful expansion. The Pennsylvania proprietors worked to dispossess squatters as well as Indians as they endeavored to control both the land base and the process of expansion. They wanted to stop squatters from overrunning the Susquehanna, and they also feared that squatters would lease land from the Indians rather than from them as landlords.

In May 1750, Governor Hamilton issued a proclamation banning settlement on unpurchased land west of the Susquehanna. People evidently ignored it. In May, Hamilton sent provincial secretary Richard Peters, together with the German interpreter Conrad Weiser, Irish trader George Croghan, and Métis interpreter Andrew Montour, to Cumberland County, the Juniata Valley, Sherman's Creek, and Great Cove "to take proper Measures with the Magistrates to remove the Settlers over the Hills who had presum'd to stay there, notwithstanding his Proclamation prohibiting their Stay under the severest Penalties." According to Peters, "the Ranges of Country said to be seized by these vile people extend from Juniata and its Waters all along the Indians' Path thro both the Coves above half way to Allegheny." Unless his party exercised "a prudent severity" with the first people they came across and thereby intimidated the rest to remove voluntarily, he feared the job would likely take up a good part of the summer. Peters, Weiser, and Montour were accompanied by eight Cumberland County magistrates, and by five Indians to witness the evictions, including three from Shamokin and two sons of Shikellamy "who transact the business of the Six Nations with this government." "What the authority of this weak Government cannot do," wrote Peters, "It is hoped the appearance of the Indians will effect." In fact, he could think of no way to deal with resistance except "to get the Indians to burn the log houses, and what effect this will have I cannot say." The party ejected sixty-one families of squatters west of the Susquehanna and burned some forty cabins. The cabins were of no great value, they said, "being such as the Country People erect in a Day or two."[52]

The evictees were, of course, predominantly Scotch-Irish: Armstrong, Campbell, Cohoon, Cowan, Doyle, Downy, Dunlap, Gass, Jamison, Kilaugh, Kirkpatrick, Lewis, McCartie, McClare, MacDonnell, McKeeb, MacClelland, Macmean, Millican, Murray, Patterson, Scott, Stuart, as well as Simon Girty and others. Most succumbed, Peters reported; only George and William Galloway and Andrew Lycon resisted.[53] The Iroquois were appeased by the evictions. When chiefs at Onondaga asked Weiser in

September 1750 what had been done about the squatters on their land near Juniata Creek, he was able to tell them that the governor had sent his secretary and magistrates and had evicted them, and that Weiser and Indians from Shamokin had been witnesses. The chiefs said, "they were very glad that their Brother the Governor of Pennsylvania had taken Notice of their Complaint."[54] Representatives of the colonial government in Philadelphia and the Iroquois government at Onondaga had collaborated in trying to prevent the people Pennsylvania had placed on its borders from crowding out the people the Iroquois had placed on their borders.

Scotch-Irish squatters were furious and most returned to rebuild their cabins. Scotch-Irish traders, merchants, and others with ties to the proprietary government supported the measures, however. Surveyor John Armstrong of Carlisle, who had emigrated from Enniskillin in Ulster, felt he needed to bring three or four Indians with him for protection when surveying one tract of land in case he was "Stopt by the Irish with guns" as he had been before.[55]

Backcountry settlers and squatters remained a headache for the Pennsylvania authorities, and for Richard Peters in particular. Maintaining a human borderland was difficult when it was as mobile as the Scotch-Irish. In a long and rambling letter to the proprietors in March 1752, Peters fretted about the numbers who were leaving Pennsylvania. The reason, he said, was "that most of the Irish live high and fall into debt, and the Dutch [Germans] buy them out at any rate." After they had settled their debts, the Irish had little money left. As there was no vacant land nearby, nor any place within the province purchased from the Indians, they moved on to Virginia or Carolina, where they could take up land without having to pay any "consideration." Peters reckoned that three hundred families had gone away the previous year and that the trend would continue until more lands were purchased. Many people did not like the Virginia and Carolina backcountry ("detestable Places" by all accounts, said Peters) and would "risque any thing rather than go there and so flock in numbers over the Hills in spite of the Government." If these people were not punished, "the authority of the Government would be at an end," and if the Germans took their places, "there will soon be an end of the Constitution."

Peters despaired of being able to rein in the backcountry Scotch-Irish. "I suppose there is not in the world a more stubborn and perverse People than those of the County of Cumberland," he told the proprietors; "what is the Authority of a Governor at such a Distance, and where there is no Gaol and a Pack of Banditti over the Hills[?]" As the officer charged with enforcing the government's proclamations but without any support from that government, Peters was in an embarrassing situation. The "Rioters," as he called them, had powerful allies in the county. No one of influence supported the government, and the members of the assembly either sided with the people or lacked the heart to carry out the government's measures. "Add to this and which quite unmans me the Numbers of Irish who are continually going out of the County of Cumberland to Virginia and Carolina. Under these different and mortifying views of things, it is no wonder that my mind is disturbed." The only way to stem the exodus was to make an extensive new purchase of land from the Indians, in which case people would then probably come back from Virginia and Carolina "and settle like Bees." A new purchase, said Peters, was "absolutely necessary."[56]

Colonial officials often used squatting—and the Indians' complaints about it—as the pretext for purchasing more land, and they often purchased the lands, whomever they belonged to, from the Six Nations. At the Albany Congress in 1754—where Benjamin Franklin famously first floated his plan for a union of the colonies—Weiser and Peters engineered a huge sale of land on the Susquehanna from the Iroquois. Delaware and other war parties targeted settlements in the disputed area when the Seven Years War broke out the following year.[57]

Escaping the Susquehanna Borderland

As Scotch-Irish people occupied the Susquehanna Valley in growing numbers, Indian people left it in growing numbers. As colonial settlers increased in the lower valley, Delawares and Shawnees retreated to the upper valley, following the system of interlinked trails over the Allegheny Plateau to the Ohio Valley. People who functioned as borderland communities were not simply passive victims of colonial or tribal policies. Movable people were not always manageable. Whether Scotch-Irish or Indian, they negotiated, built, and severed their own relationships and occasionally refused to acknowledge the political authority of the powers—imperial, colonial, or Iroquois—that claimed to control them. As it was for the Scotch-Irish, mobility was a strategy of survival for Indian peoples seeking to preserve their independence and trying to keep distance between themselves and encroaching Europeans.[58] They were not hapless refugees, driven west like human flotsam by the flood of colonial settlers; they made calculated moves, often after several seasons of hunting, planting, or fishing in new locations; they maintained connections with related and allied groups east of the mountains; and they maintained their own clan and tribal identities even as they merged and allied with other peoples on the move.

By the 1730s, Delawares, for example, had not only moved west to the Susquehanna; they were also rebuilding communities on the Allegheny, Muskingum, and Scioto rivers in the Ohio country. Using the Allegheny Mountains as a natural barrier to colonial settlement and control, they gave themselves additional options with easier access to the French without severing their ties to the English.[59] Throughout the eighteenth century, the Wolf, Turtle, and Turkey tribes of the Delawares left their eastern Pennsylvania homelands and migrated into western Pennsylvania and the Ohio country, building new villages, and increasingly thinking of themselves as one people. Through their diaspora, they developed a new identity as the Delaware nation.[60]

As relations with traders and settlers in Pennsylvania deteriorated, Shawnees began to cross the Allegheny Mountains, as well, heading for the Ohio Valley. Both the Iroquois and Pennsylvania tried to woo them back to where they could control them. In 1731 James Logan urged the provincial council to make a treaty with the Six Nations, "who have an absolute authority as well over the Shawanese as all our Indians," to keep the Shawnees in the English interest, and to induce them to move from the Allegheny closer to the settlements.[61] The Shawnees refused to behave like tributaries of the Iroquois, however. In 1732 Governor Patrick Gordon sent them wampum belts and rum, reminded them of the alliance they had entered into with the English in Pennsylvania, and said a large tract of land had been laid out for them near Paxton, "which should always be kept for them and their Children for all time to come, or so long as any of them continued to live with us." The Shawnees replied that they were fine were they were, and "can live much better there than they possibly can any where on Sasquehannah."[62]

By the middle of the eighteenth century, the Ohio country was becoming a refuge for displaced peoples and a crossroads of cultures. There were Shawnees in the Scioto and Miami valleys; Delawares on the upper Muskingum, and Wyandots; remnants of the once-powerful Huron or Wendat confederacy, near Detroit and Sandusky. Splinter groups from the Iroquois confederacy—primarily Senecas and Cayugas but known to the English as Mingoes, derived from the Delaware word for them,

Mingwe—occupied the area between Lake Erie and the Allegheny River. Miamis, Weas, and Piankashaws from Indiana and Michigan and Kickapoos and Mascoutens from the Illinois Country in the Wabash Valley also moved in. The region, said one Cayuga, was "a Republic composed of all sorts of Nations." Unfortunately, Indian peoples who sought security and independence in the Ohio country found themselves once again on a contested borderland and in a war zone as Britain and France moved toward open conflict over the region.[63]

Like the Scotch-Irish, Delawares and Shawnees time and again lived as border peoples. John McCullough, who lived with the Delawares as a captive, said "the Delaware nation was always on the frontier."[64] After generations of movement and conflict, struggling to defend their lands, lives, and way of life in successive borderland situations, Shawnees told the British, "We have always been the frontier."[65] Scotch-Irish people could have said the same thing.

Cherokee and Catawba Buffers

In the South, Cherokee towns lay between English colonies and the French, and the Catawbas lay between the colonies and the Cherokees. Carolina sought to enlist Cherokees as allies because they were well situated to protect its western frontiers against the French and their Indian allies. "They are now our only defence on the Back parts," Thomas Nairne, a Scots trader and Indian agent, said in 1708. In 1730 Martin Bladen, Lord Commissioner of Trade and Plantations, urged the Duke of Newcastle and the Board of Trade to follow the same policy with the Cherokees in the south as with Iroquois in the north. "It may truly be said that they are our Frontier Guards there, always ready to defend our out settlements and to make war upon any other Nation whenever we require them to do so. We conceive it is at present in our Power to put the Cherikees upon the same footing." For Carolinians, the Cherokees could open a back door to French invaders or secure British passage to the Mississippi via the Tennessee River.[66]

Like the Scotch-Irish colonists who began to press up against and then pushed into their homeland in the second half of the eighteenth century, Cherokees had a history of movement. They also had experience incorporating others. Emerging from the chaos, population collapse, and political coalescence unleashed in the Southeast in the seventeenth century by European guns, slave trading, and diseases, the Cherokees in the mid-eighteenth century numbered almost 10,000 people in seven matrilineal clans, living in regional clusters of towns spread across 40,000 square miles in southern Appalachia and the Piedmont plateau. The Great Smoky and Blue Ridge mountains traversed the Cherokee homeland, and major river systems drained into the Atlantic, the Mississippi, and the Gulf of Mexico. Although a mountain people, Cherokee settlers, like incoming Scotch-Irish settlers, gravitated to the valleys. According to Antrim-born trader James Adair, the Cherokees were strongly attached to rivers, "all retaining the opinion of the ancients, that rivers are necessary to constitute a paradise." They looked to them for sustenance in fishing, fowling, and hunting, and for purifying waters.[67] As did other Indian peoples, they claimed extensive hunting grounds beyond the immediate vicinity of their villages, both as a source of food and as a border zone between themselves and other peoples. However, as enemy raiders, deerskin traders, and colonial settlers pushed deeper into their country, Cherokees eventually had to abandon practices of sharing the land and adopt the European practice of clearly marked boundaries.[68] As those boundaries shrank and were breached, Cherokees would experience further multiple migrations that shaped their history and identity.[69]

The Lower Cherokee Towns sat on the upper Savannah River in South Carolina, the Valley Towns along the foot of the Appalachians, the Middle Towns in the upper Little Tennessee Valley in western North Carolina, and the Overhill Towns west of the Appalachian crest on the headwaters of the Tennessee River. Lower Cherokee towns turned to South Carolina for trade but watched with concern as Carolina settlers encroached on their lands. The Overhill Cherokees were particularly important as a bulwark against the French and Indian nations in the west. They controlled the Tennessee River that ran through the heart of the trans-Appalachian region and with it, the gateway to the Ohio Valley. Having Indigenous allies in contested border regions through whom they could project their claims of territorial sovereignty—in their imaginations, if not in reality—was a key aspect of British and French imperial strategy. For the Cherokees, as for other Indigenous peoples occupying borderlands, maintaining relations with rival colonial powers was a key strategy of survival. Operating from a position of power, their leaders often oscillated between colonial capitals like Charleston and New Orleans, maintaining the appearance, if not the reality, of allegiance with each colony. At the same time, they conducted their own diplomatic relations and conflicts with other Native nations on their own western borders.[70]

The Cherokees loomed large in the borderland strategies of the southern colonies as war threatened with France. Governor Arthur Dobbs urged the North Carolina Council in December 1754 to make a law to regulate traders and to promote "Harmony with our Indian Neighbours and Allies." North Carolina owed the Indians Christian benevolence in return for taking possession of their country, he argued. Moreover, it would profit from their trade and make them steady friends, and by extending the alliance to distant nations "form an Impregnable Barrier" against the French and their Indian allies.[71] "The Importance of Indians is now generally known and understood," wrote South Carolina merchant and superintendent of Indian affairs Edmond Atkin in his report to the Board of Trade in 1755. "While they are our Friends, they are the Cheapest and strongest Barrier for the Protection of our Settlements; when Enemies, they are capable by ravaging in their method of War, in spite of all we can do, to render those Possessions almost useless."[72]

Just beyond the northern and western boundaries of the Waxhaws community, where the first Scotch-Irish migrants from Pennsylvania and the Shenandoah Valley settled, the Catawbas provided protection against both the Cherokees and Iroquois tribes farther to the north. When Spanish expeditions first penetrated the Carolina Piedmont—Hernando de Soto in 1540 and Juan Pardo in 1566–1567—they called it the Province of Cofitachequi and encountered chieftains of multiple villages of Catawba, Congaree, Esaw, Saraw or Charraw, Ushereee, Waxhaw, Wateree, Sugeree, Suturee, and other peoples. After Charleston was founded in 1670, smallpox and slave raiding produced population collapse in Indian country. English conflicts with the Tuscaroras in North Carolina in 1711–1713 and with the Yamasees in South Carolina in 1715–1717 brought further devastation and dislocation to the peoples of the Piedmont. Survivors from various groups relocated to the lower Catawba River, where they established new villages along trading paths and banded together for protection. The Catawbas incorporated the refugees, either admitting people into their own towns or permitting them to establish separate towns close by at the fork of the Catawba River. By the mid-eighteenth century, the Catawbas were a nation bound together by alliance and kinship ties. James Adair said in 1743 that they numbered almost four hundred warriors, "of above twenty different dialects." Their reputation as formidable fighters and willingness to serve as auxiliaries made them a valuable frontier garrison in Carolinian eyes.[73]

Then, in one historian's words, they "confronted a flood of people much like themselves," transplanted communities of Scotch-Irish settlers bound together by kinship ties and seeking a future in the Catawba River.[74] Governor Glen of South Carolina had promised the Catawbas a thirty-mile area exempt from colonial settlement around their towns, but North Carolina's government encouraged settlement and by 1754 there were about five hundred settler families within the thirty-mile zone.[75] Recurrent disease, enemy raids, and colonial pressures on their hunting and agriculture took a heavy toll on the Catawbas and diminished their value as a barrier to North Carolina.[76] They served as allies in the French and Indian War, but their effectiveness was short-lived. After smallpox struck them in 1760, the Catawbas were no longer feared as enemies or valued as friends.[77]

From Maine to the Carolinas, Indian peoples fulfilled the role Jonathan Swift attributed to Ulster immigrants in America, settling "in interjacent Tracts, as a screen against the Insults of the *Savages*" (although they would have had a different opinion than Swift as to who constituted the "savages"). Colonial governments and the Iroquois League placed groups of migrant and refugee Native people on their borderlands to protect their settlements and to affirm their control of territory. As James Logan knew, establishing a buffer of Indians or Scotch-Irish raised the value of the protected lands. Indigenous peoples in a tumultuous world of competing, overlapping, and shifting colonial and tribal rivalries accepted inducements, seized opportunities, and made alliances to settle and police borderland areas. They provided protection to their backers in expectation of receiving some protection themselves. Like the Scotch-Irish, however, they found it was often a devil's bargain.

4
Hard Neighbors

The Paxton Boys' murders with which this book opened forever gave the Scotch-Irish a reputation as Indian-killers. Later chroniclers hailed them as Indian-fighters. However, the racial violence that became ubiquitous in the second half of the eighteenth century—and features so prominently in subsequent chapters—was not so prevalent in earlier decades. According to the Philadelphia botanist John Bartram, backcountry settlers said that before things fell apart in 1755, Indians were "almost daily familiars at their houses, ate, drank, cursed, and swore together—were even intimate playmates."[1] James Logan described the Scotch-Irish during those earlier years as "hard neighbors" to the Indians, and they were. Yet even hard neighbors get along sometimes. It was coexistence with their Native neighbors, more than conflict, that caused eastern elites to portray backcountry Scotch-Irish as backward folk who were little or no better than Indians, and prompted later writers to suggest they were "much more Indianized than any other settler group."[2]

In theory and in general, settler colonialism required and effected the elimination of Native people; in reality and in detail, the process was not constant or complete. Although colonial records focus primarily on "bigger issues" of war and diplomacy, land, commerce, and politics, scattered through the documents are instances, glimpses really, of a world where Scotch-Irish and Indian people lived similar lives; they bartered, traded, and worked together; ate and drank together; shared lodgings, and met on well-traveled forest paths. For example, in 1737 the Pennsylvania German interpreter and cultural intermediary Conrad Weiser encountered an Indian warrior near Shamokin who "had squandered part of his property drinking with the Irish."[3] Ten years later, on his way up the Susquehanna, Weiser stopped at Paxton, where he found the Oneida chief and Iroquois half king Shikellamy and three other Native men at the house of Scotch-Irish colonist Joseph Chambers. He stayed two days and two nights talking with them. Chambers was one of four brothers from County Antrim and his home was a regular meeting place for colonists and Indians.[4]

Neighbors on contested borderlands did not simply settle next to one another and get on with life. Living in a tense proximity that could degenerate into violence, they had to build and cultivate relationships. Native peoples had long experience and traditions of doing so and employed various mechanisms to incorporate outsiders into their communities—making them kin, giving gifts, and engaging in trade and diplomacy—although Scotch-Irish settler colonists were an unknown quantity.[5] In a culture where giving and taking names conveyed power as well as respect, carried responsibility, and could shape one's life, Shikellamy named one, and perhaps two, of his sons Logan in honor of the provincial secretary. At least one Delaware bore the name "John Armstrong," probably in honor of the Scotch-Irish surveyor and Indian fighter; another, Job Chillaway's brother, was called "Thomas McKee" after the Scotch-Irish trader.[6]

"The Original great tye between the Indians and Europeans was Mutual conveniency," John Stuart, British superintendent of Indian affairs in the South, explained to the Lords of Trade. "This alone could at first have induced the Indians to receive White people differing so much from themselves into their Country."[7] For long periods and in many places, Native people and backcountry settlers who shared space, needs, resources, and subsistence practices made the best of the situation and got along. They lived by hunting and agriculture, lived beside each other, and lived in peace. They exchanged goods, labor, and knowledge, and for a time, they even shared land. When young Susanna Willard, who married Scotch-Irish immigrant James Johnson, arrived at Charlestown, New Hampshire, then on the northern frontier of New England, in 1744, it was a community of nine or ten families living in cabins alongside numerous Indian people who "associated in a friendly manner with the whites." Looking back in her old age, she recalled: "In these days there was such a mixture on the frontiers of savages and settlers, without established laws to govern them, that the state of society cannot easily be described."[8] As we've seen in the previous chapter, some squatters in the Susquehanna Valley paid yearly rents to Indians for planting rights that gave them a claim to the lands when government officials or absentee colonial landlords sought to eject them; to the Indians their colonial tenant farmers offered a buffer against colonial expansion. Scotch-Irish colonists sharing a drink with Iroquois warriors in a backwoods Pennsylvania tavern, or paying rent to Indian landlords in preference to and defiance of colonial landlords, created and inhabited what historian David Preston calls "a world of great ambivalence."[9]

There's little evidence as to how far and how often Native people distinguished between Scotch-Irish and other colonists. In some areas, virtually all the "whites" they encountered would have been Scotch-Irish, just as most of the "Indians" the Scotch-Irish colonists encountered in certain areas would have been Delawares, Shawnees, or Cherokees. So, most of the people who migrated, resettled, and met in the northern Susquehanna Valley were Scotch-Irish and Delawares. Not all Delaware people moved away when colonists moved onto their lands, and those who remained adopted new strategies of survival. Alienated by the actions of the Pennsylvania government and the Iroquois who had collaborated to dispossess them, they built local networks of accommodation with the settler communities with whom they competed for space.[10] Some of the settlers were English and many were German, but most were Scotch-Irish—landless people who chose to live and build homes near Indian villages. Some became tenant farmers of their Native neighbors. At Licking Creek in southern Pennsylvania, Delawares lived on one side of the stream, while Scotch-Irish people made their homes on the other.[11]

The Presbyterian religion of Scotch-Irish backcountry communities generally applied Old Testament attitudes to Indians as "Canaanites," heathens who should be purged from the land.[12] Nevertheless, even Presbyterians sent missionaries into Indian country, and their ministers included Indian people in their congregations. In the patchwork of communities on the Pennsylvania frontier, itinerant Presbyterian ministers who served Craig's Settlement and Donegal preached to Germans and Indians as well as to Scotch-Irish congregations, and Scotch-Irish people attended Baptist or Methodist services if that was all that was available.[13] The Presbyterian missionary David Brainerd settled at the Forks of the Delaware and on Sunday May 20, 1744, he "Preached twice to the poor Indians; . . . Afterward preached to the Irish people."[14] Indian people and Scotch-Irish people were living close enough that the preacher could serve them both on same day.

Where Scotch-Irish and Native communities lived in close proximity, women as well as men interacted. Scotch-Irish women and Native women shared similar duties and performed similar everyday tasks in agriculture and motherhood. In both cultures, women were predominantly responsible for providing medical care and assisting at childbirths, and they applied their knowledge and skills across social and ethnic lines. During times of peace, Scotch-Irish and Native women exchanged food, clothing, medicine, and hospitality. Such seemingly small connections often reflected and even shaped larger relationships between the groups. Although forging female friendships across ethnic lines occurred most often with Delaware and Mahican and German women in Moravian missionary settlements in Pennsylvania, it was not unknown between Scotch-Irish and other Native communities. Colonial women rarely visited Indian villages, but Native women commonly visited colonial settlements to sell their wares, and would have encountered Scotch-Irish women when Native people traveled "in droves" to trade at John Harris's trading post at Paxton. When the relationships and connections in which women were integral broke down, prospects for peace grew dim.[15]

Living like Indians

The Scotch-Irish and their Delaware neighbors had much in common as marginalized and displaced people. When Scotch-Irish people pushed into Indian country, though, they also adapted Indian ways. They learned to hunt white-tailed deer, wear deerskins, moccasins, and hunting shirts, paddle canoes, live in bark or log lodgings, and heal with folk medicines based on Indigenous knowledge and use of forest herbs. Some married Indian women. They competed for the same lands as Indian people and for similar purposes, rendering conflict inevitable, and when that happened they killed with tomahawks as well as guns and took up scalping.[16]

They entered the agrarian world of Native women who for centuries had harvested an extensive variety of plants, fruits, and nuts; cultivated different types of corn as well as beans, squash, and other crops; passed on horticultural knowledge from generation to generation; and evidently achieved higher crop yields using hoes than did European men using plows—Iroquois farmers growing maize in the seventeenth and eighteenth centuries produced three to five times more grain per acre than wheat farmers in Europe.[17] Although Scotch-Irish farmers also grew wheat, barley, oats, and rye, which they brought from the old country, they took up Indigenous farming practices and fed themselves and their livestock on Indian corn, especially the hardy flint and fast-growing, high-starch dent varieties. Corn became their staple diet in the new country. "Indian corn," wrote the Scottish-born Loyalist John Ferdinand Smyth at the end of the American Revolution, "is the great staff of life in America." Backcountry Scotch-Irish settlers ground cornmeal to make into cornbread, spoon bread, hoe cakes, and mush; made corn into whiskey; wove corn husks and leaves into hats, mops, dolls, and chair bottoms; and fed corn cobs to hogs and cattle. In the early years of settlement, they supplemented their agriculture with abundant wild plants and animals.[18]

Rather than carve their new homes and fields out of a dense forest that stretched unbroken from Maine to Georgia, Scotch-Irish and other backcountry settlers often occupied, or reoccupied, areas of open land that had been created and maintained by Indigenous people who employed fire to burn vegetation and improve pasturage. Much of the land that colonial governments offered the Scotch-Irish was attractive because Indigenous people had been managing it for centuries. They had cleared land for farming and at the end of their hunting season burned open ground to prevent it from reverting to woodland and to attract game to the grassland, creating fertile prairies. Colonists often took over cleared lands or "old fields"—as they were called—and planted them as their own. In addition to saving newcomers the time and labor of clearing new fields, the Indian fields indicated where the soil was rich and well-watered.

However, taking over cleared land meant plowing, manuring, and more intensive agriculture than was needed for family subsistence. Many Scotch-Irish settlers preferred the slash-and-burn technique used by Indigenous farmers. Beginning in the fall and continuing through the spring, they girdled and removed bark from trees, which caused the trees to wither and die in a couple of years; then they burned the underbrush and planted between and around the stumps. James Logan explained to the Pennsylvania proprietors in 1730 that as Scotch-Irish and other squatters moving across the Susquehanna frontier, "All your Lands of Value are posses'd and cut in pieces with Small Settlemt by wch the timber is destroy'd & yet the Land is not clear'd, for they only bark, & thereby Kill ye trees without felling them." Using the natural fertility of the soil, they cultivated crops for a time and then let the land revert to forest. As soils wore out, "new ground" could be cultivated, and the process began again. The technique saved time and helped delay soil exhaustion and was common in frontier areas where land was plentiful and labor in short supply. Squatters who expected to move on preferred it to fully clearing fields for planting. Settlers often started out by building a rough cabin, clearing land by "barking" or girdling trees, and planting Indian corn before diversifying their crops. Mixed farming of crops and livestock was suited to mountain areas where land was less fertile. Immigrants from Ulster were familiar with dispersed settlements, mixed farming, simple tools, and inefficient, even wasteful use of land, and herding systems practiced in the backcountry resembled systems practiced in northern British borderlands. Combining Irish agricultural traditions with slash-and-burn adaptations, Scotch-Irish backcountry farming became a mix of Scottish, Irish, and Native American practices. A seemingly unlimited supply of land in the backcountry encouraged the survival of those practices and perpetual movement. For travelers and outsiders, the partially cleared landscapes where tree stumps remained became evidence of backcountry poverty and sloth.[19]

Scotch-Irish people imported much that contributed to their so-called Indian ways. Family honor and retributive justice gave rise to blood feuds and a reputation for endemic violence.[20] Their clothing was often compared to that of Indians but was similar in many ways to dress in northern England, the lowlands of Scotland, and Northern Ireland. Men in the British borderlands commonly wore leather shirts and leggings; in America they added moccasins and breechcloths. The eighteenth-century pioneer historian Joseph Dodderidge said that many young men on the western frontiers of Pennsylvania and Virginia who had served on campaigns and scouting expeditions became fond of Indian clothing. They wore hunting shirts, leggings, and moccasins, and even adopted loin cloths. "The young warrior, instead of being abashed by his nudity, was proud of his Indian-like dress. In some few instances, I have seen them go into places of public worship in this dress. Their appearance, however, did not add much to the devotion of the young ladies."[21]

In some areas the Scotch-Irish adapted to ways of life that had already been shaped by previous encounters between Indigenous people and colonists. In the lower Delaware Valley, for example, Delaware peoples had interacted for generations with eastern Finns of Karelian and Savoan background who had comprised a substantial part of the population of the short-lived colony of New Sweden from 1638 to 1655. The Finns brought with them techniques of forest colonization and agriculture. They had long histories of encounter with Saami people in their home country and established patterns of mutual accommodation and adaptation with Indigenous people that were essential to building a successful woodland pioneer culture in their new country. Rather than adopt Indigenous crops and methods directly from Indian people, therefore, Scotch-Irish colonists in the Delaware found an agricultural system that incorporated Finnish and Native American elements and had developed half a century and more before large-scale migration from

Ulster immigration began.[22] Nor did the Scotch-Irish invent the iconic log cabins; they adapted and adopted dwellings built by Swedish, Finnish, and German immigrants who introduced them, as did Indian people. These suited families who had few possessions, were mobile, and were accustomed to a life of insecurity. Soon Scotch-Irish squatters and their Native neighbors were living in similar dwellings.[23]

And of course everyone was on the move. Indian people throughout the eastern half of North America periodically relocated their villages, taking advantage of different resources and regions and allowing the natural environment time to recover. Scotch-Irish squatters and settlers were often transient neighbors. Their settlement practices and patterns rarely complied with the expectations of government officials who hoped for stable communities built on property ownership. Scotch-Irish people established sparsely settled, and often relatively briefly settled, farming communities, rather than the kind of town-centered communities colonists had created in New England and the federal government wanted to see modeled in Ohio and other states carved out of the Northwest Territory. Scotch-Irish families dispersed to take up good land along waterways but maintained connections through intermarriage and religion. Kinship shaped the course and direction of migration as family and clan members tended to follow family and clan members and settle together.

Colonial authorities and eastern elites who wanted poor Presbyterian Scotch-Irish immigrants to move far away from their own society and closer to Indian country worried that once they were there, they degenerated by living like Indians. Reflecting on backcountry settlers' isolation and propensity for hunting, the French-American writer J. Hector St. John de Crèvecoeur in *Letters from an American Farmer* (1782) anticipated Frederick Jackson Turner's notion that the wilderness at first proved too much for the colonist, who was submerged in savagery and re-emerged as something new. "That new mode of life brings along with it a new set of manners, which I cannot easily describe. These new manners being grafted on the old stock, produce a strange sort of lawless profligacy, the impressions of which are indelible. The manners of the natives are respectable, compared with this European medley." Crèvecoeur thought the product "a mongrel breed, half civilised, half savage."[24] He was talking less about Germans, who were known for their order and industry, than about the Scotch-Irish, who were known for neither. George Washington encountered Indians, Germans, and Scotch-Irish on his first trip to the Virginia frontier in 1748 and he didn't think much of any of them. He thought the German settlers were "as Ignorant a Set of People as the Indians," and dismissed the rest as "a Parcel of Barbarians and an Uncouth Set of People."[25] For the rest of his life, Washington would have ambivalent attitudes toward these people who pushed west the Virginian and national expansion he treasured, but in doing so established a culture he disdained.

Scotch-Irish Traders in Indian Country

Scotch-Irish communities perched on the edge of Indian country, often just across a river from an Indian village, were natural jumping-off points for traders, who often preceded squatters and settlers into Indian country. The Kittanning Path, one of the main Indian trails across Pennsylvania, crossed the Susquehanna River at Paxton, making it an important center of communication. John Harris established a trading post there in 1719 that became known known as Harris's Ferry, the future site of Harrisburg.[26] Farther west, Donegal in Lancaster County became what one historian called "a sort of nursery of Indian traders," who made long journeys into Indian country.[27] For example, Lazarus Lowrey (also spelled Lowery and Lowry) migrated from the north of Ireland and settled in Donegal Township around 1729. He made frequent trading trips to the Ohio country and sometimes took his sons with him, five of whom (James, John, Daniel, Alexander, and Lazarus Jr.) also became Indian traders.[28] Many squatters, like George Girty, Sr., were also unlicensed Indian traders who built connections with their Native customers.[29]

Traders did not always have a good reputation, and they could be troublemakers. On May 1, 1734, five Delaware chiefs sent a letter complaining about abuses at the hands of traders from Donegal and Paxton. Edward Kenny, Jacob Ryatt, Timothy Fitzpatrick, William Dewlap, Jonathan Kelly, Thomas Moran, and William Palmer "come trading with us without licence, which is a hindrance to ye Licens'd Traders." Kelly "made great disturbance by raising false reports among us," and Fitzpatrick, Moran, and Palmer were quarrelsome. The Delawares asked that these traders "be kept particularly from us" and that no one be allowed to bring more than thirty gallons of rum, and only twice a year, so that their Native customers would have chance to pay off their debts. Traders should have their licenses with them and the Indians would stave the kegs and seize the goods of any others they encountered. Traders they wanted included Edward Cartlidge, Lazarus Lowrey, Francis Stevens, James Patterson, and the French-Shawnee trader Peter Chartier, "who we reckon one of us."[30] The Moravian missionary Christian Frederick Post in 1758 claimed, "There are a great numbers [sic] of *Irish* traders now among the *Indians*, who have always endeavoured to spirit up the *Indians* against the *English*."[31] Jean Lowery, who was taken captive with her children in the French and Indian War, noted other influences. Her Delaware captors could not "swear or curse in their own Language," she said; the only profanities she heard, she supposed, were learned "of our Traders, and the like." In fact, Delawares had many opportunities to borrow swear words, in the exchange of words, phrases, and meanings that accompanied their daily interactions with colonists on the Pennsylvania frontier in the years before the war.[32]

Traders were also not the only people who peddled alcohol. Settlers in Cumberland County and other backcountry areas distilled whiskey and sold it to their Native neighbors.[33] Edward Dougherty kept "an ilgoverned Tipling Hose" at Donegal where he sold rum to Indians.[34] John McAlister claimed that his backcountry neighbors generally became well acquainted with the woods and with "the Manner and Customs of several Nations of Indians." McAlister himself evidently did. In 1751 a county court indicted him for carrying "Quantities of Rum and other strong Liquors above the Quantity of one Gallon amongst the Indians at their Towns and Beyond the Christian inhabitants."[35]

Individual traders and peddlers who supplied Indians and frontier families were dependent on Philadelphia merchants for their stock in trade.[36] Those merchants employed "traveling traders" who operated between urban markets and mountain communities, carried goods to the Indians, and brought back the skins with which their Native customers purchased the goods. Beginning in the 1740s, Alexander Lowrey, son of trader Lazarus Lowrey of Donegal, mentioned above, began an association with Joseph Simon, a Jewish trader from Lancaster, that lasted forty years. His brothers, Daniel, James, and John, also worked for Simon and associates. Lancaster was a depot on the traders' route between Philadelphia and the Ohio country. Goods were provided on credit to the traveling traders, who were supposed to settle their accounts when they returned east. They were thus tied into a network of credit that extended ultimately to merchants in London or Bristol who supplied the goods, and they in turn relied on networks with Indian peoples and among themselves.[37]

Like Lancaster traders, many Carlisle merchants engaged in the fur and deerskin trade with western Indians. Established as the county seat of Cumberland in 1750–1751 and named after a town with a bloody history in the northern England borderlands (now Cumbria), Carlisle was a predominantly Scotch-Irish Presbyterian town. Surveyor Thomas Cookson fixed upon the site and purchased 1,200–1,300 acres from the six Scotch-Irishmen and one widow already settled there. Surveyor John Armstrong from County Fermanagh laid the town out on a grid plan, reflecting order and civilization. Sitting at the convergence of five Indian paths, it occupied a pivotal location between Native and colonial communities and became a rendezvous point, a depot, and a thoroughfare between Philadelphia and Indian villages on the upper Susquehanna and in the Ohio country. Carlisle merchants like Robert Callender, in partnership with Irish traders Michael Taaffe and George Croghan, traded in the Ohio country in the 1750s, acting as middlemen, shipping in goods from Philadelphia, and equipping the packhorse trains that then carried the goods into Indian country. "The town of Carlisle is a considerable place of trade, principally with the western country & the Indians," wrote the Reverend David McClure in his diary when he traveled through it, by which time the town had two Presbyterian churches.[38] In 1753 Ohio chiefs seeking better trade regulations and a reduction of tensions in the Ohio country asked to meet the governor of Pennsylvania at Carlisle rather than travel all the way to Philadelphia.[39]

Some traders who immersed themselves in Indian country developed broader intermediary roles. Thomas McKee, born around 1695, migrated from County Antrim sometime after 1707 with his father Alexander, a veteran of the Battle of the Boyne, who took up farming on the Pennsylvania frontier in Lancaster County until his death in 1740. Thomas established himself as an Indian trader. He established one post on the Susquehanna River near present-day Dalmatia, in 1740; another, McKee's Post, near present-day Dauphin, by 1742; and had a storehouse at the Shawnee town at Big Island or Great Island, at the mouth of the Juniata River on the south branch of the Susquehanna. McKee married a woman named Mary who may have been a white captive adopted by the Shawnees. Moravian missionary John Christopher Frederick Cammerhoff, traveling through the upper Susquehanna, a country he described as "populous with Indians," in the winter of 1748, stayed at McKee's, "the last white settlement on the river below Shamokin." He said McKee's wife "was brought up among the Indians, speaks but little English." McKee himself was recovering from a serious sickness and still feeble. "During the past summer, he informed us, probably one-half of the settlers living along the river died from fever and a cough, and that even now many still lay sick." Cammerhoff said McKee, who held a captain's commission from the government, "is an extensive Indian trader, bears a good name among them, and drives a brisk trade with the Allegheny Country." Provincial secretary Richard Peters informed the Pennsylvania proprietors the following year that McKee "has taken an Indian Wench & has several Children by her & they reckon him one of themselves." Thomas McKee died in 1769. His son Alexander (Mary may or may not have been his biological mother), born around 1735, followed in his father's footsteps. He became a trader, a land speculator, and then an agent with the British Indian Department, in which role he opposed American expansion until his death in Canada in 1799.[40]

Scotch-Irish traders figured prominently in the southern colonies as well. They were vital to the growth of Charleston, promoted British imperial interests, and maintained Indian alliances. Trader James Adair was born in County Antrim in 1709 and emigrated from Ulster to Charleston in 1735. He ran a tavern at Cherokee Ford in South Carolina, from which he traded with Indians. He lived with the Overhill Cherokees from 1737 to 1743, and then moved to Chickasaw country in 1744, where he operated as a trader and a diplomat, securing Indian alliances against the French, and wrote "most of the pages" of his book, *History of the American Indians*. Published in 1775, in addition to a lengthy discussion of the supposed Jewish origins of the American Indians, it contained valuable information on Native American history and life.[41]

Another Northern Ireland emigrant to the southern colonies, Thomas Brown, became a trader among the Catawbas, and married a Native woman. He interpreted for the Catawbas in negotiations with South Carolina, and Catawbas asked him to act as go-between in arranging for them to visit Charleston and meet the governor. By the time he died in 1747, Brown had also acquired extensive landholdings. His will bequeathed 361 acres of land, two slaves, and some cattle to fifteen-year-old William, "my natural son, born of a free Indian woman of the Catawba Nation." Another Irish trader, Matthew Toole, married the daughter of Catawba chief Hagler.[42]

Marrying Native women and acquiring Native land was common practice for traders, and the Scotch-Irish were no exception. George Galphin, one of the most prominent traders in the colonial South, was the eldest of six children in a poor linen-weaving family from County Armagh. He emigrated to Savannah in 1737, entered the deerskin trade, and by the 1740s joined the Augusta, Georgia, firm of Patrick Brown (from southern Ireland) and John Rae (from County Down). Galphin had abandoned his first wife in Ireland; he married a second in South Carolina who died, and then married a French woman, with whom he had two children. He also had several relationships, and children, with Native and African women. He married and had three children with Metawney, daughter of Chigelli, headman of the Creek town of Coweta, who incorporated Galphin into her matrilineal networks of family and clan. Many Creeks regarded him as one of their own, even as he enmeshed them in bonds of debt and dependency and abetted in dispossessing them of land. Galphin built an extensive network trading with the Creeks and other southeastern tribes, as well as relationships with colonial governors, imperial agents, English traders, English settlers, European merchants, Irish kinsmen, and Ulster immigrants. Together with merchants Lachlan McGillivray, John Rae, and John McQueen, Galphin dominated the Indian trade of the Southeast by mid-century. He also traded and owned slaves. He established a trading post at Silver Bluff in 1750 and maintained his estate there for thirty years as a home for all members of his family, and a meeting ground for colonists, Indians, and Africans. It was also the place to which he relocated kinsfolk from Ulster. British Indian superintendent John Stuart, at the start of the Revolution, said that Galphin "had traded in the Coweta Town upwards of 30 years and has by that means acquired a considerable fortune." In fact, Galphin became one of the wealthiest men in the South Carolina backcountry. At his death in 1780 he owned at least 14,000 and perhaps as many as 50,000 acres. His will made provision for children by a European woman, an Indian woman, and an African woman. "Give to my halfbreed Indian girl, Rose (daughter of Nitehuckey) her freedom," it stated. It also provided money for the poor of Enneskilling and Armagh.[43] Despite his transformation, Galphin apparently never forgot his roots.

Although individuals like Thomas McKee, Thomas Brown, and George Galphin stand out in the historical record, they were not exceptional in building businesses, families, and lives in Indian country. Scots and Scotch-Irish traders married into Indian societies so frequently that families of Scotch-Irish and Native American heritage became commonplace in southern Appalachia. Some of the Cherokees and Creeks who resisted later Scotch-Irish invasions of their homelands were themselves of Scotch-Irish ancestry.[44]

Contending the Land

In the histories of early America, the clash of Indians and Europeans is often depicted as a conflict between hunters and farmers, and between people who occupied land communally and people who owned property individually. Europeans generally changed the landscape and introduced new concepts of landownership to North America, treating land as a commodity to be marked out and measured, bought and sold, and owned exclusively. Indigenous peoples generally regarded land as something to be shared and utilized by the members of the community, although some groups had stronger rights to certain areas. Indians who signed deeds believing they had given colonists the right to share their land found instead that the colonists thought they had bought the land, "lock, stock, and barrel." European invaders felled trees with fire and axes, cleared and plowed fields, fenced in pastures for domesticated animals, built farms, villages, and towns, and marked property boundaries, imposing unprecedented pressures on ecosystems and producing permanent changes in the landscape.[45]

The depictions are broadly accurate, and Scotch-Irish squatters and settlers played a major role in transforming tribal homelands into colonial real estate, and later the territorial base of the United States. However, the contest for land was not a simple conflict between diametrically opposed systems and philosophies along a racially defined border. Despite John Locke's famous pronouncements in his *Second Treatise of Government* (1690)—often invoked to this day to demonstrate the differences between European notions of private property and Indigenous practices of communal landholding—capitalist concepts of landholding did not dominate the Highlands of Scotland and Ulster until the first half of the eighteenth century. Open field systems in the Scottish Highlands (*runrig*) and in Ireland (*rundale*) permitted shared farming of communal arable lands. Ulster Irish recognized common rights to the forest, including free pasture and firewood as well as hunting and fishing rights, and free access to rivers. Scotch-Irish and other emigrants from the British borderlands had their own traditions of common fields, where "common" people could graze livestock and harvest resources, and in America they assumed they had the right to use lands that appeared to them to be underused, whether by the Indigenous inhabitants or by eastern landlords. In other words, common land featured in settler as well as Native land tenure systems in the early modern period, and clashes occurred over Indigenous commons and colonial commons as well as private property and communal landholding.[46]

Landless and displaced people in motion, both Indigenous and European, took up residence on the lands of other people, often with the permission of those people, and shared access to the region's resources. By permitting squatters, Native people exerted some choice over who settled on their lands. Following the example of Pennsylvania and the Six Nations, which were trying to control Indians and Scotch-Irish squatters as they moved and resettled, Delawares and other Native nations that allowed squatters to settle on their land asserted their own sovereignty vis-à-vis Philadelphia and Onondaga.[47] Government officials blamed squatters for causing upheaval and violence by trespassing on Indian lands in defiance of regulations, but they also denounced them because their vision of orderly settlement by property owners included no place for interethnic sharing of common lands by people who lived interdependently with Indians.

The struggle for land on the frontiers of Pennsylvania in the half century before the American Revolution was a kaleidoscope of competing and overlapping groups. In addition to a three-way contest among Native people, squatters, and proprietary officials, it involved Maryland, Virginia, London, land speculators, the Six Nations, the Susquehanna Valley tribes, and the Ohio tribes. Colonial officials regarded squatters, who did not pay for land or rents or who made individual purchases from Indians, as a threat to orderly settlement, property, and investments. Squatters resisted, refused, or ignored payment and rents. James Anderson, the Scotch-Irish minister at the Presbytery of Donegal, said in 1733 they had been so oppressed and harassed by landlords in their own country that they had migrated to America "with the chief principal view of being, in this foreign world, freed from such oppression." They also objected to land speculators who bought cheap and sold dear.[48]

Deprived of landownership by landlords, speculators, and the systems they controlled, Scotch-Irish settlers invoked their rights as landless people who, they believed, could *earn* title to land simply by possession. They reputedly drew on a cluster of traditional tenant rights and customary practices in Ulster involving occupancy, labor, and service, which they asserted in backcountry Pennsylvania and carried west of the Appalachians. They refused to pay quitrents, arguing that the government had attracted them to the frontier with an implied commitment to free land and that they earned their right to it by their occupancy and their labor and by serving as defense against

Indians. They marked their claims by blazing trees ("tomahawk rights"), erecting structures ("cabin rights"), clearing and planting land ("corn rights"), and taking up "vacant" or unused land. In doing so, they clashed with the Native occupants, with colonial, federal, and state governments, and with speculators and absentee landlords who claimed ownership.[49] The Scotch-Irish were hard neighbors to Indians throughout the colonies, and they were hard neighbors to other people as well.

In many places and cases, it was precisely the similarities between Indigenous and squatter subsistence cycles and farming techniques that made them hard neighbors and rendered competition for the best lands so deadly.[50] Indians and non-Indians farmed the same rich bottomlands, fished the same streams, and hunted in the same forests. They not only shared a backwoods hunting economy, but also were tied into the larger Atlantic economy as frontier consumers of manufactured goods, often purchased with the products of the hunt.[51]

Although Scotch-Irish backcountry people and Native people used the woods in similar ways, they did so with divergent understandings and different relationships to the animals. For Native Americans, proper rituals were necessary to harvest plant and animal life and keep the world in balance. They halted at ritual stopping places to make offerings of tobacco or food. They communicated with animals, dreamed the whereabouts of their prey, and offered prayers to the spirits of the animals that gave their bodies so that the people might live. Europeans not only claimed ownership of the land; they also claimed to own the animals that fed them. Indian people often said the Creator made wild animals for them and domesticated animals for whites. "God has given you the tame creatures; we do not want to take them from you," Delawares told Christian Frederick Post. "God has given us the deer, and other wild creatures, which we must feed on."[52]

Colonists regarded wild animals and the woods as a hunting resource free for the taking, but held their own domestic animals as private property no matter where those animals might wander and graze. They often turned their animals loose to graze on forest undergrowth, rather than fencing them in and feeding them. Indian hunters had very different ideas about human ownership of nonhuman creatures and viewed unpenned livestock as, literally, fair game. As one historian points out, colonists who claimed that Indigenous resources of fish, deer, and timber were open to all, whereas their own hogs and cattle roaming the woods remained private property, were in effect asserting claims to the land itself. "You claim all the Wild Creatures, and will not let us come on your Land to hunt for them," complained the Oneida chief Saghughsuniunt, known to colonists as Thomas King. "You will not so much as let us peel a Single Tree." Unpenned livestock trampled Indian cornfields and competed with deer for grazing, making domestic animals instruments of dispossession that extended the colonial commons into Indian country. Native people understood what was going on, and they killed, and sometimes even mutilated, pigs, cattle, and sheep. But in time they adapted the new animals into their lives and economies, with repercussions on the gender-based divisions of labor in their societies. Previously, men had hunted animals in the forests while women tended crops in the fields around the villages; now domesticated livestock became part of village life.[53]

To eastern gentry and travelers in the backcountry, hunting seemed to reflect the degeneracy of people who now lived like Indians. Two Moravian missionaries traveling through western Virginia in 1749 visited primarily German communities. Crossing the mountains, they came to the outer limit of colonial settlement and met people who were not German. "The manner of living is rather poor in in this district," they wrote. "The clothes of the people consist of deer skins. Their food of Johnny cakes, deer and bear meat. A kind of white people are found here, who live like savages. Hunting is their chief occupation."[54] In European theories that explained societal evolution as a series of stages of development, hunting preceded agriculture; backcountry hunters therefore had "reverted" to a more primitive way of life. "Civilized" men lived by farming and hunted for sport; uncivilized people hunted for subsistence and delegated farming to women. What was worse, backcountry hunters learned how to hunt by emulating Native hunters in dress, techniques, and woodcraft.[55]

In actuality, however, few Scotch-Irish hunters adopted the ethics as well as the techniques of Native hunters. Although they might hunt in the same forests and adopt Indian ways, they had different relations with the animals and the natural world. Indian hunters saw spiritual forces everywhere in the forest and traveled with a light foot. White hunters did not. Native people were appalled by their profligacy and uncivilized behavior.

Simmering Tensions

Although Scotch-Irish people living in backcountry areas often found and made common ground with their Native neighbors and, at least in the first half of the eighteenth century, showed little evidence that they were predisposed by ethnicity or experience to be Indian-haters or Indian-killers, the bonds of coexistence were delicate and easily frayed. Tensions grew as numbers increased, pushing more people into competition for the same space and resources. When tensions exploded into violence, the colonial and Indigenous powers that had placed people in the contested areas struggled to contain the reverberations of intercultural murders.[56]

James Logan had encouraged Scotch-Irish settlement at Donegal in 1720 and the place grew rapidly, mainly through squatting. Ten years later, he wrote to a Lancaster County magistrate to "get the principal Inhabitants of Donegal together and particularly their Minister to make them sensible of the Consequences of the Resentment of these Peoples of the Five Nations." Indians complained that Scotch-Irish around Donegal had killed five Native people and had hidden their bodies.[57]

Rum-soaked trading encounters always carried the potential for violence and threatened to sever the tenuous ties that bound Natives and newcomers together in peace on the borderlands. Colonial authorities and Indian leaders often scrambled to prevent such killings from flaring into a broader conflict, but negotiating a response that satisfied disparate philosophies of justice could be tricky. Killings could have different meanings. Europeans demanded retribution for murder (although not for "legitimate killings" in war). For Indian people, though, identifying the individual murderer might be less important than establishing the group to which a murderer belonged. If it was an allied group, the dead could be "covered" and harmony restored by the ritual of giving and accepting appropriate gifts.[58] So, for example, when two brothers assaulted a Seneca hunter at Conestoga in 1722 in a drunken brawl over trade and left him for dead, Pennsylvania put the brothers on trial for murder, but the Iroquois insisted on reparations and reconciliation, not execution.[59] Scotch-Irish people had their own traditions of blood feud and vengeance and codes of justice that allowed little room for cultural compromise and compensation if an Indian killed one of them.

There were also problems between members of communities that operated on reciprocity and sharing and communities that respected and revered individual property rights. At a council in Philadelphia in 1736, Native delegates complained "That amongst them there is never any Victuals sold, the Indians give to each other freely what they can spare, but if they come amongst our People they can have nothing without paying." The officials explained in response "That all the White People, tho' they live together as Brethren, have each, nevertheless, distinct Properties & Interests, & none of us can demand from another Victuals or any thing of the kind without payment." Every man lived by his own labor and had a right to keep for himself what his labor produced "& all Victuals cost money."[60] The officials' explanation hardly explained social dynamics in the Scotch-Irish backcountry, where ties of community and kinship also operated to ensure that families and neighbors shared resources and labor. Nevertheless, cultural misunderstandings created grounds for conflict.

Distrust and suspicion were never far below the surface. Although relations with the Native inhabitants around Shippensburg, for example, were generally peaceful, there were warning signs. A colonist named Robert McInnis was shot in 1733. After a young colonist named Alexander Askew was killed, the settlers in 1740 began building a small fort with a well within its enclosure. "I have no confidence in the friendship of these savages," one inhabitant, Francis Campble, wrote, "and have always felt that we were warming a viper which will some day show us its fangs. Our only safety, in my opinion, depends wholly upon our vigilance and the preparation we make in our defence." Two years later, after an Indian named Bright Star, "a desperate man," was mortally wounded in a drunken brawl, Campble reiterated, "These savages will give us trouble yet." Campble served in the militia in the French and Indian War.[61]

Rumors spread quickly among people who inhabited precarious and isolated borderland areas and were prone to believe the worst about their neighbors and what they were up to. British colonial officials regularly referred to Indians who spread false reports as "bad birds." In 1743, the Iroquois half king Shikellamy reprimanded the Delawares for spreading lies among the Indians and told the Shawnees, "You believe too many Lies, and are too forward in action." At the same time, Shikellamy reminded colonial authorities, "Your Back Inhabitants are people given to Lies and raising false Stories."[62]

For more than twenty years after the first Scotch-Irish settled in the Shenandoah Valley, there was no open warfare between the Indians and the colonists. Even so, there were plenty of incidents. Bands of "roving" Indians frequently "helped themselves to whatever moveable property they took a fancy to" and sometimes burned cabins. The Reverend John Craig described such encounters in a manuscript account of his life and times. He described Augusta, Virginia, when he arrived in 1740 as "a wilderness in the proper sense, and a few Christian settlers in it with numbers of the heathens traveling among us." The Indians were "generally civil, though some persons were murdered by them about that time." They also expected hospitality from their new neighbors. "They march about in small companies from fifteen to twenty, sometimes more or less. They must be supplied at any house they call at, with victuals, or they become their own stewards and cooks, and spare nothing they choose to eat and drink."[63]

Tensions led to open violence in the valley in 1742. In July, the inhabitants of the so-called Borden's Tract—comprising most of the heavily Scotch-Irish Rockbridge County and the southern part of Augusta County—conscious of their exposed situation in the back parts of Virginia, petitioned Governor Gooch to commission John McDowell captain of militia. McDowell was born in Ireland around 1714, migrated to Virginia in 1737, and had worked to attract Scotch-Irish families to settle Borden's Tract and colonize the valley. In December 1742, according to his son, Samuel, a war party of thirty-three Delawares, heading south to raid the Catawbas, stopped by the Scotch-Irish settlement. "They were one whole day at my father's house, he treated them with whiskey." After they resumed their journey south, however, they "went to the houses of white people, scaring women and children, taking what they wanted, and shot horses running at large." McDowell and a company went after them to escort them beyond the settlement. On December 14, they caught up with the Indians and confronted them. There was a fight at the Forks of the James River in which McDowell and seven of his men were killed.[64]

Things threatened to unravel in Pennsylvania as well. In the spring of 1744, Mushemeelin, a Delaware from Shamokin, with two younger accomplices, killed John or Jack Armstrong and two employees or servants, James Smith and Woodworth Arnold, on the banks of the Juniata River. Killer and victim knew each other: Armstrong, a sharp dealing trader from Lancaster Country, apparently had seized Mushemeelin's horse in payment for an outstanding debt. With England and France on the brink of war, Shikellamy worked with colonial and Delaware leaders to craft a resolution that would defuse the situation. Mushemeelin admitted his guilt and was handed over for trial and hanged; wampum belts were exchanged to restore harmony. Although the full details of the crime, and the role of the two younger Delawares who went unpunished, remained (and remain) unclear, Pennsylvania officials, the Delawares, and the Iroquois accepted a narrative and an outcome that averted a crisis.[65]

Relations between Scotch-Irish backcountry settlers and their Native neighbors were deteriorating everywhere by the middle of the century. How they deteriorated can be seen starkly in the Carolina backcountry where the Scotch-Irish influx was accelerating rapidly. Antrim-born Governor Arthur Dobbs advocated treating Indians with fairness and justice when he first arrived in North Carolina, and even proposed that soldiers should take Indian wives.[66] But friction increased when settlers began pouring into backcountry areas after 1750. The Moravian Bishop August Gottlieb Spangenburg complained in 1752 that the conduct of the Indians in North Carolina was "quite different from that in Pennsylvania." There the Indians were to be feared only when they were drunk, he claimed. "Here they conduct themselves in such a way that the whites are afraid of them. If they enter a house & the man is not at home they become insolent & the poor woman must do as they command." Sometimes the Indians came in large groups. "This is difficult when people live alone in the woods about here; they are in danger of getting into unpleasant relations with the Indians" who were still bitter over losing their land.[67]

Across the border in South Carolina, by the time Scotch-Irish people encountered them, Catawba men and women often wore a mixture of European and Indigenous clothing along with customary Catawba jewelry. They used textiles, needles, thread, scissors, metal pots, steel weapons, muskets, ammunition, and other goods transported along the trading paths from Charleston into the backcountry. Catawba women peddled baskets and their distinctive pottery in colonial settlements. Though given little attention in colonial records, numerous face-to-face encounters and small acts of cooperation with Scotch-Irish women likely occurred when Catawba women were gathering plant foods and berries or collecting firewood in the woods, or when they went to the new settlements to barter pottery and baskets for everyday items such as salt, sugar, buttons, and thread, or for cloth, clothing, tools, and utensils.[68]

Increasingly, however, colonial settlers encroached on Catawba settlements. An influx of Scotch-Irish families fleeing Indian raids in Pennsylvania and Virginia increased the pressure on Catawba towns, fields, and resources. By 1755 the Catawba Nation was almost surrounded, with five hundred families living within thirty miles. Whereas traders needed Indian hunters and customers and adjusted to doing business in Indian country with regard for Indian ways, settlers made little effort to understand or accommodate Native people and brought with them a different understanding of the land and a desire to change the landscape. They divided up the land, built square or rectangular houses and barns, fenced and plowed fields, planted new crops of wheat, barley, oats, rye, flax, and other plants; and introduced hundreds of cattle, hogs, and sheep that degraded the environment and outcompeted the deer for grazing. The Catawba chief known as King Hagler worked so hard to maintain an alliance between Catawbas and colonists that nineteenth-century residents of the predominantly Scotch-Irish community of Camden deemed him their "patron saint" and placed an effigy of him in their Presbyterian church.[69] Nevertheless, as one historian notes, the Scotch-Irish newcomers were "no more interested in incorporating Indian ways than the Catawba were in becoming European."[70]

Amid growing competition for the same resources, drought produced periodic food shortages. In 1755, at a time when the colony was acutely aware of the Catawbas' positional significance as Anglo-French tensions escalated in the Ohio country, the North Carolina council resolved to buy corn for the Catawbas, "it being represented that the said Indians are in great want of corn at this time and subsist by begging from the neighbouring Planters and thereby Quit their families and oppress the Planters who are themselves scarce of Corn yet Dare not Deny them." Catawbas more often asked for food or helped themselves. Colonists more often refused, calling Indians beggars and thieves, and complained that they destroyed fences, killed cattle, stole horses, burgled their homes, and threatened their lives. With horse thefts rampant, an enterprising fellow named Robert McClanahan developed a lucrative little business as "stray master," rewarding Indians for any "stray" horses they "found," and then returning them to their rightful owners for a fee.[71]

When Scotch-Irish settlers complained about Catawbas stealing, Hagler and other chiefs countered with their own explanation, citing settler breaches of the reciprocity that should exist between friends and neighbors. Warriors traveling to or from raids often went to colonists' houses when they were hungry, they said. Many of the settlers were kind and courteous and shared freely, but when people hid or refused food and behaved "Churlish and ungreatful [sic]," the Indians took what they needed: "if we ask a little Victuals you Refuse us & then we Owne we Take a Loaf of bread a little meal or meat to Eat, and then You Complain and say those are Transgressions." Some young men might steal other things despite their warnings, the chiefs acknowledged, but the whites were partly to blame: "you Rot Your Grain in Tubs, out of which you take and make Strong Spirit" and sell it to the young men and "it Rots their guts."[72] Hagler said much the same at a conference in the spring of 1756: "As my people and the White people are Brethren I desire that when they go to their houses they may give them victuals to eat, some of the White People are very bad and quarrelsome and whip my people about the head, beat and abuse them but others are very good." He asked them to stop selling rum.[73] Colonists continued to encroach on Catawba lands and ignore Catawba codes of behavior, and Catawbas continued to engage in acts of unrest and resistance.[74]

As did Indigenous people elsewhere, they also had to contend with missionaries who wanted their souls, as well as settlers who wanted their lands. The Reverend William Richardson, a Presbyterian Scot educated in England, came to Virginia in 1755 and went on a mission to Cherokee country in December 1758. After two months there, he became disheartened by his "unreceptive audience" and gave up. He did not speak Cherokee, knew nothing of Cherokee culture, and resented the Cherokee ethic that expected hospitality and sharing: He did not think a missionary could live among them for less than £120 per year, no matter how frugal he was, "& why shou'd a Missionary starve[?] must he deny himself the Necessaries of Life because he undertakes that self denying Work? No."[75] Nevertheless, he started again in the Waxhaws, preaching to the largely Scotch-Irish community and the Catawbas. Catawba people who had suffered from their encounter with Scotch-Irish colonists were in no mood to convert to Presbyterianism, however.[76]

Individual relations persisted and personal bonds developed, despite the growing tensions and increasing conflicts during the period of the Seven Years War. After smallpox struck the Catawbas in 1759 and under threat of Cherokee raids, many Catawba women moved their families south along the Catawba River to a temporary refuge close to the Irish Quaker settlement at Pine Tree Hill (Camden) settlement for protection. Catawba women continued their role as itinerant potters, trading with settler families. Catawba men and women began leasing land to landless white settlers for goods and cash, and traveled from tenant to tenant, collecting lease payments. Doing so allowed them a temporary measure of control over the terms, including the amount of land rented, for how much, and to whom, and gave them a paper trail of legal documentation of land tenure.[77] Thomas Spratt was born at sea in 1731 as his family migrated from Ireland, one of eight children. His father was reputed to be the first white man to cross the Yadkin in a wheeled vehicle. In the mid-1760s, Spratt leased land twelve miles south of Charlotte from the Catawbas, who called him Kanawha or Cainhoy, ostensibly for his bravery in the battle against the Shawnees. He was said to have enjoyed good relations with the Catawbas, and was a friend of a Catawba chief, New River. He raised a young Catawba called Peter Harris, who was orphaned at age three in the 1759 smallpox epidemic (and who later served in a Catawba company on the American side in the Revolution). The chief's wife, Sally New River, was said to have lived for "weeks and months" with Spratt's family.[78]

In the first half of the eighteenth century, Scotch-Irish and Indian peoples met and mingled in borderland regions and built networks of accommodation and cautious coexistence. They turned borderlands that were intended to serve as barriers into zones of cooperation as well as competition, and sometimes they produced bicultural communities. Living close to each other and like each other did not prevent conflict and violence, however. In fact, coexistence and competition for the same land and resources often caused or heightened violence. Scotch-Irish and Indian people lacked Robert Frost's "good fences" that might have made them good neighbors. Familiarity bred contempt; trade produced debts; alcohol sparked volatility. Cultural tensions were never far from the surface. Shared cultures of masculine martial prowess guaranteed instances of violence. Yet even acts of violence sometimes revealed evidence of nonviolent relationships. A Native person killed in a tavern after too much drinking was someone who had shared space with his killers. A Nanticoke who raped a young girl in Paxton in February 1751 after being allowed into her home (and possibly given drink) violated trust as well as the girl.[79] When war broke out in 1755, raiding warriors in many cases "knew exactly whom they captured, killed, or did not kill and why." Sometimes they spoke to their victims in English or German. Sometimes captives recognized their captors.[80]

Once the French and Indian War engulfed their lives, however, instances of violence between hard neighbors gave way to unrestrained race war. Scotch-Irish and Indian people who had lived alongside each other now spattered the borderlands with each other's blood. And they would perpetrate acts that graphically and dramatically rejected their former ties and common humanity.

PART II
FIGHTING FOR AMERICA

5

We Are Now the Frontier

Britain and France had competed for domination in North America for more than half a century. By the mid-eighteenth century, that competition focused on the Forks of the Ohio, the confluence of the Ohio, Allegheny, and Monongahela rivers, which strategists saw as the key to controlling North America. France claimed the Ohio country on the basis of discoveries made in the late seventeenth century. Britain claimed it on the basis of colonial charters that granted huge swaths of land and on the fiction that the Iroquois, who claimed the region by right of conquest in the seventeenth century and had transferred it to Britain, were British subjects.

Britain and France each tried to assert their power in the Ohio country through Native proxies. The Indian peoples who lived there wanted to preserve their land and autonomy from the British, the French, and the Iroquois. The fighting that broke out there in 1755 sparked a broader North American conflict known as the French and Indian War and a global conflict known as the Seven Years War. Across large stretches of the American backcountry, it was a Scotch-Irish and Indian war (Map 5.1). It forever changed relations between the two peoples and it created an enduring history of the Scotch-Irish in America as a beleaguered and embattled people, as their ancestors had been in Northern Ireland.

"In the Utmost Danger of Dreadful Destruction"

Concerned by growing Virginian interest in Ohio land and the increasing activities of Pennsylvania traders in the area, the French in the early 1750s began building a string of forts stretching from Lake Erie to the Forks of the Ohio. In 1754 they constructed Fort Duquesne at the Forks, the site of modern-day Pittsburgh. Governor Robert Dinwiddie of Virginia sent George Washington, then a young militia officer, to demand that the French withdraw—a rather futile gesture—and then again to force their

Map 5.1 The French and Indian War in the Scotch-Irish backcountry.

withdrawal. After a messy skirmish in which Washington's men and his Indian allies killed a dozen French soldiers—murdered them, the French claimed—Washington surrendered to a superior French force at Fort Necessity and was sent packing back to Virginia.

In 1755, Britain dispatched a professional army to get the job done. General Edward Braddock's British regulars and colonial militia hacked a road through the mountains and forests into western Pennsylvania. Backcountry people hardly rallied to the flag. Benjamin Franklin had to cajole and threaten the inhabitants of Lancaster, York, and Cumberland counties to provide wagons and horses for the expedition.[1] Even so, Braddock's army had crossed the Monongahela River and Fort Duquesne was almost within its grasp when, on July 9, a sortie of Indian warriors and their French allies routed the British columns, inflicting almost one thousand casualties. Braddock took a bullet through the lungs and died a few days later; George Washington was one of the few officers to escape unharmed. Colonel Thomas Dunbar and what was left of the army retreated to Philadelphia.[2]

Scotch-Irish people who had settled on the frontiers were the first to feel the impact of the war. For them, the imperial contest that produced titanic battles in Europe, India, Canada, and on the high seas generated brutal, local, and sometimes personal assaults on their farms and families. Eastern colonists who volunteered for militia service could refuse to serve far from home in a war that many of them suspected was motivated by land speculators and to benefit wealthy elites. Colonists on the frontiers had no choice—the war came to them. Defending the backcountry required money and commitments that colonial governments were loath to make. The great planters in the Virginia assembly feared slave insurrection in the Tidewater more than Indian raids on the frontier, and the pacifist Quakers in the Pennsylvania Assembly balked at funding a war. From Pennsylvania to Georgia, the coastal representatives who dominated the legislatures attended to their own regional interests and showed less concern about families exposed to peril in the remote backcountry.[3]

Even before the rout of Braddock's army, Scotch-Irish backcountry communities sent petitions to the Pennsylvania government, begging protection and assistance. Seventy-five inhabitants of Cumberland County, the most heavily Scotch-Irish county in the colony, petitioned Deputy Governor James Hamilton in July 1754: "We are now in the most imminent Danger by a powerful Army of cruel, merciless, and inhuman Enemies, by whom our Lives, Liberties, Estates, and all that tends to promote our Welfare, are in the utmost Danger of dreadful Destruction." Inhabitants of Derry, Donegal, Paxton, and Hanover townships in Lancaster County sent similar petitions, pleading for guns and ammunition to defend themselves. The governor forwarded the petitions to the Assembly, urging them to provide protection, but pacifist Quakers controlled the Assembly and the purse strings. They felt the estates of the Penn family proprietors should be taxed to fund the war effort, something which the governor, who was appointed by the proprietors, would not and could not countenance.[4]

A year after the petition from Cumberland, the inhabitants of the Pennsylvania backcountry remained unprotected and terrified by reports of settlers being killed by Indians. Contrary to providing a formidable barrier of fighting farmers that repelled enemy attacks, Scotch-Irish communities began to crumble under the mere threat of Indian assaults. John Harris at Paxton warned interpreter Conrad Weiser at the end of June 1755 that "Upon the first Alarm of Murder being committed among us the general part or Majority of our Settlers will run off and leave their Habitations and Effects, Grain, &^{ca}; You may certainly depend on it, For in the Situation our People are they cannot make any Defence."[5] Edward Shippen, Lancaster's most prominent citizen, tried to get settlers to stand their ground, to fort up and form companies, he told William Allen. "But of all the Persons I have talked with John Harris at Pexton is the greatest Coward, and discourages the Folks most, buzzing them in the Ears of their great Danger. But I hope I have put a Stop to his silly Proceedings."[6]

Deputy Governor Robert Hunter Morris had informed General Braddock on July 6—three days before his defeat at the Battle of the Monongahela—that Indian war parties murdering inhabitants near Fort Cumberland had caused panic and that it would be difficult to get backcountry people to carry provisions to the road cutters without an escort, which the Assembly would not allow Morris to provide. Five days later, now at Carlisle, Morris wrote to Braddock again, hoping that he was in possession of Fort Duquesne. By then Braddock lay mortally wounded.[7]

A young Presbyterian minister, the Reverend Hugh McAden, kept a diary in 1755 as he made his way by horseback, preaching from Pennsylvania to North Carolina. When he first learned of Braddock's defeat, McAden was "so shocked ... that I knew not what to do." The news, and reports of daily murders on the frontiers, "struck terror into every heart" and caused "universal confusion," he wrote. "Scarcely any man durst sleep in his own house, but all met in companies with their wives and children, and set about building little fortifications to defend themselves from such barbarians and inhuman enemies, whom they concluded would be let loose upon them at pleasure."[8] At Staunton in the Shenandoah Valley, the Reverend John Craig wrote that when Braddock was defeated "our country was laid open to the enemy, our people were in dreadful confusion, and discouraged to the highest degree." Some of the wealthier inhabitants, who could take some money with them on which to live, wanted to flee to a safer part of the country, but Craig advised against it as "a scandal to our nation," one that would dishonor "our brave ancestors." Instead, they built forts, and Craig fortified churches at his own expense. The Augusta Stone Church became "Fort Defiance."[9]

Colonel Dunbar's retreat to Philadelphia with what was left of Braddock's army left the frontier exposed to assault by war parties who often used the road Braddock had cleared. After seventy-five years of peace, Pennsylvania had no militia force to defend its backcountry settlers. Governor Morris warned that they would be overrun and abandon their homes if help was not forthcoming, but the issue of frontier defense became a political standoff between the governor and the Assembly. Morris accused the Assembly of leaving the people unprotected by "an ill-timed Parsimony" and demanded a simple and straightforward answer "whether You will or will not Establish a Militia."[10]

Backcountry inhabitants sent petition after petition to the governor and Assembly describing their distressed situation in heartbreaking language and begging for arms and ammunition. "As we Dwell upon the Frontiers our case at present is Lamentably Dangerous," the inhabitants of Lurgan Township in Cumberland County wrote to the governor on August 1, "we being in such imminent Peril of being inhumanely Butchered by our Savage neighbours, whose tender Mercies are Cruelty." Other petitioners said their wives and children were scared to death by the slightest rumors and could barely be persuaded to stay. Unless something was done quickly, some predicted, their only options were to sit at home and be butchered, run away, or go out to fight as "a confused Multitude" without arms and ammunition and lacking discipline or proper officers. As Indian raiding parties destroyed horses and cattle and burned everything in their path, people fled before them, abandoning the country.[11] At Wright's Ferry on the Susquehanna River, Rhoda Barber, who was not even born at the time, remembered vividly in her old age hearing her mother describe the dreadful situation they were in, "alarm'd at the slightest noise in the night expecting every hour to see canoes coming down upon them." The community finally decided to evacuate the women and children to Philadelphia.[12]

The Reverend John Elder, the Scottish pastor of Paxton Presbyterian Church from 1738 to 1792, organized defenses and ranger companies. Writing to Secretary Richard Peters in September, Elder complained that the multiple reports of attacks and petitions sent to Philadelphia had had no effect, "so that we seem to be given into the hands of a merciless Enemy." Nearly forty people had been killed within a few weeks on the frontiers of Lancaster and Cumberland counties, with many others carried into captivity, and yet the legislature did nothing but debate. "What may be the end of these things God only knows."[13] Writing to James Hamilton and Benjamin Franklin from the infant town of Easton in December, William Parsons, an English-born major in the Northampton County militia, said that the settlers on this side of the mountain all along the river had fled and "we are now the frontier." The townspeople were exhausted watching for enemy raiding parties, and seeing no help coming from the government, they too were moving away. "Pray do something," Parsons begged, "or the country will be entirely ruined."[14]

The Quaker Assembly remained unresponsive.[15] Morris told the petitioners that his heart bled for them, but with no militia and no money at his disposal, all he could do was issue commissions for the officers they chose if they formed their own companies.[16] In other words, Scotch-Irish families on the frontier would have to defend themselves. Left "naked & defenceless" by what they called "an unnatural scheme of policy," more than one hundred frontier inhabitants sent a petition direct to King George, imploring him to intervene and protect the province.[17]

Their fears were hardly exaggerated. For more than three years following Braddock's defeat, raiding parties from the Ohio country crossed the mountains, dropped down into the valleys, and attacked the scattered and exposed farmsteads of the Scotch-Irish and their neighbors in the backcountry of Virginia and Pennsylvania. As Benjamin Franklin observed, their dispersed settlement patterns rendered them particularly vulnerable.[18] In addition, few settlers had thought it necessary to build fortifications during years of peaceful coexistence with Indian neighbors. According to Governor Morris in a speech he sent to the Six Nations, the Delawares and their allies fell upon "People whose Houses were always open to them" and who had no guns because "they thought there was no need of Arms, being Secure of the Friendship of the Indians."[19]

By the time the Seven Years War broke out, physical and cultural boundaries between Indian and colonial communities had become blurred in areas where people shared common ground. Delawares and Shawnees had traded with and worked alongside Scotch-Irish and German colonists for years, but now, so Morris claimed, French papists had won them over with false promises of restoring their country to them and were orchestrating raids on places and people the Indians knew intimately from decades of face-to-face interaction.[20] The Delawares "did us the greatest Mischief," according to another account, because they knew the location of almost every settlement on the frontier and acted as guides for the French Indians.[21] From what he could tell from the reports coming from the backcountry, Philadelphia botanist John Bartram wrote to his friend Peter Collinson, most of the Indian raiders had formerly been close neighbors of the settlers "and now, without any provocation, destroy all before them with fire, ball, and tomahawk." Unlike Collinson, Bartram had little sympathy for the Indians' accumulated grievances: must we, he asked, "have thousands of our innocent people barbarously murdered, because some of our traders made them drunk to get a skin cheap? or an Irishman settles on a bit of their land which they will never make use of?"[22]

Rolling Back the Scotch-Irish Frontier

The Scotch-Irish and other backcountry settlers had good reason to fear Indian attacks, and Indians had good reasons to attack them. The French encouraged and equipped their Native allies to wage guerrilla warfare on the western frontiers of the British colonies. With most of their regular military forces concentrated on the New York frontier and the St. Lawrence to protect Canada from invasion, they used Fort Duquesne as a base for launching Indian raids against Virginia and Pennsylvania. The strategy was to divert British energies and resources from the north and to so demoralize the backcountry inhabitants that they would seek peace.

Indian people fought for Indian reasons, however, not French. Delawares in the Susquehanna and Allegheny Valleys cited years of trade abuse, land theft, and unpunished murders at the hands of colonists. Delaware deputies told the Six Nations Council at Onondaga that the English "used us like Dogs" and would "make Slaves of us" if they let things continue as they had.[23] Cunning and covetous Pennsylvanians had already taken all the Delawares' lands on the Delaware River and most of their lands on the Susquehanna and they kept coming, "for where one of those People settled, like Pidgeons, a thousand more would settle, so that We at last offered to sell it" and moved across the Alleghenies[24] (Figure 5.1).

It was a view with which the anonymous author of *An Enquiry into the Causes of the Alienation of the Delaware and Shawanese Indians from the*

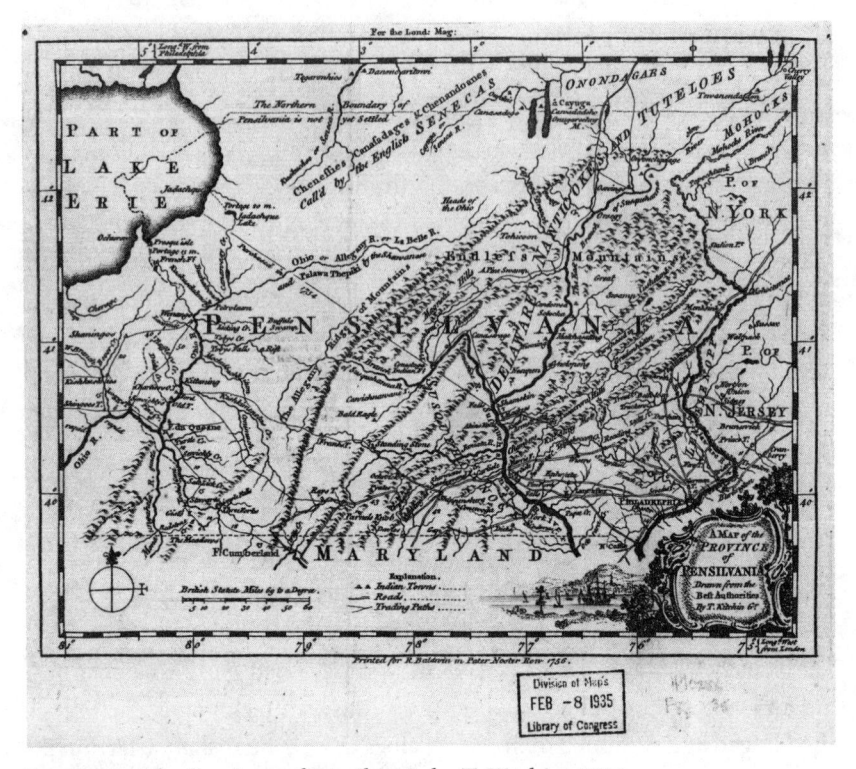

Figure 5.1 The Province of Pensilvania by T. Kitchin, 1756.
Library of Congress Geography and Map Division.

British Interest (1759) agreed, in a scathing indictment of the Pennsylvania proprietors. The author was Charles Thomson, one of three brothers from County Londonderry who were orphaned on their way to America when their widowed father died at sea. Thomson, who taught at a Quaker school in Philadelphia—and went on to sign the Declaration of Independence and serve as secretary of the Continental Congress—was an adopted Delaware who worked as an interpreter and scribe for the eastern Delaware chief, Teedyuscung.[25]

Teedyuscung could speak for himself, in English or in Lenape. He repeatedly vented his anger that lands had been taken by fraud, but he also understood that the Indians were not the only people being cheated. The Indians were not fools. "The Proprietaries who have purchased their Lands from us cheap, have sold them too dear to poor People, and the Indians have suffered for it."[26] When the war erupted, the English blamed Teedyuscung, "a noted

Delaware Indian born and bred amongst us," for instigating all the attacks on the east side of the Susquehanna. When Teedyuscung and his people met with Governor Morris and other officials at Eaton in July 1756, the townspeople observed that the Native women were wearing shirts "made of Dutch Table Cloths which it is supposed they took from People they murdered on our Frontiers." Major William Parsons described Teedyuscung as "a lusty raw bon'd Man" nearly fifty years old, with a reputation for loud talking and hard drinking, but the Delaware chief was playing a cagey game. He knew that his borderland location—"in the middle between the French and the English, quite disengaged from both sides"—offered opportunities as well as dangers. Whether he joined the English or the French, he announced, "he would publish it aloud to the World that all Nations might know it."[27]

Pennsylvania colonial officials and Sir William Johnson, Britain's agent to the Iroquois, both tried to prevail upon the Six Nations to exert their influence and rein in the Delawares and their allies. The Six Nations wanted to limit their own involvement in the conflict and minimize its impact on their league.[28] They attempted to restrain the Delawares, whom they had formerly treated "as women" and ordered to live on the Susquehanna. But the Delawares refused to be governed any longer by those who, as we saw in Chapter 3, had sold their lands from under them at Lancaster in 1744 and Albany in 1754. When the Pennsylvania government dispatched the Oneida half king Scarouady and interpreter Andrew Montour to the tribes on the Susquehanna, the Delawares "put the Six Nations to Defiance." They said they launched their attacks without provocation or warning "to shew the Six Nations that they are no longer Women, by which they mean no longer under their Subjection." They were determined to wage war against the English, no matter what the Six Nations said. Even Scarouady, "a Man of Authority among the Six Nations, and of great Experience and Eloquence, could not prevail on them," reported Paxinosa, a Shawnee chief of the community at Wyoming and one of the few to support the British. Indeed, the Delawares would not even touch the wampum belts Scarouady laid before them, but "throwed them on one side with their Pipes and gave him ill Language." Paxinosa said it was "in vain to speak one more word to our Grandfathers, the Delawares. I spoke so often to them to the same Purpose, till at last they threatened to knock me on the head."[29] By going to war themselves and asserting their independence from Iroquois control, the Delawares upended Pennsylvania's Indian policy, which was predicated on the supremacy of the Iroquois over other Native nations.[30]

Like the Delawares, the Shawnees were determined to keep their country free of the European Settlement.[31] They went to war in part because they had experienced recurrent dispossession and displacement, and in part because they were outraged by South Carolina's imprisonment of six of their warriors, one of whom died in captivity. Although Paxinosa's Shawnees were reported to be "very hearty in the English Interest" in 1756, two years later the old chief and his band joined others in moving to the Ohio country to escape English threats to their lands and lives in the Wyoming Valley.[32]

Shawnee warriors launched their earliest strikes against Virginia, and targeted Colonel James Patton. Sheriff, president of the court, county lieutenant, and militia commander in Augusta County; a member of the Virginia House of Burgesses with extensive landholdings—Patton was now a prominent figure in the colony. He had gotten his start transporting Ulster immigrants across the Atlantic to settle the Borden and Beverley tract in the Shenandoah Valley. Seeing greater prospects in the promise of Appalachian land than in continued Atlantic voyages, Patton himself emigrated in 1738, at age forty-six, and became a land speculator. He employed John Buchanan, who became his son-in-law, as surveyor. Patton and his nephew, William Preston, who was born in Londonderry County on Christmas Day, 1729, and was educated by the Reverend Isaac Craig at his Tinkling Spring congregation,[33] clashed over land titles with Patrick Calhoun and others in the Calhoun family. Indian people knew Patton as a trader, land speculator, and treaty commissioner. He attended the Treaty of Lancaster in 1744; he accompanied a Cherokee delegation to Williamsburg in 1751, and a dozen Cherokee women and children stayed at his house while the delegation was in town; and he was one of Virginia's commissioners at the Logstown Treaty in 1752, where he met with representatives of the Six Nations, Delawares, and Shawnees to try to secure their consent to opening lands beyond the Alleghanies to colonial settlement. On July 30, 1755, Shawnee raiders attacked Draper's Meadows, later known as Blacksburg, as Patton was leading a party of rangers carrying ammunition to the outpost. The Shawnees recognized him and killed and scalped him.[34]

It was a grim fall on the Scotch-Irish frontier in 1755. Indian raiders employed terror tactics and psychological warfare. Scalping, torture, and mutilations spread panic, destroyed morale, and sent backcountry settlers into full retreat, leaving an area about 150 miles in length and 20–30 miles wide, from the Potomac to the Delaware, entirely deserted. Shocking descriptions of atrocities so demoralized the people that they were unable "to make any considerable Resistance or stand against the Indians."³⁵ In other words, the Indians' tactics worked. A series of chain reactions rolled back the frontier. Flights and rumors of flights triggered more flights. Raids that devastated one region propelled settlers to abandon a neighboring area. Indians then raided farther east, targeted another region, and generated another round of flights.³⁶

At the mouth of Conococheague Creek where it joins the Potomac, William Trent reported forty people killed and a family burned to death in a house. The Indians were destroying everything in their path, he wrote, burning houses, barns, and stacks of grain, and they captured a girl named Jenny McClane near the fort. "I expect we shall soon be the Frontier." Then in a postscript he added, "the woods is alive with them; how long will those in power by their Quarrels suffer us to be massacred?"³⁷

At Paxton, John Harris continued to sound the alarm. People expected the enemy any day and, with no sign of assistance, were abandoning their farms. "The Indians is cutting us off every day," he wrote in a letter to colonial officials. Governor Morris could only reply once more that it was not in his power to help. He urged Harris and his neighbors to "act with caution and spirit" and defend their families.³⁸ William Parsons, distributing powder, lead, and bread to the refugees in his region, told Richard Peters, "It is impossible to describe the Confusion and distress of those unhappy people. Our Roads are continually full of Travellers." "Men, Women & Children, most of them barefoot, have been obliged to cross those terrible Mountains with what little they could bring with them in so long a Journey thro' ways almost impassable, to get to the Inhabitants on this side." Meanwhile, the people on this side who lived near the mountains were removing their effects to Tulpehocken; those at Tulpehocken were retreating to Reading; many at Reading were moving closer to Philadelphia, and so on. The frontier was receding quickly.³⁹

An emergency meeting of the General Council for Cumberland County at Shippensburg at the end of October resolved to build five large forts immediately for defense and as refuges for women and children.⁴⁰ By the next month, Shippensburg was full of people, with five or six families to a house. John Armstrong, now an officer in the militia, said there were no inhabitants left in the Juniata or Tuscarora valleys.⁴¹ "You cannot conceive what a vast Tract of Country has been depopulated," Governor Morris wrote to Sir William Johnson in November 1755; "all the Families from Augusta County in Virginia to the River Delaware have been obliged to quit their

Plantations on the North side of that Chain of Hills which is called the endless Mountains."[42]

The population of Augusta County, Virginia, was predominantly Scotch-Irish. Safe in Williamsburg, Governor Dinwiddie's response to the situation in Augusta was to spill a lot of ink blaming the victims. He told multiple correspondents that he had dispatched ranger companies to the frontier and had done everything in his power to help the county, and that the Indians' numbers were exaggerated. But the people were indolent, cowardly, and "supine" and, rather than stand and fight, they fled in panic. If the inhabitants had shown "Spirit and Resolution" they could have defeated the few Indian raiders and protected their women and children, he told Colonel John Buchanan, son-in-law of the deceased Patton; "but if Your People will dastardly give up their Families and Interest to a barbarous Enemy without endeavouring to assist them, they cannot expect to be assisted without their own Assistance against these Banditti." He told the Earl of Loudon, the commander of British forces in North America, that it would be difficult to raise recruits in the mountain regions "as our lower Class of People are Dastardly and [the] most inactive Mortals I ever met with."[43] To be fair to Dinwiddie, he was consistent and catholic in his defensiveness: he blamed Braddock's soldiers for their defeat at the Monongahela; Maryland and Pennsylvania for not doing their share of frontier defense; and the Virginia Assembly for not stepping up and financing the war effort.

Stationed on the Virginia frontier, George Washington realized that efforts to stem Indian raids were generally futile. "The inhabitants see, and are convinced of this; which make each family afraid of standing in the gap of danger, and by retreating one behind another, they depopulate the country, and leave it to the Enemy, who subsist upon the plunder."[44] If one Shawnee raiding party of fifty warriors in the summer of 1755 could cause such havoc and drive off almost two thousand head of cattle and horses, the minister of Fredericksville parish reported, no wonder people were terrified by the prospect of "much greater and more extensive Mischiefs." Hundreds of families had abandoned their homes, and both sides of the Alleghenies were almost entirely depopulated. People beyond the Blue Ridge mountains were fleeing to the Carolina backcountry, hoping to find safety under the shelter of the Catawbas and Cherokees, wrote the minister, where northern Indian raiders would not venture. He had heard that three hundred people in one week passed by Bedford Courthouse on their way to Carolina.[45]

Although Scotch-Irish victims viewed them as unpredictable outbreaks of savagery, Indian raids were not haphazard and random, but part of a strategy of eroding their enemies' capacity for resistance and will to fight by repeated assaults. Lacking the population, logistics, and military resources to sustain military operations year-round, Native societies were nevertheless able to mount raids year after year.[46] War parties targeted specific areas of encroachment, which meant backcountry settlements between the Susquehanna and the Appalachians in Pennsylvania, and the western valleys of Virginia, and especially lands illegally occupied. "It may be thought and said by some that the Indians are a faithless and ungrateful set of Barbarians, and will not stand by any agreements they make with us," said Irish trader George Croghan; "but it is well known that they never claimed any right to a Tract of Country, after they had sold it with the consent of their Council, and received any consideration, tho' never so trifling."[47] Morris informed Governor William Shirley of Massachusetts, who became commander-in-chief in North America on Braddock's death until replaced by Loudon, that the Indians' plan seemed to be to take possession of the Susquehanna, after which they would be free to destroy the rich country beyond the river where there were thousands of families.[48] He was right. A messenger from the Ohio Delawares told Scarouady in November 1755: "One party will go against Carlisle; One down the Sasquehannah; and I myself with another party will go against Tulpehoccan to Conrad Weiser. And We shall be followed by a Thousand French and Indians, Ottowawas, Twightwees [Miamis], Shawonese and other Delawares."[49]

The first colonists on Penn Creek, which joins the Susquehanna on the west bank of the river a few miles below Sunbury, were mostly Scotch-Irish who, according to local history, pitched their tents on the rich land around the mouth of the stream as early as 1744.[50] More Scotch-Irish settled Penn Creek after Weiser and Peters engineered the sale of a huge tract west of the Susquehanna at the Albany Congress in 1754, purchasing it from the Six Nations rather than the Delawares and Shawnees, who were furious. A war party of fourteen Delawares from the Ohio country attacked German families at Penn Creek in October 1755. Then a group of Delawares fired on trader Thomas McKee, John Harris, and forty-some Pennsylvanians who had traveled to Shamokin to investigate the attack. Petitioners living near Penn's Creek, mainly with Scotch-Irish names, wrote to tell Governor Morris that, although most of the inhabitants had fled in terror, they wanted to stay and fight, but unless supplies of arms and ammunition arrived soon, they would have to abandon the country.[51]

Many Scotch-Irish, mostly from Maryland, had entered the Great Cove Valley, situated on the west bank of the Susquehanna (in the vicinity of present-day McConnellesburg in Fulton County), and the neighboring Little Cove and Conolloways valleys by about 1740. The Iroquois complained that they were squatting on lands that had not yet been purchased, and, despite efforts by Peters, Croghan, and Weiser to expel them in 1750, the squatters returned. On November 1, 1755, the Delaware war chief Shingas and about ninety Delaware, Shawnee, and Mingo warriors attacked Great Cove, Little Cove, and the Conolloways, killing and capturing people they regarded as squatters on their land. Over the course of several days, they virtually blotted out the Great and Little Cove settlements. Great Cove was reduced to ashes; 47 of its 93 settlers were killed or captured, and the terrified survivors fled east. Charles Stuart, his wife, and two small children were among the captives. Shingas spared them because of Stuart's past acts of generosity and hospitality. In a war between former neighbors, many of the participants knew each other.[52]

Angry and frustrated that their repeated petitions to Philadelphia brought no relief, backcountry settlers tried other measures to get the government to act. In November 1755, Adam Hoops from Conococheague sent Governor Morris a tomahawk, "which was found sticking in the breast of one David McClellan." Then a group of frontiersmen drove a wagonload of frozen corpses through Philadelphia and laid them in the state house yard.[53] "There is no Order among the People; one cries one Thing, and another another Thing," Weiser and other officials warned Morris later that month. "They want to force us to make a Law, that they should have a Reward for every Indian which they kill; They demanded such a Law of us, with their Guns Cocked, pointing it towards us." The people were so incensed against the Indians and the government that "we are afeard they will go down in a Body to Philadelphia and comit [sic] the vilest Outrages. They say they will rather be hanged than to be butchered by the Indians, as some of their Neighbours have been lately."[54] It was a presage of future events.

Indian people on the Susquehanna who wanted to remain neutral or allied to Pennsylvania were caught between two fires. Fearful of Delaware and Shawnee attacks like their backcountry neighbors, they requested that a fort be constructed for them at Shamokin as a place of refuge. At the same time, they were terrified that the backcountry inhabitants would take revenge on them for the atrocities committed by Delaware and Shawnee war parties. They had heard that thousands of Pennsylvanians were coming to destroy them and that backcountry settlers were terrorizing friendly Indians, Weiser reported. When people from Paxton captured and interrogated an enemy Indian, he "begged for his Life and promised to tell what he knew to-morrow morning, but (shocking to me) they shott him in the midst of them, scalped him and threw his Body in the River." Weiser feared that the lawlessness, brutality, and ignorance of the backcountry inhabitants would bring on a general Indian war. "They curse and damn the Indian[s] and call them Murdering Dogs into their faces without distinction." Native people who remained friendly and lived close to colonial settlements were in danger of being "Killed by the Mob" and they dared not go into the woods for fear of being killed by the enemy.[55]

It seemed to the Scotch-Irish that the further from the backcountry officials lived, the less they cared about the settlers' plight. William Smith's pamphlet, *A Brief View of the Conduct of Pennsylvania, For the Year 1755*, accused the Assembly of alienating the Indians and then making light of the suffering of the backcountry folk who bore the brunt of the resulting Indian attacks. The Quakers, he wrote, seemed concerned only with maintaining their political power based on unequal representation. "The *Scotch Irish*, in particular, think that the *Quakers* have a secret Satisfaction in seeing their increasing Multitude *thinned* and *beggared* in the Back Countries," Smith wrote. He cited a "genuine Letter . . . written from a Gentleman in the Back Countries" who claimed to have heard that a member of the Assembly "replied with great Indifference, that *there were only some* SCOTCH-IRISH KILLED, *who could well enough be spared*." This, he said, was "the common Language of many of these People":

> Their Consciences are mighty tender of shedding the Blood of Indian Murderers, but hardened and seared as to shedding the Blood, at least of the Scotch-Irish. The Papists think they do God Service by killing us as Heretics. The Quakers think they do the same, by looking calmly on, while we are killed to their Hand. And where lies the Difference? Both act as their Religion dictates, and both are staunch, bigoted, and *pharisaical*.

Nathaniel Grubb, a Quaker assemblyman from Chester County, published a denial in the *Pennsylvania Gazette* that he had said the Scotch-Irish were expendable, but for Scotch-Irish people in backcountry areas the story explained the government's inaction.[56]

The prominent Philadelphia Quaker Isaac Norris and members of the Assembly took a defensive and patronizing tone. They told the governor they felt badly for those living on the frontiers and had done everything they could. They had reason to believe (although they did not say what reason) that the people suffering on the frontiers themselves did not wish them to do more. What was more, they declared, people "who would give up essential Liberty to purchase a Little Temporary safety deserve neither Liberty nor safety." Men who were ready to defend themselves but unable to purchase guns and ammunition had been supplied with both from monies provided by the last assembly. Things might have been different if the governor had not rejected their bills. In any case, experience in Virginia clearly showed that it was virtually impossible to effectively guard an extended frontier settled by individual families scattered two or three miles apart against "the insidious attacks of small parties of skulking Murderers."[57] The Scotch-Irish would have to make the best of things.

Striking Back and Striking Out

That meant they had to carry out their own defensive and offensive measures.

Scotch-Irish men fought in the French and Indian War as regular soldiers as well as backcountry militia. British regiments contained a disproportionate number of men from Scotland and Ireland. Braddock's two regiments came from Ireland, and nine of the fourteen regiments stationed in Ireland were sent to America in 1756 and early 1757.[58] In fact, the war stimulated additional Irish migration to America among soldiers and other people attached to regiments who opted to stay.[59] Regulars did not necessarily have a better reputation than militia, though. At Easton in October 1756, Major William Parsons complained, "there is in Town a Number of Irish Recruits, some of them as abandoned, drunken Fellows as ever was got together." He wished the officer had had orders not to let them mix with the Indians at all.[60]

And few regulars were stationed in the backcountry. Settlers who did not flee faced a next-to-impossible challenge with minimal assistance from their government. Many "forted up." Organizing defenses as a militia officer in Cumberland County, John Armstrong advocated establishing a chain of blockhouses along the Kittatinny Mountains. Governor Morris made a tour of the frontiers in early 1756, traveling to Carlisle and back through York County, inspecting the forts. The engineer he took with him reported that "scarce anything has been done right." Morris had four forts built beyond the Kittatinny Hills, including Fort Granville on the Juniata River.

Reporting Morris's findings to the proprietors, Richard Peters said that many of the small forts built by townships in the interior of the province were poorly situated and poorly garrisoned and were to be demolished as useless. Other forts would be built in more strategic locations with stronger defenses and garrisons of about fifty men in each. In the course of his journey, the governor had found things in general disorder and, according to Peters, "conceived a very mean, tho' it is but too just, an Opinion of the Settlers of the Back Counties," whom he thought "extremely backward." Peters hoped he would change his opinion once mistakes had been rectified and officers and men received regular pay.[61]

Virginia also built a cordon of forts on its western frontier. Eventually a chain of posts positioned at roughly twenty-mile intervals stretched across almost four hundred miles of mountainous terrain from the Potomac through the Allegheny Mountains to the borders of North Carolina. "Forts" was a misleading term for many of these structures, which were no more than fortified homes or mills, or a cluster of cabins stockaded together. Mobile Indian warriors, who had little to fear from colonial soldiers cooped up in blockhouses, skirted around them with ease. The stockades' purpose was to offer refuge to backcountry families, rather than stop Indian raids. Looking back on his service on the Virginia frontier, George Washington acknowledged that manning the forts was done to quiet the fears of the inhabitants, rather than in any realistic expectation of providing security to such an extensive line of settlements.[62]

The Scotch-Irish on the frontier were supposed to provide protection for eastern communities, not vice versa. If the purpose of placing them there had been to provide a defensive wall of hardy fighting farmers who would repel Indian attacks and emulate the heroics of their ancestors at the sieges of Londonderry and Enniskillen, as James Logan had imagined, the policy failed dismally. It has even been said that the Seven Years War was "a conflict for which the Scots-Irish did not show up."[63] Although there were at least 160 militia at Great Cove, for example, few volunteered to go out on campaign after the attack and, according to one report, the old officers hid themselves to "save their Scalps."[64] When so many inhabitants fled into other areas, it was clear that the Pennsylvania authorities could not count on them to protect their own region or to provide military service.[65]

Poorly armed, poorly prepared, and scattered through mountain valleys, Scotch-Irish in the backcountry resented those on the coast who were supposed to organize defense. Eastern elites who had expected the Scotch-Irish to perform their designated role and provide layers of protection were often bitter in their denunciations of men who evaded militia duty in order to protect their families and farms. Washington, headquartered at Winchester, was contemptuous of the frontier militia in general and those of predominantly Scotch-Irish Augusta County in particular. They were, in his view, disorganized, indolent, unruly, wasteful, and ineffective. When danger threatened, it took them so long to assemble that the enemy had time to plunder, kill, scalp, and escape before they arrived. Their lack of regulation and discipline rendered them ineffective when they did show up. Each one thought he should be in command and if not accorded respect, "takes huff, thinks his wisdom & merit affronted, and so marches off in high contempt of every social Law." Knowing they had to depend on the militia for protection, it was no wonder that backcountry settlers were alarmed and ready to run for it.[66]

Benjamin Franklin, traveling to Bethlehem in January 1756, met wagons of people moving their families and belongings from the Irish Settlement. Lehigh township and Bethlehem filled with refugees, "the Workmen's Shops and even Cellars being crowded with Women and Children." Yet when Reverends John Elder and John Craig, as well as other leading men from the Irish Settlement, came to see him and demanded more men for Craig's company, Franklin responded by threatening to disband or remove the companies already posted for the security of particular townships "if the People would not stay on their Places, behave like Men, do something for themselves, and assist the Province Soldiers."[67] Presbyterian ministers like Elder and Craig took the lead in organizing local defense, forming paramilitary bands of volunteers or rangers, who often dressed and fought like Indians.[68] Elder himself commanded the Paxtang Rangers. Captain Thomas McKee also commanded a company.[69]

From Reading, the Reverend Thomas Barton informed Richard Peters in February that the inhabitants over the hills were all fleeing, and in two or three days the North Mountains would be the frontier. All work had stopped. "In short Sir, it appears as if this part of the Country breath'd its last." Barton had been back in the country less than a year. Descended from an Anglo-Irish family that had emigrated to Ulster in Cromwellian times, he had attended university in Dublin, emigrated to Philadelphia, and then went to England to enter the priesthood. Ordained as an Anglican minister, he returned to

Philadelphia in April 1755. He became a missionary for the Society for the Propagation of the Gospel, but war broke out before he could begin his work in Indian communities. For the next three years Barton and his backcountry neighbors experienced what he called "the sad effects of Popish Tyranny and Savage Cruelty." Barton hoped that Catholics in Ireland and Indians in America might both be "civilized."[70]

In Virginia, Governor Robert Dinwiddie complained about the spineless and parsimonious populace, who neither rallied to defend the colony themselves nor voted sufficient money to keep the militia in good shape, and who seemed to be seized with panic whenever a few French and Indians appeared.[71] Washington realized that militia were no match for Native warriors and that "without Indians to oppose Indians, we may expect but small success."[72] Washington and other colonial leaders also complained about militia who refused to serve for prolonged periods. It's not hard to imagine why. Generals and politicians waged war to advance imperial interests; ordinary people often tried to avoid getting caught up in the conflicts they caused. Militia reluctance had less to do with cowardice and lack of discipline than with safeguarding families, harvesting and marketing crops, and running a family farm economy.[73]

As if to underline Dinwiddie's concerns, Major Andrew Lewis led an abortive counterstrike against the Shawnee towns. Andrew Lewis was born in Ireland in 1720, the third son of John Lewis, the pugilistic immigrant from Donegal who had partnered with William Beverley and James Patton in developing Shenandoah Valley lands by attracting settlers. John Lewis and his sons, William, Thomas, and Charles, became principals in the Greenbrier Land Company. Andrew was chief surveyor. He became a captain of militia in 1742 and county colonel in 1752. Wounded in Washington's Fort Necessity campaign in 1754, he survived Braddock's campaign the next year unhurt, serving with Dunbar's detachment, and was one Washington's chief lieutenants in his beleaguered defense of the Virginia frontier.[74] In February 1756, Lewis set out along Sandy Creek, a tributary of the Ohio in what is now West Virginia, to attack the Shawnee towns on the Ohio and Scioto River. The force comprised some 350 men, many of them Scotch-Irish, and included 100 Cherokees led by Ostenaco (who was also known as Judd's Friend, and often called by his title Outacite, or Mankiller, signifying head warrior) and Scotch-Irish trader Richard Pearis who was married into Cherokee society. Captain William Preston, whose uncle James Patton the Shawnees had killed six months before, brought a company of rangers.

Captain Archibald Alexander, who had emigrated from County Down in 1737, led another volunteer company. Craig sent the expedition off with a sermon. The campaign was a debacle. After six weeks, their progress halted by flooded rivers, Lewis and his men returned home "having done nothing essential," as Dinwiddie told Washington. "I believe they did not know the Way to the Shawnesse Towns." Eighteen years later, Lewis would learn his way and attack the Shawnee towns again.[75]

When Scarouady, half king of the Six Nations, was told the Pennsylvania Assembly would not agree to raise the necessary money to support the war effort, he was stunned. He feared it would cause all the Delawares to defect to the French, although he hoped it might not be too late if Pennsylvania showed the Delawares proper encouragement.[76] Pennsylvania tried to reach out to those Indians that were "yet our Friends." In mid-January 1756, with Croghan and Weiser interpreting, Pennsylvania held a council at Carlisle and solicited the help of The Belt, Silver Heels, Jagrea, Newcastle, Seneca George, and other prominent Iroquois chiefs in stopping "these cruel and barbarous attacks on our peaceable inhabitants." Deep in Scotch-Irish country, Carlisle was a dangerous place for the Iroquois to be.[77] Governor Morris assured Indian delegates at Philadelphia in March that Pennsylvania would always distinguish between Native people who were innocent and friendly and those who were guilty and at war.[78] It was a promise he could not keep, and the next month he implemented measures that made it even more difficult.

By April 1756, the entire frontier of the American colonies was in upheaval. At the beginning of the month, Shingas and a Delaware war party attacked McCord's Fort in Cumberland County, taking more than twenty captives.[79] On April 5, Thomas Mckee reported that John Shikellamy had told him the Indian people on the North branch of the Susquehanna were in "Great Confusion." The Delawares were moving to the Ohio and trying to persuade the Shawnees to go with them. The same day, a correspondent at Carlisle informed Governor Morris that the people there were in "the Greatest Confusion." Troops were abandoning forts and "the Country People" were huddling together in "the greatest Consternation." They were so enraged against the Assembly that he feared "they will Carry their Resentment to a Great Length."[80]

Three days later, on April 8, Morris proclaimed war against the Delawares. Benjamin Franklin and Assembly member Joseph Galloway had brokered a compromise between the governor and the Assembly in which, rather than agree to taxes, the proprietors gave a "gift" to help finance the war effort. Morris also placed bounties on Indian scalps: 130 Spanish dollars for the scalp of every adult male over twelve years old; 50 dollars for every adult female scalp. Philadelphia Quakers beseeched him to try more pacific measures before declaring war, but Morris said he had to yield to the demands of "the enraged People" because he could not afford them protection. Few bounties were paid out. Nonetheless, the premiums encouraged and rewarded military service by frontiersmen. Some Quakers were so appalled that they withdrew from politics altogether, opening the way for dramatic change in forthcoming elections.[81] Explaining his decision to Sir William Johnson, Morris wrote, "You cannot conceive the havoc in this defenseless province, the murders, or the vast extent of country laid waste." With more than three hundred people taken captive, most of them at Shingas's Town, also called Kittanning, but also in almost every Delaware town on the Susquehanna, Morris justified offering rewards for the scalps of Indian people as a necessary measure to encourage frontier inhabitants "to hunt, pursue, and attack them in their own Country, and by these means keep them at home for the Defense of their own Towns, and prevent the Total Desertion of the Back Countries."[82] In other words, by offering scalp bounties, the government outsourced Indian fighting to the same people who were begging the government for assistance against the Indians in the first place.

That same month, John Shikellamy and about ten Indian men, women, and children who were staying at Thomas McKee's place told him they were often accosted by people who told Shikellamy to his face "that they had a good mind to Scalp him." Shikellamy beat a hasty retreat from the fort near John Harris's at Paxton because "the Irish People did not use him well and threatened to kill him."[83] A few weeks later, the Moravian Reverend August Gottlieb Spangenberg worried about sending the Seneca chief Jagrea and others as messengers to the Native communities on the Susquehanna because he "thought them all in greater Dangers of being Hurt in the Irish Settlement than any where Else in all the Province."[84]

The scalp bounties had little immediate effect. Later that April, backcountry inhabitants from York and Cumberland counties met at Lancaster with the expressed intention of marching to Philadelphia to make the legislature understand the gravity of their situation and to demand the protection to which they were entitled. Hundreds of their neighbors had been either murdered and scalped or carried into captivity, and nearly two-thirds of the inhabitants of Cumberland County had already deserted their habitations, many of which had been destroyed. In York County, stables and corn houses were crowded with refugees. Men, women, and children who had formerly lived in affluence and plenty were "reduced to the most extreme Poverty and distress, flying before their merciless enemies and lacking the common necessities of life." York County kept a standing guard of 80 or 100 men on its frontiers.[85] Morris feared that if help did not arrive before the next attack, York and Cumberland counties would be completely evacuated, making the Susquehanna River the frontier.[86]

Franklin and other commissioners had always thought the best way to fight back was to invade Indian country and strike Native people where they lived, hunted, fished, and farmed. Building forts and offering scalp bounties to encourage volunteer parties had not worked. It was time to carry the war into Indian country.

The attack on Fort Granville in the summer of 1756 underscored the need (Figure 5.2). When Arthur Buchanan and four Scotch-Irish families had initially settled in the Fort Granville neighborhood on the Juniata River, the Delawares were unwilling to sell the land. Then, apparently, Buchanan, after some hard drinking, swindled the Delaware chief Tewea, also known as "Captain Jacobs," into selling land on the Juniata Valley. Tewea relocated

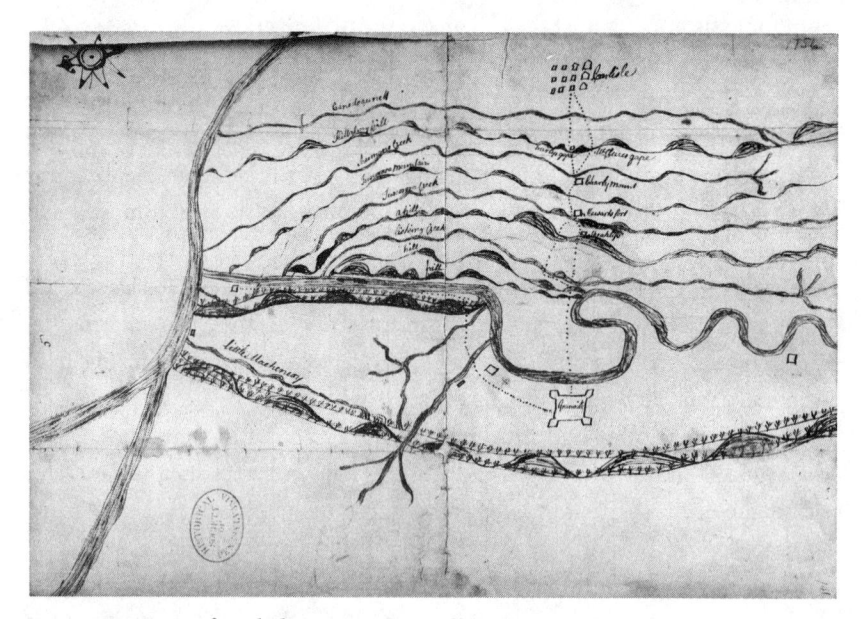

Figure 5.2 Map of Carlisle to Fort Granville, 1756.
Collection of the Historical Society of Pennsylvania. Lamberton Scotch-Irish Collection (0349).

to Kittanning, the principal Delaware town on the Allegheny River, where the war chief Shingas also lived. A refuge and rendezvous for displaced peoples, Kittanning became the stronghold of Delaware resistance. On July 30 or August 1, 1756, leading a war party of thirty-two Western Delawares and Shawnees and a couple of dozen French-Canadian allies under Louis Coulon de Villiers, who had defeated George Washington at Fort Necessity two years before, Tewea attacked Fort Granville. Seventy-five Scotch-Irish people (two dozen families) from across Cumberland County were gathered there. Tewea's warriors set the fort on fire and Lieutenant Edward Armstrong, the fort commander, and brother of John Armstrong, was killed in the fighting. Twenty-nine of the inhabitants were captured and taken to Kittanning. Among the captives was the family of Sergeant John Turner: his wife, the widow of trader Simon Girty, Sr., four sons by her previous marriage, and their own son, John. The senior Turner was tortured to death at Kittanning.[87] However, the Shawnees appear to have avoided attacking the swindler Arthur Buchanan and his family when they destroyed the fort because, as we saw in Chapter 2, a chief named Kishacoquillas had befriended him.[88]

Petitions for help from the inhabitants of Cumberland County to Pennsylvania officials resumed.[89] An expedition against Kittanning could relieve the pressure on the backcountry communities, rescue captives, and show the Indians—and Pennsylvanians—that Pennsylvania was capable of striking back.

Colonel John Armstrong led the three-hundred-man expedition. Armstrong had been born in County Fermanagh, arriving in Cumberland Valley as a surveyor for the Pennsylvania government and laying out the town of Carlisle. He built a chain of forts in the Cumberland Valley during the war. His force was recruited almost entirely from Scotch-Irish communities in Cumberland, Lancaster, and Dauphin counties. With trader Robert Callender as second-in-command and a Presbyterian minister named John Steele, it was essentially a Scotch-Irish expedition.[90] When marching on the expedition, Armstrong, according to the Reverend David McClure, "like a good Christian soldier, attended prayer, night and morning, at the head of his little band, and God was pleased to answer his request, by giving him compleat success."[91] Richard Peters called it "a glorious Expedition."[92]

It was hardly that. Kittanning had a population of perhaps 400 people, which meant fewer than 100 warriors. Armstrong's Scotch-Irish troops outnumbered them three to one. They killed Tewea and burned the town, but recovered only eleven of the more than 100 captives reputed to be held there. Only seven of these made it back, one of whom was Thomas Girty. Mrs. Alexander McAllister, who had been captured with her husband in Cumberland County three months earlier, was initially recovered by Armstrong's men, but the Delawares recaptured her and subsequently tortured her to death. After a disorganized retreat, the expedition suffered 17 killed, 13 wounded, and 19 missing. The "victory" was celebrated with fanfare, odes in the press, and a commemorative medal. Armstrong knew that he had left some 90 captives behind and that the expedition's results were "far from being satisfactory." Nevertheless, he understood that it was important to make the most of "the smallest degree of Success that God has pleased to give us." The Reverend Thomas Barton agreed: "tho' the killing of a few Indians & burning their Huts at the Kittanning is an Action not very considerable in itself, yet it is the best that has yet appear'd for this Province."[93] The expedition did demonstrate that Indian settlements west of the mountains, like colonial settlements east of the mountains, were vulnerable. To escape the expanding war zone, many Delawares pulled back from the Allegheny and moved up Beaver Creek to a cluster of towns at Kuskuski. Within a few years, Delawares were abandoning the Beaver Valley for safer locations. With the consent of the Wyandots, they settled on the headwaters of the Muskingum and Cuyahoga rivers and other locations in eastern Ohio.[94]

The Kittanning raid did not end the Indian raids. Armstrong himself informed the new governor, William Denny, in November that a raiding party near McDowell's Mill had killed and mutilated a number of people and taken some children captive. He enclosed a list of the killed and missing. The names on the list illustrated once again the toll on the Scotch-Irish: James and William MacDonald, Bartholomew McCafferty, Anthony McQuaid.[95] In a report to the Society for the Propagation of the Gospel that month, Reverend Thomas Barton said his heart bled for inhabitants reduced to poverty and distress; for lost husbands, wives, and children; and for years of labor destroyed when barns, storehouses, and wheat went up in smoke. Carlisle was all that remained of a once populous country, and the County of York was now the frontier.[96] By the end of 1756, Indian raiders had killed more than one thousand colonial settlers and soldiers, and refugees had evacuated a huge swath of territory from 50 to 200 miles wide, almost 30,000 square miles.[97]

Finding the Path to Peace

Indian raids and settlers' petitions resumed in the spring.[98] Desperate to make peace, Governor Denny made overtures to Teedyuscung. He called on Scotch-Irish expertise. Having heard that John Grey of Donegal had a reputation as a competent interpreter of Delaware and a reliable individual, Denny told George Croghan to send him with a message to Teedyuscung, "instructing him in the Indian Form and Ceremonies, furnishing him with proper Strings and Belts of Wampum, and giving him a Strict charge to take down everything that Passes in Writing."[99] Scotch-Irish trader Thomas McKee assisted in the peace process as an agent and interpreter.[100]

Talking peace with Indians while the war still raged was a tricky business in Scotch-Irish country, however. Denny ordered an escort for Teedyuscung, arguing that it was a mark of respect for the chief and also "most likely to keep both the Country People and the Indians from committing any Irruptions on one another."[101] Even as Teedyuscung negotiated at Lancaster in June 1757, Indian raiders came within thirty miles of the town, laying waste a swath of country and killing many inhabitants. As Edward Shippen wrote in a letter, "Four dead Bodies, one of which was a Woman with Child, were brought to Lancaster from neighbouring Frontiers, scalped and butchered in a most horrid Manner, and laid before the Door of the Court House for a Spectacle of Reproach to every one there."[102]

The following April, Thomas Barton reported that two families, eleven people, had been killed or captured within twelve miles of his house and that people in Lancaster and Cumberland counties were "daily alarm'd with fresh Ravages and Murders."[103] Traveling west through the lands around the Susquehanna River on a peace mission in the summer of 1758, Moravian missionary Christian Frederick Post saw so many farms deserted and destroyed that he could not help reflecting on the distress of the poor owners who once lived there in plenty. Peace was restored at the Treaty of Easton in October, when the British assured the Ohio nations that their lands would be secure once the French were defeated. Pennsylvania even promised to return the contested lands west of the Alleghenies that the Iroquois had ceded four years before at Albany. Post traveled west again with the news in company with Pisquetomen, Shikellamy, and Teedyuscung's son Captain Bull. As they passed Chambers Fort, a settlement near Big and Little Cove first established by Benjamin Chambers from County Antrim, "some of the *Irish people*, knowing some of the *Indians*, in a rash manner exclaimed against them, and we had some difficulty to get them off clear."[104] Peace overtures between the British and Indian nations did little to repair the toll the war had taken on relations between the Scotch-Irish and their Indian neighbors.

The Treaty of Easton deprived the French of their Indian allies in the Ohio country and opened the way for General John Forbes's army to advance on Fort Duquesne. Forbes had begun moving his troops forward in the spring, from Philadelphia to Carlisle and Rays Town. Carlisle, which had become the frontier after Braddock's defeat, was also a staging point for British expeditions.[105] That meant there were Cherokees in and around town. A total of eight hundred Cherokees came to Virginia's aid as allies between 1755 and 1758 and carried the war into Shawnee and Delaware country while the Virginians remained essentially on the defensive in their frontier forts.[106] Some of the Cherokees accompanied Forbes's army, which put them in a dangerous position among the Scotch-Irish of the Cumberland Valley, who were inclined to kill and scalp any Indian on sight.[107]

Forbes, a regular officer, was disappointed in the forces from Virginia and Pennsylvania. He described their officers, with few exceptions, as "broken Innkeepers, Horse Jockeys, & Indian traders," and the men as "the scum of the worst of people, in every Country, who have wrought themselves up, into a panick at the very name of Indians who at the same time are more infamous cowards than any other race of mankind."[108] Many of these men, of course, were Scotch-Irish. John Armstrong commanded Pennsylvania's first battalion in Forbes's campaign.[109] Washington sent Andrew Lewis and two hundred Virginia rangers. Lewis and his backcountry woodsmen dressed Indian style, which impressed Forbes's second in command, Colonel Henry Bouquet, and they did important work cutting Forbes's road. Lewis was captured in September when Major James Grant of the 77th Highland Regiment made an ill-advised advance on Fort Duquesne. Sent as a prisoner to Montreal, he was exchanged in December 1759.[110]

Despite his complaints about the quality of his provincial troops, Forbes succeeded where Braddock had failed. The French evacuated and blew up Fort Duquesne. Washington and Armstrong, who had argued that Indian raids had to be snuffed out at their source, were vindicated. The Treaty of Easton and the fall of Fort Duquesne effectively ended the war for the Scotch-Irish on the frontiers of Pennsylvania and Virginia, and the fighting swung north to be decided at Niagara, Quebec, and Montreal. Keeping the promises made at the Easton Treaty raised old problems, however. In the fall of 1761, Bouquet issued a military proclamation requiring squatters who had settled west of the Appalachians to leave. The following spring, he sent soldiers to burn down their cabins. Bouquet's proclamation exasperated Scotch-Irish squatters, though it also alarmed Washington and other Virginians who owned or claimed grants of land in the area.[111]

Northern and Southern Conflicts

Scotch-Irish were also at the forefront of the Seven Years War as it was being fought in northern New England and the southern backcountry. In Maine, in June 1755, a group of colonial militia led by James Cargill, whom historian Alan Taylor describes as "a sternly devout Scotch-Irish Presbyterian and a cold-blooded scalp hunter," murdered a dozen Penobscot people, including a woman and child, at Owl's Head near Rockland. Cargill's brutal act disrupted Lieutenant Governor Phips's attempts to pull the Penobscots into an alliance against the French and western Indians. In correspondence with Penobscot leaders, Phips tried to reassure them that Cargill would be brought to justice, taking a conciliatory tone in the hopes of at least maintaining Penobscot neutrality. However, with escalating tensions on the Maine frontier and growing hawkishness in Boston, Massachusetts declared war upon the Penobscots in November 1755 and offered bounties for the scalps of Indian men, women, and children. Cargill apparently served a year in jail for his murders—and then claimed the bounties on the scalps he had taken from victims who were now officially enemies.[112]

Scotch-Irish stronghold Londonderry was not attacked, although men from the town served as scouts and rangers protecting other communities on the New Hampshire frontier against Indian attacks, and some were among the New Hampshire soldiers killed or captured at the infamous "massacre" at Fort William Henry in 1757, when General Montcalm's Indian allies fell upon the British garrison after it had surrendered.[113] The most famous ranger was Robert Rogers. According to one historian, Rogers was a native of Londonderry and most of his men were from there.[114] The son of immigrant parents from County Antrim, Rogers had been born in Methuen, Massachusetts, in 1731. Eight years later, the family moved to New Hampshire. Growing up in a New Hampshire frontier town, Rogers recalled, "I could hardly avoid obtaining some knowledge of the manners, customs, and language of the Indians, as many of them resided in the neighborhood, and daily conversed and dealt with the English." Such patterns of coexistence were shattered when Anglo-French rivalry erupted into open war and Abenakis sided with the French to curtail English expansion northward. Rogers and his Scotch-Irish neighbors found themselves on the front lines of border warfare, where combatants sometimes recognized each other in battle.[115] Rogers's Rangers, as they were called, earned a reputation for fighting Indians by adopting Indian ways of fighting.

As in Pennsylvania and Virginia, colonists in New England struggled to contain Indian raids. Abenaki warriors from Missisquoi on Lake Champlain and Odanak or St. Francis near Montreal swept down into their former homelands, burned settlements, killed people and cattle, and carried off captives. Rogers raised a company of independent rangers to respond in kind in the Lake George–Lake Champlain corridor. Governor Shirley's orders were "to distress the French and their allies, by sacking burning, and destroying their houses, barns, barracks, canoes, batteaux, &c. and by killing their cattle of every kind."[116] Captain-Lieutenant Henry Pringle of the 27th Foot or Inniskilling Regiment, himself an Ulsterman, based at Fort Edward on the New York frontier in 1757, described the Rangers in a letter home to his family. They were independent companies formed to scout through the woods; "in short, they are created Indians, & the only proper troops to oppose to them. They are good men, but badly disciplined. They dress & live like the Indians, & are well acquainted with the woods. There are many of them Irish, & their Commanding Officer, Rogers (who dined with me this very day) was born in the County of Antrim."[117] (Actually, he wasn't.)

As in Pennsylvania and Virginia, New England colonists carried the war into Indian country and targeted the source of the raids. Rogers's Rangers attacked and burned St. Francis in October 1759. The community had grown up as a Catholic mission and a refuge for Abenaki peoples who retreated from growing colonial pressures to their south, and it became a center of Abenaki resistance, dispatching war parties that penned back colonists with lightning raids and guerrilla warfare. Rogers and 220 rangers ascended Lake Champlain in whaleboats, made a grueling one-hundred-mile march across land from Missisquoi Bay, and attacked the village at dawn. They burned most of the houses and destroyed the church. Some people who hid in the cellars and lofts of their houses died in the fire; others were shot down as they tried to escape across the river. General Jeffery Amherst had given orders not to kill women and children, but those orders, as one English newspaper put it, "were little attended to." Rogers claimed the Rangers killed at least two hundred Abenakis, mostly warriors; French accounts suggested they killed thirty, mostly women and children. Only a handful were taken captive. The Rangers' two-hundred-mile retreat, pursued by the French and Abenakis and reduced to starvation, became a nightmare. There were reports that the Rangers killed and ate a captive Abenaki woman and child. Like the raid on Kittanning, the raid on St. Francis was a pyrrhic victory at best, but, like Kittanning, it dealt the Indians a hard blow and gave a psychological boost to embattled colonists hungry for any measure of success.[118]

At the other end of the Scotch-Irish backcountry, the war took a rather different course. After making a tour of North Carolina's western border, Governor Dobbs gave instructions to put the frontier in the best state of defense against Indian attacks.[119] Initially, the Cherokees and Catawbas served as an effective buffer for the frontiers of North and South Carolina. "We have had no Attacks or Insults yet upon our Frontier, owing principally to our frontier Company, and Neighbourhood of the Cataubas Indians our friends," Dobbs wrote to William Pitt in January 1756, a time when the Scotch-Irish buffers protecting Pennsylvania and Virginia were near total collapse.[120] It was just as well, because relying on fighting farmers to rally to the defense of the province was as precarious in the Carolinas as in Pennsylvania, at least according to Colonel Bouquet, who struggled to raise men without success. There were enough men scattered in the Carolina backcountry, he wrote the Earl of Loudon in August 1757, but they could earn more as laborers than as soldiers "and those who inlist, being the worste, desert very Soon."[121]

Unlike backcountry colonial militia, the Cherokees and Catawbas sent their men to fight with the army far from home, on the frontiers of Virginia and Pennsylvania. There, however, the alliance began to unravel. Cherokees with Forbes's army were poorly supplied, frustrated by slow progress, treated with suspicion, and insulted by officers and soldiers alike. Warriors returning home through southwestern Virginia exchanged blows with backcountry settlers and plundered them of goods they no doubt felt were owed them for their unpaid services. Backcountry settlers murdered at least thirty Cherokees on their way home in the spring and summer of 1758, when Virginia's scalp bounties were still in effect. Cherokees appealed to Virginia and North and South Carolina for satisfaction but received none. When Governor William Henry Lyttleton of South Carolina seized and executed twenty-three Cherokee hostages, smoldering resentment exploded into open war.[122]

The Cherokees fell upon the Scotch-Irish backcountry early in 1760. They attacked settlements on the Broad River and devastated the largely

Scotch-Irish community at Long Cane or Long Canes in western South Carolina, near present-day Abbeville, where some 250 settlers and their African slaves squatted on land the Cherokees retained by treaty. Many of the inhabitants had fled to the area to escape the Indian raids to the north following Braddock's defeat in 1755, and the Long Cane Presbyterian church was established that year, along with other large congregations at Waxhaws and Saluda. The closest of South Carolina's settlements to the Cherokees' Lower Towns, Long Cane was located about sixty miles southeast of Keowee. Cherokees still hunted the area, while men from Long Cane hunted deep into Cherokee country. The settlers degraded the environment by damming and fishing the Little River and raised cattle in the salt licks that deer and buffalo had used. They also traded without licenses, peddling alcohol and other goods among the Cherokees. Cherokees had complained about the Long Cane squatters before, although their interactions produced connections as well as tensions. Local tradition recalled that a young Cherokee woman walked almost one hundred miles from the Lower Towns to warn "the white women who had been so good to her in giving her clothes and bread and butter in trading parties" that an attack was imminent.[123]

It did them little good. Early on February 1, as the settlers were evacuating Long Cane, one hundred Cherokees attacked them, killing and scattering the people, and taking thirteen captives. The Calhoun family was particularly hard hit. Patrick and William Calhoun escaped, but their brother James was killed, as was seventy-six-year-old Catherine Calhoun, the grandmother of John C. Calhoun. William's daughters, Ann and Mary, aged four and two, were taken captive, and their sister Catherine was killed. (Ann was returned to her father at Fort Keowee when peace was restored; Mary was presumed to have died in captivity.) Patrick Calhoun and a party of militia returned the next day and buried twenty-three bodies in a mass grave, although the total loss of killed and captured was closer to fifty. A number of children were said to be found wandering in the woods, and many refugees fled to the communities in the Waxhaws. Patrick Calhoun was subsequently appointed captain (without pay) of a ranger company to protect the Long Cane settlement.[124]

At the end of February, another Scotch-Irish ranger officer repulsed a Cherokee attack on Fort Dobbs, a fortified log structure which Governor Dobbs had ordered built on a tributary of the Yadkin River (near present-day Statesville) to protect backcountry settlers in Rowan County and maintain relations with the Catawbas and Cherokees. The fort commander, Hugh

Waddell, was born in Country Down and had led a company of rangers in Forbes's expedition.[125]

Smallpox compounded the wartime miseries of the Indian, white, and Black populations. Catawba warriors returning from fighting alongside the British in Pennsylvania brought the disease home with them, and Catawba raiders carried it to Cherokee country. Thousands of Scotch-Irish people fled the Cherokee attacks and many huddled in scattered backcountry fortifications, but smallpox, measles, and hunger drove them to seek refuge farther east, and they crowded into Presbyterian communities around Williamsburg, Stony Creek, Jacksonboro, and the Waxhaws. Many went as far as Charleston. Some carried the disease with them; others fell ill when they got there. The Reverend Archibald Simpson, a Scottish Presbyterian minister at Stony Creek (also called "Indian Land"), found some of "the poor distressed people" who had fled from Long Cane "to be very sober, serious, senceble religious people." However, the refugees received little sympathy or assistance from people who blamed them for having been overpowered by the enemy they were supposed to defend the colony against. Charlestonians' reserves of private charity were already taxed by the arrival of more than a thousand Acadians exiled from their homes in Nova Scotia. Once again, it seemed, eastern colonial elites seemed indifferent to Scotch-Irish suffering.[126]

The militia turned out for this war. They took part in British campaigns into Cherokee country, serving alongside Highland troops under Colonel Archibald Montgomery and Major James Grant. Grant's army burned fifteen towns and more than 14,000 acres of cornfields, driving Cherokee men, women, and children into the woods and mountains, where they faced a choice between starving and making peace. As settlers on the Pennsylvania frontier had in 1755–1756, refugee Cherokees in 1760–1761 sought safety in towns farther from the fighting.[127] Twenty-one-year-old Andrew Pickens joined a provincial regiment that served alongside Grant's campaign.[128] For economically marginalized Scotch-Irish frontier militia, plunder offered an additional incentive to leave their families and invade Cherokee country. Henry Laurens, who served on the campaign, said the Cherokee homes they burned were better made and more comfortable than many of those inhabited by "our White Brethren, the backsettlers upon North and South Carolina." Laurens, a Charleston merchant and Lowcountry planter, invested in backcountry lands after the war and co-owned a 13,000-acre plantation at Long Cane.[129]

Cherokee people rebuilt their communities in the wake of the war, as did the Scotch-Irish who pressed against Cherokee country. Cherokee leaders adopted a strategy of keeping trade paths open and placing Métis families, descended from the union of white men and Cherokee women, as a permeable but protective barrier between the core of Cherokee society and the colonies.[130] Meanwhile, at Long Cane, Ninety-Six, and Waxhaws, Scotch-Irish men who had taken a lead in the Cherokee War, such as Patrick Calhoun, Andrew Pickens (who married Calhoun's sister), and Andrew Williamson, gained political status, at the same time as they built their wealth trading with the Cherokees.[131]

The French and Indian War changed the backcountry and seared itself into the historical memory of the Scotch-Irish. In Augusta County, Virginia, the population fell by nearly 20 percent between 1755 and 1757, with the western half of the county virtually deserted. A register in William Preston's papers of persons killed, wounded, and captured in the county from 1754 to 1758 conveys the devastating impact of Indian raids on backcountry Scotch-Irish communities.[132] A list of people killed by Indians from 1755 to 1758, furnished by John McCullough, whom Delawares took captive with his brother from the Scotch-Irish settlement at Conococheague in 1756, conveys a similar picture in Pennsylvania.[133] A colony once defined by peaceful and cross-cultural interaction was transformed into a frontier war zone; coexistence gave way to racial hatred and violence.[134] By thrusting places like Carlisle into the center of imperial conflict between colonial and Native populations, the war transformed economic life; by arming the backcountry, it transformed settlers from people who, contrary to legend, generally had few guns and little expertise in using them, into a populace that was armed and dangerous—at least in dealing with Indian neighbors.[135] It drove a divide between backcountry Scotch-Irish and the government in Philadelphia, particularly the Quaker Assembly that failed to meet their needs: "what the Scotch-Irish demanded," wrote one Pennsylvania historian in the mid-twentieth century, "was not talk with folded hands, not temporizing with murderous savages, but soldiers, forts, munitions, and war to the knife against the invaders of their homes and firesides."[136] Quaker pacifists were just not cut out for wartime leadership, explained Edmund Burke in his 1758 book, *An Account of the European Settlements in America*: "As a peaceable, industrious, honest people, the Quakers cannot be too much cherished; but surely they cannot themselves complain, that when, by their opinions, they make themselves sheep, they should not be entrusted with the office, since they have not the nature of dogs."[137]

The war also established an enduring legacy of Indian-hating in Scotch-Irish country. In Cumberland County in February 1760, persons unknown burst into the cabin of a friendly Delaware called Doctor John in the middle of the night, and murdered him and his wife and child or children. Three weeks earlier, John had gotten into a heated argument, apparently about the killing of Captain Jacobs and the recent war, at a tavern in Carlisle.[138] Recognizing that the murder might reignite the war that was winding down, Governor Hamilton offered one hundred pounds reward for the apprehension of the murderers and recommended treating all Indians "with Civility and Brotherly Kindness" for the safety of the province.[139] In May, several Scotch-Irish men from Paxton and Lancaster County confessed to the murder of Doctor John and his family. Two years later, Hamilton gave gifts to the victims' relatives who had come to Philadelphia to cover the dead.[140] Covering the dead to stop an endless cycle of vengeance might still work when Scotch-Irish killed Native people, but it would not expunge the memories of Scotch-Irish blood shed by Indian warriors.

Heading as a missionary into Indian country in 1762, John Heckewelder, accompanied by the Moravian Christian Post, followed Forbes Road to Fort Pitt. As they passed Carlisle and headed to Shippensburg, "In every direction, the blackened ruins of houses and barns, and remains of chimneys met our eyes; the sad memorials of the cruelties committed by the French and Indians, during the savage warfare of 1756, and in the following years; concerning which many horrible stories were related to us by eye-witness."[141] When the Delaware war chief Shingas's wife died that same year, he asked Heckewelder and trader Thomas Calhoon, "a man of open hand and heart," to assist at the funeral, where she was buried in a coffin made by Calhoon's carpenter.[142] Such instances of shared humanity were ignored or dismissed as aberrations.

Instead, stories of danger, murder, and atrocity were told and retold for generations. They circulated in Northern Ireland as well as around Scotch-Irish firesides in America. Presbyterians in Ulster followed the wartime experiences of those who had emigrated and suffered at the hands of vicious Indian warriors, spurred on by French Catholics. From 1754 to 1764, the *Belfast News-Letter* published at least 142 accounts of Indian violence, creating empathy for the people who had left and had borne the brunt of the war, antipathy for Indian people, and enthusiasm for British imperial expansion in North America.[143]

Taking refuge in garrisoned homes and huddling around small forts changed how people lived, farmed, and harvested. Armed groups guarded men as they harvested the crops needed to feed their families.[144] Women assisted men in various defensive roles in garrisoned communities and still had responsibility for taking care of cattle, which often took them out early in the morning, making them prime targets.[145] Living in forts under the threat of death or captivity and being "worn out with constant Watchings," as Governor Morris put it, became part of the shared wartime memory of Scotch-Irish frontier families.[146] Their experiences of petitions submitted and ignored, serial flights, homes abandoned and burned, fearful nights, killings and atrocities fused backcountry people together.[147] The memories shaped Scotch-Irish attitudes toward Indians and future encounters with Indian people.

The French and Indian War was the great war for America, and it has been called the war that made America.[148] Britain wrested the interior of continent from France and, in doing so, set in motion events that would lead to the American Revolution and shape an emerging American identity. For Scotch-Irish people who suffered and survived on the front lines, the war also served as a defining event, shaping their identity as a people in conflict with Indians and at odds with government.

6

Indian-Killers

In December 1763, Scotch-Irish vigilantes from the towns of Paxton and Donegal, near modern-day Harrisburg, Pennsylvania, murdered twenty Indian people in cold blood. Horrific as this is, compared with the Pequot massacre in 1637, the systematic eradication of California Natives during and after the Gold Rush of 1849, the massacres of Shoshone people at Bear River in 1863, of Cheyenne and Arapaho people at Sand Creek in 1864, and of Lakota people at Wounded Knee in 1890, in all of which hundreds were killed, the Paxton massacre stands as a relatively minor atrocity. However, it is typically singled out as marking the ultimate descent into darkness, finally shattering patterns and policies of peaceful coexistence that William Penn had instilled in Pennsylvania. The scalped and mutilated bodies of the men, women, and children murdered at Conestoga and Lancaster killed any lingering dreams that colonial Americans and Native Americans might coexist in peace. Race hatred and violence now became the American norm, and the Scotch-Irish led the way.

In its immediate moment, however, the fallout from the massacre revealed as much about the attitudes of its Scotch-Irish perpetrators toward the eastern government and backcountry elites as toward their Indian neighbors. The social tensions fueled a new political culture, and what one historian describes as a kind of "backcountry nationalism" emerged.[1]

Indian War Redux

The Peace of Paris in 1763 ended the French and Indian War. France ceded all its territory in mainland North America east of the Mississippi to Britain, and Britain's American colonists hailed the victory as initiating a new era of freedom and expansion. Most of the ceded land was Indian country, however, and the Indigenous inhabitants viewed the developments with concern. The British had won the war in the Ohio country by promising the Native nations that their lands would be safe once the French were gone.

Now British redcoats occupied forts abandoned by French soldiers, and settler colonists streamed west along the roads built by Generals Braddock and Forbes during the war. The army tried to eject settlers who illegally squatted on Indian land, but military presence encouraged settlement more than it restrained it. At the same time, the British commander-in-chief, General Jeffery Amherst, cut costs by cutting back on the gifts and supplies that sustained alliances in Indian country. Withholding presents and sending in troops sent a clear message: Britain intended to reduce the tribes to submission and take over their land.

Meanwhile, a Delaware prophet named Neolin preached that Native people must cast off alien influences and return to traditional ways. War belts circulated through the Ohio Valley and Great Lakes and a coalition of tribes led by the Seneca chief Guyasuta and the Odawa war chief Pontiac took on the British Empire. In the spring of 1763, Native warriors captured most of the British posts west of the Appalachians and laid siege to Detroit, Niagara, and Fort Pitt.[2]

Pontiac's Revolt, as it came to be called, hit frontier inhabitants with "as rude a shock"—George Washington's description—as any they had received during the previous war. It constituted a death sentence for many Scotch-Irish people, who once again bore the brunt of Indian violence generated by British imperial policies.[3] "Our Country bleeds again under the Savage knife," reported the Reverend Thomas Barton, rector of the Episcopal church in Lancaster.[4] Dozens of traders in Indian country died, many with identifiable Scotch-Irish names.[5] In July, Indian war parties struck the Juniata, Cumberland, Tuscarora, and Sherman's valleys. As happened eight years earlier, hundreds of colonists in scattered farmsteads were killed or captured; many more sought safety in neighboring towns or farther east.

As also happened eight years earlier, correspondence and petitions from the backcountry painted a picture of devastation and despair. Newspapers printed accounts of desperate people fleeing Indian atrocities, abandoning their homes and belongings, and taking, one put it, "hardly any thing with them but their children." Inhabitants from the Juniata and other places near the Susquehanna "fled from Danger, and brought their Families, and little else, down the River in Canoes." Many refugees had gone through similar experiences in the French and Indian War and had returned to their "forsaken Habitations" once peace was made; they "were scarce able to begin the World anew" before having to take flight again.[6] With the countryside ablaze, letters from Carlisle, published in the *Pennsylvania Gazette* in July, reported scenes "shocking to humanity, and beyond the power of language to describe." Grief-stricken and frantic refugees who had lost everything filled the streets of the town, "reduced to a state of beggary and despair." Some found shelter in stables and hovels; others made fires in the nearby woods and lived "like the savages."[7]

Jane Horner was one of those who did not escape "the fury of the Savages." Born Jane Kerr in Ireland, she and her husband James Horner had migrated to America in 1734 and were among the first Scotch-Irish settlers in Allen township in Northampton County. A war party caught and tomahawked Mrs. Horner as she was carrying coals for a morning fire to a neighbor's house. She was buried in the graveyard of the Allen Township Presbyterian Church, with an inscription on her gravestone that provided the community with a permanent record and visible reminder of the violence that took the lives of hundreds of ordinary people: "In memory of Jane, wife of James Horner, who suffered death by the hands of the savage Indians October eighth, Seventeen Hundred and Sixty-three, aged fifty years."[8]

Yet, despite sympathy for "Christian Brethren" and "Fellow Subjects" on the frontier, people farther east were not keen to see them abandon their backcountry stations. One correspondent wrote from Philadelphia: "It is our Interest as well as our Duty to encourage them to stay in Cumberland Country; or even to return to their forsaken Dwellings, if it can be done in safety. For if that County shall be deserted, where shall we make a Stand? Shall Lancaster or this City be the Frontiers of this Province?"[9]

In Carlisle, Colonel John Armstrong and Thomas Wilson wrote to Colonel Edward Shippen in June, requesting powder and lead to defend the town and "our naked & much expos'd Frontier."[10] Colonel Henry Bouquet arrived in Carlisle around July 1, marching west with a hastily assembled force to the relief of Fort Pitt, which was under siege by the Delawares and Shawnees. He had hoped the town would provide supplies and sustenance; instead, refugees crowded around his tents, soliciting relief. Pushing beyond Carlisle, Bouquet passed abandoned and burned cabins in the Cumberland Valley. When he came to Shippensburg, he found it "crowded with almost 1400 terrified and starving refugees."[11] Bouquet also found in town two families of allied Cayugas, who had been growing corn peacefully on an island in the Susquehanna near Carlisle when the war began and were now being held prisoner. "It was with the utmost Difficulty, I could prevail with the enraged Multitude not to massacre them," he wrote. "I don't think them very safe in the Goal [sic]; They cannot be released as they would be torn to Pieces by our

People, or forced to join the Enemy."[12] Bouquet fended off a Delaware and Shawnee assault at the Battle of Bushy Run on August 5–6, and relieved Fort Pitt, but the military was stretched thin. The inhabitants of western counties remained "continually exposed to the Savage cruelty of a merciless Enemy."[13]

Once again, the Scotch-Irish defensive barrier on the frontier was on the verge of total collapse. Deputy Governor James Hamilton pressed the Pennsylvania Assembly to heed the appeals for help and stave off disaster.[14] The Assembly responded in July with a resolution to pay up to 700 men— 400 from Cumberland County and 100 each from Berks, Lancaster, and Northumberland counties. The Reverend John Elder of Paxton and Colonel John Armstrong were appointed to command the Lancaster and Cumberland County recruits. Local settlers had already banded together in volunteer groups—the Paxtang Rangers or Paxton Boys, who were to achieve enduring infamy, were formed in western Lancaster Country, and the Cumberland Boys west of the river—and Elder and Armstrong organized them into the militia units authorized by the Assembly.[15] Elder, an honorary colonel of militia, said the people in his neighborhood were "quite sunk & dispirited" and more likely to seek safety in flight than to fight Indians. It was vital to keep the two militia companies. If they dispersed, the frontier inhabitants would evacuate the country at the first alarm, and if the frontier settlements were broken, many of the inhabitants who escaped the Indians "must either perish by famine, or be subsisted at the expense of the publick, while the poor distressed people, in their flight, will communicate the pannick to others, and render it the more difficult to stop the encroaching Foe."[16] Armstrong told Governor John Penn in mid-December that the people who had been driven from the valleys on the north side of the Allegheny Mountains now formed the frontier and were mixed with other settlers on the south side; many had left their belongings and their crops stacked in the field. The government needed to provide ranger companies and relief.[17]

Elder and Armstrong recognized that the ranger companies performed an essential community function. From the mid-1750s to the early 1760s, Paxton was a community at war, facing recurrent Indian attacks. Its citizens repeatedly looked to the provincial government for assistance that was not forthcoming. About one hundred miles or three days' travel from Philadelphia and one day from Lancaster, Paxton—like other frontier communities—was forced to organize its own defense. Indeed, it has been argued, only then did its diverse inhabitants forge any kind of unified community. Scotch-Irish and Germans, New Lights and Old Lights, Upper and Lower Paxtonians, subsistence and commercial farmers—they all came together to fight under the common threat of Indian attack. The inhabitants repeatedly formed unofficial ranger units, usually subsidized by subscription from the community and from Presbyterian churches, rather than recognized or funded by the province. The units were intensely local in their loyalty; they volunteered to protect their own community, quickly disbanding once the immediate threat passed, and were loath to serve far from home. As they were also extralegal, they often went beyond the limits set by provincial officials. They were rarely sanctioned for overstepping bounds, establishing a precedent for illegal actions that were effectively condoned. The government that failed to meet the needs of the people also failed to punish those who broke the law. The Paxton Rangers and Paxton Boys saw themselves as the front line of frontier defense and the last line of frontier justice, in other words retribution; men who stepped forward to defend and avenge their community and the backcountry in general.[18]

For all of their vaunted sense of purpose, the men in the companies showed little appetite for combat. In August, Captain James Patterson and 114 men passed through Fort Augusta on their way to attack Indian towns farther up the West Branch of the Susquehanna. They returned two days later, having been put to flight when a Delaware war party fired on them. Instead, a group of soldiers waylaid, robbed, killed, and scalped three Native people on their way back from trading in Bethlehem. Thomas McKee told Sir William Johnson that the Indians on the Susquehanna with whom he conversed "behaved as well as any People cou'd do," but he feared that the rash killing of three friendly Indians would have severe consequences.[19] Volunteer expeditions in September against the Indian town at Great Island, a three-hundred-acre intertribal gathering place just downriver from present-day Lock Haven, were equally ineffective. Armstrong and three hundred volunteers, mainly from Cumberland and Bedford Counties, found the town abandoned and destroyed food supplies. Men eager for scalps and vengeance would have to try elsewhere.[20]

The Storm Explodes

Scotch-Irish colonists who lost farms and loved ones in what looked to them like an unprovoked war saw little distinction between enemy and friendly Indians. Their Calvinist Old Testament religion assured them they need show no mercy to any heathens who stood between them and their possession of the promised land and should in fact destroy them completely. They imagined that so-called friendly Indians, like the Conestogas and the converted Moravians, were in league with the enemy. In early October, Delaware and Shawnee warriors attacked Craig's settlement, also known as "the Irish settlement," near Bethlehem; two days later the Moravian minister at the mission village of Wechquetank had to dissuade a mob of "Irish freebooters" from killing the Native residents.[21] The provincial commissioners reported to the House that in their opinion the Moravians and their congregants were secretly supplying Indian war parties: "the said Indians having an Intercourse with our Enemies on the Frontiers, do barter and exchange with them, to the great Danger of the neighbouring Inhabitants."[22] Moravian missionary John Heckewelder wrote that Native people living on the north branch of the Susquehanna River still "traveled as usual through the settlements of the white people without fear" at the beginning of 1763, but by the end of the year, another observer said, Indian-hating "Spread like a Contagion into the Interior parts of ye province" and even to Philadelphia.[23]

Scotch-Irish colonists had a long and difficult relationship with Conestoga Manor. From the beginning of the founding of Pennsylvania, William Penn and his sons practiced a policy of reserving lands to themselves, which they called "manors." In 1718 the Commissioners of Property issued a warrant to Penn for a tract of land containing 16,000 acres on the east side of the Susquehanna River, stretching north from Conestoga Creek. This was Conestoga Manor and it soon became a source and site of contention with Scotch-Irish squatters who regarded these "sham purchases" with contempt and settled there in defiance. When "a parcel of Disorderly People" took possession of the manor in 1730, James Logan warned Thomas Penn that speedy measures were needed if he was not to lose the country. "This is the most Audacious Attack that has ever yet been offer'd. They are of the Scotch-Irish (so-called here) of whom ... you seem'd to have a pretty good Opinion but it is more than I can have tho' their Countreyman." The squatters declared, Logan continued, that "it was against the laws of God and nature that so much should be idle when so many Christians wanted it to labor on and to raise their bread" and "that they would hold it by the Sword." In an effort to eject "the Gang of Scotch-Irish," Logan dispatched the county sheriff and a posse, who pulled down and burned about thirty cabins that had been built in the previous two or three weeks. He knew this would not stop the intrusions across the Susquehanna,[24] and indeed Conestoga Manor remained a source of conflict. When the government provided the small surviving population of the once-powerful Susquehannocks with a refuge on the manor, it placed them on ground that Scotch-Irish people already coveted and contested.

Deputy Governor Robert Hunter Morris met with the Conestogas in council at Lancaster in January 1756 at the start of the French and Indian War. He asked them to provide information on enemy Indians and not to harbor any who came among them, reassuring them of the government's protection. The old chief of the Conestogas responded that he was relieved to hear it. They had heard so much violent talk that they expected to be killed, but now they could lay aside their fears. The formerly numerous Conestogas were now reduced to a handful, "and I must die soon," the old chief told Morris. "I put them under your Protection; they are all young and some meer Children and will want your Advice and Countenance."[25] During the war, with Thomas McKee interpreting for them, the Conestogas told Governor Denny they planned to move farther upriver to a safer location above the Indian town of Shamokin. Denny assured them he would protect them and persuaded them to say at Conestoga Manor.[26] In a brief meeting at Lancaster in February 1760, the old Conestoga chief Canrach Caghera, or Cuyangueerycoea, gave provincial secretary Richard Peters a wampum belt to deliver to the governor. "You may, perhaps, think I will go away," he told Peters, "but I tell you I will always stay at Conestogo, and these that are with me will stay too. You must be my mouth to the Governor, and acquaint him with our intention, and that we hope he will be as kind to us as Wm. Penn, and all the Governors to this time."[27] It was a decision that had disastrous consequences.

John Harris and John Elder repeatedly asked the colonial authorities to move the Conestogas out of harm's way because Delaware and Shawnee raids had incensed the colonists in the Paxton region. Elder told Governor John Penn in October 1763 that there could be no safety for the frontier settlements "till that Branch of the River is cleared of the Savages." He evidently meant all Indians. Penn replied that the Indians of Conestoga had the support of the governor. "The faith of this Government is pledged for their protection. I cannot remove them without adequate cause."[28] As late as November 1763, the Conestogas asked Penn to appoint their friend Thomas McKee, who lived near them and spoke their language, to take care of them "and see Justice done us."[29]

On December 14, a group of Paxton Rangers murdered and scalped half a dozen Indian people at Conestoga Town.[30] Although it occurred three years before she was born, one of Rhoda Barber's first memories was hearing people speak about the massacre. She had grown up in the area and in her old age she remembered the Conestogas as "entirely peaceable" people who seemed as afraid of the enemy Indians as the whites were. Their cabins were close by, and Rhoda and her siblings sometimes passed "whole days with them" and were fond of them. They made brooms and baskets which they bartered for food, "and often spent the night by the kitchen fire of the farms round about, they appear'd much attached to the white people calling their children after their favorite neighbours."

But then, Barber recalled, things changed, and many people thought all the Indians should be destroyed. On the morning of the massacre, five or six men stopped at her father's house, their coats covered in snow and sleet. Her father did not know them, although he apparently knew what part of the country they were from. As was customary, he let them warm themselves by the fire and gave them refreshment. They left without telling what they had done, although her two brothers, aged ten and twelve, saw bloody tomahawks tied to the saddles on their horses and a gun they recognized as having belonged to a little Indian boy named Christie ("Chrisly" in some accounts), who was about their age and a playmate. Then a messenger arrived with news of "the dreadful deed" and her father and others went to see them buried. Barber was shocked by the sight of the dead bodies, which lay among burned-out cabins "like half consum'd logs." Christie or Chrisly evidently escaped and carried the news of the massacre to Thomas McKee. It was a temporary reprieve.[31]

Writing to John Elder two days after the massacre, Edward Shippen described the murder of people known to be under government protection as "riotous behaviour of flying in the Face of the Government," and he was right.[32] Elder was the commander of the Paxton Rangers and a religious leader in the community. That same day, Elder wrote Governor John Penn, claiming that he had tried to prevent the killings which were perpetrated by "some hotheaded, ill advised persons," most likely those who had lost relatives in the Indian raids of the war.[33] Penn removed Elder from command, issued proclamations denouncing the killing of the six Conestogas, and called on the magistrates of York, Cumberland, and Lancaster counties to arrest the murderers. He also had the Moravian Indians moved for safety to Province Island in Philadelphia.[34] As Penn explained to the Assembly on December 21, as the Conestogas had been placed on the Manor by the government, and had lived there peacefully throughout the recent troubles, he would do everything in his power to bring their murderers to justice.[35]

Elder continued to divert responsibility from the perpetrators to the government. "The storm which had been so long gathering has at length exploded," he wrote Penn from Paxton on December 27. If only the government had removed the Indians from Conestoga, as he had frequently urged, the catastrophe might have been avoided. "What could I do with men heated to madness?" he asked. He tried everything, but they would not listen to reason. In private life, these were virtuous and respectable men, not cruel and merciless killers. In time, when the circumstances could be calmly weighed, "This deed, magnified into the blackest of crimes, shall be considered one of those youthful ebullitions of wrath, caused by momentary excitement, to which human infirmity is subjected."[36]

That same afternoon of December 27, fifty or sixty Paxton Boys, as they became called, rode into Lancaster in broad daylight and broke into the workhouse section of the county jail, where the city magistrates had given refuge to fourteen other Conestoga people. The Conestogas sat in a circle and prayed. The Paxton Boys shot, scalped, and hacked to pieces three old men, three women, and eight children: "Captain John, Betty, his wife; Bill Sock, Mollie, his wife; John Smith, Peggy his wife; Little John, Captain John's son; Jacob, a boy; Young Sheehays, a boy; Chrisly; Little Peter, a boy; Mollie, a little girl; a Little Girl; Peggy, a little Girl" (Figure 6.1).[37] The slaughter was over in little more than twelve minutes. The killers then rode around the courthouse "hooping & hallowing" and firing their guns in jubilant public defiance of town officials who had given refuge to the victims. There were too many of them for any of the inhabitants to interfere, said one resident; and "too many approved of the massacre." Like Edward Shippen, he recognized the attack as a blatant challenge to the authority of local government: "If these outrages are passed over with impunity all Civil Govt, is at an end. I wish better times. God knows where this will end."[38]

In Nathaniel Bacon's Rebellion in Virginia, in 1675, colonial leaders had feared that an Indian war was, as one put it, "a contagion that spread of its own accord and led directly to civil unrest." Once again, an Indian "rebellion" against colonists seemed to have infected colonists with a spirit of rebellion against their own governments.[39] Although contemporaries and historians have seen the "Paxton Riots" as a protest against the authority of provincial elites in Philadelphia, the killings were also a challenge to the local elite, in particular to Edward Shippen, the most prominent citizen and chief magistrate of Lancaster County. Shippen had wanted the Scotch-Irish on the frontier as a protective barrier for Lancaster, not for towns farther east. Initially

Figure 6.1 Lithograph depicting the Paxton massacre of the Indians at Lancaster, by Thomas Sinclair.
From *Events in Indian History* (Lancaster, PA: G. Hills & Co., 1841).

at least, the Scotch-Irish vented their anger and frustration against local elites who did nothing to help or protect them while they risked their lives protecting Lancaster. "You peacefully drink your tea and coffee etc., live carefree, and we have to stand constantly at the ready on the border expecting to be destroyed by the Indians," the pastor of Lancaster's Moravian church reported them saying.[40]

The attack on the workhouse happened while most of Lancaster's town leaders, including Shippen, were attending a delayed Christmas service with the Reverend Thomas Barton at St. James Episcopal Church. A week before the massacre, the prison keeper Felix Donnally had gone to Shippen's house in the evening and warned him that the men who killed the Indians at Conestoga Manor were gathering to kill those who had taken refuge in Lancaster. Shippen sent out spies to ascertain the truth of the reports so that the town could be placed in a state of emergency and measures taken to protect the Indians, "tho' God knows, the Inhabitants, undisciplined, & miserably armed, could have made but a poor Stand against 80 or 100 Desperadoes well armed at least, and in the dark, too, the Streets being full of Snow & ice, and the weather excessive cold." Perhaps Shippen protested too much.

At that time, he claimed in a letter to his son, written a week after the massacre, he had not heard that a detachment of the 42nd Highlanders was in the town—a remarkable statement by the chief magistrate in a town of two or three thousand inhabitants. Assured that the reports of imminent attack were unfounded, Shippen told his son, he knew nothing about the massacre until it was over.[41] The men charged with protecting the Indians failed to do so: prison keeper Felix Donnally absented himself from the scene on the afternoon of the attack and John Hay, the sheriff of Lancaster County, stepped aside or was pushed aside as the mob broke into the workhouse.

Donnally reappeared to take charge of burying the mutilated bodies of the victims in a common grave. He submitted an itemized account "For the Diet and Maintenance of the Indians" from December 14 to 27; he left blank the amount for "the Trouble & Expense of having the said Fourteen Indians carried to the Grave and interred."[42]

Writing to Governor Penn from Carlisle, John Armstrong that same day asserted that killing defenseless Indians was something few of his neighbors would condone. From what he could learn, not one person in Cumberland County—the most heavily Scotch-Irish county in Pennsylvania—"has either been consulted or concerned in that inhuman and scandalous piece of Butchery." He expressed regret that anyone would take out their anger on the "heads of a few inoffensive superannuated Savages."[43] That was not how things looked from Philadelphia or from Indian country, however. Nor from the Moravian communities where the inhabitants lived in fear that they would be next, as hundreds of backcountry settlers voiced support for the Paxton killers and damned the Moravians as "Indian lovers" who aided and abetted the enemy.[44]

Penn responded with another proclamation on January 2, 1764, offering reward for the murderers.[45] Then, hearing that the rioters intended to march on Philadelphia and kill the Delaware, Munsee, and Mohican Moravian converts, 140 or so in all, sheltering at Province Island, he wrote to General Gage, the governors of New York and New Jersey, and Sir William Johnson, informing them of the murders and asking to send the Moravian refugees to them for protection.[46] "Every good Man must look upon the Conduct of the perpetrators of these unparalleled Villanies with Abhorrence & Detestation," Penn wrote Johnson, "who at the same time that they have imbrued their Hands in innocent Blood, have set themselves above, and violated, those very Laws, under which they themselves derive the Rights of Security and protection."[47]

Johnson feared the massacre would have serious repercussions. The Conestogas were under the protection of and in alliance with the Six Nations, who would judge it a clear breach of faith. He did what he could—which was not much—to cast things in a positive light and assuage their anger. He gave Iroquois delegates to his home at Johnson Hall black wampum belts to cover the graves of the deceased and ease their grief. The Iroquois were quick to point out, as Johnson noted, "that we had often upbraided them for not keeping their people in order, which they were sorry to see, was too much our own case." They also claimed that the extinction of the Conestogas meant that the lands they had occupied now reverted to the Iroquois.[48] As for the Paxton Boys' threats against Indians under Penn's protection in Philadelphia, said Johnson, it "savors so much of Madness that I cannot acc't for them."[49]

As Thomas McKee noted to Johnson, the Paxton murders were as bad as any Indian atrocities and "leaves us no Room to find Fault with their killing our innocent People in cold Blood."[50] Sally Wilkins, a teenage girl who had been taken captive in Northampton County, returned to Philadelphia after several years living with Indian people on the upper Susquehanna. She said that when word of the massacre reached the town she was living in, the Indians were enraged, vowed to take revenge, and threatened the white captives.[51]

The killers made no secret of their intentions or of what they had done. Nevertheless, in spite of Penn's proclamations and offers of reward, no one was arrested, tried, or punished for the murders. Not one of the Paxton Boys was even identified. As Lancaster journalist Jack Brubaker noted in his reconstruction of the massacre: "All of the victims have names. None of the killers is known." Local officials and community leaders turned a blind eye, even if they did not conspire with the killers. While the frontiersmen's actions might "have been disliked by the most thinking judicious men," Elder explained to Penn, "yet the indulgence shown the savages, gives a general disgust." Even if Elder had it in his power to learn the names of the killers (some of whom, by his own account, he had tried to dissuade and doubtless knew from his church), he judged it best to say nothing. Playing the part of "Informer" was "a Character too odious for a gentleman to bear" and would tarnish his reputation as a clergyman What was more, the Presbyterians were deeply outraged at being lumped "under the name of Scotch Irish and other ill-natured titles," and resented that the Conestoga killings were being compared to the Irish massacres of old.[52]

Like it or not, the Scotch-Irish were blamed for the massacre at Conestoga Town then, and it has forever defined their role as "Indian-killers." In his sympathetic book on the Scotch-Irish in America published in 1902, Charles Hanna wrote that some people viewed the Conestoga massacre as the first instance of lynch law in America "and many blamed the Scotch-Irish for its introduction. Doubtless the odium is merited."[53]

True Savages

Telling and retelling of Indian raids and terrors turned backcountry settlers into Indian-killers and also turned them against their government.[54] Rather than showing any remorse for killing the Conestoga Indians, an armed mob from the Paxton backcountry now threatened, as Governor Penn had heard, to march on Philadelphia and repeat the same acts on the Moravian Indians taking shelter there. Quaker Benjamin Kendal, a Philadelphia merchant just back from Lancaster, warned the governor and council that 1,500 men were ready to descend on Philadelphia and another 5,000 were ready to join them. Heaven would not stop them, he said, for they were driven by the same spirit as the "blood-thirsty Presbyterians" who had cut off the head of King Charles in 1649 during the English Civil War. Penn urged the Assembly to prepare the city's defenses against rioters driven by "the same Spirit & frantic Rage."[55]

The roughly 250 Pennsylvania settlers and militia who marched on Philadelphia in February 1764—a fraction of what was feared—declared they were coming to kill the Christian Indians and Quaker Israel Pemberton, and they demanded that the legislature raise more troops to defend the frontiers. Penn had written to John Armstrong at the end of December stressing the need to end the insurrection and instructing him, a justice of the peace, to be diligent in finding the rioters, most of whom he assumed lived on the frontiers of Cumberland and Lancaster counties.[56] Instead, Armstrong joined the march on Philadelphia; he could, he wrote, "forgive everybody except the Assembly and the enemy Indians."[57] Scotch-Irish men who had served the state now threatened its legitimacy.[58] Benjamin Franklin, home from five years in London as agent of the Pennsylvania Assembly, hastily organized the residents to protect the city. The Scotch-Irish had shown themselves to be savages in slaughtering the Conestogas, and now the savages were massing outside the walls of civilization and threatening the Quakers and Indians within.[59] The crisis sparked debate about who—Indians, backcountry Scotch-Irish, or Quaker elites—were truly savage and who were civilized.

William Egle, a nineteenth-century physician and local historian, defended the "brave Paxtang boys" for taking matters into their own hands when their government refused to implement measures against the Conestogas, who had aided and abetted the enemy. He pointed out the irony of pacifist Quakers taking up arms to defend the Indian refugees who were huddled in the Philadelphia Barracks. The Lutheran missionary Henry Melchior Muhlenberg said it was "almost inconceivable" that Quakers who had refused to fight in the French and Indian wars were now forming companies and preparing to fight against "their fellow citizens and fellow Christians." Children followed one prominent Quaker down the street shouting in amazement, "Look! A Quaker carrying a musket!"[60]

Benjamin Franklin averted the crisis by meeting the rebels at Germantown and negotiating an end to the insurrection. The Philadelphia authorities agreed to hear their grievances, and the rebels agreed to "stand down" and return home. The marchers appointed Matthew Smith and James Gibson as representatives to draw up two documents outlining their complaints and submit their case to the provincial government. They reiterated their anger that the leading Quakers had taken the Moravian Indians into the city "and treated them like lords at the public expense." When it came to the "suffering frontiersmen," on the other hand, as far as the authorities were concerned they were just "a mixed crowd of Scotch-Irishmen and Germans" and it didn't matter whether they lived or died. Smith and Gibson duly presented *A Declaration* and the *Remonstrance of the Distressed and Bleeding Frontier Inhabitants* to the governor and Assembly. Penn told the Assembly he thought it would not be proper for him as governor to negotiate by responding, but the Assembly could do so if it saw fit.[61]

By then Franklin had already landed the first punch in an unfolding war of words that would generate sixty-three pamphlets and ten political cartoons, making it the most publicly debated controversy in Pennsylvania to date.[62] Franklin published *A Narrative of the Late Massacres* in January 1764, just before the negotiations at Germantown took place. The essay expressed outrage at the massacres and pictured the Paxton Boys as lawless savages. "If an *Indian* injures me," Franklin asked, "does it follow that I may revenge that Injury on all *Indians*?" The only crime of the poor Conestogas seemed to be that they had reddish-brown skin and black hair; and people with the same features had murdered colonists on the frontiers. "If it be right to kill Men for such a Reason, then, should any Man, with a freckled Face and red Hair [characteristic Scotch-Irish traits], kill a Wife or Child of mine, it would be right for me to revenge it, by killing all the freckled red-haired Men, Women and Children, I could afterwards any where meet with." "We pretend to be Christians," Franklin continued, and as such should "exceed Heathens, Turks, Saracens, Moors, Negroes, and Indians, in the Knowledge and Practice of what is right." Instead, by massacring peaceful, Christian Indians, the Scotch-Irish had showed themselves to be the true savages. The Conestogas "would have been safe in any Part of the known World," Franklin concluded, "except in the Neighbourhood of the CHRISTIAN WHITE SAVAGES of *Peckstang* and *Donegall*!"[63]

Historians have quoted Franklin far more often than other commentators on the Paxton riots and some (myself included) have quoted him and no one else, as if his moral outrage was the last word on the subject. Franklin himself, back in London the following year, sent the Scottish jurist and philosopher Lord Kames a copy of the pamphlet and confided that he wrote it "to strengthen the Hands of a weak Government by rendering the Proceedings of the Rioters unpopular and odious."[64] Some members of the provincial government condemned the Paxton Boys for challenging their authority as much as, if not more than, for killing innocent Indians. The debate became less about the Paxton Boys' actions than about their experience of government.[65]

In its epistle to London containing an account of the events, the Philadelphia Yearly Meeting of the Society of Friends pointed out "that the Rioters were mostly Presbyterians from the North of Ireland, and their descendants." It added that, to their credit, German settlers had refused to join them "in their tumultuous Proceedings."[66] Franklin was not himself a Quaker, but he represented the Assembly party and advocated making Pennsylvania a royal colony, aligning himself with the Quakers who wanted to oust chief proprietor Thomas Penn from power. He faced opposition from many Scotch-Irish Presbyterians and took a decidedly anti-Presbyterian stance. In one historian's words, he was a man of strong dislikes, and he particularly disliked Presbyterians. His defense of innocent Indians, Franklin wrote, was used "to stir up against me those religious Bigots, who are of all Savages the most brutish."[67] His public condemnation of the Paxton Boys was a thinly veiled attack on his political opponents as well as a defense of murdered Indian people.

Many Assembly writers adopted the strategy of explaining the Paxton massacres in the context of a history of insurrections sparked by Presbyterians.

They drew on a long tradition of anti-Presbyterianism in Britain, fueled by unease about the influx of Irish immigrants in Pennsylvania, and reverted to stereotyping Presbyterians as violent and rebellious people unfit to hold political power. The author of *A Looking-Glass for Presbyterians* (evidently written by a Quaker apologist and prominent member of the Assembly named Isaac Hunt) pointed out that Presbyterians had taken up arms and executed King Charles I and replaced him with Oliver Cromwell, "a Tyrant, chosen from the very Dreggs of the People." He proposed that during the Catholic rebellion in Ireland in 1641, "all the innocent Blood that was shed in that horrid Massacre" could "be justly laid to their Charge." Scotch Presbyterians had slaughtered hundreds of Irish men, women, and children on Island McGee or Magee on the east coast of County Antrim near Carrickfergus "without the least Remorse." In Scotland, this "bigoted, stiff-necked, rebellious, pedantick Crew" had imposed upon King William III and procured an order to massacre the MacDonalds at Glencoe in cold blood in 1692. They were to blame for the 1715 and 1745 Jacobite rebellions as well.

Guilty of insurrections and atrocities in the past, Presbyterians had now imported their murderous traditions to Pennsylvania. Always a threat to the British state, they now threatened civic order in Pennsylvania. The very structure of the Presbyterian church challenged social hierarchy and inspired independence and republicanism in its congregation. Had the Presbyterian clergy instead instilled "Doctrines of *Peace* and *Loyalty*" among their congregations, "people would by this time have returned to their senses." They must not be allowed to impose their church on the rest of the province or to take over the reins of government.[68] Citing the Conestoga murders, the march on Philadelphia, and the bitter disputes dividing the province, another pamphleteer suggested "the *Presbyterians* have been the Authors, and Abettors, of all the Mischief, that has happened to us, as a People."[69]

Assembly pamphleteers represented Presbyterians as fanatics in religion and politics. In one, written as a farce but deadly serious and entitled *A dialogue between Andrew Truman and Thomas Zealot*, Thomas, a Paxton man, recounts: "We shot six and a wee ane, that was in the Squaw's Belly; we sculped three; we tomahawked three; we roasted three and a wee ane; and three and a wee ane we gave to the Hogs.... We kilt them at the Mannor just as they getting out of their Beds; And the Gued Folks of Lancaster had taken away aw the Guns, Tomhawks ... from them that were in the Goal." Andrew asks: "but did you think it right, Tom, to kill the Women and the Weans?" Tom responds that some men thought it wrong until an elder in the church gave a sermon preaching otherwise. "So, you did this all in the name of the lord?" asks Andrew. "Aye, to be sure," Thomas Zealot replies. "We were Presbyterians."[70]

While colonial leaders depicted Scotch-Irish frontiersmen as savages, the Paxton protesters and their supporters tried to apply that label exclusively—and generally—to Indians, to differentiate themselves from Indians, and to position themselves within, rather than without, the British colonial world as citizens deserving its protections and privileges. With a long history of acting as human buffers between contending parties, they portrayed Indians as perpetual enemies. Bloodthirsty Indians, not distressed frontier folk, were the savages; heartless Quakers and eastern elites were the ones who lacked civility and humanity. Directing their anger and frustration onto Indians as enemy others, the Paxton Boys and their supporters attempted to reshape political institutions on the frontier and in Philadelphia to adopt a policy that excluded all Indians, rather than protected allied Indians.[71] Like American revolutionaries a dozen years later, they justified their rebellion against a government on the grounds that the government did not represent them—that in this case it seemed more inclined to protect Indians than to protect its citizens and in doing so had dissolved the bonds of allegiance.[72]

The first item on the list of grievances in Smith and Gibson's *Declaration and Remonstrance* was that "as Free-Men and English Subjects" the inhabitants of the western counties of Lancaster, York, Cumberland, Berks, and Northampton were entitled to the same representation in government as the inhabitants of Philadelphia, Chester, and Bucks counties. This was the root cause of many of their grievances, they said. As to their attacks on the Indians, they were entirely justified. Skulking parties of Indians had repeatedly ravaged the frontiers, murdering "Men, Women, and Children, without distinction," and reducing a thousand families to distress. "It grieves us to the very Heart," they said, to see refugees who had lost homes and loved ones left destitute by the public, and exposed to poverty and wretchedness, "while upwards of One Hundred and Twenty of the Savages, who are with great Reason suspected of being guilty of these horrid Barbaraties, under the Mask of Friendship, have procured themselves to be taken under the Protection of the Government, with a view to elude the Fury of the brave Relatives of the Murdered; and are now maintained at the public Expence." They portrayed a world turned upside down, one operating against the dictates of fairness and "good policy." "Who ever proclaimed War with a part of a Nation, and not with the Whole?" As far as the Paxton Boys were concerned, all Indians were enemies in a time of Indian war.[73] For them, the frontier was a racial frontier and had to be guarded and maintained as such.

An anonymous pamphlet, *The Conduct of the Paxton Men, Impartially Represented*, challenged Franklin's version of the events, vilifying the murdered Indians, and blaming Pontiac's War on the pacifist policies of the Quaker-controlled Assembly that was unwilling to allocate public funds to defend frontier settlements. The author was likely the Reverend Thomas Barton. Barton grew up in Ulster on lands his ancestors had expropriated from Irish Catholics. He spent most of his adult life in the Pennsylvania backcountry, ministering primarily to Ulster-born settlers threatened by French Catholics and by Delawares and Shawnees whose lands had been acquired by force and fraud. Having been left to their own devices in the French and Indian War, Barton stated, backcountry settlers experienced the same thing in Pontiac's War, and thousands fled eastward to escape the "dreadfulnes of Murdering, Burning and Scalping."[74] The pamphlet claimed that 90 percent of backcountry inhabitants were in sympathy with the Scotch-Irish. They had "suffered and bled in the Cause of their Country" yet were "treated as Aliens of the Commonwealth, and denied a just and proportionable Share in Legislation." They had submitted their grievances to the Assembly, only to be insulted as "A Pack of insignificant SCOTCH-IRISH, who, if they were all killed, could well enough be spared." Instead, the government afforded aid and protection to the Indians living among them. Was it any wonder, Barton asked, "if the unhappy Frontier People were really *mad with Rage*?" "In short," he concluded in direct allusion to Franklin, "it appears that they would have been safe in any Part of the known World—except in the Neighbourhood of the RELENTLESS and OBSTINATE QUAKERS OF PENNSYLVANIA."[75]

Paxtonians portrayed Quakers as frauds and lambasted the Quaker Assembly in verse for supplying murdering savages with guns while leaving backcountry folk unfed and unprotected:

> Go on good Christians, never spare
> To give your Indians Clothes to wear;
> Send 'em good Beef, and Pork, and Bread,
> Guns, Powder, Flints and store of Lead,
> To Shoot your Neighbours through the Head;
> . . .
> Of Scotch and Irish let them kill
> As many Thousands as they will.[76]

The Quakers maintained their pacifist ideals when frontiersmen were in danger, but abandoned them when their own safety, or that of the Indians they harbored, was at risk, taking up arms when the Paxton Boys marched on Philadelphia. "Tis safe and common, in a Friend's disguise/To mask hypocrisy, Deceit, and Lies" declared the title page of *A Battle! A Battle!*[77]

The Apology of the Paxton Volunteers addressed to the candid & impartial World outlined an "an unjustifiable Attachment" between the Quakers and the Indians, that took precedence over anything else. No one would believe "that the Quakers would be so liberal to Savages, & at the same Time not contribute a single Farthing as a Society to our Distress the last Summer although applied to for this Purpose when near a thousand Families of our Frontier Inhabitants were obliged to abandon out Habitations."[78]

Behind it all, the Paxton Boys and their supporters believed, was Quaker determination to deprive the Scotch-Irish of protection and political representation. *The Plain Dealer: or a few remarks upon Quaker Politics* spelled out the inequities. The three eastern counties of Pennsylvania, the Quaker stronghold, had twenty-six seats in the Assembly (the city of Philadelphia had two seats, and Philadelphia, Bucks, and Chester counties eight each), although they included little more than half the taxable inhabitants of the colony; the five interior counties, the Scotch-Irish stronghold, had just ten seats. The backcountry people, wrote author Hugh Williamson, "are depriv'd of their share in legislation; laws are made and impos'd on them, and measures are taken which they do not approve, and yet cannot prevent, because they are not fairly represented in Assembly." Quakers depriving Scotch-Irish frontier people of fair representation was the root of all the trouble. If these people had been adequately represented in government, their requests for protection would not have been ignored and the Paxton massacre and march on Philadelphia would not have happened. The biggest cause was "the people conceiving that unjust laws are imposed on them." The German and Irish inhabitants of the frontiers "have felt your scourge," Williamson declared. The Quakers had left them naked and perishing and "the Indians that you fed, had left [them] nothing but the miserable life."[79]

David James Dove, a schoolmaster and scholar with a caustic wit who had clashed with Franklin before, echoed the same theme in *The Quaker unmask'd; or, Plain truth: humbly address'd to the consideration of all the freemen of Pennsylvania*. "These compassionate and merciful Christians, so easily affected with Pity for Indians, would not grant a single Farthing

Figure 6.2 Political cartoon by James Claypoole showing a Quaker wearing a broad-brimmed hat, riding on the back of a Scotch-Irish colonist with a gun, who tries kick him off. The Quaker leads a German settler who has an Indian riding on his back with a pack of furs for, or gifts from, I. P. (Israel Pemberton), while children lie dead and farmhouses burn in the background. Benjamin Franklin stands at the left side, holding a proclamation against the Paxton Boys.
Library Company of Philadelphia.

(as a Society) for the Relief of their Fellow Subjects." Whether the affection that some principal Quakers had shown to Indians could be owing "to the Charms of their Squaws," to trade advantages, or to their use in opposing the proprietors, Dove could not say. But what was certain was that frontiersmen, unlike Indians, could stand for seats in the Assembly and so some Quakers might think it good policy "not to afford them that Protection, nor shew them that Regard they at this Time shew the Savages." When the Paxton Boys marched on Philadelphia, the so-called Quaker pacifists were "unmasked"; they took up arms to destroy the very people who had been placed on the frontier and "who protected their Lives and Properties, whilst these ungrateful People sat unmolested in their Houses, and were preserved from feeling the Severities and Contrivances of Indian Cruelty."[80]

Figure 6.3 Cartoon attributed to David James Dove. On the left, Quaker Israel Pemberton (IP) hands out tomahawks to Indians, saying "Exercise those on the Scotch Irish and Dutch [Germans] and I'll support you while I am Abel." On the right a Quaker is in sexual embrace with a Native woman who steals his watch fob.
Collection of the Historical Society of Pennsylvania. Quakers and Benjamin Franklin political cartoon, 1764. Historical Society of Pennsylvania large graphics collection (V65).

As the crisis devolved into a war of words, the Paxton Boys still remained unidentified, uninvestigated, untried, and unpunished. The code of silence that John Elder invoked proved impenetrable. Writing to his uncle Thomas Penn in September 1764, John Penn said everyone in Cumberland County seemed to belong to the Paxton party. If he had ten thousand men, he did not believe he could arrest any of the perpetrators; he could not even get their names. In the breakdown of law and order, western settlers seemed free to do as they wished.[81] In the spring after they had exterminated the Conestogas, backcountry settlers, one of whom, Robert Bow, was identified as a "Relation to the Scotts famillia in Donegall," tried to occupy the now uninhabited Indian lands at Conestoga Manor.[82]

Political Reverberations

The repercussions of the Paxton Massacre, the march on Philadelphia, and the pamphlet war were far-reaching, as Benjamin Franklin spelled out in a series of letters to Richard Jackson, a member of Parliament and political ally during his years in London. "The Spirit of killing all Indians, Friends and Foes, spread amazingly thro' the whole Country," he wrote in February 1764. Nothing good could come of it all, he added in June: "the Mob being Presbyterians, the whole Posse of that Sect, Priests and People, have foolishly thought themselves under a Necessity of justifying as well as they could their mad and bloody Brethren." Franklin had never seen the kind of political violence and animosities that had arisen, and feared there would be "civil Bloodshed" before the year was over. In September, he reported that the Irish Presbyterians, angry at the Quakers for blaming them for the Paxton riots, had joined forces with the proprietary party in hopes of ending Quaker dominance in the Assembly. He expected the approaching election to be "a warm one" and the outcome was uncertain.[83] The Paxton Boys and their frontier supporters saw the Assembly as the problem and allied with the proprietary party; Franklin saw proprietary government as the problem and advocated a new government, one based on royal authority.[84]

The general election that October generated the largest and most diverse voter turnout to that point in Pennsylvania's history. Despite the Assembly party's heavy anti-Presbyterian rhetoric, the Presbyterian "New Ticket" found support from Anglicans and Germans and won eleven of the thirty-six seats in the Assembly. The Quakers and the Assembly endorsed the proposal by Benjamin Franklin and Joseph Galloway to convert Pennsylvania into a royal colony. Franklin and Galloway both lost their seats.[85] These were alarming developments for the establishment. "For when I consider the natural Increase of the P[resbyteria]ns, and the vast numbers yearly arriving among Us, I am induced to beleive, they will have the Rule and Direction of our Election's," Quaker merchant Thomas Wharton wrote to Franklin in December.[86]

The political changes did not soon change the lives of backcountry settlers, however. In fact, only one of the grievances from the *Declaration and Remonstrance*, the call for bounties on Indian scalps during wartime, was implemented in law following the election. Proclaiming the scalp bounty in July 1764, John Penn said it would encourage His Majesty's subjects "to exert and use their utmost Endeavours to pursue, attack, take, and destroy our said Enemy Indians."[87] In other words, as it had in the French and Indian War, the government outsourced Indian fighting to the same people who were demanding that the government protect them against Indians.

It had little effect. Frustrated by the lack of Pennsylvanian support for his campaign into Indian country that year, Colonel Henry Bouquet told John Harris at Paxton that, "after all the noise and bustle of your young men upon the Frontiers" and with scalp bounties back on the table, everyone had expected them to step up as soldiers or volunteers to defend their country, as the surest way to rid themselves of the taint of killing defenseless Indians. Otherwise, "Will not People say that they have found it easier to killing Indians in a Goal [sic], than to fight them fairly in the woods?" Instead, they signed on as pack horse drivers and waggoners, "employs for which a coward is as fit as a brave man." Whereas Virginia had offered volunteers to serve on the expedition, not one man had come forward from Pennsylvania. Frankly, Bouquet concluded, "I am so much disgusted at the Backwardness of the Frontier people in assisting us in taking Revenge on the Savages who murder them daily with Impunity that I hope this will be the last time I shall venture my Reputation and Life for their sake."[88]

Men who were unable to prevent Indian raids and protect their families may have felt their male honor and patriarchy undermined. They saw themselves as victimized, and they directed their animosity against Indians and colonial officials. Striking out against any and all Native people, the Paxton Boys created a racial enemy and legitimized killing unarmed men, women, and children as an act of male valor.[89] In massacring the Conestogas, the Scotch-Irish sent a message to a legislature which they thought had failed in its duty to protect and promote the well-being of society.[90] For the Paxton Boys, it would seem from their pamphlets, killing Indians in defiance of government authority had as much to do with defying government authority as with killing Indians. For their part, by denouncing the Scotch-Irish as the instigators and perpetrators of violence against the Indians, Pennsylvania eastern elites, and the Quakers in particular, were able to absolve themselves of responsibility for the destruction of Penn's peaceable kingdom and ignore their own implication and role in the broader colonial assault on Indian country.[91]

Penn's peaceable kingdom may have been more myth than reality, and Native people and colonists in eighteenth-century Pennsylvania may not have built and sustained middle grounds of coexistence as happened in other eras and areas.[92] After all, Scotch-Irish settler colonists were positioned on Pennsylvania's frontier to act as armed guards, not cultural ambassadors and intermediaries. Nevertheless, the Indian-killers from Paxton turned Pennsylvania away from other possibilities. John Penn summed up the situation in the aftermath of the killings in a letter to his uncle in September 1764: "I am convinced the murderers deserve to be hang'd, but I am sure there is not force enough in this Government to take away any one of them." Most backcountry inhabitants were pleased to hear of the death on an Indian, whatever the circumstances. Better abandon any idea of bringing the "Rioters to Justice," he concluded.[93]

Not all eighteenth-century mobs simply defied the law; in England and America popular action was often seen as a quasi-legitimate way to advance claims and causes. The Paxton rioters differed from most popular protest movements by targeting lives rather than property. They nonetheless saw themselves acting in the tradition of resorting to extralegal means to enforce laws, demand redress, or defend the public welfare when government failed to carry out that responsibility, as the Quaker Assembly failed to provide adequate defense against Indians.[94] Some scholars view the Paxton riots and organization of Scotch-Irish leaders in protest against the Pennsylvania government in the 1760s as a rehearsal for protests against the British government in the 1770s.[95] Yet the Paxton Boys actually wanted more government. Their grievance was that they were deprived of the protection that, as colonists on the frontiers, they had a right to expect from their government.[96]

The Paxton riots signaled other, more sinister, developments. As historian James Merrell points out, the Conestoga courthouse around which the Scotch-Irish Indian-killers galloped, and the town of Lancaster where they tomahawked defenseless refugees huddled in the workhouse, had in earlier years been treaty grounds, venues of intercultural diplomacy where Native people and colonists came together to kindle council fires, talk, smoke, and eat together, iron out disagreements, and refresh friendships. Now their bloody ground represented "mute repudiation of council culture and all that it stood for." When they killed off the Conestogas, the Scotch-Irish had, in some ways, killed off an era.[97] It was not entirely their doing. Pontiac's War and the Paxton Riots both turned simmering hatreds into racial conflicts that pitched all Indians and all whites against each other.[98]

During the pamphlet war of 1764, Paxtonian defenders argued that killing Indians was a legitimate form of opposition to bad government. During the American Revolution, killing Indians became an act of patriotism. The Paxton Boys killed a small community of Indian people close at hand; Revolutionary armies waged campaigns of total war against entire tribes. Colonists struggling to find a new, shared identity as white Americans found it in distancing themselves from, dehumanizing, and destroying non-whites.

For backcountry Scotch-Irish who claimed a place in the emerging new American society, a sure way to demonstrate that they were not like their Indian neighbors was to kill Indians.[99] The Paxton Boys' brutality that was anomalous and shocking in Pennsylvania in 1763 would soon become the new normal.

7

Scotch-Irish Captives and Scotch-Irish Indians

In *A Brief View of the Conduct of Pennsylvania, For the Year 1755*, William Smith provided graphic examples of the atrocities committed by Indian warriors in their attacks on the settlements in Great Cove and Tulpehocken: stakes driven into women's private parts; men's genitalia cut off and stuck in their mouths; men, women, and children murdered, scalped, and mutilated. "Last of all, to fill up the Measure of our Sorrow," he added, the young women who were taken captives would suffer "a worse Fate than those who suffered Death in all its horrid Shapes."[1]

Such images became part of the standard lore of settler suffering in Indian warfare. Smith, an Aberdeen-born Episcopal priest, staunch Quaker critic, and the first provost of the College of Philadelphia, which became the University of Pennsylvania, was clearly no friend to Indians. Yet, a decade later, in 1765, when he described the scene as Delawares and Shawnees returned their colonial captives to Colonel Henry Bouquet and the British army after Pontiac's War, even Smith acknowledged that many of the captives, particularly women and children, kicked against their liberation. They wanted to stay with the Indians.[2]

Early captivity narratives from Puritan New England were a staple of early American literature. Returned captives who related their stories, or their editors who put their accounts into print, often portrayed conflict with Indians as a Holy War against the forces of Satan, Indian captivities as tests of Christian resolve, and survival and liberation from the hands of savages as testament to God's infinite mercy. Such narratives were eagerly consumed. Mary Rowlandson's *The Sovereignty and Goodness of God*, recounting her captivity and redemption during King Philip's War, first published in 1682, sold out so quickly that three more editions were published in the same year, the fourth in London. *The Redeemed Captive Returning to Zion*, in which the

Reverend John Williams described the French and Indian raid on Deerfield, Massachusetts, in 1704, the ordeal of the captives carried to Canada, and his own redemption, while his daughter Eunice stayed with the Kahnawake Mohawks, sold one thousand copies in the first week of its publication in 1707 and went through six more editions during the course of the eighteenth century. Dozens of publications, of varying degrees of authenticity, related other captives' experiences. Many people read each copy; first editions of captivity narratives are extremely rare because so many were literally read to pieces. Many more people listened as narratives were read aloud. The popular literature of the day, captivity narratives quickly established an image of Indians as bloodthirsty savages who scalped, tomahawked, and tortured indiscriminately and subjected women to "unspeakable horrors." Although later narratives were less infused with jeremiads and biblical morality tales, many continued to depict Indian captivity as a fate worse than death.

In fact, northeastern Native peoples took captives to assuage the grief of bereaved relatives and appease the spirits of deceased kinsfolk. As wars and diseases in the wake of European invasion took heavy tolls, captive-taking became a way to maintain population levels, as well as to patch holes torn in the social fabric of kin- and clan-based communities: an adopted captive could fill the place of a deceased relative. While we don't and can't know the precise numbers, hundreds of white people were taken captive during the wars for North America.

Always occupying the front lines in the borderlands, the Scotch-Irish constituted a substantial percentage of the captives taken when war broke out. Most of the people captured in raids on the Pennsylvania backcountry in the French and Indian War and Pontiac's War were abducted from predominantly Scotch-Irish Cumberland County, as well as from Lancaster, Berks, and Northampton counties, which had substantial Scotch-Irish populations. In the words of one early-twentieth-century Pennsylvania historian, "the great majority of them, as shown by their names, belonged to the hardy, religious Scotch-Irish families along the frontiers of Pennsylvania and Virginia."[3] Scotch-Irish people were not more susceptible to cultural conversion and more likely to become "white Indians" than were their English or German-speaking neighbors. However, many of the people who became "white Indians" were, more specifically, Scotch-Irish Delawares or Scotch-Irish Shawnees.

Taking Captives

For all the horrors of frontier warfare, Indian warriors were far more likely than British or colonial soldiers to spare the lives of their enemies. Despite colonial claims that Indians killed indiscriminately, Ian Steele, in his exhaustive study of captive-taking in the wars of 1755–1758 and 1763–1764 in the Allegheny country, found at least 2,873 people who could have been killed immediately but were not. Levels of violence varied according to time and circumstance. Indians were much more likely to kill soldiers and militiamen, but in their raids from 1754 to 1759 they captured more noncombatants (perhaps as many as 822) than they killed (765). From 1754 to 1764, the Shawnees added at least 327 captives and converts to their communities and, although most were eventually returned, more than 100 may have stayed and lived out their lives with the Shawnees.[4]

Less than a year into the French and Indian War, in April 1756, Deputy Governor Robert Hunter Morris informed Sir William Johnson that raiding parties had carried off "a Multitude of Inhabitants, of all ages and sexes." No fewer than three hundred were held in the Ohio country, most at Shingas's Town at Kittanning. John Baker, who escaped from Kittanning in the summer of 1755 by killing and scalping an Indian, said there were more than one hundred captives from Pennsylvania in the town, "whom the Indians intend to keep, in order to increase their Inhabitants."[5] Scarouady and Montour saw captives in almost every Delaware town on the Susquehanna.[6] Indians took so many captives in raids on the backcountry that in the decade from 1755 to 1765 they held more captives than at any other time. The influx of so many people into relatively small Native populations shaped diplomatic relations between colonial powers and Indigenous communities, who also began to use captives as human shields against attack. Some of the newcomers brought changes to Indian culture. Some were transformed into Indians.[7]

War parties often made raids for the specific purpose of taking captives, and they sometimes brought leather thongs, extra clothing, and moccasins for the prisoners they expected to seize. Whereas Puritan writers had usually portrayed them as faceless savages, Indian raiders during the French and Indian War and Pontiac's War sometimes knew—and were known by— the people they took captive. John McKinney was captured by a Delaware at Little Cove in Cumberland County in February 1756 after trying to make a run for it. "John you run very fast, and you run a great while too," the Delaware gasped when he finally caught him. McKinney addressed him by name and said he hoped he would not kill him. The Delaware said he would not and kept his word. He handed McKinney over to the French at Fort Duquesne, from where he was sent to Niagara. McKinney escaped in September and literally lived to tell the tale, collected along with countless other frontier reminiscences by the indefatigable nineteenth-century historian Lyman Copeland Draper.[8]

Captives' fates and experiences varied, depending on circumstances, past encounters, the character of their captors, the decisions of bereaved relatives back in the villages, and even chance happenings. Adult males who might resist, older people who might slow travel, and crying infants who might betray a raiding party's presence might be tomahawked on the trail. On the other hand, as we've seen, when Charles Stuart and his wife were captured in the raid on Great Cove in November 1755, Shingas spared Stuart's life and adopted him into his family because Stuart had shown Delaware people generosity and hospitality before the war.[9] Once a raiding party escaped pursuit, warriors often displayed considerable—and considered—kindness to those, mainly women and children, they intended to adopt into their communities and convert to their way of life.[10] In contrast, captives who attempted to escape might suffer a grisly fate as an example to others. Mrs. Alexander McAlister, who tried to escape to Armstrong's men during their attack on Kittanning, was stripped, tied to a post, and burned with hot irons; and the other captives were made to witness it. Three days later, an Englishman who had tried to escape was brought in and burned alive.[11]

Whether recounted by Puritan writers in the seventeenth century or by contemporaries such as William Smith, at the start of this chapter, horror stories of the treatment women could expect from Indian captors inspired terror in female captives, although they appear to have been fueled by rumor more than reality. Of more than 242 women who were captured during the wars, Mrs. McAlister seems to have been the only one known to have been tortured.[12] Warriors whose ritual preparations for combat included sexual abstinence and whose captives might be adopted as clan relatives were unlikely to risk compromising their war medicine or infringing incest taboos by forcing themselves on female captives. Isabella McCoy, who had moved from Londonderry to Epsom in New Hampshire and was captured by Abenakis during King George's War (1744–1748), experienced "nothing like insult or indecency" during the whole time she was with them. Susanna Johnson, who was captured with her Scotch-Irish husband and children at Fort Number

4 (Charlestown, New Hampshire) in August 1754 and taken to St. Francis (Odanak), recalled that, except for one mischievous youngster, none of their Abenaki captors "were disposed to show insults of any nature." The warriors who captured William and Elizabeth Fleming assured William they would not abuse his wife "for fear of affronting their God."[13] According to George Croghan, an experienced trader in Indian country and deputy agent to Sir William Johnson, were an Indian warrior "to indulge himself with a captive taken in war, and much more were he to offer violence in order to gratify his lust, he would incur indelible disgrace." Scotch-Irish trader James Adair acknowledged that the Indians "are said not to have deflowered any of our young women they captivated, while at war with us; . . . they would think such actions defiling, and what must bring fatal consequences on their own heads." Even the Delaware chief Tewea or Captain Jacobs, whom Adair called "that blood-thirsty villain," "did not attempt the virtue of his female captives."[14]

Hard travel in moccasins in harsh weather and over rugged terrain, irregular meals and unfamiliar diet, and separation from family and home all took a toll on captives. But these experiences also initiated them into a new way of life. Once the trek into Indian country was over, captives faced new ordeals. Arriving at a village, they might be made to run a gauntlet between ranks of people brandishing sticks and clubs, although in some cases this was a symbolic rather than physical beating. Many captive Scotch-Irish girls would have experienced similar treatment to Marie Le Roy, a Swiss immigrant, and Barbara Leininger, a German, whom Delawares captured in their attack on Penn's Creek in Cumberland County, Pennsylvania, in October 1755. Their captor "was tolerably kind, and allowed us to ride all the way, while he and the rest of the Indians walked." When they arrived at Kittanning the girls "received our welcome, according to Indian custom. It consisted of three blows each, on the back. They were, however, administered with great mercy. Indeed, we concluded that we were beaten merely in order to keep up an ancient usage, and not with the intention of injuring us." Jean Lowery, who was captured with her children at McCord's Fort in 1756, was beaten by her Delaware captives at one village, but at Kittanning she was given a turkey feather to carry through the gauntlet as a sign that she was marked for adoption and suffered only one blow. Susanna Johnson and her family likewise expected a severe beating from the Abenakis at Odanak, but "each Indian only gave us a tap on the shoulder."[15]

Although some women captives adjusted to living in Native communities, many more clung to hopes of returning home and gathering back their children. Fanny Barnett and her younger sister Susannah were captured by Shawnees in 1756, when they were about ten and six years old. Susannah adamantly insisted on returning home to Virginia the first moment she could. After twelve years with the Shawnees, according to one chronicler, eighteen-year-old Susannah walked some two hundred miles to Fort Pitt. Fanny, on the other hand, married a Shawnee, had five children, and lived her life with them. She returned briefly in 1775, but stayed with her sister only a few days before returning to her Shawnee family.[16]

Others escaped. A total of 225 captives in the Allegheny country are known to have escaped between 1745 and 1765, less than one in seven of those captured, but three times as many as those known to have stayed living as Indians.[17] Patrick Burns and George or Hugh McSwaine were captured by Shawnees in Cumberland County on a Sunday evening in October 1755. Burns managed to escape, but the Shawnees gave McSwaine to the Delaware chief Shingas. Within two weeks of his capture, McSwaine also escaped, by killing two Delawares in their sleep, and brought their scalps, guns, and matchcoats into Fort Cumberland.[18] McSwaine may have been the individual whose liberation Charles Lewis recorded in his journal on October 31, 1755: "An Irish man arrived at the Fort with two scalps." Shawnees had taken him captive the Sunday before, but he escaped by seizing an axe and "beat out the brains of the Indian next to him."[19] Shingas told John Craig, whom he captured near McDowell's Mill in Cumberland County in February 1756 and adopted, that the Indians kept their captives "to enlarge their Nations, and to repair the Losses they might sustain in the War." Shingas, however, does not seem to have been particularly good at keeping captives. Like McSwaine, Craig escaped a few weeks later, taking with him a rifle and a pistol, a French coat and leggings, two pounds of powder, and a pound of bullets.[20] Twenty-year-old Daniel McMullen and twenty-six-year-old Thomas Moffitt were captured in separate raids in Northampton County in December 1755 and March 1756, respectively. The Delawares who captured McMullen took him to Tioga and sold him to a Mohawk who, McMullen said, "used him very kindly." The Mohawk then sold him to Catherine Montour, identified as "French Margaret's Daughter." Moffitt's captors also delivered him to Montour. The two took advantage of her absence to escape together. After three days in the woods, they reached the North Branch of the Susquehanna and paddled downriver for ten days, reaching Fort Augusta at Shamokin late in September 1756, where each gave an account of his experiences.[21]

The story of Mary Draper Ingles's escape has been preserved and commemorated in history, fiction, oral tradition, drama, and legend. Mary's parents, George Draper and Eleanor Harding Draper, emigrated from Donegal in 1729. Mary was born three years later in Philadelphia. In the 1740s the family relocated to the New River Valley of Southwest Virginia, where Mary married William Ingles. Shawnee war parties on their way south to attack Catawbas usually passed by the settlements without violence, but things changed with the outbreak of war in 1755. The Shawnees attacked Draper's Meadow that year, on harvest day, when the men were at work in the fields. They killed Colonel James Patton, also from Donegal, and Mary's mother Eleanor, and took captive Mary and her two sons, four-year-old Thomas and George, who was just two. Oral tradition said that despite giving birth to a baby girl on the third night out, Mary was able to continue on horseback. The Shawnees took her to a town at the mouth of the Scioto River. Although they made the other captives run the gauntlet, Mary was spared the ordeal and, according to the account of her captivity given by one of her sons, she "was treated with considerably more lenity than the rest of the prisoners." However, the Shawnees took her children from her and assigned them to different families. Mary tried to make the best of things, even sewing shirts for the Indians and for French traders as long as she remained in the town. Then a party of Shawnees took her almost one hundred miles farther away to Big Bone Lick in Kentucky. Mary managed to escape, along with an old Dutch or German woman, by pretending to go out gathering food. She made her way to the Ohio River and followed it upstream, surviving on roots. After forty-two days, frostbitten and starving, she encountered a settler family, who took her in. She was reunited with her husband and they eventually returned to their New River land and raised three sons and two daughters together. Mary was gone about five months.[22]

Jennet or Anne Clendinnen also escaped from the Shawnees, although she had to abandon her children to do so. She was widowed and captured with her three children and about twenty neighbors when Shawnees attacked Greenbrier in Augusta County, Virginia, in July 1763. She managed to escape on the trail into captivity. The Shawnees killed her infant child the next day. Her young son died in captivity. Her daughter, Jeanne or Jane, was returned at Fort Pitt in May 1765, although it was said that her mother took a long time to form any attachment to the six-year-old girl she had abandoned two years before.[23]

Indian captors often targeted children for adoption. Joseph Barnet, who was born in County Derry in 1726, lost his son William when Indians abducted him and a neighbor's boy named Mackey near Hanover, Pennsylvania. According to local lore, as they passed an orchard, the warriors told the boys to take plenty of apples as they were the last they would get for a long time. William spent seven years in captivity.[24] James McCullough lost his son for a similar length of time. He had migrated from County Londonderry with his wife Martha, moved from Delaware to Pennsylvania's Cumberland Valley with his family in 1750, and settled near the west branch of Conocheague Creek. His diary records the mundane events of daily farming and frontier life until Braddock's defeat in July 1755. That summer, the family fled on what turned out to be a false report of Indian raiders. A year later, on July 26, 1756, his sons John and James were taken captive by a party of five Indians and one Frenchman. McCullough turned to Jeremiah 12:10: "Weep Y^e not for the dead neither bemoan him but weep sore for him that goeth away for he shall return no more nor see his native country." The next two years of the diary record a litany of Indian attacks, people killed and captured.[25]

John McCullough was eight when he and his five-year-old brother were captured. As soon as his captors reached the place where they had left their baggage, John recalled, they tied a pair of moccasins on his feet. The morning before they reached the Delaware town, they plucked all the hair from the boys' heads except for a small spot on the crown. Then the Delawares dunked John several times in the Allegheny River. He thought they were going to drown him, but when he finally waded out, "they put a new ruffled shirt on me, telling me that I was then an Indian." He lived with the Delawares for eight years. At one point, when his father tried to take him home, John "wept bitterly" and had to be tied on a horse; he escaped back to the Delawares under cover of night. He stayed with them for another year before he was finally taken to Fort Pitt under guard and delivered up, along with two hundred other captives, after Colonel Henry Bouquet marched an army into Delaware country in the fall of 1764. After relearning English and readjusting to white ways, John McCullough lived more than forty years on the family farm in the Conocheague Valley, where he wrote a memoir of his youthful captivity.[26]

Going Native

Other captives found that time and the wealth of kinship relations in Native communities healed many wounds and kept them in Indian country. Some refused to return home even when the opportunity arose. Less than 4 percent of the more than 1,700 captives taken in the Allegheny-Ohio borderlands between 1745 and 1765 are known to have remained and lived as "white Indians."[27] Nevertheless, captives who went Native were a recurrent, and for Euro-Americans a troubling, occurrence on the frontier. J. Hector St. John de Crèvecoeur, the author of *Letters from an American Farmer*, wondered: "By what power does it come to pass, that children who have been adopted when young among these people, can never be prevailed on to readopt European manners." Anxious parents going to redeem children in the last war had "found them so perfectly Indianised that many knew them no longer." Some refused to return. Crèvecoeur concluded that "there must be in their social bond something singularly captivating, and far superior to anything to be boasted of among us."[28]

Delawares had a simple explanation. "We love you more than you love us," they told missionary Christian Frederick Post during peace negotiations in 1758; "for when we take any prisoners from you, we treat them as our own children. We are poor, and yet we clothe them as well as we can, though you see our children are as naked as at the first. By this you may see that our hearts are better than yours."[29] Children in Scotch-Irish frontier families were expected to carry their weight by performing daily chores on the farm and were subject to patriarchal authority, the dictates of a stern Calvinist religion, and corporal punishment. In contrast, said missionaries who had lived with the Delawares, Indian children ran free, had minimal responsibilities, were indulged by their elder relatives, and, instead of physical punishment, were reproached with gentle words. John Heckewelder said it was "a sacred principle" that parents took care of children until they could provide for themselves, at which time grown children would repay their care with similar care for the elderly.[30] The differences in their treatment would not have been lost on older children who were taken captive or on young captives who returned to colonial society after several years living with an adoptive Native family.

Recounted in her father's best-selling tract, the most famous captivity narrative in colonial America is that of Eunice Williams who, captured as a child in the raid on Deerfield, spent the rest of her life in the Mohawk community of Kahnawake.[31] Almost as well known is that of Mary Jemison, an adopted colonial captive who lived most of her life as an Indian. Of some 2,873 people captured or missing on the Allegheny frontier between 1745 and 1765, she was the only one to provide an extensive account of her captivity experience.[32] In November 1823, when she was about eighty years old, she spent three days relating the story of her life in a series of interviews to a local physician named James Seaver, who published them as a book in 1824. Though the narrative is flawed by Seaver's intrusive influence as writer, it nevertheless provides a rare account by a Scotch-Irish woman who converted to Indian life.

Born on an immigrant ship bound for Philadelphia in 1742 or 1743, Jemison grew up on her parents' farm on Marsh Creek in western York County in Pennsylvania. In April 1758, a war party of six Shawnees and four Frenchmen attacked the farm. They killed and scalped Jemison's parents and three of her siblings but had other plans for her. They took off her shoes and stockings and made her wear moccasins on the trek to Fort Duquesne. There, they gave her to two Seneca women, who were mourning a brother killed in the war. "If they receive a prisoner," Jemison explained, "it is at their option either to satiate their vengeance by taking his life in the most cruel manner they can conceive of; or, to receive and adopt him into the family, in the place of him whom they have lost." The Seneca sisters adopted Jemison, ritually bathing her and dressing her in Indian clothing. She sat motionless, expecting to be killed at any moment. However, "in the course of that ceremony, from mourning they became serene—joy sparkled in their countenances, and they seemed to rejoice over me as over a long lost child. I was made welcome amongst them as a sister." They gave her a new name, Dickewamis.[33]

With her new name and family, Dickewamis began her long transition from a Scotch-Irish girl to a Seneca woman. Scotch-Irish women in the North American backcountry may have fared better than those who migrated to other areas of the world or stayed home, but their common lot was still hard work. In addition to bearing and raising children, they were primarily responsible for time-consuming domestic chores: cooking, baking, washing, cultivating gardens, milking cows, churning butter, spinning cloth, and making clothes. Travelers often reported that women and men routinely shared the heaviest manual labor. Both sexes worked in the fields, not just at harvest time but through the entire growing season, and women not only tended the livestock but also did the slaughtering. They also helped with forest-clearing and breaking ground for plowing.[34] Seneca women likewise raised children and planted, tended, and harvested the fields of corn, beans, and squash on which the Haudenosaunee depended. Like other Native villagers in the Ohio River valley, they also harvested an abundant variety of wild foods.[35] Yet the communal life of an Indian village could be more rewarding than isolated life on a backcountry farm. After four years living with the Senecas, Jemison told Seaver, she "had become so far accustomed to their mode of living, habits and dispositions, that my anxiety to get away, to be set at liberty, and leave them, had almost subsided." She was "warmly attached" to her new family and friends, and found that life was not unpleasant and followed a predictable rhythm. Although Indian women had to gather all the firewood, bake all the bread, and do all the cooking, she reckoned "their task is probably not harder than that of white women, who have those articles provided for them; and their cares certainly are not half as numerous, nor as great."[36]

Women in Scotch-Irish society submerged their identity in that of their husbands, who headed the household and governed the family. Seneca society, in contrast, was matrilineal. Clan membership passed through the female line. Seneca women's responsibility for giving and cultivating life, raising crops and children, gave them a status unknown to most women in Scotch-Irish society, and they enjoyed considerable freedom and influence. Jemison married two Indian husbands, first a Delaware and, after he died, a Seneca, and raised a family, naming her children after the deceased members of her Scotch-Irish family. Eventually, she had eight children (only three of whom survived her), thirty-nine grandchildren, and fourteen great-grandchildren. From the destruction of her Scotch-Irish family, she emerged as a member of an Indian family and then built her own Indian family. In time and in cultural allegiance she became a Seneca, sharing fully the lives of Seneca women. After the American Revolution, Jemison had the chance to return to white society but refused, fearing that any white relatives she found would reject her Indian children: "they would despise them, if not myself; and treat us as enemies: or, at least with a degree of cold indifference, which I thought I could not endure."[37]

Known as the "white woman of the Genesee," Jemison lived most of her life in the Genesee country of western New York, the Seneca heartland. James Seaver described her dress, demeanor, and speech reflecting the mixing of cultures that had occurred in her over the course of more than sixty years (Figure 7.1). She wore buckskin moccasins, an Indian blanket, a brown

MARY JEMISON, THE CAPTIVE.

Figure 7.1 Mary Jemison in her old age.
Depicted in Harriett S. Caswell, *Our Life among the Iroquois Indians* (1892).

flannel gown, a petticoat, and a bonnet. She still spoke English clearly, with "a little of the Irish emphasis."[38]

Mary Jemison was not the only Scotch-Irish captive to become a "white Indian." Eleanor Kincaid was widowed and captured with her three small children in a Shawnee raid on Jackson River in Augusta County in September 1756. Nine years later, they were seen in Lower Shawnee Town, near present-day Portsmouth, Ohio, and presumed to have become Indians.[39] David McClure in 1772 saw a woman named Eliot living at Wakatomica among the Ohio Delawares. She had been captured as a child fourteen years earlier and now "appeared perfectly naturalized, and conformed to the Indian customs and dress." She apparently spoke no English and "was as contented as her Indian companions." McClure concluded that "there is an unknown charm in the Indian life, which surprizingly attaches white people; those especially who have been captivated in early life."[40]

The Renick family evidently originally migrated from Germany to Scotland, then to Coleraine in Northern Ireland, then to Pennsylvania, and on to Virginia. Robert Renick was killed by Indians; his wife and children were captured by Shawnees in a raid on the forks of James River in Augusta County in July 1757. Eighteen-month-old Robert Jr. was killed on the journey to the Shawnee town of Chillicothe; five-year-old Joshua was taken to Piqua. Soon after reaching Chillicothe, Mrs. Renick gave birth to a son she called Robert after her murdered husband and child. Mrs. Renick, William, and young Robert were returned to Staunton in 1767. William became a successful farmer and a major of militia in Greenbrier County and Robert, who spent his childhood as a Shawnee named Pechyloothame, adjusted to white settler society and eventually rebuilt the family estate. Joshua, however, remained with the Shawnees, married a Native wife, and according to family tradition became "as complete an Indian as could be found among the Shawanoes." Relating the story to historian Lyman Draper one hundred years later, seventy-five-year-old William Renick of Greenbrier, son of the child born in captivity, said Joshua was raised by the parents of Tecumseh, married an Indian wife, "and became a chief of the Miamis."[41]

Bringing Captives Home

Family members agonized over the fate of loved ones in captivity. Catherine McKey submitted a petition to Deputy Governor James Hamilton of Pennsylvania in August 1762. Her husband had been killed by Indians the previous August and her eight-year-old son John had been captured "& has never since been heard of." She asked the governor to inquire of the headmen of the various tribes he was negotiating with so "that if possible Your Petitioner might hope of having her Child again, Reliv'd from Savage Bondage."[42]

John Martin's brief petition to James Hamilton, dated August 13, 1762, reads like the plot for John Ford's Western movie *The Searchers*, in which John Wayne's character spends years trying to locate and retrieve a niece held captive by Comanches. Martin, an Indian trader whose family was captured in 1755, described himself as "Bereaved of my Wife & five Children By Savage War at the Captivity of the Great Cove." Using his connections in Indian country, he managed to secure the return of his wife and youngest child, two-year-old Janet, although going through the French, they were sent first to Quebec and then to England before reuniting with John in Pennsylvania. Martin then endeavored to recover his three other children. He made many long journeys and finally went to the Indian town at Tuscarowas with letters asking the Delaware chiefs Tamaqua, also called the Beaver, and Shingas to deliver one of his daughters. He saw his daughter with Shingas. Shingas refused to give her up then, but promised to do so when he delivered the other captives to Hamilton. Martin asked the governor to intercede. The three children were finally returned two years later. Captured when they were 8, 10, and 12, they "returned as young Indians of 15, 17, and 19 years of age."[43]

Once captives were adopted, they had two families. Their Indian families were reluctant to part with adoptees whom they now regarded as relatives. At a conference in Pittsburgh in July 1759, delegates from multiple tribes gathered to confirm peace with "the English." In fact, none of the principal colonial participants was English: George Croghan, there as Sir William Johnson's deputy agent, was Irish; Croghan's assistant Captain Thomas McKee, was Scotch-Irish; and Lieutenant Colonel Hugh Mercer, commander at Fort Pitt, was Scottish, a survivor of the Battle of Culloden *against* the English. Tamaqua returned two female captives he had adopted. "Brothers," he announced to them, "I have brought with me some of your flesh and Blood; there they set. One is my mother, the other my Sister. I deliver them up to you, in the presence of all here; do not think I am tired of them; no. I love them as well as I do my own Mother and Sister. When they go to the Inhabitants do not hide them; when I go down, I shall Call and see them."[44]

Women commonly facilitated peace in Indian country, and some captives were returned as gifts at treaty councils or during visits to colonial capitals to establish good faith and restore diplomatic relations. In July 1758, the eastern Delaware chief Teedyuscung brought a captive teenager named Sarah Decker, who had been captured in Northampton County in December 1755, to a conference at Easton and handed her over to the governor of Pennsylvania as a gesture of peace.[45] On occasion, Indian people returned captives voluntarily. David Boyd, the son of an immigrant from Northern

Ireland, was captured by Delawares when he was thirteen, along with his mother and siblings, in Cumberland County in February 1756. According to his grandson, four years later Boyd's adoptive Delaware father decided to return him, took him to Carlisle at considerable personal risk, and even sold horses and furs to provide him with clothes and cash for his new life among the whites. Boyd, however, made several attempts to return to the Delawares before he married and raised a family in Shippensburg.[46]

The British did not seize every opportunity to recover captives. Hugh Mercer, commanding at Fort Pitt, told Colonel Henry Bouquet that when Indian families visited the fort with captives, "The Country People sollicit me to purchase their friends, but that method I detest, as most dishonorable." Colonel Henry Bouquet and General Jeffery Amherst shared his distaste for ransoming captives.[47] Nevertheless, the British made the return of captives a prerequisite of peace talks, although such returns did not always go smoothly. At a conference with Delawares, Iroquois, and other delegates in Easton in August 1761, the Indians returned a captive teenage girl, about thirteen years old, whom the governor committed to the care of an Irish Quaker named Susannah Hatton and another woman, Susannah Brown, who took her to their lodgings, washed her, and dressed "in a Suit of English Cloathing" (just as Native women would have washed her and dressed her in Indian clothes when she was adopted). According to the Quaker account of the conference, the girl appeared to be reconciled to parting from the Native women, and one of the Quakers was to take her home. But on the morning of the departure she slipped into the woods and escaped "and is we suppose again returned to the Indians She had before lived with." She spoke English well and remembered how the Indians had murdered her parents when they took her and her brothers captive, but the Quakers could not win her back from the Indians. Despite their many assurances that her surviving relatives would welcome her home with open arms, "She rather chose to live with the Indians and in which she does not appear to be Singular, as most of the Children which have been restored to us have manifested the Same Disposition."[48]

This may have been the girl to whom the Oneida chief Thomas King, or Saghughsuniunt, referred at Lancaster in August 1762. King brought fourteen captives and delivered them to Governor Hamilton, with the promise of more to come. He implied that captives escaping back to Indian country was due to English carelessness, not Indian collusion. "*Brother* Onas," he addressed Hamilton, using the Iroquois title for governors of Pennsylvania,

"As I have now brought your Flesh and Blood, I would have you take Care of them, and keep them fast. I brought a Girl to Easton, and she run away. When I came Home, I found her here. Bless me! Says I, there is my Wife. I was sorry that I had delivered her, but to my Surprize I found her at Home." Now he had brought another prisoner "who I love as my own Wife. I have a young Child by her. You know it is very hard for a Man to part with his Wife. I have delivered her, therefore take Care of her, and keep her safe, that she don't make her Escape."[49] On his part, Hamilton addressed the Indians' concerns that the English would make servants of the prisoners they returned and assured them that redeemed prisoners were free to join their relatives or take the best employment they could get.[50]

Indian people returned a number of captives to the governor at the Lancaster courthouse. A clerk recorded the names and tribal affiliations of the Munsees and Senecas who delivered them, but only a few of the names of the captives themselves. They included Peggy Dougherty, who was likely taken in the Delaware attack on Conococheague Creek in Cumberland County in November 1755, and Elizabeth Williams and her eighteen-year-old brother Henry, whom Delawares captured in Northampton County the following month. The clerk estimated the ages of two girls and five boys who were delivered (from a little girl to a boy of fourteen), but he was unable to give their names "as they cannot speak English, or give any account from whence they were taken."[51]

Colonel Bouquet oversaw a mass delivery of captives at the end of Pontiac's War. In a meeting with Shawnee, Delaware, and Mingo chiefs at his camp on the Tuscarawas River in late October 1764, Bouquet gave them twelve days to deliver up all their captives to him at the town of Wakatomica on the Muskingum River. Between October 25, 1764, when Bouquet's army arrived at the forks of the Muskingum, and November 9, the Indians brought in 206 captives (32 males and 58 women and children from Virginia; 49 males and 67 women and children from Pennsylvania). By mid-November, the Delawares and Mingoes had delivered all their prisoners, "& even their own children born from white women," which Bouquet insisted upon and "which considering their attachment to their children is a convincing Proof of their Sincerity & their Humiliation."

The Shawnees proved more difficult and dragged their feet. Bouquet expected they would bring in one hundred more captives, but some of the captives had been with them for so many years "that they are become Savages & they are obliged to tie them to bring them to us." The British had to post guards to prevent them from escaping. Unless the redeemed captives were "treated with Indulgence & Tenderness by their Relations," Bouquet warned, "they will certainly return to their Savage Masters."[52] Bouquet intended to send them to Carlisle.

There were scenes of anguish on all sides. William Smith, who was present, described "fathers and mothers recognizing and clasping their once-lost babes; husbands hanging around the necks of their newly-recovered wives; sisters and brothers unexpectedly meeting together after long separation, scarce able to speak the same language." At the same time, others searched frantically and in vain for lost relatives and looked stricken. Some Indian people were in tears as they parted with their adopted captives, and many captives clung to their Indian relatives. Children who had been carried off when they were young and had lived a long time among the Indians could not be expected to display any signs of joy on being restored to their parents or relatives, wrote Smith. "Having been accustomed to look upon the Indians as the only connexions they had, having been tenderly treated by them, and speaking their language, it is no wonder that they considered their new state in the light of a captivity, and parted from the savages with tears." However, Smith acknowledged, adults too parted from the Indians with the greatest reluctance, and some women found a way to escape back to the Indian towns. Others grieved for days and refused to eat.[53]

A Virginian volunteer in Bouquet's army named William Kincaid (sometimes spelled Kinkead) was reunited with his wife. Born in Ireland in 1736, Kincaid had moved with his parents to Augusta County, Virginia, where he married Eleanor Guy (or Gay), with whom he had a dozen children.[54] Eleanor had been captured along with their three children in a Shawnee raid seven months earlier, in April 1764, when she was twenty-three and pregnant. She was adopted into Tamaqua's Delaware family and well treated. She brought the three-month-old baby back with her, but their four-year-old son had been killed on the march into captivity and their seven-year-old daughter had died of disease. She called the newborn Andrew, giving him the same name as his brother who had been killed. Two-year-old Isabella had been taken from her mother and she had not seen her since. She identified a three-year-old girl who was returned with other prisoners as her missing daughter and claimed her, although the girl did not recognize her parents, clung to the skirts of her Indian mother, and spoke only Delaware.[55] Rhoda Boyd, whom Delawares had captured with her brother David in Cumberland County in February 1756, was one of the "liberated" captives who escaped and went back to her captors.[56]

The Shawnees did not bring in many of their captives until the following spring. In May 1765 a delegation of fifteen Shawnee chiefs, together with forty-five warriors and their women and children, joined Seneca and Delaware delegates in conference with the officers of the British garrison at Fort Pitt. The Shawnees came over the river with their prisoners, "beating a Drum and singing their peace song, agreeable to the Ancient Custom of their Nation." When they entered the council house, their speaker, Lawoughqua, presented forty-two captives. Others were out with hunting parties and would be brought soon. "Father, Here is your Flesh and Blood," said Lawoughqua. "They have been all tied to us by adoption, and altho' we now deliver them up to you, we will always look upon them as our relations whenever the great Spirit is pleased that we may visit them." All but five of the captives had been taken when they were under age sixteen, more than half of them had lived with the Shawnees for more than five years, and at least thirty-six had been adopted. "We have taken as much care of these prisoners as if they were our own Flesh and Blood," Lawoughqua told those gathered at the conference; "they are now become unacquainted with your Customs & manners, & therefore Fathers, we request you will use them tenderly & kindly, which will be a means of inducing them to live contentedly with you." The Shawnees knew what they were talking about; that was precisely the treatment they had employed to win over the captives to their way of life. Lawoughqua handed the British a six-row wampum belt, commending the captives to their care.[57]

Returned Captives

The return of captives in 1764–1765 effectively halted hundreds of individuals from becoming "white Indians." Liberated captives returned with Indian skills, languages, relatives, and ways of thinking and acting.[58] They faced a difficult re-entry into colonial society and some never fully made it. Many returned home permanently changed by the experience. Long after Ann Calhoun returned from her captivity among the Cherokees, family tradition said that she "longed for her wild Indian life" and would steal away to spend a day in the woods.[59] For some, captivity was a nightmare they never forgot. Others retained lasting connections in Indian communities and deep affection for the families who had adopted them. Few experienced smooth transitions back into colonial society. An unsigned petition for relief in the

Augusta Parish vestry book for October 1766 reads: "Your petitioner was taken prisoner by the Northward Indians in June 1756, and continued many years among them, since her return with two of her children she has by the industry of herself and children and the Bounty of some Benevolent persons subsisted in the best manner she could." However, reduced now to begging from door to door, the petitioner wrote, she was "worn out with Old age and Infirmities and Misfortunes, and has become a real object of Charity."[60]

Captives who had been wrenched from their families as children and then taken into the fold of Indian families and communities were wrenched away from their adoptive families when they were returned, sometimes with no certainty that they would be reunited with their original families or fully accepted in colonial society. Following the return of captives at Lancaster in the summer of 1762 and at Muskingum in the fall of 1764, the *Pennsylvania Gazette* carried advertisements describing returned children who could speak no English and had only Indian names. The paper called for relatives to claim them soon, "otherwise the Boys will be bound out to Trades, and the Girls so disposed of, as to prevent their becoming a further Expence to the Public."[61] Children who had had two families in their short lives risked having no family at all after their "liberation" and would be treated as orphans.

Some redeemed captives applied the knowledge, contacts, and experience they had acquired to construct new roles for themselves as culture brokers and exercised significant influence in the borderlands. Nineteen-year-old Gershom Hicks and his younger brother Levy were captured along with two other brothers and their mother, Barbara Hicks, in November 1755 when Delawares attacked the family's farm at Great Cove and killed their father. Barbara was retaken in the attack on Kittanning, and the two unnamed brothers were returned against their will at Muskingum in November 1764. Levy Hicks was said to have become a white Indian, but he escaped to Fort Pitt in 1762. He served as a guide for travelers going west of the Juniata River. In 1766, Hicks and Delaware Joseph Peepee accompanied Antrim-born missionary Reverend Charles Beatty as interpreters on his trip to the Ohio country to preach to "the Distressed Frontier Inhabitants ... and to the Indian Nations in their Neighborhood." After five years as a captive, Gershom Hicks became a white Delaware and even participated in Delaware raiding parties. A British commander at Venango, who hired him as a guide, described him as "a fellow who has been Prisoner with the Indians & just the same as one of themselves." When Gershom Hicks was released in 1764, however, he did not go back to live with the Delawares. Although suspected as a spy and a traitor, he fought in a Pennsylvania regiment in the Revolution and seems to have lived out the rest of his life with his brother Levy at Hicks Run in Allegheny County.[62]

James Smith (Figure 7.2) turned his captivity experience among Indians to advantage in fighting against Indians. A resident of Conococheague

Figure 7.2 Col. James Smith, artist unknown, ca. 1800–1810. After living for years as an Indian captive, James Smith became a prominent leader of the Black Boys and an advocate and exponent of using Indian ways of fighting.
Warren J. Shonert Americana Collection, Eva G. Farris Special Collections, W. Frank Steely Library, Northern Kentucky University.

and of Scotch-Irish descent, Smith had been working as a woodcutter on Braddock's expedition when he was captured by Delawares and Kahnawake Mohawks near Fort Bedford in July 1755 and adopted. He was exchanged in November 1759 and returned home to Conococheague early the next year to find that his people did not know if he was dead or alive. They received him with great joy but, as he wrote in his account of his captivity and return, "were surprised to see me so much like an Indian, both in my gait and gesture." He was appointed a captain of rangers in Pontiac's War. He chose two other former captives as his lieutenants. They had their men dress like Indians, wear red handkerchiefs instead of hats, and paint their faces red and black like Indian warriors. "I taught them the Indian discipline, as I knew of no other at that time, which would answer the purpose much better than British. We succeeded beyond expectation in defending the frontiers." In the fall of 1763, Smith participated in Armstrong's campaign that burned Delaware and Munsee towns and destroyed their cornfields on the West Branch of the Susquehanna. The next year he took part in Bouquet's campaign on the Muskingum. One of the conditions of peace was the release of anyone living in captivity.[63]

The Girty family exemplified multiple captive experiences. Simon Girty, Sr., migrated to Pennsylvania from Ireland around 1730. Although it is not known where exactly he came from, his descendants say he was Protestant and probably from the North.[64] He moved to the frontier, took up residence at the Scotch-Irish community of Chambers Mill on the Susquehanna, and found work trading with the Delawares from his home at Paxton. In 1737 he married an English girl, Mary Newtown, who bore him four sons: Thomas, Simon, James, and George. In 1749 Girty moved the family across the Susquehanna to Sherman's Creek where a dozen families had built cabins on Indian lands. When the authorities of newly formed Cumberland County attempted to remove the squatters in 1750 and burned some of their cabins, Girty and the others were bound to appear in the county court. The Girty family returned to Chambers Mill. The next year, Girty was killed in a duel or a drunken brawl with an Indian called "the Fish." His widow remarried, to a neighbor named John Turner, who moved the family back to Sherman's Creek in the summer of 1755.

Braddock's defeat and the subsequent spate of Indian raids sent the settlers scurrying for shelter to Fort Granville. When the fort was captured in 1755, Delawares took the Turner/Girty family to Kittanning. They tortured and killed John Turner in the presence of the other captives. Mary and her sons were earmarked for adoption. After only a few weeks of captivity, Thomas Girty, the eldest brother at eighteen, was among the handful of prisoners rescued when John Armstrong attacked and burned Kittanning in 1756. The rest of the family was separated as the Indians dispersed. The Delawares took Mary, her newborn child, and ten-year-old George to their towns on the Kuskusky and Shenango; the Shawnees took twelve-year-old James, and Senecas took Simon. Fifteen-year-old Simon quickly mastered the Seneca language. After General John Forbes took Fort Duquesne in 1758, the Ohio Indians made a treaty with the British in which they agreed to turn over their prisoners. The family was reunited at Fort Pitt. The brothers apparently blazed trees and claimed a large tract of land by "tomahawk right," and with numerous Virginia and Pennsylvania merchants operating out of Fort Pitt, earned livings as traders and interpreters. James married a Shawnee woman and became a trader. George married a Delaware and raised a family. Simon worked as a translator in conferences at Fort Pitt and for the British Indian department in the turbulent early 1770s. In 1784 he married a former captive, Catherine Malott.[65] A Delaware named Katepakomin took the name Simon Girty, and a Delaware named Simon Girty attended the 1765 Fort Pitt treaty. Mention of a young man called Indian George Girty could refer to someone who had taken the name or to George himself who, of all the brothers, became most completely a "white Indian."[66]

Although several hundred captives were returned in 1764–1765, something like 1,100 others were not, and most simply disappeared.[67] For those who returned, the ordeal was far from over. Four-year-old Thomas Ingles had been captured with his mother Mary and younger brother George in August 1755. Mary escaped, but George died and Thomas grew up Shawnee. He escaped one attempt to ransom him; another failed because of the outbreak of Pontiac's War. Not until 1768 was he successfully redeemed. By then the seventeen-year-old spoke no English and, according to Augusta County tradition, was "said to have been a perfect savage in appearance and manners." Ingles would periodically return to his Shawnee friends and relatives. He received an education in Virginia, however, joined the Virginian forces in Lord Dunmore's War, and became a farmer in the New River region, where he married and started a family. In 1782, during the frontier war of the Revolution, Indians attacked his farmstead while he was working in the fields and carried off his family. Ingles joined a party of militia who went in pursuit, but when they caught up with the raiding party the Indians tomahawked their captives, including Thomas's wife and two older children. Ingles is not known to have returned to the Shawnees. He apparently went west on his own, moving first to Tennessee and eventually to Mississippi.[68]

Although feared as a fate worse than death, an Indian captivity could be a passage to a new life and a new identity. Captive-taking highlighted the brutality and violence of Indian resistance against the people who invaded their land. It also revealed and created connections between Native people and Scotch-Irish people who contested the same land.[69] Captives who "went Native" upended colonial assumptions about the superiority of what was deemed civilized life and underscored the fluid and precarious nature of identity. A Scotch-Irish person might become an Indian. An Indian person might be Scotch-Irish. A person might be one and then the other and then return to their original identity. For Scotch-Irish people who were taken captive and who became white Indians if only for a time, cultural borders sometimes remained porous even as racial battle lines hardened.

8

Black Boys and White Savages

At the end of the French and Indian War in 1763, an elderly Delaware named Joseph Wipey relocated from the Kittanning Trail in southwestern Pennsylvania to a creek on the Conemagh River. He lived there alone and on friendly terms with neighboring colonial settlers, and his cabin became something of a landmark in the area. A survey six years later located another cabin on the same creek "Near Wipsey's [sic] Cabin." In 1774, Wipey was murdered, evidently by two neighbors, James Cooper and John Hinkston. Reporting the murder to Governor John Penn, Arthur St. Clair, a wealthy landowner and member of the Westmoreland County court, added: "It is the most astonishing thing in the world, the disposition of the common people in this country, actuated by the most savage cruelty, they wantonly perpetrate crimes that are a disgrace to humanity." Penn issued a proclamation calling for the arrest of the murderers, to no avail.[1]

Before the war, Indian people and colonists across large stretches of the backcountry had rubbed elbows in their daily lives—trading, exchanging news, smoking, eating, drinking, and sometimes sleeping together. The war shattered patterns of peaceful coexistence. Many people in the backcountry tried to rebuild those patterns, and some even built new ones as they moved west in the wake of war, but as Wipey's story shows, local relationships of coexistence and cooperation were increasingly difficult to sustain, and of decreasing value, in a world of escalating population, pressures, and aggression.

In the decade or so leading up to the Revolution, American colonists in East Coast cities grew disaffected from the Crown on issues of royal authority, taxation, and liberty. But the roots of revolution also lay in the West and involved Scotch-Irish borderland inhabitants who increasingly defied colonial authorities, and whose defiance increasingly revolved around killing Indians. Following hard on the heels of the French and Indian War, Pontiac's War in 1763 was an Indigenous war of independence waged against the imposition of British imperial authority in the Great Lakes region. It was also, or became, a war about the relationship of Indian peoples to the empire and their status within it.[2] Colonial leaders, who had once promoted settling Scotch-Irish and other colonists in Indian country and among Indian peoples as a protective measure, now saw that stability in those same borderland regions demanded segregation. A firm boundary was necessary to keep peace.[3] Many tribal leaders agreed. Scotch-Irish people in the borderlands, however, resented and resisted the government's efforts to restrict their access to Indian lands and to regulate their dealings with Indian people, especially since, in their eyes, those efforts appeared to favor Indians at their expense. As we've seen, Arthur St. Clair was not the first colonial official and member of the eastern elite to view the Scotch-Irish and their neighbors as lawless "white savages" and to blame them as much as the Indians for the violence and disorder that permeated the frontier.

Contrary to backcountry settlers' complaints that the British government did nothing to protect them, the imperial government took measures that it believed would do just that. It kept an army of ten thousand troops in America to protect those backcountry settlers from Indians—and Indians from them—and it tried to keep peace and order on the frontier by keeping them apart. The Royal Proclamation in October 1763 was intended to halt colonial expansion at the Appalachian Mountains and reserve the territory between the Appalachians and the Mississippi for the Native peoples who lived there. Colonists who had crossed the mountains and who were now squatting illegally on Indian land were supposed to leave immediately and might be removed by British troops. Only the Crown's representatives acting in formal council with Native nations could negotiate land transfers. Indian relations were to be directed from London by a government with an imperial vision of American affairs, not by individual colonies pursuing local agendas, and much less by people living cheek by jowl with Indian people on the same lands.

Intended to remove "all just Cause of Discontent, and Uneasiness" among the tribes, the Proclamation generated outrage among Scotch-Irish backcountry settlers: the imperial government seemed to be favoring the Indians over the people who had borne the brunt of the Indians' raids. They were not alone in their outrage. Land speculators who had been poised after the war to reap the fruits of victory beyond the mountains could not rent or sell the land they owned or claimed there unless they had clear title to it, and now title to the land derived from the Crown, not from the Indians. Lacking legal title, speculators could not extract payment from or evict people who squatted on the lands they claimed. At the same time, the government asked the colonists to help shoulder the financial burden of maintaining the military establishment in North America. In 1765, Parliament passed the Stamp Act, a measure that is often considered the first step in the imperial crisis that led to the American Revolution.[4] Presbyterians, who had gained influence in the Pennsylvania Assembly after the Paxton Boys' show of strength undermined the Quakers' political position, took the lead in opposing the Stamp Act and moving toward independence.

The 1763 Proclamation aimed to create a line running down the spine of the Appalachians, one that would keep frontier settlers in place and in check, subject to imperial authority, and connected to British trade, but many colonists ignored it and continued to push onto Indian land. Despite the bloodletting of the previous eight years, some moved west into the eastern Ohio Valley as Indians moved there, recreating interethnic relationships with Native people at the very time the British government was trying to segregate them.[5] Scotch-Irish immigrants who had resented English laws at home were unlikely to obey them now that they were three thousand miles away. They were accustomed to ignoring governmental mandates; there were no courts beyond the line, and the British army lacked the resources to patrol and maintain it. In effect, the Proclamation created a kind of no-man's land beyond the line. To Scotch-Irish in the West, Britain's management of its new empire seemed designed to appease and protect Indians but withheld protection from its subjects, or at least those who crossed the line.[6]

The Black Boys

While colonial governments worried about Scotch-Irish settlers moving west, Scotch-Irish settlers in Cumberland County, Pennsylvania, worried about traders going west to supply the Indians. The French and Indian War had put Carlisle at the center of imperial conflict as a supply point and launching pad for military campaigns as well as a refuge for fleeing families, bringing new economic opportunities as well as fear and violence. Even after the war, the Scotch-Irish community was not united in its hatred of Indian people. Traders, merchants, retailers, packhorse men, wagon drivers, and others who depended on the Indian trade had to rebuild the frontier exchange economy and the relationships with Indian people it involved. Carlisle became the commercial and cultural capital of Scotch-Irish communities west of the Susquehanna, and Scotch-Irish merchants were among the town leaders. However, as trade followed Indian peoples who moved west across the mountains, fewer individual residents of Carlisle wanted or were able to participate. With the resources and organization to sustain long-distance trade, the Philadelphia mercantile firm of Bayton, Wharton, and Morgan took over the lion's share of the western fur business, anxious to recoup wartime losses and to open new markets in the interior, despite (and sometimes in violation of) increasing regulations and restrictions on their activities. Carlisle merchant Robert Callender successfully negotiated the waves of change. He was first a fur trader, then an Indian fighter at Kittanning, then a wagon master for the Forbes campaign, then a partner of Bayton, Wharton, and Morgan, and after that, their rival in the Illinois trade. Colonel Henry Bouquet, who employed him as a messenger to the tribe, said the Delawares "seem to like the man."[7]

However, fear and loathing of Indians among the general population in places such as Carlisle made merchants like Callender and companies like Bayton, Wharton, and Morgan suspect: what were they up to and what were they trading? Peddling guns and ammunition to Indians threatened the lives of people on the frontier, and the merchants' business links to Philadelphia conjured up suspicions that they were part of the Quaker-Indian conspiracy of which Scotch-Irish backcountry folk felt they were victims.

In March 1765 a group of vigilantes calling themselves the Black Boys attacked a wagon train carrying thousands of pounds of goods as it made the long and arduous climb up Sideling Hill in southwestern Cumberland County. The convoy was on its way from Philadelphia to Fort Pitt, where George Croghan was going to meet with tribal delegates to establish the peace and order envisioned by the Royal Proclamation. Local inhabitants, still smarting from the government's inattention to their suffering in Pontiac's War, saw this as more evidence that the Indians were receiving preferential treatment from, even being armed by, the colonial government. As commander-in-chief General Thomas Gage reported the event, "The People of the Frontiers, exasperated at Seeing Supply carried to the Indians, rose in Arms, disguised themselves, and pursued the Convoy in the Woods, where they killed some Horses, and burned and destroyed fourscore Horse-loads of goods, amongst which, were the Presents that had been provided by Mr. Croghan." Consciously associating the Black Boys with the Indian-killers of 1763, Samuel Wharton called them "the Paxton & other Rioters" and said they seized and destroyed $3,000 worth of goods at Sideling Hill. Robert Callender, who also petitioned for compensation for losses sustained in

Pontiac's War, lost a pack train of goods to the Black Boys and tried to have British troops bring them to justice.[8] Shocked by an action he denounced as "Illegal, Ill tim'd, & Ill judg'd," Scotch-Irish magistrate John Armstrong told Croghan that it was "Chiefly parpetrated [sic] by our Country-Men." There was widespread support among settlers on both sides of the Susquehanna for stopping the goods and "the Vulgar and common people all along the Frontier declare according to report, that none of the trespassers shou'd suffer Death."[9]

One of the leaders of the Black Boys was James Smith, the former captive whose rangers had dressed and painted like Indians when fighting Indians. Now they "blacked and painted" themselves again when they attacked the wagon train at Sideling Hill, and they kept a guard on the frontiers to prevent goods being sent to Indians.[10] In 1768, three years after Sideling Hill, Joseph Rigby, a backcountry agent for Bayton, Wharton, and Morgan, reported to his employers that the traders were "Surrounded by Ja-b-t-s [Jacobites?] who are continually prying into every Waggon and package that comes to the Gate to know the Contents, and often ask whether, there is any powder or Lead going back to kill the Sc-th Irishmen?"[11]

In fact, the Black Boys were more ethnically diverse than the Paxton Boys. They drew support from groups other than the Scotch-Irish, and from Maryland and Virginia as well as western Pennsylvania. The movement spread into a broader protest against government authority, with clashes against British troops at Fort Loudon, which John Armstrong had built as part of a line of defenses to protect settlers during the French and Indian War, and continued efforts to prevent traders from supplying Indians. Like the Paxton Boys, the Black Boys disputed the legitimacy of a government that appeared to do more for Indians than it did for them, although they demanded a renegotiation of political power on the frontier, not an overthrow of imperial government.[12] Government officials often regarded the Scotch-Irish as rebellious by nature, but their radicalism grew from their frontier experience and their conflicts with both Pennsylvania and trans-Atlantic hierarchies. Cumberland County's Black Boys resembled their Scotch-Irish counterparts in Northern Ireland—the Oakboys or Hearts of Oak, a protest movement of farmers and weavers that began in Country Armagh in 1761, and the Steelboys, or Hearts of Steel, a rent protest movement that started in Antrim in 1769—in rejecting British domination that had marginalized them and deprived them of political rights.[13]

Scotch-Irish people who had been encouraged to move to the frontier as instruments of colonial policy to prevent or at least contain Indian war now resisted and undermined a colonial policy that sought to secure peace and order. In the eyes of colonial officials, Scotch-Irish defiance and Indian-hating went hand in hand. "These Paxton, or Frontier People having a great inveteracy to all Indians, may possibly do some more mischief, as they have for a good while past, laid Aside all obedience to the Laws, or public Authority," wrote Sir William Johnson.[14] Thomas McKee, himself a Scotch-Irish trader and agent located at Paxton, met with a delegation of Delaware, Shawnee, Munsee, and Nanticoke chiefs at Fort Augusta or Shamokin in the spring of 1765 to restore peace and trade, and other Indians on the upper Susquehanna asked to meet with him. However, he informed Johnson, "such has been, and is the ungovernable, and riotous Disposition of the frontier Inhabitants that I dare not move a Step from my house, otherwise I should most certainly fall a Victim to their Rage, and Infatuation." He was convinced that any Native people who came close would be murdered, while settlers from Cumberland County continued to encroach on their land, cutting down trees and building cabins, which caused the Indians "real Disgust, and uneasiness."[15] There were disturbances in Cumberland County that spring.[16] A letter from Carlisle reported that a group of residents had gone to kill the Indians at Shamokin, which caused the Native people to flee from that place.[17]

Scotch-Irish antipathy toward Moravian Indian converts continued long after the Paxton march on Philadelphia in 1764. At the mission village of Friedenshütten (German for "Tents of Peace") in Bedford County near Bethlehem, a couple of hundred Native and non-Native Moravians lived in a dozen huts and forty houses "built of wood in the European manner" and surrounded by gardens and cornfields. In 1765 the community ran short of bread and a party of the brethren set out for Fort Allen to fetch corn provided by the government of Pennsylvania. Halfway there, they were obliged to turn back, "hearing that the white people in the Irish settlement were again exasperated against them." Two men had been murdered there and the Scotch-Irish blamed the Christian Indians. As Moravian minister George Henry Loskiel wrote in 1789, it had been common since the French and Indian War to regard the Moravians as "snakes in the grass."[18]

British officers and officials feared that Indian-hating backcountry settlers would scuttle efforts to preserve peace. There was little point in making treaties "if this Disposition of the People of the Frontiers, of killing every defenceless Indian met with" continued, General Gage told Bouquet.[19] Sir William Johnson shared Gage's antipathy toward frontier people, his attitudes perhaps sharpened by inherited Irish prejudices against Scotch-Irish Presbyterians. Complaining to Gage and to Governor Colden of New York about the "licentious Conduct of the Frontier People" of Pennsylvania, Johnson confessed he was sick and tired of people's ignorance and prejudices regarding Indian affairs which, "Exclusive of [the] riotous Conduct of persons worse than Savages," threatened to undo all peace efforts and to unite the tribes in a general war.[20] He had no doubt about which people were responsible. In February 1766, a party of Six Nations chiefs traveled to North Carolina to accompany a delegation of Tuscaroras back to Johnson Hall. As the chiefs passed through York County, the inhabitants abused them and made several attempts to murder them. The chiefs returned with the Tuscaroras in December. They were well treated by the inhabitants throughout their journey northward "until they came to *Paxton*," where the people "used them ill" and stole horses from them.[21]

The strategy of settling Indians near colonists as a buffer no longer worked if the colonists killed all the Indians. Backcountry Scotch-Irish now seemed to do so in defiance of the government as an assertion of their independence and autonomy. The Black Boys were revolutionaries, but their rebellion does not fit easily with the usual narratives about a struggle for liberty, or work well as a morality tale or a founding legend. While colonists in the East protested against taxation and resisted imperial restraints, the Black Boys were motivated by fear and loathing of Indians as much as by ideals of rights and liberty. They wanted to be free of Indians as much as to be free of imperial authority. Resentful of eastern elites who seemed to govern in their own interests and of British officials who seemed to put Indian land and Indian trade before the safety of frontier families, the Black Boys echoed the claims of the Paxton Boys. They justified their actions in fighting Indians and corrupt officials as acts of patriotism, and they wanted to create a frontier society that excluded Indians, not one that included them.[22] The provincial government proved no more able to punish the Black Boys than it had the Paxton Boys.

Too Lawless and Licentious Ever to Be Restrained

Anti-Indian actions generally went unpunished on the Scotch-Irish frontier in Virginia as well as in Pennsylvania. Upper Shenandoah Valley leaders tried to distinguish between friendly and unfriendly Indians and to avoid action that might turn friends into enemies. Local settlers rarely drew such careful distinctions and were often suspicious of those who did.[23]

In May 1765, ten Overhill Cherokees on their way to Fort Cumberland stayed with Colonel Andrew Lewis of the Augusta militia at Staunton. He hosted them for two nights and furnished them with passes for safe conduct to Winchester, but the morning after they left, twenty or thirty locals ambushed and murdered five of the Cherokees. Lewis promptly arrested two of the perpetrators, James Clendinning and Patrick Duffy. He said the killers were "poor blinded creatures who have not considered that in consequence of what they have done our frontier inhabitants who are innocent of the crime may be cut to pieces by a nation of Indians who otherwise would have lived in amity with us." Unfortunately, Lewis's neighbors did not see things that way. Clendinning was rescued before he even got to jail, and an armed mob broke down the doors of the prison with axes and freed Duffy. They declared "that they had most of the County to back them, and that they would never suffer a man to be confined or brought to justice for killing Savages." Calling themselves the Augusta Boys, they issued a proclamation condemning the Virginia government for failing to protect the frontier and offered £1,000 for Lewis's head. Governor Francis Fauquier issued a proclamation condemning the act and sent a copy to the Cherokees to show them he was doing everything he could to bring the criminals to justice. However, he told the Board of Trade, he feared the people on the frontiers would rather be at war with Indians than live in peace with them and he did not have the military resources to enforce obedience to the law. Lewis moved away from Staunton to a new home on the Roanoke River.[24]

The next summer the Cherokee chief Attakullakulla asked "why the Governor and his beloved men, did not catch the rogues." If the British could not catch them, he said they must send large presents for the relatives of the victims. Colonial officials discussed reparations but failed to provide them. In the winter of 1766–1767, Cherokees supposedly murdered a dozen traders from Virginia; General Gage suspected the killings were committed by "Relations of those Cherokees who were put to Death in Virginia two years ago."[25]

Military officers and colonial officials tried to stem the invasion of those occupying unpurchased Indian lands. They knew that "if Rascals from the Frontiers are allowed to come and take possession of the Indians Country before it is purchased from them, it will be impossible to prevent a Rupture with the Indians in which the Innocent may suffer as well as the Guilty." Governor Fauquier issued proclamations ordering settlers to evacuate lands west of the Alleghenies. If they failed to do so, they could expect no protection or mercy from the government and would be "exposed to the revenge of the exasperated Indians," he warned. But he was no more able to keep frontier settlers off Indian lands than he was to stop them from murdering Indian people.[26]

Squatting and the attendant possibility of racial violence that threatened British imperial policy were particularly acute at places like Redstone Creek, a tributary of the Monongahela River, which had long been a meeting ground and a contested ground for hunters, farmers, and fighters from various colonies and Indian nations. In violation of the Royal Proclamation, hundreds of families from Pennsylvania, Virginia, and Maryland settled in the fertile bottomlands of the Redstone, Monongahela, and Cheat valleys, on lands that had not been purchased from the Indians. A fortified Scotch-Irish settlement was established at the junction of Redstone Creek and the Monongahela in 1765. Gage ordered detachments of British troops from Fort Pitt to expel them. At Redstone Creek in June 1766, Captain Alexander Mackay, with a company of soldiers and "in the presence of some Indian Chiefs now along with me," issued a notice ordering the squatters to return to their colonies without delay. If they remained where they were, he would seize their goods and merchandise, the Indians would be encouraged to mete out justice themselves, and "you lawless People must look upon yourselves as the Cause of whatever may be the consequence hurtful to your Persons and Estates."[27]

Many, if not most, of the people being given fair warning were Scotch-Irish. The person giving the warning was a Scotsman. Mackay commanded a unit of the 42nd Regiment, more famously known as the Black Watch. Highland soldiers of the Black Watch had earned a reputation for heroism and sacrifice in the Seven Years War, and in Pontiac's War they had marched with Colonel Henry Bouquet, a Swiss officer, to the relief of Fort Pitt, fending off Shawnee and Delaware warriors in a two-day battle at Bushy Run. The Black Watch had helped secure the lands west of the Appalachians for the British Empire and, it must have seemed to Scotch-Irish people on the frontier, for settlement. Now, with Indian chiefs in attendance, Black Watch officers served notice on Scotch-Irish squatters to vacate those lands in accordance with a Proclamation issued in London. When historians use terms like "Anglo-Indian relations" or the "Indian-white frontier," we obscure the layered complexities of such colonial encounters.

Mackay was pursuing a lost cause, and the British government could not stem the flood. Notwithstanding all the efforts to remove the people settled on Redstone Creek and the Cheat River, George Croghan was convinced there were twice as many people in those two settlements in October 1767 than ever before.[28] Laws to remove squatters and prevent others from settling on unpurchased Indian lands proved ineffective. Driving settlers off the land and "destroying a parcel of vile Hutts" was little use, Gage told Shelburne, because they received no punishment and simply returned in greater numbers.[29]

And Scotch-Irish murders of Indian people continued. In 1766 a fifty-year-old man named James Annin and a teenager named James McKinsey or McKenzie were hanged for murdering Hannah and Catherine, two Native women, one of whom was pregnant, whom they attacked with intent to rape as the women walked home from shopping in Moorestown, New Jersey.[30] Their punishment was an exception to the general rule. Governors Penn and Fauquier struggled in vain to bring Indian-killers to justice because so many backcountry people regarded killing Indians as a meritorious act. The murderers were generally "Vagrant Persons, beyond the settled parts of the Country" and beyond the reach of the law. If they were apprehended, they were likely to be freed from jail by an angry mob. If they went to trial, they were unlikely to be convicted. "The Difficulties of bringing those lawless Ruffians to punishment encourages them to every Excess," wrote General Gage. Penn said that orders to remove squatters carried little weight with "a People who had the hardiness to Settle in a Country of Savages, and lay themselves continually exposed to their Fury and Resentment." He was at a loss to know what else the civil authorities could do "to compel these lawless People to Obedience" and hoped Gage would apply military force. Fauquier told the Earl of Shelburne he found it baffling that the very people who screened Indian-killers from justice were the first to be exposed to Indian attack, "in so much that I am confident they desire and wish for nothing so much as an Indian War."[31]

The message of government impotence in the face of backcountry violence was reinforced when Frederick Stump, a thirty-three-year-old German settler, and his nineteen-year-old servant John Ironcutter murdered ten Indian people, including three women and three children, on Middle Creek in Cumberland County in 1768. Captain William Patterson and a posse of twenty men apprehended Stump and put him in the Carlisle jail, but a predominantly Scotch-Irish mob of seventy or eighty armed men stormed the jail and freed him, despite the efforts of Colonel John Armstrong and the magistrates to block entry. The "ignorant & giddy Crowd who have committed this hasty flagrant violation of the established course of justice," Armstrong informed the governor, were under the mistaken impression that Stump was to be taken to Philadelphia for trial and were determined to prevent it. They complained that the government always showed "greater concern at the killing or Death of an Indian than at the Death or killing of one of them"; that it made no such efforts to apprehend Indians who murdered frontier people; "that their Wives & Children must be threatened & insulted by the Indians, and that a Number of them must receive the fatal Blow before they dare say it is War." Efforts to persuade "these piteous & distracted People" that their actions only made things worse proved futile, Armstrong wrote. "These Madmen" kept Stump and his servant hidden "somewhere beyond the Mountains."[32] Stump moved on. He was one of the first white settlers in the Cumberland country near Nashville, and the Stump family became one of the wealthiest in the region.[33]

Like other Native nations, the Iroquois were deeply concerned about the Stump murders.[34] No sooner were the murders committed than Thomas McKee went to Shamokin and spent two days doing everything he could to reassure and appease them.[35]

Gage knew that nothing was more likely to spark conflict with the Indians than invading their lands. Justice and self-interest alike meant it was better to protect their lands and to trade with them, while confining settlers within the present colonies would keep them more closely tied to British commerce and more closely regulated by British law and government. He thought there was room enough for them to spread "for a century to come." Unfortunately, backcountry settlers did not share Gage's sentiments. Neither the government's efforts nor fear of the Indians kept them within bounds, he told Lord Hillsborough. They were "too Numerous, too Lawless and Licentious ever to be restrained."[36]

In what became a pattern, repeated time and again, the violence that erupted along the frontier when colonists defied the government's authority and breached the boundary gave the same government leverage in persuading Native leaders to move the boundary. In the fall of 1768, John Stuart, the British superintendent of Indian affairs in the South, negotiated a treaty with the Cherokees at Hard Labor in South Carolina. It moved the boundary established by the Proclamation west to the Kanawha River but left Kentucky and southwestern Virginia to the Cherokees.[37] Meanwhile, in the North, Sir William Johnson met with some two thousand Iroquois at Fort Stanwix in New York. The home government had authorized Johnson to secure an extension of the boundary down the Ohio River as far as the Kanawha River, where it would meet up with Stuart's new boundary. Instead, Johnson obtained a land cession that stretched another four hundred miles down the Ohio to the mouth of the Cherokee or Tennessee River, opening Kentucky and the common hunting ground of the Cherokees and Shawnees to invasion. The new boundary lines formed by the Fort Stanwix and Cherokee treaties drove a huge wedge into the heart of Indian country. The lines did not hold, and neither did the peace.[38]

As colonists pushed west onto lands the Shawnees and Cherokees still regarded as theirs, in April 1769, Pennsylvania opened a land office for the sale of lands in the areas purchased at Fort Stanwix. Southwestern Pennsylvania and the Forks of the Susquehanna were opened to settlers.[39] Large numbers of Scotch-Irish, American-born from the Cumberland Valley as well as new arrivals from Ulster, applied for land warrants. They crossed the mountains on the road General Forbes had constructed in his 1758 campaign against Fort Duquesne, formed a chain of settlements along the length of the road, and established farms near Fort Pitt. Hanna's Town was founded in 1758 when Scotch-Irish immigrant Robert Hanna built a log house there, thirty miles from Fort Pitt. Located on Forbes's Road, Hanna's structure served as a tavern and boarding house. By 1769, Hanna had mapped out a town of seventy plots covering 370 acres. By 1773, Hanna's Town was the county seat of Westmoreland County.[40] Encouraged by Governor Lord Dunmore and the Ohio Company, another stream of migrants, many of whom were also Scotch-Irish, flowed into the area from Virginia, producing clashes as magistrates, militia, and settlers of the rival colonies vied for control.[41]

Rival colonists also clashed in the Wyoming Valley, and some of the Paxton Boys moved there and continued to defy Pennsylvania's authority and oppose its land policies. Although many Delaware people lived in the region, the Iroquois claimed jurisdiction over it. At the Albany Congress in 1754, agents of Connecticut land companies had purchased millions of acres in the upper Susquehanna and Delaware valleys from Iroquois delegates in dubious circumstances. At the same time, Pennsylvania's delegation had acquired a deed from the Iroquois to much of the same land. Delaware anger at the cessions fueled their attacks and determined many of their targets during the French and Indian War. At the end of the war, Connecticut's Susquehanna Company began sending settlers to occupy the

Wyoming Valley. Teedyuscung, who led Delaware opposition to the occupation, was burned to death in his sleep when arsonists set fire to his village. Teedyuscung's son, known as Captain Bull, led vengence raids, and the British government tried to stop the Connecticut invasion for fear it would provoke conflict with the Iroquois.

Nevertheless, the intrusions continued. Pennsylvania and the Connecticut land companies intensified their struggle for possession after the Treaty of Fort Stanwix in 1768 ostensibly extinguished Indian title to the region. The next year, Lazarus Stewart made a deal with the Susquehanna Company. Stewart, from Donegal, Pennsylvania, was the grandson of Ulster emigrants and a member of the Paxton Boys; according to one report, he was the ringleader in the assault on the Lancaster jail.[42] Disaffected with Pennsylvania's land policies, which they felt deprived frontier settlers of equitable access, he and his followers agreed to rid the Wyoming Valley of Pennsylvanian claimants in return for promises of a grant of land along the North Branch of the Susquehanna. In 1770 Stewart and about fifty Scotch-Irish men from Lancaster Country, including his brother, three sons, and other kinsmen, relocated to northeastern Pennsylvania and joined forces with the Connecticut colonists, igniting open violence and destruction of property. Whites were now fighting whites instead of Indians for the land, though men on both sides dressed and painted like Indians, blaming the bloodshed and damage on "White Indians." Pennsylvania governor John Penn reminded his uncle Thomas that Stewart's "banditti" were the same "lawless villains" who had massacred the Conestoga Indians at Lancaster. Proclamations were issued for Stewart's arrest, but after much fighting and looting, Stewart's men and the Susquehanna Company prevailed and the Pennsylvania claimants withdrew—to the chagrin of both Pennsylvania and the Six Nations, whose southern door no longer seemed secure.[43]

Scotch-Irish colonists moved into the "New Purchase" lands transferred by the Treaty of Fort Stanwix and they squatted on the West Branch of the Susquehanna.[44] Instances of wary coexistence with Indian people in the region continued—as Philip Vickers Fithian, a tutor traveling through the area, found to his alarm when staying with a Scotch-Irish family whose home Indian people felt free to enter without knocking.[45] Nevertheless, increasing population intensified the pressure on Indian lands and simultaneously reduced the need for settler communities to maintain networks of cooperation with Native communities.[46] On New Year's Day 1770, George Croghan reported to General Gage that so many settlements had been made on the East and West branches of the Susquehanna as a result of the Fort Stanwix cession that the Native people there "have no hunting grounds left." The Wyandots in northwestern Ohio had agreed to give the displaced people lands on which to plant and hunt, and trader Alexander Mckee, who lived among the Shawnees, said he had already seen about fifty families of Delawares and Shawnees moving west; the rest planned to depart in the spring. One Delaware chief informed his Quaker friends that he intended to leave his present settlement at Great Island on the Susquehanna and move to Kuskusky, a town on a branch of the Ohio River, because his people had "no Right to Lands on Susquehanna River" and it was "discouraging to work the Land of Others."[47] The Shawnees began to build a confederacy of Indigenous allies alienated by the collusion of the Six Nations and the British at Fort Stanwix. They called the Iroquois "slaves of the white people."[48]

Pushing In

Scotch-Irish colonists poured into the wedge of territory beyond the Appalachians created by the Treaties of Hard Labor and Fort Stanwix and pushed deep into Indian country. They occupied the new lands much as they had previous lands. Speculators had to establish their claims to large tracts of land by going through the proper channels and having the lands surveyed and registered. Squatters employed less formal and more violent methods of establishing ownership. They cleared fields and built fences and cabins with the axe, defended their new property with the gun, and often defied and disputed the legal claims and surveys of their "betters."[49] They knew from long and hard experience by this point that imperial policies were often multifaceted and contradictory, that local interpretations of the law usually mattered more than imperial ones, and that wealthy and well-connected colonists tended to take advantage of such contradictions to enrich themselves at the expense of ordinary folk who hoped to own their own land. Their physical occupation of the land gave them a claim to title amid competing and messy land policies.[50]

Like other colonists, they not only encroached on Indian lands; they also encroached on the deer and other game that Indians claimed as their own. They followed prey across boundary lines and claimed that game-rich country like Kentucky constituted common hunting territory, not an Indian reserve. By the 1760s, in the heavily Scotch-Irish region at the headwaters of Holston River in southwestern Virginia, parties of backcountry men congregated each fall to make "long hunts" across the mountains. These "long hunters" were no more inclined to observe Indigenous hunting ethics than they were to observe British proclamations.[51] Daniel Boone, born to an English Quaker family in Pennsylvania in 1734, is commonly credited with leading the colonial advance into Kentucky, although according to the nineteenth-century historian Lyman Draper, Boone's "precursor and pilot" to Kentucky was the Irish-born Indian trader John Finley or Findley, who had emigrated to the Scotch-Irish settlement around Carlisle, Pennsylvania, and served with Boone on Braddock's campaign. Findley apparently turned up at Boone's home on the upper Yadkin in the winter of 1768–1769 with stories of the rich hunting to be found in Kentucky. Findley, Boone, and other Yadkin neighbors began making hunting trips to the region, to the chagrin of the Shawnees, who caught and expelled Boone and his companions and confiscated their hauls of furs.[52] "The Elks are our horses, the Buffaloes are our cows, the deer are our sheep, & the whites shan't have them," the Delaware chief Killbuck told the Reverend David McClure. White hunters ignored Indigenous hunting rituals and slaughtered game wastefully. Shawnees said they were "like crazy people and want to shove us off our land entirely."[53]

They were not all crazy, but they kept coming. "Long hunters" pushed into Tennessee as well as Kentucky. Eastern Tennessee consists of a great forested valley that runs from northeast to southwest, between the Cumberland range to the west and the Great Smoky Mountains and the Unaka Mountains that straddle the border with North Carolina to the east. As had happened elsewhere, the first movements of settler colonist populations paralleled rather than crossed the mountain ranges, and followed the watercourses of the Clinch, Holston, Watauga, Nolichucky, and French Broad rivers down as they flowed into the Tennessee River.[54] James Knox, John Montgomery, and James Dysart were all young Scotch-Irish hunters who had emigrated from Northern Ireland.[55] Knox, who had emigrated when he was fourteen, led a party of some forty hunters from southwestern Virginia to the Cumberland region. (He later rose to the rank of major, settled in Kentucky, where he married the widow of Benjamin Logan, and became a wealthy member of the state legislature.)[56] John Montgomery was in his early twenties when he went to the Cumberland. (He later fought in the border warfare of the Revolution, served on George Rogers Clark's expedition into the Illinois country, and founded Clarkesville on the Cumberland River. He was killed by Indians at the mouth of the river in 1794.)[57] James Dysart, an orphan, migrated to Philadelphia in 1761 when he was fourteen and then gradually worked his way south and west to the heavily Scotch-Irish area on the Holston. From there, he hunted the Cumberland.

Colonists began settling Tennessee in the 1770s. Tennessee historians long assumed and asserted that Scotch-Irish settlers played a dominant role in defining the character of the state. The First Families of Tennessee project, however, indicates that few of the earliest settlers arrived direct from Ireland; most came via Pennsylvania, Virginia, and Maryland, and most were children or grandchildren of Irish-born immigrants. There were also English, Germans, Scots, Welsh, French, and Dutch. From their earliest years, French Lick, near Nashville, and other places farther west were much more ethnically and culturally mixed than the Scotch-Irish world of the Holston Valley.[58]

Nevertheless, Scotch-Irish people and people from Scotch-Irish communities were at the forefront. William Bean, a Scot, and his wife, Lydia, selected a homestead in Tennessee's Watauga Valley in 1769, then part of North Carolina, which became known as Bean's Station. James Robertson (1742–1814) (Figure 8.1) followed the Bean family across the mountains two years later. Born in Brunswick County, Virginia, Robertson was the eldest son of a Scotch-Irish immigrant father. After his father's death, James in his youth moved with his family down the Valley of Virginia to Wake County, North Carolina, where he married Charlotte Reeves, with whom he had eleven children. He moved his growing family west to Orange County, North Carolina, around 1766. From there, in 1770, he crossed the mountains alone to the Watauga Valley in Tennessee, planted corn in an old Indian field, and then returned home. The next year he led his own and several other families to the Watauga. Like many men on the backcountry, Robertson wanted land for his family.[59]

In defiance of both the Royal Proclamation of 1763 and the Treaty of Hard Labor in 1768, and beyond the control of Virginia and North Carolina, groups of Scotch-Irish people settled in the Watauga Valley near the Overhill Cherokee towns (Map 8.1). The Cherokees refused to sell land to the people on the Watauga but allowed them to rent the land and to harvest the crops they planted, on condition that they then move back across the boundary. According to Moses Fisk, a Dartmouth graduate, professor, and minister who moved to Tennessee in 1795 to pursue a career as a lawyer and land speculator, the squatters lived in harmony at this time with the Cherokees, "the only power by which they were recognized." By 1772,

Figure 8.1 James Robertson. Often called the "father of Middle Tennessee," Robertson was a leader in both the Watauga and Cumberland settlements and a prominent figure in relations with the Cherokees and Chickasaws.

Portrait of James Robertson, commissioned after the general's death and attributed to Washington B. Cooper, 1835; courtesy of Tennessee State Museum.

there were about one hundred predominantly Scotch-Irish farms on the banks of the Watauga and Holston Rivers. That year, the colonists established the Watauga Association, organizing a government for their mountain community and to manage land affairs. They also negotiated a ten-year lease with the Cherokees. The Cherokees tolerated them as a source of trade,

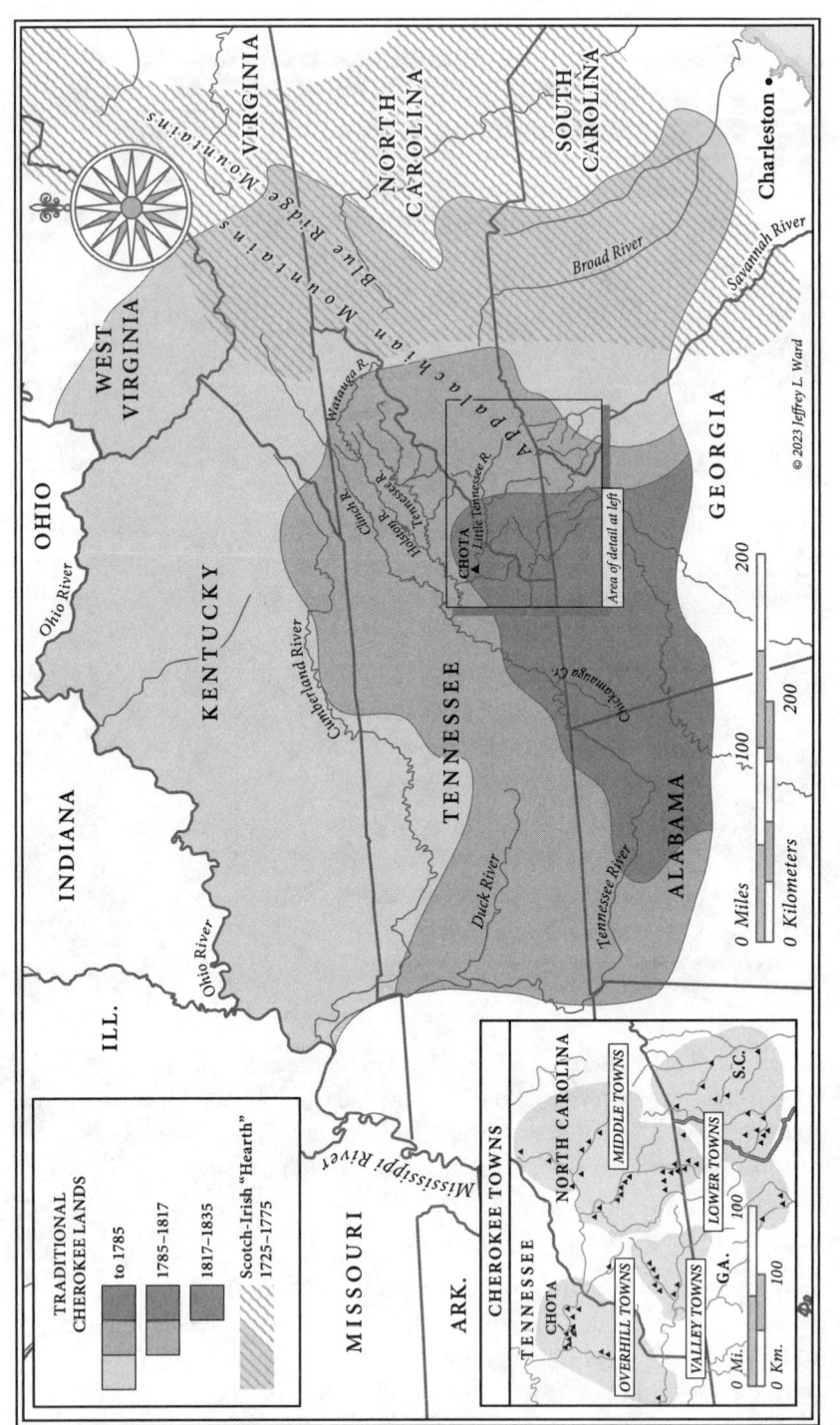

Map 8.1 Scotch-Irish settlement areas in the Upland South and Cherokee country.

though they grew increasingly uneasy at the encroachment on their hunting grounds. Oconostota, an Overhill Cherokee war leader, told Colonel Andrew Lewis and William Preston in July 1774 that he wanted peace, but that they must stop their people from breaching the boundary line. British Indian agent Alexander Cameron warned the Wataugans to remove from the Cherokees' hunting grounds or be driven off by force. The settlers, however, stayed put.[60] Writing to Lord Dartmouth, Governor Dunmore of Virginia described them as "a set of People" who "finding they could not obtain titles to the Land they fancied," formed their own ruling structures and effectively created a separate state, upsetting the peace and setting "a dangerous example to the people of America of forming governments distinct from and independent of His Majesty's Authority." In Theodore Roosevelt's words, in his book *The Winning of the West*, written in the 1880s but published in 1902, the Wataugans were people who "bid defiance to outside foes."[61]

Scotch-Irish colonists who flouted government regulations of the land as property also ignored Indigenous occupation of it as homeland. "The white people upon the frontier are all inveterate against the Indians because they have any land left them," Alexander Cameron, a Scot and British Indian agent among the Cherokees, told John Stuart, another Scot and British Indian superintendent in the South.[62] Just back from Indian country in April 1771, the Carlisle merchant Robert Callender warned Governor John Penn that an Indian war was brewing. The Ohio nations were furious that the Six Nations at Fort Stanwix had sold lands that were not theirs to sell. The Shawnees were working to build multi-tribal resistance and had robbed some Virginia traders. Callender feared for the safety of settlers west of the mountains. Although the people at Redstone had murdered one of their men, the Delawares reassured Callender that they understood that there were foolish and ungovernable people among the whites, just as there were among Indians.[63] Killbuck conveyed a more ominous message, however. "We find your people are very fond of our rich land," he told the governors of Virginia, Pennsylvania, and Maryland. Whites had swarmed "over the Great Mountains and settled throughout this Country" and would soon be crossing the Ohio. If the governors could not restrain their people, the chiefs would not be able to control their young men, who had seen nation after nation destroyed and realized "it must be soon their turn also to be exterminated."[64] George Croghan conceded in a letter that this was likely true, and that frontier people had "too great a Spirit ... for killing Indians."[65]

Things deteriorated when Britain withdrew imperial authority in the West. After Parliament in 1766 repealed the Stamp Act, which had been intended to finance the military presence necessary to protect settlers from Indians and Indians from settlers, the government evacuated all but the most vital western posts and abandoned Fort Pitt in 1772.[66] General Gage hoped the Indians would act as a check on western settlers, and if the latter continued to "force the Savages into Quarrels by using them ill," he wrote Viscount Barrington, "let them feel the Consequences, we shall be out of the scrape."[67]

In fact, the withdrawal of British troops confirmed western settlers' beliefs that the government was abandoning them to their savage enemies, and rendered it even less likely that assaults on Indians would be punished. Richard Penn, acting as governor while his brother was in England, informed the Pennsylvania Assembly in January 1773 that the evacuation of Fort Pitt "greatly alarmed the Inhabitants of this Province settled beyond the Allegheny Mountains, who have been used to look upon that Fortress as their Safeguard against the Incursions of the Indians." They had sent many petitions expressing concern at the dangerous situation they were in and asking the government for relief.[68] British failure to protect the frontiers became a central argument for independence.[69] It was a familiar story for Scotch-Irish people in the backcountry.

Hundreds of families were on the move across the Appalachians into the Ohio country, where they competed for resources in Indian homelands and hunting grounds.[70] An Indian interpreter saw thirty or forty people settled on the banks of the Ohio, many of whom, Gage told Lord Hillsborough, "were half-naked, chiefly covered with loose, coarse, linen frocks, such as the Frontier People manufacture for themselves, and paint or colour with bark, and they differ little from the Indians in their manner of life." With no means to purchase clothing except by bartering skins, they were induced to live by hunting, intruding on the Indians' lands, and that led to "quarrels and murthers."[71]

In the diary he kept of his travel through western Pennsylvania, across the Appalachians, and into the Ohio country in 1772–1773, Reverend David McClure noted that most of the people on the move were Scotch-Irish, people from the north of Ireland or their descendants, who had moved from the middle colonies. McClure's own grandparents had emigrated to Boston from the north of Ireland, descendants of Scots Highlanders who had settled there in the reign of King James I. Stopping in Carlisle, McClure noted: "The people principally scotch-irish. Two presbyterian churches." When he passed through McCallister's Gap to the west side of the Appalachians, he found "the inhabitants of this country, many miles around, are Scotch-Irish," with more moving daily into the region. In the Ligonier Valley the settlement consisted of "about 100 families, principally Scotch & Irish." With no permanent minister or church west of the Appalachians, McClure worried, "Truly the people here, in this new country, are as sheep scattered upon the Mountains, without a Shepherd." McClure, a Congregationalist, noted they were chiefly Scotch-Irish Presbyterians. He repeated the observation on returning from the Ohio country, in the area of Shippensburg, where he preached to a congregation of about three hundred families. "The people of this settlement are almost all of scotch irish descent. Immigrants from the North of Ireland, or descendants of such. They are presbyterians, well instructed in the principles of religion." Like many eastern visitors, McClure described the people living on the frontiers as "generally white Savages," who subsisted by hunting and lived like the Indians. "Murders between them and Indians, when they meet in hunting, are said sometimes to happen," he added.[72]

McClure penned a sympathetic portrait of these families on the move. Near Ligonier, he overtook several families who were relocating to the western country from older settlements in Pennsylvania, Maryland, and New Jersey. "Their patience and perseverance in poverty and fatigue were wonderful. They were not only patient, but cheerful, and pleased themselves with the expectation of seeing happy days beyond the mountains." He described one large family—twelve in all. "The man carried an ax and gun on his shoulders—the Wife, the rim of a spinning wheel in one hand, and a loaf of bread in another." The children meanwhile carried what they could. "Two poor horses, each heavily loaded with some poor necessaries, on the top of the baggage of one, was an infant, rocked to sleep in a kind of wicker cage, lashed securely to the horse." They had a cow "destined to bear her proportion of service, a bed-cord was wound around her horns, and a bag of meal on her back." In all, the portrait is one of "poor and enterprising people, who leave their old habitations and connections, and go in quest of lands for themselves and children, & with the hope of the enjoyment of independence, in their worldly circumstances, where land is good & cheap."[73]

In 1763, few Europeans lived west of the Proclamation line; by 1774, just over a decade later, as many as 50,000 did.[74] In 1768, when the Treaty of Fort Stanwix opened the region to colonial settlers, few white people lived in Kentucky. Scotch-Irish were among the first. In 1773, while James Harrod led a group of colonists from Pennsylvania, and Daniel Boone and William Russell led another from North Carolina, James, Robert, and George McAfee and a small party from Virginia traveled cross-country to the Salt River. The McAfee brothers seem representative. Their ancestors had migrated from the Scottish Lowlands between Glasgow and Edinburgh and settled in Antrim and Armagh in the reign of James I or Charles II. The family migrated to Newcastle, Delaware, in 1739 and settled on the Susquehanna. The Irish trader Richard Butler sent the McAfee party a letter from Chillicothe, warning that the Shawnees claimed "an absolute rite to the country you are about to settle" and which the Iroquois had no power to sell. Nevertheless, Butler continued, "I do assure you that it lies in your power to have good neighbors or bad, as they are a people very capable of discerning between good treatment and ill. They expect you to be friendly with them, and endeavor to restrain the hunters from destroying the game." Butler anticipated that should pose no problem, since the McAfees intended to cultivate the land rather than hunt it. The McAfee party planned to return to Kentucky in 1774 to build cabins and plant corn, establishing their claims to the land by occupying and improving it. By then, however, Lord Dunmore had declared war between Virginia and the Shawnees, and the trip had to be postponed until the following year. In 1774, the McAfee brothers joined Andrew Lewis's army that marched against the Shawnees.[75]

Lord Dunmore's War

Often portrayed as born warriors, Indian people faced Scotch-Irish frontiersmen who, according to some writers, were "born fighting." Often portrayed as nomads with no fixed attachment to the land, Indian people faced Scotch-Irish invaders who, according to colonial officials, acted like nomads. Lord Dunmore and his elite Virginian associates had their eyes, and soon their hands, on Shawnee lands, but, to hear Dunmore tell it, it was "the emigrating Spirit" of the people on the frontiers that caused conflict. Mainly Scotch-Irish and Germans, they moved "as their avidity and restlessness incite them. They acquire no attachment to Place: But wandering about Seems engrafted in their Nature," always imagining that "Lands further off, are Still better than those upon which they are already Settled." Such people could not conceive that government had any right to stop them from taking possession of territory that was uninhabited or occupied only by a few scattered tribes of Indians, or that they need respect treaty pledges made to people they considered as "little removed from the brute Creation." In Dunmore's view, backwoodsmen were "Hunters like the Indians and equally ungovernable." Unruly frontier people like the Scotch-Irish offered Dunmore a ready excuse as he tried to explain to the home government in London why a war, appropriately named after him, happened.[76] Colonial authorities commonly initiated policies and generated conflicts that spawned violence, and then distanced themselves from the violence and denounced the people who, they claimed, were responsible for it.[77]

In the spring of 1774, Michael Cresap, the son of the combative and controversial Thomas Cresap, and a posse of frontier militia attacked some Shawnee chiefs returning from Pittsburgh.[78] Then, at the mouth of Yellow Creek, a settler named Daniel Greathouse and another group of thugs murdered a family of Native people, including the wife, youngest son, and daughter of Shikellamy, and the Shawnee wife of Shikellamy's son, Logan. Logan's sister Koonay was carrying a baby, about two months old, whom the killers carried off. Logan's grief became immortalized in various versions of a speech attributed to him, especially the one recorded by Thomas Jefferson in *Notes on the State of Virginia*, first published in Paris in 1785. Recruiting Shawnee and Mingo warriors to his cause, Logan vowed to exact vengeance.[79]

Despite its horrific details, the Yellow Creek massacre revealed evidence of coexistence as well as violence. It occurred at Baker's Bottom, a settlement located directly across from a Shawnee and Mingo town on Yellow Creek. Socializing between the communities was not unusual, and the Indian people apparently suspected nothing amiss when their neighbors invited them to come over and drink rum. One Native woman was evidently "in the habit" of crossing the Ohio River to get milk from Mrs. Baker, who gave her milk for her two small children. As the killers went about their bloody business, Logan's sister begged mercy for her baby, telling them that "it was a Kin to themselves." The baby was eventually returned to its father, John Gibson of Carlisle.[80]

John Gibson was born in Lancaster, Pennsylvania, in 1740, where his father, a Scotch-Irish immigrant from Stewarts Town in Ulster, ran the Hickory Tree Tavern, which was frequented by local Indian people.[81] John entered the Indian trade and served as a soldier in the French and Indian War and in General Forbes's campaign against Fort Duquesne. He was captured by Delawares at the outbreak of Pontiac's War with two companions, both of whom were tortured to death. Gibson was spared by an old woman, who adopted him in the place of a son she had lost. Returned with other captives to Colonel Henry Bouquet at Muskingum the next year, he resumed trading at Pittsburgh. He lived with and may have married Logan's sister. According to one account, it was Gibson who translated Logan's speech into English and wrote it down. Despite his personal loss, Gibson served in Dunmore's War, fighting against the Indians.[82]

Once again, Scotch-Irish and other frontier settlers recoiled from the impending Indian attacks. "It is lamentable to see the multitudes of poor people that are hourly running down the country," reported one correspondent from Bedford at the end of May; "such as stay, are building forts; God knows how it will turn out with them." Shawnees said they had nothing against Pennsylvania, only Virginia, but Pennsylvanians expected to feel their wrath once the fighting started.[83] Once again, the anticipated horrors of an Indian war sparked petitions, rumors, and false alarms.[84] Writing to William Johnson in June, Governor John Penn reported panic spreading "to such a Degree that there is just Reason to apprehend a total Desertion of that Country." He asked Johnson to get the Six Nations to act as mediators with the Shawnees and Delawares. Unfortunately, Johnson died on July 11, in the middle of a council urging the Indians to restrain from war. General Gage told Lord Dartmouth a week later that the frontier people, especially in Virginia, had "taken so much Pains to bring on an Indian War," brutally slaughtering a number of Indians, that only Johnson's skill and influence had prevented every tribe from joining the war.[85]

As soon as Alexander McKee learned of the killings, he dispatched former captive Simon Girty to try to stop tribes from going to war. Girty escorted the Delaware chief White Eyes and his family to and from a meeting at Fort Pitt, where McKee and the Seneca chief Guyasuta assured each other that the Baker's Bottom murders and Shawnee retaliations did not reflect the disposition of the majority of settlers, nor that of the Delawares and Six Nations.[86] This was more than just rhetoric; it reflected the complexity of the border country, where people's actions often followed local grievances and loyalties rather than racial lines. Yet, increasingly, race hatred drove people to violence. Trader Richard Butler, who was with the Shawnees at Pittsburgh, declared in an affidavit that, whatever their intentions for the future, the Shawnees did not want war at the time, although the cold-blooded murders were "sufficient to bring on a war with a Christian instead of a Savage People." He feared the actions and prejudices of the majority of "the White People in this part of the Country" would cause a general Indian war because there was little effort "to restrain the common people whose prejudice leads them to greater lengths than ought to be shown by civilized people."[87] Born in Dublin, Butler had migrated with his family and grew up in Lancaster and Carlisle. He knew the people he was talking about.

Logan took his revenge by killing thirteen settlers and then declared his vengeance satisfied. The murders, however, played into the hands of men who coveted Shawnee lands. An Indian war not only provided justification for a land grab, but would also send squatters scurrying east to safety, leaving the field open for wealthy speculators to amass large holdings, which they could rent to settlers once the war was over. Whether or not Dunmore and Virginian land speculators manufactured the war, as Pennsylvanians then and many historians since have argued, they seized the opportunity to punish and dispossess the Shawnees.[88] Many Virginians had been waiting for a chance like this.[89]

Although Dunmore's War was named after a Scottish governor, the muster rolls suggest it was largely a Scotch-Irish fight. For example, when Indians attacked a militia company sent in pursuit of Logan's raiding party at Ten Mile Creek, a tributary of the Monongahela, they killed and scalped Captain Francis McClure, and wounded his lieutenant, Samuel Kinkade.[90]

The war offered a number of prominent Scotch-Irish men the opportunity to demonstrate military leadership and enhance their tatus in western communities.[91] Many were connected by blood or marriage. Thomas Lewis, son of John Lewis, was born in County Donegal. He became Augusta County surveyor in 1746, laid out the town of Staunton, acquired large landholdings, and was active in political and Indian affairs. Colonel Andrew Lewis, commander of the southwestern militia, had fought alongside Washington in the French and Indian War. Lewis sent expresses to his younger brother Charles, county-lieutenant for Augusta County, and to his friend William Preston to prepare for an expedition as the surest method of "reducing our inveterate enemies to reason." Staunton area recruits gathered under Charles Lewis. Fourteen companies arrived. Fincastle County men assembled under Colonel William Christian.[92] The county lieutenant of Fincastle, charged with defending its frontiers, was Colonel William Preston. Born on Christmas 1729 in Londonderry County, he had migrated with family to Augusta County in the Shenandoah Valley when he was about ten and was educated by Reverend Craig. After his father died when he was seventeen, Preston's maternal uncle Colonel James Patton became his guardian. He served as a captain of rangers during the French and Indian War; took part in the abortive Sandy Creek expedition; and was the first surveyor for Fincastle County. In a circular calling for volunteers, Preston urged men to rally to the defense of their lives and properties. Never again perhaps would they have such a good opportunity to stop the Shawnees' attacks, drive them from their country, burn their towns, and destroy their cornfields. There would be valuable plunder and the Shawnees had "a great Stock of Horses." The volunteers would be led by their own officers and assisted by others "raised behind the Mountains"; in other words, more Scotch-Irish frontiersmen.[93] Captain William Campbell, who was born in Augusta County and was baptized at Tinkling Spring Presbyterian Church (and who married the sister of the later legendary patriot orator Patrick Henry), served under Andrew Lewis. Many of these officers also fought in the Revolution.

Dunmore ordered Andrew Lewis to march against the Shawnees and "destroy their Towns & Magazines and distress them in every other way that is possible."[94] Lewis advanced down the Kanawha with a force of 1,000 men that included the McAfee brothers. Chief Cornstalk and some 600 Shawnee warriors made their stand at the junction of the Great Kanawha and Ohio rivers. The Battle of Point Pleasant on October 10, in the words of historian James Leyburn, was "a battle primarily of Scotch-Irish against Indians."[95]

The battle involved individual conflicts and family tragedies. John Ward, who had been captured in 1758 at three years of age and adopted by the Shawnees, married an Indian woman, and had three children, fought against the Virginians. His natural father was killed in the battle. George Collett also fought with the Shawnees, exhorting them to fight on against "the white Damnd. Sons of bitches." After the battle, Collett was found among the fallen warriors. His brother, who was in the Virginian army, identified the body.[96] Charles Lewis, who commanded the Augusta men, died in the fighting. His son John was wounded. Also among the wounded was one John McKinney, who "was disabled by two balls, which passed through the thick muscles of his left thigh and tore and lacerated them in a great degree." An invalid for the rest of his life, he was still drawing an annual pension of £15 sixteen years after the battle.[97]

Outnumbered and outgunned, the Shawnees inflicted more casualties than they sustained, but after a hard-fought, daylong struggle they were forced from the field. After the battle, when his army reached Camp Charlotte, Dunmore sent three men with connections in Indian country, John Gibson, Simon Girty, and Matthew Elliott, with a message of peace.[98] The Mingoes were reluctant, and Dunmore dispatched William Crawford on an expedition against their towns.[99] Cornstalk and the Shawnees grudgingly accepted Dunmore's peace terms, giving up their lands south of the Ohio, and in October, Andrew Lewis was sent to Fort Pitt to conclude the negotiations Dunmore had started. Meanwhile, however, in a further move to restrict settlement from the seaboard colonies, Parliament in June 1774 had passed the Quebec Act, transferring jurisdiction over the territory between the Ohio and the Mississippi to Quebec, in effect making it part of Canada. The Ohio River became a barrier, rather than an opportunity.[100]

The Southern Backcountry

While Scotch-Irish in Virginia pushed into Shawnee country and battled Shawnee warriors, many of their relatives and countrymen followed the path of migration that led them southwest into Catawba, Cherokee, and Creek country. Others arrived by sea, especially after the government of South Carolina offered incentives in the 1760s for poor Protestants to settle on the frontier. The population of the South Carolina backcountry increased by about 50 percent in the four years after the Anglo-Cherokee War of 1759–1761.

The influx of Scotch-Irish Presbyterians into the South alarmed government officials who were concerned about their incursions on Indian land and their political disruptiveness, and ministers of rival denominations who were concerned about their clannishness, nonconformity, and immorality. For example, acting governor James Habersham advised the Georgia Council in 1772 to issue a proclamation ordering removal of "a Parcel of stragling [sic] northward People" who had settled on Indian lands and whose numbers were likely to grow. The next year, John Stuart informed Lord Dartmouth that the great numbers of emigrants from Virginia and the northern colonies on their way to the Mississippi were destroying game as they passed through Cherokee, Creek, and Chickasaw hunting grounds, giving "great umbrage to these three Nations."[101]

Theodorus Swaine Drage was a missionary for the Society of the Propagation of the Gospel and rector of St. Lukes Parish in Rowan County in the North Carolina backcountry. He described it as a "promised land ... originally possessed by the Cananites," but he struggled with Presbyterian dominance and confronted an influx of dissenters from the North. In a long letter to Benjamin Franklin in 1771, Drage complained that "when the late Governor Dobbs came over here, he brought a colony from his neighbourhood in Ireland, to be here provided for." They were given positions, made attorneys, and allowed "to live like soldiers upon free Quarter." North Carolina therefore became, in Drage's words, "an asylum for Thieves and cheats from the Northward, character was no exception against their being well received by their Countrymen." The first settlers "lived by the gun so were ferocious in their manners." Many were hunters, volunteers in expeditions into Indian country, and Indian traders. In recent years, migrants from Conococheague, and York and Cumberland counties, as well as "more civilized People" from Maryland, Virginia, and Pennsylvania, had arrived, seeking land for their children to settle. As for St. Lukes Parish, wrote Drage, "Mr. Dobs's Friends, and all the Scotch Irish are clanned in one Settlement together [and] had Interest enough to get the County Town adjacent." The town was "full of them" and they dominated the county government "exclusive of all others." He described them as "Dissenters by Profession" of various sects whose only teachers had been "Itinerant Preachers from the North."[102]

The Reverend Charles Woodmason was even more critical of the Scotch-Irish Presbyterians he encountered. A newly ordained Anglican minister with strong opinions, Woodmason left Charleston in 1766 to work for six years in the southern backcountry settlements, traveling more than 3,000 miles a year. He found himself in country that "has been settled within these 5 Years by Irish Presbyterians from Belfast, or Pennsylvania."[103] The Scotch-Irish and their neighbors were, he said, "set down here just as a Barrier between the Rich Planters and the Indians, to secure the former against the Latter."[104] Woodmason had an antipathy toward frontier settlers in general, toward the Scotch-Irish in particular, and especially toward Presbyterians who caused him constant trouble and disrupted his services. He wrote some of the most oft-quoted descriptions and generated some of the most enduring stereotypes of backcountry Scotch-Irish as "white savages." The people around Pine Tree (Camden), he wrote, were "of abandon'd Morals and profligate Principles." Ignorant and void of manners, they were "of all Sects and Denominations—A mix'd Medley from all Countries and the Off Scouring of America." All new settlers, they were extremely poor; they "Live in Logg Cabbins like Hogs—and their Living and Behaviour as rude or more so than the Savages."[105] The fine land of the Cheraws region at the head of Peedee River was "occupied by a Sett of the most lowest [sic] vilest Crew breathing—Scotch Irish Presbyterians from the North of Ireland."

They swapped wives and lived "in a State of Nature, more irregularly and unchastely than the Indians."[106]

Woodmason didn't temper his opinions. In his role as an itinerant minister in the woods, he had to deal with "the lowest vilest Scum of Mankind" and the Scotch-Irish were "certainly the worst Vermin on Earth." Their children ran naked and the Indians were "better Cloathed and Lodged." The Presbyterians were "a Sett of Vile unaccountable Wretches" who would lie, cheat, and rob you. "They were as rude in their Manners as the Common Savages, and hardly a degree removed from them." They differed from Indians only in complexion. They possessed the finest country in America but lived in poverty because of "their extreme Indolence." "They delight in their present low, lazy, sluttish, heathenish, hellish Life, and seem not desirous of changing it." On the west side of the Wateree River, the government had recently expended good money to bring over five or six thousand "Ignorant, mean, worthless, beggarly Irish Presbyterians, the Scum of the Earth, and Refuse of Mankind." The women went barefoot and barelegged and wore indecent dresses that accentuated their curves. They rubbed their hair with bear's grease and tied it up behind in a bunch like the Indians, "being hardly one degree removed from them." The men wore moccasins. North Carolina backcountry people were no better: "the Out Casts of all the other Colonies who take Refuge there."[107]

Clearly a man with all sorts of issues, Woodmason compared Scotch-Irish Presbyterians unfavorably with their Catawba neighbors. In 1763, northern Indians had raided the settlements on the Broad and Catawba rivers, and killed the Catawba headman, Hagler, "almost in the middle of the Waxsaw settlement."[108] In December, Catawbas "complained that the White People had settled their Land all round and even into their Town." With game scarce, and their numbers reduced by perpetual war with the northern Indians and by smallpox, the Catawbas asked for a reservation fifteen miles square, and the right to hunt in unsettled parts of North and South Carolina.[109] The colony used the Catawbas to maintain racial boundaries. After many enslaved people fled into the swamps around Christmas 1765, there were fears of conspiracy and insurrection. The governor, in addition to placing the militia on alert, called on Catawba Indians "to come down and hunt the negroes in their different recesses almost impervious to White Men at that season of the year." The Catawbas' tracking abilities, plus the terror of their name, did the job: some of the runaways were apprehended, and the rest surrendered rather than risk falling into Catawba hands. A report on the boundary line between North and South Carolina in 1769 stated: "It would be convenient and reasonable that the Catawba Indians should be comprehended in the proposed Boundary as a very useful Body of Men to keep our numerous Negroes in some awe."[110] The Catawbas were to be a temporary buffer, however; the government did not expect them to stay on their tiny reservation more than ten years because white people were settling fast around them and deer and other game were already very scarce.[111]

When Minister Woodmason was in the Waxhaws in 1767–1768, he encountered sectarian hostility from Presbyterians who, he said, insulted and threatened him. At Hanging Rock, just south of the Waxhaws, he was preaching to a mixed audience of whites and Catawbas when a crowd of people, "2/3 of them Presbyterians" made "a great Noise" in an effort to disrupt the service. The Catawbas "behaved more quiet and decent than the lawless Crew" of backcountry settlers. They "resented their affronts and fought with several of them, which only made more Noises."[112]

Woodmason traveled through the backcountry at a time when a group known as the "Regulators" were active in the area. Like the Black Boys in Pennsylvania, many settlers in the Carolina backcountry felt deprived of political power and the benefits of government which seemed to be confined to the East Coast, and like that movement, the Regulator rising was predominantly, although not exclusively, Scotch-Irish.[113] In South Carolina, the Regulators were backcountry slave-owning planters, better off than the poorest settlers. Angry at the lack of adequate courts and jails in the interior, they took matters into their own hands and organized vigilante groups to apprehend and punish bandits and criminals. In other words, they protested against *lack* of government.[114] The more extensive Regulator movement in North Carolina's piedmont began in Orange County in 1766, when a reform group petitioned the government in New Bern to repeal punitive taxes, curtail excessive legal fees, and investigate corrupt local officials whom they accused of embezzling funds. Small and middling farmers seeking economic independence on the frontier often found that access to the means of economic advancement was controlled by the elites. Confronting ruthless agents and officials who kept lands in the hands of the wealthy, these backcountry settlers disputed the titles of absentee landlords and invoked squatters' rights. They also felt themselves burdened by taxes and debts to merchants and speculators. When their complaints were ignored, the movement grew. In the British tradition of "purposeful riot," they resorted to violence to provoke the government to address their demands. The Black Boys, who disguised their faces with soot, came from the Presbyterian communities of Rocky River and Sugar Creek in Mecklenburg County, which were heavily Scotch-Irish. The inhabitants had migrated south from Pennsylvania and Virginia, not west from coastal North Carolina, and so had few ties to the centers of political and economic power there. They heard rumors that Governor William Tryon planned to unleash Indians against them, a chilling prospect for survivors of the French and Indian War. Fearing that the settler movement's momentum might culminate in a full-scale backcountry revolt, Tryon led a force of militia, including men from Mecklenburg, against the Regulators and defeated them at the Battle of Alamance in the spring of 1771, killing 30 men, wounding 200, and executing 7 for treason.[115]

Like the Paxton Boys and the Black Boys in the Pennsylvania backcountry, the Regulators in the Carolina backcountry added political rebelliousness to eastern perceptions of the Scotch-Irish. Lieutenant Governor William Bull informed Lord Dartmouth in the summer of 1774 that the South Carolina Assembly, expecting him to prorogue it, met without his knowledge and, among other things, sent him a request to purchase arms to be given to "many poor Irish and others in our Western Frontiers, with Ammunition, upon the apprehensions of an Indian War." Bull intended to do everything he could to enable them to defend themselves, though he recognized that the Scotch-Irish on his frontiers drew on a long history of defying government. He thought it likely that many of the poor Irish had been members of the White Boys, Oak Boys, or Steel Boys, movements of agrarian protest in Ireland in the 1760s. Having "been accustomed to oppose Law & Authority in Ireland," he feared they "may not change their Disposition with their Climate, and may think of other Objects than Indians." If their expectations were not met, he warned Dartmouth, they might carry things to extremes.[116]

Although outsiders like the Reverend Woodmason saw surface similarities between Scotch-Irish border people and Indians—savages, all—they said little about what distinguished them. As we've seen, the Scotch-Irish did not have the same relationships with animals and the land that Native people did, and they did not deal with people in the same way as Indian people dealt with each other. The Scotch-Irish had a heritage of clans in Scotland and Ireland, and the Cherokees had seven clans, but backcountry Scotch-Irish people went into Indian country to hunt, to get land, to trade, and if necessary to kill Indians, not usually to build and sustain webs of clan-based kinship relations with them.[117]

Even Scotch-Irish traders who lived in Indian towns and built networks of relationships pursued personal fortunes in trade and land and promoted settlement in Indian country. By 1765, according to the Philadelphia botanist John Bartram, who traveled through Georgia and the Carolinas on his way to Florida, George Galphin employed four hundred packhorses trading through the Creek, Chickasaw, Choctaw, and other southern nations.[118] Galphin also encouraged Scotch-Irish migration to South Carolina and Georgia. As did South Carolina in 1731 and 1761, Georgia in 1764–1766 made land grants to attract Ulster Protestants and other colonists to frontier regions. Galphin financed the immigration of hundreds of poor Ulster families in the 1760s and 1770s. He advertised for immigrants in the *Belfast News-Letter*, subsidized their voyages, gave each head of family one hundred acres, and provided them with cattle and tools to build a farm. The settlers paid an annual tax, shopped at Galphin's store, and in many cases sought employment in Galphin's firm to supplement their income from farming. In other words, Galphin enmeshed them in bonds of debt and dependency, as he did his Creek customers. He settled them on lands ceded by the Creeks at the Treaty of Augusta in 1763 (a treaty he helped to engineer; the Creeks ceded more than two million acres), creating Queensborough, a township of Protestant families from the north of Ireland.[119]

Galphin partnered with John Rae from County Down in promoting and organizing Ulster colonization along the Ogeechee River. Rae emigrated to Savannah in 1734 with his wife, Catherine, and settled on the Georgia frontier, where he became a prosperous rancher and, like Galphin, an Indian trader with the Creeks and Cherokees, investing in land, slaves, and cattle. Rae and Galphin promptly secured land grants totaling about 80,000 acres on the Ogeechee and began promotional efforts in Ireland. Matthew Rea acted as middleman for his brother in recruiting immigrants and indentured servants. In a letter to Matthew back home in County Down in May 1765, which was published in the *Belfast News*, John wrote, "Now, Brother, if you think a Number of good industrious Families will come over here I will [do] every Thing in my Power to assist them." Nothing, he wrote, would give him "more Satisfaction than to be the Means of bringing my Friends to this Country of Freedom; there are no Rents, no Tithes here, only the King's Quit Rent [a small rent paid to the landlord], which is only two Shillings Sterl, per hundred Acres." Moreover, he boasted that there was a "firm" peace with the Indians and because of the Treaty of Augusta, clear boundaries between them—"so that all is settled with them." He added that he was looking for poor to middling families, and didn't expect his brother to come, "nor would I advise any Person to come here that lives well in Ireland." There was more to eat and drink in Georgia, but "there is not the Pleasure of Society that there is there, and the Comfort of the Gospel preached."[120]

Despite Rae's confidence in a firm peace and firm boundaries, the Scotch-Irish settlers generated conflict with the Native peoples on whose land they settled. The Queensborough township was not a great success. In 1768 the British government disallowed the Georgia law that had granted Rea and Galphin lands. Some settlers sent back unfavorable reports, and their aggressive behavior toward the Indians produced violence.[121] A complaint from the son of the Creek chief Handsome Fellow, presented in the Council Chamber at Savannah in October 1771, alleged that "bad White People" caught two Creeks who had stolen horses, whipped one and killed the other. One of the men was named McNeal and, a deponent said, "these People are Chiefly of the Irish Settlement." They were heard to say among themselves "that they would not suffer themselves to be taken into Custody for killing Indians who stole their Horses."[122]

Immigrants, and Galphin himself, encroached on other Creek lands, sparking violence and animosity, and Queensborough Irish threatened to kill the first Indian that came into their settlement. Galphin used his influence to engineer a second treaty at Augusta in 1773, where the Creeks ceded another three million acres, largely to pay off traders' debts, and he continued to secure land for his family. As another wave of immigrants followed, tension between Queensborough and the Creek town of Coweta led to open conflict in 1774, destroying the network of relationships Galphin had built and closing the Queensborough settlement. Many of the immigrants went to Pennsylvania and South Carolina. Galphin sided with the Americans in the Revolution. The British seized Silver Bluff in 1779. Galphin died the following year.[123]

By the eve of the American Revolution, relations were fracturing along the 1,500-mile arc of Scotch-Irish incursion into Indian country. As Sir William Johnson said, "These settlers generally set out with a general Prejudice against all Indians and the young Indian Warriors or Hunters are too often inclined to retaliate."[124] British attempts to restrict access to Indian land pushed many colonists to embrace revolution; fears of the "white savages" who constantly invaded their lands pushed many Indians into the arms of the British. Scotch-Irish people once again were on the front lines when the Revolution in the West became a race war. So, of course, were Indian people.

9

Indian-Killers to Patriots

James Caldwell emigrated from County Antrim to Philadelphia in 1769. Writing to his brother back home five year later, he explained the emerging divisions in the American colonies. The Scots, with few exceptions, remained loyal to King George III and seemed anxious to atone for the Jacobite rebellions of 1715 and 1745, "but among the Irish," he added, "nine tenths espouse the American Cause, and our Countrymen of the North add the sagacity and calmness of the calculating Scotch Lowlander, to the enthusiastic chivalry of the native of the Emerald Isle."[1] James Galloway informed New Jersey Governor William Franklin in March 1775 that almost all Presbyterians in Pennsylvania were "truly independents" and wanted no political connection with Britain. General Thomas Gage, in Boston six months later, informed Lord Dartmouth that Irish emigrants disembarking at Philadelphia immediately had guns put into their hands and there were "many Irish in the rebel army, particularly amongst the riflemen brought here from the frontiers of Virginia and Pennsylvania" (although Gage maintained they took every opportunity to desert to the British). Nearly half the soldiers who fought in the Continental Army and Pennsylvania militia units were of Irish birth or descent, and in some companies as many as 75 percent—in other words, they were predominantly Scotch-Irish. The rosters of the First Regiment of the Pennsylvania Line, heavily recruited from the Cumberland Valley, contained so many Irish names that at least one researcher described it as "an Irish regiment." A Hessian officer serving with the British wrote to a friend that the American Revolution was "nothing more than a Scotch Irish Presbyterian rebellion."[2]

The Hessian may have exaggerated, but he had a point. For instance, Thomas McKean, an ardent voice for independence in Delaware and Pennsylvania, was the son of immigrant parents from Antrim. Samuel Thompson, a revolutionary insurgent born in Brunswick, Maine, to Scotch-Irish parents, may have drawn on his Ulster heritage to shape his politics, reflecting long-standing grievances against Britain and the Parliament that had passed trade laws that undermined Ulster's economy. Although most of the time, old betrayals in Ireland lay buried in the past, they were, in historian Tim Breen's words, "dry seeds of a shared identity capable under certain conditions of energizing resistance in a new land." Reactions in Ireland were ambivalent, yet many Irish people on both sides of the Atlantic saw revolution against Britain in America and the bid for a republic in Ireland as two sides of the same struggle.[3]

The Revolution was a key event in making the Scotch-Irish into Americans. That was certainly the view expressed by the "English gentleman" who translated the Marquis de Chastellux's *Voyages*, a travel book about United States in the early 1780s. Commenting on the Marquis's encounter in the Blue Ridge Mountains of Virginia with a recent Irish immigrant who had served on several campaigns, the translator added his general observation that "an Irishman, the instant he sets foot on American ground, becomes ipso facto, an American: this was uniformly the case during the whole of the late war."[4] The question of whether Ulster colonists were still "Irish" or had become "American" by 1776 cannot be answered simply, however. Second- and third-generation Ulster Americans, especially in urban areas, largely assimilated, whereas recent immigrants who settled in predominantly Irish areas retained aspects of Irish culture and identity longer. At the top of Ulster-American society were merchants, lawyers, newspapermen, and other professionals; then a prosperous middle class of shopkeepers, artisans, traders, and commercial farmers. These men were on the cutting edge of commercialization, offered prototypes for later myth makers, and served as political and cultural spokesmen for the great majority of Ulster-Americans. But that majority tended to be subsistence farmers, better off than if they had stayed home but still working the land much as they would have in Ireland, and still living in identifiably Scotch-Irish towns named Londonderry, Donegal, and Colerain.[5]

If Scotch-Irish and Presbyterians led the revolutionary fight in Pennsylvania and the Middle Colonies, the story was much more varied in other regions. Although support for the Revolution was nearly unanimous among Scotch-Irish farmers and frontier people in New Hampshire and Pennsylvania, many more recent Scotch-Irish immigrants in the backcountry regions of New York, Georgia, and the Carolinas were ambivalent, and some actively opposed the rebellion.[6] In the southern backcountry, kinship ties shaped the causes, course, and consequences of Revolutionary war—in claiming Indian lands, enlisting and fighting in militia units, and determining military and political leadership.[7] Scotch-Irish people in the

South inhabited multiple enclaves, more isolated from each other and from centers of power than in the North. There were pockets of loyalism on the South Carolina frontier, and a strong correlation throughout America between very recent immigration and loyalism.[8]

Individuals from Northern Ireland fought on both sides in the Revolution, which was also a civil war. Elite Anglo-Irish colonial families in Ulster supported the Crown and more than one-third of the British officer class were Irish Protestants.[9] Officers from Northern Ireland served in both the redcoat and rebel armies. In December 1775, General Richard Montgomery was killed leading an American army in a disastrous attack on Quebec. Sir Guy Carleton led the opposing British forces. Carleton and Montgomery were both from County Tyrone and had served together at the British capture of Quebec from the French in 1759.[10] Lieutenant Colonel John Caldwell, later Sir John Caldwell, 5th baronet of Caldwell Castle in County Fermanagh, served in the 8th (King's) Regiment of Foot at Fort Niagara and Detroit in the early years of the Revolution and as a negotiator with the surrounding tribes.[11]

The Revolution meant different things to Scotch-Irish people in different places. For Oliver Pollock, the choices he made during the Revolution had more to do with commercial opportunities than with anti-British sentiment or commitment to revolutionary principles. Born in Londonderry around 1737, Pollock migrated to America in 1760 with his widowed father and brothers. As a Scotch-Irish Presbyterian, he became active in Pennsylvania's Scotch-Irish merchant network and settled in the Scotch-Irish backcountry near Carlisle before moving to Philadelphia and working for major mercantile houses in the city. In that capacity, he went to Cuba in 1762, but there he represented himself as Celtic Irish and Roman Catholic to better position himself with Alejandro O'Reilly, an Irish general in the Spanish service. Following O'Reilly to New Orleans in 1769, and receiving contracts from the general, Pollock built a successful business importing goods and slaves to Spanish Louisiana, and acquired land and plantations. Having benefited from his status as both a British citizen and a resident of Spanish Louisiana and having presented himself as Scotch-Irish, Celtic Irish, Presbyterian, and Roman Catholic depending on the circumstances, he shifted allegiance and identity again when the Revolution broke out. Although he had lived only briefly in one of the colonies from which the United States was born, he had developed substantial connections with American merchants. He supplied American forces during the war and by the end of the Revolution he became an American.[12]

For many Scotch-Irish Presbyterians in the East, the Revolution meant asserting political power. For many Scotch-Irish families in the West, it meant renewed Indian war. The collapse of an old imperial order and the birth pangs of an expansive new nation brought upheaval and new levels of violence. Local struggles for power, authority, and resources often took precedence over the larger conflict between the Crown and the colonies. Frontier populations that rebelled against the king also contested the government of eastern elites and struggled to build new societies on their own terms.[13] In some regions, backcountry people embraced the Revolutionary cause only after the broader colonial struggle became identified with a frontier war against Indians.[14]

In western Pennsylvania, where tribes, empires, and now states and the federal government all competed to assert their authority, settlers asserted their autonomy. The Scotch-Irish inhabitants of Hanna's Town, still little more than a log-cabin community, issued the first direct challenge to British authority in the colonies in May 1775 when they drew up the so-called Westmoreland Declaration, pledging their opposition against Britain's oppressive acts. On July 4, 1776, Scotch-Irish at Pine Creek, unaware of was happening in Philadelphia that day, drew up their own declaration of independence from Britain.[15] Western counties sent 64 of the 96 representatives to the convention to frame a new Pennsylvania government, and the majority of the Assembly was composed of frontier representatives, including the former captive and Black Boy leader James Smith, elected by Westmoreland County, and Matthew Smith, author of the *Declaration and Remonstrance* in 1764. Scotch-Irish backcountry leaders drafted Pennsylvania's democratic constitution in 1776.

Yet, although Scotch-Irish people in the backcountry embraced the goals of the Revolution and supported American conceptions of liberty, they looked to the new government to provide security, stability, and access to land more than liberty and equality. Driven by grievances from earlier Indian wars, they withdrew their allegiance from the imperial government that had failed to protect them and to remove Indians, and they demanded the new government provide that defense and assistance now.[16] Scotch-Irish settlers in western Pennsylvania defied distant government authority not primarily because of some inherent ethnic disposition, frontier unruliness, or democratic leanings, but because they had never had effective government that met their needs. Unfortunately, the new federal and state governments also neglected them, left them vulnerable to Indian attack, and failed to provide the stability and security they demanded.[17]

Seven Continental battalions, more than five thousand men, served under Scotch-Irish Cumberland County commanders, from Quebec to Carolina and throughout the war.[18] Yet the military goals of Continental commanders did not always mesh with those of militia who were fighting local wars for survival and autonomy, rather than a national war for independence. They expected Continental commanders to assist them in *their* war, and their war was primarily against Indians.[19] Competing goals rendered Fort Pitt, the western hub of operations, a site of contestation between the government, the military, and the local Scotch-Irish population, as well as between Americans and Native Americans.

The Revolution in the backcountry unleashed violence between neighbors with bloody histories and scores to settle. The Declaration of Independence accused King George III of unleashing "on the inhabitants of our frontiers, the merciless Indian Savages whose known rule of warfare, is an undistinguished destruction of all ages, sexes and conditions." American assaults on Indian villages during the Revolution also were marked by "an undistinguished destruction of all ages, sexes and conditions." The best way to defend the backcountry from Indian attack was to invade Indian country; it was also the best way to lay claim to Indian land. Western settlers sought to secure land as the basis of their own economic independence and that meant ridding the land of Indian neighbors. Speculators ached to get their hands on the best western lands. Congress and the individual states needed land to fulfill the bounties and warrants they issued in lieu of pay during the war. Most Native Americans saw the aggressive people pushing on their borders as a greater threat than a distant king; some said the Americans were intent on destroying them.[20]

No matter what the Declaration of Independence said, Native Americans did not fight against freedom in the Revolution, any more than did Scotch-Irish frontiersmen who refused to comply with orders from Revolutionary governments and commanders. Indian people and Scotch-Irish people both fought for land, life, and liberty in the Revolution. In the borderland regions they shared and contested, and the world as they saw it, that meant they killed each other in the process.

Paths to War

In the months leading up to the outbreak of war, Patriot leaders and the press boosted revolutionary unity by circulating rumors and reports that Indian war parties and insurrectionist slaves, instigated by the British, were poised to unleash savage warfare against the colonists.[21] Scotch-Irish people on the backcountry needed little prompting to conjure up fears of another Indian war. Some saw parallels and precedents in history when Stuart kings had unleashed Roman Catholic "savages" on their ancestors in Northern Ireland.[22] Indian people, however, were not unthinking tools of the British. Their decisions to go to war, and on which side, depended on region and circumstances.

Richard Henderson, whom North Carolina Regulators reviled as a slippery lawyer and rapacious land speculator, outdid himself at the Treaty of Sycamore Shoals on the Watauga River in March 1775. With a group of North Carolina land speculators known as the Transylvania Land Company, and in defiance of both British and Cherokee law, he got Attakullakulla, Oconostota, the Raven of Chota, and other prominent Cherokee headmen to sell twenty-seven thousand square miles of land between the Kentucky and Cumberland rivers. The cession comprised most of modern Kentucky and a slice of today's northern Tennessee. Attakullakulla's son, Dragging Canoe, stormed from the treaty council in disgust. He told the British he had no hand in the sale and blamed it on the older chiefs who caved in under pressure. He and the younger warriors "were determined to have their land."[23] Two days after the treaty with Henderson, Cherokees made another transaction at Sycamore Shoals, selling the Wataugans the lands they had earlier leased to them and the entire Watauga River valley.[24] Daniel Boone threw in his lot with Richard Henderson and his associates, as did Robert, George, and William McAfee.[25]

Creating buffer zones of ceded territory while at the same time keeping trade contacts open was a common borderland strategy, and the older chiefs had done it before. In this instance, though, they claimed Henderson had deceived them as to what they were signing. The Raven of Chota told British agent Henry Stuart:

> we suffered the people who first settled on our lands on Watauga to remain there some years, they paying us annually in guns, blankets and rum, etc. But we are informed lately that they gave out publicly that we sold the land

to them forever and gave them a paper for it. If they have a paper of this kind, it is of their own making, for we have never given them any, as it was contrary to our thoughts.[26]

Although the Sycamore Shoals land purchases were illegal under the Proclamation of 1763, they unleashed a wave of immigration. Henderson and his associates attracted colonists "very fast," and about one thousand people from Virginia occupied the lands by September.[27]

British Superintendent of Indian Affairs John Stuart reported to Secretary of State Lord George Germain that "amazing great settlements" were being made on Cherokee land by individuals "taking advantage of their wants and poverty, or by forgeries and frauds of different sorts in which the nation never acquiesced." The Cherokees would never cede any land "without the consent of the nation obtained in general council."[28] According to Scottish trader and British agent Alexander Cameron, Scotch-Irish trader and agent Richard Pearis was one of those guilty of "forgeries and frauds." Cameron reminded the Cherokees of the many occasions when Pearis had defrauded them of their lands "by lies and forgeries." The Cherokee chief Keanitah denounced Pearis as "a rogue and a devil and could never speak truth." Pearis worked to win over his Cherokee wife's people to the American cause, but it was an uphill struggle.[29]

Cherokee warriors were especially enraged by the squatters in the Watauga and upper Holston valleys, many if not most of whom were Scotch-Irish, and British agents struggled to restrain them from attacking the settlements that lay on the wrong side of the boundary. In May 1776, fourteen delegates from the Shawnees, Delawares, Mohawks, Nanticokes, and Odawas arrived at Chota on the Little Tennessee River. They brought a nine-foot wampum belt, painted red as a sign of war, and urged the Cherokees to unite with the other tribes against the Americans. Older chiefs remembered that British troops had burned Cherokee crops and villages the last time they went to war, and they did not want war with the Americans now. Younger men had not had their fathers' opportunities to demonstrate their masculinity and achieve standing through war and hunting and were infuriated by the recurrent sales of land. Asserting their independence from the older chiefs who would normally have guided the Cherokees in such critical decisions, Dragging Canoe and his followers accepted the war belt and seized the opportunity to expel the squatters. Their authority eroded, the chiefs sat by, "dejected and silent," while the warriors plunged the nation into war.[30]

The Cherokees' southern neighbors were not drawn so quickly into the war. At first, according to South Carolina planter and Continental officer William Moultrie, the Catawbas "were alarmed, and could not tell what to make of it," but then they sided with their American neighbors. Dispersed through colonial settlements in North and South Carolina, it was, as John Stuart realized, "no wonder that they should be practiced upon and seduced by the Inhabitants with whom they live." Catawbas fought alongside Waxhaw militiamen in the Revolution; according to some accounts, all sixty Catawba warriors served with the rebels.[31]

While Cherokee warriors took up the hatchet, Creeks in May 1776 resisted the efforts of Stuart and other British agents to get them to fight against the Americans. Headmen from Coweta and Cussita cited their connections to the Scotch-Irish traders George Galphin and Robert Rae, whom the Continental Congress appointed Indian commissioners in the summer of 1775. "I look upon Messrs Galphin and Rae not only as my Elder brothers but as my father and mother," said one. "I considered Stuart as out of his senses to ask such a thing."[32] Stuart blamed the two Scotch-Irish traders-turned-agents, "acting under the usurped authority of declared rebels," for trying to win over the Creeks and Cherokees with presents and lies. David Taitt, British agent to the Creeks, called Galphin "a most infamous man" who had tried to bribe Indians to murder both him and Alexander Cameron.[33]

In the Ohio country, American agents at Fort Pitt competed with British agents operating out of Detroit for the allegiance of the Indian nations. Andrew Lewis and other Virginian commissioners met with the tribes at Fort Pitt in the fall of 1775 to confirm the Treaty of Camp Charlotte the year before, when the Shawnees had ceded their lands south of the Ohio to Lord Dunmore, and to allay their concerns. Shawnee chiefs, who saw Virginians building forts and settling in Kentucky, hunting north of the Ohio, and driving away the game, feared they were determined to "deprive us entirely of our whole Country" and that "there is no resting place for us."[34] Cornstalk had led Shawnee warriors at the Battle of Point Pleasant, but when the Revolution began, he worked for peace with the Americans and tried to remain neutral. Unfortunately, neutrality was not a viable option for the Shawnees.[35] Cornstalk told American agent George Morgan to tell Congress, "We never sold you our Lands which you now possess on the Ohio between the Great Kanawha and the Cherokee River, and which you are settling without ever asking our leave, or obtaining our consent."[36] Like his Cherokee counterparts, Cornstalk could not prevent younger warriors from contesting the invasion of tribal lands. In October 1777, American militia seized Cornstalk under a flag of truce at Fort Randolph on the Kanahwa River. A month later they murdered him, together with his son and another Shawnee whose body was "terribly mangled." Colonial authorities denounced the deed, but the backcountry militia effectively propelled the Shawnees into the arms of the British.

In this moment of choosing sides, some Scotch-Irish also went over to the British. In April 1776 the West Augusta Committee of Safety at Fort Pitt made Alexander McKee sign a parole that he would not transact any business with the Indians on behalf of the Crown or communicate with any of the Crown's officers without the committee's consent.[37] The son of Thomas McKee and his Shawnee or adopted Shawnee wife, Mary, McKee also had a Shawnee wife and family. He spoke multiple Indigenous languages and worked for George Croghan as an interpreter and deputy. Two years later, Colonel John Proctor in Westmoreland County reported that "Capt. Alexander McKee with seven other Vilons is gon to the Indians."[38] McKee defected on the night of March 28, along with his cousin Robert Surphit, Simon Girty, Matthew Elliott, a man named Higgins, and two enslaved men. A proclamation of attainder against persons adjudged guilty of high treason, issued on June 15, 1778, included George Croghan, Alexander McKee, Simon and James Girty, and Matthew Elliott. It was a long list and included plenty of Scotch-Irish names.[39] The Reverend Thomas Barton, who had written a defense of the Paxton Boys in 1764, was also expelled from Pennsylvania in 1778 as a Tory.

When McKee reached Detroit, the British made him a captain in the Indian department, with a substantial annual salary of £200. Lieutenant Governor Henry Hamilton described him as "a man of good character" who had "great influence with the Shawanese" and knew the country well.[40] Simon Girty, another on the list, had become increasingly alienated from the Patriot cause after he was denied the captain's commission which he felt his services warranted and became suspected of Tory sympathies. He served in the British Indian department as an interpreter, scout, and messenger, and led Indian raiding parties. The Americans offered $800 for his scalp.[41] Margaret Handley Erskine, who was held captive by Shawnees for much of the war, said the Indians "thought a great deal of McKee and Girty." So did she. McKee was "a gentlemanly man," she recalled, and Girty had reassured her that she need have no fear of being forced into marriage by the Shawnees, "as they were not the people to compel any one to such a course."[42] Born in County Donegal, probably in 1739, Matthew Elliott emigrated to Pennsylvania in 1761. He entered the fur trade in partnership with Alexander Blaine of Carlisle and developed connections and influence among the Shawnees. He served in Bouquet's expedition in 1764 and in Dunmore's War, and after the Battle of Point Pleasant he acted as an intermediary to arrange peace talks between Dunmore and the Shawnees. When the Revolution broke out, Elliott, like the Shawnees, found he could not remain neutral. He threw in his lot with McKee and Girty and fled to Detroit, where he was employed in the British Indian department.[43]

At the Treaty of Fort Pitt in September 1778, the first formal treaty between the new United States and an Indian nation, the negotiations were largely conducted by Scotch-Irish and Delaware people who already knew each other. Like their Shawnee neighbors, Delawares were divided in their responses to the Revolution. Reluctant to give direct military assistance to either side, they initially endeavored to maintain their traditional role as peacemakers and alliance-builders. White Eyes, war captain of the Turtle clan, and Gelemend or John Killbuck, chief of the Turtle clan, favored a neutral and then a pro-American stance and took the lead in the making the treaty. Buckongahelas and Hopocan, also known as Captain Pipe, of the Wolf clan were much more distrustful of the Americans.[44]

Andrew and Thomas Lewis served as the American commissioners, although Andrew felt that a treaty with the Indians was unlikely to accomplish anything "before they are heartyly drubbed into a peacifick disposition."[45] William Crawford, Arthur Graham, Joseph and John Finley, John Campbell,[46] and John Gibson also attended. Gibson knew Indian languages and customs, and White Eyes requested, as a Moravian minister wrote in his diary at the time, that he "be appointed to have the charge of all matters between you & us. We esteem him as one of ourselves, he has always acted an honest part by us, & we are convinced he will make our common good his chief study, & not think only how he may get rich."[47] The Lewis brothers and White Eyes made a defensive alliance at Fort Pitt, although other Delawares complained that the written treaty misrepresented what they had agreed to and contained "Declarations and Engagements they never intended to make or enter into." Two months later, during Continental General Lachlan McIntosh's campaign against Detroit, American militia murdered White Eyes. Like the Shawnees in the wake of Cornstalk's murder, most Delawares made Britain's war their own.[48]

Racial war drenched the frontiers of Pennsylvania and Virginia in blood after the middle of the century. Nonetheless, patterns of coexistence and cultural accommodation between colonial and Indian communities had persisted on the borders of Iroquoia.[49] But the Revolution shattered the peace of the region and the unity of the League. Mohawks, led by war chief Joseph Brant, supported the Crown, due in no small measure to the influence of Sir William Johnson before his death in 1774. The Mohawks' neighbors, the Oneidas, sided with their colonial neighbors, due in no small measure to Samuel Kirkland, their Presbyterian missionary, who favored breaking with the Church of England.[50] By the end of 1778, from western New York to the Carolina backcountry, the borderland regions inhabited by Scotch-Irish and Native Americans were war zones once again.

Revolutionary War in the Backcountry

The Revolution in the backcountry was generally a war of attrition, fought by proxy in short brutal campaigns against noncombatants, not in conventional battles like Saratoga or Yorktown. British commanders armed and instigated Native allies to ravage American frontier settlements; George Washington and his commanders mobilized local militia to burn Indian villages and cornfields.[51] On the Pennsylvania frontier, Indian and white inhabitants practiced guerrilla warfare and waged what could be termed "total war"— killing noncombatants and burning homes and crops in racially charged raids and counter-raids.[52] Many Scotch-Irish men had suffered personal losses in previous Indian attacks on frontier communities and had scores to settle, and militia units fought in accordance with *lex talionis*, the law of retaliation, rather than European cultural restraints on the conduct of war. Atrocities begat atrocities, and the vicious border warfare of the Revolution reaffirmed pre-war views of all Indians as merciless savages and vindicated treating them as such.[53]

No incident had more impact than the killing of Jane McCrea, a murder made infamous by John Vanderlyn's famous painting of 1804 (Figure 9.1), but firmly established in anti-Indian attitudes long before. The McCrea family originated in the Scottish Highlands. Jane's great-grandfather moved to Ulster in the mid-seventeenth century, and her grandfather took his family and migrated to New Castle on the Delaware. Her father, James McCrea, a Presbyterian minister, married Mary Graham, whose family originated in the Scottish borderlands. They had seven children. Jane was born in 1751 or 1752. After Mary died at age thirty-one in 1753, James remarried and had five

Figure 9.1 John Vanderlyn, *The Murder of Jane McCrea*, 1804. Oil on canvas, 32.5 × 26.5 in. (82.6 × 67.3 cm), height × width.

Wadsworth Atheneum Museum of Art, Hartford, CT. Purchased by Subscription, 1855.4.
Photography credit: Allen Phillips/Wadsworth Atheneum.

more children. During the Revolution, the Reverend McCrea's older sons served on the American side, although his children with his second wife, who was English, leaned toward the Crown. At the time of General John Burgoyne's invasion from Canada in 1777, Jane was living in her brother's house in the upper Hudson Valley near Albany. She was also engaged to a Loyalist officer serving with Burgoyne's army. The details of her death are not clear, although most versions agree she was captured near Fort Edward by Indian warriors attached to Burgoyne's army, who then killed and scalped her. Most of Burgoyne's Native allies were recruited from towns such as Kahnawake and Akwesasne on the St. Lawrence, although Jane's captors appear to have recently joined from the Great Lakes. They evidently killed her in a dispute as to whose prisoner she was.

The American general Horatio Gates seized on the murder as a powerful piece of anti-British propaganda. Newspapers picked up, circulated, and embellished the story of Jane's death. The story and the image of a fair-skinned Scotch-Irish girl being brutally murdered on the eve of her wedding became an enduring symbol of savagery and provided powerful justification for subsequent American dispossession and treatment of all Indian people.[54]

The experiences of Scotch-Irish families and their backcountry neighbors in the early years of the war were eerily similar to those in the French and Indian War and Pontiac's War. Defensive measures were poorly funded, poorly organized, and reactive. Reports, petitions, and pleas for help from Westmoreland, Northampton, and Bedford counties in Pennsylvania told of terror, distress, and confusion: war parties striking at will; families abandoning their farms and crops; and lack of ammunition. Many people fled; others did not know whether to leave or stay.[55] With rumors and false alarms swirling, many of those who stayed were immobilized by fear; in the daytime they dared not work in their fields; at night they lay awake listening to every sound.[56]

Congress established a military department at Pittsburgh but diverted few troops or resources from the main theater of war in the East, leaving the burden for defense on the shoulders of the inhabitants and the local militia.[57] Residents of the Juniata Valley found themselves acting as a bulwark between enemy Indians and the more settled regions of Pennsylvania. They erected lines of stockades that afforded enough security that they were barely able to hang on, and they helped to limit the extent and impact of Indian strikes in other areas.[58] Frontier militia in the Revolution were generally more effective than their colonial predecessors had been and rendered service neither the state nor the regular army could dispense with. States made significant improvements in organizing, mobilizing, and, in some cases, arming militia units.[59] Nevertheless, militia often were still poorly prepared, ill equipped, and reluctant to leave their families. Not one in ten of the militia was armed, petitioners from Bedford wrote in November 1777, "and for all the defence that can be made here the Indians may do almost what they please."[60]

Even when reports of Indian attacks reached Carlisle, which had been a hub of military operations in the previous war, the citizens there displayed little desire to fight Indians. Many Cumberland Valley men opted to stay home rather than serve on campaign.[61] Major General John Armstrong, the hero of Kittanning, petitioned Benjamin Franklin and the committee of safety to raise a battalion in Cumberland County. He acknowledged that many of the militia were a scandal to the military profession.[62] With refugees from rumored and actual Indian raids streaming into Carlisle, Armstrong requested additional militia to defend the backcountry and arms and ammunitions so that the settlers living on the farthest reaches of the counties could protect themselves. Defensive measures were needed to save the harvest, but the best way to stop Indian raids was to attack Indian towns; "any Indian Town in reasonable reach, on either Branch of the Susquehanna" could probably be destroyed without too much preparation, he wrote. Even so, he looked to Congress to solicit divine assistance, hoping it would declare "another day of general humiliation & prayer."[63]

At Fort Pitt, General Edward Hand (an Irishman, although not an Ulsterman) called out the militia but could not get them to do duty at the fort or assemble in sufficient force to mount a campaign into Indian country.[64] In February 1778, he led five hundred men in an abortive expedition that killed one old man, four Indian women, and a boy, and became known derisively as the "squaw campaign."[65] In May, Washington appointed Brigadier General Lachlan McIntosh to succeed Hand. Two regiments were stationed at Fort Pitt: Colonel Daniel Brodhead commanded the 8th Pennsylvania, and Washington sent Colonel John Gibson to take temporary command of the 13th Virginia. McIntosh found things in a bad way at Fort Pitt. There were no more than one hundred men in the garrison, Indian attacks ravaged the frontier settlements, and the militia was dispirited and deserting.[66]

Perched on the upper Susquehanna on the southern border of Iroquoia, colonists at Wyoming, in the words of a later petition to Congress, "stood as a shield to all the settlements below us."[67] On July 3, 1778, that shield was destroyed when several hundred Iroquois warriors and Loyalists routed the militia at the Battle of Wyoming. Lazarus Stewart, who had participated in the killings at the Lancaster workhouse fifteen years earlier, was killed. The so-called Wyoming Massacre prompted "the Great Runaway" of settlers from the west branch of the Susquehanna.[68] William MacClay, the son of immigrants from Antrim and who later became the first U.S. senator from Pennsylvania, left Sunbury and brought his family to Paxton. "I never in my Life saw such Scenes of distress," he reported. "The River and the Roads leading down it were covered with men, women and children, flying for their lives, many without any Property at all, and none who had not left the greatest part behind." If the enemy followed up on the blow they delivered at Wyoming, they would have no difficulty penetrating to Carlisle, he said. As they had twenty years earlier, the people in the backcountry feared nothing would be done to protect them.[69] MacClay recommended using horsemen and dogs to hunt down Indian war parties.[70]

There was worse to come. Cherry Valley in central New York by 1769 had 40–50 families, "mostly of those called Scotch Irish," according to a traveler through the region, as well as Germans and others in the area. By 1775, it had almost three hundred residents. In the Revolution, Scotch-Irish in the Cherry Valley region joined Germans and Dutch from the Mohawk Valley to form the Tryon County Militia. Joseph Brant of the Mohawks and Loyalist Captain Walter Butler attacked Cherry Valley in November 1778, killing about fourteen soldiers and thirty civilians, and taking seventy or more prisoners. There were Scotch-Irish people on both sides and caught in the middle. William McClellan begged the raiders to spare his house, barn, and belongings because he was a king's man; the Indians burned them anyway, saying that if they did not, the Americans would know he was a Loyalist and burn them.[71] Mary Jemison saw captives from Cherry Valley brought to the Seneca village where she was living.[72] After twenty years with the Senecas, it is not clear whether she viewed these people as fellow captives or enemy prisoners.

The Cherry Valley "massacre" hastened plans for an invasion by the Continental Army of Iroquois country, although withdrawing troops from garrisons on the Susquehanna for the campaign left that part of the frontier without adequate defenses. On July 28, 1779, Captain John McDonald, a Loyalist commanding a force of British and three hundred Senecas, attacked Fort Freeland in Northumberland County, where many settlers had gathered for safety. They killed or captured 108 people, although McDonald allowed fifty-four women and children and four old men to go free.[73] Colonel Matthew Smith and "60 Paxton Boys" with volunteers from the neighboring towns tried to catch up with the enemy, whose progress was slowed by the cattle they had taken, but the enemy burned everywhere they went, leaving the people in great distress. Joseph Reed, president of Pennsylvania's Supreme Executive Council, considered placing a bounty on Indian scalps and urged the inhabitants of Northumberland County to call out the militia as their best defense.[74]

After the murder of Cornstalk, the Ohio River became a war zone, one which Shawnee and Kentucky raiders crossed and recrossed, burning villages, plundering homes, and lifting scalps with equal ferocity. In Kentucky and southern Ohio, people gravitated to small forts called stations—some housing as many as thirty families behind substantial defenses, others consisting of a few cabins huddled together—and endeavored to carry out basic subsistence activities while constantly on the alert for Indian attacks.[75]

Boonesborough found itself in the thick of the border skirmishes. Although the settlement, of course, was named after Daniel Boone, of English Quaker ancestry, most of its first inhabitants appear to have come from County Antrim.[76] Simon Kenton, who grew up in a poor Scotch-Irish farming family in Virginia (his father was born in Northern Ireland in 1701 and emigrated to Virginia; his mother was Scots-Welsh), moved to Boonesborough in 1775. His life and storied frontier exploits in many ways paralleled those of the more famous Boone. Like Boone, he was captured by the Shawnees during the war. His former friend Simon Girty evidently used his influence among the Shawnees to save Kenton from being killed, and he was taken to Detroit in a prisoner exchange with the British.[77]

The war did not stop Scotch-Irish migrations deeper into Indian country. In 1779–1780, James Robertson joined John Donelson in establishing a settlement at the Cumberland Bluffs, now Nashville, Tennessee. Robertson and two hundred men drove livestock overland from the Holston River in East Tennessee along the Wilderness Road and through the Cumberland Gap to the French Lick. Reaching the site of the Cumberland settlement by Christmas, they built log cabins for their families, who arrived in the spring after traveling with Donelson in a flotilla of forty boats down the Holston and Tennessee and up the Cumberland, an odyssey of nearly one thousand miles. The Cumberland settlers were intruding on hunting grounds of Chickamauga Cherokees, Chickasaws, and Shawnees, and endured small-scale attacks, horse thefts, and individual killings for the rest of the war.[78]

Chickasaw hostility foiled the first attempt to establish an American settlement on the Mississippi, with disastrous results for one Scotch-Irish family. Anne and Andrew McMeans were both born in the Scotch-Irish backcountry. Their fathers had both migrated from Northern Ireland. Anne and Andrew married in Lancaster in 1762. In 1778 they sold their farm in Pennsylvania and moved to Kentucky. In early 1780, they traveled down the Ohio and joined some forty other families in George Rogers Clark's scheme to establish the town of Clarksville and Fort Jefferson on the east bank of the

Mississippi. Lack of supplies and a Chickasaw raid in August prompted many of the settlers to leave in September. The extended McMeans family joined the flotilla of refugees floating down the Mississippi to Natchez. Sickness—probably malaria—broke out on the McMeans' boat and they were unable to keep up. Snagged on a sandbar, they ran out of provisions. Andrew died, leaving Anne with seven children. His elder sister died. Two of the children died, possibly from eating poisonous plants. According to Anne's account, only the timely assistance of some passing Indian people saved the party from resorting to cannibalism. Anne survived and made it to Natchez, but it took her months to recover from the ordeal. In 1782 she and her surviving children found passage on a vessel back to Pennsylvania. Anne published a self-consciously religious account of "her weary pilgrimage" in 1824.[79]

As in the French and Indian War, some Scotch-Irish people in the new Tennessee settlements endured the ordeal of Indian captivity. Mary Neely was one of ten children, the daughter of William and Margaret Neely. Her father was born in Ireland and migrated first to South Carolina, then to Eastern Tennessee. He accompanied Robertson on the winter journey to French Lick and settled with his family at Mansker's Station, a dozen miles from French Lick. In August 1780, he and Mary were attacked by Shawnees when they ventured from the protection of the fort. The Shawnees tomahawked and scalped William, dragged Mary into a canoe, and paddled down the Cumberland River. After two years, and a bout of smallpox—during which she was blind for several days—Mary managed to escape while her Shawnee captors were visiting the British fort at Detroit. She was reunited with her brother, married George Spears in 1785, and lived first in Kentucky and then in Illinois. She became a local celebrity in her old age, known for her healing skills she had learned from the Indians. "Granny Spears" died in 1852.[80]

Despite the sufferings and sacrifices of backcountry settlers in the border warfare of the Revolution, East Coast officials continued to hold ambivalent attitudes about them and to blame them for the bloodshed on the frontier. "These people are, we own, difficult to manage," the Pennsylvania Council informed the Delegates to Congress.[81] Reporting on conditions in Westmoreland, Northampton, and Bedford counties in May 1778, Timothy Pickering told George Washington that many disaffected inhabitants mingled with Indians in committing barbarities. They were "a wild ungovernable race, little less savage than their tawny neighbours; and by similar barbarities have in fact provoked them to revenge; but the innocent are now involved in one common calamity with the guilty."[82] Washington shared such attitudes toward people who squatted on his lands, disputed his title, and refused to show him due deference. At the same time, like other land speculators and government officials, he relied on settler families to brave the dangers of frontier warfare and to help secure lands he intended to develop.[83] As commander-in-chief during the Revolution, he outsourced much of the fighting in the West to frontiersmen, who collected bounties on Indian scalps and furnished militia for expeditions against Indian villages, which, Washington, John Armstrong, and others were convinced, was the only way to win an Indian war.[84]

Waging War on Indian Fields and Families

For Scotch-Irish people throughout the backcountry, the immediate enemy was not British regulars but Tories and Indians, who threatened their families and their Presbyterian vision of social order. General William Campbell and Scotch-Irish militia from over the mountains are famously credited with the pivotal victory over Major Patrick Ferguson's Loyalists Scots at King's Mountain on the border of North and South Carolina in October 1780. King's Mountain and the brutality of the war in the southern backcountry helped unify inhabitants, while at the same time fueling outsiders' perceptions of "the Back Water men," as they derogatorily called them, as barbarians.[85] Scotch-Irish commanders and militia figured prominently in campaigns against Indian people, who had plenty of reason to agree with that characterization.

Virginia Governor Patrick Henry sent arms and ammunition to the frontier and appointed men like his brother-in-law William Christian and William Preston to defend the West against British-instigated Indian attacks.[86] Christian was born in 1742, two years after his family migrated from Ireland; Preston was born in Northern Ireland.[87] The Continental Congress appointed Andrew Lewis a brigadier-general and he took command of Virginia's volunteer units. Lewis died of "bilious fever" on September 26, 1781.

As soon as Dragging Canoe's warriors launched their attacks on the settlements at Watauga, Nolichucky, and Long Island, militia armies from Virginia, North and South Carolina, and Georgia swept through Cherokee country. As usual, there was a heavy Scotch-Irish presence. Although encroachments on Indian land were the root cause of the so-called Cherokee

War, revenge was a powerful force driving the retaliatory expeditions.[88] North Carolina's delegates to the Continental Congress urged the North Carolina Council of Safety to retaliate swiftly against the Cherokees, "to carry fire and Sword into the very bowels of their country and sink them so low that they may never be able to rise again and disturb the peace of their Neighbours."[89]

In August and September, General Griffith Rutherford and two thousand North Carolinians rendezvoused with Colonel Andrew Williamson and an army from South Carolina, guided by a contingent of twenty Catawba scouts, and destroyed the Lower and Middle Cherokee towns. The orphaned son of Scotch-Irish immigrants, Rutherford had moved to the Waxhaws from Pennsylvania in the 1750s and made a place for himself as a land speculator, local politician, and backcountry strongman. A veteran of the French and Indian War, he was appointed a brigadier general of the militia for the western frontier of the state in April 1776. He quickly earned a reputation for brutality against both Indians and Loyalists. He was convinced, he told the North Carolina Council of Safety, that the "finel Destruction of the Cherroce Nation" was necessary.[90] William Christian and 1,800 Virginians attacked the Overhill towns. They spared Chota, where the Raven sent a flag of truce as the Virginian army approached, but burned Big Island Town, Tellico, Chilhowee, and Settico and destroyed 50,000 bushels of potatoes and 40,000–50,000 bushels of corn, leaving the Cherokee inhabitants without food and shelter for the coming winter.[91]

Charles Cummings and Joseph Rhea both served as chaplains on the 1776 Cherokee campaign. Born and raised in County Donegal, Cummings migrated to Pennsylvania as a ministerial student, married the daughter of a Virginia planter, and became the first resident minister in the Holston area of southwestern Virginia. Known as the "Fighting Parson," he carried his rifle and shot pouch to church and organized settlers in defense against Indian attacks. His colleague Joseph Rhea was also a Donegal native and a pastor in Ulster before he emigrated with his wife and seven children in 1769 and settled in southwest Virginia near the Tennessee line.[92]

Faced with massive destruction, older Cherokee chiefs reasserted their influence and sued for peace. At the Treaty of DeWitt's Corner with Georgia and South Carolina in May 1777 and the Treaty of Long Island on the Holston with Virginia and North Carolina in July, the Cherokees lost more than five million acres as the price of peace.[93] William Christian and William Preston served as commissioners for Virginia at the treaty talks. The Cherokee chief

Old Tassel referred to Preston as "my old friend the Elk."[94] After the treaty of 1777, James Robertson was appointed Indian agent for North Carolina and went to live at Chota.[95] The Cherokees asked that the Watauga settlements be removed, but by then North Carolina had extinguished Indian title to the land the Wataugans had occupied for several years and passed a law authorizing sales of 640 acres to each settler at fifty shillings per 100 acres. A new wave of migration ensued, not least among militiamen who had eyed fertile lands as they campaigned through Cherokee country.[96]

Dragging Canoe stayed away from the treaty talks. He and his followers moved lower down the Tennessee River, built new towns along Chickamauga Creek, and kept up the fight. Fears of Cherokee raids and Loyalist plots kept backcountry militia on the alert and, in General Rutherford's words, "employed in the suppression of the Savages and other inhuman wretches who have their livelihood from Carnage and rapine."[97] Reports of massacres, plundering, and battles "stirred" Reverend James Hall, a Scotch-Irish minister near the Catawba River, to persuade his congregation to form a company of cavalry. As in the campaigns against the Cherokees, fighting between local Tory and Whig militia in backcountry areas where Scots and Scotch-Irish people were familiar with traditions of blood vengeance degenerated into "savage warfare."[98]

After the Battle of King's Mountain, Lord Cornwallis fell back on his Native allies for support and ordered his agents to direct Cherokee attacks against the mountain settlements. The attackers came from Chickamaugua, but American forces often retaliated against towns that were more easily accessible. In 1780, Jefferson dispatched John Sevier and Arthur Campbell and "the Wattago men" against the Overhill Cherokee towns on the Hiwassee and Little Tennessee Rivers. Sevier, a renowned Indian fighter from Tennessee, was of French Huguenot descent, although a nineteenth-century source promoting the importance of the Scotch-Irish opined that he "was born and reared among the Scotch-Irish, and no doubt caught some of their spirit."[99]

Arthur Campbell (William Campbell's cousin) was born in Augusta County in 1743. His father, David, was one of the region's earliest Scotch-Irish settlers. At age fifteen, Arthur was captured by Wyandots. After four years in captivity near Like Erie, he was released in 1760 when the British took Detroit, and he returned to southwest Virginia. In 1776 he was chosen as county lieutenant for Washington County (named after the general), an office he held for thirty years.[100] In December 1780, Campbell burned Settico, Tuskegee, Chota, and other towns, destroying about 1,000 houses and 50,000 bushels of corn, a massive blow to the Cherokees in the dead of winter. The Raven told the British the next year that the Virginians "dyed their hands in Blood of many of our Woman and Children, burnt 17 towns, destroyed all our provisions by which we & our families were almost destroyed by famine this Spring."[101]

Southern Scotch-Irish commanders faced the same problems as their Pennsylvania counterparts in raising militia and securing supplies for campaigns. Men with families in remote areas were reluctant to turn out for militia duty for fear the Indians would come when they were absent—on one occasion, Colonel William Preston in Montgomery County informed Governor Benjamin Harrison of Virginia, many of the militia were "skulking in the mountains."[102] Arthur Campbell was frustrated by lack of financial and material support from the government and the Continental Army, which limited his ability to launch offensive operations against the Cherokees. "They have struck the first blow, and are not going to desist until the terms of war are carried to their Country," he wrote Colonel William Davies in April 1782. The northern Indians had joined them in attacking the frontiers, and things were likely to get worse if measures were not taken against them. "Pardon this intrusion!" Campbell added. "I am insensibly led into discussions to men living in security, which may let affecting scenes pass with indifference."[103] Campbell enjoyed no such security himself. Hearing that a war party had been seen ten days before within twenty miles of his house, he wrote on June 5, 1782, he intended to ask leave to go home by the end of the week.[104]

By the end of the war, the Cherokees' miseries defied description, Christian told Governor Harrison. Men, women, and children were almost naked; their crops were worse than ever and their supplies of corn and potatoes would soon be exhausted, and they needed ammunition for hunting. Hundreds would die of hunger unless Virginia did something. He urged the government to buy and distribute corn to them.[105] After Christian was killed by Indians in 1786, the Cherokee chief Old Tassel remembered him as a good man who took care of everybody. "I loved Col. Christian, and he loved me," he told treaty commissioners from the state of Franklin.[106]

Like Christian, Andrew Pickens (Figure 9.2) also displayed a measure of mercy in the wake of the devastation he brought to Cherokee people. As a boy in the early 1750s, Pickens migrated with his own and other Scotch-Irish families from Virginia down the Great Wagon Road to the Waxhaws. He became a merchant, planter, justice of the peace, church elder, and Indian-fighting militia officer in the Ninety-Six District of western South

Figure 9.2 Andrew Pickens. Born in Pennsylvania to Scotch-Irish parents from Antrim, who moved the family down the Shenandoah Valley via the Great Wagon Road to Virginia and then to the Waxhaws on the South Carolina frontier, Pickens led campaigns against the Cherokees in both the Anglo-Cherokee War and the American Revolution.

From the New York Public Library. NYPL Digital Collections. https://digitalcollections.nypl.org/items/510d47da-30de-a3d9-e040-e00a18064a99.

Carolina. He served on the campaign against the Cherokees in 1760–1761 and he invaded Cherokee country again in the Revolution. In one fight, he said he and his troops fought until "every white man was literally covered with blood." In the 1781–1782 campaigns he helped destroy fifteen Cherokee towns and kill more than one hundred warriors, and in October 1782 he extorted a punitive Cherokee land cession.[107] Named "Sky-a-gun-sta," "great warrior" or a "good white warrior," Pickens also persuaded South Carolina to aid the Cherokees and bought two hundred pounds of supplies for starving Cherokee villages in the winter of 1782–1783.[108]

In the North, in 1779 Washington dispatched John Sullivan, an Irish American general from New Hampshire, to conduct a scorched-earth campaign through Iroquois country. "The immediate objects are the total destruction and devastation of their settlements and the capture of as many prisoners of every age and sex as possible," he instructed Sullivan. "It will be essential to ruin their crops now in the ground and prevent their planting more." Washington had long believed that striking Indians in their homes was the only way to stamp out their raids; now he was determined that Iroquoia would "not be merely overrun but destroyed." He forbade Sullivan to listen to any peace overtures until he had "very thoroughly completed the destruction of their settlements."[109] In town after town, from Chemung on the upper reaches of the Susquehanna to Chenussio on the Genesee River, the soldiers burned houses, cornfields, and stores of food, and cut down orchards. Sullivan estimated he destroyed forty towns, 160,000 bushels of corn, and vast quantities of fruit trees and vegetables.[110]

Many of the officers and men on Sullivan's expedition were Scotch-Irish. So was one of the Seneca people who experienced the ravages of the campaign. Mary Jemison and other Seneca women fled their villages as the army approached. When they returned, they found their homes destroyed and "not a mouthful of any kind of sustenance left, not even enough to keep a child one day from perishing with hunger." When winter came, the weather turned bitterly cold and snow fell to a depth of five feet, killing the game. The Senecas were reduced, Jemison recalled, "almost to a state of starvation through that and three or four succeeding years."[111] Iroquois refugees crowded around the British garrison at Fort Niagara. But Niagara stood at the end of a long supply line that was closed during the winter months when vessels from Montreal and Quebec could not navigate the ice-bound Great Lakes. The refugees endured exposure, starvation, sickness, and misery during one of the coldest winters on record.[112]

Initially, Sullivan's expedition seemed to have succeeded. There had been no sign of Indian war parties since the expedition returned, Colonel Matthew Smith reported to Pennsylvania President Reed from Paxton in late November 1779.[113] The following spring, however, Iroquois warriors resumed their attacks on the frontiers of New York and Pennsylvania with renewed vigor, to take grain and cattle as much as scalps and captives.[114]

In areas like Westmoreland County in Pennsylvania, the burden of defense—which often meant offense—continued to fall on the local communities. "The Savages are continually making depredations among us; not less than forty people have been killed, wounded, or captivated this Spring, and the Enemy have killed our Creatures within three hundred yards of this Town," Lieutenant Colonel Archibald Lochry informed President Reed from Hanna's Town in May 1779, adding in answer to Reed's inquiry that, yes, the inhabitants would appreciate a bounty on Indian scalps.[115] After giving much thought to the state of the frontiers, and anxious to relieve them, Reed issued "a Proclamation encouraging the young Fellows to turn out in small parties as the Enemy do."[116] It had little effect. Lochry struggled to raise men for the First Battalion of the Westmoreland militia, and the Second and Third Battalions of Westmoreland Militia were unable to raise any volunteers for an expedition because men on the frontiers dared not leave their families unprotected. Lochry feared that if the Indians knew how bad things were, they might easily drive the people over the Youghiogheny River.[117]

Like Washington, John Armstrong, and George Rogers Clark, Lochry and other Westmoreland County officers advocated offensive operations as the only sure way to snuff out Indian raids. Clark hoped to coordinate their efforts with his expedition against the Shawnee, Delaware, and Sandusky towns.[118] Westmoreland County sent militia to join Clark in the summer of 1781, but as Lochry and his party of eighty-three men descended the Ohio, they were ambushed near the mouth of the Miami River. Lochry was killed and scalped by a Shawnee warrior. Clark, with the support of Governor Patrick Henry, raised men from Kentucky, thereby weakening their home defenses, but instead of attacking Detroit and the Shawnee towns he headed for the Illinois country, where Henry and other Virginian land speculators hoped to establish claims. Yet again, elites with Scotch-Irish ancestry evidently had few qualms about manipulating people of Scotch-Irish ancestry for their own ends.[119] Despite Lochry's death and Clark's failure, offense remained the best means of defense. Writing to William Irvine after Lochry's defeat, William Moore, who had succeeded Reed as president, suggested that "the disposition of the people of Westmoreland county to emigrate into the Indian country" might be "diverted and applied" to launching an invasion.[120]

A village of Moravian Delawares at Gnadenhütten in the upper Muskingum Valley offered an easy target (Gnadenhütten means "huts of grace" in German).

The Delawares had rejected the missionary efforts of David McClure and David Jones in 1772—they apparently told Baptist missionary Jones that they associated Presbyterians with the violence and land hunger of the backcountry Scotch-Irish. However, some Delawares turned instead to Moravians, or at least tolerated them.[121] The Delaware Moravian converts were pacifists, but their neutrality rendered them suspect in the eyes of militants on both sides. As evidenced by their murder of White Eyes in 1778, few backcountry settlers distinguished among different groups of Delawares who took different positions in the war. When the Pennsylvania government offered scalp bounties, Colonel Brodhead at Fort Pitt feared it would "be construed into a License to take off the scalps of some of our friendly Delawares, and produce a general Indian War."[122] When Brodhead in 1780 recruited forty Delaware warriors to fight against the British, he had to assign regulars to guard them and their families when they camped outside the fort because Scotch-Irish from Hanna's Town attempted to kill them all, men, women, and children.[123]

Tragedy played out around Fort Pitt, where William Irvine (Figure 9.3) was in command. Born in 1741 near Enniskillen, County Fermaugh, and educated at Trinity College, Dublin, Irvine served as a British navy surgeon during the Seven Years War. After the war he emigrated to America and settled in Carlisle, likely drawn there by John Armstrong, a friend and fellow Enniskillen immigrant. Irvine practiced medicine and at thirty-three married sixteen-year-old Ann Callender, the eldest daughter of Scotch-Irish trader, merchant, land speculator, and militia captain Robert Callender. They had ten children. Irvine gave up practicing as a physician and became a military and political leader and land speculator, effectively forging a new American identity on the frontier. When the Revolution broke out, the Cumberland County Committee of Correspondence organized what Congress designated the Sixth Pennsylvania Battalion, with Irvine as commander, which went on campaign to Canada. Captured when a British army under Governor Guy Carleton defeated units of the Continental Army at the Battle of Three Rivers in Quebec in June 1776, Irvine was exchanged. The remnants of his force and new recruits were organized into the Seventh

Figure 9.3 Brigadier General William Irvine; etching by H. B. Hall, 1870. Born in Enniskillen in County Fermanagh, Irvine commanded the Western Department at Fort Pitt at the time of the Gnadenhütten massacre and the rout of William Crawford's expedition.
Collection of the Historical Society of Pennsylvania. Simon Gratz Autograph Collection (0250B).

Pennsylvania Regiment under his command, which remained in existence until early 1781. Irvine served as a colonel and brigadier-general in the Continental Army, and replaced Brodhead as commander at Fort Pitt from 1781 to 1783.[124]

When Irvine assumed command in November 1781, he reported to Washington that everything was in such a wretched state that there was little he could do. "I never saw troops cut so truly a deplorable, and at the same time despicable, a figure. Indeed, when I arrived, no man would believe from their appearance that they were soldiers; nay, it would be difficult to determine whether they were *white men*."[125] Short of men and ammunition, Irvine had to rely on the local militia. When he left Fort Pitt to go to Carlisle, Irvine delegated much of the day-to-day operation at the fort to Colonel John Gibson, as acting commander. He handed Gibson a volatile situation.

According to Spencer Records, a former resident of the area, looking back some sixty years later when he was eighty years old, "it came to pass that the devil entered into one Colonel Williamson."[126] Born in Carlisle in 1752, David Williamson was colonel of the 3rd Battalion of Washington County militia. Accusing the Moravian Delawares of aiding and abetting enemy raiding parties, in March 1782, Williamson and two hundred militiamen marched to Gnadenhütten. Gibson sent a warning to the village, but the messenger arrived too late. The previous month, Indian warriors had attacked the home of Robert Wallace on Raccoon Creek while he was absent, killed his wife Mary and youngest child, captured his surviving son, and slaughtered his cattle. According to one source, the militia found a woman at Gnadenhütten wearing Mary Wallace's dress. Their suspicions confirmed, they rounded up the inhabitants, separated the men and the women and children, and debated how to put them to death. A proposal to set fire to the houses and burn them alive was rejected; some thought it "too Barbarous," others "did not think it tormenting enough." Instead, the next day, the militia bound the Delawares together in pairs and, while their victims knelt and sang hymns, systematically bludgeoned them to death with wooden mallets. Then they scalped and burned them. Ninety-six men, women, and children perished. The militia headed back to Pittsburgh with a haul of furs, horses, and other plunder, killing several more peaceful Indians on the way.[127] On Sunday morning, March 24, a couple of weeks after Gnadenhütten, Scotch-Irish settlers on Chartiers Creek attacked friendly Delawares living on Smoky Island under the protection of Fort Pitt and killed several more people. Before they left for home, they sent word to Gibson threatening to scalp him, his Indian wife, and children for protecting the Delawares.[128]

A report detailing the atrocities of the Gnadenhütten massacre was submitted to Congress and communicated to the governments of Pennsylvania and of Virginia.[129] Another letter announced: "The Moravian Indian Congregation at Sandusky is butchered, as it is reported by the *Scotch*."[130] Once again, Indian-hating Scotch-Irish frontiersmen perpetrated a massacre that appalled Indians and whites alike. Not all Scotch-Irish people hated Indians or condoned the killers' actions, of course. Lieutenant Colonel Edward Cook of Westmoreland County was one of the few to risk the wrath of his Scotch-Irish neighbors and condemn the massacre. He assured President Moore that reports that "every man on this side the Mountains" approved of the massacre were false; in fact, most people believed that "the Perpetrators of that wicked Deed" ought to be brought to justice and that unless the government did something, it would "Disgrace the Annals of the United States, and be an Everlasting Plea and Cover for British Cruelty."[131] Spencer Records maintained that he never heard anyone mention the massacre without expressing their abhorrence, "except one poor old Scotchman, James Greenlee." Greenlee apparently told Records that Williamson's men did the right thing, "but he did not receive any sanction of his approval from his neighbors."[132]

However, the local political culture made dissent difficult, and people looked the other way.[133] Back in command at Fort Pitt, William Irvine did nothing. In a letter to his wife, he said the perpetrators spared neither age nor sex. "What was more extraordinary, they did it in cold blood, having deliberated three days, . . . fell on them while they were singing hymns and killed the whole. Many children were killed in their wretched mothers' arms. Whether this was right or wrong, I do not pretend to determine." Irvine understood that people who had had "fathers, mothers, brothers or children, butchered, tortured, scalped by the savages" felt very differently about killing Indians than did people who lived farther east in "perfect safety." He implored Ann, whatever her own opinions might be, to keep them to herself, lest any sentiments she expressed be attributed to him. "No man knows whether I approve or disapprove of killing the Moravians," he said.[134] The Supreme Executive Council of Pennsylvania ordered Irvine to investigate the massacre. He interrogated Williamson and several of his officers and found popular sentiment overwhelmingly in favor of the massacre. Best to let the matter rest, he reported.[135]

Unlike the Paxton Boys, whose identities were never revealed, the identities of the Indian-killers at Gnadenhütten were known and acknowledged. A partial list of the names of men from Washington County who took part in the massacre was published in 1888, edited by an amateur local historian named William H. Egle, M.D., who wrote, "It is not our purpose to extenuate or censure the Pioneers of Western Pennsylvania, who in their efforts to secure peaceful homes, found the necessity to exterminate the red man prowling the frontiers." He acknowledged that the list was incomplete, as there were at least 160 men under "the brave Williamson."[136]

When George Croghan's son, William, arrived at Fort Pitt in April, he found that the people in the surrounding countryside talked of "Nothing but killing Indians, & taking possession of their lands."[137] Succumbing to pressure, Irvine launched another campaign into Indian country. Three months after Gnadenhütten, he dispatched an expedition with orders to destroy the Indian town and settlements at Sandusky in northern Ohio with fire and sword, "by which we hope to give ease and safety to the inhabitants of this country."[138]

The Sandusky expedition comprised 480 mounted volunteers, mostly Scotch-Irish. Colonel William Crawford, a friend and land business associate of George Washington, commanded; David Williamson was second-in-command. Many of the militia had been with Williamson at Gnadenhütten. The British commander at Detroit dispatched a force of rangers, under Captain William Caldwell, and Indian warriors led by Matthew Elliott. Like Elliott, Caldwell was a Scotch-Irish trader from Pennsylvania. Born around 1750 in County Fermanagh, he emigrated to Pennsylvania in 1773, and served in Dunmore's War. At Detroit, he and Elliott became partners in the fur trade and land business, as well as on campaign against the Americans.[139] The Pennsylvanian militia fared very differently when facing armed warriors ready for battle instead of unarmed pacifists surprised in their homes.

The Delawares and their allies routed the expedition and captured and ritually tortured Crawford. Hopocan, who had attended the Treaty of Fort Pitt with Crawford four years earlier, presided over his execution. According to an eyewitness account, Crawford begged Simon Girty to shoot him. Girty intervened to help and even save captives on other occasions during the war—Samuel Murphy, Margaret Handley Erskine, John Burkhart, and his old friend Simon Kenton—but he could do nothing to save Crawford. The Delawares were culturally obligated to exact revenge for the slaughter of their relatives at Gnadenhütten. Girty refused, saying he had no gun, and asked, "how can you expect any other—this in Retaliation for the meravians [moravians] that was murdered last Spring." The story of Girty's refusal was fundamental to his evil reputation.[140] Reports of Crawford's grisly fate provided powerful anti-Indian propaganda long after the war, while Native resistance leaders for generations invoked memories of Gnadenhütten as testimony to the white man's perfidy and genocidal intentions toward Indian people.[141]

The Continuing War on the Scotch-Irish Frontier

Lord Cornwallis's surrender at Yorktown in October 1781 effectively ended the fighting in the East between American, British, and French forces. The story was very different for Scotch-Irish and Indian people in the West, where the war continued, and indeed heated up. The "Township of Ardmaugh is, at this Time, the nearest Frontier to the Indians in that Quarter, and is quite exposed to the Incursions of the Savages, no Troops whatever being stationed among them," complained petitioner William Brown from Cumberland County in April 1782, begging for state troops or militia and ammunition.[142] While Washington decried the continuing violence, he also wanted the United States to lay claim to as much of the Ohio country as it could before the peace terms ending the war were decided. Whether conducted by federal forces or local militias, military strikes that drove Indian people from their homes and fields helped to establish the new nation's claim to their lands.[143] The continuing war in the West was a war for Indian land, with the Scotch-Irish at the heart of the conflict.

Native Americans ramped up their attacks after the grisly murders at Gnadenhütten. On July 13, 1782, Guyasuta, who had worked hard to stay out of the war when it started, attacked Hanna's Town with about one hundred Seneca warriors and sixty Canadian rangers. The town was now the county seat of Westmoreland. It consisted of about thirty log houses, with a stockade fort at its northern end. Guyasuta burned it to the ground, an event, William Irvine informed Pennsylvania President Moore, that "put the people generally into great confusion for some days."[144]

The attack was a traumatic event in the hard life of Elizabeth Brownlee Guthrie. Elizabeth was born in Derry in 1755. Her father emigrated to America in 1771 and two years later moved with his wife and six children to Hanna's Town, where he became a prominent member of the Scotch-Irish community. During the Revolution, Elizabeth's first husband, William Brownlee, served in the Eighth Pennsylvania Regiment. The Brownlees and their neighbors were attending a wedding at Miller's Station a couple of miles from town when the attack happened and were captured. The Indian warriors knew Brownlee and "on hearing his name, instantly fell on him and murdered him and his son, together with nine other persons," Elizabeth recalled in a petition to the Pennsylvania legislature in February 1829, nearly forty-seven years later. "Your petitioner with her little child in her arms was dragged along as prisoners." Taken to the Seneca town of Cattaraugus and near death, she and her daughter were sold to the British at Niagara, transferred to Montreal, and finally returned home after an ordeal of thirteen months. She married her second cousin, William Guthrie, who had also served in the Eighth Regiment and commanded a company of rangers. Guthrie's "habits of life" rendered him inept at farming or any other business, and his attempts at land speculation in the 1780s and 1790s failed. The family moved to more remote regions, where they settled as squatters and lived "in great want of the indispensable necessaries of life." William received a pension from Pennsylvania. After he died in a wagon accident in 1828, Elizabeth, "destitute of everything that could make her comfortable" in her old age, petitioned the Assembly to grant the same pension to her. Her request was granted.[145]

In Kentucky, Shawnee war parties ranged the frontier in the summer of 1782. In August, a force of two or three hundred Indians and thirty rangers, led again by William Caldwell and Matthew Elliott, attacked Bryan's Station at present-day Lexington. At Blue Licks on the Licking River, they ambushed a force that included Daniel Boone, killing more than seventy of them, including Boone's son, Israel. Hugh McGary was evidently largely to blame for the disaster. McGary had scores to settle. Indians had ambushed a party of sugar makers from Harrodsburg in 1777 and killed his stepson. In a clash with Shawnees the next day, McGary himself was wounded, but he killed, or found dead, a Shawnee wearing the stepson's hunting shirt. McGary reportedly hacked the Shawnee's body to pieces and "fed him to the dogs." At Blue Licks he impulsively urged the Kentuckians forward into the Shawnee trap.[146] "Never was the lives of so many valuable men lost more shamefully than in the late action of the 19th of August, and that not a little thro' the vain and seditious expressions of a Major McGreary," Colonel Arthur Campbell, the veteran commander of an expedition against the Cherokees, wrote Colonel William Davies. "How much more harm than good can one fool do[?]." For Campbell, the disaster confirmed the need for capable officers and for militia to adapt to Indian fighting.[147]

The effects of the disaster at Blue Licks reverberated through countless lives in close-knit backcountry communities. Ann Wilson Pogue Lindsey McGinty was born Ann Kennedy in Virginia in the 1730s. She lost her first husband John Wilson and their only child in the early 1760s. In 1762 she married William Pogue, with whom she had five children in Virginia and two more after they migrated to Kentucky. The Pogues were among the first families at Boonesborough. When Boonesborough became too dangerous, they moved to Fort Harrod, but William died there during an Indian siege in 1778 or 1779. A few years later, Ann married John Lindsey, a former trader who had moved to Kentucky after serving with George Rogers Clark. Lindsey was killed at Blue Licks. Five years later, Ann married James McGinty in 1787, but he became abusive and they separated. Ann then supported herself by running a tavern and raised her children and ran the household on her own.[148]

In the fall, George Rogers Clark retaliated by invading Shawnee country. Boone and Simon Kenton participated in the campaign, which burned five villages, destroyed corn, "and spread desolation through their country," as Boone wrote in his journal. The Shawnees said "the white Savages Virginians" committed atrocities.[149] Clark was not to blame for his men's actions, Colonel Joseph Crockett wrote Governor Harrison of Virginia; he had "*strain'd every nerve* in his power" to raise enough men and could not subject those he had to good order.[150] Many Shawnees pulled back from the Ohio River, where they were vulnerable to such assaults and congregated with their allies in towns on the Auglaize and Maumee rivers in northeastern Ohio, multiethnic refugee communities that became the center of the continuing Indian war for independence.[151] Other Shawnees migrated beyond the Mississippi, and many Delawares continued their westward movement. About sixty Delawares passed through the Cumberland country in the winter of 1780 on their way to settle on Bear Creek on the Tennessee River, and by 1785 there were some five hundred Delawares living in Chickasaw country.[152]

While the British and Americans went about the business of negotiating peace in Paris, backcountry settlers continued to invade Indian lands and attack Indian villages. Brigadier Allan Maclean, the British commander at Fort Niagara, was trying to stop his Native allies from going to war. However, the Americans, he said, "were preparing to cut the throats of the Indians."[153] Indians responded in kind and their raids continued unabated. The settlements on Clinch, Bluestone, and New River expected Indian war parties to be "upon them" as usual in the spring, as soon as the season permitted them to penetrate the mountains, William Preston wrote Governor Harrison in February 1783. Many of the inhabitants were already preparing to leave for the interior.[154] Frontier counties continued to pepper Harrison with requests for assistance. Little had changed: he ordered militia from adjacent counties, but that was often ineffectual. Meanwhile, Clark insisted that Indians could never be kept quiet except by invading their country.[155]

Writing to Washington from Carlisle at the end of the war in April 1783, William Irvine said the renewed raids exacerbated "a temper already pretty prevalent among backcountry settlers, never to make peace with Indians." He feared there could be no peace until all the western tribes were driven beyond the Mississippi and the lakes. Although it would take time and expense, it was much more effective than throwing money away on treaties.[156] Major Isaac Craig echoed and amplified his commander's views. Craig had emigrated from County Down as a young man, served throughout the Revolution as an artillery officer, and was now stationed at Fort Pitt. Despite their promises, the British had not restrained the Indians, and families were being murdered every day, Craig wrote Irvine. "Prospects of peace on this side of the mountains seem to vanish." He hoped Congress would send an expedition "to extirpate or at least properly chastise these marauding rascals" and looked forward to "the pleasure of battering the Wyandot blockhouses in the course of the ensuing summer and perhaps of taking possession of Detroit."[157]

As the fighting continued and revenge killings multiplied, Indian-hating and Indian-killing dominated the attitudes of the Scotch-Irish and their neighbors who had lost relatives and property. Washington blamed the "wanton Barbarities" on frontier inhabitants, both Indian and white.[158] Racial violence became the new normal in the West, and Indian killing became almost a way of life and an article of faith, supplanting more moderate policies advocated by U.S. Indian agents, Congress, and the military.[159] John Ferdinand Smyth, a Scottish-born Loyalist writing just after the Revolution, said Americans' antipathy toward Indians was widespread "and nothing is more common than to hear them talk of extirpating them totally from the face of the earth, men, women, and children."[160] Such widely held sentiments continued to gain ground and culminated decades later, in 1828, when another Scotch-Irish commander from the backcountry entered the White House.

As in the French and Indian War and Pontiac's War, stories of Indian attacks and atrocities during the Revolution multiplied and endured in community memories. For example, Shawnees captured Rachel McCutchen and killed her child. Rachel eventually escaped, but "she was crazy after she returned," a neighbor remembered. "Went about with a rake, turning over the leaves in the fence corners, looking for her son."[161] In western Pennsylvania the threat and reality of Indian raids encouraged communal reliance in Presbyterian congregations as people came together for prayer and protection. Experiences during the frontier warfare of the Revolution also gave rise to an enduring folklore of Scotch-Irish daily life and worship in a world of danger.[162] Thomas Mellon, the father of Andrew Mellon, migrated to America with his family in 1818, following family members and settling in Westmoreland County. As a youth there in the 1820s, Thomas heard the stories:

> The old people yet living when we came there never tired of relating the local horrors of the settlement: how certain families were massacred and burned in their cabins; how at one time when the Indians had come suddenly upon the settlement and the children were at school, the teacher dismissed them to hide in the woods and thickets as best they could, and fled to take his chances for life or death under similar conditions.

Events such as the burning of Hanna's Town, Mellon said, "formed an exhaustless source of conversation among the old people," who called to mind "similar atrocities in the massacres in Ulster by the native Irish, in 1641."[163] Mellon's experience was common. Philip Vickers Fithian, a Presbyterian missionary, reported that all the people in the back settlements were "very taleful of the Indian Wars."[164]

The Scotch-Irish may never have been natural frontiersmen, as some writers have claimed, but they were frontiersmen by the end of the Revolution as they pushed west over the Alleghenies, into the Ohio country, through the Cumberland Gap, into Alabama and Mississippi and beyond.[165] As Scotch-Irish immigrants carried stories of Irish atrocities to western Pennsylvania when they arrived, so subsequent generations carried stories of Indian atrocities with them as they traveled west. In *Sketches of History, Life, and Manners in the West*, first published in 1857, James Hall likened the intense hatreds that developed on American frontiers to "the history of the borders of England and Scotland." American pioneers, born and raised on successive frontiers from generation to generation, found themselves in the same situation in relation to Indians and their own government. "Every child thus reared, learns to hate an Indian, because he always hears him spoken of as an enemy.... Every family can number some of its members or relatives among the victims of a midnight massacre.... With persons thus reared, hatred towards an Indian becomes a part of their nature, and revenge an instinctive principle." The children of Scotch-Irish families who had endured the frontier fighting of the Revolution were primed for conflict with Indian people they met elsewhere.[166] At the same time, in the same way, Delaware and other Indian people migrating west carried with them stories of the Paxton massacre, the murders of Cornstalk and White Eyes, and Gnadenhütten.

In general, in the Revolution the Scotch-Irish managed to shed many of the negative characteristics commonly attributed to them as Irish Presbyterians, and their historical associations with republicanism appeared in a more positive light. However, Scotch-Irish responses to the Revolution varied, and acceptance in American society was neither immediate nor unanimous. Complaining to Virginian legislator and future president James Monroe around 1780 about the transformation of politics in Virginia and other states, Major General Charles Lee—who had been born in Great Britain—fumed that state assemblies had fallen into the wrong hands; instead of monarchy, aristocracy, or democracy, "it is rather a Mac-ocracy by which I mean a banditti of low Scotch-Irish whose names generally begin with Mac—and who are either the sons of Imported Servants or themselves imported Servants." On the whole, however, unlike Highland Scots who had fought for absolute monarchy in the Jacobite Rebellions of 1715 and 1745 and now apparently did so again, the Scotch-Irish, it seemed now, naturally fought in the cause of republicanism, allowing them to redefine their position in American society and to redefine their identity as Americans.[167]

Before the Revolution, backcountry Scotch-Irish and their frontier neighbors were generally seen as troublemakers who ignored regulations, defied legitimate government and their betters, and were in many ways worse than the Indians they lived next to and fought against. Their lack of deference to authority and unruly behavior persisted, but the Revolution depicted all Indians as enemies of American independence and turned Indian-killing into a patriotic duty. With some notable exceptions, it unified the Scotch-Irish against British Tories and Indians and helped them achieve shared identity as white Americans fighting a common enemy.[168] Before the Revolution, the fears and realities of Indian warfare contributed to the development of a white racial consciousness, in which disparate groups of European colonists shared pervasive anti-Indian sentiments.[169] During the Revolution, the fears and realities of Indian warfare contributed to the development of an American white racial consciousness.[170] Backcountry Scotch-Irish—likened to "savage" Indians by Anglo-American elites from the very beginning of their immigration—distanced themselves from Indians by killing Indians. In short, they became American by killing Indians.[171] Invoking their own history of combating savagery and royal tyranny in Northern Ireland, Scotch-Irish joined other Americans in crafting an identity for themselves as an exceptional people who vanquished tyranny and turned an uncivilized land into an empire of liberty that excluded "the merciless Indian Savages" whom, as the Declaration of Independence stated, a tyrannical king had unleashed on the inhabitants of the frontiers.[172] Their contributions to winning the Revolution enabled the Scotch-Irish and their descendants to take their place as Americans in the new nation.[173]

For Scotch-Irish Americans on the nation's frontiers, however, the freedoms and opportunities they had helped to win during the Revolution often remained elusive.

PART III
SCOTCH-IRISH AMERICANS AND AN EXPANDING NATION

10

Fighting Landlords, Indians, and Taxes

In September 1784, George Washington set out to tour his western lands. At the close of the Revolution, he owned approximately 58,000 acres west of the Alleghenies: 4,695 acres in southwestern Pennsylvania, 9,744 along the Ohio River, and 43,466 along the Great Kanawha.[1] At Miller's Run, in an area of western Pennsylvania the state had named Washington County, he came across several Scotch-Irish families squatting on his land. Rather than tamely defer to the general who had just won America's independence, they challenged the legality of his title and defiantly asserted that they had earned the right to settle there. When the squatters reluctantly offered to buy, Washington offered them 999-year leases or sale over three years with interest. When they asked him to extend the purchase period and forgo the interest, he refused. Washington hired Thomas Smith, a Carlisle attorney, and two years later a court found in Washington's favor. The Scotch-Irish squatters moved away rather than pay rent to an absentee landlord, no matter who he was.[2]

There was more to the incident than tight fists and hard heads. The Revolution on the frontier had involved conflicts over lands between Indian peoples and Scotch-Irish colonists. Those conflicts continued after the Revolution and were accompanied by ongoing clashes between settlers and landlords over property, who held it, and on what terms. Backcountry settlers aggressively sought land and the economic independence it brought, and they believed they could and should earn title by occupying, clearing, planting, and building on the land.[3] In the cutthroat scramble for land in the early Republic, however, they found that landlords, land speculators, and governments often stood in their way, and agrarian unrest spread across the post-revolutionary frontier, as it had on previous frontiers when common people seeking land-based autonomy confronted gentlemen who controlled access to the land.[4] The Scotch-Irish may have achieved unity with other Americans fighting British and Indians in the Revolution, but old fractures of region and class resurfaced as the new nation built itself on Indigenous lands.[5] Frontier conflicts after the Revolution involved a reshuffling of relationships among multiple groups and a tangled triangular contest of Scotch-Irish settlers, eastern governments, and Indian nations.

Pennsylvania's Scotch-Irish generally enjoyed an improved situation after the Revolution. They had proved themselves as Americans in the war and they now dominated the state's government. Writing to London bookseller William Strahan in August 1784, Benjamin Franklin said, "It is a fact, that the Irish emigrants and their children are now in possession of the government of Pennsylvania by their majority in the Assembly, as well as of a great part of the territory."[6] Even so, like the families ejected from Miller's Run, many Scotch-Irish in western Pennsylvania experienced frustration and hardship where Washington and other absentee landlords found profit. Eighty "Scotch-Irishmen" signed a memorial to the Pennsylvania Assembly in 1785 on behalf of widow Katherine Smith. Left with ten children, Smith had taken three hundred acres at the mouth of White Deer Creek on the West Branch of the Susquehanna. She borrowed money and built a sawmill and grist mill, completed in 1775. Four years later, Indians burned the mills. Her eldest son was killed fighting (Indians, she believed) on the frontier. After the war, Smith returned with her family and began rebuilding the mills. But then Claypoole and Morris, Philadelphia land buyers and speculators who claimed the land, sent agents who ordered her off the land. Her Scotch-Irish neighbors rallied to her support in the memorial, but it was unsuccessful.[7] In the minds and experiences of people like Katherine Smith, eastern elites were sometimes as big a threat as Indians.

Some historians maintain that the Scotch-Irish in America ceased to be Scotch-Irish after the Revolution, easily taking their place as Americans in the new nation they had helped to create. This is partly true. They may have won acceptance when they helped win the independence that, among other freedoms, secured access to trans-Appalachian lands, but their distinctive identity and local loyalties did not disappear so easily in the backcountry.[8] And their pursuit of land and economic independence on the frontier continued to pit them against East Coast governments and elites as well as Indians in the early years of the Republic. They and their Native neighbors not only shared and contested borderland regions, they also, increasingly, shared a borderland culture of race hatred and endemic violence which the federal government struggled to control and adjudicate as it tried to implement an orderly process of transforming Native homelands into American property.[9] Many backcountry Scotch-Irish Americans opposed the creation of a strong federal government, which they suspected was controlled by eastern elites.[10] For their part, the French delegate in Philadelphia, Guillaume Otto, reported in 1790, eastern elites generally regarded American emigrants on the frontiers as "the scum of mankind and infinitely more ferocious, more perfidious and more intractable than the savages themselves." The federal and state governments did what they could to restrain them, and the troops stationed on the frontiers were there "to check the Americans rather than the savages."[11]

New Immigrants and Continuing Migration

The flow of migration from Ulster to America stuttered and stalled during the Revolution but resumed and increased afterward. The war's end unleashed a small flood of Irish emigration to the new United States—at least 5,000 in 1783, perhaps 15,000–20,000 in 1784, and then between 3,000 and 5,000 every year until the War of 1812. Between 100,000 and 150,000 Irish people emigrated between 1780 and 1814. More migrated to America in the fifty years following the Revolution than had done so in the one hundred years preceding it. Although they came from southern Ireland as well as the north, at least two-thirds of the immigrants were from Ulster, primarily Presbyterians of Scottish ancestry.[12]

The first United States census in 1790 recorded a population of almost 4 million. Of the white population, between 440,000 and 517,000, roughly comprising 14 to 17 percent, were of identifiable Irish extraction. Most of those, upward of 350,000, were of Scotch-Irish descent, although how many actually were born in Ireland is unknown. Scholars broadly agree that somewhere around 10 percent of the white population were Scotch-Irish.[13] The British consul in Charleston wrote Lord Grenville in late December 1791 that although the population growth was attributable to natural increase, it was also the case that "many thousands" had come from the north of Ireland and Highlands of Scotland. Eight hundred had arrived just at Charleston from Larne and Londonderry.[14] The new immigrants who arrived from Ulster in large numbers after the Revolution did not jettison their identities at the quayside.

As they had before, and as letters written by trans-Appalachian migrants demonstrate, many followed in the wake of relatives who had gone before.[15] Immigrants sent letters back to Ireland, and western settlers sent letters to eastern friends, relatives, and business associates. John Breckenridge, whose grandfather had emigrated from Ulster to Pennsylvania and then moved on to Augusta County, Virginia, corresponded for almost a decade with friends and family members about lands and conditions in Kentucky. He also did his own tour of inspection in 1789, before he sold his Virginia plantation and moved west in 1793, settling his household and twenty slaves on six hundred acres of prime agricultural land on the North Fork of Elkhorn Creek.[16] Most Scotch-Irish American migrants were not as well-heeled as Breckenridge. They went for reasons that would have been familiar to many Ulster emigrants—to escape high rents, heavy taxes, and poor or depleted soil, and to find economic independence in farmland.

Not all who had fought Indians in the Revolution moved west, however. Military warrants—scrip for claims to western land—were used during the Revolution in lieu of pay, as war bounties, and as incentive payments to encourage soldiers to re-enlist. Many veterans expected their warrants would give them a fresh start and the chance for economic security. Yet individuals who lacked the opportunity or the means to relocate often sold them for a pittance to wealthier men who offered ready cash. Job Johnson, a poor rural schoolmaster who had migrated from Ulster in the early 1760s, wrote home touting the benefits of Pennsylvania as "As Good a Country as any Man Needs to Dwell In." He served throughout the Revolution, in New Jersey, for three years in the border warfare in Pennsylvania and Ohio, and at Yorktown. In a letter to his brother after the war, Johnson said that most of the time he served as a deputy commissary general in the western department he was "out against the Indians." He declined to say much about "that Savage people that we had to fight against, and their Cruelty to us when in their power," or about the battles, casualties, and hardships they suffered in Indian country, "as it would swell My letter that I would write Nothing else." Although Johnson bought or was granted 1,500 acres in Fayette County, Kentucky, after the war, he remained in Philadelphia teaching school, probably because his health had suffered too much to allow him to move west. He died in 1790, directing that his lands be sold to cover his debts and funeral expenses. Unfortunately, his Kentucky deeds were probably worthless because Virginia's government had granted and sold more lands than existed, creating a maze of uncertain titles that all too often benefited lawyers and speculators and left ordinary settlers landless.[17]

Nevertheless, Scotch-Irish Americans continued to move west in growing numbers. Thousands of Scotch-Irish from Pennsylvania, mostly from the Cumberland Valley and the southwestern area of the state, migrated to Ohio between 1780 and 1820, where they created settlements and established counties.[18] Colonel Josiah Harmar, who as commander of the First American Regiment, was charged with evicting squatters as well as establishing a military presence in the Ohio country, recorded "almost incredible" numbers of people traveling down the Ohio River, as hundreds of boats, several hundred wagons, and almost twelve thousand people, with several thousand horses and hundreds of cattle and hogs, passed by his post between October 1786 and June 1788.[19] Although there are no figures regarding what proportion of this human flood was Scotch-Irish, it was substantial. Others pushed into Kentucky and Tennessee, and historians describe the 250,000 people who passed through Cumberland Gap between 1775 and 1800 as primarily "of Ulster stock."[20] Although one survey of Tennessee country population in 1790 estimated that only about 11 percent were Scotch-Irish, Tennessee had nearly 106,000 people in 1800, about one-third of whom were of Scotch-Irish descent. The children and grandchildren of emigrants who had settled first in Pennsylvania, Virginia, Maryland, and other states, they lived mainly in the mountainous east, along the tributaries of the Tennessee River.[21]

Between 1780 and 1840, as territory west of the Blue Ridge and Allegheny Mountains opened to "legal" white settlement, a new society developed in southwestern North Carolina, composed primarily of English, German, and Scotch-Irish. The 1790 census listed three hundred nuclear families named "Alexander" in Catawba County, North Carolina. As people in motion, the Scotch-Irish were not always fully represented in census data, however; they tended to dominate the first phase of frontier settlement and then often moved on.[22] From North Carolina, they went south and west into Georgia and Tennessee and beyond.

As they pushed deeper into the interior, they continued to congregate around areas of settlement and establish regional cultures. It stands to reason, though, that those settlements and cultures became less distinctively Scotch-Irish as migrants moved farther and mixed with other peoples. One historical geographer, considering the folk culture and landscape of the Upland South, identified various Scotch-Irish "hearth areas" that developed over time and space: a primary one in the Lower Delaware Valley, Chesapeake Tidewater, and Carolina Low Country; a secondary area in the Shenandoah Valley, North Carolina Piedmont, and Carolina Upcountry; a tertiary hearth area in the Watauga area; and a quaternary in Middle Tennessee. A regional culture coalesced in the quaternary Middle Tennessee hearth of the Upland South by around 1790–1815. By then, however, the blending of English,

Scotch-Irish, Welsh, German, Swedish, Finnish, and Indigenous peoples and cultures had produced an entirely new population. The process was illustrated by southern notched-log cabin construction, which derived from Pennsylvanian models but exhibited colonial continuities, Indigenous selections, and backcountry modifications that gave it its own regional character. From Tennessee, migrants spread to Arkansas, Missouri, and Texas, where Tennesseans were a major presence as early as 1820s.[23] People who traveled as Virginians, Pennsylvanians, and North Carolinians became Kentuckians, Tennesseans, Georgians, Missourians, and Texans in their new locations. Mingling with other westward-moving Americans, they became Americans themselves in the process.[24]

And yet, identities, attitudes, old habits, and shared experiences as backcountry Scotch-Irish were not quickly or easily shed. In some cases, they appear to have been reinforced as subsequent generations in new places shared and invoked the same defining experiences as their parents and grandparents in dealing with Indian neighbors, eastern elites, and unresponsive governments. Backcountry Scotch-Irish communities retained distinctive characteristics, even if they were no longer distinctive to Ulster. Travelers from the East and from Europe recorded familiar impressions of the Scotch-Irish people they encountered in the West.

Virginian Arthur Lee, one of three commissioners sent to make treaties with the Ohio Indians in 1784, stopped at Carlisle on his journey west. Cumberland County, he wrote in his journal, "is peopled almost entirely with Scotch and Irish, who have become rich by farming; the land producing wheat, which is their staple commodity." When he reached Pittsburgh, he found it "inhabited almost entirely by Scots and Irish, who live in paltry log-houses, and are as dirty as in the north of Ireland, or even Scotland." He doubted Pittsburgh would ever amount to much.[25] Traveling in the region of Hillsborough, North Carolina, John Ferdinand Smyth, a Scottish-born American Loyalist, asked the locals for directions without success. The German inhabitants could not speak English, and those who could were "chiefly natives of Ireland, most wretchedly ignorant and uncivilized."[26] Traveling from Philadelphia in 1787 with a party of emigrants heading to Kentucky, Mary Dewees described the people at Cherry's Mill in southwestern Pennsylvania as "Scotch-Irish, exceedingly kind but surprisingly dirty."[27]

Philadelphia physician and signer of the Declaration of Independence Dr. Benjamin Rush sketched a portrait of the backwoods settler that sounds a lot like a passage by Frederick Jackson Turner: "As he lives in the neighbourhood of Indians, he soon acquires a strong tincture of their manners," and "is nearly related to an Indian in his manners." Rush noted the growth of class distinctions and the emergence of a backcountry Scotch-Irish elite; a dinner at the home of Jonathan Montgomery in Carlisle was as "plentiful, elegant, and as well attended as any dinner I ever was at in a Gentleman's house in Philadelphia." Nevertheless, Rush regarded the Scotch-Irish in general as dirtier and lazier than the Germans. He suggested that the reason they always migrated southward from Pennsylvania was because the soil and climate in the western parts of Virginia, the Carolinas, and Georgia afforded an easier living for lazy farmers than did the hard soils of Pennsylvania. In fact, he concluded, Pennsylvania was "the great outport of the United States," acting as "a sieve by detaining all those people who possess the stamina of industry and virtue, it allows the passage to the rest to those states which are accommodated to their habits of indolence and vice."[28] Colonel John May of Boston, traveling in the Ohio country in 1789, wrote in his journal: "Sunday, 27th. Feel no better. Where the devil did this accursed Scotch Irish itch come from?" The itch was likely scabies, an infestation of microscopic insects picked up from people with poor personal hygiene, and often associated with Scotch-Irish backcountry folk.[29]

Foreign visitors echoed Americans' opinions. Johann David Schoepf, a German doctor who traveled west to Pittsburgh in 1783, recorded the customary European impression of frontier inhabitants who lived in log cabins, grew corn, had a few pigs and cattle, hunted, and wore leggings and fringed hunting shirts: "These hunters or 'backwoodmen' live very like the Indians and acquire similar ways of thinking. They shun everything which appears to demand of them law and order, dread anything which breathes constraint."[30] A young Swiss traveler passing through the settlements between the mouth of the Cumberland and Nashville in 1785 noted that officials and leading citizens like James Robertson had "in some degree polished these rough dwellers of the wilderness, who, in their lonely and distant fastness, had in truth begun to live very much like the Indians."[31] Traveling in western Tennessee in May 1797, Louis-Philippe, the future king of France, complained in his diary that the settlers in the region made his trip "absolutely unbearable." In contrast to the Cherokees who treated the French traveler and his companions with boundless hospitality, they were crude, lazy, and inhospitable. "They are the most villainous breed of men I have ever come across. By and large they are the scum of Ireland and America." Even so, he added, "Whatever my prejudice against the Irish settlers, I always found them more hospitable and less disgusting than the American settlers."[32] William Strickland, an English farmer visiting America around 1800, wrote "none emigrate to the frontiers beyond the mountains, except culprits, or savage backwoodsmen, chiefly of Irish descent . . . a race possessing all the vices of civilized and savage life without the virtues of either . . . the outcasts of the world, and the disgrace to it."[33] In the American laboratory for testing the theory that human societies evolved from a state of savagery to an age of reason, squatters and backwoodsmen seemed to succumb to Nature, regress to savagery, and defy "the concept of property on which civilization was based."[34]

In the eyes of outsiders, backcountry Scotch-Irish Americans evidently were still distinguishable as Scotch-Irish and barely distinguishable from Indians.

For their part, emigrants who pushed west drew on their parents' and grandparents' past experiences with Indians. Many carried with them memories of the brutal warfare of the Revolution and had come to regard Indians—all Indians—as a savage race occupying lands that belonged by right to white men. Many also remembered their grievances against colonial and imperial governments that had protected Indians and their lands when they should have been removing them and opening their lands to settlers.

The Scotch-Irish and the Limits of Federal Power

In June 1789, Iroquois delegates who were gathered in council at Buffalo Creek in northwestern New York sent a letter to the new president of the United States. They began by congratulating Washington "upon Your New System of Government, by which you have one Head to Rule Who we can look to for redress in all disputes which have arose or which may arise between Your people and ours." They looked forward to doing business with a more orderly and centralized system of government and they hoped the president would control his "Disobedient Children" so that they could live in peace with their white neighbors.[35] President Washington no doubt shared their hopes. Unfortunately, as Arthur St. Clair, governor of the Northwest Territory, informed him three months later, people on the frontier did not. They were "in the habit of retaliation, perhaps without attending precisely to the nations from which the injuries are received." They might appeal to him as governor, but would take matters into own hands rather than wait for redress, "and the government will be laid prostrate."³⁶ Many Americans shared the hopes and expectations of the backcountry Scotch-Irish rather than the Iroquois. They did not want the new government to exert its new power to mediate between Indians and whites and protect Indian lands; they wanted it to control, punish, dispossess, and, if necessary, destroy Indians.

Post-Revolutionary contests for land—between Indians and Americans, between speculators and squatters, between land companies and individual farmers, and between states and the federal government—highlighted the ambivalent relationship between Scotch-Irish people on the frontiers and governing elites in the East.

Scotch-Irish Americans were at the forefront of these contests, and they endeavored to dispossess Native Americans in a range of roles, capacities, and situations, by both peaceful and violent means. To acquire land, they had to deal with both the Indian peoples who lived on it and the governments who regulated, surveyed, and sold it as real estate. The federal government in the early Republic adopted a policy of expansion in the trans-Appalachian West that in some ways satisfied and harnessed western settlers' expectations and supported their land hunger and abetted their anti-Indian sentiments. Rather than impose strict prohibitions, as Britain had done, it sought to implement a program of managed federalized expansion.³⁷

However, the federal government envisioned national expansion as an orderly process in which lands would be systematically surveyed in townships and then sold and settled by the "right" sort of people, and that entailed regulating access and restricting rights to Indian land. In the post-Revolutionary mania for Indian land, well-placed and well-heeled speculators used their political connections and financial clout to get a head start, and Congress collaborated with them in their pursuit of profits. State and federal governments forged reciprocal relationships with land companies and increasingly turned to them to distribute public land.³⁸ Federalist land policy favored speculators over settlers, mandating a minimum price of $2 per acre and a minimum purchase of 640 acres, with the price paid in full at time of purchase. Most settlers instead had to buy 160-acre farms on credit from wealthy land speculators who made money from them, and who the federal government expected would act as community leaders.³⁹ Speculators purchased vast tracts of land on credit, in anticipation that once the Native inhabitants were removed, they could quickly resell lands to settlers and generate the cash for future payment. They also bought up at a fraction of their face value the unpaid notes of the Continental

Congress, veterans' land bounties, and military warrants, and used them to buy land.

The federal government often struggled to assert its authority and execute its policies in the West. For good reason. It had to secure the loyalties of western farmers and consumers who were vital to the growth of the nation's economy and who served as buffers against Spain, Britain, and multiple Native nations. It acquired land from the tribes and then surveyed and used the land to pay the nation's debts, reward veterans, satisfy land companies, and create new states. It encouraged settlers to move to frontier regions and occupy Indian lands and endeavored to shape the pace and patterns of their settlement. However, backcountry settlers disputed both Indigenous and federal claims to the land, routinely ignored the government's restrictions, and defied state and federal authorities who did not do enough to defeat and dispossess the Indians. They took matters into their own hands with bloody results, and then complained about lack of government action when their actions triggered Indian resistance. Unauthorized raids into Indian country threatened federal authority as well as Native villages. The government needed to subdue unruly backcountry settlers as well as resistant Indians, even as it absorbed takeovers of Indian land, often sanctioned or turned a blind eye to murders of Indian people, and invoked on-the ground "settler sovereignty" to exert jurisdiction and control over Indian country.[40]

Federal and state officials continued to regard Scotch-Irish and other frontier settlers with disdain as "worse than the Indians," decried squatters who violated treaties, and denounced Indian-hating frontiersmen who committed murders. People who lived "remote from the seat of government," wrote Secretary of War Timothy Pickering, "do not deem Indians entitled to the common rights of humanity" and "murder & plunder Indians whenever they can."[41] Chief Alexander McGillivray described the Americans encroaching on Creek country as people of a "turbulent & restless disposition."[42]

In truth, the fledgling national government lacked the power to enforce its will over unruly citizens on distant frontiers. It also lacked the power to implement national expansion without the support of those citizens, depending on them to buy land and turn it into farms, to provide manpower for militia companies, and to establish republican governments that would develop territories into states as the country grew along the lines outlined in the Northwest Ordinance of 1787. The Ordinance created the nation's first territory west of the Appalachians, established the methods by which states formed from the territory would be admitted to the union as their populations grew, and laid out a blueprint for orderly westward expansion. However, as tribal civil chiefs struggled to restrain their warriors from committing violence, so federalist officials struggled to restrain backcountry settlers. The United States could not expect Indian leaders to "govern their own people better than we do our's," said Washington.[43]

"Sundry persons are preparing to settle upon lands within the U.S which have not been purchased from the Indian natives," a congressional committee had reported in 1783.[44] Two years later, Governor Patrick Henry of Virginia issued a proclamation prohibiting the survey and settlement of lands north of the Ohio River and down to the Tennessee.[45] Federal officials tried to enforce Congress's ban on unauthorized settlements. Secretary of War Henry Knox instructed Colonel Josiah Harmar that "the first object" for the few hundred federal soldiers stationed along the Ohio was to remove "all intruders" from federal lands. Throughout 1785 and 1786, detachments of federal soldiers ranged the Ohio, ordering settlers to leave their cabins and burning the homes and crops they left behind. Major John Armstrong was one of the officers carrying out Harmar's orders. Despite his record and reputation defending his Scotch-Irish neighbors and fighting Indians, settlers frequently defied Armstrong: some just laughed when he read his orders. One fellow named Ross, after casting aspersions on Congress, insisted that he "was determined to hold his possession." Armstrong had Ross arrested and hauled off in chains. Others armed themselves, backing down only when Armstrong threatened to fire on any armed party. When Armstrong entered the intruders' homes, he discovered loopholes for shooting through and barricades erected for defense.[46]

In its efforts to secure clear title to the lands transferred by Britain at the Peace of Paris in 1783, the United States government appointed George Rogers Clark and Irish trader Richard Butler to treat with the Indian nations. Born in Dublin and raised in Scotch-Irish areas of Pennsylvania, Butler entered the Indian trade at Pittsburgh about 1770 and when the Revolution broke out served as an Indian agent for the Middle Colonies and then as an officer in the Pennsylvania line.[47] At the Treaty of Fort McIntosh in 1785, Clark and Butler told the Ohio Indians that they claimed the country by right of conquest and intended to make peace "upon such conditions as seem proper to Congress." At the Treaty of Fort Finney a year later, they rode roughshod over the rituals of wampum diplomacy and offered the Shawnees in attendance a blunt choice between acquiescence and destruction.[48] Such tactics had little chance of securing lasting peace, even among a population that wanted peace, and many Scotch-Irish, it seemed, did not. In March 1786, Colonel James MacFarlane and a group of Washington County leaders upbraided Butler on the futility of making treaties and declared that frontier people had an "absolute determination to be at war with the Indians."[49]

The treaties did little to change Clark's insistence that nothing would bring peace but a punitive campaign into Indian country.[50] Less than a year after the Treaty at Fort Finney, Colonel Benjamin Logan (Figure 10.1) and the Kentucky militia invaded Shawnee country. Born in Pennsylvania or in Augusta County, Virginia, in 1743, Logan was the son of Scotch-Irish parents. At age fourteen, he took over support of the family when his father died. He served with Henry Bouquet in 1764 and as a lieutenant at Point Pleasant ten years later. He removed to Kentucky in 1775; his family followed the next year, and he built Logan's Station, ten miles from Boonesborough. During the Revolution he was second-in-command in Colonel John Bowman's expedition of Kentucky militia against the Shawnee villages in 1779, and he brought a relief party to Blue Licks in 1782 but arrived too late.[51] Daniel Boone and other survivors of Blue Licks accompanied him on this campaign, as did Simon Kenton. They burned several villages. Lieutenant Ebenezer Denny, who was born in Carlisle, Pennsylvania, and had fought in the Revolution, said, "Logan found none but old men, women and children in the towns; they made no resistance; the men were literally murdered."[52]At the village of the Shawnee chief Moluntha, the old man met them carrying a copy of the treaty he had signed at Fort Finney just months before, while his people hoisted an American flag. As the Kentuckians were rounding up their prisoners, Hugh McGary pushed his way forward and demanded to know if Moluntha had been at Blue Licks. Many people blamed McGary for the disaster at Blue Licks, and one fellow Kentuckian called him "a fractious ill tempered man, hated by the people & constantly engaged in fights and affrays."[53] Moluntha apparently did not understand what McGary said, and simply nodded and smiled. McGary buried his hatchet in the old man's skull and the Kentuckians destroyed the town. McGary was court martialed and suspended for a year.[54]

South of the Ohio, state governments struggled to contain the same forces that plagued federal efforts north of the river. "It is not easy for those who are unacquainted with our Frontiers, to judge of the evils & calamities which threaten to arise from the licentious & ungovernable conduct of the People there" and "the vindictive Spirit of the Indians," said Colonel Joseph Martin, who served as Indian agent for Virginia and then for North Carolina. He

Figure 10.1 General Benjamin Logan. Born in Augusta County, Virginia, the eldest son of Scotch-Irish immigrants, Logan campaigned against the Shawnees with the Virginia militia in Bouquet's expedition in 1764, in Lord Dunmore's War in 1774, and during the Revolution. Oil on canvas. Artist unknown.
General Benjamin Logan (CHS.1967.7); provided courtesy of the Cincinnati Museum Center.

justified his own involvement in purchasing Cherokee land on the Tennessee River as a measure to help bring order out of chaos and create a double barrier against both Indians and unruly frontier folk by settling "a number of respectable Gentlemen" in the area.[55] Martin's efforts to establish boundaries as a path to peace won him few friends and many enemies among backcountry settlers, who thought he "takes the part of the Indians." As the Moravian brother Martin Schneider found when he traveled through the heavily Scotch-Irish region of the French Broad and Holston rivers on his way to the Cherokees, the inhabitants "would rather like to extirpate them altogether, & take their Land themselves; they scarce look on upon them as human creatures, which I often could perceive in their Conversations."[56]

Even so, conflict and coexistence often went hand in hand in borderlands. Just back from the Cherokee towns in July 1784, Joseph Martin informed Governor Harrison that starving frontier settlers in Virginia and Carolina were forced to ask Indians for corn, "and some Hundreds have been plentifully supplied upon moderate Terms." This traffic gave villains opportunities to travel to and from the Cherokee towns under pretense of buying corn, instead stealing Cherokee horses and causing disruption. He feared the Indians would turn to Spain for help.[57]

Congress selected Andrew Pickens as one of its four treaty commissioners tasked with bringing order in the South, and the Treaty of Hopewell in 1785 ostensibly secured Cherokee boundaries. Pickens had previously fought against the Cherokees; now he became their advocate and they gave him the name Skiagunsta, after a Cherokee peacemaker.[58] There was little he could do, however. The Overhill Cherokee chief Old Tassel asked the commissioners to eject the "three thousand souls" squatting between the forks of the French Broad and Holston. If Congress could defeat the king of Great Britain, why could it not remove its own citizens? he asked.[59] Congress was no more successful in maintaining the boundaries after the treaty than before. A series of treaties after the Revolution opened Cherokee country to invasion by settlers from the Virginia and North Carolina Piedmont, a large proportion of whom were of Ulster ancestry. An estimated 43 percent of the nearly nine hundred families settled along the Swannanoa and French Broad rivers in 1800 were Scotch-Irish.[60] In effect, the federal government left the Cherokees to defend themselves against Scotch-Irish and other backcountry folk, who also felt they had been left to defend themselves.

People on the North Carolina backcountry who felt vulnerable to Indian attacks and neglected by their state government looked to their own leaders for protection and access to Indian lands. Separatist leaders in the upper Tennessee Valley formed their own State of Franklin in 1784 with a view to becoming the fourteenth state. Far removed from the eastern parts of North Carolina and separated from them by "high & almost impassable Mountains," they came to believe, as one put it, "that our Interest is also in many respects distinct from the inhabitants on the other Side & much injured by a Union with them." Anticipating an Indian war in the summer of 1785, John Sevier predicted, "it is the Western people alone that must Suffer and Undergo all the Hardships & Cruelties That Usually attend a savage and bloody War." Like members of Pennsylvania's Quaker Assembly in 1763 who allegedly regarded the Scotch-Irish on the frontier as expendable, some members of the North Carolina General Assembly were reported to have said that those same people "are the off scourings of the Earth, fugitives from Justice, & we will be rid of them at any rate." Little wonder that backcountry settlers felt they were "taxed to support Government, while they were deprived of the blessings of it."[61] Franklin proved short-lived, but during its four-year existence Franklinites pursued a policy of unrestrained encroachment on Indian lands that put them at odds with the policies proposed by the federal government and North Carolina.[62]

Petitioners from the western counties (a long list that included many notably Scotch-Irish names) reminded the North Carolina General Assembly of their sufferings in the Revolutionary War. They had lost friends and relatives defending the country against Indians and other enemies, and North Carolina had benefited "from our alertness in taking & securing a Country."[63] A memorial to Congress from freemen living west of Appalachians requesting a new state bore the signatures of eighteen representatives, most if not all of them Scotch-Irish names (Cummins, three Campbells, Jameson, Buchanan, Wiley, Tate, Finley, Kinard, Christian, Anderson, Looney, Adair). "In our present settlements we have maintained our ground during the late perilous War, and frequently gave effectual aid to our Bretheren to the South and Eastward," they said. They described themselves as "first occupants and aboringers [sic] of the Country, freemen claiming natural Rights, and the priviledges of American Citizens."[64] By occupying and defending the land against Indian attack, Scotch-Irish settler colonists had replaced Native Americans as Indigenous inhabitants.[65]

Exercising what the petitioners understood as their rights and privileges involved trampling the rights of others. Settlers poured into the land between French Broad and the Tennessee River "to the great disquiet of the

Indians," Joseph Martin informed Governor Edmund Randolph of Virginia in 1787, and "seem to take every step that seems most productive of a war with them people."[66] The lands between French Broad and Tennessee included the beloved Cherokee town of Chota, which Cherokee chiefs tried to protect.[67] Speaking to Martin at Chota, Old Tassel and Hanging Maw said, "we always find that your people settle much faster shortly after a Treaty than Before." Tuskegetchee, known also as the Long Fellow, added, "you love our Land, and know we are not able to fight for it. You Suffer your People to settle to our Towns and say nothing about it." Tuskegetchee said he lived in "the Middle Ground between Chota and Chickamogga," and stood "like a wall between Bad people and my Brothers, the Virginians. Both Creeks and Chickamoggas has been turned back from doing mischief by me."[68] The Chickamaugas were Cherokees who had separated from their relatives and more compliant chiefs farther east during the Revolution and continued the fight from the new towns they built on Chickamauga Creek in western Tennessee. Scotch-Irish backcountry settlers saw themselves as a buffer between eastern settlements and the Cherokees; Cherokees saw themselves as a buffer between backcountry settlements and Indian nations farther south and west.

As always, the Scotch-Irish buffer was precarious. Backcountry settlers feared that unless their government provided assistance, they would be forced to abandon their homes "and thus expose to the savages the more interior parts of the frontier."[69] Colonel Arthur Campbell, who as an adoptive Indian captive for two years and had "a peculiar opportunity to study their language, customs and manners," feared that frontier militia were no match for Indian raiders who approached "as secretly as a Wolf in search of his prey." Campbell had burned Cherokee towns during the Revolution, but the more he thought about it, he told Governor Randolph in December 1787, there had to be a better way, and lives could be saved. "It is a wrong policy at this day, and in the present circumstances of the United States, to wish to extirpate whole Tribes of Indians."[70]

Like their Indian neighbors and enemies, frontier militia were part-time soldiers. In Tennessee, Cumberland settlers' enthusiasm for militia service was limited by their half-agricultural, half-military way of life.[71] The almost constant fighting on the Cumberland for fifteen years produced a grim record of killings. The reality and threat of Indian violence shaped the lives of men, women, and children. Farms were often makeshift forts, and people risked death going about their daily business. As had happened farther east during the French and Indian War and the Revolution, stories and experiences of Indian fighting became part of family and community lore.[72]

Hugh Rogan survived the fighting. Born in County Donegal in 1747 and described as fair-skinned with blue eyes and yellow hair, Rogan married Nancy Duffy when he was twenty-six and she was sixteen, and their son was born in 1774. The next year, Rogan and his brother-in-law sailed for America and went as traders to the upper Yadkin country. The plan was to scout out and prepare a place and then bring over their families. The outbreak of the Revolution delayed things, but Rogan was entitled to a grant of land on the Cumberland by North Carolina after the war and set out to bring over his family from Ireland. Being misinformed that his wife had remarried, "he turned back and slowly retraced his steps into the wilderness," a changed man. In 1787 in a skirmish at the mouth of Duck River, "that brave Irishman Hugh Rogan" was shot through the body, the bullet passing below the right collar bone and coming out below the left shoulder blade. He thought the wound was mortal and "a judgment upon me for leaving my poor wife and child in Ireland." In fact, Rogan made it back to Nashville and recovered. He became a scout and Indian fighter. In 1794 he finally managed to return to Ireland and brought his wife, who had waited for him, to settle on his land grant on Bledsoe Creek.[73]

James Brown was not so fortunate. He migrated from the north of Ireland when he was seven, was raised in Culpeper County, Virginia, and married Jane Gillespie there. He served in the Revolutionary War and acquired certificates for his services with which he secured several tracts of land in the Nashville region. As he traveled down the Tennessee River with his family in the spring of 1788, Chickamaugas attacked the boat. They killed Brown and took Jane and five children captive, dividing them with their Creek allies. The eldest son, Joseph, and two of his sisters were released after almost a year in captivity. Alexander McGillivray intervened to secure the release of Jane and her daughter Elizabeth after seventeen months in captivity with the Creeks. "I am under many obligations to you for the kindnesses you have done for me when my calamities threw me upon your mercy. They shall never be forgotten," Jane Brown wrote McGillivray when she was back at Cumberland and reunited with four of her five children. She asked him to do what he could to secure the return of her younger son, George. George, who was eight when he was captured, remained with the Indians for five years and could not speak a word of English when he returned. Joseph Brown subsequently acted as a guide for an expedition against the Chickamauga towns of Nickajack and Running Water in 1794 and fought in the Creek War at the battles of Tallahatchee and Talladega in 1813.[74]

Cycles of vengeance played out in the mountains of western North Carolina. In May 1788, a Cherokee named Slim Tom killed the wife and ten relatives of John Kirk who were squatting on Cherokee land. When James Sevier called for volunteers to attack the Cherokee towns on the Little Tennessee in June, Kirk enlisted in a militia company commanded by Major James Hubbard, a noted Indian-hater and fighter.[75] Sevier led attacks on several towns and killed thirty people in retaliation for killing of the Kirk family. At Chilhowee, calling Old Tassel and several other neutralist chiefs together for peace talks in a cabin, Hubbard posted guards at the door, handed Kirk a tomahawk, and told him to take his revenge. Kirk murdered Old Tassel and the others under a white flag, an act that even Sevier denounced as inhuman. Cherokee war parties in turn avenged Old Tassel's murder by killing seventeen white men. Sevier's militia burned more Cherokee towns in the winter.[76]

The Franklinites and Cherokees agreed to a truce early in 1789, and the State of Franklin dissolved soon after. But there was no respite for the Cherokees. "We are so Distrest By the No. Carolina People that it seems Like we sho'd soon become no People," they told Patrick Henry that May. "They have got all our Land from us. We have hardly as much as we can stand on, and they seem to want that little worse than all the Rest."[77] When North Carolina ceded its western lands to Congress that year—some 29 million acres lying between the Alleghenies and the Mississippi—the Scotch-Irish and other "over-mountain" people came under federal jurisdiction. They expected that by ceding land claims to the federal government they would "obtain a more ample protection than they have heretofore received."[78]

Scotch-Irish Presbyterian frontiersman James White, whose father had emigrated from Londonderry, founded Knoxville, Tennessee, and named it after the secretary of war in 1791.[79] Secretary Henry Knox was the son of Scotch-Irish parents from County Derry. From modest origins, he rose through military service in the Revolution to a position of wealth and power. Up to his ears himself in land schemes in Maine, he regarded squatting by common folk as a threat to order, status, and property.[80] Relations between Knox and Tennesseans, therefore, were ambiguous, if not testy. Multiple issues strained the fragile national loyalties of new citizens in the West, particularly those concerning Indian policy, access to Indian lands, and conduct of Indian wars, all of which fell under the authority of the secretary of war. Conscious of being neglected while federal forces launched campaigns north of the Ohio, backcountry people south of the river questioned what loyalty they owed a government that left them to their fate, and Knox knew it. He informed Governor of the Southwest Territory William Blount in August 1791 that he would have to rely on the militia because the federal government was focused on fighting the Indians northwest of the Ohio.[81]

The government needed to show that it had the power to preserve peace and order on the frontier. "The population of the lands lying on the Western waters is increasing rapidly," Knox told Washington in January 1791. "The inhabitants request and demand protection; if it be not granted, seeds of disgust will be sown; sentiments of separate interests will arise out of their local situation, which will be cherished, either by insidious, domestic, or foreign emissaries." A year later, in his report to Congress on the causes of Indian hostilities, he stressed that providing protection against lawless violence was a basic purpose of government and "a frontier citizen possesses as strong claims to protection as any other citizen." A country's frontiers were its most vulnerable areas, and the U.S. government had a sacred obligation to protect the inhabitants of its western frontier as well as those of the Atlantic frontier. The federal government could not long refrain from applying its power in the conflict between backcountry settlers and Indians.[82]

Knox's words would have been music to the ears of backcountry residents like those who warned General James Robertson in February 1792 that "the Frontiers will break unless some speedy method is taken to secure them from the Inroads of the Savages."[83] Still, the federal government was not yet ready to throw its entire weight behind them. Secretary of State Thomas Jefferson explained to Judge David Campbell the next month that the United States would not risk incurring an Indian war "merely to gratify a few intruders with settlements which are to cost the other inhabitants of the U.S. a thousand times their value in taxes for carrying on the war they produce."[84] Jefferson would somewhat change his tune as president.

In its early years, the federal government struggled to curb frontier violence against Indians without generating frontier unrest. Alexander McGillivray complained vociferously about intrusions on Creek lands by white people from Cumberland, but the federal government could not check what southern agent James Seagrove described as "the insatiable rage which our frontier brethren have for extending their limits." Writing to Knox, he lamented that "the United States, like most other countries, is unfortunate in having the worst class of people on her frontiers."[85] Acting governor Daniel Smith echoed his pessimism. "This Spirit for war against Indians pervades people of all Ranks so far that no order of Government can stop them," he told Knox.[86]

As in the French and Indian War and the Revolution, Scotch-Irish people in the backcountry had a siege mentality during the 1790s. Attacks by Creeks and Chickamauga Cherokees took an increasing toll, and Cumberland settlers saw themselves maintaining a foothold in occupied territory with minimal assistance from the federal government. Their settlements provided a buffer for Kentucky and other regions against the Indians and the Spaniards, who in turn tried to use the Indians as a barrier against the Americans.[87] Spanish officials kept a wary eye on the Cumberland settlements. "There are there about four thousand souls," wrote one, "one fourth of whom possess arms and are supplied with rifles which they handle very expertly, since most of them are hunters." Furthermore, since they had "been obliged to use force" to settle on the lands they had taken from the Indians, "their manner of life is very harsh."[88] Andrew Pickens, attending treaties in the western country with Blount in 1792, told the governor of South Carolina that Creek and Chickamauga raids had reduced the whole area, and Cumberland in particular, to "a most pitiable and distressed situation." Blount told Knox that the Cumberland settlers spent any free time they had building blockhouses and stockades to protect their families.[89]

Help for these settlers was at hand, but it came from the Chickasaws rather than the federal government. At a time when the Chickamaugas and Creeks threatened the Cumberland settlements, the Creeks threatened the Chickasaws. The Chickasaws' location and competition with the more powerful Creeks led them to ally with the Cumberland settlers, and their conflict with Creeks helped to divert Creek attention and attacks from the settlements. According to a Chickasaw chief at a council at French Lick near Nashville in November 1783, with the English no longer there to incite them, there was no need for the Chickasaws and settlers to be "like two puppies thrown together and provoked to fight."[90] James Robertson, a loyal supporter of Governor Blount as well as his land agent in the area, was appointed temporary agent to the Chickasaws at an annal salary of $400.[91] Robertson cultivated good relations with Piominko (Mountain Leader) and other Chickasaw chiefs.[92]

The bloodletting between Indians and whites on the frontier is often described as lawless violence, but federal officials attributed it less to the absence of law than to invoking the wrong kind of law—*lex talionis*, the law of vengeance and blood for blood. Horse stealing—by Indians and whites—was a major cause of hostilities. Settlers on the Cumberland River complained repeatedly about horse thefts by Indians.[93] Governor Blount struggled to restrain settlers from exacting satisfaction by killing the perpetrators. It was a world where Indians and whites alike resorted to similar forms of retaliatory punishment, he explained to Knox:

> Every Indian Nation is divided into families or Clans and it is a law among them that each clan shall protect and take satisfaction for all injuries offered to the person of each individual of it whatever his offences may be except that of killing an Indian of another Clan and then if the injured Clan or any of its members take satisfaction it is well and the matter ends.[94]

Rather than allow people take matters into their own hands, hold entire groups responsible for the actions of individuals, and perpetuate an endless cycle of vengeance, Knox wanted to establish federal authority over Indians and U.S. citizens alike in an effort to arbitrate frontier violence, but he struggled to replace the law of retaliation with federal law.[95]

Questions of Indian status and federal power became inseparable. Federal officials who attempted to prosecute territorial citizens for crimes committed against Native people and in Indian country faced angry and sometimes violent reactions from people who resented such heavy-handed federal interference as much as they hated Indians.[96] In June 1793, Captain John Beard and a party of fifty mounted infantry carried out an unprovoked attack on Hanging Maw's house near the Tennessee River, killing and wounding several Cherokee people. In his report on the southern tribes to the president, communicated to the Senate six months later, Secretary Knox called Beard's assault an outrage "disgraceful to the United States," one of many in which the perpetrators would be unlikely to be punished. No peace could be made with the Cherokees until effective means existed to punish those who violated it, he said. The United States could hardly demand that "banditti Indians" be punished when guilty whites escaped with impunity.[97]

Officials' assurances that the government would do everything in its power to bring the perpetrators to justice carried little weight with Cherokees. The dead had to be avenged. In September a war party of nearly one thousand Chickamaugas and Creeks, led by John Watts (Kunoskeeskie) and Doublehead, set out to destroy Knoxville. Thwarted, they attacked a nearby fortified farmstead known as Cavett's Station. The Cavett family originated in France and moved through England to settle in Ulster. Richard Cavett joined the exodus of Scotch-Irish emigrants to America, settled in Paxton Township in 1711, and then moved his growing family to Virginia. After he was killed by Indians in 1757, family members continued to move south. Two of his sons, Alexander and Moses, settled in the Holston country of Tennessee and were in Knox County by 1790, where Alexander built Cavett's Station. The war party destroyed the station, killed the cattle, sheep, and hogs, and murdered Cavett and his family: thirteen men, women, and children.[98]

As in earlier conflicts, Indian war and civil disorder were intertwined, and each fed on the other.[99] In echoes of Scotch-Irish anger at Philadelphia elites and Quaker pacifists, frontier settlers and speculators continued to distrust a distant government that seemed willing to do more for Indians than for them. Disenchanted with Federalist administration, Tennesseans turned to their growing political antagonists, the so-called Democratic-Republicans, to deliver what they wanted: security against Indians and unfettered access Indian land.[100]

Kentucky and the Scotch-Irish Frontier Myth

Thousands of Scotch-Irish people joined the migration across the Appalachians in the early Republic. Kentucky was touted as a good poor man's country, where cheap and abundant land, game-filled forests, and limitless opportunities awaited adventurous and industrious white males and their families eager to establish farmsteads and get ahead in the world. Writing to his mother back home in Londonderry from Lexington, Kentucky, in 1817, David Robinson painted a rosy picture of his own health and of prospects in his adopted country, compared to starving conditions in Ireland. "I wish all the inhabitants of Ireland were in the back woods of America, where they could obtain a sufficiency of every thing their heart could wish," he wrote; "the millions of uncultivated acres would give employment to all them who wished it." "We are all free here, and all possess a spirit of independence."[101] Realities on the ground in Kentucky did not match its lure as a promised land, however. Many Scotch-Irish emigrants found, yet again, that eastern land speculators and lawyers, as well as Indian warriors, stood between them and their dreams of economic independence. The disparities of wealth they had hoped to escape were replicated in the backcountry, where inequalities in distribution of landed wealth were common. There was plenty of land in western North Carolina, Tennessee, and Kentucky, but a few families held most of it.[102]

The Scotch-Irish and other early migrants could be seen as "storm troopers of civilization" in Kentucky.[103] North of the Ohio, wrote Theodore Roosevelt in his multi-volume history *The Winning of the West*, "the regular army went first" and settlements often grew up in the shadow of protection from federal troops. In Kentucky and Tennessee, "the early settlers acted as their own army" and carried out the invasion of Indian country themselves.[104] Migrants to Kentucky saw a clear difference in how the federal government approached and managed Indian affairs north and south of the Ohio River; the Indians saw it too, they said. Kentuckians received no help and were treated as if they were a separate people.[105] They had a point.

After the Revolution, in 1783 or 1784, a large party people from Augusta County, bearing Scotch-Irish names such as Allen, Moffett, Trimble, and others, followed in the wake of the McAfee brothers and removed to Kentucky via the Wilderness Road, which ran from southwest Virginia through the Cumberland Gap and on to the Ohio country.[106] Simon Kenton moved his entire family, including his aged father, from Virginia to Kentucky in 1783.[107] William Kinkead, whose wife and children had been captured by Shawnees in 1764, moved his family to Kentucky in 1789.[108] Kentucky had twelve thousand white inhabitants in 1783; two years later, it had thirty thousand, half of them from Virginia.[109] Two distinct groups of settler colonists emerged: people from the eastern Virginia lowlands were called "Tuckahoes" (derived from an Indigenous name for a root), while "Cohees" (from "quo he," an abbreviated form of "quoth he," once frequently used in Scots and Scotch-Irish speech) were primarily Scotch-Irish from western Virginia, Pennsylvania, or the Carolinas, described as "Backwoods Virginians and Northward men, Scotch, Irish, &c." By 1790, between a quarter and one-third of Kentucky's population of 74,000 was of Irish or Scotch-Irish birth or descent.[110]

Shawnees and Cherokees, whose Kentucky hunting grounds had been sold from under them by the Iroquois at the Treaty of Fort Stanwix in 1768, resisted the invasion. It was the same old story for Scotch-Irish people on the Kentucky frontier. In the summer of 1784, Indians killed and scalped Walker Daniel, Attorney General for the Kentucky District, and "a merchant from Ireland by the name of George Keightley," and escaped pursuit. A companion who narrowly escaped with a glancing wound related the details of the attack to Governor Benjamin Harrison of Virginia, adding that war parties ranged the country "fearless of Danger, while in trembling Crowds, the men, women & children once more leave their little Farms."[111] Escalating Indian raids produced more widows and orphans, more cases of poverty, and more demands on poor relief. As usual, the reluctance and poor reputation of Kentucky militia stemmed in large part from their refusal to leave their homes and families exposed to attack.[112] With insufficient federal troops and forts, families faced the prospect of abandoning their homes, Samuel McDowell told Governor Beverley Randolph of Virginia in July 1789.[113] Federal defense efforts were hampered by more than lack of troops and resources: President Washington asked Secretary of War Knox to get him a map of Kentucky and the western parts of Virginia because, according to Knox, "the maps which are in the public possession are totally wanting in the division of the western counties, which occasions considerable perplexity in ascertaining the information of the Depredations of the Indians in that quarter."[114]

Emigrants to Kentucky struggled against land speculators and wealthy investors as well as Indians. Attracted by the promise of land, claiming rights to land by occupancy and improvement, and hoping to become economically independent, they found instead that the agents, lawyers, and officials who managed the land system had many ways to keep lands in the hands of the wealthy and the well-connected. Virginia's land laws that governed Kentucky before it became a state rendered titles there so uncertain "that the Chance is at least three to One, that a Man who purchases there must defend his Title by a Lawsuit, the Expense of which will ruin a new Settler." Instead of becoming independent property owners, most Kentucky settlers remained landless tenant farmers, paying rent or laboring for wages. Hearing on his way to the Treaty at Fort Finney that the Virginia House had voted for separating Kentucky, Richard Butler worried what might happen if Congress did not move quickly to acknowledge Kentucky as a state. "One of the evils we apprehend is, that there is scarce a tenth man in Kentucky who has land with certain title." When Kentucky became the fifteenth state in 1792, two-thirds of adult white male residents owned no land; they lived as tenants on enormous landholdings belonging to distant landlords or, in the words of one pioneer, they squatted on lands, "not knowing or caring who claimed to own them."[115]

Many migrants who moved to Kentucky in search of land and independence found neither. Some landless men worked at Bullitts' Lick saltworks south of Louisville on land that belonged to William Christian. Christian had developed the operation into a substantial business and moved to Kentucky with his family in 1785. After he was killed by Indians in April 1786,[116] his wife Annie took over management of the operation. The salt workers hardly fit the model of independent frontiersmen. Often transient laborers, they worked alongside hired slaves and at the end of the day handed their income over to a female tavern owner in payment for rent and equipment. They were a dependent labor force who lacked status, economic security, and patriarchal authority. For white men who were conscious of their failure to succeed in a land of opportunity, violence against Indians offered another way to demonstrate their manhood and status.[117]

Resentful Kentuckians demanded self-government and separation from Virginia. The Black Boy James Smith had migrated from Pennsylvania to Kentucky, settled on new lands in Bourbon County, helped draft Kentucky's state constitution, and served in the legislature. The creation of a new state founded on democratic principles represented a culmination of the frontier revolution the Black Boys and others had led. Now that frontier people held government power, they were free to achieve the independence they sought by taking Indian land and removing Indian people.[118] Kentucky finally resolved the tensions that divided white men by adopting a constitution and building a system of government and society in which rights for white men depended on excluding white women, African Americans, and Native Americans.[119]

Nevertheless, although they had helped win the Revolution by fighting Indians and had earned status as white Americans by defining them as racial inferiors, Scotch-Irish migrants to Kentucky lost the fruits of the Revolution to the wealthy.[120] The population of Kentucky soared to 220,000 by 1800.[121] Yet the richest 10 percent of taxpayers still owned about 30 percent of privately owned Kentucky lands; more than a third of adult white males held less than two hundred acres, and more than half owned no land at all.[122] By then, many Scotch-Irish Americans had left Kentucky and moved elsewhere.

Indian War and Whiskey Rebellion

Between 1791 and 1794, backcountry Scotch-Irish played central roles in the so-called Whiskey Rebellion. In 1791, Congress passed Alexander Hamilton's excise tax of 25 percent on whiskey, to generate revenue for paying off debts incurred during the Revolutionary War. The first domestic excise tax imposed by the new federal government, it applied to all distilled spirits, but hit hardest were western farmers who distilled surplus rye, barley, wheat, and corn to make whiskey and often used whiskey as a medium of exchange. A resistance movement that echoed Revolutionary actions in opposing taxation without representation spread the length of the backcountry. It was most intense in western Pennsylvania, where protesters used violence and intimidation to prevent federal officials from collecting the tax, which became a test case for the assertion of federal authority over popular protest.[123] In Kentucky, where backcountry settlers balked at paying taxes to a federal government that failed to provide protection against Indians or secure cooperation from Spain, civil disobedience took a less overt form in massive tax evasion.[124] Westerners' grievances during the Whiskey Rebellion also included land speculation; believing that lands taken from Native people should be theirs for the taking, they protested against sales of land in large quantities to companies and "favorites of government."[125] As in other agrarian protests, some Whiskey rebels painted their faces and donned Indian clothing. Government officials later referred to them as "White Indians."[126]

The tax also seemed to be a test of eastern elites' rights to ride roughshod over poor people's rights as they enriched themselves at their expense. During the Revolutionary War the cash-poor Continental Congress had resorted to issuing paper bonds, IOUs, to pay soldiers and compensate farmers for requisitioned crops and livestock. With banker Robert Morris at the financial helm, the state of Pennsylvania then announced it would no longer accept the bonds as payment for taxes. Left holding nearly worthless notes, veterans and farmers had little chance but to sell them for whatever they could get, usually at a fraction of their face value. Wealthy speculators bought them up until some four hundred individuals held over 96 percent of Pennsylvania's war debt, almost half of it by Morris's friends and business partners. When Morris and his protégé Alexander Hamilton assumed control of the federal government's financial policy, they had the government buy back the worthless bonds at face value plus interest, with payment in silver and gold, ensuring that their bond-speculating friends and associates made a killing. The expensive plan was to be financed by new federal excise taxes that fell most heavily on poor people, many of whom had been given and then sold the worthless congressional notes in the first place.[127]

Multiple issues and grievances fueled the protest movement, many of them familiar to backcountry Scotch-Irish people who yet again felt themselves neglected and underrepresented. For example, the population of Pennsylvania's three western counties grew by around 87 percent between 1783 and 1790, yet the number of landowners fell and the number of absentee landlords increased, producing class stratification and a relative decline in status for most backcountry inhabitants. Western Pennsylvania was experiencing social and economic turmoil, but for backcountry settlers nothing was more important than Indian war.[128] Backcountry Scotch-Irish saw themselves as bearing the burden of both an unjust tax and an Indian war.

Scotch-Irish settlers, whose imported expertise in domestic distilling was changing the national drink from rum—cane whiskey imported from the Caribbean or distilled from imported molasses—to grain whiskey, distilled in individual or community stills, felt the tax targeted them particularly. "All the backcountry of America is very favorable to the growth of rye," wrote William Strickland; "this grain is entirely consumed in the distillation of whisky, chiefly for the consumption of the Irish frontier-men." The Englishman claimed that admirers of French democracy had "got among the people inhabiting to the West of the Allegheny Mountains on the frontiers of Pennsylvania and Virginia and worked them up into a state of insurrection; those countries are inhabited intirely by Irish, the most ignorant and savage race imaginable as all their proceedings testify."[129]

Despite their reputation for hard drinking, however, Scotch-Irish people in the backcountry did not embrace the rebellion because of a propensity for alcohol. They did so because the government imposed its domestic excise tax on the most important item of trade on the frontier, where it fell disproportionately on the poor and vulnerable inhabitants. Frontier settlers had two main demands of the federal government: acquire access to the Mississippi River so farmers could get their agricultural produce to market; and provide military protection against the Indians whose lands they occupied. The government did neither. People resisted taxation without representation, but they particularly resented being taxed to support a government that failed abysmally to protect them against the Indians.[130]

Backcountry settlers saw themselves, yet again, left to fend for themselves by a government that was insensitive to their danger and deaf to their pleas. The government ignored petitions asking for rejection of Hamilton's excise tax, just as it ignored petitions asking for protection against Indian attacks, and the excise was adopted. Meanwhile, an Indian war continued to rage in the Northwest Territory, and farmers still lacked a profitable outlet for their agricultural produce.[131] Western Pennsylvania's leading politician, William

Findley, who emigrated from Ulster around 1763 in his early twenties, settled in Carlisle, moved west to Westmoreland County after the Revolution, and avoided getting caught up in the Whiskey Rebellion. He nonetheless sympathized with his Scotch-Irish constituents and defended them in his *A History of the Insurrection in the Four Western Counties*, published in 1796, which placed their grievances in the context of a recurrent intercolonial competition, government neglect, and Indian wars.[132]

As multiple Native nations in the Northwest Territory confederated to repel American expansion beyond the Ohio River, Scotch-Irish and other colonists encroaching on Indian land were the first to feel their wrath. The petitions came flooding in, expressing the same fears and complaints found in petitions in 1755, 1763, and 1777. Recognizing that its attempt to secure acquiescence in the conquest of Indian lands by treaty had failed, the federal government turned to armed invasion and assaults on Indian villages, the tactic repeatedly invoked as the only sure way to defeat Indians. Washington ordered territorial governor General Arthur St. Clair to avoid war with the Indians "by all means consistently with the security of the frontier inhabitants, the security of the troops, and the national dignity," but "to punish them with severity" if they persisted in their resistance, which they did.[133]

The center of Native American resistance was a complex of Miami, Shawnee, and Delaware towns around Kekionga in northwestern Ohio. In 1790, Knox dispatched Brigadier General Josiah Harmar with 320 regulars and 1,133 militia from Pennsylvania and Kentucky to destroy Kekionga. Many of the militia were old men and young boys hardly able to bear arms, with an "indifferent" assortment of muskets; many of them had never fired a rifle in their lives.[134] They confronted a formidable multi-tribal alliance led by the Miami war chief Little Turtle, Blue Jacket of the Shawnees, and the Delaware Buckongahelas. Harmar's army left Fort Washington at Cincinnati in September and burned Kekionga and five other towns in October, but by the time it limped back into Fort Washington, it had suffered more than two hundred casualties, lost a third of its packhorses, and abandoned much of its equipment. The campaign was a humiliating failure.[135] A court of inquiry exonerated Harmar and blamed the militia.[136] Senator William Maclay of Pennsylvania was not fooled. "The ill-fortune of the affair breaks through all the coloring that was given to it," he wrote in his journal. Maclay was convinced that Washington and his government created the Indian war as "the Pretext for raising an Army meant to awe our Citizens into Submission."[137] Indian raids intensified in the wake of Harmar's defeat.

Pressured by impatient land speculators, the United States launched another invasion the next year. In a campaign plagued by bad planning, bad weather, repeated delays, and contractor fraud, Arthur St. Clair led a poorly prepared and poorly equipped army to an even more devastating defeat. Routed by Little Turtle and Blue Jacket's warriors on November 4, 1791, the army lost 630 killed and more than 280 wounded, in addition to noncombatants and captives. Most of the officers fell, including Richard Butler, tomahawked and scalped by Shawnee warriors, and George Gibson, brother of John Gibson, whose Shawnee wife had been murdered by backcountry thugs years before. A congressional committee of investigation absolved St. Clair of responsibility for the defeat, placing the blame instead on delay in apportioning funds for the campaign, the lateness of the season, mismanagement, and, again, the behavior of soldiers who lacked discipline and experience.[138]

Alarmed at the prospect of being left defenseless, as they had been in the wake of Braddock's defeat in 1755, frontier families renewed their calls for protection, fled their homes, and looked in vain for federal assistance.[139] John McCullough or McCullock, a captain of the Ohio County Rangers, complained to Governor Henry Lee of Virginia in March 1793 that the protection they got from the federal army was so inconsiderable as to be "not worth mentioning." Things were quieter in the fall, but McCullough kept scouts out.[140] Lee would lead a substantial federal force into the backcountry the following year—but against Whiskey Rebels, not Indians.

A new American army, rebuilt, reorganized, and refinanced, finally delivered the results western settlers craved when General Anthony Wayne defeated the Indian confederation at the Battle of Fallen Timbers in northwestern Ohio in August 1794. Confederation chiefs at the Treaty of Greenville the next year ceded most of Ohio to the United States.

Alexander McKee, Matthew Elliott, and Simon Girty, and other Scotch-Irish in the British Indian department at Detroit, continued to aid and abet Indian resistance. Girty operated as an interpreter, fought with the Indians in the destruction of St. Clair's army, and played a key, and perhaps subversive role in abortive peace negotiations between the United States and the Indians. Henry Knox told Washington the Indians considered Girty "one of themselves" and that he was the only white man they admitted into their councils. William Caldwell led a contingent of fifty Detroit militia alongside the Indians at the Battle of Fallen Timbers. After Fallen Timbers, Girty took refuge in Canada.[141] His former friend Simon Kenton, who served with Wayne but did not fight in the battle, moved his family to Ohio in 1798.[142]

In the South, where militant Chickamaugas continued to raid the settlements on the Cumberland River, General James Robertson applied the tried and tested strategy of snuffing out Indian raids by destroying Indian homes. In defiance of federal authority, he dispatched a force of 550 Kentucky and Tennessee militia to attack the town of Nickajack on the Tennessee River, near present-day Chattanooga, in September 1794, killing seventy of the inhabitants. Some people were shot down as they tried to escape across the river. Militiaman Jonathan Ramsey recalled that he and Samuel McCutchen found a canoe in which a woman was lying dead. "A lad shot through the bowels and was in great agony, and talking to his dead mother in his native language. I had not the heart to throw the wounded boy into the river. We left him in the canoe. We took a small Indian girl some ten years old with a flesh wound, and we placed her among the prisoners." As a consequence of his unauthorized expedition, Robertson resigned his military commission, but it was no more than a formality and he continued to serve. In fact, authorizing an attack on the Chickamauga towns *and* defying federal authority to do so validated his authority among Middle Tennesseans.[143]

Wayne's victory demonstrated that the government finally could raise a military force capable of providing the security that frontier people had long wanted and lacked. It was no coincidence that the Whiskey Rebellion collapsed at the same time.[144] At the beginning of August 1794, thirty years after the Paxton Boys had marched on Philadelphia, some seven thousand Appalachian Pennsylvanians marched on Pittsburgh, the commercial and cultural center of western Pennsylvania and home of a regional elite of wealthy merchants and land speculators who had grown rich while common folk suffered hardship and deprivation, threatening to burn it to the ground.[145] President Washington and the federal government, whose efforts to defeat the Indians seemed puny by comparison, responded with a massive display of federal power and sent an army of thirteen thousand militia under Governor Henry Lee to defeat its own citizens. The rebellion ended with a whimper.

There were Scotch-Irish on both sides. William Irvine commanded the Pennsylvanian militia under General Mifflin.[146] Major Isaac Craig, the emigrant from County Down who served as deputy quartermaster and military storekeeper at Fort Pitt after the Revolution, also participated in suppressing the rebellion.[147] Nevertheless, the Scotch-Irish were tarnished again with the brush of rebellion. "Our Army under Wayne has beat the Indians, and the Militia under Governor Lee, have Subdued the Insurgents, a miserable though numerous rabble of Irish & Scotch Emigrants and Redemptioners, chiefly imported Since 1783," John Adams wrote to John Quincy Adams in December 1794.[148]

Relations with Government and Indians at the Turn of the Century

The Scotch-Irish "rabble" did not have to face the disdain of Federalists like John Adams for much longer. Political crisis and persecution drove much of the Irish emigration in the 1790s. Inspired by the ideals of the French Revolution, Protestant radicals in Belfast and Dublin, under the leadership of Theobold Wolfe Tone, organized the Society of United Irishmen, in the hope of bringing Protestants and Catholics together and establishing a democratic republic through a French-backed revolution. When the rebellion collapsed in 1798, thousands of embittered emigrants from Northern Ireland fled to the United States. They joined with earlier Ulster Presbyterians in embracing the "republican principles" of Thomas Jefferson and rejected the "aristocratic" government and pro-British policies of the Federalists, whom they equated with the ruling Tories in England. Many joined relatives in established communities and built lives in a country that was becoming increasingly industrialized and urbanized. Jefferson's election in 1800, achieved with overwhelming Irish American support, validated Irish revolutionary ideals and made America a home fit for Irish political refugees.[149]

On the frontiers, the intertwined challenges and problems of relations with Indians and government remained, but now Scotch-Irish advocates of Indian removal found themselves increasingly in step, rather than at odds, with government policy. Scotch-Irish prejudices and practices had become an established part of life and death in the backcountry and even of U.S. Indian policy. The language of savagism that angry Scotch-Irish on the mid-Atlantic frontier had employed in the midst of a brutal war became part of the everyday talk of white Americans, justifying dispossession.[150] White people on the frontier continued to seize land by force or fraud from their Indian neighbors, Secretary of War Henry Knox lamented in his end-of-year report to Congress in 1794, and there could be no lasting peace until the Indians could rely with confidence on the United States to protect their lands. As it was, "the feeble advice of the old men," as Knox put it, could not stop Indian warriors from murdering white people encroaching on their lands, and the United States lacked an adequate policing force to prevent or punish the depredations of its own unruly citizens. Knox wished he could say American justice treated the murder of Indians the same way as it did the murder of whites, but that was not the case. "The irritated passions on account of savage cruelty are generally too keen in the places where trials are had, to convict and punish for the killing of an Indian."[151]

George Washington acknowledged that there was as much need for a force "to restrain the turbulent & disorderly people" on the frontier from disturbing the peace as there was for protection against the Indians.[152] It was the same old problem: the government tried to protect its citizens by preventing trespass on Indigenous lands that provoked Indian wars; Scotch-Irish and other frontier settlers ignored and defied the government which seemed to be coddling Indians when it should be fighting them and opening their lands to settlers.

The Federalist government wanted national expansion to proceed in an orderly process of obtaining land by treaties, and having it surveyed, parceled out, and sold to settlers holding legitimate title. Instead, a morass of competing and overlapping land claims made for a chaotic situation in the territories, where tribes and states contested authority and settler colonists asserted ownership on the basis of clearing, planting, and building on land. The practice commonly employed by Scotch-Irish squatters on the frontier had become a well-established principle of occupancy and, in fact, codified in state land laws. During the Revolution, states like Virginia and North Carolina granted rights to purchase land to settlers who had occupied and improved them. Preemption rights encouraged Americans to invade Indian country in the belief that when (not if) the lands were purchased from the Indians, they would have the first claim. "All our acts of No. Carolina seem to favour intruders," Senator Benjamin Hawkins noted, by granting them title "under the appellation of occupants." So it was, Hawkins lamented, "that by violating a solemn treaty these people could acquire this *right of occupancy*." Settlers who defied federal and state proclamations prohibiting settlement and claimed occupancy rights did not see themselves as lawless banditti.[153]

The triangular relationship of backcountry settlers, Cherokees, and the federal government continued to dominate affairs after Tennessee was admitted into the Union in 1796, the first federal territory to achieve statehood. Not surprisingly, many of Tennessee's leading men had the same goals that Scotch-Irish had fought for on successive frontiers: unrestricted access to Indian land; government protection against Indian attacks; and limited government control over their conduct of Indian affairs. State leaders developed a broad-based state role in Indian policy with a philosophy of limited federalism. Along with other western Americans, they depicted Indigenous nationhood and federal power over Indian affairs as incompatible with states' rights, and degraded the Cherokees from a Native nation to tenants at will, setting the stage for the Trail of Tears.[154]

Thomas Dillon, a native of Maryland, visited Tennessee's Cumberland County in the spring of 1796 as the prospects of lasting peace and soaring migration into the area promised to drive up the price of land. It was, he informed his friend and Secretary of War James McHenry, "the best Land Speculation that will occur in our time." He hoped the investments would be safe. Although many of the settlers were "disorderly & licentious and would be very glad to seek an opportunity of kicking up a dust with the Indians," they were people who had nothing to lose or were squatting on Indian land; "the more respectable & thinking" people were averse to anything that might lead to war.[155] Francis Baily, an Englishman traveling through Tennessee and Cherokee country in the summer of 1797, said the Indians disputed "every inch of ground with the Americans," were very particular in abiding by treaties and asserting their rights, and kept an eagle eye on surveyors when they ran a boundary. Bailey also encountered a group of squatter families waiting in the wings for the business to be completed. They had encroached on Indian country before and the government had ordered them to remove, and even sent a detachment of troops to enforce the order. "This," said Baily, "was the bone of contention, which was the subject of conversation in every place I went into." People living within the limits of U.S. territory shared the squatters' outrage, "as they all hate the Indians, and think a little deviation from justice is a thing to be overlooked where their two interests clash with each other."[156]

Washington and the Federalists wanted national expansion to be orderly and measured. Jefferson and the Republicans wanted it to be much more rapid. Where Washington had complained about frontier settlers as peace breakers, Jefferson harnessed their role as hard neighbors and active participants in the process of expansion. As he wrote to Washington, "a society taking possession of a vacant country, and declaring they mean to occupy it, does thereby appropriate to themselves, as prime occupants, what was before common." Understanding that frontier people would "settle the lands in spite of everybody," Jefferson thought it best "to give way to the torrent" and make land more affordable and accessible. The Jefferson administration reduced the minimum purchase acreage to 160 acres and offered land on credit for four years with just 5 percent ($16) down payment.[157] Henry Knox had declared that the United States would not "support the expenses of a war brought on the frontiers by the wanton blood thirsty disposition of our own people."[158] Jefferson, on the other hand, would not only do it; he saw it as an effective way for the government to dispossess Indian people without shouldering the blame for waging war against them. In Jefferson's thinking, the government could and should do little to regulate the frontier and protect Indian lands. When Indians fought back against the intruders, however, the government had no choice but to protect its citizens and invade Indian country. It would suppress the uprising, dictate treaties in which the defeated tribes signed away more land, and set the stage for the process to repeat itself.

Jefferson's strategy for acquiring Native lands resulted in some thirty treaties with a dozen or so tribal groups and the cession of almost 200,000 square miles of Indian territory in nine states. Jefferson and the Republicans sought to "civilize" Indians, and "civilization" and dispossession worked hand in hand to achieve the main goal of turning Indian lands over to American farmers. Scotch-Irish frontiersmen who had been stigmatized as outlaws who violated Federalist Indian policies could join "God's chosen people" in Jefferson's vision of American expansion.[159] Knox's vision of applying justice equally to Indians and U.S. citizens waned, and U.S. policy became a full-frontal assault on tribal autonomy and lands. Federal sovereignty, in the words of legal historian Gregory Ablavsky, morphed into settler sovereignty.[160]

Frontier violence in the 1780s and 1790s fueled Indian-hating and a racialized white identity. The Scotch-Irish and their neighbors on post-Revolutionary frontiers were perhaps no more unified than were the Shawnees, Delawares, and others who opposed them. However, Scotch-Irish, Germans, and Anglo-Americans all became Americans when opposed to Indians, just as Shawnees, Delawares, and Miamis became Indians when opposed to backcountry settlers.[161] Settlers on the Cumberland who had experienced "forted life" and had lost relatives, homes, crops, and livestock shared what the novelist and historian Harriette Simpson Arnow termed a "bond of remembered danger" that transcended cultural differences and promoted a common identity.[162]

Backcountry settlers also demonstrated their common identity as white Americans by striking back. As in the Revolution, by killing Indians, they distanced themselves from Indians with whom eastern elites frequently compared them. In defeating savage enemies, they demonstrated their masculinity, patriotism, and civilization. If they committed atrocities like their savage adversaries, that, as Frederick Jackson Turner pointed out in 1893, was a temporary regression necessary to triumph over savagery. Put simply, by fighting Indians, "the Scots-Irish became white." At same time, attacking Indians and breaking treaties in defiance of federal policies struck back at eastern elites who wanted an orderly transformation of Indian lands into real estate and seemed more inclined to protect Indians than to help backcountry settlers.[163] The federal government in the early 1790s spent tens of thousands of dollars every month on territorial militia defense, and paid thousands more in claims, even for unauthorized expeditions against Indian villages. Nevertheless, backcountry settlers demanding federal aid ritually employed the narrative of a government that neglected its own citizens and coddled Indians who were butchering innocent people.[164]

Contrary to what the Scotch-Irish and their fellow-sufferers may have believed, their complaints did have an effect.[165] The powerfully emotive trope of women and children sacrificed by their own government to Indian tomahawks was one that Andrew Jackson, a son of Scotch-Irish immigrants and raised in a Scotch-Irish community, grew up with, invoked, and fueled.

11

Andrew Jackson and the Triumph of Scotch-Irish Indian Policy

In the early nineteenth century, Scotch-Irish colonists continued to move into Indian country and to act as buffers between contending powers. As national expansion gathered momentum and the federal government passed from the Federalists to the Jeffersonian Republicans to Andrew Jackson's Democrats, policies that had sought, or at least claimed, to restrain backcountry settlers' invasions of Indian lands gave way to policies that harnessed and promoted those invasions. Scotch-Irish and other frontier settlers ignored federal treaties with Indian tribes and ignored treaty boundaries with Indian country. They trespassed on Indian lands, expecting that the resulting conflict would result in the Native inhabitants being expelled. Cherokees told the future French king Louis-Philippe that white neighbors who were angry about the last treaty wanted "a war with Indians so a new treaty c[ould] strip them of the coveted lands."[1]

This was Jeffersonian and Jacksonian Indian policy in action, and the Scotch-Irish and their neighbors were its cutting edge. With the rise to power of Andrew Jackson (Figure 11.1), Scotch-Irish frontiersmen became less aggressive disrupters of U.S. policy than embodiments of aggressive U.S. policies of dispossession and removal. Once the alleged outlaws of federal Indian policy, the Scotch-Irish became its willing instruments.

In *Albion's Seed*, the historian David Hackett Fischer described Jackson as "a Border Chieftain in the White House." Rooted in the political folkways of the backcountry with overwhelming support in the South and West, Jackson demonstrated "a political style characterized by intensely personal leadership, charismatic appeals to his followers, demands for extreme personal loyalty, and a violent antipathy against all who disagreed with him."[2] Fischer and others portrayed the first western president as a product and personification of Scotch-Irish borderland culture and experiences, the archetype of the combative Scotch-Irish frontiersman, and "that most Scotch-Irish of Presidents."[3]

Figure 11.1 Major General Andrew Jackson, painted by Thomas Sully; engraved by James B. Longacre, ca. 1820. Born to Ulster immigrants in the predominantly Scotch-Irish Waxhaws region on the border of North and South Carolina, Jackson moved to Tennessee as a young man. He made a name for himself as an Indian fighter, built a political career and a fortune in acquiring Indian lands, and made Indian removal a national policy.
Library of Congress Prints and Photographs Division.

Andrew Jackson's grandfather was a weaver and merchant from Carrickfergus in County Antrim, where Williamite and Protestant forces had laid siege to a Jacobite and Catholic garrison in 1689. Jackson's father, a well-to-do farmer who held property near the town of Castlereagh, led a party of immigrants to Pennsylvania in 1765, followed the migration path southward, and settled in the Waxhaws region on the border of North and South Carolina. He died in 1767, just before Andrew was born, forcing his wife and children to move in with relatives. The tight-knit Waxhaws community was predominantly Scotch-Irish, and immigrants from Antrim, Down, and Tyrone kept arriving. Scotch-Irish families seeking kinship and security followed each other to the area, until the Waxhaws and the communities to the west constituted one extensive Irish Presbyterian settlement.[4] Jackson grew up in that environment. His biographer and future secretary of war, John Henry Eaton, told how Jackson's mother would spend winter evenings recounting to her sons the sufferings of their grandfather at the siege of Carrickfergus, the oppressions by the Irish nobility, and the need to defend the natural rights of man. She sent Andrew to be educated for the ministry at the academy in the Waxhaws meetinghouse.[5] Reflecting his heritage and early education, Jackson in his correspondence occasionally substituted "they" for "the" and routinely substituted "the" for "they," in accordance with archaic Scotch-Irish usage.[6] Young Jackson was part of an extended Scotch-Irish kin network.[7]

Yet Jackson himself had little to say about his origins, and clear evidence of his Scotch-Irish identity is hard to find. During his presidency, he was criticized for ignoring his Irish roots in a controversial case in which he let an Irish criminal hang but pardoned his American accomplice. James Porter was executed in Philadelphia on July 2, 1830, in front of a crowd of forty thousand, many of them Irish and angry. Jackson defended his actions: "The absurdity that I should have pardoned Wilson because he was an american, and permitted Porter to be hung, because he was an Irishman is too palbable to deserve one single comment from me, when it is known my parents were Irish," he wrote.[8] Thanking his vice president Martin Van Buren for sending him a genealogy of the Jackson family in 1832, Jackson wrote simply, "the statement made of the time when my father came from Ireland, and the names of his children, are correct. This is stated in the Biography of Jackson, wrote by Eaton, & may have been taken from that, or it may be really true."[9]

Contrary to David Hackett Fischer and other writers, historian Kevin Kenny argues that Jackson did not regard himself as Irish in any meaningful sense, and neither did his countrymen. His antipathy to Britain stemmed from the Revolution, when he lost his mother and brothers to disease and was slashed in the face by a British officer's sword, and from the War of 1812, rather than from a tradition of Ulster dissent. There was nothing unusual about Jackson's ambiguous relationship with his Scotch-Irish heritage. John C. Calhoun, a forceful spokesman for the slave-holding South who crossed swords with Jackson on the question of South Carolina's nullification of the tariff, was, like Jackson, a second-generation Ulsterman, the son of Scotch-Irish immigrants who had settled in a Scotch-Irish frontier community that experienced Indian attacks and suffered family losses. Calhoun was also a nephew of the Scotch-Irish Indian-fighting general Andrew Pickens. Nevertheless, Kenny notes, Calhoun "seems to have been no more consciously Irish than his sometime ally and political enemy, Andrew Jackson."[10]

Contrary to the image of Jackson as personifying and taking to the White House the characteristic traits of the backcountry Scotch-Irish, he was in many ways the antithesis of the Waxhaw community where he grew up. Born into a world of family farms, he disdained farming. Baptized by the Reverend William Richardson, he was raised by a pious mother in an intensely religious community, though one would not know it from his youthful behavior and his worldly ambitions. And in a society knit together by kinship ties, Jackson was born fatherless, lost both his brothers and his mother, and was left on his own by age fifteen. Leaving the Waxhaws may have done more to shape his life and character than growing up there.[11] He came of age in a backcountry Scotch-Irish culture of confrontation and violence, but he rarely mentioned the Waxhaws except in reference to the events that occurred there during the Revolution.[12] Jefferson Davis, the future president of the Confederate States of America, in 1845 wrote simply that the seventh president of the United States "was descended from an Irish family of obscure history but as far as I can learn distinguished by a love of liberty, a hatred of tyranny, and defiance of oppression."[13]

The image of Jackson as archetype of the Scotch-Irish frontiersman is clearly overblown, yet his attitudes and actions toward Indians reflected and replicated those of two or three generations of Scotch-Irish frontiersmen. The memory of an elderly former neighbor that "Mrs. Jackson and her son Andrew . . . were inveterate haters of the Indians, on account of their barbarities" does not appear to have referred to their own experiences, although young Jackson would certainly have heard plenty of stories.[14] Educated by a Presbyterian minister, he subscribed to the Calvinist doctrine of collective punishment and eye-for-an-eye atonement in blood in dealing with Indian resistance. The Paxton Boys and the Black Boys had advocated removing Indians from the settlements.[15] So had previous administrations to Jackson's. However, these latter had resisted, restrained, and denied backcountry Scotch-Irish attitudes and actions as they struggled to forge and implement policies that dispossessed Native people with minimal violence and with minimal cost. That meant that, like Philadelphia elites and London imperial officials in the eighteenth century, Washington elites in the early nineteenth century stood accused by Scotch-Irish frontier folk of coddling Indians and neglecting poor whites who needed and deserved their lands.

Jackson harnessed and represented these concerns, advocated and executed removal practices, and rendered them less distinctively Scotch-Irish by incorporating them into the nation's Indian policy. Jackson was a westerner, a southerner, a slave holder, a soldier, a politician, and a president. The adjective "Scotch-Irish" could be placed in front of all of these, not because that was his governing identity, and instead because it was part of who he was.[16] Similarly, to trace Scotch-Irish influences in Jackson's Indian policies is not to claim that they governed U.S. Indian policy, and rather to recognize that they were part of the stream of influences that shaped it.

Making a Name in Tennessee

Following in the footsteps of hundreds of Scotch-Irish people from the Waxhaws and other regions, Jackson as a young man made his way west to Tennessee. He arrived at the height of the land grab and inserted himself into a network of land grabbers that included the Blounts, Donelsons, Sevier, and the Polks. Clan connections dominated Tennessee politics, and Jackson married well when he married a daughter of Colonel John Donelson, who had led one of the two expeditions that founded the town that became Nashville. The extended Donelson family dominated the region's land-speculation business. They positioned themselves as surveyors, lawyers, local government officials, and justices on county and state courts, used their kinship networks to promote and protect their investments, and built fortunes acquiring land from Indians. Marrying into the Donelson family gave Jackson an entrée into the land business and the right connections as he started to climb the ladder of Tennessee society from lawyer to landowner to politician with local, state, and national ambitions.[17]

At the same time, although Jackson invoked the Revolution and Indian fighting, he was keenly aware that he was too young to have fought in the Revolution and came too late to the Tennessee frontier to fight Indians. Unlike his older political rivals John Sevier or James Robertson, Jackson's dealings with Indian people at this point in his life were as a lawyer and land speculator. Appointed District Attorney for the Southwest Territory early in 1791, he was responsible for enforcing the U.S.-Cherokee boundary established by the Treaty of Holston that summer and removing squatters from Cherokee land.[18] This was not the kind of action likely to launch a successful political career in Tennessee. Jackson needed a war against the British or the

Indians to elevate him to the status he craved. Meanwhile, in the absence of war, he engaged in private quarrels and, for the moment, his hunger for Indian land fueled harsh words rather than harsh actions.[19]

The settlements on the Cumberland River in Tennessee confronted stiff resistance from the Chickamauga Cherokees, who continued their own war of independence after the Revolution.[20] Their raids prompted the same fears, frustrations, and fury that Scotch-Irish backcountry settlers had experienced and expressed on previous frontiers. Jackson quickly became a mouthpiece for the beleaguered settlers, albeit with a bullhorn. In response to a raid on Knoxville in 1793, he warned that the Cumberland settlements would dissolve if Congress did not send more help, and the settlers would have to look for support from another source, namely Spain. In what was to become a pattern, he railed against Indians and Congress alike. Writing to Indian agent John McKee, a man with close connections to the Chickamaugas, in May 1794, Jackson fumed at the federal government for what seemed to him a policy of appeasement in dealing with Indians who murdered settlers with impunity. "I fear that their Peace Talks are only Delusions; and in order to put us off our Guard," he wrote. Why make treaties with them? Did not experience show that treaties served no purpose other than to open "an Easy door for the Indians to pass thorough to Butcher our Citizens"? He was at a loss to understand Congress's motives in pursuing pacific policies toward the tribes; "some say humanity dictates it; but Certainly she ought to Extend an Equal share of humanity to her own Citizens." In Jackson's opinion, Cherokees who failed to hand over those responsible for the killings broke their treaty commitments and gave their tacit consent to the bloodshed, and so the whole nation should be "Scurged."[21]

Fueled by righteous Calvinist fury, Jackson routinely, almost reflexively, conjured up images of innocent white women and babies killed by Indians to incite and justify mass retaliation. Invoking biblical revenge for the butchery of the tomahawk and the scalping knife was common rhetoric among men we might call backcountry warlords. They saw themselves as instruments of God's will, and their revenge was justified. The government could leave the retribution to the frontiersmen, although it should foot the bill.[22] For men like James Robertson (son-in-law of a Presbyterian minister), William Rutherford, and Jackson, only Cherokee blood, and lots of it, could atone for the murder of innocent men, women, and children. Jackson did not take part in the fighting when Robertson dispatched an unauthorized expedition against the Chickamauga towns in 1794 that destroyed Nickajack, but he used fighting words. Employing the language of self-defense to obscure his own aggressive intentions was a rhetorical tactic he would employ often.[23]

After Tennessee achieved statehood in 1796, Jackson was named as a representative to the United States Congress. He moved to the Senate a year later. When Tennessee militiamen submitted petitions to Congress appealing for reimbursement for expenses incurred during their unauthorized expeditions against Indian villages, Jackson, in opposition to the secretary of war, supported the petition and Congress approved payment.[24] Returning home, he became a major general in the Tennessee militia, and served as judge for the Tennessee Superior Court from 1798 to 1804. He had definite ideas about the role the federal government should play in relations with Indians, as he made clear to John Sevier, the first governor of his home state, in 1797. He commended Sevier for arresting and bringing to trial citizens who had committed depredations against Indians because such actions if left unpunished could cost innocent lives and endanger the safety of the state. Such powers belonged exclusively to the states, he added, and should never "on any account" be surrendered to the national government. The moment the federal government rode roughshod over the sovereignty of the individual states, "we may bid adieu to our freedom."[25]

Jackson's resistance to the assertion of federal authority manifested itself in a clash with Silas Dinsmoor. Dinsmoor came from a Scotch-Irish family that had settled in Londonderry, New Hampshire. Appointed as agent to the Cherokees by President Washington in 1794, he worked closely with Benjamin Hawkins in promoting the government's "civilization program" among the southern tribes and, according to his son, won over the influential Cherokee chief Bloody Knife to the cause. Fired by President John Adams, Dinsmoor was recalled to the Indian service by Thomas Jefferson and in 1802 was appointed agent to the Choctaws in southern Mississippi, a post he held for twelve years.[26] In 1805, Secretary of War Henry Dearborn sent Dinsmoor and James Robertson as treaty commissioners to deal with the Chickasaws and Choctaws. They acquired a huge tract of land, stretching from Kentucky to Alabama, from the Chickasaws and more than four million acres in south central Mississippi from the Choctaws.[27] Nevertheless, his son said, Dinsmoor "considered himself in honor bound to look after the interests of the tribe over which he was placed, as well as over the interests of the United States." He worked to protect Choctaw lands and became a friend of the Choctaw chief, Pushmataha.

Andrew Jackson, in contrast, was intent on driving the Choctaws out. "The Indians were in possession of excellent land, and some speculative white men wanted to get hold of it," Dinsmoor's son recalled. "Andrew Jackson was in their interests, but the agent watched the corners so closely as to be a thorn in their sides." This may have been the cause of a duel with another Irishman, "fought with pistols while at the dinner table," in which, not surprisingly in the circumstances, Dinsmoor was wounded.[28]

The Trade and Intercourse Act of 1796 required U.S. citizens south of the Ohio to obtain a passport from the Indian agent before entering Indian lands guaranteed by treaty. Dinsmoor ran afoul of Jackson by insisting that anyone going into the Indian nations, including Jackson, carry a passport in compliance with treaty provisions. He had Jackson stopped when he was transporting slaves across the Choctaw nation in 1811, which sent Jackson into apoplexy. The government should be assisting American citizens emigrating to that country to help strengthen the frontier, not alienating them with heavy-handed actions, he fumed to Governor Willie Blount in January 1812, in an unusually long letter recounting the affair. Jackson told the deputy agent who had halted him that "being a citizen of the United States the only passport I carried was, an honest face and a good reputation—that I might have been a subject of Spain had it not have been for such despotism—and bid him farewel—this was communicated to his high mightiness, Silas, who issued his Bull against me."

Arming his party, Jackson proceeded on his way, and the show of force apparently did the trick. Dinsmoor must be removed, Jackson told Blount, "or our citizens will rise and burn his Tavern and Store with Silas in the midst of them." Westerners would not put up with such despotism. It was intolerable that citizens peacefully traveling a road ceded by solemn treaty should be threatened with arrest and confinement, and "that the savages and Indian-countrymen should be assembled to carry these threats into execution." Dinsmoor, Jackson thundered, "is a barbarian, and delights in alarming women by threats that he dare not himself to carry into execution." If he was not removed from office, Jackson would have him indicted for his dealings in trade with the Indians.[29]

In March, Secretary of War William Eustis informed Dinsmoor that the laws regulating trade and intercourse with the Indians were designed to prevent trespasses and encroachments on the Indian Territory, "but are not construed to authorise the stopping of any person travelling through the country in a peaceable manner on the public road or high way; *you will therefore refrain from the exercise of any such authority hereafter.*"[30] When it suited him, Jackson was quick to depict government authority as a threat to liberty.[31]

War against the Creeks

Jackson commonly appealed to honor and masculine pride to defend the republic against its enemies, who included his political opponents, the British, Spain, slaves, and, of course, Indians. Seeing British or Spanish intrigue behind every act of Indian resistance, he issued loud denunciations of merciless savages spurred on by British tyranny. Reacting to rumors (unfounded, as it turned out) of a "massacre" at Duck River in Tennessee in the spring of 1808, Jackson lectured President Jefferson: "These horrid scenes bring fresh to our recollection, the influence, during the revolutionary war, that raised the scalping knife and Tomhawk, against our defenceless weomen and children."[32] When the charismatic Shawnee war chief Tecumseh and his brother Tenskwatawa, the Shawnee Prophet, mobilized a multi-tribal resistance movement, Jackson was enraged by news of the Battle of Tippecanoe, where the governor of Indiana Territory, General William Henry Harrison, launched a preemptive strike against the Prophet's village. As Major General of the 2nd Tennessee Division, Jackson offered to march one thousand Tennesseans to Harrison's aid. "The *blood* of *our murdered Countrymen must be revenged*," he cried. "That banditti ought to be swept from the face of the earth."[33]

When Creek Indians killed and scalped two families near the mouth of Duck River and captured Martha Crawley in the spring of 1812, Jackson conjured up images of wives and children "wallowing in their gore" and called for vengeance and retaliation on a massive scale. Any man who could "see the infant babe of nine days old torn from the arms of its mother and beat to the pieces upon the walls of the house" and did not demand vengeance, was no man at all, he told militia. He informed Governor Willie Blount he was ready to march to the nearest Creek towns, demand they hand over those guilty at bayonet point, and "lay their Towns in ashes" if they refused. The safety of the entire frontier demanded an immediate response, and Jackson thought himself justified "in laying waste their villages, burning their houses, killing their warriors and leading into Captivity their wives and Children—untill I do obtain a surrender of the Captive, and the Captors are delivered up."[34]

Faced with a more serious conflict—Congress declared war against Great Britain in June—the secretary of war preferred to secure the captives' release by negotiation rather than direct assault. An article, probably written by Jackson, in the *Democratic Clarion* declared that if the federal government did not permit an expedition against the Creeks, the people of Tennessee would have to take matters into their own hands. Past experience showed that defensive actions by ranger companies were ineffective. Their only recourse was to emulate the expedition against Nick-a-Jack which had at one stroke terminated the war that had plagued the infant settlements of Tennessee for so long. Like Armstrong and Robertson before him, Jackson was determined to carry the war to the Indians: "Citizens! hold yourselves in readiness: it may be but a short time before the question is put to you: *Are you ready to follow your general to the heart of the Creek nation.*" In the event, Creek chiefs themselves stepped up to ensure the perpetrators were executed and Mrs. Crawley, traumatized and feeble, was released.[35]

Jackson was clearly itching for a fight, and the outbreak of the Creek War in 1813 gave him the occasion and opportunity to put his rhetoric of mass retaliation into action. Like many settler colonists, Jackson believed that the violence of Native people was not a consequence of colonization but inherent in their nature, and a justification for taking their land in the first place, and that the only defense against Native violence was more violence. Whereas Jackson and his men fought to defend their homes, families, and honor, "the savage," he wrote, "goes to war, only that he may gather scalps, & . . . only because he delights in blood."[36] Jackson fueled and harnessed animosity toward Indians that Tennesseans harbored from previous generations of vicious border warfare, and his campaigns during the Creek War echoed and applied the ideology developed earlier that defending the frontier meant eliminating Indians.[37]

The Creeks or Mvskokes (Muskogees) were a loose confederacy of 15,000–20,000 ethnically and linguistically diverse people. More than fifty autonomous Creek towns or *talwas*, and satellite towns, *talofas*, stretched across northern Florida, western Georgia, northern Alabama, and eastern Mississippi.[38] The confederacy was divided into the Upper Creek towns on the Tallapoosa, Coosa, and Alabama rivers in present-day Alabama, and the Lower Creeks on the Ocmulgee, Chattahoochee, and Flint rivers in Georgia.[39] Creeks who had migrated into northern Florida in the course of the eighteenth century had established themselves as an increasingly independent Seminole nation.[40] Many Creek people, especially in the Lower

Towns, accommodated to American ways as the best way to survive in the new nation. They wore European styles of clothing, plowed fields and fenced lands, and cultivated corn and cotton. Influential sons of Scottish traders and Creek mothers—men like Alexander McGillivray at Little Tallassee and William McIntosh at Coweta—had inculcated property values and reoriented Creek society toward a market economy.[41]

Encouraged by U.S. Indian agents, Creek people attempted to diversify their economy to include farming and ranching. However, loss of land, cultural assault, and the inroads of American assimilationist policies generated divisions. Tensions escalated after Tecumseh traveled to the Southeast in 1811, preaching his message of united Indian resistance. Upper Creek towns, called "Red Stick towns" from the color of their ceremonial war clubs, tended to adopt a militant stance in dealing with the United States; Lower Creek towns tended to advocate peace and accommodation. A conflict within the nation that was also a spiritual revolt against the erosion of Creek territory, culture, and identity erupted into a Creek civil war, and the civil war spilled over into attacks on American settlers.[42]

In August 1813, the Scots-Creek chief William Weatherford, who went by the name Red Eagle, and seven hundred Creek warriors attacked Fort Mims, north of Mobile on the Alabama River. Many of the four hundred or so people crowded inside the fort were recent immigrants to Mississippi Territory from Georgia, the Carolinas, and Virginia. Although often described as "of English descent," many were clearly of Scotch-Irish descent. Others were Métis, like Vicey McGirt, former wife of Alexander McGillivray, who was taken captive with her five daughters. An Irish-Creek named Barney O'Riley carried news of the disaster to U.S. Indian agent Benjamin Hawkins two weeks after the attack, and Zachary or Zachariah McGirth, who at first believed his wife and children had been killed, served as an express rider, dressed and painted like a Creek warrior, before joining the American forces. (His family in fact had been saved by a Creek warrior, and McGirth was reunited with them at the end of the war.) Whatever the ethnic backgrounds of the victims, Jackson and others saw Fort Mims as a national tragedy that had to be avenged and an opportunity to seize vast amounts of land from the perpetrators.[43]

In the second year of the War of 1812 with Britain, the United States government was preoccupied with fighting along the Canadian border and lacked the troops to respond effectively to an Indian war on the southern frontier. Tennesseans had had plenty of experience fighting Indians in the South while the government focused its efforts in the North.[44] The Reverend

Thomas Craighead in Nashville invoked memories of Tennesseans' past experiences fighting off Indians without national support. "Hundreds of our fellow-brethren of the Mobile have fallen beneath the Savage Tomahawk," he declared. "The martial sons of Tennessee will do well to recollect the time when they and their fathers were isolated from the rest of the American family, and exposed to the incursions of the same barbarians that now depredate on the Mississippi Territory. You can remember how many members of your individual families have fallen in defense of their altars and firesides."[45] Jackson immediately called out the Tennessee Volunteers to defend their homes against invasion. "Time is not to be lost. We must hasten to the frontier, or we will find it drenched in the blood of our fellow-citizens." His strategy was clear and appealing: only by waging war in the heart of the enemy's country could Tennesseans protect their own frontiers.[46]

David Crockett was among those who remembered and responded to the call. Although the exact genealogy is unclear, it seems that his grandfather was born in 1725 in Ulster or aboard an immigrant ship. His grandparents and parents had moved from Virginia down the Shenandoah Valley to North Carolina and on to the Watauga/Holston settlements in Tennessee, where the grandparents were killed by Creeks and Chickamaugas in 1777. Crockett joined a company assigned to the 2nd Regiment of Volunteer Mounted Riflemen, part of General John Coffee's brigade.[47]

The well-worn rhetorical tactic of depicting white people as innocent victims of savage slaughter and foreign intrigue united Americans in inflicting massive destruction on the Creeks. Armies invaded Creek country from Mississippi and Georgia as well as Tennessee, and turned the Creek civil war into a war to destroy the Creeks. Two armies, one from East Tennessee under General John Cocke and the other from West Tennessee led by Jackson, merged and, under Jackson's overall command, marched south to the junction of the Coosa and Talapoosa Rivers.[48] Jackson led a force of some 2,500 volunteer Tennessee infantry. General John Coffee joined him with 1,300 cavalry. Coffee, a friend and business associate who was also of Scotch-Irish descent, was married to Jackson's niece, Mary Donelson. Jackson and Coffee drew on their kinship network to place trusted family members in key positions in their army.[49] Scotch-Irish Presbyterian James White, the founder of Knoxville, brought 850 men.[50]

On November 3, Coffee and nine hundred mounted troops attacked and destroyed the town of Tallushatchee. They killed almost two hundred warriors and many women and children. "We shot them like dogs," David

Crockett recalled. When desperate Creeks took refuge in a house, we "set the house on fire, and burned it up with the forty-six warriors in it." The next day, hungry soldiers ate potatoes they found in the cellar of the house, although "they looked like they had been stewed with fat meat" from the bodies burned the day before. Even some of the Tennesseans were repulsed by the carnage. Coffee said that the soldiers could not avoid killing some women and children because the warriors fled to their houses and mingled with their families, a claim John Henry Eaton repeated in the biography of Jackson he published in 1817.[51] A ten-month-old infant, found in his dead mother's arms, was brought to Jackson, who named him Lyncoya and sent him home to the Hermitage, where he lived with the family until his death in 1828. Six days after the slaughter at Tallushatchee, Jackson's Tennesseans killed more than three hundred poorly armed Creeks at Talladega.[52] The Hillabee people sued for peace with Jackson, but General White's force, unaware of the situation, attacked and destroyed the Hillabee towns, driving the Hillabees back into the Red Stick alliance, where they fought to the death in subsequent engagements.[53]

The armies from Georgia and Mississippi also made bloody inroads into Creek country. Some Creek and Scotch-Irish men who had rubbed shoulders in the borderlands before the war met each other in combat. Samuel Dale, who began his life-and-times narrative declaring, "I am of Scotch-Irish extraction," was the son of Scotch-Irish parents in Rockbridge County, Virginia, who moved to Georgia. Dale became a trader among the Creeks and Cherokees. In the war, he killed Creeks he knew, including one in hand-to-hand combat who called him out by name in the "Great Canoe Fight" in November 1813.[54]

Jackson's war against the Creeks culminated at the Battle of Topoheka or Horseshoe Bend on March 27. Bolstered by the arrival in February of the 39th Regiment of U.S. Infantry, comprising primarily men of English and Scotch-Irish descent recruited in Knoxville and the surrounding area,[55] Jackson now commanded an army of about 5,000 men, including some 600 Cherokee and Creek allies. He deployed 3,000 troops against an estimated 1,000 Red Stick warriors who had fortified the neck of a bend on the Tallapoosa River. "*Determining to exterminate them*" (emphasis added), Jackson wrote the day after the battle, he dispatched Coffee and most of the Indian allies "to surround the bend in such a manner, as that none of them should escape by attempting to cross the river." Jackson's artillery bombarded the Creeks' position for two hours, and then his troops stormed their defenses. Outgunned and outnumbered and with no other option, the Creeks fought a desperate last stand. "The carnage was dreadful," Jackson told his wife, Rachel. "It was dark before we finished killing them." Officers counted 557 dead (Jackson had his men cut the noses off the corpses to get an accurate count) and Coffee estimated that 200–300 more were killed trying to swim across the Tallapoosa. About 250 women and children were taken prisoner. The mortality rate of roughly 90 percent made Topoheka one of the deadliest Native American battles against the United States.[56] "The fiends of the Tallapoosa will, no longer murder our women & children, or disturb the quiet of our borders," Jackson announced in his address to his troops.[57] Creeks called him Sharp Knife.

While a second-generation Scotch-Irish general commanded operations, and another cut off the Creeks' escape, a second- or third-generation Scotch-Irish officer, twenty-five-year-old Major Lemuel Montgomery in the 39th Infantry, was reputed to be the first to scale the breastworks and died as he did so. His grandfather Hugh Montgomery and perhaps his parents had immigrated from Londonderry.[58] Sam Houston, a lieutenant in the 39th, was wounded in the battle. Houston's grandfather had emigrated from County Antrim. Crockett, Houston, and other veterans of the Creek War later participated in the colonization of Texas. A scattering of Creek Métis individuals of Scots and Scotch-Irish descent were found on the other side of the carnage as well.

By the spring of 1814, 1,600 Creeks had died in battle. Sixty Creek towns and settlements had been abandoned or destroyed.[59] Creek people were starving. Their chiefs were ready for peace, but they were not ready for the terms that Sharp Knife imposed. For Jackson, taking Indian territory opened fertile land for American farms and plantations; it was also essential to strengthening the nation's borderlands against foreign powers who, he knew, lay behind every Indian war. The country west of the Coosa and north of the Alabama River might indemnify the government for the expense of the war, and justice required that the friendly Lower Creeks should be left in peaceful occupation of their towns and with sufficient woodland, he wrote. Nevertheless, the government must connect the settlements of Georgia with those of the Mississippi Territory and Tennessee, forming a bulwark against foreign invasion, and preventing foreign influence from corrupting the minds of the Indians (Map 11.1). The settlements would divide the strength of the Creek nation and keep them peaceful.[60]

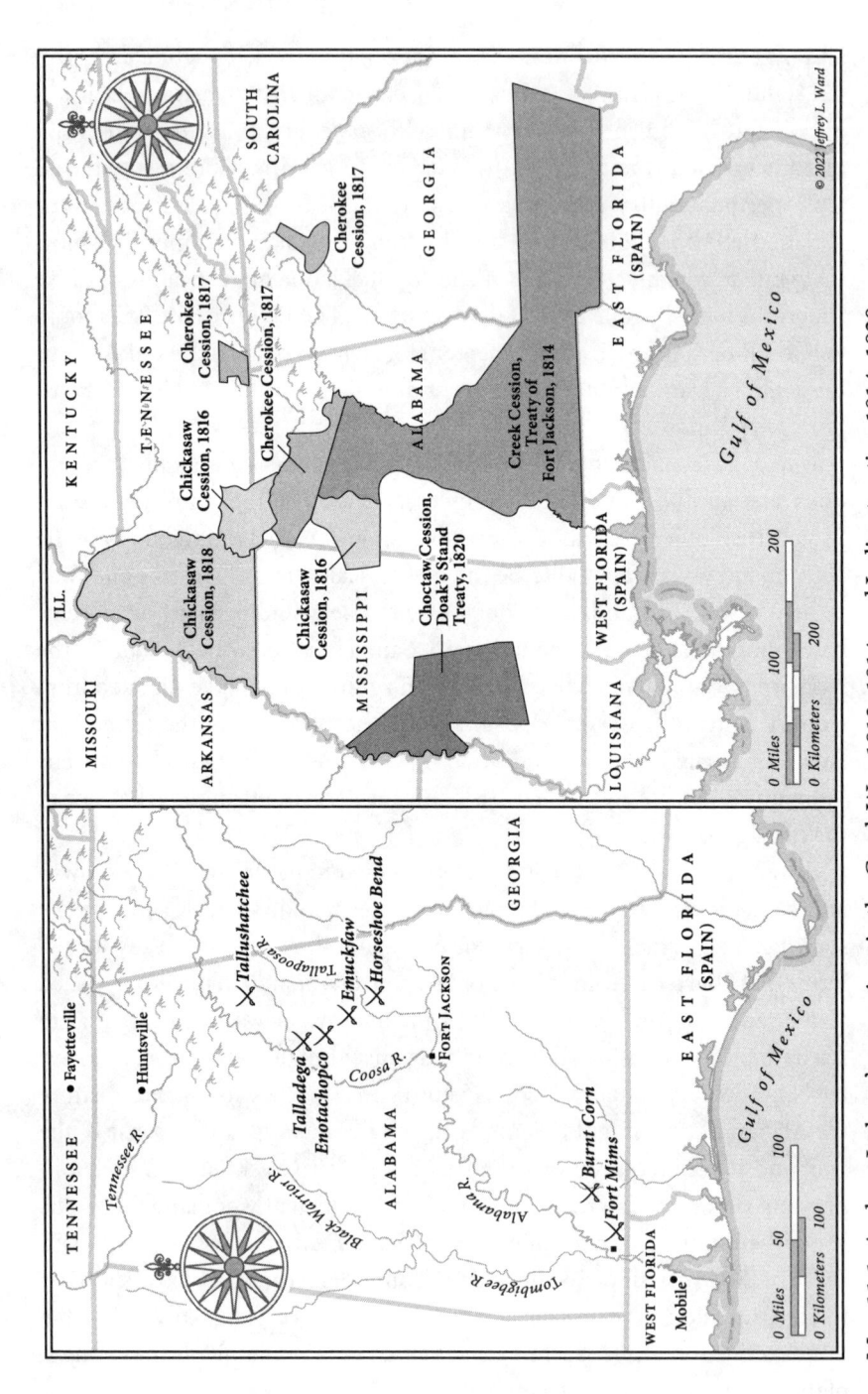

Map 11.1 Andrew Jackson's campaigns in the Creek War, 1813–1814, and Indian treaties, 1814–1820.

In August, he admonished the Creeks for having "followed the counsel of bad men," and made war on a part of their own nation and the United States. The war had cost the United States a large amount and they must yield enough land to pay for it. Moreover, "it must be taken from your whole nation, in such a manner as to destroy the communication with our enemies every where."[61] The Creek chief Big Warrior, who had helped Jackson secure his victory, protested against treaty terms that punished allies as well as enemies. Jackson was adamant that such measures were justified and necessary to protect the United States from its enemies.[62]

Jackson intended to destroy the Creek Nation. "Sensitive to the land greed of westerners, and conditioned by environment and heritage to disregard Indian rights," wrote one biographer, he prepared to strip them of their land.[63] Unlike other treaties that began with conventional platitudes and the ritual language of peace, the Treaty of Fort Jackson in August 1814 began by justifying the massive land cession as punishment for "an unprovoked, inhuman, and sanguinary war" waged by hostile Creeks against American homes and families.[64] Contrary to the instructions that Secretary of War John Armstrong, Jr., the son of General John Armstrong of Carlisle, sent to Pinckney and Hawkins in peace discussions with the Creeks, Jackson imposed a draconian treaty of conquest, taking almost 23 million acres— three-fifths of modern Alabama, one-fifth of Georgia, and more than half of what had been the Creek Nation. It was largest amount ever ceded by Indian people to the United States in a single treaty. Most Red Stick chiefs had fled to Florida; only one of the thirty-five chiefs Jackson browbeat into signing the treaty was a Red Stick; the rest were Jackson's allies. The late Robert Remini, a biographer so sympathetic to Jackson that he often sounded like an apologist, said the friendly Creeks experienced "the awful dimension of Sharp Knife's vindictiveness."[65]

The treaty deprived Creeks of any land contiguous to Spanish Florida. Jackson wanted to quickly populate that land with "a hardy race that would defend it," as he put it in a letter to fellow Tennessean John Williams, who had served with him in the Creek War and at Horseshoe Bend, giving a "preference right ... to those who conquered it at two dollars per acre of three hundred and twenty acres."[66] Although men who fought the Creeks as Tennesseans or Americans may have subsumed their Scotch-Irish identity, they were to be assigned the same role as their Scotch-Irish parents and grandparents.

Jackson's lopsided victory over the British at the Battle of New Orleans in January 1815 secured his status as a military hero and laid the foundations for his subsequent election to the White House.[67] He had inflicted crushing defeats on what he regarded as the two most dangerous threats to his country: the Indians and the British. The next month, the U.S. Senate ratified the Treaty of Fort Jackson. In March, however, news arrived that the Treaty of Ghent ending the War of 1812 had been signed in Belgium on Christmas Eve, 1814, two weeks before the Battle of New Orleans. Britain abandoned its Indian allies once again, as it had at the Treaty of Paris in 1783, but it insisted on including a flimsy pretense of protection in the treaty. Article IX stipulated that the United States agreed to end hostilities with the Indians and restore them to the *status quo antebellum*, including all the lands taken from them since 1811. The Treaty of Ghent effectively nullified the Treaty of Fort Jackson. Jackson would have none of it. The Treaty of Ghent did not apply to *his* treaty, he insisted, and proceeded to implement its punitive terms. The two governments who had agreed to the Treaty of Ghent did nothing.[68]

Jackson met with delegates of the Creeks, Cherokees, Chickasaws, and Choctaws in 1816, using threats, bribery, and intimidation, facing down any opposition, and even defying Secretary of War William H. Crawford, to secure the boundary lines he wanted. The following year, acting as a treaty commissioner for the United States, he secured two million acres of land in Tennessee, Georgia, and Alabama from Cherokees who agreed to move west, and he stripped the Chickasaws of their remaining lands in Kentucky and Tennessee.[69] Scotch-Irish immigrant David Robinson reported a "vast emigration" as the newly acquired lands were opened up for sale.[70]

Jackson had little patience with Indian treaties, even when they gobbled up Indian land. He told Rachel that he resented having to conduct treaties to "regain by tribute" what he had already "purchased by the sword."[71] He was anxious to get the newly acquired lands on to the market, consolidate the nation's frontiers, and settle them with people who would form a defensive buffer against Indian and foreign enemies. The notion that Indian tribes were nations should be dispensed with, he told the new president, James Monroe, in March 1817. "I have long viewed treaties with the Indians an absurdity not to be reconciled to the principles of our Government." Indians were subjects of the United States, inhabiting its territory and acknowledging its sovereignty, and he thought it "absurd for the sovereign to negotiate by treaty with the subject." Indians had only a "possessory right to the soil," they stood in the way of his drive for national growth and unity, and national security demanded removing them. The federal government could assist and implement the process and should not stand in the way of the states and its citizens.[72] John C. Calhoun agreed. Indians were not "independent people" and should not be considered as such. Instead, he told the Senate, the government should take them under its guardianship "and our opinion, and not theirs, ought to prevail, in measures intended for their civilization and happiness."[73]

Jackson's unwavering goal was to defend the sovereignty of white Americans against their enemies. Those enemies included Indians, foreign powers, even their own government.[74] As long as Spain remained in the region, Jackson believed, it would foment Indian wars against innocent American settlers. After the Creek War, many Red Sticks joined their Seminole relatives in northern Florida, then a Spanish province, and Seminoles continued to raid across the border and resist American settlement. The day after Christmas, 1817, Calhoun, then secretary of war, ordered Jackson, as major general of the Army's Southern Division, to assume direct command of troops on the southern frontier and suppress the Seminoles. Calhoun's directive to Jackson referred to orders sent ten days earlier to General Edmund P. Gaines, his predecessor in field command, which authorized pursuing the Seminoles into Florida but forbade attacking the Spaniards there without further instruction. As Remini noted, however, "the administration must have been out of its mind if it expected Jackson to content himself solely with pursuing Indians."

In the spring of 1818, Jackson campaigned through Florida, with five hundred regular troops, some Georgia militia, and about one thousand Tennessee volunteers, as well as a large force of Creek warriors led by William McIntosh, who had fought with him at Horseshoe Bend. Jackson attacked and destroyed Seminole villages, assaulted and captured Spanish forts at St. Marks and Pensacola, and summarily executed two British agents, Alexander Arbuthnot and Robert Ambrister, as well as a Red Stick prophet called Josiah Francis or Hidlis Hadjo, and a war chief named Homathlenico. Monroe's Cabinet considered privately whether to discipline him for transgressing orders but decided against it. Subsequently the administration, including Calhoun, publicly defended Jackson against heated criticism in Congress, foreign embassies, and newspapers, justifying his conduct as a response to Spanish provocation in inciting the Indians. Jackson himself claimed that he acted out of military necessity and had full authority from the administration for everything he did. Unable to defend or control the territory, Spain agreed to cede Florida to the United States in the Adams-Onís Treaty of 1819.[75]

Indian Removals

Between 1815 and 1845, almost one million Irish people migrated to America. After the eruption of the Mount Tambora volcano in Indonesia in 1815 produced a global ecological crisis and a "year without summer" in 1816, emigration surged. About fourteen thousand emigrants made the voyage in 1816–1817 and twenty thousand more in 1820, two-thirds of them sailing from the Ulster ports of Belfast, Newry, and Derry. Irish emigration climbed steadily from the 1820s, though it became increasingly southern and Catholic.[76] The Irish joined a growing flood of migrants from Europe and came looking for land in a country that, it seemed to them, had plenty to spare once the original occupants were removed.

Like the Black Boys and other inhabitants of the Scotch-Irish backcountry world in which he moved, Jackson regarded the dispossession and removal of Indian people as essential to the safety and prosperity of frontier families.[77] In pursuing a relentless assault on Indian lands and criticizing Washington elites who coddled Indians and neglected poor whites, he believed he was carrying on the legacy of the Revolution.[78] He also appealed to his southern and western—and Scotch-Irish—base. Jeffersonian policies had promoted the voluntary removal of Indian peoples, even if it was achieved by the kind of coercive tactics and nefarious means employed by William Henry Harrison.[79] Scotch-Irish and other backcountry farmers demanded forced expulsion.[80] At the same time, many people who were sympathetic to Native people also favored removal as the only way to protect them from their rapacious white neighbors.

Jackson was the driving force behind Indian removal even before he became president. With a very few personal exceptions, from his earliest days in Tennessee he advocated and anticipated expelling all Native people and opening their homelands to white settlers.[81] From 1814 to 1824, eleven treaties were made with southern Indian nations. Jackson was responsible for all but two of them and was present at six. His treaties acquired three-quarters of Alabama and Florida, one-third of Tennessee, one-fifth of Georgia, and parts of Kentucky and North Carolina. He told the tribes that the government could not protect them from annihilation if they insisted on remaining in their homelands; only removal treaties could save them.[82] He worked with Coffee to bribe, intimidate, and coerce Choctaws, Chickasaws, and Cherokees—people who had fought as allies of the United States—into making treaties. With Jackson as commissioner at the Treaty of Doaks Stand in 1820, Pushmataha and the Choctaws ceded much of their homelands in Mississippi to the United States and accepted new lands in the West in return.

Jackson was not interested in incremental dispossession and not overly concerned about the means employed. Concentrating the southern tribes in an area west of the Mississippi, "and thereby strengthening our Southern border with the white population which will occupy their lands . . . required some attention to the Indian character," he explained to Chickasaw agent John Dabney Terrell in 1826. It was "useless to attempt to prepare the minds of the Chickasaws for the surrender of a part of their lands. From my knowledge of their character I have no doubt that an entire exchange will be effected with less difficulty than a partial one." The best plan was to tell them bluntly that so long as they remained where they were, they would always be exposed to encroachments from the white people who were constantly harassing the president to allow them to occupy the Indians' lands. Terrell "must be prepared to give assurances of permanency of title, and dwell upon the idea that they will never be asked to surrender an acre more." He might even suggest the possibility of uniting with the Creeks and Choctaws "as a speedy means of making them a great, powerful, & happy people, &, when their children shall be educated, of enabling them to become a member of the United states, as Alabama & Mississippi are."[83]

The election of 1828 landed the leading proponent of removal in the White House. Jackson was elected president on a mandate to remove Native Americans from the lands desired and demanded by white Americans. "Our conduct toward these people is deeply interesting to our national character," he declared in his First Annual Message to Congress in December 1829, with considerable understatement and more insight than he intended. Reflecting on Jackson's role in Indian removal after his own retirement from the presidency, Martin Van Buren wrote, "There was no measure, in the whole course of his administration, of which he was more exclusively the author than this."[84] Although Jackson decried making treaties with people who, he claimed, lacked sovereign rights, during his two terms as president he oversaw the ratification of seventy treaties that together secured roughly 100 million acres of land and displaced forty-six thousand people.[85]

In May 1830, after extensive debate and a close vote in both houses, and despite widespread opposition from church and reform groups throughout much of the country, Congress passed the Indian Removal Act, authorizing the president to negotiate treaties of removal with all Indian tribes living east of the Mississippi. Indian removal was now national policy.

David Crockett (Figure 11.2) voted against the Removal Act. Perhaps even more than Jackson, Crockett embodied the western-style hero. Both men were Indian fighters of Scotch-Irish heritage and backwoods origins, and Crockett supported Jackson in 1828. But then they diverged. Crockett enjoyed a national reputation manufactured by Whig politicians to counter the appeal to the "common man" of Jackson the Democrat and was even considered a presidential possibility. Opposing Jackson on Indian removal ended his political career.[86] Crockett had been a squatter himself, advocated for squatters' rights, and took up the cause of the landless poor. Jackson did not support squatters' rights, and he did not hesitate to employ the military to remove them. He justified white possession of land because whites cleared and improved it. Indians who did not and who resisted assimilation were to be treated like squatters and removed.[87] Not for the last time in American politics, people opted for a politician who claimed to speak for them, rather than one who actually did. Crockett burned his political fences and went to Texas.

In his first State of the Union address to Congress in December 1830, Jackson basked in the successful passage of the Indian Removal Act and urged its speedy implementation as beneficial to the United States, to the individual states, and to Indian people themselves. In addition to the financial benefits it would bring, the removal policy would put an end to the danger of collision between the U.S. government and state governments over the conduct of Indian affairs. It would "place a dense and civilized population in large tracts of country now occupied by a few savage hunters," and by opening the whole territory between Tennessee on the north and Louisiana on the south to white settlers, it would strengthen the southwest frontier and the adjacent states against future invasions. It would relieve the whole of Mississippi and the western part of Alabama of Indian occupancy, and enable those states to advance rapidly in population, wealth, and power. And it would even benefit the people being driven from their homes:

> It will separate the Indians from immediate contact with settlements of whites; free them from the power of the States; enable them to pursue

Figure 11.2 David Crockett. The grandson of Scotch-Irish immigrants, Davy Crockett became popularized as the iconic frontiersman. The real David Crockett, pictured here and attested to by Crockett himself, was an aspirant Tennessee politician as well as an Indian-fighter, in an area where the two careers often went hand in hand.
Tennessee State Library and Archives.

happiness in their own way and under their own rude institutions; will retard the progress of decay, which is lessening their numbers, and perhaps cause them gradually, under the protection of the Government and through the influence of good counsels, to cast off their savage habits and become an interesting, civilized, and Christian community.

Humanity wept over the fate of the continent's Indigenous inhabitants, and no one had more friendly feelings toward Indian people than Jackson—said Jackson. However, history showed that the decline and fall of nations to make way for newer, stronger nations was inevitable and there was no stopping progress. Although Jackson knew the settled and agriculturally based Creeks and Cherokees firsthand—after all, many of them had served as allies in his campaigns—he depicted them as wandering hunters: Who would not prefer "our extensive Republic, studded with cities, towns, and prosperous farms" and "occupied by more than 12,000,000 happy people" to "a country covered with forests and ranged by a few thousand savages"?

He invoked his own ancestors' displacement and emigration as the natural course of things. It would no doubt be painful for Indian people to leave the graves of their fathers, but that was no more "than our ancestors did or than our children are now doing." "To better their condition in an unknown land our forefathers left all that was dear in earthly objects. Our children by thousands yearly leave the land of their birth to seek new homes in distant regions." Was it to be supposed, Jackson asked, "that the wandering savage has a stronger attachment to his home than the settled, civilized Christian?" Rather than weep at these painful separations, humanity should rejoice that America afforded scope for its young population to progress.[88]

Thomas Jefferson had regarded Indians as culturally inferior but capable of improvement with the proper instruction; Jackson regarded Indians as racially inferior and incapable of change. In Jackson's view, even the so-called civilized tribes were, in fact, "savages." They did not put the land to good use, and they could not be allowed to deny that land to American farmers. "Civilization" and "progress" demanded that they be removed. In the 1830s and 1840s, the United States deported more than eighty thousand Native people from their eastern homelands.

Jackson presented himself as the straight-talking father who knew what was best for his Indian children and would tell them the hard truth. They had no realistic alternative but to leave their homelands and move west, he said. "Where you now are, you and my white children are too near to each other to live in harmony and peace. Your game is destroyed and many of your people will not work and till the Earth." If they stayed, they must succumb to the jurisdiction of the states in which they lived, and the United States government could not protect them. Beyond the Mississippi, however, there was plenty of land, the government would protect them, and they would never have to give up territory again. "There your white brothers will not trouble you; they will have no claim to the land, and you can live upon it, you and all your children, as long as the grass grows or the water runs, in peace and plenty. It will be yours for ever."[89]

Addressing the Choctaws in late August 1830, a few weeks before the Treaty of Dancing Rabbit Creek, Jackson told them they had to make a choice: "remove—seek a home beyond the Mississippi, or else remain, where you are, under the laws of the State." They had no other option.[90] When the Choctaws during the negotiations suddenly balked at removing, John Eaton charged them with deceit and threatened to break off the talks and leave them to their fate under Mississippi's laws.[91] At the Treaty of Dancing Rabbit Creek, Choctaws ceded 11 million acres in Mississippi in exchange for 15 million acres in Indian Territory. Reflecting on the treaty with Chickasaws that same year, Robert Remini wrote: "Jackson never for a moment paused over the human wreckage he left in his wake."[92]

Cherokee removal stood as the most enduring example of Jackson's removal policies in action. The Cherokee homeland lay adjacent to and overlapped with the Scotch-Irish hearth area in northern Georgia, western North Carolina, and Tennessee (see Map 8.1 in Chapter 8), and Georgia settlers put the pressure on Cherokees to bring them to the treaty table, especially after gold was discovered in Cherokee country. John Coffee, veteran of the Creek War and Jackson's right-hand man on many occasions, understood the situation. "The pioneers and frontier settlers are so clamourous, that the authorities of the state feel bound to urge their claim even beyond the sober dictates of their better judgments," he wrote to the president in March 1830; "indeed it seems proverbial that a man in office in Georgia, must clamour on this subject, or be driven out of Office—for although some may and do differ in opinion, yet such must be silent, or be hunted down by the vociferous part of the community." Coffee also understood how to resolve the situation. Deprive the chiefs of their power, take away their code of laws, and reduce them to plain citizenship, and they would soon agree to move. Georgia would take care of things if the United States did not intervene, "for if Georgia extends her laws over the nation, and take away the authority of the

Chiefs, ... they will instantly withdraw when they find that neither Congress or the Executive will interfere." That being the case, Coffee continued, the United States should be liberal in making treaties with the Indians, affording them protection and maintaining good relations. That would "have a happy effect on the feelings of the civilized world" and silence critics at home. "It may indeed turn them loose upon Georgia, but that matters not, it is Georgia who clamour for the Indian lands, and she alone is entitled to blame if any there be."[93]

The same month, George Lowry (Lowery) and other Cherokee chiefs in Washington, DC, wrote to Jackson from Brown's Hotel, which specialized in lodging Indian delegations, about the alarming increase in people searching and digging for gold in the Cherokee Nation. The number of intruders was variously estimated at one to two thousand, "which we cannot but consider as depriving us of property for which the faith of the Govt. is pledged for our protection."[94] It could hardly have been news to Jackson. The next month the *Cherokee Phoenix* reprinted a statement by settlers who claimed that U.S. officers and government officials had encouraged them to intrude into the Cherokee Nation.[95]

Pushing frontier settlers onto Indian land and then citing the subsequent disturbance as a pretext for taking the land was by now a long-standing government strategy. Its antecedents stretched back to William Penn's time, and Jefferson had made the trespass-leads-to-treaty tactic semi-official policy. Yet again, trespassers were doing the work of disrupting and dismantling—in this case, the advance work of removal. Despite a landmark Supreme Court decision in *Worcester v. Georgia* in 1832, which stated that the State of Georgia had no authority in Cherokee country, the assault on Cherokee land, people, and rights continued unabated. Jackson would not employ federal troops to enforce existing treaties. Federal troops would be employed, however, to enforce removal under a new treaty.

In 1835, U.S. commissioner John Schermerhorn signed the Treaty of New Echota with a minority group of Cherokees who agreed to move west voluntarily. The "Treaty Party" included Major Ridge, John Ridge, Elias Boudinot, his brother Stand Watie, and others who had formerly resisted removal but now, given Jackson's stance, felt they had no alternative but to emigrate. Principal chief John Ross denounced the treaty as fraudulent; it squeaked through ratification in the Senate by just one vote, and fourteen thousand Cherokees signed a petition protesting against it. Undeterred, Jackson signed the treaty and professed that it expressed the will of the Cherokee people, "the real Indians," not the self-interested "half breeds." In 1838, federal troops rounded up most of the Cherokee people, placed them in stockaded internment camps, and then deported them across the Mississippi. About one-quarter of the Cherokees, including Ross's wife, died on the "Trail of Tears."

Jackson is famous for his refusal to enforce John Marshall's decision in *Worcester v. Georgia*, but his stance was consistent: he insisted that the federal government had no power over the states' dealings with Indians and he repeatedly told Indian people that the federal government could, and he would, do nothing to protect them if they remained in the states. He didn't do much to protect them when they left, either. Native families moving west were threatened, fleeced, and abused by frontier settlers, speculators, and contractors, often with the collusion of corrupt Indian agents who had been appointed for their loyalty to the president and his policies. Jackson turned a deaf ear to the complaints of Indian people who arrived in the West to find they had been deceived. As usual, he attributed their suffering to their inherent characteristics—their racial incapacity, in other words—or to the "designing white men" and "half breeds" living among them.[96] As biographer Jon Meacham acknowledges, Jackson believed in removal with all his heart and refused to consider any other scenario; "he was as ferocious in inflicting harm on *a* people as he often was in defending the rights of those he thought of as *the* people."[97]

It may be an overstatement to say that Jackson's election brought a border chieftain to the White House, and a distortion to suggest that he governed as a Scotch-Irish president, driven by Scotch-Irish experiences and prejudices to apply Scotch-Irish Indian policies. Jackson is often portrayed as the archetypical Scotch-Irish American; Scotch-Irish Presbyterians lent their considerable support to his election in 1828, and Irish voters helped to transform the politics of deference that had elected presidents from Massachusetts and Virginia for forty years. By 1832, however, Scotch-Irish Presbyterians in Pennsylvania were turning away from Jackson and turning toward his opponents, the future Whigs. Some were dissatisfied with Jackson's Indian policy, but many wanted to distance themselves from Irish Catholics, who strongly supported Jackson. Some would later gravitate toward the nativist Know-Nothing Party and its anti-immigrant, anti-Catholic platform.[98] And not even Andrew Jackson could entirely remove backcountry suspicions and ambivalence toward the federal government. In the Treaty of Cusseta in 1832, the Creeks ceded their remaining tribal lands east of the Mississippi, all of which lay in Alabama, and the United States provided allotments for

Creek people who chose to stay in Alabama. Jackson incurred the wrath and resentment of settlers when in his role as president he tried to apply the treaty provisions that offered a measure of protection to Creek lands; Alabama settlers accused the architect of Indian removal of siding with the Indians over them.[99]

Still, contemporaries and historians recognized that Jackson's presidency brought significant changes in American democracy, presidential power, and Indian policy, and contained elements that reflected Scotch-Irish frontier experiences and expectations. Jackson appealed to a base who felt betrayed by eastern elites and by a federal government that tried to limit their access to lands they felt they had won by right of conquest. With Jackson at the helm, attitudes and practices that were formerly associated with backward and aggressive Scotch-Irish frontier settlers were now entrenched in national policies. In the colonial and early national era, Scotch-Irish on the backcountry were instruments of Indian policies—whether formulated by colonial governments, the British imperial government, or the United States government—and at the same time obstacles to the successful implementation of those policies. Scotch-Irish people had often felt they were fighting on two fronts, against Indians who resisted their presence and trespass, and against an eastern government that seemed to do more to protect Indians from them than it did to protect them from Indians. With Andrew Jackson in the White House, their attitudes, experiences, and aspirations now seemed to be represented in national policies of westward expansion and Indian removal. Rather than feeling alienated from it, Scotch-Irish backcountry inhabitants could finally identify with their national government.

With Jackson's presidency, the frontier squatter replaced Jefferson's yeoman farmer as the mythological personage at the backbone of America. Always a contested figure, by the 1830s and 1840s, the squatter came to symbolize partisan politics and epitomize Jacksonian democracy. Jacksonian democracy, though, and Jackson's presidency were less concerned with establishing equality among the people than with unleashing an aggressive national expansion for the people. Seizing land and clearing it of potential threats, be they British, Spanish, or Indian; employing violence if necessary; and acting without legal authority, Jackson incorporated squatter practices into national policy.[100] White supremacy was an essential part of Jacksonian democracy; expansion was for white males at the expense of Indians and other peoples.[101] The national identity that Jackson forged and that shaped

American politics for the next generation was grounded in westward expansion and Indian removal and, ultimately, in violence.[102]

Jackson repeatedly appealed to and invoked the support of his base in the South and West. Like previous government officials, he claimed to decry the actions of squatters who trespassed on Indian land. As an affluent slaveholding planter and aspiring southern gentleman, he shared the contempt of his class for frontier "roughs" who robbed and murdered Indians. Yet he exploited their trespasses and aggressions to persuade Indian people of their urgent need to sell out and move west.[103] He grew rich speculating in lands, and his friends and relatives received patronage appointments created by treaties as Indian agents, land agents, commissioners, surveyors, and traders. He opened up the Deep South to the expansion of the Cotton Kingdom and plantation slavery, which drove economic growth in the United States and England but meant that poorer people on the frontier found, as they had elsewhere, land prices inflated and their own opportunities stifled. As Tennessee historian Thomas Perkins Abernethy wrote almost one hundred years ago, "Jackson never really championed the cause of the people; he only invited them to champion his."[104] It is, perhaps, not surprising that Donald Trump placed a portrait of Andrew Jackson in the Oval Office.

12

Across the Mississippi

In 1803 the United States bought 828,000 square miles of territory west of the Mississippi from France and doubled the nation's size. In the years that followed the Louisiana Purchase, the American population bulged west from Kentucky, Tennessee, and other Appalachian regions and spilled across the Mississippi. The majority of the first migrants from the Appalachians were of Scotch-Irish descent.[1] As their parents and grandparents had followed river valleys to western Pennsylvania, Virginia, the Carolinas, Kentucky, and Tennessee, families from the Old Northwest and upland South traveled down the Ohio, Cumberland, and Tennessee valleys to their junction, funneled into Missouri, settled there, and passed through as they pushed farther west.[2] Everywhere they went, Scotch-Irish Americans who crossed the Mississippi encountered Indian people. Contrary to stereotypical depictions of white settlers dispossessing Native people who had inhabited their homelands from time immemorial, Scotch-Irish Americans in Missouri and Arkansas often found themselves sharing and contesting lands with Native peoples that they or their ancestors had met before and who, like them, were on the move.

Immigrant Buffers and Ambiguous Loyalties

People had been crossing the Mississippi long before Louisiana became American territory. In the wake of the Revolution, Britain and Spain feared American expansion beyond the borders of the United States, and they recruited settlers from the new nation to form buffers for their own thinly settled colonies. The British drew Mohawk allies from New York to settle on reserves at Grand River and Tyendinaga in Ontario and offered land grants to lure Americans across the border. They also hoped that a neutral Indian state might be constructed as a barrier between their own territory and that of the United States, a dream that flickered brightly when the Northwest Indian confederacy routed General Arthur St. Clair's army in 1791, died down after Anthony Wayne's victory at Fallen Timbers three years later, flared again when Tecumseh preached his vision of a united Indigenous state, and was finally snuffed out in the peace negotiated at the end of the War of 1812.[3]

Spain, after the American Revolution, tried to make the Mississippi a barrier for its northern provinces, and ultimately its Mexican silver mines. Confronted with aggressive Americans and displaced Indians, Spain built alliances with the Creeks, Choctaws, Chickasaws, and Cherokees as its first line of defense in the Southeast; west of the Mississippi, with the Osages, Quapaws, Shawnees, and Delawares as a second line of defense. Like the British, Spanish officials also welcomed American immigrants as a buffer against colonial rivals and Indian raiders. They preferred Catholics, although they accepted Protestants, provided they brought no clergy. To help encourage conversions, Spain recruited English-speaking Irish priests to serve in Louisiana.[4] Immigrants from Kentucky and Tennessee flooded in. During the 1780s and early 1790s, about 20,000 Americans, including Daniel Boone, crossed the Mississippi and settled in Louisiana as Spanish subjects.[5]

Even before the United States won its independence and launched renewed assaults on Indian lands, Shawnees, Delawares, and other Native migrants were crossing the Mississippi and taking up Spanish offers to settle there. Beginning around 1779, Shawnee chiefs Yellow Hawk and Black Stump led some 1,200 of their people to Missouri and settled on lands near Cape Girardeau. Iroquois, Shawnee, Cherokee, Creek, and other delegates in St. Louis in the summer of 1784 told the Spanish governor that Americans were spreading, as one put it, "like a plague of locusts," in the Ohio Valley.[6] Hundreds more Native emigrants crossed the Mississippi to escape the ongoing violence in Ohio country and settled in southwest Missouri. Francisco Luis Hector de Carondelet, the Spanish governor of Louisiana, described the Americans in 1793 as a "vast and restless population, driving the Indian tribes continually before them and upon us."[7]

Delawares, who had moved from the Delaware Valley to the Susquehanna, on to the Allegheny, and then to the Ohio country, continued to move after the Revolution, part of a tribal diaspora that took Delaware people north to Canada, west to Indiana, Missouri, and Kansas, and southwest to Spanish Louisiana and Texas.[8] A young Swiss traveler who encountered large numbers of Delawares encamped at the mouth of the Wabash in 1785 wrote: "This nation, the whole of whose territory has been taken possession of by the whites, has now no home, and live in the country of the Chickasaws."[9] The main body of Delawares, about one thousand people, settled in at least nine villages on the White River in Indiana.[10] Others joined Shawnees seeking territory and refuge in Missouri. Some settled at Cape Girardeau; some in villages on the White and St. Francis rivers.

By 1787, about 1,800 emigrant Indians, mainly Delawares and Shawnees, had settled in towns along the Mississippi, accompanied by, among others, Louis Lorimier and his Métis family. The Spanish government set aside a tract of 750 square miles for Indian emigrants south and west of Ste. Genevieve near Cape Girardeau. By the 1790s there were at least six new villages, with about 1,200 Shawnees and 600 Delawares, mostly along Apple Creek, and several hundred Cherokees farther south. Indian groups also passed through the area as they moved farther west. In 1793, Spain granted Louis Lorimier a trading monopoly among the emigrant Indians; in return he was to bring as many of them as possible over to the Spanish side of the Mississippi and settle them "as conveniently as may be to our settlements, ... with a view to their rendering us aid in case of war with the whites as well as with the Osages." After the United States took over, Lorimier became agent for the Delawares and Shawnees.[11]

Nicolas de Finiels, an expatriate French engineer working for the Spanish colonial government in Louisiana, described the Shawnee villages along Apple Creek near Cape Girardeau in the late 1790s as well laid-out, solidly constructed, and surrounded by fields "fenced around in the American style." He esteemed the Shawnees more highly than other immigrant Indians and had no doubt that, with some encouragement and without giving up their hunting economy, they "could become a stable agricultural people and would be useful residents of Upper Louisiana."[12] Modern archaeological excavations along Apple Creek found little to distinguish Shawnee and Delaware sites from American sites because the material remains—clothing, household goods, implements—were much the same.[13] According to Amos Stoddard, the first U.S. commandant of the district of Upper Louisiana, the Delawares and Shawnees were "considered as a safe-guard to the whites," protecting new American settlements. For their part, however, the Delawares and Shawnees asked the U.S. government to protect them against American families who "settled promiscuously" on their lands by confirming them in possession of the lands they had been granted by Spain or assigning them "another place out side of the Settlements."[14]

More Delawares moved west after the Treaty of St. Mary's in 1818, when they agreed to give up their lands in Indiana to the United States and to move west within three years. Their chief, William Anderson, Kithtuleland, led the first contingent of about 800 people in 1820, first to Illinois and then to the James Fork of the White River in southwestern Missouri. By 1822, almost 2,500 Delawares lived in villages west of the Mississippi.[15] The statistical table of Indian populations appended to Jedidiah Morse's report to the secretary of war in 1822 listed 1,383 Shawnees at Cape Girardeau and the Meramec River, and 1,800 Delawares on Current River and the east bend of White River.[16]

Whereas Europeans and Americans in their colonial contests treated the Mississippi River as a border, Native Americans more often used it as a corridor. Eastern Indian peoples who moved across the Mississippi adjusted to a new environment of prairie grasslands, a different climate, and alien peoples, in an area which was a confluence of peoples. Exiled Delawares and Shawnees with a history of movement into and away from borderlands found themselves in a familiar situation; border people once again, they functioned as buffers between contending colonial powers and competing Indigenous peoples and tried to preserve their autonomy in an area of ambiguous and overlapping sovereignties. Faced with declining options and resources, they adapted traditional subsistence practices, shared resources and trade networks, and rebuilt intertribal alliances, as they had east of the Mississippi.[17]

Like Pennsylvanian officials before them, Spanish colonial officials believed that farmers occupying their own lands provided an effective military defense against outside threat. They hoped that American immigrants who took an oath of loyalty to Spain in return for grants of land would assimilate and form a protective buffer against other land-hungry Americans. Bringing in Americans as a defense against Americans was a calculated risk at best, however.[18] Thomas Jefferson knew better how these things worked. Referring to Spanish attempts to attract American settlers to Florida, he wrote George Washington in April 1791, "I wish a hundred thousand of our inhabitants would accept the invitation. It will be the means of delivering to us peaceably what may otherwise cost a war." For expansion-minded politicians like Jefferson, settling Americans in borderland areas was the first step toward U.S. acquisition of those areas.[19]

Making the Ozarks Common and Contested Ground

Thousands of people whose dreams of landed independence had been frustrated by speculators, lawyers, and officials in Kentucky and Tennessee

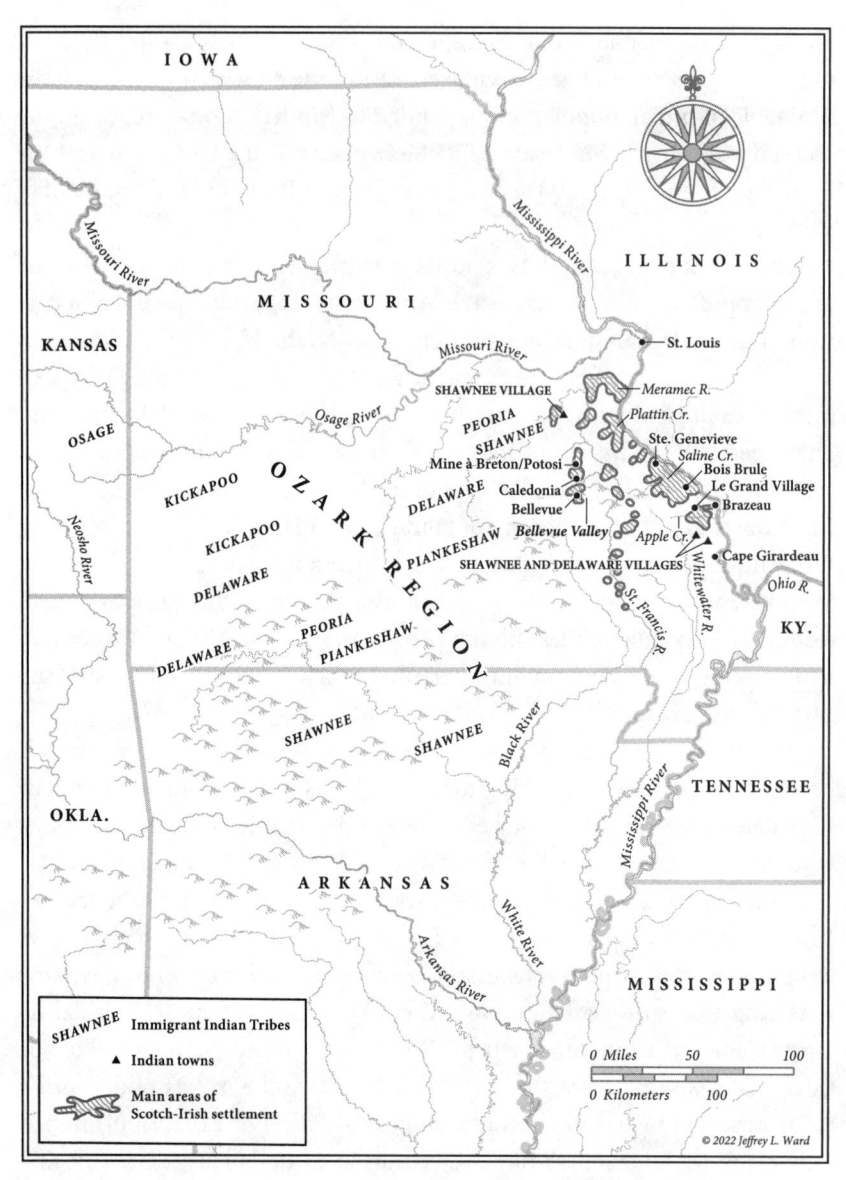

Map 12.1 Scotch-Irish and immigrant Indians in the Ozarks.

migrated to Missouri and the Ozarks in the early nineteenth century.[20] Writing to his mother in Londonderry, Ireland, David Robinson reckoned that seven thousand people had emigrated from Kentucky to the Missouri country in the space of just three months in the fall of 1816.[21] Given the geographic regions and demographic reservoirs from which the migrants came, it is likely that many, if not most, of the Tennesseans, and many of the Kentuckians, who settled in the Ozarks were of Scotch-Irish descent. Establishing dispersed farmsteads and hamlets along rivers and creeks, they settled in the St. Francis region, the Bellevue and Acadia valleys, and the interior.[22]

The Ozark Plateau, some sixty thousand square miles of upland, encompasses southern Missouri and northern Arkansas and reaches into northeastern Oklahoma and the southeastern part of Kansas. Although the eastern Ozarks held valuable mineral resources such as lead, iron ore, and salt, much of the Ozarks consisted of poor soils and rough terrain that had little appeal to most farmers, as had been the case in the Appalachians. On the other hand, Ozark forests offered rich hunting and ample forage for free-ranging livestock. Migrants from Kentucky, Tennessee, and Appalachia would have found the environment quite familiar.[23]

They also encountered Native peoples who would have seemed quite familiar, as they joined the inflow of emigrant Shawnees, Delawares, and Cherokees into the region (Map 12.1). Shifting colonial and tribal contests for dominance and survival made the Ozarks a borderland zone in constant flux. In the first decades of the century, it was also an international Indigenous world where multiple groups jostled for position and competed for resources.[24]

Such competition had been going on for centuries among successive occupants of the region who regarded it as their native ground, and created, contested, shared, and negotiated borders with other peoples. Immigrant Americans and Native Americans came across earthen mounds that were visible remainders of Casqui, Pacaha, and other chiefdoms the Spanish expedition of Hernando de Soto had encountered when it pushed up the Arkansas Valley in 1541.[25]

Two hundred years after De Soto, the most powerful people in the region were the Osages. They had moved there in the 1600s in a migration of Dhegiha Siouan peoples down the Ohio River that also carried Quapaws, Omahas, Poncas, and Kansas across the Mississippi. With a population of around ten thousand, the Osages dominated the prairies between the Missouri and Arkansas rivers and controlled the Ozarks, especially the interior and western areas. Osages supplemented their hunting, gathering, and farming economy with trading. They planted fields near their villages in spring, dispersed to hunt buffalo on the plains in the summer, returned to harvest, dry, and store crops of corn, beans, and squash in the fall, and wintered near the forests. They acquired horses by 1690 and were among the first peoples on the lower Missouri to obtain firearms from the French, with whom they traded and established kinship ties. They largely dictated the terms of their relationships with traders, and they bullied and denied trade to rival tribes. When Spain took over Louisiana, the Osages fended off Spanish attempts to subdue or control them. When the United States took over and Thomas Jefferson dispatched Meriwether Lewis and William Clark to explore the new territory, he warned the captains that the Osages were "the great nation South of the Missouri . . . as the Sioux are great North of that river."[26]

However, the Osages' power and way of life was coming under increasing pressures, and they were a different force by the time Scotch-Irish Americans began to penetrate their world in the early decades of the nineteenth century. More immigrant tribes from the East joined those who had settled on Apple Creek, the St. Francis River, and elsewhere near Cape Girardeau to act as a buffer for Spain against the Osages. The Quapaws on the southern border of the Ozarks invited Cherokees to move south to the Arkansas River and settle on the St. Francis River as an ally and barrier against the Osages. Osages sometimes clashed with Quapaws and sometimes used them in turn as a barrier against Chickasaws and Cherokees. Osages terrorized trespassers into their hunting territory and plundered traders, but they could do little to slow the relentless advance of American settlers up the river valleys. "They brought their oxen and their dogs and their children and their women, and they built their cabins," wrote tribal historian John Joseph Matthews. In 1808 Pawhuska and other Osage chiefs "touched the feather" at a treaty with William Clark, ceding fifty thousand square miles of land between the Missouri and Arkansas rivers, including most of the Ozarks, to the United States. Having acquired the Ozarks from Osages, the United States encouraged more migration by eastern tribes, who slowly pushed Osages west, where they clashed with Pawnees, Kiowas, and Comanches. More eastern peoples moved west after the War of 1812. William Clark in 1817 reported 1,200 Shawnees, 600 Delawares, 200 Piankeshaws, 60 Peorias, and about 6,000 Cherokees on the lower Arkansas, as well as around 6,000 Osages. The Osages ceded more land by treaty in 1818 and 1825. Caught between immigrant and western tribes and dependent on the United States for guns and ammunition to defend their territory, they struggled in vain to maintain their hegemony in the 1820s and 1830s.[27]

In particular, the Osages had to contend with Cherokees migrating west from the southern Appalachians, where Scotch-Irish settlements pushed up against their towns. Cherokees had begun crossing the Mississippi in the second half of the eighteenth century to winter hunting grounds along the St. Francis, White, and Arkansas rivers. By the end of the eighteenth century, some Cherokees requested and received Spanish permission to settle on the St. Francis River in northeastern Arkansas. Between 1790 and 1820, some five thousand Cherokees crossed the Mississippi to build farms and ranches in the Arkansas Valley and hunt farther west. As divisions grew within the Cherokee nation in the east over how to respond to intensifying American pressure on their land and culture, more Cherokees crossed into the Ozark region. The trickle grew into a flood after the relocation policy initiated by Thomas Jefferson. In early 1810, Duwali, also called the Bowl, headman of Little Hiwassee town in western North Carolina, and several other Cherokee chiefs led their followers west and settled on the St. Francis. In 1817, the Western Cherokees agreed to give up their land rights in the east in exchange for a permanent reserve in northern Arkansas. By 1819, the Western Cherokees numbered more than three thousand people.[28]

Whereas multiple tribes and American settlers hunted and shared the St. Francis Valley, the Osages regarded the Arkansas and White rivers as theirs and viewed Cherokees as squatters and poachers. The Cherokees endeavored to build an anti-Osage coalition among other tribes. They also played on American assumptions and shaped American perceptions of their conflict with the Osages. Taking a leaf from the settler colonist playbook, they bolstered their claim to the Arkansas Valley by depicting themselves to the U.S. government as "civilized" farming people who used the land productively and the Osages as "savage" hunters who wasted it. "It is not we that are in the wrong it is the Osages," they told William Clark in 1817. The next year, Secretary of War John C. Calhoun instructed Clark to make peace between the two tribes on terms favorable to Cherokees, as President Monroe was "anxious to hold out every inducement to the Cherokees, and other Southern nations of Indians, to emigrate to the West of the Mississippi." Peace between the Cherokees and Osages proved elusive, however. Arkansas Cherokee chiefs reminded the president that when "the white people of Tennessee coveted our delightful country, the land of our nativity," and the Cherokees agreed to move from the Tennessee Valley to the Arkansas Valley, the government had promised to protect them in their new lands. The Osages and the immigrant tribes each saw the other as a greater threat than the United

States, a situation that may have helped make the Ozarks a safer place for Scotch-Irish American immigrants, although officials feared that American settlers might get caught up in the continuing hostilities between the tribes.[29]

The western movements of the Cherokees were paralleled by the migrations of American settlers and traders. The best documented example of a consciously Scotch-Irish community on the edges of the Ozark region was in the fertile Bellevue Valley south of Mine à Breton (Potosi), a thriving mining village that produced nearly ten million pounds of lead between 1798 and 1818. William Reed, from Greene County, Tennessee, was reputed to be the first settler in the valley around 1798, with his wife and two children. Ananais McCoy, Benjamin Crow, and other Scotch-Irish pioneers settled there. When John McNeal arrived in Upper Louisiana in 1797 and took up residence at Potosi, the country called Bellevue was already settled by Reed and others. Almost all the early settlers were of Protestant Irish descent; many brought enslaved African Americans with them. The first group of migrants to the Valley in 1803 came predominantly from the Scotch-Irish region on the Upper Holston in Greene County, Tennessee, with neighbors from Rutherford County, North Carolina. Another migration came from the Scotch-Irish communities on the upper Catawba in western North Carolina. Some thirty Scotch-Irish Presbyterians arrived from South Carolina in 1807. In 1818, Alexander Craighead, a Scot or Scotch-Irish from Tennessee, purchased one of the first lots of the town he named Caledonia.[30]

Many early immigrants to the region followed similar paths and patterns. Among the first Americans to cross the Mississippi and take up Spanish land grants were Michael Burns, his three sons, eight sons-in-law, and their families, who in the 1790s took up land in the Bois Brule Bottom, a rich alluvial floodplain in present Perry County, Missouri. Born in Ireland and listed as a Catholic, Burns was more likely Scotch-Irish and became nominally Catholic to qualify under Spanish immigration policy. Other members of the Burns clan were Scotch-Irish Americans, with names like McConnochie and Murdoch, from Virginia, Pennsylvania, Kentucky, and Illinois. Most did not stay at Bois Brule; in the fifteen years or so after the American cession in 1803, they sold the lands they had cleared and improved and moved on to the mining country or to other lands in the Ozarks.[31] Peter McCormick, an Irish-born Methodist, served in the Revolutionary War and led his family through Virginia and Kentucky to Missouri. After the Louisiana Purchase, a group of his relatives or followers were among the first to settle the Plattin Valley between Ste. Genevieve and the Meramec River.[32] Ulster-born John

Lafferty was a hunter and keelboat man who migrated from the North Carolina Piedmont to Tennessee's Cumberland Plateau in the late eighteenth century. Then he explored the upper White River and in 1810 led a group of interrelated families to the area, where they were generally recognized as the first American settlers.[33] Extended families of Scotch-Irish ancestry from the North Carolina Piedmont established settlements at Brazeau and Abernethy in the eastern Ozarks by 1820.[34]

Romanticized portrayals of Scotch-Irish and their progeny as hardy folk who retained supposed ethnic traits that uniquely equipped them for hardscrabble hill farming and frontier existence persisted in the Ozarks as elsewhere. Yet the likelihood that Scotch-Irish identity and cultural characteristics survived west of the Appalachians among American-born second- and third-generation Scotch-Irish was slim. Even the Bellevue Valley community hardly fit the stereotype of a marginal and ethnic backcountry culture. Nevertheless, immigrants from earlier areas of Scotch-Irish settlement left their imprint on the settler culture of the Ozarks. They found themselves in a mix of other nationalities, including Germans and Indian nations, and they adapted to and shaped the physical and cultural environment. They brought horizontal log construction, slash-and-burn agriculture, open-range livestock raising, small-patch farming, and an amalgam of home remedies and medicine from both European and Native American sources. They also brought a "culture of migration" that had become a central feature of Scotch-Irish life. With less fear of Indian attacks than their forebears on the Cumberland and other regions had faced, they lived in widely dispersed farmsteads, often miles from their nearest neighbors.[35]

Some brought another presumed trait or marker—a reputation as Indian-haters and Indian-fighters. Edmund Jennings was reputed to be the first white man to explore southwest Missouri and was said to carry scalps on his belt. Born in Bedford County, Virginia, around 1751, he fought at Point Pleasant in 1774 and went with Boone to Kentucky in 1775. He fought Indians during the Revolutionary War, served on Clark's campaign, and drove cattle to French Lick in 1779 with James Robertson. His father was killed by Indians in 1780, and his brother was scalped "and rendered incapable of getting his living." According to one account, Jennings was also probably at Blue Licks, in Clark's campaign in 1782, in the attack on Nickajack in 1794, "and was out in the Creek War." He crossed the Mississippi from Tennessee and traveled west to the Ozarks, where he lived and trapped with Indian people for about fifteen years. He returned to Tennessee around the end of the 1820s, where his descriptions of the country prompted "a colony of Tennessee people" to migrate to Missouri in the 1830s. At one point Jennings was keeping a ferry on a small river in Arkansas. He died in December 1840.[36]

Shawnees and Delawares had fought Scotch-Irish invaders for decades in the Ohio Valley. Scotch-Irish and other migrants from Appalachia had experienced or heard about recurrent conflict with Cherokees. But in the Ozark region, despite the presence of some confirmed Indian-killers, early interactions appear to have been relatively peaceful. The American settlers' numbers were not yet great, fewer than their Indian neighbors, and they lived in scattered farms and small communities. As they had with French, Spanish, and other tribes, Native people in the Arkansas Valley pulled the newcomers into their networks of diplomacy, exchange, and land use.[37] Traders followed eastern Indian migrants to their new homes in Missouri, pursuing economic opportunities, and in some cases making their fortunes. Native people with cash annuities to spend after treaties were more valuable customers than cash-poor settlers.[38] In the 1810s and 1820s, immigrant Native Americans and immigrant Scotch-Irish Americans coexisted, with refugee Indian communities interspersed among clusters of American farms. Shawnees in Missouri Territory even stayed on peaceful terms and helped mount defense during the War of 1812, rejecting Tecumseh's call to arms, and in 1814, Governor William Clark sent Delawares and Shawnees to protect settlers in the Boone's Lick region from the Osages.[39]

Osages plundered, threatened, and occasionally killed hunters who overstepped bounds, and they killed a trader named Alexander McFarland in 1814.[40] For the most part, however, they tolerated settlers and traders. The settlers were few and traders were useful. Osages said they preferred whites to Cherokees as neighbors, because whites would act as a buffer between them and the Cherokees. As they had in the upper Susquehanna Valley, colonists and Natives developed "frontiers of inclusion" with affiliations, intermixing, and even intermarriage between their communities, before they gave way to exclusion.[41] Interdependency was a source of strength in borderland regions like the Ozarks.

It also meant that emigrant Indians and emigrant Americans grew more alike in their ways of life. As had happened in earlier borderland areas, settlers dressed like Indians, hunted like them, and grew and ate Indian crops; Indian people raised livestock, fenced their fields, and built log cabins.[42] Stephen Austin remembered Shawnees and Delawares visiting his father's store; others recalled hunting, horse racing, gambling, drinking, dancing, and socializing with immigrant Indians.[43] Some Missouri Shawnees sent their children to the Choctaw Academy in Kentucky, the first national Indian boarding school in the United States and, at a time when the United States was moving toward creating a biracial society based on exclusion, the site of experimental intercultural and interracial community. Other Shawnee children attended the school established for Indian and white students by Baptist missionary John Mason Peck at the Shawnee village of Rogerstown on the Meramec River in 1817.[44] Pioneer Ozark folklorist Silas Claiborne Turnbo gathered stories in the late nineteenth century that told of daily intercourse between early settlers and bands of emigrant Shawnees, Delawares, and Cherokees along the St. Francis, Whitewater, White, and Arkansas rivers. The Cokers, one of the earliest white families in northwest Arkansas, were descendants of Irish immigrants originally from County Cork who made their way to the Ozarks via northern Alabama. Joseph Coker was remarkable not for having a Native wife, but for having two. After his first wife died, he married a Cherokee woman called Aney and brought her and their children with him when he moved to White River in 1814. He then married a second wife, Cynthia Rogers (identified as either the daughter of captive John Rogers and his Cherokee wife or as a Shawnee woman).[45]

The travels and experiences of the family of Samuel Watson (1754–1838), a stone cutter from York County, Pennsylvania, illustrate the migrations and varied interactions with Indian peoples by many families from Scotch-Irish communities. Samuel was born in York County in 1754, the youngest of eight children. After Indians destroyed nearby McCord's Fort in April 1756, his father, David Watson, led the family south and bought land west of the Catawba River on the border of North and South Carolina. During the Revolution, Samuel served in the militia, including two campaigns against the Cherokees. After the war, he married, and he, too, had eight children. In 1808, the Watson family joined a dozen other families migrating to Missouri Territory. Watson took up a farm on Buffalo Creek in Pike County (where he died in 1838).

Fears that British agents were arming the Osage, Ho-Chunk (Winnebago), Iowa, and Sauk and Fox tribes in 1811 caused the settlers to build Buffalo Fort, two miles south of the present-day town of Louisiana, Missouri. During the War of 1812, they took refuge in St. Louis County and stayed there five years. Polly Watson, who was a child at the time, later wrote an account of their lives after they returned to Buffalo Creek in 1817. Despite the family's past troubled relations with Indians, her recollections were generally warm.

When a couple of Native people visited her grandfather's house, she "was afraid of them at first, but they gave us a lot of pecans" and she found she "rather liked them." In fact, "I think I may safely say that from that day I have always liked Indians." The next year, when Indian people camped one mile from her father's house, she played with the children and grew fond of an elderly man she called an "old chief" who was kind to her. Subsequent generations of the Watson family migrated by ox-wagon to Oregon, where they settled on the north bank of the Umpqua River near Mount Scott. According to a later family member, "There was a tribe of several hundred Indians about the settlement, with whom my grandfather managed always to have kept on good terms." Looking back over the Watson family's trajectory, she said they "seem to have always lived on the frontier."[46]

The Watson family's experience on different frontiers was shared by other Scotch-Irish descendant families on the move across the decades, and whose experiences streamed together to forge recurrent invasions of Indian country and sometimes also produced individuals who figured prominently in the assault on Native lands and peoples. In 1700, Alexander Carson, a Presbyterian minister in Dumfriesshire in southwest Scotland, migrated to Ulster. Sometime between 1738 and 1748, he migrated again with his family to Lancaster County, Pennsylvania. Alexander's son William and his wife Sarah Elizabeth migrated to North Carolina. Their son Lindsey was born in Rowan County in 1754. In 1792 or 1793, Lindsey moved his family from North Carolina to Kentucky. His first wife, Sarah, died within the year, and in 1796 he married Rebecca Robinson. Lindsey had five children with Sarah and ten with Rebecca. The sixth, a boy named Christopher, was born on Christmas Eve, 1809. A year or so later, the family moved to Boone's Lick at the farthest edge of white settlement in central Missouri, where Christopher spent his boyhood on the family farm and, it was said, played with Indian children, either Sauk and Fox, who still claimed the land, or visiting Osages. After his father's death and his mother's remarriage, Christopher left home when he was about sixteen and traveled to New Mexico on the Santa Fe Trail, beginning a storied life as the frontiersman Kit Carson.[47]

Both Scotch-Irish Americans, and Native Americans with whom previous generations of Scotch-Irish people had shared and contested borderlands, sought new lands and opportunities to rebuild their lives and communities. As they had in the past, they found themselves in borderland regions between competing colonial and tribal powers. Scotch-Irish and other Americans also encroached on the emigrant Indians' lands and became their new neighbors, even as the tribes endeavored to rebuild their own homes and communities.

From the 1810s to the 1840s, as landed gentry bought up real estate and pushed subsistence farmers out of their landholdings in Tennessee, Kentucky, and other regions of Appalachia, Scotch-Irish people migrated in their thousands and settled in the Ozarks and neighboring territory. Many, reported Major Stephen Long, "expended all their property in moving to this wilderness country" and had to rely on hunting until they could raise their first crops.[48] Many became subsistence hill farmers growing tobacco and hemp. Like the Native people they met in the Ozarks, they adapted to the region and its other inhabitants. They wore mixtures of Indian and European clothing, learned Native languages to facilitate trade, and sometimes intermarried. Indian people and first-generation settlers shared subsistence practices; they grew corn, raised livestock, went hunting.[49] They also lived in similar homes, similarly furnished. "The houses of all the villages are built of logs, some of them squared, and well interlocked at the ends, and covered with shingles," observed Amos Stoddard. "Many of them are two stories high; and attached to them are small houses for the preservation of corn, and barns for the shelter of cattle and horses, with which they are well supplied. Their houses are well furnished with decent and useful furniture." Stoddard left similar descriptions of white settlers' farmsteads, but in this instance he was describing the Shawnee and Delaware villages on Apple Creek.[50]

Like their forebears who had pushed into the Appalachians, migrants in the Ozarks who adopted Native clothing, trade, and customs did not become less Scotch-Irish as a result. Grafting aspects of Native American culture and life onto their existing and enduring culture shaped by heritage, class, and kinship, they developed a distinctive Ozark culture that set them apart from other regions of the country, and some would say still does. Some of them had previously intermarried and established personal and economic ties with Cherokees, Delawares, and Shawnees, and many re-established old connections and alliances with the relocatees. "The Ozarkian is not just Scotch-Irish but also Cherokee, Shawnee, Delaware, Kickapoo, Osage, and Quapaw," writes one historian, himself of multi-tribal descent. Scotch-Irish Americans in the Ozarks became tribalized by their associations and alliances with Native peoples, which meant, of course, that they also became tribalized in the eyes and language of outsiders, who conjured up anew the century-old stereotypes of Scotch-Irish frontier people as no better than the "savages" among whom they lived.[51]

As had happened in western Pennsylvania and throughout Appalachia, travelers commented on the rough and rude lifestyle they witnessed among the backcountry hunter-herders, fueling stereotypical images of the people.[52] Henry Brackenridge was shocked at the indolence of backcountry folk he met in Missouri country before the War of 1812. One did not know the name of the president and didn't give a damn about finding out, he wrote; in stark contrast, a Shawnee man who offered Brackenridge good food and lodging in a comfortable house not only knew the name of the president, but also asked for news about U.S. relations with France and England.[53]

In 1818, Henry Rowe Schoolcraft set out from Potosi to document lead mines in the interior of the Ozarks. Traveling more than nine hundred miles in ninety days, he witnessed and recorded scenes of frontier life. The families he met lived by hunting, herding, and farming. At one house he tried to engage the wife and daughter in small talk, but found they "could only talk of bears, hunting, and the like. The rude pursuits, and the coarse enjoyments of the hunter state were all they knew." He received a hospitable welcome from a man named McGary, who lived in a log house opposite the junction of the Little North Fork and the White River, where he grew several acres of corn and had several horses, cows, and hogs. McGary warned him to watch out for the Osages, who were "habitual robbers and plunderers." Farther up the White River, Schoolcraft met another family who subsisted by hunting and agriculture, which meant a staple diet of corn and wild meat, especially bear, although their limited diet may have been due in large part to the winter season. "In manners, morals, customs, dress, contempt of labour and hospitality, the state of society is not essentially different from that which exists among the savages," he commented, echoing elites' descriptions of Scotch-Irish folk in the Susquehanna backcountry generations before. He thought the frontier settlers "a hardy, brave, independent people, rude in appearance, frank, and generous," who could subsist anywhere in the woods and who, as expert riflemen, would be an effective military force in frontier warfare. He also noted the usual sources of conflict with the Indians: they hunted the same woods and used the same hunting techniques as their Indian neighbors, but did not observe the same hunting ethics:

> The Indian considers the forest his own, and is careful in using and preserving every thing which it affords. He never kills more meat than he has occasion for. The white hunter destroys all before him, and cannot resist the opportunity of killing game, although he neither wants the meat,

nor can carry the skins.... This is one of the causes of the enmity existing between the white and the red hunters of Missouri.[54]

Schoolcraft's biased and anecdotal comments painted a bleak picture and an enduring image of Ozark settlers.[55] They contrasted with Yorkshireman Thomas Nuttall's description of well-fed and well-clothed Cherokee families living on the banks of the Arkansas River about the same time: "their dress was a mixture of indigenous and European taste, yet in their houses, which are decently furnished, and in their farms, which were well fenced and stocked with cattle, we perceive a happy approach towards civilization." Industrious and growing in population, the Cherokees could prove a dangerous enemy to the frontiers of the Arkansas Territory, said Nutall, and should immediately be confirmed in their lands "so as to preclude the visits of land speculators, which excite their jealousy."[56]

Sam Houston (Figure 12.1) had personal ties to the Arkansas Cherokees. Born in Rockbridge, Virginia, Houston moved with his family to Tennessee when he was a teenager. In 1809 or 1810 he ran away to live with Cherokees along the Hiwassee River near his home in Blount County. He was adopted by chief John Jolly (Ahuludegi), given the name "Raven," and stayed with them for about three years. After fighting with Andrew Jackson in the Creek War, Houston worked as an Indian sub-agent. In 1818, when he led a delegation to Washington to meet President Monroe, he donned Cherokee dress. John C. Calhoun was outraged and reprimanded Houston, who resigned shortly after. With Jackson's support, Houston was elected to the U.S. House of Representatives in 1823 and as governor of Tennessee in 1827. Then, in 1829, he divorced his wife, resigned from office, and moved to Arkansas Territory, where Jolly had already relocated and had become principal chief of the Western Cherokees. "The fate of Houston must have surprised you as much at Washington as it did us here," William Carroll wrote to Jackson in May 1829. "His conduct, to say the least, was very strange and charity requires us to place it to the account of insanity." Houston himself wrote Jackson the same month. He said he was "the most unhappy man now living," wandering among the Indians. Nevertheless, he would do his best to improve their condition, promote peace with the United States, and protect the Cherokees from corrupt agents. And he promised to send Jackson some buffalo meat for Christmas dinner. The next year, Houston married Talihina or Diana, daughter of Jolly's brother, John Rogers, and described himself as "a citizen of the Cherokee Nation."[57]

Figure 12.1 Sam Houston. Daguerreotype by Mathew Brady, ca. 1848–1850.
Library of Congress, Prints & Photographs Division, Daguerreotypes Collection.

Remaking a Land without Indians

Just as patterns of buffering and coexistence that had marked the history of the invasion of Indian territory from Maine to Georgia and Pennsylvania to Tennessee were replicated in and around the Ozarks, so too was the pattern of intrusion as prelude to dispossession. Settlers moving westward from Cape Girardeau and southward from Ste. Genevieve into the St. Francis Valley encircled the Shawnee-Delaware tract on its back side. A settlement that began as a haven under the Spanish regime became besieged under the American regime as the people from whom the Indian occupants had fled once again became hard neighbors and pushed onto their lands.[58] As early as 1808, white people were reported to be marking trees and squatting wherever they pleased on the St. Francis River, with the United States government unable and the local militia disinclined to stop them.[59] After the War of 1812, according to missionary John Mason Peck, there was a torrent of emigration. Some families came in 1815, but the next year they came "like an avalanche." It seemed to Peck as if Kentucky and Tennessee were "breaking up and moving" west.[60]

It was an avalanche. The numbers of non-Indian settlers in Arkansas rose from fewer than 400 in 1803 to more than 14,000 in 1820 and 30,000 by 1830. Some of the newcomers established cotton plantations along the region's rivers, and 15 percent of the population in 1830 were enslaved.[61] The non-Indian population in Missouri Territory tripled between 1810 and 1820, rising from 19,783 to 66,596. By 1830, Missouri, now a state, had 140,455 people, 90 percent of whom were American, and most of whom came from Tennessee and Kentucky, with others from Virginia and North Carolina and the Ohio Valley. By 1840, the population was 383,702.[62] The avalanche swept away the networks of intercultural relations people had built in earlier decades.[63]

The early settlers came to hunt, trade furs, and raise a few crops for themselves and possibly for local sale. They lived much like their Indian and French neighbors, they did not disrupt older methods of land division, and the Osages preferred them to the Cherokees. The new settlers came to make their fortune from agriculture, wanted exclusive use of the land, and had little interest in perpetuating preexisting patterns of coexistence. As their numbers grew, they no longer needed to accommodate or even tolerate Native people sharing the land, and they subscribed to increasingly racist views.[64] That meant they did not want federal government to move more Indians there. At the Treaty of Doak's Stand, 1820, Choctaws exchanged land in Mississippi for a large tract of territory on the south bank of the Arkansas. The three thousand settlers who had already settled on those lands refused to leave, and there was a storm of protest against the government's plan to dispossess white settlers and turn "their" land over to Indians. Residents of Miller County in southwestern Arkansas Territory petitioned the president. "To be forced and driven by our own Government from the farms and improvements we have labored for years to make, for the support of our families, in order to give place to Indians," they said, was "so unjust and unprecedented" and so ruinous to the settlers that its enforcement "would produce the greatest possible excitement." Having already been displaced to make way for emigrant Cherokees, settlers in Arkansas Territory saw themselves as "the victim of indian negotiations."[65]

The election of Alexander McNair as Missouri's first governor after it became a state reflected the shifting attitudes. William Clark, the territorial governor, had tried to protect emigrant Indians' rights and in 1815, in accordance with government policy, he had responded to squatters' encroachments on lands occupied by Delawares and Shawnees around Apple Creek by issuing a proclamation warning them to leave or be removed by the military. McNair, the head of the territorial militia, refused to remove the squatters.[66] The grandson of an immigrant from County Donegal, McNair war born in Derry Township in Lancaster County, Pennsylvania, in 1774. He served as lieutenant in a company from Dauphin County in the Whiskey Rebellion and in 1799, through the influence of Senator William Maclay, whose parents came from Antrim, he secured appointment as a lieutenant in the U.S. Army. McNair went to Missouri Territory in 1804 and served several years as U.S. Commissary at St. Louis. He was a colonel in the Missouri militia in the War of 1812, then a merchant. Better attuned than his rival to the new racial and political climate, McNair attacked Clark for being soft on Indians and defeated him easily in 1820. McNair served as the first governor of Missouri from 1820 to 1824, and then held a position in the Indian department until he died in 1826.[67] Missourians voted for Jackson by a landslide in 1828.

Calls for Indian removal gathered momentum in the 1820s. Delawares, Shawnees, and other tribes continued to live in friendship with the white people crowding around them, but in the increasingly racialized climate, federal officials were inclined to see Indians as potentially hostile savages, rather than as farmers and ranchers living peacefully alongside their American neighbors.[68] The federal government was no more successful in asserting its will on settlers west of the Mississippi than it had been in the East. Squatters occupied unpurchased Indian lands, Indians protested, and the government made futile token efforts to evict the trespassers or turned a blind eye to their trespasses. Squatters stole Indian lands and improvements with impunity. As happened elsewhere, the failure or refusal of state and federal governments to protect Indian people from squatter violence drove tribal leaders to make treaties in which they sold lands to buy space and safety. More and more Delawares, Shawnees, and Kickapoos abandoned their villages in eastern Missouri and dispersed into smaller settlements farther west in the Ozarks, on the edges of Osage territory, and then signed treaties ceding lands in Missouri for lands on the Kansas River.[69]

U.S. Indian agent John Johnston played a major role in bringing more Delawares to Missouri and then removing all Delawares from Missouri.

Johnston was born in Ballyshannon in County Donegal in 1775. His father was a Scot, and his mother a Huguenot. When he was eleven, Johnston's family migrated and settled in Cumberland County, Pennsylvania. Family members served in the Revolution and Jefferson appointed him as an Indian agent, in which capacity he assisted the U.S. commissioners in negotiating the Treaty of St. Mary's whereby the Delawares on the White River in Indiana agreed to give up their remaining land in the state and join their relatives in Missouri. As Johnston later revealed, they bribed the Delaware chiefs Anderson and Big Bear. After the Delawares were reunited in Missouri, he was responsible for removing, as he wrote in his memoirs, "the whole Delaware tribe, consisting of twenty-four hundred souls, to their new home southwest of Missouri river, near the mouth of the Kansas, in the year of 1822 and '23." Johnston had no doubt that the relocated Delawares would "communicate to the wild tribes of that country the over-reaching craft, cunning and deceit of the white man." He had good reason for his prediction.[70]

Appointed superintendent of Indian Affairs by President Monroe in 1822, William Clark negotiated a string of treaties that removed Indian people from Missouri into what is now Kansas. In 1825, he negotiated a treaty with the Shawnees around Apple Creek, who gave up the remainder of their Spanish land grant in exchange for a fifty-square-mile tract near the junction of the Kansas and Missouri Rivers, just beyond the western border of Missouri, on lands the United States bought from the Osages that year. Other Shawnees from the Apple Creek region resettled at Rogerstown on the Meramec, or at Shawnee villages along the St. Francis River, and on the White River on the border with Arkansas. Rogerstown Shawnees moved to Kansas in 1828. In the foothills of the Ozarks where the land was less desirable to squatters, amicable relations between Indians and Americans persisted longer, but those places offered only temporary asylum. And as more people took refuge in the Ozarks, pressure on the area's resources made sustenance difficult on the White River. Although the Shawnees and Delawares wanted to remain there, settlers could not wait to get rid of them. In October 1832, Clark negotiated a treaty in which the Shawnees and Delawares "late of Cape Girardeau" relinquished all their lands in the State of Missouri and moved west to a tract of land on the Kansas River.[71]

As history repeated itself and settlers killed their game, built farms, and planted fields "as if it were their intention never to quit the Country," Arkansas Cherokee chiefs protested to the government and asked that the squatters be removed.[72] Instead, the government backed the squatters and pressured the

Cherokees to cede their land and move west onto what were formerly Osage lands. At the Treaty of Washington in 1828, the Cherokees ceded their lands in Arkansas Territory in exchange for lands in what became Indian Territory, along the eastern border of present-day Oklahoma. By doing so, the treaty stated, they "freed themselves from the harassing and ruinous effects consequent upon a location amidst a white population."[73] Relieving Native people from settler encroachment by relieving them of their land was now standard practice and policy.

There was little relief for them, however. Refuting a petition that asked for more troops to protect settlers against alleged Indian threats, Captain John Stuart, the post commander at Fort Smith, told Secretary of War Lewis Cass in 1833 that the Indian people in the region lived quietly and on friendly terms with the whites, "and according to my opinion the Cherokees are a more orderly and respectable people, than three fourths of their white neighbours of the Arkansas Territory." Stationing more troops in the territory would only lead to problems because "the depraved portion of the Whites, feeling themselves Protected by the Military will commence their Lawless outrages on the Indians, by Killing and Stealing their property and often by molesting their person."[74]

Five years later, thousands more Cherokee people were forced west under the Indian Removal Act. Along with other deported tribes, they also ended up on lands that had been recently taken from the Osages.[75] Most of the Cherokee parties who made the overland trek along the Trail of Tears in 1838–1839 followed much the same route by which most of the Scotch-Irish and other American settlers traveled into the Ozarks, and many of the whites they interacted with as they passed through the region were themselves recent immigrants from the southern Appalachians.[76] But even before they arrived, Americans were expelling Indian people, ridding the land of its former cultural complexity, and turning what had for a time been common ground into a land only for white Americans.[77]

Gateway to the Fur Trade

Most Scotch-Irish Americans who migrated to Missouri and Arkansas did so in search of landed independence. However, the new lands of the Louisiana Purchase also opened commercial opportunities and possibilities for some

Scotch-Irish Americans who entered the fur trade via the gateway to the Missouri River at St. Louis.

As in the quest for Indian land, there were no guarantees of success in the Indian trade. John Nevin had joined the United Irishmen in 1798 and fled County Antrim with a price on his head after the revolt was defeated. Smuggled in a barrel to County Derry, he took ship for America disguised as a sailor. According to family tradition, he landed in Charleston, South Carolina, and then moved to Knoxville, the capital of the new state of Tennessee, which had a population of only about one thousand but a lively frontier trade. Nevin became an Indian trader, licensed by the War Department to trade along the Tennessee River with the Cherokees and Creeks. Writing to his brother in April 1804 (his only letter home that has survived), he explained that he traveled down the Tennessee with a boat loaded with flour and other goods, sold them to the Indians, and bought steers from them which he stall fed and then drove to Charleston. "No Dout you will think that a Dreadful Business to Tread with the Ingins But you are Intirely Missinformed Respecting the Tread," he wrote. "You Expect that we that Go there must have Ingin wifes—True the white Men that Lives in the Nation has mostely red women but that is their Pleasure." Since the United States had acquired Louisiana Territory, "We are Now in this Country Under a Real Republickan Government and the Best in the World And has got into Possession of a New and Extensive Country which Ireland would not be a Garden to [i.e., in comparison with]—the river I go Down Goeth into it and perhaps I May Visit it Er I return [to Ireland]." He never did—he died in Nashville two years later.[78]

Robert Campbell, on the other hand, made his fortune in the vast new country beyond the Mississippi. Born in Tyrone County in 1804 to a well-to-do family, he was the youngest son and one of twelve children, which meant he stood to inherit little. When he was eighteen, he followed his older brother Hugh, who had migrated to North Carolina four years earlier. Through Hugh's connections, Campbell landed a position in St. Louis, the hub of the western fur trade. Having been advised to lead an outdoor life because he suffered from tuberculosis, in 1825 Campbell joined Jedediah Smith on an expedition backed by William H. Ashley and the Rocky Mountain Fur Company. He spent the next four years in the mountains, working alongside Iroquois trappers in Crow, Blackfoot, Gros Ventre, and Flathead country. After a trip home to Ireland in 1830–1831 to take care of family business matters, he returned to the fur trade and joined trapper William H. Sublette.

At the Battle of Pierre's Hole against the Blackfeet in 1832, Campbell saved, or at least was credited with saving, Sublette's life. That same year, the two men became partners in the supply trade, aided by brother Hugh in Philadelphia, and they constructed trading posts in the upper Missouri and Yellowstone region in direct competition with John Jacob Astor's American Fur Company. Recognizing that the Rocky Mountain fur trade was dying, Campbell and Sublette focused on dry goods and river trading, and diversified their investments into banking, real estate, and other companies. Both men made fortunes. After ten years, they dissolved their partnership but not their friendship. Campbell's experiences in Indian country and his extensive knowledge of Indian affairs led to his appointment as one of the U.S. commissioners at the multi-tribal Fort Laramie Treaty of 1851. President Grant appointed him as an Indian commissioner again in 1869, in which capacity he negotiated with the Oglala leader Red Cloud.

Campbell became one of the wealthiest men in Missouri, extending his real estate empire as far as El Paso and Kansas City, serving as president of the Merchants National Bank, and managing the Southern Hotel, reputed to be the finest hotel in St. Louis. He and his wife Virginia Kyle, whom he married in 1841, had thirteen children. Only three lived to survive their parents, as diseases like cholera, diphtheria, and measles took their toll. Campbell continued to diversify his business interests and prosper until he died in St. Louis in 1879.[79] Many Scotch-Irish Americans who migrated west no doubt experienced family tragedies similar to Campbell's, but none enjoyed his great fortune.

Despite his wealth, Campbell was surpassed in fame by Thomas Fitzpatrick. Born in County Cavan in 1799 to a moderately well-to-do Catholic family, Fitzpatrick migrated when he was sixteen and made his way to St. Louis by the winter of 1822–1823. He joined Ashley's expedition upriver to the Arikara villages and then accompanied Jedediah Smith on exploratory ventures in the West that included the so-called discovery of South Pass in southwestern Wyoming, furnishing a route through which settler emigrants funneled west across the Rocky Mountains, as they had through Cumberland Gap in the Appalachians. After a lengthy career as a fur trapper and guide, he became an Indian agent. In 1849 he married Margaret Poisal, the teenage daughter of trader John Poisal and MaHom or Snake Woman, sister of the Southern Arapaho chief, Left Hand. At the Treaty of Fort Laramie, Fitzpatrick and his friend Robert Campbell re-drew the map of tribal boundaries on the northern plains. His relations with the government during his tenure as Indian agent were often testy, and his attitudes about Indian policies and toward Indian people were often paternalistic—he named his son Andrew Jackson—but he managed to keep the lid on Indian affairs on the Plains. Dying in 1854, he did not live to see things unravel in bloodshed as the United States ramped up its campaigns to confine, defeat, and dispossess the Native peoples of the Plains in the 1860s and 1870s.[80]

As the vast territory west of the Mississippi became the new land of opportunity after the Louisiana Purchase, thousands of Scotch-Irish Americans migrated to Missouri and the Ozarks in search of land and independence. Like those for whom the fur trade opened commercial opportunities and possibilities, the migrants found themselves once again sharing and contesting lands with Native peoples, many of whom had also migrated from the East and had barely unpacked before Scotch-Irish Americans began to arrive. For Native American migrants, their time in the region proved to be short-lived. The growing settler population forced them farther west and south into another borderland region in Texas, where they once more found themselves with hard neighbors and the process of settlement, coexistence, and dispossession began again.

13

To Texas and Beyond

By about 1830, people of varying degrees of Scotch-Irish ancestry and identity had spread west from the Appalachians across much of the south-central United States. They had occupied Illinois, pushed into northern Alabama, and crossed the Mississippi into Missouri and Arkansas. Now they were beginning to settle in the Hill Country of northern Texas, at a moment of escalating political and interethnic turmoil. Second-, third-, and fourth-generation Scotch-Irish people who migrated to Texas joined a growing stream of migration typically described by historians as "Anglo-American." "Anglo" as an abbreviation for Anglo-Saxon included people presumed to be of English or British descent. Increasingly it came to include non-Hispanic white people in a region and society where individuals were categorized as members of the Anglo, Mexican, or Black "race." Whoever they were, the newcomers moved into a region of intersecting, overlapping, and porous borderlands, one in which Mexicans, Tejanos, Americans, Comanches, Wichitas, Cherokees, Shawnees, Delawares, and other Indigenous peoples competed for land and often found themselves or positioned themselves between competing entities. It was a place where identities were ambiguous. Natives and newcomers were more concerned with their immediate surroundings and everyday lives than about national boundaries, and allegiances were in constant flux.[1]

Spanish Texas was the size of Spain, France, and Holland put together, but from a Spanish perspective it was a sparsely populated backwater province.[2] It was the northern borderland of a Hispanic Catholic world, and also a region of multiple Indigenous homelands wracked by violence. Apaches, Caddos, Wichitas, Karankawas, Tonkawas, and other peoples had lived in Texas for centuries. Caddo and Wichita farming villages nestled in the timbered valleys of the Brazos, Trinity, and Red rivers in central and northeastern Texas. In the course of the eighteenth century, Comanches arrived. They established their equestrian buffalo-hunting way of life on the plains of northern and western Texas, made themselves a dominant force in the region, and expanded their power southward into Mexico, even as Pawnees,

Osages, Apaches, and other Native groups challenged them to the north and east. The Indigenous peoples of Texas experienced catastrophic population losses to imported epidemics, and the Comanches suffered heavy losses to smallpox in 1781, 1800, and 1816. Nevertheless, some thirty thousand Indian people inhabited Texas in 1820, far outnumbering the few thousand Spanish inhabitants.[3]

Spanish Texas attracted some Scotch-Irish forays. Philip Nolan, who became an almost legendary figure in early Texas history, was thought by many contemporaries to have been born in Kentucky, although a census done in Nacogdoches in 1794 lists Don Felipe Nolan as born in Belfast, Ireland, in 1771. An employee and associate of General James Wilkinson, notorious in American history for various shady activities—including attempts in the 1780s to separate Kentucky and Tennessee from the United States and deliver them to Spain and involvement in Vice President Aaron Burr's conspiracy in 1806 to create an independent nation of the southwestern United States and part of Louisiana Territory—Nolan engaged in some shady activities of his own. Traveling into Texas illegally, he rounded up horses and drove them to Natchez and Kentucky to sell, and he lived for a couple of spells with the Comanches. Spanish troops caught up with him on one of his forays in 1801 and killed him. Nolan's filibustering activities are sometimes credited with setting Texas on the path to revolution and independence.[4]

Boston-born William Augustus Magee, the twenty-four-year-old son of an immigrant from County Down, was more directly involved in a movement for revolution and independence. In 1812, Magee resigned his military commission in the U.S. Army and accepted command of "the Republican Army of the North," which José Bernardo Maximiliano Gutiérrez organized to invade Texas and assist Mexican revolutionaries. Magee took Nacogdoches without a fight, but died early in 1813 before the revolutionary movement was defeated and brutally suppressed.[5]

After Mexico won independence from Spain in 1821, Scotch-Irish Americans went to Texas in large numbers, and they went to stay. Texas in the 1820s and 1830s exerted a pull on them similar to that exerted by Tennessee and Kentucky in the 1780s and 1790s and Missouri in the 1810s and 1820s.[6] Once again, Scotch-Irish and other immigrants on someone else's borderlands found themselves at odds with the government that invited them there, and this time it generated another revolution.

The migrants followed some ten thousand eastern Indian people— Cherokees, Chickasaws, Choctaws, Creeks, Delawares, Kickapoos,

Shawnees, and Seminoles—who relocated to northeastern Texas in the 1810s and 1820s. In the winter of 1819–1820, the first Cherokees known to have settled permanently in Texas crossed the Red River from Arkansas, probably led by the chief Duwali, known as the Bowl. Moving into an area north of Nacogdoches, some three hundred Cherokees settled and cleared old Caddo fields on the upper branches of the Sabine, Neches, and Angelina rivers. Other Indian people, who had been pushed to the southwest corner of Missouri, moved to eastern Texas. Two hundred seventy families of Shawnees crossed into Texas in 1824, and two hundred fifty Delaware families settled in the province by 1827. Alarmed by the influx of Delaware, Shawnee, Kickapoo, Choctaw, and other Native peoples on the move, the U.S. agent at the Red River Indian Agency at Caddo Prairie, where the northwestern border of Louisiana abuts Arkansas and Texas, described the region in a letter to the secretary of war in 1827 as a "whirlpool" that was sucking in "the restless and dissatisfied, of all nations and languages," where "parties of broken up tribes are continually pouring in." Many of the immigrant Indians dressed and lived more like the American settlers who pushed them west than the Indigenous people they encountered in Texas. They supported themselves by American farming practices and livestock, as well as hunting and gathering like other frontier inhabitants; they grew cotton and traded with Hispanic and American settlements. Having carved out spaces for themselves in earlier borderlands, they did so again on the Texas borderland.[7]

Cherokees who had mixed with other peoples in the Ozarks continued to do so in Texas and incorporated fellow immigrant Delawares, Shawnees, Kickapoos, Quapaws, and Scotch-Irish into their communities.[8] As in the Ozarks, however, the rapid influx of American settlers into Texas swept away the patterns of coexistence, exchange, and accommodation that borderland peoples built. With what must have been feelings of déjà vu, Cherokee chiefs in the early 1820s complained to the *alcalde* of Nacogdoches about Americans settling illegally on Indian lands.[9]

In the spring of 1821, the Spanish governor of Texas had recommended resettling Cherokee, Choctaw, Miami, Kickapoo, and other Native immigrants on the edge of Comanche country, where they could form a barrier protecting east Texas settlements. Six months later, Mexico won its independence from Spain. Like Spain, Mexico struggled to defend its northern frontiers against Comanches and other Plains tribes. The Mexican government continued to offer land grants to attract both Indian and American settlers as buffers against both the *Norteños*, or northern Indians, and the advancing American frontier. Some officials hoped the immigrant Indians might offset the growing influence of American immigrants. As Sam Houston later described the situation, "The Indians had come to this country by invitation from the Mexican government at a time when the Americans were looked upon as intruders." Cherokees who had contested the Osages in the Ozarks now contended with Comanches and Lipan Apaches, who raided Cherokee as well as Hispanic and American settlements.[10] Descendants of Delaware people and Scotch-Irish people who had served as buffers and proved hard neighbors in colonial Pennsylvania repeated the experience in Texas.

The Mexican government implemented liberal land colonization policies and turned them over to the state governments in the 1820s. The Federal Constitution of the Republic of Mexico in 1824 established Coahuila and Texas as one state and allowed states to admit foreigners as settlers. John Norton, an adopted Mohawk who claimed to be of Cherokee and Scottish descent and who already had made a name for himself as a cultural mediator in London, convinced the authorities in Coahuila-Texas to grant the Shawnee immigrants land just above the Great Bend of the Red River. The 1825 Coahuila and Texas Colonization Law offered settlers a league (4,428.4 acres) for a nominal fee. Foreigners were eligible if they became citizens, converted to Catholicism, and demonstrated good character. Settlers from the United States thus received almost five thousand acres of free land in Mexican Texas, paid no taxes, and even had representation in the government of Coahuila-Texas. Military service was voluntary, and although Mexico was Catholic, the mostly Protestant settlers were left pretty much to their own religion. State legislators envisioned new communities composed of Mexicans, foreigners, and Indians across the entire territory of Texas, although American immigrants initially established their communities along the coast and the Texas Louisiana border, with commercial ties to New Orleans.[11]

Taking advantage of Mexico's land colonization policies, Moses Austin contracted with the Mexican government to recruit settlers in return for large grants of land. When Moses died in 1821, his son Stephen F. Austin took over the role of intermediary agent or empresario. With a series of land grants from Coahuila-Texas, he began to build a colony by offering immigrants large farms at low prices. At a time when the U.S. government sold land at $1.25 per acre and the cotton boom was driving the price of prime lands higher in Alabama, Mississippi, and Louisiana, poor farmers who were willing to brave reports of Indian raids and migrate to Texas could secure lands at a fraction of the cost. According to Austin's cousin Mary Austin Holley, who visited the colony in 1831, the Austins were "the movers, either directly or indirectly, of the whole North American and Irish emigration to this country."[12]

In December 1826, a coalition of American and Cherokee immigrants declared themselves the *Republic of the Red and White People*. The Fredonia Republic, as it is generally known, was quickly suppressed, but represented a first challenge to Mexican sovereignty by immigrant Americans and Indians attempting to carve out their own independent space within Mexican territory. As in other places, a government that attracted immigrants because it lacked the power to control its borders found that it also lacked the power to control the immigrants it placed on those borders. The phenomenon proved central to the story of how Mexico's Far North became the American Southwest.[13]

A century earlier, the planter and landowner William Byrd had likened the Scotch-Irish migrating into Virginia from the north to the Goths and Vandals who had invaded the Roman Empire. Mexican officials now viewed immigrant Americans, Native and non-Native, in the same terms. Despite the risks of inviting foreigners to settle in Mexican territory, officials in Mexico City in the early 1820s were convinced it was necessary to populate Texas; otherwise, the growing population of the United States would expand and annex Texas, Coahuila, and Neuvo Leon "like the Goths, Visigoths, and other tribes assailed the Roman Empire." An American leader employed the same imagery to warn the Mexican authorities in 1827 that if the Indian immigrants from the north were allowed to remain, they would "swarm in Texas as the Goths and Vandals swarmed in Italy."[14]

José Maria Sánchez, a Mexican officer investigating conditions in Texas in 1828, found that American immigrants had taken possession of most of eastern Texas, usually without permission from the authorities. Like a frustrated colonial official in the eighteenth-century Pennsylvania backcountry, he complained, "They immigrate constantly, finding no one to prevent them, and take possession of the *sitio* [location] that best suits them without either asking leave or going through any formality other than that of building their homes." Traveling on to Austin's colony, Sánchez came to the village at San Felipe de Austin, forty or fifty wooden houses on bank of the river, with a population of nearly two hundred people growing corn on small farms.

He thought them "lazy people of vicious character." Another two thousand people, families Austin had brought in, were scattered in the rolling hills beyond the village. "In my judgment," Sánchez wrote, "the spark that will start the conflagration that will deprive us of Texas, will start from this colony. All because the government does not take vigorous measures to prevent it. Perhaps it does not realize the value of what it is about to lose."[15] He was right. Far from securing the northeastern frontier, as historian Alan Taylor points out, American settlers in Texas became "a wedge that blew open Mexico, allowing the United States to sweep to the Pacific."[16]

A steady stream of people headed to Texas, hoping to get out of debt, acquire land, and prosper. Emigrants from the Deep South tended to colonize east Texas, establishing slave plantations in the Brazos Valley; those from Appalachia settled the north-central areas. The first American immigrants were mostly poor farmers from the upper South. Immigration after 1823 tripled the colonial population of Texas in a decade. Nearly thirty thousand "Anglo-Americans" arrived in the 1820s and 1830s.[17] Many were illegal immigrants. Many, in fact, were Irish and Scotch-Irish Americans.

More than two dozen empresarios tried to replicate Austin's success with land grants in Texas, although none succeeded.[18] The extended family of General James Robertson participated in the American colonization of Mexican Texas. His nephew Sterling Clark Robertson acquired a twenty-thousand-square-mile tract of land along the Brazos River and settled some six hundred families in the "Robertson Colony." He was a delegate to the convention that declared Texan independence; he fought at the Battle of San Jacinto, established a company of rangers to fight Indians, and won election to the senate of the Texas republic. He also clashed with rival empresario Stephen Austin.[19] Noah Smithwick, who left Kentucky in 1827 when he was nineteen and traveled to Texas as a recruit for Robertson's colony, recalled that the colonists lived huddled together for security against the neighboring Karankawas, although the Indians were not openly hostile, just unfriendly, and that the women bore the brunt of the isolation and hardships.[20]

Four native Irishmen in two separate partnerships applied to the State of Coahuila and Texas for authority to bring colonists from Ireland to Texas and established two Irish colonies adjacent to each other on the east bank of the Neuces River (Map 13.1). James Power, an Irishman, and James Hewetson, an Irish-born citizen of Mexico, got approval to establish a settlement on the coast, but many of the emigrants they brought from Ireland were struck with cholera when they reached New Orleans, and others lost

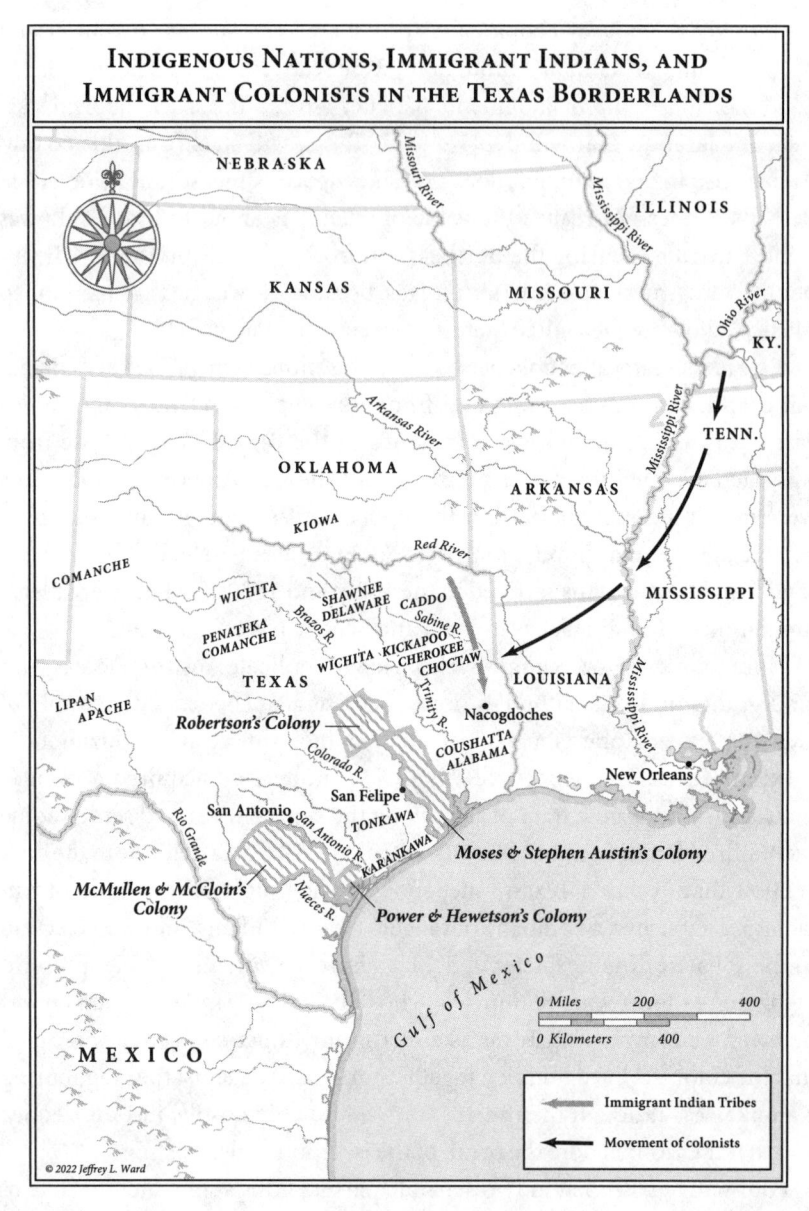

Map 13.1 Indigenous Nations, immigrant Indians, and immigrant colonists in the Texas borderlands.

most of their possessions when the two schooners carrying them on to Texas went aground. John McMullen, born in Donegal, and his son-in-law James McGloin from Sligo, both residents of Matamoros, Mexico, also applied for an empresario contract, stating that it was their intention "to introduce and settle, in the section of the country designated, Two Hundred families from Ireland, and from the United States." They received a land grant from the Mexican government in 1828 and established the "Irish colony" north of the Power and Hewetson grant, between the Guadalupe and Nueces rivers. They mainly recruited immigrants from Irish families who had already crossed the Atlantic and were living in New York and other eastern cities. "Never was there a more inviting asylum for Irish emigrants, than is presented by the colonies on the Nueces," wrote Mary Austin Holley, with an optimism that hardly reflected the realities.[21]

Many families of Irish and Scotch-Irish descent who left the United States did so in search of better fortunes, as generations had done before. Entering a borderland region where identities were fluid and ambiguous, third- and fourth-generation immigrants, already subsumed under a larger "Anglo-American" identity, transferred their allegiance and became "voluntary Mexicans," increasingly viewed themselves as Texans, fought in the Texan war of independence, and then became Americans.[22] Ben and Henry McCulloch, for example, were descended from Scottish borderland families with a tradition of military service in Ireland. Neighbors of David Crockett in Tennessee, they followed him to Texas in 1835, served in the war for independence, joined the Texas Rangers, and entered state politics.[23] Commissioned a brigadier-general in the Civil War, Ben McCulloch died leading the Confederate right wing at the Battle of Pea Ridge in Arkansas in 1862. The battle secured Missouri for the Union and opened Arkansas to occupation.

The newcomers also transformed Texas from a vast multiracial borderland where various peoples competed and coexisted into a world for white men.[24] In Texas as elsewhere, dispossessing and fighting Indians played a role in the emergence of white men's identity. Like Crockett and Houston, most of the immigrants came from the upper South. They brought attitudes toward Indians that had been forged in those regions and, influenced by Celtic and southern traditions, they adhered to a code of honor and violent retribution. Their aggressiveness, racism, and land hunger made conflict almost inevitable and, as violence toward Blacks, Indians, and Tejanos escalated, racial hatred became compatible with honor. The new Texans needed lands on which to farm, grow cotton, and ranch, not to share with Native neighbors, however "civilized" and friendly those neighbors might be. Many equated killing Indians—any Indians—with male honor.[25]

Securing Texas from Mexico and from Indians

Soon after taking office in 1829, President Andrew Jackson scribbled a note to himself in his personal memorandum book to give "early attention" to the boundary line between the United States and Mexico "as by it part of our citizens are thrown into the province of Texas."[26] In Jackson's view, the Adams-Onís Treaty of 1819 had given away to Spain the lands west of the Sabine River, and those lands should be reannexed now that Mexico had won its independence. He employed a well-worn tactic: frontier emigrants who pushed beyond the border, whether to Indian country or to Mexico, justified adjusting the border to accommodate and reintegrate them. "It is fortunate that our boundery has not been run and marked, and from the deranged state of the finance of Mexico, I hope we may be able to obtain an extension of our Southwestern limits as defined by the late Treaty with Spain, so important to the safety of New [O]rleans," he wrote to longtime associate and advisor John Overton in June 1829. "I shall keep my eye on this object, & the first propitious moment make the attempt to regain the Territory as far south & west, as the great Desert."[27] Jackson had manufactured boundary disputes after the Creek War, and he did so again in Texas in the 1830s. Like Scotch-Irish settlers on multiple frontiers, Jackson had complained loudly about the failure of governments to protect their citizens from Indian attack. He did so again now, with a twist. If Mexico could not stop its Indians from attacking American citizens, "the law of nations and of self-defense" justified the United States in doing so.[28]

Part of the Texas creation myth promoted in Congress and elsewhere held that since Mexico made land grants to early settlers for the dual purpose of cultivating the wilderness and protecting the inhabitants of its interior states by creating a barrier against the Comanches and other Plains tribes, the Texas settlers had a just title to the territory; they had held it against the Indians when Mexico could not and they defeated the Indian menace.[29] John C. Calhoun, who would have been well aware of his Scotch-Irish ancestors' employment and experiences in similar situations, said, "They came there as invited guests; not invited for their own interests, but for those of Spain and Mexico, to protect a weak and helpless province from the ravages of wandering tribes of Indians; to improve, cultivate and render productive wild and almost uninhabited wastes, and to make that valuable which was before worthless."[30] In fact, although the Comanches continued to harass Mexican ranches in the west, they recognized the immigrants in Texas as a separate people from the Mexicans and, with Indigenous enemies of their own to deal with, gave the settlements north and east of San Antonio little trouble. As they extended their raids deeper into Mexico, Comanches also sold thousands of stolen horses and mules north of the border.[31]

As more Indian peoples were deported across the Mississippi under United States removal treaties, Mexicans increasingly saw their migrations as an invasion. Minister José María Tornel protested about "the uncivilised tribes of Indians from the United States" who were advancing toward the frontiers of Mexico in the direction of the Red River and Arkansas. Shawnees, Kickapoos, Delawares, and Cherokees had already penetrated Mexican territory, and eight hundred Cherokee and seven hundred Creek families had recently arrived. Jackson responded in a memorandum that the Delawares, Shawnees, and Kickapoos had lived west of the Mississippi since "time out of mind"; the Cherokees had settled north of the Red River immediately after the United States acquired title to Louisiana and had been there ever since; the Choctaws had occupied territory north of the Red River since their treaty in 1820; and the Creeks were settled north of them also by treaty. None of these tribes were within the borders of Mexico. Closely paraphrasing Jackson's memorandum, Vice President Martin Van Buren told Tornel it was well known ("notorious") that the western tribes had long resided where they now were, in areas never claimed by Spain or Mexico.[32] The Mexicans evidently suspected that the United States was doing with the Indian peoples it relocated to Mexico's borders what it had done with the Scotch-Irish on other borders.

Writing privately to Anthony Butler, chargé d'affaires to Mexico, in February 1832, Jackson urged him to push the negotiation of a new boundary with all his energy. The president had been shown an anonymous letter that left "no doubt upon my mind but a revolution in Texas is intended, and people are emigrating to that country with a view to this thing, and it will be attempted shortly." He expected the insurrection to occur within six months. Jackson would do what he could to prevent American citizens from taking part in it, he assured Butler, "but you know we cannot prevent them from emigrating to that country, and each soldier has the right to take his rifle with him, to defend himself against the Indians, & thousands will go, & it will be impossible to restrain them." Jackson knew well the patterns and processes of intrusion and dispossession. Mexico would not be able to put down the insurrection and regain the country once it was lost, "and a government composed of all kindred & tongues on our borders, plundering, & murdering our good citizens at will, and exciting the Indians to make war upon us, & on our borders... may compel us, in self defence to seize that country by force and establish a regular Government, *there*, over it." Jackson did not want to see that happen, of course, and would deplore it if it occurred; therefore, the United States should try to purchase the territory and "prevent this very unpleasant emergency."[33] In October, he told Butler to tell Mexican officials they should acquiesce to U.S. demands because "We cannot restrain our citizens from emigrating to any country they please."[34]

The Texas Revolution occurred, as Jackson predicted, three years later. It upended Mexico's policy of enlisting eastern Indians to curtail Plains Indian raids.[35] It also threw into disarray the lives of immigrant Indian people who had moved to Texas in hopes of finding security and building a future on the land grants Mexico offered. The birth of the Texas Republic and its annexation by the United States brought turmoil and bloodshed for Native people and resulted in their expulsion from the state to make way for American settlers and slave-based cotton plantations.[36]

Mexicans and Texans both wooed the immigrant tribes as allies during the conflict. In 1833, Sam Houston left his Cherokee family in Indian Territory and went to Texas. (His wife Talihina briefly remarried to Samuel D. McGrady and died of pneumonia in 1838.[37]) Early that year, Houston met with Comanches at San Antonio on behalf of President Jackson.[38] In the war of independence he tried to enlist three hundred emigrant Indians.[39] Duwali and other Cherokee leaders endeavored to negotiate and maneuver their way through a perilous situation.[40] Echoing the grievances of Scotch-Irish colonists on earlier frontiers, colonists in Texas claimed that the Mexican government had invited them there to colonize the wilderness but had reneged on its promises to protect them; echoing the Declaration of Independence sixty years earlier, they accused the Mexican government of inciting "the merciless savage, with the tomahawk and scalping knife, to massacre the inhabitants of our defenceless frontiers."[41] Several communities formed companies of rangers—militia units—to fight Indians. Rangers from Robertson's colony launched an unprovoked attack on a village of Kichai Caddos in the spring of 1835, burning the town, killing people, and driving off fifty horses.[42]

In February 1836, anxious to secure their neutrality if not their allegiance, Houston negotiated a treaty with the emigrant Cherokees, Delawares, Shawnees, Kickapoos, and other tribes who had been living in eastern Texas for more than a decade, setting aside a one-million-acre territory for them between the Sabine, Neches, and Angelina Rivers. The Texan cause looked bleak in March when General Santa Ana's Mexican army took the Alamo and killed all the defenders, including David Crockett. After Houston won a lopsided victory at San Jacinto in April and independence was secure, however, the Texas Senate refused to ratify the treaty. Indeed, the new republic refused to honor any previous land agreements with the Indian settlers. Many Senate members argued that Indians who were not indigenous to Texas had no rights to land there, no matter what agreements Mexico had made with them.[43]

Houston was elected the first president of the Republic of Texas. He tried to employ negotiation rather than force and maintain good relations with Native peoples, especially the immigrant Cherokees, Shawnees, and Delawares, who he hoped might form a buffer between Texan settlements and raiding Plains tribes. But he was unable to control the situation. Writing to the Texas Senate in May 1838, he described history repeating itself: "The Indian lands are forbidden fruit in the midst of the garden; their blooming peach trees, their snug cabins, their well-cultivated fields, and their lowing herds excite the speculators, whose cupidity, reckless of the consequences which would ensue to the country, by goading the Indians to desperation, are willing to hazard everything that is connected to the safety, prosperity, and honor of the country."[44] In 1838, Mireau B. Lamar became president. Lamar, from Georgia, despised Houston and his conciliatory Indian policy and initiated a policy of ethnic cleansing instead. Indian people and white people could not live side by side, said Lamar; the only policy to be pursued toward the barbarian race was to drive them all out of Texas.

Angered by Texan refusal to honor past land agreements, some Cherokees supported Mexican efforts to reconquer Texas, which only increased Texans' demands that all immigrant Indians be expelled. In a letter to the Shawnees in May 1839, Lamar told them he had long suspected that Cherokees were "our Secret enemies" and now their treachery was confirmed; they were "holding dark councils with the Mexicans." "We can no longer permit Such vipers to remain amongst us." Lamar announced his intention to remove the Cherokees from Texas.[45] They must be removed immediately, he told his vice president, David Burnet, the next month. The Delawares, Shawnees, and other tribes who had shown themselves to be peaceful could remain for the present if they gave assurances of good conduct, but any evidence of hostility on their part would "cause their immediate punishment and expulsion."

They must be given no hope of being "allowed to identify themselves with the Country, or to claim any right in the Soil."[46]

In a proclamation to the citizens of Liberty County, Lamar stated that his government was determined "to remove beyond our territorial limits every Indian tribe that has no rightful claim to reside in Texas." Once the emigrant tribes were removed, the few Indians who claimed the right to remain would not give much trouble and could be easily dealt with. But, he warned, it would be impossible to carry out this policy if our own people used every pretense to make war on neighboring tribes.[47] It was the same old story. As had happened in Pennsylvania, Ohio, Kentucky, and Tennessee, even Indian-haters had trouble controlling Indian-haters.

Caught between the Mexicans and Texans, Duwali tried appeasement. Younger militants preferred to fight alongside Mexicans. "You are between two fires [and] if you remain you will be destroyed," General Thomas Jefferson Rusk told Duwali and other Indian delegates in July 1839. That same month, Texan troops attacked the Cherokees on the Neches River and killed or wounded about one hundred people. Duwali died in the battle. Many Cherokees were driven back across the Red River into Indian Territory as refugees, where they reunited with other Cherokee groups, including the thousands of eastern Cherokee people who had recently been relocated along the Trail of Tears.[48] Now that "the *friendly* Cherokees, who have formed a barrier between the people of the east and the wild Indians" had been driven out, Houston admonished the Texas House in December, settlers were left exposed to the tomahawks and scalping knives of the wild tribes.[49]

Other emigrant Indian groups fared better, for a while. A Standing Committee reported in 1837 that the tribes usually termed "Northern Indians"—the Kickapoo, Shawnee, Delaware, Potawatomi, and Menominee—"all are excellent hunters and marksmen well armed about 500 in number and roam the Prairies in perfect confidence." They had been in Texas about eight years and were friendly to the whites.[50] Texas made a treaty with the Shawnees in August 1839.[51] The Delaware and Shawnee villages on the Red and Sabine Rivers north of Nacogdoches acted as a buffer between Americans in Texas and the Penateka Comanches and other so-called wild Indians. The inhabitants traded and carried messages to Comanches and endeavored to stay on good relations with both Texans and Comanches.[52] Some Delaware leaders were of mixed Scotch-Irish ancestry and some bore Scotch-Irish names. A Delaware chief named McCulloch appeared at multiple councils.[53]

Nevertheless, Delawares and Shawnees who had lived south of the Red River without conflict since the 1820s found themselves embroiled in a series of deadly clashes with American colonists after independence.[54] Noah Smithwick recalled an incident in 1837 when a "wild Irishman" named Felix McClusky killed, scalped, and robbed a Delaware, sparking a fight between his companions, who condemned him for his reckless and ruthless deed, and Delawares intent on revenge.[55] In July 1844, a party of white men attacked a Delaware hunting party on the Trinity, killed two of them, wounded others, and stole their horses and property, although, remarkably, "the murderers were pursued by the good Citizens of the Vicinity, were captured and executed by summary process."[56] Texas made it clear to the Comanches and other tribes that it assumed the right to dictate the conditions by which they resided within its limits, and that its citizens had the right to occupy vacant lands and must not be interfered with.[57]

Elected to a second term late in 1841, Sam Houston made treaties with the various Native groups left in Texas. He believed that peace with all the tribes on the borders could be secured at less than a quarter of the cost annually expended fighting them.[58] After lending his weight to the annexation of Texas by the United States in 1845, Houston served as U.S. senator from Texas from 1846 to 1859 (when he returned as the seventh governor of Texas). He defended the rights of the Cherokees in particular and Indians in general, pointing out the fraud and duplicity of whites who broke treaties and preyed on Native people: "If they would let the Indians alone the Indians would let them alone," he told the Senate in 1853. However, his was a lone voice and he knew it. He realized, he said in a long speech against the Kansas-Nebraska Bill in 1854, "that in presenting myself as the advocate of the Indians and their rights, I shall claim little sympathy from the community at large, and that I shall stand very much alone."[59]

He was certainly a lone voice in the Lone Star State, where the fighting dragged on. The usual causes of conflict and the usual inability of governments to control their people produced the usual scenes of violence and heartbreak and the usual complaints that the government was not doing enough to protect its citizens. Indian raiders took captives and captives sometimes found their way home. In December 1845, for instance, a white boy who had been captured in an Indian raid that killed his parents nine years before was recovered and turned over to Neill McClennan. McClennan, a Scottish immigrant from the Isle of Skye, had made his way via North Carolina and Florida to Robertson's Colony, where he had settled with his two brothers and their families in 1835. He recognized the boy as his nephew but had to communicate with him through an interpreter.[60]

As usual, a government that could not keep the peace by restraining its own citizens or protecting Indian lands restored peace by dispossessing and deporting Native people. Settlers taking over Indian land caused trouble, but so did land speculators and surveyors; Indian people always regarded the chain and the compass as "emblems of fraud and usurpation," Lieutenant Governor Albert C. Horton told President James Polk in 1846.[61] Writing in September 1847 to Texas Secretary of State David Burnet about the Comanches and other tribes and the policy to be pursued toward them, Henry Schoolcraft, who since exploring Missouri as a young man had served as an Indian agent in Michigan and was now at work on a multivolume history and survey of the Indian tribes of the United States, explained that chiefs led by personal influence, example, and advice, and had limited authority. "One captain will lead his willing followers to robbery and carnage, while another, and perhaps the big chief of all, will eschew the foray, and profess friendship for the victims of the assault. Hence treaties made with these untutored savages are a mere nullity." Burnet had lived with the Comanches for a year when he was a young man and may not have needed the tutorial.[62] Schoolcraft could have been talking about the United States government and its frontier citizens.

Hardin Richard Runnels, governor of Texas from 1857 to 1859, informed the Senate that ranger companies should be sufficient for protecting the frontier, but that the great extent of frontier required a permanent mounted force of several hundred men, unless an expedition could be dispatched to strike Indians in their homes. It was the duty of the federal government to provide the protection, rather than an expense with which the state should be encumbered.[63] The frontier between the Colorado and Brazos rivers was in danger of collapsing in the fall of 1858, reports said. The residents had formed a volunteer company to ward off the tomahawk and scalping knife but were almost destitute of firearms, and families were fleeing the area. "The country is in such a condition that it is bound to be abandoned unless something is done and that very soon."[64] The landscape was very different, but Indian fighting in Texas sounded a lot like Indian fighting in Pennsylvania a hundred years earlier, and the settlers' experiences and frustrations were much like those that had given rise to the Paxton Boys.

Back in Austin—as the state's capital was named; Stephen Austin had died in 1836—Runnels issued a proclamation to citizens of counties adjoining the Indian reserve, warning against attacks on friendly Indians and the dire consequences that could ensue.[65] Texas briefly experimented with Indian reserves in the 1850s, and settled Delawares and Shawnees with bands of Caddos, Wichitas, and Tonkawas on the reservation on the Brazos River. As on previous frontiers, however, colonists who transformed the borderlands into an American state had no use or place for Indians. They expelled Indigenous and immigrant Indians to make way for white settlers and Black slaves—and to assert their identity as white men.[66]

As elsewhere, early land speculators and squatters acquired title to lands while the Indigenous inhabitants were denied property rights. John Linn, who was born in Antrim County in 1798, had migrated to New York City and then made his way to New Orleans and to south Texas as part of the Hewetson and Power colonization project. He bought a lot and ran a store in Victoria. He recalled a difficult conversation with a local Tonkawa man who asked him from whom he had bought his land. When Linn told him, the Tonkawa remarked ruefully that God had given this country to the original Indian inhabitants, but they would soon be dispossessed by white people who bought and sold their lands without any regard to their rights. "If I wish to buy something from your store I must do so with your consent, and pay you whatever amount you ask for the article; but if the white man wants a piece of the Indian's land he goes to another white man, and the trade is made." When the Tonkawa asked Linn if he thought the actions of his countrymen were honest, Linn "would fain have made some ethical defence, but could only say that I had paid for all I possessed, but, alas, *to a white man!*[67]

Few Texans shared Linn's discomfort. Most viewed reservations as temporary and increasingly demanded the removal or extermination of all Indians in the state. Ranger companies attacked Waco and Tawakoni towns. Delawares and Shawnees moved back north into Indian Territory, opening more lands for settlement.[68] The genealogy of the famous Texas Ranger and Indian fighter John Coffee Hays, generally known as Captain Jack, illustrated patterns of Scotch-Irish migration westward that merged into the American stream of settler colonialism in Texas and beyond. Hays's great-grandfather migrated from Ireland in the 1740s. His grandfather, Robert Hays, was born in Virginia, served in the North Carolina Infantry during the Revolution, and after the war migrated to Tennessee, where he married Jane Donelson, making him brother-in-law of Andrew Jackson. Robert's son, Harmon Hays, served with Sam Houston and General John Coffee in the Creek War. Born in Tennessee in 1817, Jack Hays worked as a surveyor in Mississippi in his youth before joining a group of volunteers from Kentucky, Mississippi, and Louisiana who went to fight for Texan independence in 1836. Houston appointed him to the Texas Rangers in 1839 and in the next decade he led companies of rangers, which often included Indians and Hispanos as well as Americans, against Comanches and other Indians, and served in the war with Mexico. Following the gold rush to California in 1849, he became a successful businessman, rancher, politician, and sheriff of San Francisco. He also took time to lead a campaign against the Paiutes in Nevada.[69]

Beyond Texas

Following David Crockett's death at the Alamo in March 1836, the American media increased its coverage of Crockett, the frontier hero. Along with Houston and Jackson, Crockett exemplified not only the Tennessee frontier, but also the larger national story of the American frontier.[70] They also exemplified the Scotch-Irish frontier and the now time-honored process of pressuring and dispossessing Indians. Scotch-Irish attitudes and actions toward Indians became increasingly indistinguishable from broader American attitudes and actions the farther west they went. As happened so often before, possibilities of lifeways built around coexistence dissolved as Americans—and Scotch-Irish Americans like Crockett, Houston, Jackson, and Kit Carson—created a country for white men.

Carson (Figure 13.1) worked as trapper and mountain man in the western fur trade, where he associated with Thomas Fitzpatrick and with migrant Delaware and Shawnee trappers. He served as a guide for explorer John C. Fremont in the war against Mexico, and as an Indian agent at Taos, New Mexico, where Ute and Jicarilla Apache people visited him "daily," as he later wrote in his memoirs.[71] Like his father, Kit Carson had a large family. Like Houston, he married a Native wife. He had two daughters with his Northern Arapaho wife, Waa-Nibe. (One died in childhood; the other, Adeline, died at 21.) He then married a Southern Cheyenne woman named Making Out Road, who divorced him. In 1843 he married a fourteen-year-old New Mexican girl named Josefa Jaramillo at Taos, leaving the Presbyterian Church and joining the Catholic Church to do so. The couple lived together for twenty-five years and had eight children (the first died in infancy). They also adopted and raised three Navajo children ransomed from the Utes. Josefa died at forty, shortly after the birth of their last child; Carson died a

Figure 13.1 Kit Carson. Born to Scotch-Irish parents in Missouri, Christopher Carson pursued a career as a trader, scout, Indian fighter, and Indian agent.
Library of Congress, Manuscript Division, Brady-Handy Collection.

month later, in May 1868. Extended and multiethnic families like the one Carson created were common in North American borderland regions that for long periods were shaped by intermarriage, kinship, and multiethnic communities, but they were marginalized and erased in a world for white men, dominated by race and blood, that Carson himself helped to create.[72]

Despite his close associations and family ties with Native people, Carson earned a reputation as an Indian-fighter and an Indian-killer. His own life story, dictated in the 1850s, is a litany of Indian fights. Acting as guide for John C. Fremont's expedition to California in 1846, Carson accompanied a party of sixty white men and nine Delawares, dispatched in response to rumors that Indians on the upper Sacramento River in northern California were preparing to attack settlements. The Americans, each armed with a long-range Hawkens rifle, two pistols, and a butcher knife, wrought havoc among the Wintu people they attacked. When the survivors took flight, Carson and the Delawares pursued them on horseback, tomahawking them as they fled. Hundreds of Wintu people died in the Sacramento River Massacre. Carson said it was "perfect butchery."[73]

During the American Civil War, working with General James Carleton, Carson conducted a scorched-earth campaign into Navajo country, burning villages, destroying crops, and slaughtering livestock. He then rounded up eight thousand Navajo people and marched them three hundred miles from their Arizona homelands to the Bosque Redondo reservation in New Mexico, where it was hoped they would create a buffer for New Mexican colonists against Comanche raids. The Navajos endured four years of incarceration, disease, malnutrition, drought, bad water, and rations that were sometimes unfit to eat. As many as two thousand people died before the U.S. government signed the Treaty of 1868 that permitted the Navajos to return home.

Descendants of Scotch-Irish and Indian peoples who had met in Pennsylvania, Tennessee, and other borderlands met again in the West. As Scotch-Irish Americans moved farther west, so did Delawares (Map 13.2). Relocated to Kansas by the American government, Delawares fought with the Sioux, Pawnees, Cheyennes, and Comanches. "No other tribe on the Continent has been so much moved and jostled about by civilized invasions," wrote the artist George Catlin, who met them in the 1830s; finding themselves placed once again "on the borders of new enemies," they were forced to "take up their weapons in self-defence and fight for the ground they have been planted on." Francis Parkman, who met a hunting party of Delawares during his travels in the West in 1846, wrote that the once-peaceful Delawares who had greeted William Penn were "now the most adventurous and dreaded warriors upon the prairies" and sent war parties as far as the Rocky Mountains and into the Mexican territories.[74]

Migrant Delawares worked as scouts and guides for the U.S. Army. Captain Randolph Marcy extolled their guiding skills in his *Hand-book*

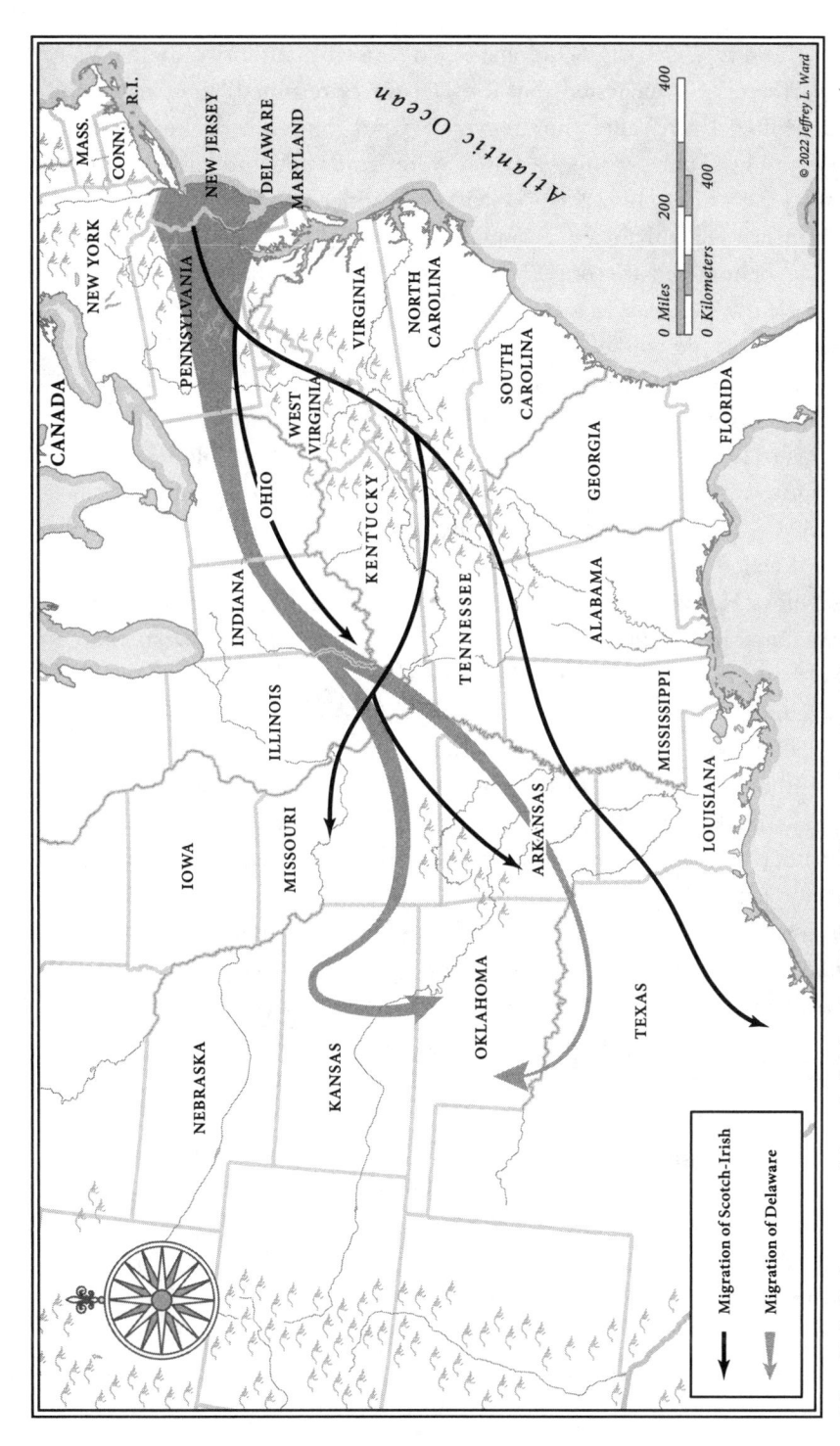

Map 13.2 Delaware and Scotch-Irish migrations from Pennsylvania to Texas.

for Overland Expeditions, published in 1859 by authority of the War Department. He suggested that the Delawares regained "their naturally independent spirt" after they moved beyond the reach of the Iroquois. Penetrating all parts of the West, they were "among the Indians as the Jews among the whites," he wrote; "essentially wanderers." Marcy was particularly impressed with Sekettu Maquah, or Black Beaver (Figure 13.2). Black Beaver epitomized the ongoing Delaware diaspora. Born in Illinois in 1806, he traveled west as a young man. Along with many other Delawares and Iroquois, he worked as a trapper in the Rocky Mountain fur trade. He never learned to read or write, but mastered the sign language of the Plains and spoke several Indian languages, as well as English, French, and Spanish. He served as interpreter for an expedition led by Colonel Richard Dodge to the Red River country of the Comanches, Kiowas, and Wichitas in 1834. A dozen years later, he scouted for the U.S. Army during the war with Mexico and commanded a company of thirty-five Delawares and Shawnees. He guided Marcy in establishing a route to Santa Fe and leading a wagon train of five hundred emigrants across the Southwest. Marcy wrote that Black Beaver "had visited nearly every point of interest within the limits of our unsettled territory.... His life is that of a veritable cosmopolite, filled with scenes of intense and startling interest, bold and reckless adventure." In the 1850s, Black Beaver worked as a farmer, trader, as well as a guide. By the Civil War, he had a ranch on the Wichita Agency in Indian Territory. Along with many other Delawares, he served the Union. As a result, Confederates seized his cattle and horses and destroyed his ranch. He acted as an interpreter in negotiations with the tribes of the southern Plains, and in 1872 he was a member of an Indian delegation from the Wichita Agency to Washington, D.C. Toward the end of his life he became a Baptist minister. The ubiquitous Delaware died in 1880.[75]

Other Delawares and Shawnees joined James "Santiago" Kirker (Figure 13.3), who made a career and a business killing Apaches. Born in County Antrim, Kirker had emigrated to New York when he was sixteen to avoid conscription in the British Navy. Instead, in the War of 1812, he became an American privateer raiding British ships. He married Catherine Donigan and had a son, although in 1817 he abandoned them and moved to St. Louis, where he went into business with the merchant firm of John McKnight and Thomas Brady, who were leaders of the Irish community.[76] In the spring of 1822, Kirker appears to have joined William Henry Ashley's fur-trapping

Figure 13.2 Black Beaver. The itinerant Delaware in many ways exemplified the diaspora of Delaware people that both preceded and paralleled that of the Scotch-Irish who had helped to push them west.

Photograph by Alexander Gardiner. National Archives and Records Administration.

expedition up the Missouri. In 1824, following the Santa Fe Trail from Missouri to New Mexico, he trapped and traded beaver pelts in the southern Rockies and worked at the Santa Rita mine near Silver City. He traded with

Figure 13.3 James Kirker, 1847. The inscription along the bottom of the daguerreotype by Thomas M. Easterly (reversed because this is likely a duplicate plate) reads, "Don Santiago Kirker, King of New Mexico."
Missouri History Museum (N17199).

Apaches, and some people accused him of gun running. In 1833, he married Rita Garcia, with whom he had three sons and a daughter, and in 1835 he became a Mexican citizen. He became known in Mexico as Santiago Querque or Quirque.

As the Mexican states of Chihuahua and Sonora struggled to contain Apache raids, they gave Kirker a contract in 1839 to fight Apaches. With a force that included Americans, Mexicans, African Americans who had escaped slavery, as well as Shawnees, Creeks, and Delawares, and with a Shawnee named Spybuck as his second-in-command, he carried out campaigns that killed and captured Apaches. In the war against Mexico, he served as a scout for Colonel Doniphan's army and participated in the American invasion of northern Mexico. At Galena in Chihuahua in 1847, assisted by local Mexicans, his men massacred 130 peaceful Apache people, many of them intoxicated and unarmed. In an 1847 interview, Kirker claimed that he and his mercenaries had killed a total of 487 Apaches and lost only three men, which suggests much about his tactics. In 1848, he was a scout on another American expedition against the Apaches and Utes. The next year he guided a wagon trail to California, where he settled with his family. He died in 1852.[77]

Lionized by Americans, like Crockett, Houston, and Jackson on their frontiers, Kirker on the U.S.-Mexican-Apache frontier exemplified larger national processes. "Despite his Scotch-Irish heritage," notes historian Brian DeLay, "Kirker was seen as eminently American in his deeds and prowess."[78] Ingrained in the nation's expansion and dispossession of Native peoples, Indian-killing paved the way to becoming fully American.

Kirker was not the only Scotch-Irish Indian-killer on a southwestern borderland where Indian-killing was part of the culture. Born in Derry in 1833, James Lee emigrated to the United States as a young man and made his way to Arizona. By 1871, he was a prominent citizen of Tucson; he owned a ranch and a grain mill and was part owner of a lucrative silver mill which, he testified, he was prevented from working on account of the hostility of the Apaches. He was also one of half a dozen Americans who in April 1871 led 47 Mexicans and 92 Tohono O'odham (Papagos) to Aravaipa Canyon, where they murdered 150 Apache people, most of them in their sleep. The victims were living supposedly under the protection of the U.S. Army at nearby Camp Grant, which had been named after General Ulysses Grant. Now president, Grant denounced the killings as pure murder.

The Camp Grant Massacre prompted a federal investigation, debates in the press, and a criminal trial of one hundred of the perpetrators, but, as had happened after massacres of innocent Indian people in Pennsylvania a hundred years earlier, the killers were vindicated rather than punished. Defended by Pima County District Attorney J. E. McCaffrey, they invoked the by now well-worn defense that they had no choice but to take matters into their own hands because the distant U.S. government had failed to protect them against Apache attacks. The U.S. District Court judge essentially instructed the jury to acquit the defendants on the grounds of self-defense; they were protecting innocent citizens against savage attack. Moreover, argued the judge, an attack need not actually be taking place in order to take steps to prevent it. The very fact that most of the victims at the Camp Grant massacre were women and children was proof in itself that the men were off committing nefarious deeds elsewhere. The jury took less than twenty minutes to return a verdict of not guilty.[79]

Violence against Native people accompanied the so-called winning of the West everywhere. Thousands of individuals of Scotch-Irish descent joined the mass invasion of California during the gold rush, and some participated in the genocide that followed.[80] John Orr, the son of a Presbyterian minister in Portaferry, County Down, emigrated to America and settled in Chicago. When gold was discovered in California, he left a profitable business in Chicago and joined thousands of others traveling west in wagon trains, passing through Fort Laramie, Wyoming. His wagon train suffered outbreaks of cholera, dysentery, and scurvy, and cholera spread from the immigrant trains to the Cheyennes and other Native peoples. Like most emigrants on the overland trails, Orr encountered little or no conflict with Indians on the Plains.[81] When he reached California, he reported "some little disturbance" with Indians north of Sacramento in 1850, which was easily dealt with by U.S. troops and miners who "chastised them pretty severely," killing three to four hundred while they only lost three men killed. Orr himself died of cholera in Sacramento later that year.[82]

Despite being primed for violence by generations of memories of Indian atrocities back East, few travelers on the overland trails encountered open hostility. More often, they met Native people who acted as guides, provided information, worked as transporters, demanded tribute, charged tolls for crossing rivers, traded, pilfered, and stole horses. In some cases, Indian people even carried mail for immigrants writing to their families back home. An estimated ten thousand people died on the overland trails between 1840 and 1860. Large numbers died from drowning, diseases, or accidental gunshot wounds; a mere 4 percent died at the hands of Indians. Overland immigrants killed fewer than five hundred Indians, and Indians killed fewer than four hundred immigrants. Most years there was just a handful of homicides.[83]

The family of James Frazier Reed accompanied a wagon train that headed west from Springfield, Illinois, in April 1846. Reed was a Scotch-Irish Protestant from County Armagh who had immigrated to Virginia with his family when he was young and made his way to Illinois. His stepdaughter, Virginia Reed, who was twelve years old at the time, recalled in later life that she had been brought up on tales of Indian ferocity by her septuagenarian maternal grandmother, whose aunt had been taken captive by Indians from a frontier settlement in Virginia. "When I was told we were going to California and have to pass through a region peopled by Indians, you can imagine how I felt," she wrote. But the Indians they encountered "were not like grandma's Indians." The first were Kaw or Kansa people, who ran a ferry and took them across the Kansas River. Passing Fort Laramie, the wagons became strung out and the emigrants endured several anxious days as a large Sioux war party, on its way to fight the Crows or Blackfeet, passed by. They "could have massacred the whole party without much loss to themselves," Virginia wrote, but "never showed any inclination to disturb us." As it turned out, the emigrants had more to fear from the weather and from each other than from Indians. The Reeds were members of the Donner party that succumbed to snow and cannibalism in the Sierra Mountains. They were one of the few families to survive the ordeal intact.[84]

Continuing the search for landed independence that had brought emigrants from Ulster to America for a century and a half, Scotch-Irish Americans pursued opportunities to acquire land cheaply on the Great Plains, and joined the tide of American settlers who took up grants of land under the Homestead Act of 1862. The debates in Congress over the proposed Homestead bill produced arguments familiar to the Scotch-Irish. Andrew Johnson of Tennessee argued that opening western lands to settlers would create "an army on the frontier composed of men who will defend their own firesides, who will take care of their own homes." Andrew Greenlees from County Antrim first tried his hand at farming in Michigan in 1861, without much success. He tried again in 1874 on a grant of 80 acres of free land in Kansas awarded under the Homestead Act and succeeded. Edward Hanlon, the son of a farmer from County Down, bought 215 acres of land in Nebraska in 1870. When his brother contemplated giving up the family farm in Ireland and joining him, Hanlon suggested they look to Kansas and southern Nebraska, where they would both be eligible for 160 acres of government land.[85]

Increasingly, though, the Scotch-Irish Americans in Indian country became dwarfed by the flood of Irish Americans, as mass migrations of Catholic Irish in the wake of the Great Famine flooded into Boston and New York. Between 250,000 and 300,000 Irish people arrived in America by 1847; by 1855, one and a half million had. More Irish came to America in the fifteen years between 1845 and 1860 than in all the years before.[86] Most exchanged a rural agrarian life in Ireland for an urban industrial life in America, and they furnished much of the manpower of the industrial revolution in the United States. As industrializing America pushed west after the Civil War, though, other Irish immigrants moved west as well. They played a significant but subordinate role as "blunt instruments" in the conquest of the West, rather than conquerors themselves.[87] Irish labor powered the construction of the Union Pacific Railroad, and much of the infrastructure of American empire-building. Irish miners turned Bodie and Butte, Montana, into Irish towns.[88]

Irish miners in the West came from all areas of Ireland. Those from Northern Ireland were not all predisposed by their history at home to be Indian-killers. In fact, some found it predisposed them to be Indian sympathizers. Micheal MacGowan was born into poverty in Donegal in 1865, the eldest of twelve children. He moved to Scotland for work and then emigrated to America. After a stint in the steel mills in Bethlehem, Pennsylvania, he made his way across country and mined silver in Montana with a group of other Donegal men. With Blackfeet to the north and Flatheads to the west, relations between miners and Indian people were sometimes tense. Seeing how Native people had been deprived of their lands, however, MacGowan said that he and his companions "had a great deal of pity for them—the same thing happened to ourselves home in Ireland. We knew their plight well. We understood their attachment to the land of their ancestors and their desire to cultivate it as well as their wish to keep their own customs and habits without interference from the white man." He joined the Klondike gold rush to Yukon fields in the 1890s, where again "[t]here were a lot of us from every part of Ireland," and where again they rubbed shoulders with the neighboring Native people. After making his fortune in the Klondike goldfields, and after seventeen or eighteen years in America, MacGowan sailed home to Donegal, where he lived prosperously until his death in 1948.[89]

Irish immigrants constituted a sizable component in the Indian-fighting U.S. Army. In the period between the Mexican War and the outbreak of the Civil War, immigrants in the army outnumbered native-born Americans more than two to one, and more than half of those immigrants were Irish. John Finerty, war correspondent for the *Chicago Times*, who himself had emigrated from Ireland in 1864, said the majority of the rank-and-file soldiers in the Indian-fighting army were of Irish or German birth or parentage. At the time of Custer's defeat at the Little Bighorn in June 1876, 15 percent of the Seventh Cavalry (almost 140 out of a total of 800) were Irish immigrants. Most, of course, were refugees from the devastating potato famine and Catholic, but some were from Northern Ireland, while second- or third-generation Scotch-Irish Americans in the ranks were not counted as foreign recruits. The army not only played a role in absorbing Irish immigrants into American life; it also distributed them along the frontier when their enlistments were up.[90] Yet Irishmen did not fill the ranks of the western army because they wanted to kill Indians; they did so because they were poor, and the poor fight nations' wars.[91]

General Philip Sheridan was the son of Catholic Irish immigrants from County Cavan. As commander of the Department of the Missouri, later expanded to the Department of the West, and the nation's preeminent Indian fighter, Sheridan waged total war against Native peoples in the late 1860s and 1870s, attacking villages in winter, destroying food supplies, and slaughtering horse herds. He is widely credited with saying that "the only good Indian is a dead Indian."[92] Similar sentiments expressed by Scotch-Irish vigilantes from Paxton in 1763, even after eight years of vicious frontier war, had shocked contemporaries who attributed their bloody deeds to their Scotch-Irish identity and heritage. Now, Sheridan's Ulster heritage mattered little. Whether or not he spoke the words attributed to him, the sentiments reflected U.S. Indian policy and widespread American attitudes.

14

How the Scotch-Irish Became Americans and Americans Became Scotch-Irish

As the Scotch-Irish and their descendants moved into every part of Native America, they became part of the fabric of American society, living their daily lives even as they were caught up in momentous developments in American history.[1] Merging into the larger population, their culture and outlook became less distinctive, and they became more American.[2] Many Presbyterians turned to the Baptist and Methodist churches, and the attitudes and actions of Scotch-Irish invaders of Indian country blurred into larger American patterns and projects of subjugation.

Yet even as these developments were taking place in the mid- and later nineteenth century, other Americans of Scotch-Irish descent, primarily in the East, were working hard to establish a distinctive Scotch-Irish identity and role in the history of the United States. They reasserted their Scotch-Irish identity in a way that both distinguished them from other Americans and gave them a special claim to be Americans. The eulogists broadened the reach of the term to include not only American Ulster Scots of Presbyterian descent, but also those of Irish Anglican, Quaker, or other Protestant antecedents, and even people of Gaelic-Irish descent who were no longer Catholic. Their goal was to place the Scotch-Irish alongside the Pilgrims and Puritans as founding figures in the history of the nation.[3] "The Scotch Irish, or as you call him, the Ulster Irish, has identified himself with his new country, America, more deeply than any but the first immigrant group," Henry Noble MacCracken, the president of Vassar College, declared to the Ulster-Irish Society of New York in 1939.[4]

Once the children and grandchildren of immigrants felt secure in their place in society, they could afford to cultivate and reconstruct an identity based on memories of the old country and their experiences in the new country, rather than just the origins of their parents and grandparents.[5] As Scotch-Irish Americans reread their history, their ancestors went from being outsiders whose story did not fit neatly in the narrative of American progress to being quintessential Americans whose story and contributions were essential to building the nation. They were there at the creation, when the struggle for freedom and the future was fought against Indians as much as against Britain. Reimagined, their Scotch-Irish ancestors were no longer people at the margins and at odds with the centers of power that used them but failed to protect or reward them; quite the contrary, in their frontier values, resolve, sacrifices, and fierce independence, the Scotch-Irish were the heart and soul of American nation-building.

In the Early Republic, the United States created what scholars have termed "borders of belonging" as it developed its criteria for citizenship. Those who did not belong—notably Native Americans and African Americans—were subject to removal to make room for those who did—free, able-bodied white men.[6] Belonging for some was achieved through the subordination or exclusion of others, and any member of any group within the colonizing population occupied a superior status to any and all Native Americans.[7] Unlike other immigrants from the British Isles, the Irish, and especially Catholic Irish, had to succeed as a group and construct an image of themselves that would gain them entry and acceptance in mainstream society.[8] The Scotch-Irish descendants knew the answer. In the late nineteenth century, when Americans imagined the frontier as a powerful symbol of national identity and the source of national character, they locked down their American identity by capturing for their Protestant backcountry ancestors the role of frontier pioneers.[9] The myth of the frontier, the need for it, and the Scotch-Irish place in it grew out of the age of industrialization when the frontier environment and the virtues and values it generated appeared to some to be disappearing.[10]

Scotch-Irish Americans also sought to distinguish and distance themselves from the masses of Catholic Irish immigrants. At least 1 million people left Ireland between 1815 and 1845; another 3 million between 1845 and 1870.[11] Every year between 1847 and 1854, 200,000 Catholic Irish flooded into the United States—almost as many each year as the total influx of Scotch-Irish. Between 4 and 5 million arrived within a century.[12] In the late eighteenth and early nineteenth centuries, Ulster immigrants and their descendants in Kentucky, Tennessee, Texas, and elsewhere took their place in American society in opposition to Indians and Africans; in the late nineteenth and early twentieth centuries, they reaffirmed their place in opposition to Irish Catholic immigrants, described by one scholar as "the first unwanted aliens in the new republic." Portrayals of Irish Catholics as rural people in

Ireland who became city people in the United States and "the pioneers of the American urban ghetto" are overblown. They also experienced nothing like the violence and structural constraints imposed on African Americans. Nevertheless, they faced formidable challenges and dehumanizing caricatures and stereotypes.[13] Catholic Irish immigrants in the cities were regarded as the laboring poor of the industrial revolution and faced an uphill struggle in establishing an American identity. Even a millionaire like Joe Kennedy, father of the president, found it exasperating. "Goddam it. I was born in this country. My children were born in this country," he exploded when a Boston newspaper described him as Irish. "What the hell does someone have to do to become an American?"[14]

Some writers have argued that nineteenth-century Irish Catholic immigrants became white by rejecting their common economic and political bonds to African Americans, with whom white Americans often compared them. They defined themselves by what they were not—enslaved Black laborers—and gained acceptance into white American society by opposing the abolition of slavery and African American rights in general. Others point out that the central theme of the story of the Irish in America is not "how they became white but how they stayed Irish."[15]

In a 1984 essay, the late Edward Said wrote that exiles feel "an urgent need to reconstitute their broken lives, usually by choosing to see themselves as part of a triumphant ideology or restored people."[16] Immigrants who were safely established as triumphant white Americans often found that their ethnic identity was actually seen as a defining characteristic of becoming American, rather than an obstacle to assimilation.[17] For Scotch-Irish Americans, their ethnic identity was very much forged in nation-building. If fighting Indians was the way to become "white," a history of fighting Indians—and the courage it required—was the way for people of Scotch-Irish descent to lay claim to distinctly American characteristics and contributions. Contemporary accounts from the colonial, Revolutionary, and early national eras contained few if any triumphal and patriotic narratives about "winning the West"; most were full of fear and loathing, ambiguities and anxieties.[18] But later generations were able to step up and claim for their ancestors the role of heroic pioneers fighting for freedom and a better life and building a nation in the process.

In *A Tribute to the Principles, Virtues, Habits and Public Usefulness of the Irish and Scotch Early Settlers of Pennsylvania*, published in 1856, Scotch-Irish descendant George Chambers lamented the negative reputation given the Scotch-Irish and the aspersions cast on their character by earlier writers; it was time to rehabilitate their reputation and recognize their role, he said.[19] Later in the century, with a growing consciousness of their history and confronted with alarming influxes of new immigrants from southern and western Europe, more Americans began to identify distinctive contributions by national groups, extolling the virtues of particular "stocks" of people, and indulging in adulation of their ancestors. In public addresses and other venues, patriotic descendants of Scotch-Irish immigrants attributed much of what was best in the American political tradition to their forebears, who were not only hardy and courageous, but also helped forge democracy, fought for liberty, and established a republican form of government.[20] Traits that were predominantly ascribed to the Scotch-Irish and qualities that were touted as fundamentally "American"—freedom-loving, self-reliant, forward-looking, hardworking—became almost indistinguishable.

The journey from a late-eighteenth-century "Irish" to a nineteenth-century "Scotch-Irish" identity was long and involved. Even Andrew Jackson's identity had been subject to debate and change.[21] Now, however, Jackson and other notable national leaders were lionized because of their Scotch-Irish heritage and their reputed Scotch-Irish character. What had once been "backward" and aggressive characteristics were now proud marks of patriotism.

Although in many parts of the country the term "Scotch-Irish" rarely appeared before the aftermath of the American Civil War, it seems to have emerged earlier in New Hampshire, even before large-scale Irish Catholic immigration. Ulster migration to New Hampshire virtually ceased after the Revolution, and by end of the eighteenth century, casual observers saw little difference between Londonderry farmers and their Congregationalist neighbors. But descendants of Londonderry's Presbyterian settlers began to use the term in the period from 1790 to 1820—likely as part of an effort to gain acceptance by American elites as not United Irishmen, for instance— and in the early to mid-1800s the Scotch-Irish emerged as a distinct ethnic group. Early Ulster settlers had often been confused with "Irish papists" by Congregationalists, and they needed to distance themselves even further once Catholic Irish started arriving in growing numbers. In centennial celebrations and town histories, they argued that their forebears were not "Irish" but "Scotch-Irish."[22] Furthermore, New Hampshire town histories and community leaders emphasized the Scottish roots of their Scotch-Irish ancestors, displayed a reverence for Scottish culture, and portrayed the Irish period as a testing time that prepared subsequent generations to settle the American wilderness: the people who survived the siege of Londonderry in Northern Ireland had the mettle to settle Londonderry, New Hampshire.[23]

The "Londonderry Celebration" of June 10, 1869, included multiple invocations of Scotch-Irish courage, endurance, and success. The keynote address, given by Horace Greeley, declared:

> The Scotch Irish were eminently men of conviction. They saw clearly; they reasoned fearlessly; and they did not hesitate to follow wherever truth led the way. Migration to Ireland cracked the shell of their insular prejudice; removal thence to America completed their emancipation. Liberalized by crossing a strait, the passage of a stormy ocean made them freemen.... No haughty prelacy can domineer over a Bible-loving, Bible-reading people; and the spirit of John Knox lives and reigns today in the hearts of the Scotch Irish in America.

Another address by Republican Congressman James W. Patterson of New Hampshire concluded, "The substratum of the Scotch Irish character was laid in the stern and stormy life of early Scotch history; but its distinctive traits were brought out and confirmed in the long and bloody conflicts which they waged in Ireland against ecclesiastical and royal tyranny."[24] Once used as a term of reproach, Scotch-Irish "has become a synonym of enterprise, intelligence, patriotism, and religious fervor," wrote William Henry Egle, the local historian of Dauphin County, Pennsylvania, in 1883.[25]

In May 1889, the Scotch-Irish Society of the United States of America was founded and held its first congress in Columbia, Tennessee. Over the next dozen years, it held annual congresses whose purpose was "to preserve the history and perpetuate the achievements of the Scotch-Irish race in America." Branch societies were subsequently established all across the country, in California, Pennsylvania, Tennessee, Virginia, North Carolina, Georgia, Kentucky, and Iowa, although by 1949 only the one in Pennsylvania survived. (The Scotch-Irish Foundation was formed that year to preserve its history and records, especially genealogical materials.[26]) The Society published volumes of papers and addresses celebrating the achievements of the Scotch-Irish in America.[27] At one of its meetings, a member quipped, "Well, if the Scotch-Irish have done all these things with which they are credited, I wonder what in the world all the rest of mankind have been doing meanwhile." Nevertheless, the Society was assiduous in its efforts to demonstrate that "no other race has had equal influence on the course of American history during the last two-hundred years."[28]

It also had another clear purpose: to demonstrate that the Scotch-Irish were not Irish. The notion that they were "a mongrel breed, partly Scotch and partly Irish" was totally wrong, wrote the Reverend John Walker Dinsmore, a prominent minister in the Presbyterian Church. "Whatever blood may be in the veins of the genuine Scotch-Irishman, one thing is certain, and that is that there is not mingled with it one drop of the blood of the old Irish or Kelt." Unlike their Highland neighbors, the Lowland Scots who colonized the north of Ireland were not Celts; they were of Teutonic or Anglo-Saxon origin, and they were Calvinists and Presbyterians, "almost to a man and to the marrow." They "had no scruple about rooting out the old Irish from Ulster." They mingled and intermarried with English Protestants and French Huguenots who also settled there, but never with Irish Catholics.[29] Put simply, in the words of Massachusetts senator, statesman, and historian Henry Cabot Lodge, the Scotch-Irish "regarded themselves as Scottish people who had been living in Ireland."[30]

So pervasive was the "Scotch-Irish myth" by the early twentieth century that Michael O'Brien, historiographer and chief contributor to the *Journal of the American Irish Historical Society*, devoted tireless research and multiple articles to exploding it and showing that the people who were so prominent in the affairs of the colonies and the early Republic were Irish, not "Scotch-Irish" or "Ulster Irish." Scotch-Irish, in O'Brien's view, was a new racial designation, intended to credit achievements to people of dubious Scots or English ancestry and deprive the Gaelic Irish of their due recognition.[31]

The predominantly Catholic Irish immigrants of the nineteenth century congregated in eastern and midwestern cities that became centers of the country's economic growth. The Protestant Scotch-Irish who had pushed into and across the Appalachians in the eighteenth century left descendants concentrated in the economically backward Appalachian South, where old patterns of speech, music, and custom endured.[32] Elite Scotch-Irish Americans who distinguished themselves from the Catholic Irish also distanced themselves from the emerging stereotype of southern Appalachian folk as in-bred, hard-drinking, feuding hillbillies, mired in poverty and ignorance. They did so by ignoring contemporary southern Appalachia and concentrating instead on the hardy independent pioneers and buckskin-clad frontiersmen of earlier times—the Kit Carsons and David Crocketts—who had led the westward march of civilization.[33]

They promoted a racial identity that they, and all Americans, could be proud of because Scotch-Irish traits were becoming American traits. Speaking to the members of the Scotch-Irish Congress as one of their own, Governor of Ohio and future president William McKinley (whose ancestors had left Country Antrim generations before) declared that the Scotch-Irishman "should be photographed by history's camera" before he lost his racial distinctiveness and individuality, "although for long years to come, his identity will manifest itself in the composite presentment of the future typical American." That identity had Ulster roots, but it was forged in America. "The Americanized Scotch-Irishman," McKinley told his audience, "is the perfection of a type which is the commingling and assimilation process of centuries."[34]

Colonists in the seventeenth and eighteenth centuries traced their roots to the Anglo-Saxons of early England, whom they credited with establishing political and individual freedoms which the Revolution restored and secured. In the nineteenth century, as the United States expanded west across the continent, the term "Anglo-Saxon" became less precise, more inclusive, and increasingly racialist, embracing a broader range of English-speaking peoples, and excluding Africans, Indians, Spaniards, Mexicans, and Asians. At the same time, other people, many of them politicians of Irish or Scotch-Irish ancestry, like James Buchanan, the fifteenth president and the son of Ulster Scot immigrants from County Donegal, took things a stage further and promoted the idea that *Americans* were now a distinct race. In their view, the American race exhibited all the best qualities of the Anglo-Saxons but was also "a unique blend of all that was best in the white European races," including Germans, Irish, Scotch-Irish, and French, and far superior to other, darker races whom it was destined to displace and replace.[35] Promoters of the Scotch-Irish myth were determined to show that they, not Anglo-Saxons, were the most influential in the development of this new American "race" and in the founding and building of the United States. The Scotch-Irish were not only Americans; they were the best kind of Americans. It was a position that appealed to many people at a time when the term "Anglo-Saxon" was coming under criticism.[36]

However, another part of the Scotch-American image, and a significant part of the imagined Scotch-Irish American identity of the late nineteenth century, rested on their historic encounters and conflicts with Indians. Ironically, at the same time, Anglo-Saxon Americans who felt threatened by the masses of new immigrants crowding the nation's shores looked to historic

American Indians as epitomizing "American" characteristics of courage and freedom, and adopted what they regarded as "Indian symbols" as markers of national identity, on public buildings, coins, and publications.[37]

As the Scotch-Irish Congress began extolling the virtues of their ancestors and their role in defeating the Indians and taming the continent, the U.S. Census Bureau in 1890 declared that the frontier no longer existed. Shortly after, in his address on "The Significance of the Frontier in American History," delivered at the World's Columbian Exposition in Chicago in 1893, Frederick Jackson Turner argued that the frontier experience, repeated as successive waves of Americans moved west into new areas of "free land," explained American development and shaped the national character. As the quintessential backcountry pioneers, the Scotch-Irish, it now seemed, epitomized the frontier experience that, Turner said, defined America.[38] Writing in the *Proceedings of the American Antiquarian Society* just two years after Turner's essay appeared in print, Samuel Swett Green asserted, "The Scotch-Irish emigrants to this country were, generally speaking, men of splendid bodies and perfect digestion." Frugal, virtuous, industrious, daring, passionate about civil and religious liberty, "they took up their abode on our frontiers and defended us from the depredations of Indians, and did a large portion of the fighting required in our wars." The American Antiquarian Society is located in Worcester, Massachusetts, a town that had driven out Scotch-Irish immigrants in the early eighteenth century. Now, at the end of the nineteenth century, Puritan New England owed them a tribute and the country owed them a debt of gratitude.[39]

In his multi-volume history, *The Winning of the West*, Theodore Roosevelt valorized the Scotch-Irish as "a bold and hardy race," who "formed the kernel of the distinctively and intensely American stock who were the pioneers of our people in their march westward." They pushed beyond the settled regions to form "a shield of sinewy men thrust in between the people of the seaboard and the red warriors of the wilderness" and they formed "the vanguard of the army of fighting settlers who, with axe and rifle, won their way from the Alleghanies to the Rio Grande and the Pacific."[40]

In the view of early-twentieth-century historian Henry Jones Ford, the rapid expansion of the United States from a coastal strip to continental dominance was "largely a Scotch-Irish achievement."[41] In the emerging mythology of the frontier, the Colt revolver and the Winchester '73 rifle became the guns that won the Old West, and the Scotch-Irish the people who won the West. Winning the West entailed winning it from someone else. Unstated but implicit in such assertions was that it involved killing Indians.

Self-identified Scotch-Irish descendants and propagandists in the nineteenth century not only made themselves American; they also shaped what it meant to be American. At a time when the national identity was still emerging, they emphasized the traits of courage, fearlessness, and individualism displayed by their ancestors. "They alone, of the various races of America were present in sufficient numbers in all of the colonies to make their influence count," wrote historian Charles Hanna in 1902; "and they alone of all the races had one uniform religion; had experienced together the persecutions by State and Church which had deprived them at home of their civil and religious liberties; and were the common heirs to those principles of freedom and democracy which had been developed in Scotland as nowhere else."[42] Dr. Maude Glasgow, an Irish immigrant pioneer in public health and preventive medicine, as well as an activist for equal rights for women, noted in 1936:

> Strong and brave, staunch and valiant, self-reliant, self-respecting, industrious, and orderly, hating sham and pretense, truthful and law-abiding, they have shone in all walks of life, and achieved success, not only with the ax which made clearings in the forest but with the plow and the loom. Their desire for education coupled with their intellect and intelligence has placed them in the most important and honorable positions in the country of their adoption.[43]

Maligned in the eighteenth century, the Scotch-Irish now epitomized the characteristics that made them entirely American. The Paxton Boys were now "Our Boys."

As the United States expelled Indigenous people from the land and then from its history, it created room for other people to make the claim that they, not the Indians, were the first Americans. The Scotch-Irish stepped forward to claim that role. Most Americans could not invoke any legitimate connections with the Mayflower Pilgrims, but most could find a connection, real or imagined, to Scotch-Irish pioneers who wrested the continent from savage Indians and helped to win independence from the tyrannical British. Settler sovereignty depended on staking a claim to be the first real settlers, and in reimagining the past, settler colonists replaced Indians as the Indigenous people of the country, the people who built it and who really belong here. This "replacement narrative" operated in New England in the nineteenth century; it also operated in rural Appalachia and rural Oklahoma in the twentieth century. Inhabitants of economically depressed Appalachia presented themselves as "Indigenous mountain people," victims of capitalist exploitation of the area and its resources and fighting back against, for example, absentee coal mining companies. Okie descendants of people who had trekked from frontier to frontier in search of landed independence found instead landless lives as tenant farmers, sharecroppers, migrant laborers, miners, and oil field workers. "Oklahoma was where the American dream had come to a halt." Nevertheless, writes Roxanne Dunbar-Ortiz, who grew up there, "We consider ourselves to be the true native-born Americans, the personification of what America is supposed to be, and we know that means being Scots-Irish original settlers, those who fought for and won the continent."[44]

In this version and vision of the nation's past, white Americans, not Native Americans, become the first real Americans and the actions, characteristics, and attitudes attributed to people like Scotch-Irish frontiersmen are celebrated as foundational values. After all, fighting Indians and taking their land was what made America white and what made the Scotch-Irish Americans. With settler colonists now the original inhabitants of the land and asserting white settler masculinity as a core value, many modern-day Americans were attracted to the bellicose white nationalism of those who promised not only to restore America to greatness, but also to stop it from being "stolen."[45]

Donald Trump won massive support in areas of the country where Scotch-Irish people and their descendants had settled and where the current inhabitants' sense of their identities, their attitudes to others and to government, and their grievances bore remarkable similarities to those of the Scotch-Irish on the backcountry. James Webb, the author of *Born Fighting*, described the Scotch-Irish as people for whom, as for modern-day Americans who claim to perpetuate and defend their legacy, "putting themselves at the mercy of someone else's collectivist judgment makes about as much sense as letting the government take their guns."[46] Ten years before the insurrection at the Capitol Building on January 6, 2021, the journalist and writer Colin Woodward, depicting Appalachia as one of eleven regional cultures that have essentially constituted separate nations, wrote: "proud, independent, and disturbingly violent, the Borderlanders of Greater Appalachia have remained a volatile insurgent force within North American society."[47]

In the twenty-first century, growing numbers of festivals celebrating "Scotch-Irish" heritage in the United States spread out of the southern highlands traditionally associated with the eighteenth-century settlement of migrants from Ulster and gave "Scotch-Irish" newfound visibility, even though the festivals often conflated Scotch-Irish and Highland Scots (perhaps because the latter have the more colorful paraphernalia and Americans tend to follow the "one drop" rule when imagining their Scottish identity). The cultural revival owed much to the genealogy boom, and cultural heritage tourism is a useful economic development strategy in depressed areas. It also represents in part a white ethnic backlash against multiculturalism, the advances made by African Americans (even in attaining the White House) and other minorities, and enduring stereotypes of "rednecks," "hillbillies," and "crackers" that continue to misrepresent and infuriate real people making lives in tough circumstances.[48]

For three hundred years, Scotch-Irish and Indian people were pushed together by colonial, political, and economic forces. In many areas they intermarried and shared economic deprivation. Nevertheless, large numbers of people from those old core areas of Scotch-Irish settlement have felt robbed of their just deserts in modern America by an unholy alliance between white elites and people of color. Most expressed their discontents in their votes. Some, like the Paxton Boys in 1763, struck out in violence against people of color and a government that did more for others than it did for them. They were, they said, fighting for the values that had made America great.

Notes

Terminology

1. Kerby A. Miller, "Ulster Presbyterians and the 'Two Traditions' in Ireland and America," in *Making the Irish American: History and Heritage of the Irish in the United States*, ed. J. J. Lee and Marion R. Casey (New York: New York University Press, 2006), 259–60.
2. Michael Montgomery, "Scotch-Irish or Scots-Irish: What's in a Name," *Tennessee Ancestors* 20 (2004), 143–50, available at http://www.ulsterscotslanguage.com/en/texts/scotch-irish/scotch-irish-or-scots-irish/.

Introduction

1. Jefferson Cowie, *Freedom's Dominion: A Saga of White Resistance to Federal Power* (New York: Basic Books, 2022).
2. Quoted in James G. Leyburn, *The Scotch-Irish: A Social History* (Chapel Hill: University of North Carolina Press, 1962), 192, and *Presbyterian Magazine* 6 (1856), 512.
3. Leyburn, *Scotch-Irish*, 314.
4. Peter Silver, *Our Savage Neighbors: How Indian War Transformed Early America* (New York: W. W. Norton, 2008); Kevin Kenny, *Peaceable Kingdom Lost: The Paxton Boys and the Destruction of William Penn's Holy Experiment* (New York: Oxford University Press, 2009); James H. Merrell, *Into the American Woods: Negotiators on the Pennsylvania Frontier* (New York: W. W. Norton, 1999); Jane T. Merritt, *At the Crossroads: Indians and Empires on a Mid-Atlantic Frontier, 1700–1763* (Chapel Hill: University of North Carolina Press, 2003).
5. Roxanne Dunbar-Ortiz, *Red Dirt: Growing Up Okie* (New York: Verso, 1997), 44–45.
6. Richard White, *The Middle Ground: Indians, Empires, and Republics in the Great Lakes Region, 1650–1815* (Cambridge: Cambridge University Press, 1991).
7. Patrick Griffin, "The Irish, Scots and Scotch-Irish and Lessons from the Early American Frontier," *Journal of Irish and Scottish Studies* 3 (Autumn 2009), 75–97 (implicated at 77).
8. See, for example, "Forum: Settler Colonialism and Early American History," *William and Mary Quarterly* 76 (July 2019).
9. *Penn. Archives*, 1st ser. 1: 505–6.
10. Richard Lyman Bushman, *The American Farmer in the Eighteenth Century: A Social and Cultural History* (New Haven, CT: Yale University Press, 2018), 183–84.
11. Henry J. Ford, *The Scotch-Irish in America* (Princeton, NJ: Princeton University Press, 1915), 19; Leyburn, *Scotch Irish*, 135; Forrest McDonald and Ellen Shapiro McDonald, "The Ethnic Origins of the American People, 1790," *William and Mary Quarterly* 37 (1980), 179–99. On the dangers, difficulties, and disagreements involved in relying on family names to determine country of origin and as "a surrogate for ethnic data," see Donald Harman Akenson, "Why the Accepted Estimates of Ethnicity of the American People, 1790, Are Unacceptable," *William and Mary Quarterly* 41 (1984), 102–19, and "Commentary," 119–35.
12. Bernard Bailyn, *The Peopling of British North America: An Introduction* (New York: Alfred A. Knopf, 1985), 34. French Protestants who migrated first to the Rhineland migrated again to the Kennebec River in Maine, where they were referred to as "Germans." Dutch-speaking emigrants from the Netherlands who migrated first to Germany and then to Pennsylvania became lumped together, ironically, with other "Pennsylvania Dutch" (i.e., *Deutsch*—Germans).
13. Timothy J. Meagher, *Becoming Irish American: The Making and Remaking of a People from Roanoke to JFK* (New Haven, CT: Yale University Press, 2023), 4–7; Kerby A. Miller, "'Scotch-Irish,' 'Black Irish' and 'Real Irish': Emigrants and Identities in the Old South," in *The Irish Diaspora*, ed. Andy Bielenberg (Harlow, UK: Longmans, 2000), quote at 141.
14. Gene Allen Smith and Sylvia L. Hilton, eds., *Nexus of Empire: Negotiating Loyalty and Identity in the Revolutionary Borderlands, 1760s–1820s* (Gainesville: University Press of Florida, 2010).

15. Patrick Griffin, *The People with No Name: Ireland's Ulster Scots, America's Scots Irish, and the Creation of a British Atlantic World, 1689–1764* (Princeton, NJ: Princeton University Press, 2001); Patrick Griffin, "'Irish' Migration to America in the Eighteenth Century? Or the Strange Case of the 'Scots/Irish,'" in *The Cambridge History of Ireland*, 4 vols., ed. Thomas Bartlett (Cambridge: Cambridge University Press, 2018), 3: 593–616; David Noel Doyle, "Scots Irish or Scotch-Irish," in *Making the Irish American: History and Heritage of the Irish in the United States*, ed. J. J. Lee and Marion R. Casey (New York: New York University Press, 2006), 151–70, and in *The Encyclopedia of the Irish in America*, ed. Michael Glazier (Notre Dame, IN: University of Notre Dame Press, 1999), 842–51; Kerby A. Miller, "'Scotch-Irish' Myths and 'Irish' Identities in Eighteenth- and Nineteenth-Century America," in *New Perspectives on the Irish Diaspora*, ed. Charles Fanning (Carbondale: Southern Illinois University Press, 2000), 75–92; Michael Montgomery, "Scotch-Irish or Scots-Irish: What's in a Name," *Tennessee Ancestors* 20 (2004), 143–50, available at http://www.ulsterscotslanguage.com/en/texts/scotch-irish/scotch-irish-or-scots-irish/; Kevin Kenny, *The American Irish: A History* (Harlow, UK: Longman, 2000), 27.
16. Kevin L. Yeager, "The Power of Ethnicity: The Preservation of Scots-Irish Culture in the Eighteenth-Century American Backcountry," Ph.D. diss., Louisiana State University, 2000.
17. Barry Vann, "Irish Protestants and the Creation of the Bible Belt," *Journal of Transatlantic Studies* 5 (2007), 87–106; Barry Aron Vann, *In Search of Ulster-Scots Land: The Birth and Geotheological Imagings of a Transatlantic People, 1603–1703* (Columbia: University of South Carolina Press, 2008) ch. 6; Fiona Ritchie and Doug Orr, *Wayfaring Strangers: The Musical Voyage from Scotland and Ulster to Appalachia* (Chapel Hill: University of North Carolina Press, 2014).
18. Miller, "'Scotch-Irish,' 'Black Irish' and 'Real Irish,'" 152.
19. David Noel Doyle, "The Irish in North America, 1776–1845," in *Making the Irish American: History and Heritage of the Irish in the United States*, ed. J. J. Lee and Marion R. Casey (New York: New York University Press, 2006), 175.
20. Donald Harman Akenson, "Irish Migration to North America, 1800–1920," in *The Irish Diaspora*, ed. Andy Bielenberg (Harlow, UK: Longmans, 2000), 112.
21. Carlton Jackson, *A Social History of the Scotch-Irish* (Lanham, MD: Madison Books, 1993), 95. For example, Tennessee history long asserted that the state's first settlers were predominantly Scotch-Irish, but more recent research suggests that few of those people were Irish-born; most were the children or grandchildren of Irish emigrants who settled first in one or more other states—Pennsylvania, Virginia, Maryland. Michael Montgomery and Cherel Henderson, "Eighteenth-Century Emigrants from Ireland to Tennessee: A Report Using First Families of Tennessee Files," *Journal of East Tennessee History* 76 (2004), 88–99.
22. Akenson, "Why the Accepted Estimates of Ethnicity of the American People, 1790, Are Unacceptable," 107. An expanded version of the essay appears in Donald Harman Akenson, *Being Had: Historians, Evidence, and the Irish in North America* (Port Credit, Ontario: P. D. Meany, 1985), ch. 2.
23. Wilma Dykeman, *The French Broad* (Newport, TN: Wakestone Books, 1955), 43–44, quoted in Ritchie and Orr, *Wayfaring Strangers*, 168.
24. James Muldoon, *Medieval Irish Frontier: Degenerate Englishmen, Wild Irishmen, Middle Nations* (Gainesville: University Press of Florida, 2003); Stuart Hall and Paul Du Gay, eds., *Questions of Cultural Identity* (London: Sage Publications, 1996), 4; Michael Montgomery, "The Problem of Persistence: Ulster-American Missing Links," *Journal of Scotch-Irish Studies* 1 (Spring 2000), 105–19 (esp. 105–7); Leroy V. Eid, "Irish, Scotch, and Scotch Irish, A Reconsideration," *American Presbyterianism* 64 (Winter 1986), 211–25; David Hackett Fischer, *Albion's Seed: Four British Folkways in North America* (New York: Oxford University Press, 1993), 618, 621; Kenneth W. Keller, "What Is Distinctive about the Scotch-Irish?" in *Appalachian Frontiers: Settlement, Society, and Development in the Preindustrial Era*, ed. Robert D. Mitchell (Lexington: University Press of Kentucky, 1991), 69–86; Daniel W. Patterson, *The True Image: Gravestone Art and the Culture of Scotch Irish Settlers in the Pennsylvania and Carolina Backcountry* (Chapel Hill: University of North Carolina Press, 2012), 18.
25. Griffin, *People with No Name*, 6–7 (quote); Warren Hofstra, ed., *Ulster to America: The Scots-Irish Migration Experience, 1680–1830* (Knoxville: University of Tennessee Press, 2012), xvi, xx; Doyle, "Scots Irish or Scotch-Irish," 158, 163; Peter N. Moore, *World of Toil and Strife: Community Transformation in Backcountry South Carolina, 1750–1805* (Columbia: University of South Carolina Press, 2007), chs. 1–2; Ritchie and Orr, *Wayfaring Strangers*.
26. Audrey J. Horning, "Myth, Migration, and Material Culture: Archaeology and the Ulster Influence on Appalachia," *Historical Archaeology* 36, no. 4 (2002), 129–49.

27. Donald M. MacRaild, Tanja Bueltmann, and J. C. D. Clark, eds., *British and Irish Diasporas: Societies, Cultures and Ideologies* (Manchester, UK: Manchester University Press, 2019), 1.
28. Stuart Hall, "Cultural Identity and Diaspora," in *Identity and Difference*, ed. Katherine Woodward (London: Sage Publications, 1997), 51–52; Paul Gilroy, "Diaspora and the Detours of Identity," in ibid., 301, 304, 315.
29. Ritchie and Orr, *Wayfaring Strangers*, 143.
30. Cf. J. Edward Townes, "The Nature of Loyalty: Antonio Gil Ibarvo and the East Texas Frontier," in *Nexus of Empire*, 164–97, and David M. Emmons, *Beyond the American Pale: The Irish in the West, 1845–1910* (Norman: University of Oklahoma Press, 2010), 25.
31. Ned C. Landsman, "Ethnicity and National Origin among British Settlers in the Philadelphia Region," *Proceedings of the American Philosophical Society* 133 (1989), 170–77. For hearth areas, see Terry G. Jordan-Bychkov, *The Upland South: The Making of an American Folk Region and Landscape* (Santa Fe, NM: Center for American Places; Charlottesville: University of Virginia Press, 2003).
32. Hubertis M. Cummings, *Scots Breed and Susquehanna* (Pittsburgh: University of Pittsburgh Press for the Presbyterian Historical Society, 1964), 53; Richard K. MacMaster, *Scotch-Irish Merchants in Colonial America* (Newtonards, N. Ireland: Ulster Heritage Foundation, 2009), 173.
33. James Webb, *Born Fighting: How the Scots-Irish Shaped America* (New York: Broadway Books, 2004); Linda Colley, *Britons: Forging the Nation 1707–1837* (New Haven, CT: Yale University Press, 1992), 6, 9.
34. Kariann Akemi Yokota, *Unbecoming British: How Revolutionary America Became a Postcolonial Nation* (New York: Oxford University Press, 2011); Andrés Reséndez, *Changing National Identities at the Frontier: Texas and New Mexico, 1800–1850* (Cambridge: Cambridge University Press, 2005).
35. Rowland Berthoff, "Celtic Mist over the South," *Journal of Southern History* 52 (1986), 523–46.
36. Thomas Daniel Knight, "A Scotch-Irish Clan in Middle Georgia: The Migration and Development of a McCarty Family across Two Centuries," *Journal of Family History* 45 (2020), 39–63, argues that elements of Scottish and Irish kinship systems were to be found in a central Georgia community in the nineteenth and twentieth centuries, an area far removed from the main regions of Scots, Scotch-Irish, and Irish settlement.
37. Walter Durham, "Ulster Immigrants and the Settlement of Tennessee," *Journal of East Tennessee History* 77 (2006), 30–44 (quote at 30, note 2).
38. Wilma A. Dunway, *Women, Work, and Family in the Antebellum Mountain South* (Cambridge: Cambridge University Press, 2008), ch. 1.
39. Leyburn, *Scotch Irish*, 190–91; L. H. Butterfield, ed., "Dr. Benjamin Rush's Journal of a Trip to Carlisle in 1784," *PMBH* 74 (1950), 450–51, 456; Larry J. Hoefling, *Scots and Scotch Irish: Frontier Life in North Carolina, Virginia, and Kentucky* (Riverside, CA: Inlandia Press, 2009), 19.
40. *The Journals of Henry Melchior Muhlenberg*, ed. Theodore G. Tappert and John W. Doberstein, 3 vols. (Philadelphia: Muhlenberg Press, 1942), 2: 391.
41. "Though rooted largely in the collective experience of the Scotch-Irish," it remained no more "confined to those of Scotch-Irish descent than the 'general American' mentality has remained confined to Anglo-Americans." Rodger Cunningham, *Apples on the Flood: The Southern Mountain Experience* (Knoxville: University of Tennessee Press, 1987), 91, 142.
42. Jordan-Bychkov, *The Upland South*.
43. Aidan O'Sullivan, "Crannogs: Places of Resistance in the Contested Landscapes of Early Modern Ireland," in *Contested Landscapes: Movement, Exile and Place*, ed. Barbara Bender and Margot Winer (New York: Berg, 2001), 87.
44. Robert Ross, quoted in Margot Winer, "Landscapes, Fear and Land Loss on the Nineteenth-Century South African Colonial Frontier," in *Contested Landscapes*, 257.
45. Eric Hinderaker, *Elusive Empires: Constructing Colonialism in the Ohio Valley, 1673–1800* (Cambridge: Cambridge University Press, 1997), 258–59; Moore, *World of Toil and Strife*, 33; Matthew C. Ward, *Making the Frontier Man: Violence, White Manhood, and Authority in the Early Western Backcountry* (Pittsburgh: University of Pittsburgh Press, 2023).
46. Hastings Donnan, "Material Identities: Fixing Ethnicity in the Irish Borderlands," *Identities: Global Studies in Culture and Power* 12, no. 1 (2005), 69–105, esp. 96. Donnan focused on the contested borderland landscape of south Armagh. See also Donna K. Flynn, "'We

Are the Border': Identity, Exchange, and the State along the Bénin-Nigeria Border," *American Ethnologist* 24 (1997), 311–30.
47. Fintan O'Toole, *The Lie of the Land: Irish Identities* (London: Verso, 1997), xv.
48. Patterson, *True Image*, 397.
49. John Anthony Caruso, *The Appalachian Frontier: America's First Surge Westward* (1959; Knoxville: University of Tennessee Press, 2003), 13.
50. Richard Slotkin, *Regeneration through Violence: The Mythology of the American Frontier, 1600–1860* (Middletown, CT: Wesleyan University Press, 1973), quotes at 4, 269.
51. Frederick J. Turner, "The Significance of the Frontier in American History," *Annual Report of the American Historical Association*, 1893, 197–227, and multiple reprints.
52. Thomas Perkins Abernethy, *From Frontier to Plantation in Tennessee: A Study in Frontier Democracy* (Chapel Hill: University of North Carolina Press, 1932), 359.
53. Patrick Griffin, "Irish Migration to the Colonial South," in *Rethinking the Irish in the American South*, ed. Bryan Albin Giemza (Jackson: University of Mississippi Press, 2013), 54–55.
54. Ford, *Scotch-Irish in America*, 157, 211, 274. After their experiences with rent hikes in Ulster in the eighteenth century, for example, Ford described their opposition to paying rent, however small, "as a racial characteristic"!
55. Although much of the information is redundant, and not always reliable, the series, published in Belfast and in Greenville, South Carolina, by Causeway Press includes: *The Scots-Irish in the Hills of Tennessee* (1995), quote at 180; *The Scots-Irish in the Shenandoah Valley* (1996); *The Scots-Irish in the Carolinas* (1997); *The Scots-Irish in Pennsylvania and Kentucky* (1998); *Faith and Freedom: The Scots-Irish in America* (1999); *Heroes of the Scots-Irish in America* (2001); *The Making of America: How the Scots-Irish Shaped a Nation* (2001).
56. Webb, *Born Fighting*, 20, 138, 140.
57. Dunbar-Ortiz, *Red Dirt*, 44.
58. Fischer, *Albion's Seed*, 630–32.
59. Webb, *Born Fighting*; Grady McWhitney, *Cracker Culture: Celtic Ways in the Old South* (Tuscaloosa: University of Alabama Press, 1988), ch. 6; Emily R. Berthelot, Troy C. Blanchard, and Timothy C. Brown, "Scots-Irish Women and the Southern Culture of Violence: The Influence of Scots-Irish Females on High Rates of Southern Violence," *Southern Rural Sociology* 2 (2008), 157–70. On more complex patterns, see Bruce E. Stewart, ed., *Blood in the Hills: A History of Violence in Appalachia* (Lexington: University Press of Kentucky, 2012).
60. Doyle, "Scots Irish or Scotch-Irish," 158.
61. James Belich, *Replenishing the Earth: The Settler Revolution and the Rise of the Anglo-World, 1783–1939* (New York: Oxford University Press, 2009), 23, 41–42.
62. Linda H. Matthews, *Middling Folk: Three Seas, Three Centuries, One Scots-Irish Family* (Chicago: Chicago Review Press, 2010), 329.
63. Patrick Spero, *Frontier Country: The Politics of War in Early Pennsylvania* (Philadelphia: University of Pennsylvania Press, 2016).
64. Pamela Clayton, *Enemies and Passing Friends: Settler Ideologies in Twentieth Century Ulster* (London: Pluto Press, 1996), quote at xiv.
65. See, for example, Gregory Ablavsky, *Federal Ground: Governing Property and Violence in the First U.S. Territories* (New York: Oxford University Press, 2021).
66. Cowie, *Freedom's Dominion*.
67. Adam Dahl, *Empire of the People: Settler Colonialism and the Foundations of Modern Democratic Thought* (Lawrence: University Press of Kansas, 2018), quote at 1–2.
68. Patrick Wolfe, "Settler Colonialism and the Elimination of the Native," *Journal of Genocide Research* 8 (2006), 387–409.
69. Alan Taylor, *Liberty Men and Great Proprietors: The Revolutionary Settlement on the Maine Frontier, 1760–1820* (Chapel Hill: University of North Carolina Press, 1990), 9; Bushman, *American Farmer in the Eighteenth Century*, x–xi, 5, 17–22, 63–64, 153.
70. Joseph Hawley advised John Adams in 1774 that he could expect to meet "diverse Gentlemen in Congress who are of Dutch or Scotch or Irish Extract. Many more there are in those Southern colonies of those descents than in these New England Colonies and Many of them very worthy, learned men." Adams should be careful to not make any aspersions that might give affront since "that which disparages our family ancestors or Nation is apt to Stick by us if cast up in Comparison and their Blood you will find is as Warm as Ours." Joseph Hawley to John Adams, 25 July 1774, Founders Online, National Archives, https://founders.archives.gov/documents/Adams/06-02-02-0028. Original source: *The Adams Papers*, Papers of John Adams, vol. 2, *December 1773–April 1775*, ed. Robert J. Taylor (Cambridge, MA: Harvard University Press, 1977), 117–21.

71. Ford, *Scotch-Irish in America*, ch. 10.
72. Silver, *Our Savage Neighbors*, 159–60; Rob Harper, "Looking the Other Way: The Gnadenhutten Massacre and the Contextual Interpretation of Violence," *William and Mary Quarterly* 64 (2007), 621–44; Rob Harper, *Unsettling the West: Violence and State Building in the Ohio Valley* (Philadelphia: University of Pennsylvania Press, 2018); Bushman, *American Farmer in the Eighteenth Century*, 160–62.
73. "Journal of a French Traveler in the American Colonies, 1765," *American Historical Review* 26 (1921), 726–47, quote at 737.
74. Cunningham, *Apples on the Flood*, xxi–xxiii, 21.
75. Shannon Lee Dawdy, *Building the Devil's Empire: French Colonial New Orleans* (Chicago: University of Chicago Press, 2008), 19.
76. November 16, 1765: C.O. 5/66: 300.
77. Allan Greer, *Property and Dispossession: Natives, Empires and Land in Early Modern North America* (Cambridge: Cambridge University Press, 2018), 10–11.
78. Daniel H. Usner, Jr., *Indians, Settlers, and Slaves in a Frontier Exchange Economy: The Lower Mississippi Valley before 1783* (Chapel Hill: University of North Carolina Press, 1992); Melissah J. Pawlikowski, "The Plight and the Bounty: Squatters, War Profiteers, and the Transforming Hand of Sovereignty in Indian Country, 1750–1774," Ph.D. diss., Ohio State University, 2014.

Chapter 1

1. John Heckewelder, *History, Manners, and Customs of the Indian Nations Who Once Inhabited Pennsylvania and the Neighboring States* (Philadelphia, 1876; reprint, New York: Arno Press, 1871), 250; John Bierhorst, *Mythology of the Lenape: Guide and Texts* (Tucson: University of Arizona Press, 1995); Daniel G. Brinton, *The Lenape and Their Legends* (Philadelphia: D. G. Brinton, 1885); C. Hale Sipe, The *Indian Wars of Pennsylvania* (Harrisburg, PA: Telegraph Press, 1929), 34–37; Dawn Marsh, "Creating Delaware Homelands in the Ohio Country," *Ohio History* 116 (2009), 26–40; Richard S. Grimes, *The Western Delaware Indian Nation, 1730–1795: Warriors and Diplomats* (Bethlehem, PA: Lehigh University Press, 2017); C. A. Weslager, *The Delaware Westward Migration: With the Texts of Two Manuscripts, 1821–22, Responding to General Lewis Cass's Inquiries about Lenape Culture and Language* (Wallingford, PA: Middle Atlantic Press, 1978).
2. Bernard Bailyn, *The Peopling of British North America: An Introduction* (New York: Alfred A. Knopf, 1985).
3. Henry Noble MacCracken, "Address to the Ulster Society of New York, 1939," in *Making the Irish American: History and Heritage of the Irish in the United States*, ed. J. J. Lee and Marion R. Casey (New York: New York University Press, 2006), 287.
4. James Muldoon, *Medieval Irish Frontier: Degenerate Englishmen, Wild Irishmen, Middle Nations* (Gainesville: University Press of Florida, 2003), vii–viii, 111.
5. M. Perceval-Maxwell, *The Scottish Migration to Ulster in the Reign of James I* (London: Routledge and Kegan Paul, 1973), 2; Lawrence J. McCaffrey, *The Irish Diaspora in America* (Bloomington: Indiana University Press, 1976), 11–16.
6. James O'Neill, *The Nine Years War, 1593–1603: O'Neill, Mountjoy and the Military Revolution* (Dublin: Four Courts Press, 2017); Nicholas P. Canny, *The Elizabethan Conquest of Ireland: A Pattern Established* (New York Harper & Row, 1976); David Beers Quinn, *The Elizabethans and the Irish* (Ithaca, NY: Cornell University Press, 1966); former soldier Thomas Gainsford's Description of Ireland at 163–69, quotation at 165–66.
7. R. F. Foster, *Modern Ireland, 1600–1972* (New York: Penguin, 1989), 9.
8. George MacDonald Fraser, *The Steel Bonnets: The Story of the Anglo-Scottish Border Reivers* (London: HarperCollins, 1995), 21.
9. Fraser, *Steel Bonnets*, 373.
10. David Hackett Fischer, *Albion's Seed: Four British Folkways in North America* (New York: Oxford University Press, 1993), 630.
11. Graham Robb, *The Debatable Land: The Lost World between Scotland and England* (New York: W. W. Norton, 2018).
12. N.a., *The Scotch-Irish of Northampton County, Pennsylvania* (Easton, PA: The Northampton County Historical and Genealogical Society, 1926), 1.
13. Derek Hirst, *Dominion: England and Its Island Neighbours, 1505–1707* (Oxford: Oxford University Press, 2012), chs. 5–6; James G. Leyburn, *The Scotch-Irish: A Social History* (Chapel

Hill: University of North Carolina Press, 1962), ch. 6; William M. Mervine, "The Scotch Settlers in Raphoe, County Donegal, Ireland: A Contribution to Pennsylvania Genealogy," *PMHB* 36 (1912), 257–72.

14. Perceval-Maxwell, *Scottish Migration to Ulster*, 83, 87; Philip S. Robinson, *The Plantation of Ulster: British Settlement in an Irish Landscape, 1600–1670* (New York: St. Martin's Press, 1984); Ron Chepesiuk, *The Scotch-Irish: From the North of Ireland to the Making of America* (Jefferson, NC: McFarland, 2000), 38 (outposts); Foster, *Modern Ireland*, 61.
15. Quoted in Theodore W. Allen, *The Invention of the White Race*, Vol. 1: *Racial Oppression and Social Control*, 2nd ed. (London: Verso, 2012), 1: 121.
16. Nicholas Canny, "The Permissive Frontier: The Problem of Social Control in English Settlements in Ireland and Virginia, 1550–1650," in *The Westward Enterprise: English Activities in Ireland, the Atlantic, and America, 1480–1650*, ed. K. R. Andrews, N. P. Canny, and P. E. H. Hair (Detroit: Wayne State University Press, 1979), 16–44, quote at 23.
17. Perceval-Maxwell, *Scottish Migration to Ulster*, 278.
18. Kerby A. Miller, *Emigrants and Exiles: Ireland and the Irish Exodus to North America* (New York: Oxford University Press, 1985), 20; Perceval-Maxwell, *Scottish Migration to Ulster*, 289; Samuel K. Fisher, *The Gaelic and Indian Origins of the American Revolution: Diversity and Empire in the British Atlantic, 1688–1783* (New York: Oxford University Press, 2022), 48–51.
19. Perceval-Maxwell, *Scottish Migration to Ulster*, 310; Karl S. Bottingheimer, "Kingdom and Colony: Ireland in the Westward Enterprise, 1536–1660," in *The Westward Enterprise: English Activities in Ireland, the Atlantic, and America, 1480–1650*, ed. K. R. Andrews, N. P. Canny, and P. E. H. Hair (Detroit: Wayne State University Press, 1979), 56–57; Foster, *Modern Ireland*, 60 ("spilling"), 73.
20. Perceval-Maxwell, *Scottish Migration to Ulster*, ch. 12.
21. Kerby A. Miller, "'Scotch-Irish' Myths and 'Irish' Identities in Eighteenth- and Nineteenth-Century America," in *New Perspectives on the Irish Diaspora*, ed. Charles Fanning (Carbondale: Southern Illinois University Press, 2000), 76–77.
22. *Calendar of State Papers, relating to Ireland of the reign of James I*, Vol. 3: *1608–10*, ed. C. W. Russell and John P. Prendergast (London, 1874), 3: 64.
23. Canny, *Elizabethan Conquest of Ireland*, esp. 160–63; Nicholas P. Canny, "The Ideology of English Colonization: From Ireland to America," *William and Mary Quarterly* 30 (1973), 585; Bernard W. Sheehan, *Savagism and Civility: Indians and Englishmen in Colonial Virginia* (Cambridge: Cambridge University Press, 1980); Robert A. Williams, *The American Indian in Western Legal Thought: The Discourses of Conquest* (New York: Oxford University Press, 1990); David Harding, "Objects of Colonial Discourse: The Irish and Native Americans," *Nordic Irish Studies* 4 (2005), 37–60; Perceval-Maxwell, *Scottish Migration to Ulster*, 2; Patrick O'Farrell, *Ireland's English Question: Anglo-Irish Relations, 1534–1970* (New York: Schocken Books, 1971), 25; Allen, *Invention of the White Race*, 1: 121–22; Ronald Takaki, "The Tempest in the Wilderness: The Racialization of Savagery," *Journal of American History* 79 (1992), 893–95. See also the forum of essays on the work of Nicholas Canny, marking the fiftieth anniversary of "The Ideology of English Colonization: From Ireland to America," *William and Mary Quarterly* 80 (July 2023).
24. Leyburn, *Scotch-Irish*, 95.
25. Foster, *Modern Ireland*, 75.
26. Eric Richards, *Britannia's Children: Emigration from England, Scotland, Wales and Ireland since 1600* (London: Hambledon and London, 2004), 9–10, 53. *IILC* 24 suggests between 80,000 and 130,000 Scots immigrants by 1690.
27. Miller, *Emigrants and Exiles*, 19.
28. Bailyn, *Peopling of British North America*, 26; Perceval-Maxwell, *Scottish Migration to Ulster*, 313.
29. John Gibney, *The Shadow of a Year: The 1641 Rebellion in Irish History and Memory* (Madison: University of Wisconsin Press, 2013); S. J. Connolly, *Divided Kingdom: Ireland 1630–1800* (New York: Oxford University Press, 2008), ch. 3.
30. Miller, *Emigrants and Exiles*, 19–20; Chepesiuk, *Scotch-Irish*, 93; R. J. Dickson, *Ulster Emigration to Colonial America 1718–1775* (London: Routledge and Kegan Paul, 1966), 2; Timothy J. Meagher, *Becoming Irish American: The Making and Remaking of a People from Roanoke to JFK* (New Haven, CT: Yale University Press, 2023), 26.
31. Foster, *Modern Ireland*, 14.
32. Leyburn, *Scotch-Irish*, 107; Dickson, *Ulster Emigration to Colonial America*, 2–3.

33. McCaffrey, *Irish Diaspora in America*, 23; James Livesey, *Civil Society and Empire: Ireland and Scotland in the Eighteenth-Century Atlantic World* (New Haven, CT: Yale University Press, 2009), 72; Gibney, *Shadow of a Year*, ch. 1.
34. Barry Aron Vann, *In Search of Ulster-Scots Land: The Birth and Geotheological Imagings of a Transatlantic People, 1603-1703* (Columbia: University of South Carolina Press, 2008), ch. 3.
35. Miller, *Emigrants and Exiles*, 39.
36. Kevin Kenny, *The American Irish: A History* (Harlow, UK: Longman, 2000), 17.
37. Peter E. Gilmore, *Irish Presbyterians and the Shaping of Western Pennsylvania, 1770-1830* (Pittsburgh: University of Pittsburgh Press, 2018), xix-xx.
38. Miller, *Emigrants and Exiles*, 137-38, 149-50, 152-53, 159-61; Maldwyn A. Jones, "The Scotch-Irish in British America," in *Strangers within the Realm: Cultural Margins of the First British Empire*, ed. Bernard Bailyn and Philip D. Morgan (Chapel Hill: University of North Carolina Press, 1991), 287, 292-93; *IILC* 5.
39. Meagher, *Becoming Irish American*, 30; Connolly, *Divided Kingdom*, 381.
40. Marianne S. Wokeck, *Trade in Strangers: The Beginnings of Mass Migration to North America* (University Park: Pennsylvania State University Press, 1999), xix.
41. Wokeck, *Trade in Strangers*, 37.
42. John B. Frantz, "Franklin and the Pennsylvania Germans," *Pennsylvania History* 65 (1998), 21-34.
43. Carla J. Munford, *Benjamin Franklin and the Ends of Empire* (New York: Oxford University Press, 2015), 96-104, 109-10, 122-23.
44. Fischer, *Albion's Seed*.
45. Miller, *Emigrants and Exiles*, 139.
46. *Correspondence between William Penn and James Logan, secretary of the province of Pennsylvania, and others, 1700-1750*, 2 vols. (Philadelphia: Historical Society of Pennsylvania, 1870-1872), 1: 230.
47. *IILC* 24; Wokeck, *Trade in Strangers*, ch. 5; Bernard Bailyn, *Voyagers to the West: A Passage in the Peopling of America on the Eve of the Revolution* (New York: Alfred A. Knopf, 1986), 25.
48. Kenny, *The American Irish*, 14; Leyburn, *Scotch-Irish*, 175 (200,000), 179-83; Wayland F. Dunaway, *The Scotch-Irish of Colonial Pennsylvania* (Chapel Hill: University of North Carolina Press, 1944; Baltimore, MD: Genealogical Publishing, 1979) (250,000); Bailyn, *Voyagers to the West*, 26 (155,000-205,000); Fischer, *Albion's Seed*, 608-9; Dickson, *Ulster Emigration* (114,000); Patrick Griffin, *The People with No Name: Ireland's Ulster Scots, America's Scots Irish, and the Creation of a British Atlantic World, 1689-1764* (Princeton, NJ: Princeton University Press, 2001), 1 (more than 100,000); *IILC* 656-57 (perhaps "up to 250,000 or more"); David Noel Doyle, "Scots Irish or Scotch-Irish," in *Making the Irish American: History and Heritage of the Irish in the United States*, ed. J. J. Lee and Marion R. Casey (New York: New York University Press, 2006), 161-62; Connolly, *Divided Kingdom*, 380; Meagher, *Becoming Irish American*, 29.
49. Hector St. John de Crèvecoeur, *Letters from an American Farmer* (London: J. M. Dent, 1971), 58.
50. Marianne S. Wokeck, "Irish Immigration to the Delaware Valley before the American Revolution," *Proceedings of the Royal Irish Academy: Archaeology, Culture, History, Literature* 96C, no. 5 (1996), 103-35; Patrick Griffin, "'Irish' Migration to America in the Eighteenth Century? Or the Strange Case of the 'Scots/Irish,'" in *The Cambridge History of Ireland*, 4 vols., ed. Thomas Bartlett (Cambridge: Cambridge University Press, 2018), 3: 593-616.
51. Líam Kennedy and Martin W. Dowling, "Prices and Wages in Ireland, 1700-1850," *Irish Economic and Social History* 24 (1997), 62-104.
52. Dickson, *Ulster Emigration to Colonial America*, 6-10; Miller, *Emigrants and Exiles*, 29, 40 ("rural proletariat"); H. Tyler Blethen and Curtis W. Wood, Jr., *From Ulster to Carolina: The Migration of the Scotch-Irish to Southwestern North Carolina* (Raleigh: North Carolina Department of Cultural Resources, Division of Archives and History, 1998), 21; Richard K. McMaster, *Scotch-Irish Merchants in Colonial America* (Newtownards, N. Ireland: Ulster Historical Foundation, 2009), chs. 1-4 (rhythm at 17); Wokeck, *Trade in Strangers*.
53. Leyburn, *Scotch-Irish*, 169.
54. Miller, *Emigrants and Exiles*, 152; Chepesiuk, *Scotch-Irish*, 99; Dickson, *Ulster Emigration to Colonial America*, 24, 31.
55. Dunaway, *Scotch-Irish of Colonial Pennsylvania*, 34; and quoted in Leyburn, *Scotch-Irish*, 170, citing Jonathan Dickinson, Copy Book of Letters, HSP, 163, 288.
56. Leyburn, *Scotch-Irish*, 170.
57. Dickson, *Ulster Emigration*, 32.

58. *Letters Written by His Excellency Hugh Boulter, D.D. Lord Primate of All Ireland &c to Several Ministers of State in England and Some Others, containing An Account of the most interesting Transactions which passed in Ireland from 1724 to 1738*, Vol. 1 (Dublin: Faulkner and Williams, 1770), 202, 209, 216–17, 224, 230–31; E. R. R. Green, ed., "The 'Strange Humors' That Drove the Scotch-Irish to America, 1729," *William and Mary Quarterly* 12 (1955), 113–123 ("sorely distressed" at 121); Dickson, *Ulster Emigration*, 33, 97 (1729 famine); Miller, *Emigrants and Exiles*, 153; Wokeck, *Trade in Strangers*, 176–77 (6,000).
59. *Col. Recs. Penn.* 3: 359–60.
60. Leyburn, *Scotch-Irish*, 172, 206–07; Dickson, *Ulster Emigration*, 52; Connolly, *Divided Kingdom*, 346.
61. Miller, *Emigrants and Exiles*, 154.
62. *The Works of the Rev. John Wesley* (London: John Jones, 1816), 3: 257.
63. Meagher, *Becoming Irish American*, 31.
64. Wokeck, *Trade in Strangers*, 179; Dickson, *Ulster Emigration*, 55–56.
65. Dickson, *Ulster Emigration*, 69–81; Miller, *Emigrants and Exiles*, 155; Bailyn, *Voyagers to the West*, 26; Foster, *Modern Ireland*, 216.
66. *DAR* 4:403–04; 5: 133 (quote).
67. Arthur Young, *A Tour in Ireland, 1776–1779, with General Observations on the Present State of that Kingdom made in the years 1776, 1777 and 1778* (Cambridge: Cambridge University Press, 1925), 38, 42–45, 50, 192–93.
68. Michael Montgomery, "On the Trail of Early Ulster Emigrant Letters," in *Atlantic Crossroads: Historical Connections between Scotland, Ulster and North America*, ed. Patrick Fitzgerald and Steve Ickringill (Newtownards, N. Ireland: Colourpoint Books, 2001), 24.
69. Dickson, *Ulster Emigration*, ch. 8.
70. "Sketch of Col. James Patton. Born Londonderry Co., 1692," Draper 21U37.
71. Dickson, *Ulster Emigration*, 98; Deirdre M. Megeean, "Emigration from Irish Ports," *Journal of American Ethnic History* 13 (1993), 10.
72. Maurice J. Bric, *Ireland, Philadelphia and the Re-invention of America, 1760–1800* (Dublin: Four Courts Press, 2008), 111.
73. Bric, *Ireland, Philadelphia and the Re-invention of America*, 111; Fischer, *Albion's Seed*, 612.
74. Michael O'Brien, *Irish Settlers in America: A Consolidation of Articles from "The Journal of the American Irish Historical Society,"* 2 vols. (Baltimore, MD: Genealogical Publishing, 1979, 1993), 1: 130.
75. *IILC* 90–93.
76. On the notorious case of the *Nancy*, see Richard K. MacMaster, "From Ulster to the Carolina: John Torrans, John Greg, John Poaug, and Bounty Emigration, 1761–1768," in *The Irish in the Atlantic World*, ed. David T. Gleeson (Columbia: University of South Carolina Press, 2010), 262–64; Philip M. Hamer, ed., *The Papers of Henry Laurens* (Columbia: University of South Carolina Press, 1968–1980), 6: 149–50; partially quoted in MacMaster, 264; Fischer, *Albion's Seed*, 612; C.O. 5/114:36; C. O. 5/661:35.
77. Bric, *Ireland, Philadelphia and the Re-invention of America*, 110, 116.
78. Kerby A. Miller, "'Scotch-Irish,' 'Black Irish' and 'Real Irish': Emigrants and Identities in the Old South," in *The Irish Diaspora*, ed. Andy Bielenberg (Harlow, UK: Longmans, 2000), 145–49; *IILC* 94–101.
79. Miller, *Emigrants and Exiles*, 139, 155; Dickson, *Ulster Emigration*, 85–87, 90; *IILC* 253–54 (percentages); Griffin, *People with No Name*, 93–94; Kenny, *American Irish*, 21 (100,000). Wokeck doubts that most Irish immigrants to the Delaware Valley were indentured servants, although they "remained a regular and integral part of the Irish trade." Wokeck, *Trade in Strangers*, 214, 218.
80. David Noel Doyle, *Ireland, Irishmen, and Revolutionary America, 1760–1820* (Dublin: Mercier Press, 1981), 66 (529), 95 (Scotch-Irish masters); Michael Tepper, ed., *Emigrants to Pennsylvania, 1641–1819: A Consolidation of Passenger Lists from the Pennsylvania Magazine of History and Biography* (Baltimore, MD: Genealogical Publishing, 1977), 61, 102–14, 155. See also "Account of Servants Bound and Assigned Before James Hamilton, Mayor of Philadelphia," *PMHB* 30 (1906), 31 (1907), 32 (1908).
81. Bric, *Ireland, Philadelphia and the Re-invention of America*, 124–25.
82. *IILC* 4.
83. Foster, *Modern Ireland*, 216.
84. *IILC* 7, 656–59.

85. *IILC* 4–5.
86. Rankin Sherling, *The Invisible Irish: Finding Protestants in the Nineteenth-Century Migrations to America* (Montreal: McGill-Queens University Press, 2016).
87. Peter Gilmore and Kerby A. Miller, "Searching for 'Irish' Freedom—Settling for 'Scotch-Irish' Respectability: Southwestern Pennsylvania, 1780–1810," in *Ulster to America: The Scots-Irish Migration Experience, 1680–1830*, ed. Warren Hofstra (Knoxville: University of Tennessee Press, 2012), 165.
88. Miller, *Emigrants and Exiles*, ch. 6.
89. Foster, *Modern Ireland*, 323–24, 345.
90. Kevin Kenny, "Diaspora and Comparison: The Global Irish as a Case Study," *Journal of American History* 90 (2003), 134–62.
91. Alexis de Tocqueville, *Democracy in America*, ed. J. P. Mayer; trans. George Lawrence (New York: Doubleday/Anchor, 1969), 281 (quote), 408–12.

Chapter 2

1. Lisa Brooks, *The Common Pot: The Recovery of Native Space in the Northeast* (Minneapolis: University of Minnesota Press, 2008), xxxv.
2. Bernard Bailyn, *Voyagers to the West: A Passage in the Peopling of America on the Eve of the Revolution* (New York: Random House, 1986), 26.
3. Maldwyn A. Jones, "The Scotch-Irish in British America," in *Strangers within the Realm: Cultural Margins of the First British Empire*, ed. Bernard Bailyn and Philip D. Morgan (Chapel Hill: University of North Carolina Press, 1991), 293; Cynthia Cumfer, *Separate Peoples, One Land: The Minds of Cherokees, Blacks, and Whites on the Tennessee Frontier* (Chapel Hill: University of North Carolina Press, 2007), 159.
4. Patrick Griffin, "Irish Migration to the Colonial South," in *Rethinking the Irish in the American South*, ed. Bryan Albin Giemza (Jackson: University of Mississippi Press, 2013), 53.
5. *IILC* 435–37; Charles Knowles Bolton, *Scotch Irish Pioneers in Ulster and America* (Boston: Bacon and Brown 1910), 106–8; Rory Fitzpatrick, *God's Frontiersmen: The Scots-Irish Epic* (London: Weidenfeld and Nicolson, 1989), 52–55; McGregor also in R. J. Dickson, *Ulster Emigration to Colonial America 1718–1775* (London: Routledge and Kegan Paul, 1966), 26–28; George H. Smyth, "The Scotch-Irish in New England," *Magazine of American History* 9 (March 1883), 153–67; Henry J. Ford, *The Scotch-Irish in America* (Princeton, NJ: Princeton University Press, 1915), ch. 7; Marsha L. Hamilton, "The Irish and the Formation of British Communities in Early Massachusetts," in *The Irish in the Atlantic World*, ed. David T. Gleeson (Columbia: University of South Carolina Press, 2010), 229–50.
6. Dickson, *Ulster Emigration to Colonial America*, 23; James G. Leyburn, *The Scotch-Irish: A Social History* (Chapel Hill: University of North Carolina Press, 1962), 17.
7. Bolton, *Scotch Irish Pioneers*, ch. 9; *Journals of the House of Representatives of Massachusetts, 1718–20* (Boston: Massachusetts Historical Society, 1921), 2:106, 172, 175.
8. *Collections of the Massachusetts Historical Society*, 6th series, 5 (1892), 387n; Ford, *Scotch-Irish in America*, 222–23.
9. Charles E. Clark, *The Eastern Frontier: The Settlement of Northern New England, 1610–1763* (New York: Alfred A. Knopf, 1970), 169–73.
10. Charles A. Hanna, *The Scotch-Irish, or the Scot in North Britain, North Ireland, and North America*, 2 vols. (New York: G. P. Putnam's Sons, 1902), 2: 17–24; Bolton, *Scotch Irish Pioneers*, ch. 10; Ford, *Scotch-Irish in America*, ch. 7; Leyburn, *Scotch-Irish*, 236–42; Richard Hofstadter, *America at 1750: A Social Portrait* (New York: Vintage Books, 1973), 25–27.
11. *Journals of the House of Representatives of Massachusetts, 1718–1720*, 2: 65, 83, 91–92, 104; Bolton, *Scotch Irish Pioneers*, ch. 11; names of the original 16 or 20 at 251–54; Rev. Edward L. Parker, *The History of Londonderry, N. H.* (Boston: Perkins and Whipple, 1851), 36–45; Leonard A. Morrison, *The History of Windham in New Hampshire (Rockingham County), 1719–1833, a Scotch Settlement (commonly called Scotch-Irish) embracing nearly one third of the ancient settlement and historic township of Londonderry, N.H, with the History and Genealogy of its First Settlers and their Descendants* (Boston: Cupples, Upham and Co., 1883), 23–25.
12. Clark, *Eastern Frontier*, 175–76, 188–90, 199; Ralph Stuart Wallace, "The Scotch-Irish of Provincial New Hampshire," Ph.D. diss., University of New Hampshire, 1984, ch. 5 (on the boundary issues); *IILC* 438; *Journals of the House of Representatives of Massachusetts, 1718–1720*: 134, 212, 288, 293–94, 315–16, 318, 321, 345; "Narrative of the People of Londonderry concerning their Boundaries," March 17, 1729/30, *Baxter Manuscripts: Documentary History*

of the State of Maine (Portland: Collections of the Maine Historical Society, second series, 1869–1916), 11: 18–20 (dispute with Haverhill); Parker, History of Londonderry, 56 (not wrested by force); IILC 437–39.
13. Gordon M. Day, The Identity of the St. Francis Indians (Ottawa: National Museum of Canada, 1981); Colin G. Calloway, The Western Abenakis of Vermont, 1600–1800: War, Migration, and the Survival of an Indian People (Norman: University of Oklahoma Press, 1990).
14. Wallace, "Scotch-Irish of Provincial New Hampshire," ch. 6 (growth); Parker, History of Londonderry, 46; Ford, Scotch-Irish in America, 237; IILC 439–40, 445 (Vaudreuil); Clark, Eastern Frontier, 196; Arthur Latham Perry, Scotch-Irish in New England (Boston: J. S. Cushing, 1891), 24; Diary of David McClure, 1748–1820, ed. Franklin B. Dexter (New York: Knickerbocker Press, 1899), 145. McClure's grandfather was Samuel McClure: Bolton, Scotch Irish, 169n.
15. IILC 67 (MacSparran), 128.
16. Wallace, "Scotch-Irish of Provincial New Hampshire," ch. 8; Clark, Eastern Frontier, 189–90, 206, 220–21, 239–44; The Diary of Matthew Patten of Bedford, N. H. (Concord, NH: Rumford Printing Co., 1903); IILC 547–59; Ford, Scotch-Irish in America, ch. 7; Smyth, "Scotch-Irish in New England," 164; Parker, History of Londonderry, 180–208; Morrison, History of Windham in New Hampshire; William Copeley, "Scotch-Irish Settlers in New Hampshire, 1719–1776," Historical New Hampshire 50 (1995), 213–28, provides a preliminary list of first-generation Scotch-Irish immigrants to New Hampshire before the Revolution. On Patten, see also Richard Lyman Bushman, The American Farmer in the Eighteenth Century: A Social and Cultural History (New Haven, CT: Yale University Press, 2018), 12–17.
17. Wallace, "Scotch-Irish of Provincial New Hampshire," chs. 9–10; Clark, Eastern Frontier, 227, 230; Parker, History of Londonderry, 48–49.
18. Philip Zea and Donald Dunlap, The Dunlap Cabinetmakers: A Tradition in Craftsmanship (Mechanicsburg, PA: Stackpole Books, 2007).
19. Calendar of State Papers, Colonial Series: America and West Indies, ed. W. Noel Sainsbury (London: Printed for H.M.S.O. by Eyre and Spottiswoode, 1889–1939), 42: 297, 313.
20. William Willis, "Scotch-Irish Immigration to Maine and a Summary History of Presbyterianism," Collections of the Maine Historical Society, 1st ser. 6 (1859), 1–37.
21. New England Historical and Genealogical Register, 32 (1878), 21–25; Michael O'Brien, Irish Settlers in America: A Consolidation of Articles from "The Journal of the American Irish Historical Society," 2 vols. (Baltimore, MD: Genealogical Publishing, 1979, 1993), 1: 109–10; IILC 129; Bolton, Scotch Irish Pioneers, 228–33 (list of people warned out from Boston).
22. James McGregor et al. to Duke of Newcastle and Robert Walpole, Boston, January 22, 1727. C.O. 5/898 part 1: 38.
23. Jeffers Lennox, Homelands and Empires: Indigenous Spaces, Imperial Fictions, and Competition for Territory in Northeastern North America, 1690–1763 (Toronto: University of Toronto Press, 2017), 88–90.
24. Lennox, Homelands and Empires, 90–93; C.O. 5/4 part 2: 8; C.O. 5/192, part 2: 19; C.O. 5/871, part 2: 3; Calendar of State Papers, America and the West Indies, 36: 628i, 630–31i, 705, 948, 1005; 37: 197, 215, 528; 38: 44; Baxter Manuscripts: Documentary History of the State of Maine, 10: 440 ("many hundred"), 466, 468–69; 11: 66–68, 86; Ian Saxine, Properties of Empire: Indians, Colonists, and Land Speculators on the New England Frontier (New York: New York University Press, 2019), 114–17.
25. Baxter Manuscripts: Documentary History of the State of Maine, 11: 44–46.
26. Baxter Manuscripts: Documentary History of the State of Maine, 10: 449.
27. Baxter Manuscripts: Documentary History of the State of Maine, 10: 442.
28. Baxter Manuscripts: Documentary History of the State of Maine, 10: 446–47.
29. Baxter Manuscripts: Documentary History of the State of Maine, 10: 458–68; 11: 5, 11. "They are a poor Miserable people," Dunbar informed the Duke of Newcastle, "having no settled habitations, & even their food uncertain, their dress is frightful and upon extraordinary Occasions they make themselves hideous with red paint, they clean their hands in their hair & make large holes thro their Ears in which they put scutts [sic] of hares, long feathers & long tobacco pipes."
30. Baxter Manuscripts: Documentary History of the State of Maine, 11: 41 (message), 77, 79.
31. C.O. 5/879: 8; Saxine, Properties of Empire, ch. 6.
32. Calendar of State Papers, America and the West Indies, 42: 375d.
33. IILC 129–30, 131–32.
34. IILC 68.

35. Richard Smith, *A Tour of Four Great Rivers: The Hudson, Mohawk, Susquehanna and Delaware in 1769*, ed. Francis W. Halsey (Port Washington, NY: Ira J. Friedman, 1964), lviii.
36. Leyburn, *Scotch-Irish*, 244.
37. Fintan O'Toole, *White Savage: William Johnson and the Invention of America* (New York: Farrar, Straus, and Giroux, 2005), 282–83, 303–13; *WJP* 8: 613–14.
38. Phyllis R. Blakeley, "McNutt, Alexander," in *Dictionary of Canadian Biography*, vol. 5, University of Toronto/Université Laval, 2003–, accessed September 22, 2022, http://www.biographi.ca/en/bio/mcnutt_alexander_5E.html; Sketch of Alexander McNutt, Draper 21U113–17; Dickson, *Ulster Emigration*, 53–54, 134–52; Joseph A. Waddell, *Annals of Augusta County, Virginia*, 2nd ed. (Staunton, VA: C. Russell Caldwell, 1902), 228–31; Thomas Peace, *The Slow Rush of Colonization: Spaces of Power in the Maritime Peninsula, 1680–1790* (Vancouver: UBC Press, 2023), 228–33.
39. Robert O'Driscoll and Lorena Reynolds, eds., *The Untold Story: The Irish in Canada*, 2 vols. (Toronto: Celtic Arts of Canada, 1988), 1: 186, 219–20; Donald Harman Akenson, "Irish Migration to North America, 1800–1920," in *The Irish Diaspora*, ed. Andy Bielenberg (Harlow, UK: Longmans, 2000), 121.
40. Edmund Burke, *An Account of the European Settlements in America*, First American Edition (Boston: Wilkins and Co. and Hillard, Gray, and Co., 1835), 274.
41. Jane T. Merritt, *At the Crossroads: Indians and Empires on a Mid-Atlantic Frontier, 1700–1763* (Chapel Hill: University of North Carolina Press, 2003), 25–28.
42. Leyburn, *Scotch-Irish*, 198–99.
43. Peter Silver, *Our Savage Neighbors: How Indian War Transformed Early America* (New York: W. W. Norton, 2008), 7.
44. Jean R. Soderlund, *Lenape Country: Delaware Valley Society before William Penn* (Philadelphia: University of Pennsylvania Press, 2015), 175. On Logan's manipulations and control of Indian trade and land titles, see Francis Jennings, "The Indian Trade of the Susquehanna Valley," *Proceedings of the American Philosophical Society* 110 (1966), 406–24. *Correspondence between William Penn and James Logan, secretary of the province of Pennsylvania, and others, 1700–1750*, 2 vols. (Philadelphia: Historical Society of Pennsylvania, 1870–1872), 1: liv (Indian guests); *Col. Recs. Penn.* 4: 580 ("fast friend").
45. Logan to James Steele, November 18, 1729, HSP, Penn Mss., Official Correspondence, 2: 101, and (slightly different version) Logan Family Papers, box 10, folder 47; also quoted in Leyburn, *Scotch-Irish*, 191–92; Wayland F. Dunaway, *The Scotch-Irish of Colonial Pennsylvania* (Chapel Hill: University of North Carolina Press, 1944; Baltimore, MD: Genealogical Publishing, 1979), 144.
46. Quoted in U. J. Jones, *History of the Early Settlement of the Juniata Valley* (Philadelphia: Henry B. Ashmead, 1856), 39.
47. Logan to the Penns, November 1 and December 15, 1725, HSP, Penn Mss., Official Correspondence, 1: 185; Allan Kulikoff, *From British Peasants to Colonial American Farmers* (Chapel Hill: University of North Carolina Press, 2000), 153 (Penn's prices), 159 (Paxton purchasers).
48. James Logan to John Penn, November 25, 1727, HSP, James Logan Letterbooks, vol. 6: 153–54 and in *Penn. Archives*, 2nd ser. 7: 96–97. See also Excerpts from Mrs. Logan's Copy Book, No. 5, James Logan Letterbooks, vol. 8: 148.
49. *Penn. Archives*, 2nd ser. 7: 132.
50. *Penn. Archives*, 1st ser. 1: 505–6. On the border conflict between Pennsylvania and Maryland, see Patrick Spero, *Frontier Country: The Politics of War in Early Pennsylvania* (Philadelphia: University of Pennsylvania Press, 2016), ch. 4; Patrick Spero, "The Conojocular War: The Politics of Colonial Competition, 1732–1737," *PMHB* 136 (2012), 365–403, and "Papers relating to the Boundary Dispute between Pennsylvania and Maryland, 1734–1760," *Penn. Archives*, 2nd ser. 7: 301–400. For more on Cresap and his family see Robert G. Parkinson, *Heart of American Darkness: Bewilderment and Horror on the Early Frontier* (New York: W. W. Norton, 2024).
51. Amy C. Schutt, *Peoples of the River Valleys: The Odyssey of the Delaware Indians* (Philadelphia: University of Pennsylvania Press, 2013), 83–84; Merritt, *At the Crossroads*, 19, 34–37; *The Scotch-Irish of Northampton County, Pennsylvania* (Easton, PA: The Northampton County Historical and Genealogical Society, 1926), 18–19, 46, 166, 221–22, 269–70; Rev. John C. Clyde, *Genealogies, Necrology, and Reminiscences of the "Irish Settlement," or A Record of those Scotch-Irish Presbyterians Families who were the First Settlers in the "Forks of the Delaware,"*

now Northampton County, Pennsylvania (published by the author, 1879), 18, 214; *The Journals of Henry Melchior Muhlenberg*, ed. Theodore G. Tappert and John W. Doberstein, 3 vols. (Philadelphia: Muhlenberg Press,1942), 3: 455.
52. Jack Brubaker, *Down the Susquehanna to the Chesapeake* (University Park: Pennsylvania State University Press, 2002), 227–29.
53. *Col. Recs. Penn.* 3: 274–76.
54. Logan to Captain Civility, August 19, 1727, HSP, James Logan Letterbooks, vol. 6: 106.
55. Burke, *Account of the European Settlements in America*, 279.
56. Hanna, *Scotch-Irish*, 2: 63; Leyburn, *Scotch-Irish*, 171; Logan to "Honoured Friend," June or August 13, 1729, HSP, Penn Mss., Official Correspondence, 2: 83, and James Logan Letterbooks, vol. 6: 304–5; Logan to John Penn, July 21, 1729, HSP, James Logan Letterbooks, vol. 6: 302–3.
57. Logan to John Wright and Blunston, July 2, 1730, HSP, Logan Family Papers, box 1, folder 95.
58. Spero, *Frontier Country*, 39.
59. Richard K. MacMaster, "Donegal Springs, Pennsylvania, 1720s–1730s," in *Ulster to America: The Scots-Irish Migration Experience, 1680–1830*, ed. Warren Hofstra (Knoxville: University of Tennessee Press, 2012), 51–76; *IILC* 143–44.
60. Logan to James Steele, November 18, 1729, HSP, Penn Family Papers, Official Correspondence, 2: 101; Logan to Thomas Penn, December 18 and 22, 1730, Penn Mss., Official Correspondence, 2: 145; Logan to Penns, November 14, 1731, Penn Mss., Official Correspondence, 2: 213; Leyburn, *Scotch-Irish*, 192.
61. *Penn. Archives*, 2nd ser. 7: 92–96.
62. *Penn. Archives*, 2nd ser. 7: 229–31, quote at 230.
63. Merritt, *At the Crossroads*, 171 (quote).
64. George W. Franz, *Paxton: A Study of Community Structure and Mobility in the Colonial Pennsylvania Backcountry* (New York: Garland, 1989), esp. ch. 5; Peters to Thomas Penn, February 2, 1763, HSP, Penn Mss. Official Correspondence, 9: 190. On squatter rights, practices, and improvements in one predominantly Scotch-Irish community in the Revolutionary era, see Marcus Gallo, "'Fair Play Has Entirely Ceased, and Law Has Taken Its Place': The Rise and Fall of the Squatter Republic on the West Branch of the Susquehanna River, 1768–1800," *PMHB* 136 (2012), 405–34.
65. HSP, Rhoda Barber, "Journal of Settlement at Wright's Ferry on the Susquehanna River" (1830), 5–6.
66. Ford, *Scotch-Irish in America*, 268.
67. Richard K. MacMaster, "Searching for Community: Carlisle, Pennsylvania, 1750s–1780s," in *Ulster to America: The Scots-Irish Migration Experience, 1680–1830*, ed. Warren Hofstra (Knoxville: University of Tennessee Press, 2012), 77; *IILC* 146 (5,000 and "handful"), 318–19 (Campble); Dunaway, *Scotch-Irish of Colonial Pennsylvania*, 59.
68. Brubaker, *Down the Susquehanna to the Chesapeake*, 140; Tim H. Blessing, "The Upper Juniata Valley," in *Beyond Philadelphia: The American Revolution in the Pennsylvania Hinterland*, ed. John B. Frantz and William Pencak (University Park: Pennsylvania State University Press, 1998), 153–54.
69. U. J. Jones, *History of the Early Settlement of the Juniata Valley* (Philadelphia: Henry B. Ashmead, 1856), 39.
70. Jones, *History of the Early Settlement of the Juniata Valley*, 91–92.
71. Guy S. Klett, "Scotch-Irish Presbyterian Pioneering along the Susquehanna River," *Pennsylvania History* 20 (1953), 170.
72. Jones, *History of the Early Settlement of the Juniata Valley*, 69, 76, 84, 91, 207; Blessing, "The Upper Juniata Valley," 156; Robert McKeen, "The Scotch-Irish of the Juniata Valley," *The Scotch-Irish in America: Proceedings of the Scotch-Irish Congress* 8 (1897), 110–29.
73. *Penn. Archives*, 1st ser. 1: 629–30.
74. *Penn. Archives*, 4th ser. 2: 159–60.
75. James T. Lemon, *The Best Poor Man's Country: A Geographical Study of Early Southeastern Pennsylvania* (Baltimore, MD: Johns Hopkins University Press, 1972), ch. 2, on settlement patterns of the various ethnic and religious groups, and 55 (settle before survey).
76. Franz, *Paxton*, 90, 99.
77. Figures from Peter C. Mancall, *Valley of Opportunity: Economic Culture along the Upper Susquehanna, 1700–1800* (Ithaca, NY: Cornell University Press, 1991), 73.
78. Franz, *Paxton*, 22–23. Map of growth at 23.

79. William Henry Egle, *History of the Counties of Dauphin and Lebanon in the Commonwealth of Pennsylvania* (Philadelphia: Everts and Peck, 1883), 31.
80. Wayland Fuller Dunaway, "Pennsylvania as an Early Distributing Center of Population," *PMHB* 55 (1931), 142.
81. Dunaway, "Pennsylvania as an Early Distributing Center," 142; Terry G. Jordan and Matti Kaups, *The American Backwoods Frontier: An Ethnic and Ecological Interpretation* (Baltimore, MD: Johns Hopkins University Press, 1989), 234–35; Ford, *Scotch-Irish in America*, 260–61; Leyburn, Scotch-Irish, 185; T. R. Fehrenbach, *Lone Star: A History of Texas and the Texans* (New York: Macmillan, 1968), 104.
82. Warren R. Hofstra, "Land Policy and Settlement in the Northern Shenandoah Valley," in *Appalachian Frontiers: Settlement, Society, and Development in the Preindustrial Era*, ed. Robert D. Mitchell (Lexington: University Press of Kentucky, 1991), 106.
83. Warren R. Hofstra, The Planting of New Virginia: Settlement and Landscape in the Shenandoah Valley (Baltimore: Johns Hopkins University Press, 2004); *IILC* 147.
84. Robert W. Ramsey, *Carolina Cradle: Settlement of the Northwest Carolina Frontier, 1747–1762* (Chapel Hill: University of North Carolina Press, 1964), 142–43.
85. Warren Hofstra, "Searching for Peace and Prosperity: Opequon Settlement, Virginia, 1730s–1760s, in *Ulster to America: The Scots-Irish Migration Experience, 1680–1830*, ed. Warren Hofstra (Knoxville: University of Tennessee Press, 2012), 105–22, esp. 108–10.
86. Samuel Kercheval, *A History of the Valley of Virginia*, 3rd ed. (Woodstock, VA: W. N. Grabill, 1902), 45; Parke Rouse, Jr., *The Great Philadelphia Wagon Road from Philadelphia to the South* (New York: McGraw-Hill, 1973); Warren R. Hofstra, "The Colonial Road," in *The Great Valley Road: Shenandoah Landscapes from Prehistory to the Present*, ed. Warren R. Hofstra and Karl Raitz (Charlottesville: University of Virginia Press, 2010), ch. 3; John Alexander Williams, *Appalachia: A History* (Chapel Hill: University of North Carolina Press, 2002), 48, 62; Bailyn, *Voyagers to the West*, 14.
87. Witham Marshe, *Journal of the Treaty of Lancaster in 1744 with the Six Nations* (Lancaster, PA, 1844), 10.
88. Williams, *Appalachia*, 62.
89. Waddell, *Annals of Augusta County*, 25–26.
90. Warren R. Hofstra, "Land, Ethnicity, and Community at the Opequon Settlement, Virginia, 1730–1800," *Virginia Magazine of History and Biography* 98 (1990), 423–48; Warren R. Hofstra and Robert D. Mitchell, "Town and Country in Backcountry Virginia: Winchester and the Shenandoah Valley," *Journal of Southern History* 59 (1993), 626; Warren R. Hofstra, "Ethnicity and Community Formation on the Shenandoah Valley Frontier, 1730–1800," in *Diversity and Accommodation: Essays on the Cultural Composition of the Virginia Frontier*, ed Michael J. Puglisi (Knoxville: University of Tennessee Press, 1997), ch. 2; Hofstra, Planting of New Virginia.
91. *Calendar of Virginia State Papers*, 1: 217.
92. Leyburn, *Scotch-Irish*, 203–6; Draper 21U37 (sketch of Patton).
93. Ramsey, *Carolina Cradle*, 143; Dunaway, "Pennsylvania as an Early Distributing Center," 143–46; *IILC* 153–54; Ron Chepesiuk, *The Scotch-Irish: From the North of Ireland to the Making of America* (Jefferson, NC: McFarland, 2000), 123; Fitzpatrick, *God's Frontiersmen*, 65; June Lee Mefford Kinkead, *Our Kentucky Pioneer Ancestry: A History of the Kinkead and McDowell Families of Kentucky and Those Families Associated by Marriage* (Baltimore, MD: Gateway Press, 1992), 13, 177–84; Joseph A. Waddell, "Scotch-Irish of the Valley of Virginia," in *The Scotch-Irish in America: Proceedings of the Scotch-Irish* 7 (1895), 82 (McDowell); Turk McClesky, "Rich Land, Poor Prospects: Real Estate and the Formation of a Social Elite in Augusta County, Virginia, 1738–1770," *Virginia Magazine of History and Biography* 98 (1990), 472–74 (McDowell family).
94. Charles E. Kemper, "The Settlement of the Valley," *Virginia Magazine of History and Biography* 30 (1922), 175–77, 179; Robert D. Mitchell, *Commercialism and Frontier: Perspectives on the Early Shenandoah Valley* (Charlottesville: University Press of Virginia, 1977), 43, 45; Robert D. Mitchell, "The Shenandoah Valley Frontier," *Annals of the Association of American Geographers* 62 (1972), 470–72.
95. *IILC* 381–400; Waddell, *Annals of Augusta County*, 48–51.
96. *IILC* 154; McClesky, "Rich Land, Poor Prospects," 449–86; Albert H. Tillson, Jr., *Gentry and Commonfolk: Political Culture on a Virginia Frontier, 1740–1789* (Lexington: University of Kentucky, 1991), chs. 2–3.

97. *William Byrd's Natural History of Virginia, or the Newly Discovered Eden*, ed. R. C. Beatty and W. J. Mulloy (Richmond, VA: Dietz Press, 1940), xxi–xxii; William Byrd, "Letters of the Byrd Family," *Virginia Magazine of History and Biography* 36 (1928), 354.
98. Leyburn, *Scotch-Irish*, 206–7.
99. Burke, *Account of the European Settlements in America*, 285.
100. *IILC* 62–63.
101. Leyburn, *Scotch-Irish*, 210.
102. Richard R. Beeman, *The Evolution of the Southern Backcountry: A Case Study of Lunenburg County, Virginia 1746-1832* (Philadelphia: University of Pennsylvania Press, 1984), 22, 56–58.
103. Rod Andrew, Jr., *The Life and Times of General Andrew Pickens* (Chapel Hill: University of North Carolina Press, 2017), 1–9.
104. Rev. William Henry Foote, *Sketches of North Carolina* (New York: Robert Carter, 1846), 77.
105. *NCCR* 5: 1214, 1225; Foote, *Sketches of North Carolina*, 78–79.
106. *NCCR* 4: 162–64.
107. Duane Meyer, *The Highland Scots of North Carolina, 1732-1776* (Chapel Hill: University of North Carolina Press, 1961), 90 (Mesopotamia), 101, 116–17.
108. *NCCR* 5: xl.
109. Harry Roy Merrins, *Colonial North Carolina in the Eighteenth Century: A Study in Historical Geography* (Chapel Hill: University of North Carolina Press, 1964), 53 (from 30,000–35,000 to 65,000–70,000, and then to 175,000–185,000), 63.
110. *NCCR* 4: xxi (figures) 1073 (overstocked); Marjoline Kars, *Breaking Loose Together: The Regulator Rebellion in Pre-Revolutionary North Carolina* (Chapel Hill: University of North Carolina Press, 2002), 15 ("Waggons by Land").
111. *NCCR* 4: 1148.
112. *NCCR* 5: 24.
113. Patrick Walsh, "Free Movement of People?: Responses to Emigration from Ireland, 1718-30," *Journal of Irish and Scottish Studies* 3 (2009), 223–28.
114. Leyburn, *Scotch-Irish*, 215.
115. *NCCR* 5: 149.
116. *NCCR* 5: 318.
117. *NCCR* 5: 353, 355–56; C.O. 5/297, part 2: 15.
118. Leyburn, *Scotch-Irish*, 172, 216; *NCCR* 5: 472.
119. *NCCR* 4: 1312. William Peters, Pennsylvania's provincial secretary, claimed that many of the people who migrated south did so "from a lazy disposition . . . because they can to the Southward support their stock all Winter without the trouble of providing Fodder in the Summer." Peters to Thomas Penn, February 2, 1763, HSP, Penn Mss. Official Correspondence, 9: 190.
120. Larry J. Hoefling, *Chasing the Frontier: Scots-Irish in Early America* (Lincoln, NE: iUniverse, 2005), 52–53, 55; Ramsey, *Carolina Cradle*, 36–37; map showing the original land grants and table listing the original grantees of the Irish and Trading Camp settlements, 1747–1762, 108–9; "Growth of the Irish Settlement, 1752–1767" (ch. 10), (117).
121. Bailyn, *Voyagers to the West*, 15.
122. *NCCR* 6: 1037.
123. *NCCR* 7: 248.
124. Quoted in Merrins, *Colonial North Carolina in the Eighteenth Century*, 59.
125. Peter N. Moore, *World of Toil and Strife: Community Transformation in Backcountry South Carolina, 1750-1805* (Columbia: University of South Carolina Press, 2007), 22, Appendix 2 at 115–17.
126. David Hackett Fischer, *Albion's Seed: Four British Folkways in North America* (New York: Oxford University Press, 1993), 760; maps of settlement patterns at Yadkin Forks and Catawba River, 761. Johann David Schoepf, *Travels in the Confederation*, 2 vols. (New York: Burt Franklin, 1968), 2: 103 said North Carolina farms were scattered in the woods and often 15–20 miles apart.
127. Moore, *World of Toil and Strife*, 19, 23–26.
128. Robert L. Meriwether, *The Expansion of South Carolina, 1729-1765* (Kingsport, TN: Southern Publishers, 1940), chs. 2, 7–11; Michael Montgomery, "Searching for Security: Backcountry Carolina, 1760s–1780s," in *Ulster to America: The Scots-Irish Migration Experience, 1680-1830*, ed. Warren Hofstra (Knoxville: University of Tennessee Press, 2012), 150; Moore, *World of Toil and Strife*, 27.
129. *IILC* 135–42 (quote at 139–40).

130. *The Colonial Records of South Carolina: The Journal of the Commons House of Assembly, 1736–1757*, 13 vols. (Columbia: Historical Commission of South Carolina, 1951–1989), 1736–1739: 430, 432–33, 439–40, 443, 457, 466–69, 471–72.
131. *The Colonial Records of South Carolina: The Journal of the Commons House of Assembly*, 1739–1741: 53–56, 124–25, 127, 131.
132. *The Colonial Records of South Carolina: The Journal of the Commons House of Assembly*, 1742–1744: 346–67.
133. *The Colonial Records of South Carolina: The Journal of the Commons House of Assembly*, 1744–1745: 36, 44–45.
134. *The Colonial Records of South Carolina: The Journal of the Commons House of Assembly*, 1749–1750: 317, 394, 396–97; 1752–1754: 106–7.
135. George Howe, D.D., *The Scotch-Irish, and their First Settlements on the Tyger River and Other Neighboring Precincts in South Carolina. A Centennial Discourse, delivered at Nazareth Church, Spartansburg District, S.C., September 14, 1861* (Columbia, SC: Southern Guardian Stem-Power Press, 1861).
136. Billy Kennedy, *The Scots-Irish in the Carolinas* (Belfast and Greenville, SC: Causeway Press, 1997), 21.
137. Hobert W. Burns, *The Life of Anne Calhoun Mathews* (Palo Alto, CA: privately published, 1988; in the South Caroliniana Library at the University of South Carolina; copy kindly provided by Todd Hoppock), 1–2, 23–24 (migrations and Colquhoun to Calhoun); A. S. Salley, Jr., "The Calhoun Family of South Carolina," *South Carolina Historical and Genealogical Magazine* 7 (April 1906), 83–84; Irving H. Bartlett, *John C. Calhoun: A Biography* (New York: W. W. Norton, 1993), 20–33. For a genealogical chart of the Calhouns of Long Canes, see Fischer, *Albion's Seed*, 648.
138. Kerby A. Miller, *Emigrants and Exiles: Ireland and the Irish Exodus to North America* (New York: Oxford University Press, 1985), 161; Moore, *World of Toil and Strife*, 51; Jean Stephenson, *Scotch-Irish Migration to South Carolina, 1772 (Rev. William Martin and His Five Shiploads of Settlers)* (Strasburg, VA: Shenandoah Publishing House, 1971), provides a 1772 list of people who applied for land grants. Robert L. Meriwether, *The Expansion of South Carolina, 1729–1765* (Kingsport, TN: Southern Publishers, 1940), 256, 260 ("entirely immigrants" from Northern Ireland); Maurice J. Bric, *Ireland, Philadelphia and the Re-invention of America, 1760–1800* (Dublin: Four Courts Press, 2008), cultural stamp at 32.
139. Richard K. MacMaster, *Scotch-Irish Merchants in Colonial America* (Newtonards, Northern Ireland: Ulster Heritage Foundation, 2009), ch. 6, esp. 143–46; Richard K. MacMaster, "From Ulster to the Carolinas: John Torrans, John Greg, John Poaug, and Bounty Emigration, 1761–1768," in *The Irish in the Atlantic World*, ed. David T. Gleeson (Columbia: University of South Carolina Press, 2010), 251–74.
140. Moore, *World of Toil and Strife*, 18 (229%); Dickson, *Ulster Emigration*, 57.
141. "The Letters of Hon. James Habersham, 1756–1775," *Collections of the Georgia Historical Society* 6 (1904), 184, 199, 201, 204.
142. Hanna, *Scotch-Irish*, vol. 2: front (map), ch. 5 (settlements listed); Lester J. Cappon et al., eds., *Atlas of Early American History: The Revolutionary Era, 1760–1790* (Princeton, NJ: Princeton University Press, 1976), 98; Bailyn, *Voyagers to the West*, 27; Jones, "Scotch-Irish in British America," 294; Leyburn, *Scotch-Irish*, 185; Fitzpatrick, *God's Frontiersmen*, 110–11 (map); Chepesiuk, *Scotch-Irish*, 122 (90%); Fischer, *Albion's Seed*, 636–37; Jordan and Kaups, *American Backwoods Frontier* (map).
143. Jordan and Kaups, *American Backwoods Frontier*, 221–22.

Chapter 3

1. Jonathan Swift and Thomas Sheridan, *The Intelligencer*, ed. James Woolley (Oxford: Clarendon Press, 1992), 211–12. Thanks to Benjamin Bankhurst, *Ulster Presbyterians and the Scots Irish Diaspora, 1750–1764* (New York: Palgrave Macmillan, 2013), 17, for directing me to Swift's comment.
2. Colin G. Calloway, *White People, Indians, and Highlanders: Tribal Peoples and Colonial Encounters in Scotland and America* (New York: Oxford University Press, 2008), ch. 4; Geoffrey Plank, "Deploying Tribes and Clans: Mohawks in Nova Scotia and Scottish Highlanders in Georgia," in *Empires and Indigenes: Intercultural Alliance, Imperial Expansion, and Warfare in the Early Modern World*, ed. Wayne E. Lee (New York: New York University Press, 2011), 221–49; Matthew P. Dziennik, *The Fatal Land: War, Empire, and the Highland Soldier in British*

America (New Haven, CT: Yale University Press, 2015); Wayne E. Lee, "Subjects, Clients, Allies, or Mercenaries?: The British Use of Irish and Amerindian Military Power, 1500–1800," in *Britain's Oceanic Empire: Atlantic and Indian Ocean Worlds, c. 1550–1850*, ed. H. V. Bowen, Elizabeth Mancke, and John G. Reid (Cambridge: Cambridge University Press, 2012), 179–217.

3. Lewis Evans, *Geographical, Historical, Political, Philosophical and Mechanical Essays. The First containing an Analysis of a General Map of the Middle British Colonies in America; And of the Country of the Confederate Indians...* (Philadelphia: B. Franklin and D. Hall, 1755), 11

4. On borderlands, see Joaquín Rivaya-Martínez, ed., *Indigenous Borderlands: Native Agency, Resilience, and Power in the Americas* (Norman: University of Oklahoma Press, 2023); Danna A. Levin Rojo and Cynthia Radding, eds., *The Oxford Handbook of Borderlands of the Iberian World* (New York: Oxford University Press, 2019); "lived spaces" at 1; Pekka Hämäläinen, "The Shapes of Power: Indians, Europeans, and North American Worlds from the Seventeenth Century to the Nineteenth Century," in *Contested Spaces of Early America*, ed. Juliana Barr and Edward Countryman (Philadelphia: University of Pennsylvania Press, 2014), 31–68; Brian DeLay, ed., *North American Borderlands* (New York: Routledge, 2013); Pekka Hämäläinen and Benjamin H. Jonson, eds., *Major Problems in the History of North American Borderlands* (Boston: Wadsworth Cengage Learning, 2012); Jeremy Adelman and Stephen Aron, "From Borderlands to Borders: Empires, Nation-States, and the Peoples in between in North American History," *American Historical Review* 104 (1999), 814–41; Evan Haefeli, "A Note on the Use of North American Borderlands," *American Historical Review* 104 (1999), 1222–25; John R. Wunder and Pekka Hämäläinen "Of Lethal Places and Lethal Essays," *American Historical Review* 104 (1999), 1229–34; Pekka Hämäläinen and Samuel Truett, "On Borderlands," *Journal of American History* 98 (2011), 338–61; Alan Taylor, *The Divided Ground: Indians, Settlers, and the Northern Borderland of the American Revolution* (New York: Alfred A. Knopf, 2006); Andrew K. Frank and A. Glenn Crothers, eds., *Borderland Narratives* (Gainesville: University Press of Florida, 2017); Jeffers Lennox, *Homelands and Empires: Indigenous Spaces, Imperial Fictions, and Competition for Territory in Northeastern North America, 1690–1763* (Toronto: University of Toronto Press, 2017); David G. McCrady, *Living with Strangers: The Nineteenth-Century Sioux and the Canadian-American Borderlands* (Lincoln: University of Nebraska Press, 2006); Benjamin Hoy, *A Line of Blood and Dirt: Creating the Canada-United States Border across Indigenous Lands* (New York: Oxford University Press, 2021); Elizabeth. N. Ellis, *The Great Power of Small Nations: Indigenous Diplomacy in the Gulf South* (Philadelphia: University of Pennsylvania Press, 2022).

5. An idea also explored in Ed White, *The Backcountry and the City: Colonization and Conflict in Early America* (Minneapolis: University of Minnesota Press, 2005); Ellis, *Great Power of Small Nations*.

6. E.g., Kristofer Ray, "Cherokees, Empire, and the Tennessee Corridor in the British Imagination, 1670–1730," in *Before the Volunteer State: New Thoughts on Early Tennessee, 1540–1800*, ed. Kristofer Ray (Knoxville: University of Tennessee Press, 2014), 35–63; and Ray, *Cherokees, Europeans, and Empire in the Trans-Appalachian West, 1670–1774* (Norman: University of Oklahoma Press, 2023).

7. Colin G. Calloway, *The Western Abenakis of Vermont: War, Migration, and the Survival of an Indian People, 1600–1800* (Norman: University of Oklahoma Press, 1990); Gordon M. Day, *The Identity of the St. Francis Indians* (Ottawa: National Museum of Man, 1981).

8. Timothy J. Shannon, *Iroquois Diplomacy on the Early American Frontier* (New York: Penguin, 2008), 68–73; Daniel K. Richter, *The Ordeal of the Longhouse: The Peoples of the Iroquois League in the Era of European Colonization* (Chapel Hill: University of North Carolina Press, 1992), 239 (Tuscarora numbers); David L. Preston, *The Texture of Contact: European and Indian Settler Communities on the Frontiers of Iroquoia, 1667–1783* (Lincoln: University of Nebraska Press, 2009); *Col. Recs. Penn.* 6: 116 ("invite all such to come").

9. Paul A. Raber, ed., *The Susquehannocks: New Perspectives on Settlement and Cultural Identity* (University Park: Pennsylvania State University Press, 2019); H. Frank Eshelman, *Annals of the Susquehannocks and Other Indian Tribes of Pennsylvania, 1500–1763* (1908; reprint, Lewisburg, PA: Wennawoods, 2000), part 1; Smith quotes at 8; Francis Jennings, "Susquehannock," in *Handbook of North American Indians*, Vol. 15: *Northeast*, ed. Bruce G. Trigger (Washington, DC: Smithsonian Institution Press, 1978), 362–67; Barry C. Kent, *Susquehannah's Indians* (Harrisburg: Pennsylvania Historical and Museum Commission, 1993), 26–29.

10. Matthew Kruer, *Time of Anarchy: Indigenous Power and the Crisis of Colonialism in Early America* (Cambridge, MA: Harvard University Press, 2021); Eshelman, *Annals of the Susquehannocks*; 37 (1,300 warriors), 39; 75 (300 warriors); Francis Jennings, *The Ambiguous Iroquois Empire: The Covenant Chain Confederation of Indian Tribes with English Colonies from Its Beginnings to the Lancaster Treaty of 1744* (New York: W. W. Norton, 1984), ch. 7; Kent, *Susquehannah's Indians*, 45–58; *EAID* 1: 232 (Penn quote); Jane T. Merritt, *At the Crossroads: Indians and Empires on a Mid-Atlantic Frontier, 1700–1763* (Chapel Hill: University of North Carolina Press, 2003), 23 ("Bulwarke" quote).
11. Kruer, *Time of Anarchy*.
12. *EAID* 1: 99, 107; John Smolenski, *Friends and Strangers: The Making of a Creole Culture in Colonial Pennsylvania* (Philadelphia: University of Pennsylvania Press, 2010), 200–4, 210–11.
13. Kent, *Susquehannah's Indians*, 70–78 (quote at 70).
14. C. A. Weslager, *The Delaware Indians: A History* (New Brunswick, NJ: Rutgers University Press, 1972), ch. 2; Amy C. Schutt, *Peoples of the River Valleys: The Odyssey of the Delaware Indians* (Philadelphia: University of Pennsylvania Press, 2007), ch. 1.
15. Jean R. Soderlund, *Lenape Country: Delaware Valley Society before William Penn* (Philadelphia: University of Pennsylvania Press, 2015).
16. Thomas J. Sugrue, "The Peopling and Depeopling of Early Pennsylvania: Indians and Colonists, 1680–1720," *PMHB* 116 (1992), 3–31, esp. 26–27.
17. Sugrue, "Peopling and Depeopling of Early Pennsylvania," quotes at 20–21; Howard Williams Lloyd, ed., "Philadelphia in 1698," *PMHB* 18 (1894), 247; Gabriel Thomas, "A Historical and Geographical Account of Pensilvania and of West New-Jersey" [1698], in *Narratives of Early Pennsylvania, West Jersey and Delaware, 1630–1707*, ed. Albert Cook Myers (New York: Scribners, 1912), 344.
18. Weslager, *Delaware Indians*, 192–93; Schutt, *Peoples of the River Valleys*, 64–65; Kevin Kenny, *Peaceable Kingdom Lost: The Paxton Boys and the Destruction of William Penn's Holy Experiment* (New York: Oxford University Press, 2009), 20.
19. Sugrue, "Peopling and Depeopling of Early Pennsylvania," 28; *EAID* 1: 303.
20. The Shawnees traditionally comprised five divisions, although it is not certain whether these divisions originally constituted different tribes, which came together to form the Shawnees, or if they developed during their migrations. Each division came to have specific responsibilities. The Chillicothe and Thawekila divisions took care of political affairs affecting the whole tribe and generally supplied tribal political leaders; the Mekoches were concerned with health and medicine and provided healers and counselors; the Pekowis were responsible for matters of religion and ritual, and the Kispokos generally took the lead in preparing and training for war and supplying war chiefs. These divisions seem to have functioned as semi-autonomous political units, each with their own chief. They moved together, occupied particular towns (often named after the division), possessed their own sacred bundles, and sometimes conducted their own foreign policies with other tribes. Thomas Wildcat Alford, *Civilization and the Story of the Absentee Shawnees* (Norman: University of Oklahoma Press, 1936), 44; Vernon Kinietz and Erminie W. Voegelin, eds., *Shawnese Traditions: C. C. Trowbridge's Account* (Ann Arbor: University of Michigan, 1939), 16–17.
21. Reuben G. Thwaites, ed., *The Jesuit Relations and Allied Documents*, 73 vols. (Cleveland: Burrows Bros, 1896–1901), 59: 144–45; James H. Howard, *Shawnee!: The Ceremonialism of a Native American Tribe and Its Cultural Background* (Athens: Ohio University Press, 1981), 5.
22. On the southeastern Indian slave trade and the fluctuating fortunes of the participants, see Paul Kelton, *Epidemics and Enslavement: Biological Catastrophe in the Native Southeast, 1492–1715* (Lincoln: University of Nebraska Press, 2007).
23. Stephen Warren, *The Worlds the Shawnees Made: Migration and Violence in Early America* (Chapel Hill: University of North Carolina Press, 2014), chs. 6–7; Sami Lakomäki, *Gathering Together: The Shawnee People through Diaspora and Nationhood, 1600–1870* (New Haven, CT: Yale University Press, 2014), chs. 1–2, "living promiscuously" quote at 30; Charles A. Hanna, *The Wilderness Trail; or, The Ventures and Adventures of the Pennsylvania Traders on the Allegheny Path*, 2 vols. (New York: G. P. Putnam's Sons, 1911), 1: 18 (settled in 1699 quote); *Correspondence between William Penn and James Logan, secretary of the province of Pennsylvania, and others, 1700–1750*, 2 vols. (Philadelphia: Historical Society of Pennsylvania, 1870–1872), 2: 83 (Shawanois and Ganawois).

24. Joseph E. Johnson, ed., "A Quaker Imperialist's View of the British Colonies in America: 1732," *PMHB* 60 (1936), 97–130, esp. 107 (reservation) and 124 (Jealous Eye quote). Although the copy of the memorial is in Benjamin Franklin's handwriting, authorship is attributed to Logan.
25. Peter C. Mancall, *Valley of Opportunity: Economic Culture along the Upper Susquehanna, 1700–1800* (Ithaca, NY: Cornell University Press, 1991), 32–39; Barry C. Kent, Ira F. Smith, and Catherine McCann, "A Map of 18th Century Indian Towns in Pennsylvania," *Pennsylvania Archaeologist* 51, no. 4 (1981), 1–18.
26. James H. Merrell, "Shamokin, 'the very seat of the Prince of darkness': Unsettling the Early American Frontier," in *Contact Points: American Frontiers from the Mohawk Valley to the Mississippi, 1750–1830*, ed. Andrew R. L. Cayton and Fredricka J. Teute (Chapel Hill: University of North Carolina Press, 1998), 16–59; Hanna, *Wilderness Trail*, 1: 195–96 (Brainerd); Jack Brubaker, *Down the Susquehanna to the Chesapeake* (University Park: Pennsylvania State University Press, 2002), 122 (routes); Kent, *Susquehanna's Indians*, 100 ("veritable capital").
27. Shannon, *Iroquois Diplomacy on the Early American Frontier*; Richard Aquila, *Iroquois Restoration: Iroquois Diplomacy on the Colonial Frontier, 1701–1754* (Lincoln: University of Nebraska Press, 1983); *Calendar of State Papers, America and the West Indies*, 1714–1715: 345; quoted in Jennings, *Ambiguous Iroquois Empire*, xvi.
28. Shannon, *Iroquois Diplomacy on the Early American Frontier*, 69–70.
29. *Col. Recs. Penn.* 3: 99–100.
30. *Penn. Archives*, 1st ser. 1: 322–33.
31. *Col. Recs. Penn.* 4: 90 ("one people"); *EAID* 1: 311 ("absolute Authority"), 428 ("one people"); Paul Wallace, *Indians in Pennsylvania* (Harrisburg: Pennsylvania Historical and Museum Commission, 1961), 144 ("strengthen the hands"); Jennings, *Ambiguous Empire*, 323; Weslager, *Delaware Indians*, 182–84; Richard S. Grimes, *The Western Delaware Indian Nation, 1730–1795* (Bethlehem, PA: Lehigh University Press, 2017), 70.
32. Merritt, *At the Crossroads*, 5–6.
33. *EAID* 1: 431; *Col. Recs. Penn.* 4: 93.
34. Shannon, *Iroquois Diplomacy*, 111.
35. *David Zeisberger's History of the North American Indian*, ed. Archer Butler Hulbert and William N. Schwarz (Columbus: Ohio State Archaeological and Historical Society, 1910), 34–35; Gunlög Fur, *A Nation of Women: Gender and Colonial Encounters among the Delaware Indians* (Philadelphia: University of Pennsylvania Press, 2009); Roger M. Carpenter, "From Indian Women to English Children: The Lenni-Lenape and the Attempt to Create a New Diplomatic Identity," *Pennsylvania History* 74 (2007), 1–20.
36. *EAID* 1: 455–59; *WJP* 3: 795–818; Rev. John C. Clyde, *Genealogies, Necrology, and Reminiscences of the "Irish Settlement," or A Record of those Scotch-Irish Presbyterians Families who were the First Setters in the "Forks of the Delaware," now Northampton County, Pennsylvania* (published by the author, 1879), 217–25.
37. *EAID* 2: 24.
38. *EAID* 2: 24–25; Weslager, *Delaware Indians*, 187–91.
39. *Col. Recs. Penn.*, 4: 575–76, 579–80; *EAID* 2: 45–46; 3: 313.
40. *EAID* 3: 149.
41. *EAID* 3: 154.
42. Michael N. McConnell, "Before the Great Road: Indian Travelers on the Great Warriors' Path," in *The Great Valley Road: Shenandoah Landscapes from Prehistory to the Present*, ed. Warren R. Hofstra and Karl Raitz (Charlottesville: University of Virginia Press, 2010), ch. 2; William N. Fenton, *The Great Law and the Longhouse: A Political History of the Iroquois Confederacy* (Norman: University of Oklahoma Press, 1998), 404; *EAID* 3: 640 ("since we were created"); James H. Merrell, "'Their Very Bones Shall Fight': The Catawba-Iroquois War," in *Beyond the Covenant Chain: The Iroquois and Their Neighbors in Indian North America, 1600–1800*, ed. Daniel K. Richter and James H. Merrell (Syracuse, NY: Syracuse University Press, 1987), 115–33.
43. Witham Marshe, *Journal of the Treaty of Lancaster in 1744 with the Six Nations* (Lancaster, PA, 1844), 10.
44. *Penn. Archives*, 4th ser. 1: 841–42.
45. Patrick Spero, *Frontier Country: The Politics of War in Early Pennsylvania* (Philadelphia: University of Pennsylvania Press, 2016), 107.

46. James H. Merrell, ed., *The Lancaster Treaty of 1744 with Related Documents* (Boston: Bedford/St. Martin's, 2008); "List of Indians present at Treaty of Lancaster," *Penn. Archives*, 1st ser. 1: 656–57.
47. *EAID* 2: 147.
48. *EAID* 2: 204; *Col. Recs. Penn.* 5: 399–400.
49. Mancall, *Valley of Opportunity*, 69–74.
50. *Penn. Archives*, 4th ser. 1: 7: 846; Kent, *Susquehanna's Indians*, 75–77.
51. *EAID* 2: 204–05; *Col. Recs. Penn.* 5: 399–401.
52. *Col. Recs. Penn.* 4: 570, 572; 5: 389, 394–95, 431, 440–49; Richard Peters to the Proprietors, May 5, 1750, HSP, Penn Mss., Official Correspondence, 5: 3–7 ("vile people"; "appearance of the Indians," and get the Indians to burn the cabins); David L. Preston, "Squatters, Indians, Proprietary Government, and Land in the Susquehanna Valley," in *Friends and Enemies in Penn's Woods: Indians, Colonists, and the Racial Construction of Pennsylvania*, ed. William A. Pencak and Daniel K. Richter (University Park: Pennsylvania State University Press, 2004), 195–97; Kenny, *Peaceable Kingdom Lost*, 50–51. For more on Shikellamy's sons, see Robert G. Parkinson, *Heart of American Darkness: Bewilderment and Horror on the Early Frontier* (New York: W. W. Norton, 2024).
53. *Col. Recs. Penn.* 5: 440–49.
54. *Col. Recs. Penn.* 5: 479.
55. Judith Ridner, *A Town In-Between: Carlisle, Pennsylvania, and the Early Mid-Atlantic Frontier* (Philadelphia: University of Pennsylvania Press, 2010), 49.
56. Peters to Proprietors, March 16, 1752, HSP, Penn Mss., Official Correspondence, 5: 217–20.
57. Preston, "Squatters, Indians, Proprietary Government, and Land in the Susquehanna Valley," 193–94, 197–98.
58. Schutt, *Peoples of the River Valleys*, 101.
59. Schutt, *Peoples of the River Valleys*, 104.
60. Grimes, *Western Delaware Indian Nation*.
61. *Col. Recs. Penn.* 3: 403.
62. *EAID* 1: 336, 338–39, 363–66, quotes at 366.
63. Michael N. McConnell, *A Country Between: The Upper Ohio Valley and Its Peoples, 1724–1774* (Lincoln: University of Nebraska Press, 1992), chs. 1–5; Richard White, *The Middle Ground: Indians, Empires, and Republics in the Great Lakes Region, 1650–1815* (Cambridge: Cambridge University Press, 1991), ch. 5; Cayuga quote in *NYCD* 10: 206.
64. Archibald Loudon, *A Selection of Some of the Most Interesting Narratives, of Outrages, Committed by the Indians, in Their Wars with the White People*, 2 vols. (Carlisle: A. Loudon, 1808), 1: 284.
65. Correspondence and Papers of Governor General Sir Frederick Haldimand, 1758–1791, British Museum, London, Additional Manuscripts, 21782: 302.
66. Tom Hatley, *The Dividing Paths: Cherokees and South Carolinians through the Era of Revolution* (New York: Oxford University Press, 1993), ch. 6; Ray, "Cherokees, Empire, and the Tennessee Corridor in the British Imagination, 1670–1730," 35–63; Nairne quote at 43; Bladen quote at 47; Ray, *Cherokees, Europeans, and Empire*, ch. 2.
67. Samuel Cole Williams, ed., *Adair's History of the American Indians* (London, 1775; New York: Promontory Press, 1930), 239.
68. Tyler Boulware, "'It Seems like Coming into Our Houses': Challenges to Cherokee Hunting Grounds, 1750–1775," in *Before the Volunteer State: New Thoughts on Early Tennessee, 1540–1800*, ed. Kristofer Ray (Knoxville: University of Tennessee Press, 2014), 65–81.
69. Gregory D. Smithers, *The Cherokee Diaspora: An Indigenous History of Migration, Resettlement, and Identity* (New Haven, CT: Yale University Press, 2015).
70. Daniel J. Tortora, *Carolina in Crisis: Cherokees, Colonists, and Slaves in the American Southeast, 1756–1763* (Chapel Hill: University of North Carolina Press, 2015), 26; Ray, *Cherokees, Europeans, and Empire*; Colin. G. Calloway, *"The Chiefs Now in This City": Indians and the Urban Frontier in Early America* (New York: Oxford University Press, 2021), 82–84.
71. *NCCR* 5: 214–15.
72. Wilbur R. Jacobs, ed., *The Appalachian Indian Frontier: The Edmond Atkin Report and Plan of 1755* (Lincoln: University of Nebraska Press, 1967), 3–4.
73. James H. Merrell, *The Indians' New World: Catawbas and Their Neighbors from European Contact through the Era of Removal* (Chapel Hill: University of North Carolina Press, 1989); Brooke M. Bauer, *Becoming Catawba: Catawba Indian Women and Nation-Building, 1540–1840* (Tuscaloosa: University of Alabama Press, 2023), ch. 2; Blair A. Rudes, Thomas J. Blumer, and

J. Alan May, "Catawba and Neighboring Groups," in *Handbook of North American Indians*, Vol. 14: *Southeast*, ed. Raymond D. Fogelson (Washington, DC: Smithsonian Institution, 2004), 301–18; Mary Elizabeth Fitts, *Fit for War: Sustenance and Order in the Mid-Eighteenth-Century Catawba Na*tion (Gainesville: University of Florida Press, 2017), esp. chs. 3–4; Williams, *Adair's History of the American Indians*, 235; Robert L. Meriwether, *The Expansion of South Carolina, 1729–1765* (Kingsport, TN: Southern Publishers, 1940), 13 (frontier garrison).
74. Peter N. Moore, *World of Toil and Strife: Community Transformation in Backcountry South Carolina, 1750–1805* (Columbia: University of South Carolina Press, 2007), 17.
75. Fitts, *Fit for War*, 113: *NCCR* 5: 124.
76. Merrell, *Indians' New World*, 134–43.
77. *NCCR*, 5: xlvii; see also John F. D. Smyth, *A Tour in the United States of America: containing an account of the present situation of that country; the population, agriculture, commerce, customs, and manners of the inhabitants; with a description of the Indian nations, ...*, 2 vols. (London: Printed for G. Robinson, 1784), 1: 184–95; Bauer, *Becoming Catawba*, 141–46.

Chapter 4

1. *A Tribute to the Memory of Peter Collinson. With some notice of Dr. Darlington's Memorials of John Bartram and Humphry Marshall* (Philadelphia: William H. Michell, 1851), 28; also, *The Correspondence of John Bartram, 1734–1777*, ed. Edmund Berkeley and Dorothy Smith Berkeley (Miami: University Press of Florida, 1992), 400.
2. Rory Fitzpatrick, *God's Frontiersmen: The Scots-Irish Epic* (London: Weidenfeld and Nicolson, 1989), 71 (quote).
3. David L. Preston, "Squatters, Indians, Proprietary Government, and Land in the Susquehanna Valley," in *Friends and Enemies in Penn's Woods: Indians, Colonists, and the Racial Construction of Pennsylvania*, ed. William A. Pencak and Daniel K. Richter (University Park: Pennsylvania State University Press, 2004), 190.
4. *Penn. Archives*, 1st ser. 1: 750–51; *EAID* 2: 155, 479n.
5. Elizabeth Elbourne, *Empire, Violence, and Kinship: Family Histories, Indigenous Rights and the Making of Settler Colonialism, 1770–1842* (Cambridge: Cambridge University Press, 2023); Joshua A. McGonagle Altoff, "Managing Settlers, Managing Neighbors: Renarrating *Johnson v. McIntosh* through the History of Piankashaw Community Building," *Journal of American History* 100 (2024), 625-42, describes these practices as "neighbor management."
6. *EAID* 2: 322, 328–29, 480n (Shikellamy); "Journal of James Kenny, 1761–1763," ed. John W. Jordan, *PMHB* 37 (1913), 12, 42, 192, (Armstrong); *Col. Recs. Penn.* 8: 489 (McKee). According to Robert Parkinson, Shikellamy honored James Logan by giving his name to two of his sons. Robert G. Parkinson, *Heart of American Darkness: Bewilderment and Horror on the Early Frontier* (New York: W. W. Norton, 2024), xix.
7. C.O. 323/17: 266 (Stuart).
8. "A Narrative of the Captivity of Mrs. Johnson," in *North Country Captives: Selected Narratives of Captivity from Vermont and New Hampshire*, ed. Colin G. Calloway (Hanover, NH: University Press of New England, 1992), 48.
9. David L. Preston, *The Texture of Contact: European and Indian Settler Communities on the Frontiers of Iroquoia, 1667–1783* (Lincoln: University of Nebraska Press, 2009), 2–5; Preston, "Squatters, Indians, Proprietary Government, and Land in the Susquehanna Valley," 185, 188.
10. Jane T. Merritt, *At the Crossroads: Indians and Empires on a Mid-Atlantic Frontier, 1700–1763* (Chapel Hill: University of North Carolina Press, 2003), 49.
11. Melissah J. Pawlikowski, "The Plight and the Bounty: Squatters, War Profiteers, and the Transforming Hand of Sovereignty in Indian Country, 1750–1774," Ph.D. diss., Ohio State University, 2014.
12. Francis Jennings, *The Ambiguous Iroquois Empire: The Covenant Chain Confederation of Indian Tribes with English Colonies from Its Beginnings to the Lancaster Treaty of 1744* (New York: W. W. Norton, 1984), 350.
13. Merritt, *At the Crossroads*, 93.
14. Jonathan Edwards, *The Life of Rev. David Brainerd, Chiefly Extracted from His Diary* (Grand Rapids, MI: Baker Book House, 1978), 93.
15. Alison Duncan Hirsch, "Indians, *Métis*, and Euro-American Women on Multiple Frontiers," in *Friends and Enemies in Penn's Woods: Indians, Colonists, and the Racial Construction of Pennsylvania*, ed. William A. Pencak and Daniel K. Richter (University Park: Pennsylvania State University Press, 2004), 79, 84. James H. Merrell, "The Other 'Susquehannah Traders': Women

NOTES 435

and Exchange on the Pennsylvania Frontier," in *Cultures and Identities in Colonial British America*, ed. Robert Olwell and Alan Tully (Baltimore, MD: Johns Hopkins University Press, 2006), 197–219; "in droves" at 204.

16. E. Estyn Evans, "The Scotch-Irish: Their Cultural Adaptation and Heritage in the American Old West," in *Essays in Scotch-Irish History*, ed. E. R. R. Green (1969; reprint, Belfast: Ulster Historical Foundation, 1992), 69–86; John B. Rehder, *Appalachian Folkways* (Baltimore, MD: Johns Hopkins University Press, 2004), 224–29; John F. D. Smyth, *A Tour in the United States of America: containing an account of the present situation of that country; the population, agriculture, commerce, customs, and manners of the inhabitants; with a description of the Indian nations,* . . . 2 vols. (London: Printed for G. Robinson, 1784), 1: 179–83.

17. Susan Sleeper-Smith, *Indigenous Prosperity and American Conquest: Indian Women of the Ohio River Valley, 1690–1792* (Chapel Hill: University of North Carolina Press, 2018), ch. 1; Jane Mt. Pleasant, "The Paradox of Plows and Productivity: An Agronomic Comparison of Cereal Grain Production under Iroquois Hoe Culture and European Plow Culture in the Seventeenth and Eighteenth Centuries," *Agricultural History* 85 (2011), 487–88.

18. Smyth, *A Tour in the United States of America*, 1: 292; James T. Lemon, *The Best Poor Man's Country: A Geographical Study of Early Southeastern Pennsylvania* (Baltimore, MD: Johns Hopkins University Press, 1972), 31–32, 40; Harriette Simpson Arnow, *Seedtime on the Cumberland* (New York: Macmillan, 1960), 322–24 (dependence on corn); John Alexander Williams, *Appalachia: A History* (Chapel Hill: University of North Carolina Press, 2002), 118.

19. Maldwyn A. Jones, "The Scotch-Irish in British America," in *Strangers within the Realm: Cultural Margins of the First British Empire*, ed. Bernard Bailyn and Philip D. Morgan (Chapel Hill: University of North Carolina Press, 1991), 300–1; Timothy Silver, *A New Face on the Countryside: Indians, Colonists, and Slaves in South Atlantic Forests, 1500–1800* (Cambridge: Cambridge University Press, 1990), 105; James G. Leyburn, *The Scotch-Irish: A Social History* (Chapel Hill: University of North Carolina Press, 1962), 206; H. Tyler Blethen and Curtis W. Wood, Jr., *From Ulster to Carolina: The Migration of the Scotch-Irish to Southwestern North Carolina* (Raleigh: North Carolina Department of Cultural Resources, Division of Archives and History, 1998), 40, 44–45, 59; Warren R. Hofstra, "Land Policy and Settlement in the Northern Shenandoah Valley," in *Appalachian Frontiers: Settlement, Society, and Development in the Preindustrial Era*, ed. Robert D. Mitchell (Lexington: University Press of Kentucky, 1991), 114; Harry Roy Merrins, *Colonial North Carolina in the Eighteenth Century: A Study in Historical Geography* (Chapel Hill: University of North Carolina Press, 1964), 192–93; *IILC* 215 (Joseph Wright, writing home to parents in County Wexford from Ohio in 1803); Williams, *Appalachia*, 104, quoting Logan to Thomas Penn, October 19, 1730, HSP, Thomas Penn Papers.

20. David Hackett Fischer, *Albion's Seed: Four British Folkways in North America* (New York: Oxford University Press, 1993), 668, 765–71.

21. Fischer, *Albion's Seed*, 681, 734; Samuel Kercheval, *A History of the Valley of Virginia* (3rd ed., 1833), 257; Joseph Doddridge, *The Settlement and Indian Wars of the Western Parts of Virginia and Pennsylvania, 1763–1783* (Pittsburgh, 1912; reprint, Bowie, MD: Heritage Books, 1988), 92–93, and extract from Doddridge in *The Olden Time: A Monthly Publications devoted to the Preservation of Documents and other Authentic Information in relation to the Early Explorations and the Settlement and Improvement of the Country around the Head of the Ohio*, ed. Neville B. Craig, 2 vols. (1848; reprint, Cincinnati: Robert Clarke & Co., 1876), 1: 141–42.

22. Terry G. Jordan and Matti Kaups, *The American Backwoods Frontier: An Ethnic and Ecological Interpretation* (Baltimore, MD: Johns Hopkins University Press, 1989), esp. 118, and 233.

23. Fischer, *Albion's Seed*, 655–61; Jordan and Kaups, *American Backwoods Frontier*, chs. 6–7; Rehder, *Appalachian Folkways*, 79–81.

24. J. Hector St. John de Crèvecoeur, *Letters from an American Farmer* (London: J. M. Dent, 1971), 52.

25. *The Papers of George Washington: Colonial Series*, ed. W. W. Abbot, Dorothy Twohig, et al., 10 vols. (Charlottesville: University Press of Virginia, 1983–1995), 1: 43–44; see also Warren R. Hofstra, "'A Parcel of Barbarians and an Uncouth Set of People': Settlers and Settlements of the Shenandoah Valley," in *George Washington and the Virginia Backcountry*, ed. Warren R. Hofstra (Madison, WI: Madison House, 1998), 87–114.

26. George W. Franz, *Paxton: A Study of Community Structure and Mobility in the Colonial Pennsylvania Backcountry* (New York: Garland, 1989), 108.

27. Wayland F. Dunaway, *The Scotch-Irish of Colonial Pennsylvania* (Chapel Hill: University of North Carolina Press, 1944), 178.
28. Charles A. Hanna, *The Wilderness Trail, or The Ventures and Adventures of the Pennsylvania Traders on the Allegheny Path*, 2 vols. (New York: G. P. Putnam's Sons, 1911), 1: 177–78; *Collections of the Michigan Pioneer and Historical Society* 19 (1892), 683.
29. Preston, "Squatters, Indians, Proprietary Government, and Land in the Susquehanna Valley," 184–85.
30. *Penn. Archives*, 1st ser. 1: 425.
31. *EAID* 3: 416.
32. Jean Lowery, *A Journal of the Captivity of Jean Lowery and Her Children* (Philadelphia: William Bradford, 1760), 13; Jane T. Merritt, "Metaphor, Meaning, and Misunderstanding: Language and Power on the Pennsylvania Frontier," in *Contact Points: American Frontiers from the Mohawk Valley to the Mississippi, 1750–1830*, ed. Andrew R. L. Cayton and Fredricka J. Teute (Chapel Hill: University of North Carolina Press, 1998), 60–87.
33. *Penn. Archives*, 1st ser. 2: 219; *Col. Recs. Penn.* 6:149.
34. Patrick Griffin, *The People with No Name: Ireland's Ulster Scots, America's Scots Irish, and the Creation of a British Atlantic World, 1689–1764* (Princeton, NJ: Princeton University Press, 2001), 113.
35. Griffin, *People with No Name*, 114 (quoting John McAlister to Richard Peters, March 28, 1754, HSP, Lamberton Scotch-Irish Collection, I: 15), 166.
36. Richard K. MacMaster, "Donegal Springs, Pennsylvania, 1720s–1730s," in *Ulster to America: The Scots-Irish Migration Experience, 1680–1830*, ed. Warren Hofstra (Knoxville: University of Tennessee Press, 2012), 65–67.
37. H. Tyler Blethen and Curtis Wood, "A Trader on the Carolina Frontier," in *Appalachian Frontiers: Settlement, Society, and Development in the Preindustrial Era*, ed. Robert D. Mitchell (Lexington: University Press of Kentucky, 1991), 150–65; Jerome H. Wood, Jr., *Conestoga Crossroads: Lancaster, Pennsylvania, 1730–1790* (Harrisburg: Pennsylvania Historical and Museum Commission, 1979), 115–16.
38. Judith Ridner, *A Town In-Between: Carlisle, Pennsylvania, and the Early Mid-Atlantic Frontier* (Philadelphia: University of Pennsylvania Press, 2010); Richard K. MacMaster, "Searching for Community: Carlisle, Pennsylvania, 1750s–1780s," in *Ulster to America: The Scots-Irish Migration Experience, 1680–1830*, ed. Warren Hofstra (Knoxville: University of Tennessee Press, 2012), 83–85; Richard K. MacMaster, *Scotch-Irish Merchants in Colonial America* (Belfast: Ulster Historical Foundation, 2009), 110–12; *The Diary of David McClure, 1748–1820*, ed. Franklin B. Dexter (New York: Knickerbocker Press, 1899), 36.
39. The treaty is in *EAID* 2: 282–301.
40. Larry L. Nelson, *A Man of Distinction among Them: Alexander McKee and British-Indian Affairs along the Ohio Country Frontier, 1754–1799* (Kent, OH: Kent State University Press, 1999), 24–28; *EAID* 2: 218 ("Indian Wench"); "Deposition of Thomas McKee," *Col. Recs. Penn.* 4: 630; "Bishop J. C. F. Cammerhoff's Narrative of a Journey to Shamokin, Penna., in the Winter of 1748," ed. John W. Jordan, *PMBH* 29 (1905), 167, 169.
41. Samuel Cole Williams, ed., *Adair's History of the American Indians* (London, 1775; reprint, New York: Promontory Press, 1930), "most of the pages" at xxxv.
42. *EAID* 13: 331, 398n; James H. Merrell, *The Indians' New World: Catawbas and Their Neighbors from European Contact through the Era of Removal* (New York: W. W. Norton, 1989), 85–87, 137; Ian Watson, "Catawba Indian Genealogy," *Papers in Anthropology*, no. 4 (Department of Anthropology, State University of New York at Geneseo, 1995), 17 (will); Brooke M. Bauer, *Becoming Catawba: Catawba Indian Women and Nation-Building, 1540–1840* (Tuscaloosa: University of Alabama Press, 2023), 63–64.
43. Michael Montgomery, "Searching for Security: Backcountry Carolina, 1760s–1780s," in *Ulster to America: The Scots-Irish Migration Experience, 1680–1830*, ed. Warren Hofstra (Knoxville: University of Tennessee Press, 2012), 151–60; will at 158–60; Bryan C. Rindfleisch, *George Galphin's Intimate Empire: The Creek Indians, Family, and Colonialism in Early America* (Tuscaloosa: University of Alabama Press, 2019); Michael P. Morris, "Profits and Philanthropy: The Ulster Immigration Schemes of George Galphin and John Rae," *Journal of Scotch-Irish Studies* 1 (2002), 1–11; R. J. Dickson, *Ulster Emigration to Colonial America 1718–1775* (London: Routledge and Kegan Paul, 1966), 164–73 (on Matthew Rae); *DAR* 11: 164 (Stuart on Galphin).

44. James E. Doan, "How the Irish and Scots Became Indians: Colonial Traders and Agents and the Southeastern Indian Tribes," *New Hibernia Review* 3 (Autumn 1999), 9–19; Michael Toomey, "Children of Two Clans," *Journal of Scotch-Irish Studies* 3, no. 1 (2009), 39–51; Michelle LeMastre, *Brothers Born of One Mother: British-Native American Relations in the Colonial Southeast* (Charlottesville: University of Virginia Press, 2012), although she obscures the role of Scots and Scotch-Irish by labeling them English, as does Natalie R. Inman, *Brothers and Friends: Kinship in Early America* (Athens: University of Georgia Press, 2017), 149n3, by including them as "Anglo-Americans."

45. William Cronon, *Changes in the Land: Indians, Colonists, and the Ecology of New England* (New York: Hill and Wang, 1983); Silver, *A New Face on the Countryside*; Carolyn Merchant, *Ecological Revolutions: Nature, Gender, and Science in New England* (Chapel Hill: University of North Carolina Press, 1989); Strother E. Roberts, *Colonial Ecology, Atlantic Economy: Transforming Nature in Early New England* (Philadelphia: University of Pennsylvania Press, 2019).

46. Pawlikowski, "The Plight and the Bounty"; Cynthia Cumfer, *Separate Peoples, One Land: The Minds of Cherokees, Blacks, and Whites on the Tennessee Frontier* (Chapel Hill: University of North Carolina Press, 2007), 217–20; Allan Kullikoff, *From British Peasants to Colonial American Farmers* (Chapel Hill: University of North Carolina Press, 2000), 2; Allan Greer, *Property and Dispossession: Natives, Empires and Land in Early Modern North America* (Cambridge: Cambridge University Press, 2018), 242.

47. Pawlikowski, "The Plight and the Bounty," 64.

48. Preston, *Texture of Contact*, ch. 3 (Anderson at 122); Preston, "Squatters, Indians, Proprietary Government, and Land in the Susquehanna Valley," 180–200, esp. 182–84, and citing Patrick Griffin, "The People with No Name: Ulster's Migrants and Identity Formation in Eighteenth-Century Pennsylvania," *William and Mary Quarterly* 58 (2001), 587–614 (Anderson at 593).

49. Cumfer, *Separate Peoples*, 211–14; Kullikoff, *From British Peasants to Colonial American Farmers*, 150–62. For squatters' rights in Ulster: Jordan and Kaups, *American Backwoods Frontier*, 70; E. Estyn Evans, "The Scotch-Irish: Their Cultural Adaptation and Heritage in the American Old West," in *Essays in Scotch-Irish History*, ed. E. R. R. Green (1969; reprint, Belfast: Ulster Historical Foundation, 1992), 84.

50. Cf. James D. Rice, *Nature and History in the Potomac Country: From Hunter-Gathers to the Age of Jefferson* (Baltimore, MD: Johns Hopkins University Press, 2009).

51. E.g., Elizabeth A. Perkins, "The Consumer Frontier: Household Consumption in Early Kentucky," *Journal of American History* 78 (1991), 486–510.

52. *EAID* 3: 416 (Delaware quote).

53. *EAID* 3: 446 (Thomas King quote); Virginia DeJohn Anderson, *Creatures of Empire: How Domestic Animals Transformed Early America* (New York: Oxford University Press, 2004), 139–40, 171; Greer, *Property and Dispossession*, 253–54, 261–62, 268; Preston, "Squatters, Indians, Proprietary Government, and Land in the Susquehanna Valley," 188. See also Andrea L. Smalley, *Wild by Nature: North American Animals Confront Colonization* (Baltimore, MD: Johns Hopkins University Press, 2017).

54. William J. Hinke and Charles E. Kemper, eds., "Moravian Diaries of Travel through Virginia," *Virginia Magazine of History and Biography* 11 (October 1903), 123.

55. Stephen Aron, *How the West Was Lost: The Transformation of Kentucky from Daniel Boone to Henry Clay* (Baltimore, MD: Johns Hopkins University Press, 1996), ch. 1; Stephen Aron, "Pigs and Hunters: 'Rights in the Woods' on the Trans-Appalachian Frontier," in *Contact Points: American Frontiers from the Mohawk Valley to the Mississippi, 1750–1830*, ed. Andrew R. L. Cayton and Fredricka J. Teute (Chapel Hill: University of North Carolina Press, 1998), 175–204.

56. Robert M. Owens, *Killing over Land: Murder and Diplomacy on the Early American Frontier* (Norman: University of Oklahoma Press, 2024).

57. Franz, *Paxton*, 96; HSP, Logan Letterbook, 3: 302.

58. Richard White, *The Middle Ground: Indians, Empires, and Republics in the Great Lakes, 1650–1815* (Cambridge: Cambridge University Press, 1991), 76–77.

59. Nicole Eustice, *Covered with Night: A Story of Murder and Indigenous Justice in Early America* (New York: Liveright/W. W. Norton, 2021).

60. *Col. Recs. Penn.* 4: 93–94.

61. *IILC* 319–20, 322–323.

62. *Col. Recs. Penn.* 4: 649. For a broader discussion of such issues, see Gregory Evans Dowd, *Groundless: Rumors, Legends, and Hoaxes on the Early American Frontier* (Baltimore, MD: Johns Hopkins University Press, 2015).
63. Joseph A. Waddell, *Annals of Augusta County, Virginia*, 2nd ed. (Staunton, VA: C. Russell Caldwell, 1902), 39–40, 69; *IILC* 390.
64. Waddell, *Annals of Augusta County*, 44–47, 49; *EAID* 5: 35; Draper 21U29–35; June Lee Mefford Kinkead, *Our Kentucky Pioneer Ancestry: A History of the Kinkead and McDowell Families of Kentucky and Those Families Associated by Marriage* (Baltimore, MD: Gateway Press, 1992), 181–86. It was the first of many clashes between the McDowell family and the Indians that stretched across three generations. Born two years before his family had migrated from Ireland to Virginia, Samuel McDowell in 1754 married Mary McClung, who had migrated a few years before. In 1755 Samuel fought in and survived Braddock's defeat; in 1774 he fought under Andrew Lewis at the Battle of Point Pleasant, and he served in the Revolution, before moving to Kentucky where he became a judge and political leader. Members of subsequent generations of the McDowell family served as volunteers in Scott's campaign against the Wabash Indians in 1792 and William Henry Harrison's campaign against Tecumseh that culminated at the Battle of the Thames in Ontario in October 1813, from which all returned but some succumbed to the fever they brought home. Kinkead, *Our Kentucky Pioneer Ancestry*, 189–95, 396–97, 402.
65. *Penn. Archives*, 1st ser. 1: 643–52; James H. Merrell, *Into the American Woods: Negotiators on the Pennsylvania Frontier* (New York: W. W. Norton, 1999), 42–53; David C. Hsiung, "Death on the Juniata: Delawares, Iroquois, and Pennsylvanians in a Colonial Whodunit," *Pennsylvania History* 65 (1998), 445–77.
66. *NCCR* 5: ix.
67. *NCCR* 4: 1313–14.
68. Bauer, *Being Catawba*, esp. chs. 4–5.
69. Merrell, *Indians' New World*, ch. 5; Bauer, *Being Catawba*, 40–41; James H. Merrell, "'Minding the Business of the Nation': Hagler as Catawba Leader," *Ethnohistory* 33 (1986), 55–70.
70. Peter N. Moore, *World of Toil and Strife: Community Transformation in Backcountry South Carolina, 1750–1805* (Columbia: University of South Carolina Press, 2007), 17.
71. *NCCR* 5: 141–44, 655 ("Dare not Deny"); Merrell, *Indians' New World*, 169, 184, 188–89.
72. The complainants were William Morrison, John Armstrong, William Young, and William McNight. *NCCR* 5: 141–44, quotes at 142–43; *EAID* 13: 349–53.
73. *NCCR* 5: 581.
74. *NCCR* 5: 579–81, 784; 7: 879–80.
75. Quoted in Daniel W. Patterson, *The True Image: Gravestone Art and the Culture of Scotch Irish Settlers in the Pennsylvania and Carolina Backcountry* (Chapel Hill: University of North Carolina Press, 2012), 290; *The South Carolina Diary of Reverend Archibald Simpson*, ed. Peter N. Moore, 2 vols. (Columbia: University of South Carolina Press, 2012), 1: 135.
76. Richardson baptized Andrew Jackson. His nephew and inheritor, William Richardson Davie, was a prominent military officer and led Jackson's first regiment. Richardson evidently died by suicide. His Scotch-Irish wife Agnes found him hanging "on his knees." Peter N. Moore, "The Mysterious Death of William Richardson: Kinship, Female Vulnerability, and the Myth of Supernaturalism in the Southern Backcountry," *North Carolina Historical Review* 80 (2003), 279–96; Moore, *World of Toil and Strife*, 1–3, 36.
77. Brooke Bauer, "Catawba Women and Imperial Land Encroachment," in *The Early Imperial Republic: From the American Revolution to the U.S.-Mexican War*, ed. Michael Blaakman, Emily Conroy Krutz, and Noelani Arista (Philadelphia: University of Philadelphia Press, 2023), ch. 4; Bauer, *Being Catawba*, 113–14, 127–36, 154–64. In 1840 South Carolina purchased the Catawbas' land, ending their legal ownership of the 144,000 acres guaranteed them by Treaty of Augusta in 1763.
78. Patterson, *True Image*, 269–73; Bauer, *Being Catawba*, 4–5.
79. Louis M. Waddell, "Justice, Retribution, and the Case of John Toby," in *Friends and Enemies in Penn's Woods: Indians, Colonists, and the Racial Construction of Pennsylvania*, ed. William A. Pencak and Daniel K. Richter (University Park: Pennsylvania State University Press, 2004), 129–43.
80. Merritt, *At the Crossroads*, 8–9, 177–78; "The Examination of George Hutchinson," November 15, 1755, HSP, Penn Mss., vol. 2, Indian Affairs, 2: 42. (On one occasion, Delaware warriors driving children together spoke to them in high Dutch, "be still we wont hurt you," but then

killed and scalped a woman and some of the children while the others fled. *Penn. Archives*, 1st ser. 2: 512).

Chapter 5

1. Advertisement of B. Franklin for "Waggons," April 26, 1755, and address to inhabitants of Lancaster, York, and Cumberland counties, *Penn. Archives*, 1st ser. 2: 294-96; *The Papers of Benjamin Franklin*, ed. Leonard W. Labaree et al., 43 vols. to date (New Haven, CT: Yale University Press, 1959-), 6: 19-22; *The Autobiography of Benjamin Franklin, with Related Documents*, ed. Louis P. Masur (Boston: Bedford Books), 1993, 130-33.
2. David Preston, *Braddock's Defeat: The Battle of the Monongahela and the Road to Revolution* (New York: Oxford University Press, 2015).
3. Fred Anderson, *Crucible of War: The Seven Years' War and the Fate of Empire in British North America, 1754-1766* (New York: Alfred A. Knopf, 2000), 160.
4. *Col. Recs. Penn.* 6: 130-132, 134-35.
5. *Col. Recs. Penn.* 6: 458.
6. *Col. Recs. Penn.* 6: 459-60.
7. *Penn. Archives*, 4th ser. 2: 424-26, 429; *Col. Recs. Penn.* 6: 461-62.
8. Extracts and narrative in *NCCR* 5: 1200-1212, quotes at 1202; Rev. William Henry Foote, *Sketches of North Carolina* (New York: Robert Carter, 1846), 161-76, quotes at 163; Joseph A. Waddell, *Annals of Augusta County, Virginia*, 2nd ed. (Staunton, VA: C. Russell Caldwell, 1902), 105.
9. Waddell, *Annals of Augusta County*, 109; *IILC* 386, 394; photo of Old Stone Church, 384.
10. *Penn. Archives*, 4th ser. 2: 438, 430-33, 484; *Pennsylvania Gazette*, August 14, 1755.
11. *Col. Recs. Penn.* 6: 533 (Lurgan), 550-51, 590-91 (wives and children); *Penn. Archives*, 1st ser. 2: 385-86, 448, 450.
12. HSP, Rhoda Barber, "Journal of Settlement at Wright's Ferry on the Susquehanna River (1830)," 10.
13. *Col. Recs. Penn.* 6: 704-5; *The Paxton Papers*, ed. John R. Dunbar (The Hague: Martinus Nijhoff, 1957), 10.
14. *Col. Recs. Penn.* 6: 761.
15. *Col. Recs. Penn.* 6: 546.
16. *Col. Recs. Penn.* 6: 590-91.
17. "To the Kings most Excellent Majesty," 1755, HSP, Penn. Mss., vol. 2, Indian Affairs, 2: 55. The petitioners included John Harris and William Smith.
18. Warren R. Hofstra, "'A Parcel of Barbarians and an Uncouth Set of People': Settlers and Settlements of the Shenandoah Valley," in *George Washington and the Virginia Backcountry*, ed. Warren R. Hofstra (Madison, WI: Madison House, 1998), 92; *Papers of Benjamin Franklin*, 6: 231.
19. Melissah J. Pawlikowski, "The Plight and the Bounty: Squatters, War Profiteers, and the Transforming Hand of Sovereignty in Indian Country, 1750-1774," Ph.D. diss., Ohio State University, 2014, 52; Morris's Instructions and speech to Scarouady and Andrew Montour, December 1755, HSP, Penn Mss., vol. 2, Indian Affairs, 2: 54.
20. *Col. Recs. Penn.* 6: 671.
21. *The Papers of Henry Bouquet*, ed. S. K. Stevens, Donald H. Kent, and Autumn L. Leonard. 6 vols. (Harrisburg: Pennsylvania Historical and Museum Commission, 1972-1994), 4: 405.
22. *A Tribute to the Memory of Peter Collinson. With some notice of Dr. Darlington's Memorials of John Bartram and Humphry Marshall* (Philadelphia: William H. Michell, 1851), 24, 29.
23. *Col. Recs. Penn.* 7: 71; *EAID* 3: 2, 19: Report of Scarouady and Andrew Montour at a Council held in the Council Chamber, March 27, 1756, HSP, Penn Mss., vol. 2, Indian Affairs, 2: 77.
24. *EAID* 3: 423-25.
25. [Charles Thomson], *An Enquiry into the Causes of the Alienation of the Delaware and Shawanese Indians from the British Interest, and into the Measures Taken for Recovering Their Friendship* (London: J. Wilkie, 1759); J. Edwin Hendricks, *Charles Thomson and the Making of a New Nation, 1729-1824* (Teaneck, NJ: Fairleigh Dickinson University Press, 1979), 1-3, 14-23; James H. Merrell, "'I desire all that I have said ... may be taken down aright': Revisiting Teedyscung's 1756 Treaty Council Speeches," *William and Mary Quarterly* 58 (2006), 777-826.
26. *Col. Recs. Penn.* 7: 324-25; *EAID* 3: 149 (see also Moses Tatamy's account of Delaware claims, *EAID* 3: 163-64).

27. Extract of a Letter from Mr. Peters, August 4, 1756, HSP, Penn Mss., 2: Indian Affairs, 2: 99; *Penn. Archives*, 1st ser., 2: 724–25.
28. Timothy J. Shannon, "War, Diplomacy, and Culture: The Iroquois Experience in the Seven Years' War," in *Cultures in Conflict: The Seven Years' War in North America*, ed. Warren R. Hofstra (Lanham, MD: Rowman and Littlefield, 2007), 79–103.
29. *Penn. Archives*, 1st ser. 3: 193 (Defiance); *WJP* 9: 310 ("no longer Women"); *Col. Recs. Penn.* 6: 701 (no longer Women); 7: 12–14 (Scarouady) 7: 49 (Paxinosa: "Man of Authority" and pushed Scarouady's belt aside "in a contemptuous Manner"); *EAID* 3: 15; "Treaty Talks at Fort Johnson," December 1755–February 1756, HSP, Penn Mss., vol. 2, Indian Affairs, 2: 65–71; Minutes of a Council held in the State House, February 24, 1756, Penn Mss., vol. 2, Indian Affairs, 2: 74.
30. *EAID* 3: 7, 213; Richard S. Grimes, "We 'Now Have Taken up the Hatchet against Them': Braddock's Defeat and the Martial Liberation of the Western Delawares," *PMHB* 137 (2013), 227–59; C. A. Weslager, *The Delaware Indians: A History* (New Brunswick, NJ: Rutgers University Press, 1972), 231.
31. Michael A. McDonnell, *Masters of Empire: Great Lakes Indians and the Making of America* (New York: Hill and Wang, 2015), 170–71, 177; Daniel P. Barr, "'This Land Is Ours and Not Yours': The Western Delawares and the Seven Years' War in the Upper Ohio Valley, 1755–1758," in *The Boundaries between Us: Natives and Newcomers along the Frontiers of the Old Northwest Territory, 1750–1850*, ed. Daniel P. Barr (Kent, OH: Kent State University Press, 2006), 30–37; Colin G. Calloway, "Red Power and Homeland Security: Native Nations and the Limits of Empire in the Ohio Country, 1750–1795," in *Facing Empire: Indigenous Experiences in a Revolutionary Age*, ed. Kate Fullager and Michael A. McDonnell (Baltimore, MD: Johns Hopkins University Press, 2018), 145–62.
32. Eric Hinderaker, "Declaring Independence: The Ohio Indians and the Seven Years' War," in *Cultures in Conflict: The Seven Years' War in North America*, ed. Warren R. Hofstra (Lanham, MD: Rowman and Littlefield, 2007), 105–25; Ian K. Steele, "Shawnee Origins of Their Seven Years' War," *Ethnohistory* 53 (2006), 657–87; *NYCD* 10: 423; *EAID* 3: 218, 383–84 (Paxinosa) 445; C.O. 5/1328: 28–29; *Papers of Henry Bouquet*, 4: 405; Memorandum of a conversation between Conrad Weiser and John Tachnedorus, February 22, 1756 ("hearty in the English Interest"), Message from the Governor to the Susquehannah Indians, April 26, 1756, and Council held at Philadelphia, June 8, 1756, HSP, Penn. Mss., vol. 2, Indian Affairs, 2: 73, 81, 90.
33. Draper 21U58.
34. Waddell, *Annals of Augusta County*, 110–13; *The Official Records of Robert Dinwiddie, Lieutenant-Governor of the Colony of Virginia, 1751–1758*, ed. R. A. Brock, 2 vols. (Richmond: Virginia Historical Society, 1883–1884), 2: 132–33; *EAID* 5: 115, 129, 133; Patricia Givens Johnson, *James Patton and the Appalachian Colonists* (Verona, VA: McClure Press, 1973), 112–19, 201–6; Draper 12U159–72 (Meadows attack); 21U37 (sketch of Patton).
35. "A brief Narrative of the incursions and ravages of the French Indians in the Province of Pennsylvania," October–December 1755, HSP, Penn Mss., vol. 2: Indian Affairs, 2: 34; *Col. Recs. Penn.* 6: 766–68.
36. Peter Silver, *Our Savage Neighbors: How Indian War Transformed Early America* (New York: W. W. Norton, 2008), ch. 4; Matthew C. Ward, *Breaking the Backcountry: The Seven Years' War in Virginia and Pennsylvania, 1754–1765* (Pittsburgh: University of Pittsburgh Press, 2003), 45–58; Matthew C. Ward, "'The European Method of Warring Is Not Practiced Here': The Failure of British Military Policy in the Ohio Valley, 1755–1759," *War in History* 4 (1997), 247–63; Barr, "'This Land Is Ours and Not Yours,'" 30–31. French summaries of the Delaware and Shawnee raids are in *NYCD* 10: 423–25, 435–37, 469–70, 481–82, 486.
37. *Col. Recs. Penn.* 6: 641–42.
38. *Col. Recs. Penn.* 6: 655, 661.
39. *Penn. Archives*, 1st ser. 2: 444.
40. "At a meeting of the General Council for Cumberland County," October 30, 1755, HSP, Lamberton Collection on the Scotch-Irish Settlements in Cumberland County, folder 23.
41. *Penn. Archives*, 1st ser. 2: 445, 458.
42. *Penn. Archives*, 4th ser. 2: 528.
43. *Official Records of Robert Dinwiddie*, 2: 92–93, 110–12, 132–33, 154–55 (Buchanan quote), 198–99, 239, 345, 356, 369, 403, 498 (Loudon quote), 533, 564.
44. *The Papers of George Washington: Colonial Series*, ed. W. W. Abbot, Dorothy Twohig, et al. 10 vols. (Charlottesville: University Press of Virginia, 1983–1995), 5: 33.

45. "Letter of Rev. James Maury to Philip Ludwell, on the Defence of the Frontiers of Virginia, 1756," *Virginia Magazine of History and Biography* 19 (2011), 293, 295–96.
46. Wayne E. Lee, *The Cutting-Off Way: Indigenous Warfare in Eastern North America, 1500–1800* (Chapel Hill: University of North Carolina Press, 2023).
47. *Penn. Archives*, 2nd ser. 6: 620.
48. *Penn. Archives*, 1st ser. 2: 457.
49. *EAID* 2: 430; "At a Council held at Philadelphia," November 8, 1755, HSP, Penn. Mss., vol. 2: Indian Affairs: 37.
50. John Franklin Meginness, *History of the West Branch Valley of the Susquehanna* (1888; Alpha Editions reprint, 2021), 112.
51. *EAID* 2: 423; 3: 1, 48n; "A brief Narrative of the Incursions and Ravages of the French Indians in the Province of Pennsylvania," October–December 1755, HSP, Penn. Mss., vol. 2: Indian Affairs, 2: 34; "The Petition of us the Subscribers living near the Mouth of Penn's Creek," October 20, 1755, Penn. Mss., vol. 2, Indian Affairs, 2: 32; *Col. Recs. Penn.* 6: 647–48 (petition).
52. C. Hale Sipe, *The Indian Wars of Pennsylvania* (Harrisburg, PA: Telegraph Press, 1929), 217–29; David L. Preston, "Squatters, Indians, Proprietary Government, and Land in the Susquehanna Valley," in *Friends and Enemies in Penn's Woods: Indians, Colonists, and the Racial Construction of Pennsylvania*, ed. William A. Pencak and Daniel K. Richter (University Park: Pennsylvania State University Press, 2004), 180–81, 197–98; *Col. Recs. Penn.* 6: 673–77; *Penn. Archives*, 1st ser. 2: 462–63; 4th ser. 2: 517–18; "A brief Narrative of the Incursions and Ravages of the French Indians in the Province of Pennsylvania"; William Maxwell to [?], November 3, 1755, HSP, Lamberton Collection on Scotch-Irish Settlements in Cumberland County, folder 23.
53. *Penn. Archives*, 1st ser. 2: 475–75 (tomahawk); *Paxton Papers*, 11 (frozen corpses). See also *The Journal of John Woolman*, ed. John G. Whittier (Boston: James Osgood and Co., 1871), 128.
54. *Penn. Archives*, 1st ser. 2: 511–12.
55. "A Message to the Governor from the Assembly," November 5, 1755, HSP, Penn. Mss., vol. 2: Indian Affairs: 36; "At a Meeting of the Aughquageys, Tuscaroros, etc," February 29, 1756, Penn. Mss., vol. 2: Indian Affairs, 2: 66; Memorandum of a conversation between Conrad Weiser and John Tachnedorus, February 22, 1756, HSP, Penn. Mss., vol. 2, Indian Affairs, 2: 73; Minutes of Councils held in the State House, February 24, March 4, March 27, 1756, Penn Mss., vol. 2, Indian Affairs, 2: 74, 76, 77; *Col. Recs. Penn.* 6: 763; *EAID* 3: 12–13.
56. William Smith, *A Brief View of the Conduct of Pennsylvania, For the Year 1755* (London: R. Griffiths, 1756), 54–61; *Pennsylvania Gazette*, June 10, 1756; *Papers of Benjamin Franklin*, 6: 457n; Patrick Spero, *Frontier Country: The Politics of War in Early Pennsylvania* (Philadelphia: University of Pennsylvania Press, 2016), 132–33.
57. *Col. Recs. Penn.* 6: 692–96 (quote at 695).
58. Stephen Brumwell, *Redcoats: The British Soldier and War in the Americas, 1755–1763* (Cambridge: Cambridge University Press, 2002), 73–74, 318–19.
59. Benjamin Bankhurst, *Ulster Presbyterians and the Scots Irish Diaspora, 1750–1764* (New York: Palgrave Macmillan, 2013), 27–28.
60. *Col. Recs. Penn.* 7: 288.
61. *Penn. Archives*, 1st ser. 2: 451–53, 569–70; Peters to Proprietors, October 30, 1756, HSP, Penn Mss., Official Correspondence, 8:187.
62. James Titus, *The Old Dominion at War: Society, Politics, and Warfare in Late Colonial Virginia* (Columbia: University of South Carolina Press, 1992), 94–95, 102; Ian K. Steele, *Setting All the Captives Free: Capture, Adjustment, and Recollection in Allegheny Country* (Montreal: McGill-Queens University Press, 2012), 117; David Humphreys, *"Life of General Washington,"* with *George Washington's "Remarks,"* ed. Rosemarie Zagarri (Athens: University of Georgia Press, 1991), 20.
63. Warren Hofstra, ed., *Ulster to America: The Scots-Irish Migration Experience, 1680–1830* (Knoxville: University of Tennessee Press, 2012), xxiii.
64. *Col. Recs. Penn.* 6:674.
65. Extract from Philadelphia to William Penn, August 1756, HSP, Penn Mss., vol. 2, Indian Affairs, 2: 83.
66. *Papers of George Washington: Colonial Series*, 4: 11–18, quote at 14.
67. *Penn. Archives*, 1st ser. 2: 548–50; *Papers of Benjamin Franklin*, 6: 357–58.
68. Kevin Kenny, *Peaceable Kingdom Lost: The Paxton Boys and the Destruction of William Penn's Holy Experiment* (New York: Oxford University Press, 2009), 76.
69. *Penn. Archives*, 1st ser. 2: 553–54, 563–64.

70. *Penn. Archives*, 1st ser. 2: 563; *IILC* 487; 491 (quote); James P. Myers, Jr., *The Ordeal of Thomas Barton, Anglican Missionary in the Pennsylvania Backcountry* (Bethlehem, PA: Lehigh University Press, 2010).
71. *Official Records of Robert Dinwiddie*, 2: 116–18, 155.
72. *Papers of George Washington: Colonial Series*, 2: 333–35, 338; 3: 45.
73. Warren Hofstra, "Searching for Peace and Prosperity: Opequon Settlement, Virginia, 1730s–1760s," in *Ulster to America: The Scots-Irish Migration Experience, 1680–1830*, ed. Warren Hofstra (Knoxville: University of Tennessee Press, 2012), 114–15; Richard Lyman Bushman, *The American Farmer in the Eighteenth Century: A Social and Cultural History* (New Haven, CT: Yale University Press, 2018), 232–36.
74. Waddell, *Annals of Augusta County*, 127–33; Patricia Givens Johnson, *General Andrew Lewis of Roanoke and Greenbriar* (privately published; printed by Southern Printing Co., Blacksburg, VA, 1980), 44–55; Thomas A. Lewis, *West from Shenandoah: A Scotch-Irish Family Fights for America, 1721–1781* (Hoboken, NJ: John Wiley and Sons, 2004); Draper 21U6–21 (sketch of Andrew's life and military services), 21U22–25 (John's landlord brawl).
75. *Official Records of Robert Dinwiddie*, 2: 292, 294–96; 314, 320–22, 336–37, 382 ("nothing essential"); *Papers of George Washington: Colonial Series*, 2: 214, 235, 278, 290, 334, 344; Douglas McClure Wood, "'I Have Now Made a Path to Virginia': Outacite Ostenaco and the Cherokee-Virginia Alliance in the French and Indian War," *West Virginia History*, new ser. 2 (Fall 2008), 39–43; Ward, *Breaking the Backcountry*, 104–5. Draper 21U58 (Preston's birth and education); Preston's company of rangers, listing their nationality, age, and trade, is at Draper 1QQ92 and 21U110–12; his diary of the expedition at Draper 1QQ96–123 and 21U85–104. Waddell, *Annals of Augusta County*, 122 (Alexander), 127–33.
76. *Col. Recs. Penn.* 6: 692.
77. *Col. Recs. Penn.* 7: 1–7.
78. *Col. Recs. Penn.* 7: 56.
79. Steele, *Setting All the Captives Free*, 100.
80. *Penn. Archives*, 1st ser. 2: 623, 615–16.
81. *Col. Recs. Penn.* 7: 74, 76, 78, 84–85 (sense of duty), 88–90, 98 ("enraged People"); *Penn. Archives*, 1st ser. 2: 619; 4th ser. 2: 594–97; *EAID* 3: 20–21, 25–27; Sipe, *Indian Wars of Pennsylvania*, 281–83; Henry J. Young, "A Note on Scalp Bounties in Pennsylvania," *Pennsylvania History* 24 (1957), 209–11; Silver, *Our Savage Neighbors*, 161–68; Anderson, *Crucible of War*, 161–62 (compromise and Quaker reaction).
82. *Penn. Archives*, 4th ser. 2: 601.
83. *Penn. Archives*, 1st ser. 2: 634; *Col. Recs. Penn.* 7: 244.
84. *Col. Recs. Penn.* 7: 118–19.
85. Report of Benjamin Chew, Alexander Stedman, William West, and Edward Shippen, Philadelphia, April 21, 1756, HSP, Penn Mss., vol. 2, Indian Affairs, 2: 80.
86. *Col. Recs. Penn.* 7: 120; *Penn. Archives*, 4th ser. 2: 608–09.
87. Sipe, *Indian Wars*, 294–96, 317; *Col. Recs. Penn.* 7: 231–33; Brady Crytzer, *War in the Peaceable Kingdom: The Kittanning Raid of 1756* (Yardley, PA: Westholme, 2016), 137–42; U. J. Jones, *History of the Early Settlement of the Juniata Valley* (Harrisburg, PA: Harrisburg Publishing Co., 1889), 82–87; Steele, *Setting All the Captives Free*, 122–23; Samuel L. Russell, trans. and ed., *Coulon De Villiers: An Elite Military Family of New France* (Savannah, GA: Russell Martial Research, 2018), 76–77, 145.
88. Jane T. Merritt, *At the Crossroads: Indians and Empires on a Mid-Atlantic Frontier, 1700–1763* (Chapel Hill: University of North Carolina Press, 2003), 181.
89. *Penn. Archives*, 1st ser. 2: 757–59.
90. Wayland F. Dunaway, *The Scotch-Irish of Colonial Pennsylvania* (Chapel Hill: University of North Carolina Press, 1944), 150. For example, James Potter, a Major-General in the Revolution, was born in County Tyrone in 1729, migrated with his family when he was twelve and moved to Cumberland County, and served on the expedition as an ensign. Dan McClenahen, "Major-General James Potter," in *Proceedings of the Northumberland County Historical Society* 28 (1980), 33–100 (Kittanning expedition, 34).
91. *Diary of David McClure, 1748–1820*, ed. Franklin B. Dexter (New York: Knickerbocker Press, 1899), 117.
92. Richard Peters to Unspecified, September 22, 1756, HSP, Penn Mss., Official Correspondence, 8: 165.

93. John Armstrong, "Scheme of an Expedition to Kittanning," ca. 1755 (notes and roughly drawn map describing Armstrong's attack), American Philosophical Society, Neg 1023; William W. Betts, *Rank and Gravity: The Life of General John Armstrong of Carlisle* (Westminster, MD: Heritage Books, 2011). Armstrong's account of the expedition is in *Col. Recs. Penn.* 7: 257–63 and *Penn. Archives*, 1st ser. 2: 767–75 (list of casualties, 773–75; prisoners recaptured, 775); reprinted in Sipe, *Indian Wars of Pennsylvania*, 305–12, with list of killed and prisoners 312–14, and in *The Olden Time: A Monthly Publications devoted to the Preservation of Documents and other Authentic Information in relation to the Early Explorations and the Settlement and Improvement of the Country around the Head of the Ohio*, ed. Neville B. Craig, 2 vols. (1848; reprint, Cincinnati: Robert Clarke & Co., 1876), 1: 76–82. Crytzer, *War in the Peaceable Kingdom*, ch. 7; Armstrong and Barton quotes at 201, 203; Daniel P. Barr, "Victory at Kittanning? Reevaluating the Impact of Armstrong's Raid on the Seven Years' War in Pennsylvania," *PMHB* 131 (2007), 5–32; John S. Fisher, "Colonel John Armstrong's Expedition against Kittanning," *PMHB* 51 (1927), 1–14; Steele, *Setting All the Captives Free*, 202 (Mrs. McAllister).

94. Helen Hornbeck Tanner, ed., *Atlas of Great Lakes Indian History* (Norman: University of Oklahoma Press, 1987), 46–47, 62; Steele, *Setting All the Captives Free*, 105; Michael N. McConnell, "Kuskusky Towns and Early Western Pennsylvania History, 1748–1778," *PMHB* 116 (1992), 50–53; Charles A. Hanna, *The Wilderness Trail, or The Ventures and Adventures of the Pennsylvania Traders on the Allegheny Path*, 2 vols. (New York: G. P. Putnam's Sons, 1911), 1: 340–51.

95. *Penn. Archives*, 1st ser. 3: 40.

96. Myers, *Ordeal of Thomas Barton*, 165–71.

97. Ward, *Breaking the Backcountry*, 70 (one thousand); Ward, "'The European Method of Warring Is Not Practiced Here,'" 247–48 (casualties and territory abandoned); Steele, *Setting All the Captives Free*, 99 (50–200-mile swath).

98. *Penn. Archives*, 1st ser. 3: 158–59 (from Hanover and Derry), 164, 174–75, 284–85, 321–22, 357–60 (from Northampton).

99. *Penn. Archives*, 4th ser. 2: 806.

100. E.g., *Col. Recs. Penn.* 7: 597–98.

101. *Penn. Archives*, 4th ser. 2: 790.

102. *Penn. Archives*, 1st ser. 3: 194; Col. Shippen to James Burd, May 19, 1757, *Letters and Papers relating chiefly to the Provincial History of Pennsylvania* (Philadelphia: privately printed, 1855), 78.

103. *Penn. Archives*, 1st ser. 3: 377.

104. "Journal of Christian Frederick Post," in *Early Western Journals, 1748–1765*, ed. Reuben Gold Thwaites (Lewisburg, PA: Wennawood, 1998), 188, 238; *IILC* 157 (Chambers from Antrim).

105. Richard K. MacMaster, "Searching for Community: Carlisle, Pennsylvania, 1750s–1780s," in *Ulster to America: The Scots-Irish Migration Experience, 1680–1830*, ed. Warren Hofstra (Knoxville: University of Tennessee Press, 2012), 86–90.

106. Paul Kelton, "The British and Indian War: Cherokee Power and the Fate of Empire in North America," *William and Mary Quarterly* 69 (2012), 763–92; Daniel J. Tortora, *Carolina in Crisis: Cherokees, Colonists, and Slaves in the American Southeast, 1756–1763* (Chapel Hill: University of North Carolina Press, 2015), 44–46; Wood, "'I Have Now Made a Path to Virginia.'"

107. Sipe, *Indian Wars of Pennsylvania*, 249–50; *Col. Recs. Penn.* 7: 303–5; 8: 110–12.

108. *The Writings of General John Forbes relating to his service in North America*, ed. Alfred Proctor James (Menasha, WI: Collegiate Press, 1938), 205; Hugh Cleland, *George Washington in the Ohio Valley* (Pittsburgh: University of Pittsburgh Press, 1955), 199.

109. Sipe, *Indian Wars*, 389, lists the officers, from *Penn. Archives*, 5th ser. 1: 178–85.

110. Johnson, *General Andrew Lewis of Roanoke and Greenbriar*, 82–89.

111. Anderson, *Crucible of War*, 524–26; *Papers of Henry Bouquet*, 5: 355, 437, 844 (proclamation), 847; 6: 39–40, 44–45; *George Mercer Papers: Relating to the Ohio Company of Virginia*, ed. Lois Mulkearn (Pittsburgh: University of Pittsburgh Press, 1954), 614–15; *Executive Journals*, 6: 205; *The Official Papers of Francis Fauquier, Lieutenant Governor of Virginia, 1758–1768*, ed. George Reese, 3 vols. (Charlottesville: University Press of Virginia, 1980–83), 2: 663–66.

112. Alan Taylor, *Liberty Men and Great Proprietors: The Revolutionary Settlement on the Maine Frontier, 1760–1820* (Chapel Hill: University of North Carolina Press, 1990), 19; Neil Rolde, *Unsettled Past, Unsettled Future: The Story of Maine Indians* (Gardiner, ME: Tilbury House, 2004), 123–27.

113. Leonard A. Morrison, *The History of Windham in New Hampshire (Rockingham County), 1719–1833, a Scotch Settlement (commonly called Scotch-Irish) embracing nearly one third of the ancient settlement and historic township of Londonderry, N.H, with the History and Genealogy of its First Settlers and their Descendants* (Boston: Cupples, Upham and Co., 1883), 53, 58; Ian K. Steele, *Betrayals: Fort William Henry and the "Massacre"* (New York: Oxford University Press, 1990), 135, 139, 197.
114. Henry J. Ford, *The Scotch-Irish in America* (Princeton, NJ: Princeton University Press, 1915), 244.
115. Robert Rogers, *Journals of Major Robert Rogers* (London, 1765; Readex Microprint, 1966), vi; Colin G. Calloway, *The Western Abenakis of Vermont: War, Migration, and the Survival of an Indian People* (Norman: University of Oklahoma Press, 1990), 25–26.
116. Rogers, *Journals*, 15.
117. Quoted in Stephen Brumwell, *White Devil: A True Story of War, Savagery, and Vengeance in Colonial America* (London: Weidenfeld and Nicholson, 2004), 101.
118. Rogers, *Journals*, 147–58; Brumwell, *White Devil*, chs. 6–7 (newspaper quote at 197; cannibalism at 229–30); Calloway, *Western Abenakis*, 175–78.
119. *NCCR* 5: 419–20.
120. *NCCR* 5: 560.
121. *Papers of Henry Bouquet*, 1: 215.
122. Samuel Cole Williams, ed., *Adair's History of the American Indians* (1930; New York: Promontory Press, reprint, n.d.), 259–61; The Headquarters Papers of Brigadier-General John Forbes Relating to the Expedition against Fort Duquesne in 1758, University of Virginia Library; microfilm copy at the David Library of the American Revolution, reel 2: items 234, 237, 239, 277, 303; *Writings of General John Forbes*, 256–57; *Official Papers of Francis Fauquier*, 1: 89–90 (killings), 292–94 (hostages); Kelton, "The British and Indian War," 789–90.
123. Tom Hatley, *The Dividing Paths: Cherokees and South Carolinians through the Era of Revolution* (New York: Oxford University Press, 1993), 86–87, 89; Tortora, *Carolina in Crisis*, 104–5. The warning is in "Memoirs of Mrs. Ann Mathews," 2, and Hobert W. Burns, *The Life of Anne Calhoun Mathews* (Palo Alto, CA: privately published, 1988), 28–29, both in the South Caroliniana Library at the University of South Carolina, and copies of which were kindly provided by Todd Hoppock.
124. Tortora, *Carolina in Crisis*, 105; William L. McDowell, ed., *Documents Relating to Indian Affairs 1754–1765* (Columbia: South Carolina Department of Archives and History, 1970), 495; Burns, *Life of Anne Calhoun Mathews*, 17–20, 25–30; "Memoirs of Mrs. Ann Mathews," 2–3, 6; A. S. Salley, Jr., "The Calhoun Family of South Carolina," *South Carolina Historical and Genealogical Magazine* 7 (April 1906), 83–90; George Howe, *The Scotch-Irish, and their First Settlements on the Tyger River and Other Neighboring Precincts in South Carolina. A Centennial Discourse, delivered at Nazareth Church, Spartanburg District, S.C., September 14, 1861* (Columbia, SC: Southern Guardian Steam-Power Press, 1861), children in the woods at 18; Peter N. Moore, *World of Toil and Strife: Community Transformation in Backcountry South Carolina, 1750–1805* (Columbia: University of South Carolina Press, 2007), 26; *South Carolina Gazette*, February 9, February 10, February 16 (children found wandering in the woods), February 23, 1760; *Pennsylvania Gazette*, March 20, 1760.
125. *NCCR* 6: 229–30; Tortora, *Carolina in Crisis*, 108.
126. Hatley, *Dividing Paths*, 127–29; Tortora, *Carolina in Crisis*, 34–35; 87, 113–15; *The South Carolina Diary of Reverend Archibald Simpson*, ed. Peter N. Moore, 2 vols. (Columbia: University of South Carolina Press, 2012), 1: 149–54, quotes at 153. On the disease among the Cherokees, see Paul Kelton, *Cherokee Medicine, Colonial Germs: An Indigenous Nation's Fight against Smallpox, 1518–1824* (Norman: University of Oklahoma Press, 2015), 114–29.
127. Paul David Nelson, *General James Grant: Scottish Soldier and Royal Governor of East Florida* (Gainesville: University Press of Florida, 1993), ch. 3; *The Papers of Henry Laurens*, ed. Philip M. Hamer et al., 16 vols. (Columbia: University of South Carolina Press, 1968–2003), 3: 275–355; Duane H. King and E. Raymond Evans, eds., "Memoirs of the Grant Expedition against the Cherokees in 1761," *Journal of Cherokee Studies*, Special Issue, 2 (September 1977).
128. Rod Andrew, Jr., *The Life and Times of General Andrew Pickens* (Chapel Hill: University of North Carolina Press, 2017), 15–17. In later life, Pickens said that he was "much out" in the Cherokee War.

129. *Papers of Henry Laurens*, 3: 342; Hatley, *Dividing Paths*, 146, 171 (plantation).
130. Hatley, *Dividing Paths*, 205–8; John Alexander Williams, *Appalachia: A History* (Chapel Hill: University of North Carolina Press, 2002), 64.
131. Hatley, *Dividing Paths*, 173–75.
132. Steele, *Setting All the Captives Free*, 99 (20 percent drop); Draper 21U118–24; register kept by William Preston, October 1754–May 1758 of people killed or captured in Augusta County, Preston Papers, Draper 1QQ83; reprinted in Waddell, *Annals of Augusta County*, 154–58.
133. Archibald Loudon, *A Selection of Some of the Most Interesting Narratives, of Outrages, Committed by the Indians, in Their Wars with the White People*, 2 vols. (Carlisle: A. Loudon, 1808), 2: 195–98; reprinted in C. Hale Sipe, *A Supplement to the First Edition of the Indian Wars of Pennsylvania* (Harrisburg, PA: Telegraph Press, 1931), 42–44.
134. Merritt, *At the Crossroads*, 184–88; Amy C. Schutt, *Peoples of the River Valleys: The Odyssey of the Delaware Indians* (Philadelphia: University of Pennsylvania Press, 2007), 114; Steele, *Setting All the Captives Free*, 95–96; Spero, *Frontier Country*, 112–18.
135. Matthew C. Ward, "The 'Peaceable Kingdom' Destroyed: The Seven Years' War and the Transformation of the Pennsylvania Backcountry," *Pennsylvania History* 74 (2007), 247–79.
136. Dunaway, *Scotch-Irish of Colonial Pennsylvania*, 120–21.
137. Edmund Burke, *An Account of the European Settlements in America*, 1st American ed. (Boston: Wilkins and Co. and Hilliard, Gray, and Co., 1835), 277–78.
138. *Col. Recs. Penn.* 8: 455–56, 650, 709–12; *Penn. Archives*, 2nd ser., 7: 262; *EAID* 3: 492; Spero, *Frontier Country*, 142–46.
139. *Penn. Archives*, 4th ser., 3: 19–22; *Col. Recs. Penn.* 8: 456; *EAID* 3: 533–34.
140. *Col. Recs. Penn.* 8: 709, 712–13.
141. *Thirty Thousand Miles with John Heckewelder, or Travels among the Indians of Pennsylvania, New York and Ohio in the Eighteenth Century*, ed. Paul A. W. Wallace (1958; reprint, Lewisburg, PA: Wennawoods, 1998), 38.
142. *Thirty Thousand Miles with John Heckewelder*, 59, 65 ("open hand").
143. Bankhurst, *Ulster Presbyterians and the Scots Irish Diaspora*.
144. *Penn. Archives*, 1st ser. 2: 719, 3: 213, 290; 448; 4: 146–47; Joseph Doddridge, *The Settlement and Indian Wars of the Western Parts of Virginia and Pennsylvania, 1763–1783* (Pittsburgh, 1912; reprint, Bowie, MD: Heritage Books, 1988), 94–96.
145. Gina M. Martino, *Women at War in the Borderlands of the Early American Northeast* (Chapel Hill: University of North Carolina Press, 2018); Cynthia Cumfer, *Separate Peoples, One Land: The Minds of Cherokees, Blacks, and Whites on the Tennessee Frontier* (Chapel Hill: University of North Carolina Press, 2007), 161.
146. "Watchings": *Col. Recs. Penn.* 7: 120; *Penn. Archives*, 4th ser. 2: 608–9; Moore, *World of Toil and Strife*, 31.
147. Ed White, *The Backcountry and the City: Colonization and Conflict in Early America* (Minneapolis: University of Minnesota Press, 2005), 64.
148. Fred Anderson, *The War That Made America: A Short History of the French and Indian War* (New York: Penguin, 2006).

Chapter 6

1. On the massacre, see *The Paxton Papers*, ed. John R. Dunbar (The Hague: Martinus Nijhoff, 1957); Kevin Kenny, *Peaceable Kingdom Lost: The Paxton Boys and the Destruction of William Penn's Holy Experiment* (New York: Oxford University Press, 2009), chs. 13–14; James H. Merrell, *Into the American Woods: Negotiators on the Pennsylvania Frontier* (New York: W. W. Norton, 1999), 285–88; Jane T. Merritt, *At the Crossroads: Indians and Empires on a Mid-Atlantic Frontier, 1700–1763* (Chapel Hill: University of North Carolina Press, 2003), 283–94; Peter Silver, *Our Savage Neighbors: How Indian War Transformed Early America* (New York: W. W. Norton, 2008), 174–90; *Penn. Archives*, 1st series, 4: 147–49, 151–55, 160–62; 4th series, 3: 256–76; Patrick Spero, *Frontier Country: The Politics of War in Early Pennsylvania* (Philadelphia: University of Pennsylvania Press, 2016), 125; Patrick Spero, ed., "1763: Pontiac and Paxton," Special Issue, *Early American Studies* 14 (Spring 2016); Ed White, *The Backcountry and the City: Colonization and Conflict in Early America* (Minneapolis: University of Minnesota Press, 2005), 117 ("Backcountry nationalism"), and Jack Brubaker, *Massacre of the Conestogas: On the Trail of the Paxton Boys in Lancaster County* (Charleston, SC: The History Press, 2010).

2. On the causes and course of Pontiac's War, see Gregory Evans Dowd, *War under Heaven: Pontiac, the Indian Nations, and the British Empire* (Baltimore, MD: Johns Hopkins University Press, 2002); David Dixon, *Never Come to Peace Again: Pontiac's Uprising and the Fate of British Empire in North America* (Norman: University of Oklahoma Press, 2005); and Richard Middleton, *Pontiac's War: Its Causes, Course and Consequences* (New York: Routledge, 2007).
3. *The Papers of George Washington: Colonial Series*, ed. W. W. Abbot, Dorothy Twohig, et al., 10 vols. (Charlottesville: University Press of Virginia, 1983–1995), 7: 230–31, 236–37, 257–60.
4. *IILC* 496.
5. "List of Indian Traders and Their Servants Killed or Captured by Indians," September 5, 1763, *The Papers of Henry Bouquet*, ed. S. K. Stevens, Donald H. Kent, and Autumn L. Leonard, 6 vols. (Harrisburg: Pennsylvania Historical and Museum Commission, 1972–1994), 6: 412–13; "List of Traders Killed by Indians," December 1763, ibid., 6: 489–90; see also list at 412–13; Patrick Griffin, *American Leviathan: Empire, Nation, and Revolutionary Frontier* (New York: Hill and Wang, 2007), 63 (Patrick Dunn, John Farrell, Patrick Guin, William Lunehehan, Matthew McCrea, William McGuire).
6. For example: Armand Francis Lucier, comp., *Pontiac's Conspiracy and Other Indian Affairs: Notices Abstracted from Colonial Newspapers, 1763–1765* (Bowie, MD: Heritage Books, 2000), 20 (children quote), 26, 33 (canoes and "World anew").
7. Lucier, *Pontiac's Conspiracy and Other Indian Affairs*, 37; also quoted in C. Hale Sipe, *The Indian Wars of Pennsylvania* (Harrisburg, PA: Telegraph Press, 1929), 437.
8. *The Scotch-Irish of Northampton County, Pennsylvania* (Easton, PA: Northampton County Historical and Genealogical Society, 1926), 49, 237.
9. Lucier, *Pontiac's Conspiracy and Other Indian Affairs*, 34.
10. *Penn. Archives*, 1st ser., 4: 108–9.
11. Sipe, *Indian Wars of Pennsylvania*, 440–41.
12. Ian K. Steele, *Setting All the Captives Free: Capture, Adjustment, and Recollection in Allegheny Country* (Montreal: McGill-Queens University Press, 2012), 175–76; *Papers of Henry Bouquet* 6: 308.
13. *Penn. Archives*, 4th ser., 3: 209–10, 216–18; *Penn. Archives*, 1st ser., 4: 120.
14. *Penn. Archives*, 4th ser., 3: 202–5; *Col. Recs. Penn.* 9: 31–33.
15. *Penn. Archives*, 1st ser., 4: 114–15, 116–17; Kenny, *Peaceable Kingdom Lost*, 119–20.
16. To Gov. Hamilton, October 25, 1763, and to Col. Joseph Shippen, November 5, 1763, *Penn. Archives*, 1st ser., 4: 127, 132–33.
17. *Penn. Archives*, 1st ser., 4: 146–47.
18. George W. Franz, *Paxton: A Study of Community Structure and Mobility in the Colonial Pennsylvania Backcountry* (New York: Garland, 1989), 82, 106 (distances), 269–271.
19. Merritt, *At the Crossroads*, 273; *WJP* 13: 297–98.
20. Kenny, *Peaceable Kingdom Lost*, 125–28; Sipe, *Indian Wars*, 450–52; Lucier, *Pontiac's Conspiracy and Other Indian Affairs*, 90–91.
21. Rachel Wheeler, "A View from the Philadelphia Barracks: Religion in the Mid-Atlantic," in *A Companion to American Religious History*, ed. Benjamin E. Park (Newark, NJ: Wiley and Sons, 2021), 31–32; George Henry Loskiel, *History of the Mission of the United Brethren among the Indians in North America* [1789], trans. Christian Ignatius Latrobe, 3 parts (London: Brethren's Society for the Furtherance of the Gospel, 1794), 2: 209–10 ("freebooters").
22. Kenny, *Peaceable Kingdom Lost*, 133; *Paxton Papers*, 21.
23. Silver, *Our Savage Neighbors*, 131; "Fragments of a Journal kept by Samuel Foulke, of Bucks County," *PMHB* 5 (1881), 67 ("Contagion"); Paul A. W. Wallace, ed., *Thirty Thousand Miles with John Heckewelder or Travels among the Indians of Pennsylvania, New York and Ohio in the 18th Century* (1958; reprint, Lewisburg, PA: Wennawoods, 1998), 71.
24. James G. Leyburn, *The Scotch-Irish: A Social History* (Chapel Hill: University of North Carolina Press, 1962), 192; Charles A. Hanna, *The Scotch-Irish, or the Scot in North Britain, North Ireland, and North America*, 2 vols. (New York: G. P. Putnam's Sons, 1902), 2: 63; Logan to Thomas Penn, December 18 and 22, 1730, HSP, Penn Mss., Official Correspondence, 2: 145, 147; Logan to Unspecified, December 29, 1730, Penn Mss., Official Correspondence, 2: 147; Logan to John, Thomas, and Richard Penn, February 17, 1731, HSP, James Logan Letterbooks, vol. 6: 339; Franz, *Paxton*, 92–94.
25. *Col. Recs. Penn.* 7: 7–9; *EAID* 2: 463.
26. *EAID* 3: 344, 376–77.
27. *EAID* 3: 533–35.

28. *Paxton Papers*, 23–24; Kevin Yeager, "Rev. John Elder and Identity in the Pennsylvania Backcountry," *PMHB* 136 (2012), 470. Penn's reply quoted in Henry J. Ford, *The Scotch-Irish in America* (Princeton, NJ: Princeton University Press, 1915), 308.
29. *Col. Recs. Penn.* 9: 89; *EAID* 3: 666.
30. The coroner's inquisition on the six Conestoga Indians is in *Penn. Archives*, 1st ser., 4: 147–48.
31. Rhoda Barber, "Journal of Settlement at Wright's Ferry on the Susquehanna River" (1830), 10–12, HSP and Digital Paxton. Barber said fourteen Indians were killed in this initial slaughter, rather than six. Brubaker, *Massacre of the Conestogas*, 23 (Chrisly's escape).
32. Edward Shippen to Rev. John Elder, December 16, 1763, Digital Paxton.
33. *Paxton Papers*, 26; *Penn. Archives*, 1st ser., 4: 148–49.
34. *Paxton Papers*, 25; *Col. Recs. Penn.* 9: 95–96; *EAID* 3: 667–69; *Penn. Archives*, 4th series, 3: 251–52, 254–56.
35. *Penn. Archives*, 4th series, 3: 252–54.
36. Quoted in William Henry Egle, *History of the Counties of Dauphin and Lebanon in the Commonwealth of Pennsylvania* (Philadelphia: Everts and Peck, 1883), 63; Hubertis M. Cummings, *Scots Breed and Susquehanna* (Pittsburgh: University of Pittsburgh Press for the Presbyterian Historical Society, 1964), 108.
37. *Col. Recs. Penn.* 9: 89–90, 92–96, 100–12. Names of Indians killed: *Col. Recs. Penn.* 9:103–04; *EAID* 3: 673–74; *Paxton Papers*, 57–58; Lucier, *Pontiac's Conspiracy and Other Indian Affairs*, 162–65 (names at 163).
38. D. A. Henderson, "Account of the Indian murders," December 27, 1763, Digital Paxton.
39. Matthew Kruer, *Time of Anarchy: Indigenous Power and the Crisis of Colonialism in Early America* (Cambridge, MA: Harvard University Press, 2021), 114.
40. Scott Paul Gordon, "The Paxton Boys and Edward Shippen: Defiance and Deference on a Collapsing Frontier," *Early American Studies* 14 (2016), 319–47; Scott Paul Gordon, "The Paxton Boys and the Moravians: Terror and Faith in the Pennsylvania Backcountry," *Journal of Moravian History* 14 (2014), 119–52; Albrecht Ludolph Russmeyer to Nathaniel Seidel, January 2, 1764, p. 3, Digital Paxton.
41. Edward Shippen to Joseph Shippen, January 5, 1764, American Philosophical Society, Shippen Papers, and Digital Paxton.
42. HSP, "Account for Maintaining Indians at Lancaster, Dec. 27, 1763"; Brubaker, *Massacre of the Conestogas*, 42.
43. *Penn. Archives*, 2nd ser., 4: 152.
44. Gordon, "Paxton Boys and the Moravians."
45. *Col. Recs. Penn.* 9: 107–08; *Penn. Archives*, 4th ser., 3: 260–62.
46. *Penn. Archives*, 4th ser., 3: 256–60, 262–67, 269–70; *WJP* 11: 1–2. For the backstory on the Moravian Indian refugees, see Wheeler, "A View from the Philadelphia Barracks," 25–43.
47. *WJP* 4: 284–85.
48. *WJP* 4: 310, 323–24; 11: 38; *Penn. Archives*, 1st ser., 4: 162.
49. *WJP* 11: 18–19.
50. *WJP* 11: 55–57.
51. Lucier, *Pontiac's Conspiracy and Other Indian Affairs*, 213–14
52. John Elder to Shippen, February 1, 1764, reprinted in Francis Parkman, *The Conspiracy of Pontiac and the Indian War after the Conquest of Canada*, 2 vols. (originally published 1851; reprint of revised 1870 edition, Lincoln: University of Nebraska Press, 1994), Appendix E, 2: 347–48, and quoted in Franz, *Paxton*, 76 and 77. Brubaker, *Massacre of the Conestogas*, chs. 11–13, presents a persuasive case for the complicity of men like Elder and Shippen; quote at 113. Yeager, "Rev. John Elder and Identity in the Pennsylvania Backcountry," 470–71.
53. Hanna, *Scotch-Irish*, 1: 60.
54. Richard Lyman Bushman, *The American Farmer in the Eighteenth Century: A Social and Cultural History* (New Haven, CT: Yale University Press, 2018), 160–62.
55. *Col. Recs. Penn.* 9: 126, 133; *Penn. Archives*, 4th ser., 3: 273–74.
56. *Penn. Archives*, 1st ser., 4: 155; *The Journals of Henry Melchior Muhlenberg*, ed. Theodore G. Tappert and John W. Doberstein. 3 vols. (Philadelphia: Muhlenberg Press, 1942), 2; 18–24.
57. Spero, *Frontier Country*, 168.
58. Kenny, *Peaceable Kingdom*, ch. 15 (march on Philadelphia), 137 (threat to state).
59. Fintan O'Toole, "Going Native," in *The Lie of the Land: Irish Identities* (London: Verso, 1997), 23.

60. Egle, *History of the Counties of Dauphin and Lebanon*, 59–78; *Journals of Henry Melchior Muhlenberg*, 2: 19–20.
61. *Penn. Archives*, 4th ser., 3: 276–77; *Journals of Henry Melchior Muhlenberg*, 2: 23 ("like lords").
62. On the pamphlet war, see Kenny, *Peaceable Kingdom*, chs. 16–18; Silver, *Our Savage Neighbors*, 161–226; Spero, *Frontier Country*, 156–69; Alison Olsen, "The Pamphlet War over the Paxton Boys," *PMHB* 132 (1999), 31–55; Jeremy Engels, "Equipped for Murder: The Paxton Boys and 'the Spirit of Killing all Indians' in Pennsylvania, 1763–1764," *Rhetoric and Public Affairs* 8 (2005), 355–81; Nathan Kozuskanich, "'Who Ever Proclaimed War with Part of a Nation, and Not with the Whole?': The Paxton Riots and Perceptions of Civil Society in Pennsylvania," *Journal of Scotch-Irish Studies* 2 (2004), 45–63; Nicole Eustace, "The Sentimental Paradox: Humanity and Violence on the Pennsylvania Frontier," *William and Mary Quarterly* 65 (2008), 29–64; White, *The Backcountry and the City*, 114–21; Brubaker, *Massacre of the Conestogas*, ch. 6; Judith Ridner, "Unmasking the Paxton Boys: The Material Culture of the Pamphlet War," *Early American Studies* 14 (2016), 348–76, and the collection of pamphlets, broadsides, political cartoons, and correspondence assembled by the Pennsylvania Historical Society at Digital Paxton: A Digital Archive and Critical Edition of the Paxton Pamphlet War; http://digitalpaxton.org/works/digital-paxton/index.
63. Benjamin Franklin, "A Narrative of the Late Massacres, in Lancaster County," in *Paxton Papers*, 57–75, quotes at 63, 64, 72; also in *The Papers of Benjamin Franklin*, ed. Leonard W. Labaree, 37 vols. to date (New Haven, CT, and London: Yale University Press, 1959–), 11: 42–69, and "A Narrative of the Late Massacres, [30 January? 1764]," *Founders Online*, National Archives, https://founders.archives.gov/documents/Franklin/01-11-02-0012.
64. Colin G. Calloway, *The Scratch of a Penn: 1763 and the Transformation of North America* (New York: Oxford University Press, 2006), 78; *Papers of Benjamin Franklin*, 12: 160; Egle, *History of the Counties of Dauphin and Lebanon*, 68.
65. Merritt, *At the Crossroads*, 287; White, *The Backcountry and the City*, 114.
66. "Epistle from the Philadelphia Yearly Meeting, 1764," Digital Paxton.
67. Kenny, *Peaceable Kingdom*, 173–74; *Papers of Benjamin Franklin*, 11: 434.
68. Isaac Hunt, *The Scribbler, Being a Letter From a Gentleman in Town* (Philadelphia, 1764), 7–8; *A Looking-Glass for Presbyterians* (Philadelphia, 1764), in *Paxton Papers*, 241–55; quotes at 247–49 Benjamin Bankhurst, "A Looking-Glass for Presbyterians: Recasting a Prejudice in Late Colonial Pennsylvania," *PMHB* 133 (2009), 317–348; Samuel Fisher, "Fit Instruments in a Howling Wilderness: Colonists, Indians, and the Origins of the American Revolution," *William and Mary Quarterly* 73 (2016), 662–64.
69. *An Answer to the Pamphlet Entitled "The Conduct of the Paxton Men, Impartially Represented"* (Philadelphia, 1764), in *Paxton Papers*, 317–37, quote at 314.
70. *A Dialogue, Between Andrew Trueman, And Thomas Zealot; About the killing the Indians at Cannestogoe and Lancaster*, in *Paxton Papers*, 89–90.
71. Merritt, *At the Crossroads*, 12–13, 267–68, 288–94; Spero, *Frontier Country*, 158–64, 172; Kozuskanich, "'Who Ever Proclaimed War with Part of a Nation?'"; Eustace, "Sentimental Paradox."
72. Samuel K. Fisher, *The Gaelic and Indian Origins of the American Revolution: Diversity and Empire in the British Atlantic, 1688–1783* (New York: Oxford University Press, 2022), 220–23.
73. *A Declaration and Remonstrance of the Distressed and Bleeding Frontier Inhabitants of the Province of Pennsylvania, Presented by them to the Honourable Governor and Assembly of the Province, Shewing the Causes of their late Discontent and Uneasiness and the Grievances Under which they have labored, and which they humbly pray to have redress'd*, in *Paxton Papers*, 99–110, quotes at 105–8.
74. IILC 487, 496–97; James P. Myers, Jr., *The Ordeal of Thomas Barton, Anglican Missionary in the Pennsylvania Backcountry* (Bethlehem, PA: Lehigh University Press, 2010).
75. *The Conduct of the Paxton-Men, Impartially Represented* (Philadelphia, 1764), in *Paxton Papers*, 265–98, quotes at 271–72, 293, 296.
76. *The Cloven-Foot discovered*, in *Paxton Papers*, 85.
77. *Paxton Papers*, 173.
78. *Paxton Papers*, 190–91.
79. Hugh Williamson, *The Plain Dealer: or a few remarks upon Quaker Politics* (Philadelphia, 1764), in *Paxton Papers*, 339–51, quotes at 341, 343, 344; Patrick Spero, *Frontier Rebels: The Fight for Independence in the American West, 1756–1776* (New York: W. W. Norton, 2018), 41 (allocation of seats).

NOTES 449

80. David James Dove, *The Quaker unmask'd; or, Plain truth: humbly address'd to the consideration of all the freemen of Pennsylvania* (Philadelphia, 1764), in *Paxton Papers*, 205–15, quotes at 208, 211, 212.
81. Penn quoted in Spero, *Frontier Country*, 167; Kenny, *Peaceable Kingdom Lost*, 205.
82. Jacob Whistler letter, March 12, 1764, and Jacob Whistler to William Peters, April 9, 1764, Digital Paxton.
83. *Papers of Benjamin Franklin*, 11: 77, 239, 326–31.
84. Spero, *Frontier Country*, 166–69.
85. Alexandra Mancini, "The Paxton Boys and the Pamphlet Frenzy: Politics, Religion, and Social Structure in Eighteenth-Century Pennsylvania," *Concept* 30 (2007), 11; Kenny, *Peaceable Kingdom Lost*, 202. On the emerging German political influence, see Daniel Crown, "'A Breach That Must Be Healed': Immigration, Politics, and Voter Suppression in Late Colonial Pennsylvania," *PMHB* 146 (2022), 103–33.
86. *Papers of Benjamin Franklin*, 11: 485.
87. *Col. Recs. Penn.* 9: 190–92, quote at 191; Lucier, *Pontiac's Conspiracy and Other Indian Affairs*, 227.
88. "Bouquet Papers," *Collections of the Michigan Pioneer Historical Society* 19 (1892), 268.
89. Krista Camenzind, "Violence, Race, and the Paxton Boys," in *Friends and Enemies in Penn's Woods: Indians, Colonists, and the Racial Construction of Pennsylvania*, ed. William A. Pencak and Daniel K. Richter (University Park: Pennsylvania State University Press, 2004), 201–20, esp. 204; Matthew C. Ward, *Making the Frontier Man: Violence, White Manhood, and Authority in the Early Western Backcountry* (Pittsburgh: University of Pittsburgh Press, 2023).
90. Maurice J. Bric, *Ireland, Philadelphia and the Re-invention of America, 1760–1800* (Dublin: Four Courts Press, 2008), 51–60, esp. 59.
91. Joanna Brooks, "Held Captive by the Irish: Quaker Captivity Narratives in Frontier Pennsylvania," *New Hibernia Review / Iris Éireannach Nua* 8, no. 3 (Autumn 2004), 31–46.
92. Daniel P. Barr, "Did Pennsylvania Have a Middle Ground? Examining Indian-White Relations on the Eighteenth-Century Pennsylvania Frontier," *PMHB* 136 (2012), 337–63.
93. John Penn to his uncle, September 1, 1764, HSP, Penn Mss., Official Correspondence, 9: 252.
94. Pauline Maier, "Popular Uprisings and Civil Authority in Eighteenth-Century America," *William and Mary Quarterly* 27 (1970), 3–35, quote at 8; Paul A. Gilje, *Rioting in America* (Bloomington: Indiana University Press, 1996), ch. 1. As Robert Parkinson has suggested, the January 6 riot at the U.S. Capitol may lead historians to think differently about the "extra institutional" nature of eighteenth-century riots. Comments delivered at the session "The 1776 Problem in U.S. History," Annual Meeting of the Organization of American Historians, April 2, 2022.
95. Bric, *Ireland, Philadelphia and the Re-invention of America*, 59–60.
96. Spero, *Frontier Country*, 163–64.
97. Merrell, *Into the American Woods*, 287.
98. Daniel K. Richter, *Facing East from Indian Country: A Native History of Early America* (Cambridge, MA: Harvard University Press, 2003), 207–8.
99. Kenny, *Peaceable Kingdom Lost*, 5, 231.

Chapter 7

1. William Smith, *A Brief View of the Conduct of Pennsylvania, For the Year 1755* (London: R. Griffiths, 1756), 46–47.
2. William Smith, *Historical Account of Bouquet's Expedition against the Ohio Indians in 1764* (Cincinnati, OH: Robert Clarke Co., 1907), 62–67.
3. Matthew C. Ward, "Redeeming the Captives: Pennsylvania Captives among the Ohio Indians, 1755–1765," *PMHB* 125 (2001), 161–89, esp. 163; George P. Donehoo quoted in C. Hale Sipe, *The Indian Wars of Pennsylvania* (Harrisburg, PA: Telegraph Press, 1929), 405.
4. Ian K. Steele, *Setting All the Captives Free: Capture, Adjustment, and Recollection in Allegheny Country* (Montreal: McGill-Queens University Press, 2012), ch. 4 (figures at 115–16), 183, 430.
5. *Pennsylvania Gazette*, April 1, 1756.
6. *Col. Recs. Penn.* 7: 97–98.
7. Ward, "Redeeming the Captives," 183 (human shield), 188. For broader consideration of the influence of captives on captors, see Catherine Cameron, *Invisible Citizens: Captives and Their Consequences* (Salt Lake City: University of Utah Press, 2008); Cameron, "Captives and Culture Change," *Current Anthropology* 52 (2011), 169–209.

8. Steele, *Setting All the Captives Free*, 509; Jared C. Lobdel, ed., with notes by Lyman Copeland Draper, *Indian Warfare in Western Pennsylvania and North West Virginia at the Time of the American Revolution* (Bowie, MD: Heritage Books, 1992), 29.
9. Beverly W. Bond, Jr., ed., "The Captivity of Charles Stuart, 1755–57," *Mississippi Valley Historical Review* 13 (1926), 62; Steele, *Setting All the Captives Free*, 394–95.
10. Steele, *Setting All the Captives Free*, ch. 4.
11. An account of the captivity of Hugh Gibson, in Archibald Loudon, *A Selection of Some of the Most Interesting Narratives, of Outrages, Committed by the Indians, in Their Wars with the White People*, 2 vols. (Carlisle: A. Loudon, 1808), 2: 181–88, torture at 182; "Narrative of Marie Le Roy and Barbara Leininger," in *Crossroads: Descriptions of Western Pennsylvania, 1720–1829*, ed. John W. Harpster (Pittsburgh: University of Pittsburgh Press, 1938), 54–55; *Penn. Archives*, 2nd ser., 7: 405.
12. Steele, *Setting All the Captives Free*, 202, 204–5.
13. Colin G. Calloway, ed., *North Country Captives: Selected Narratives of Captivity from Vermont and New Hampshire* (Hanover, NH: University Press of New England, 1992), 19 (McCoy), 62 (Johnson); William Fleming and Elizabeth Fleming, *A Narrative of the Sufferings and Surprizing Deliverances of William and Elizabeth Fleming* (Boston: Greene and Russell, 1756) 5–8.
14. "Opinions of George Croghan," *PMHB* 71 (1947), 157; Samuel Cole Williams, ed., *Adair's History of the American Indians* (1930; reprint, New York: Promontory Press, n.d.), 172.
15. *Penn. Archives*, 2nd ser., 7: 403–12, quote at 404; Ruth Ann Denaci, "The Penn's Creek Massacre and the Captivity of Marie Le Roy and Barbara Leininger," *Pennsylvania History* 72 (2007), 307–32; Steele, *Setting All the Captives Free*, 207; Jean Lowery, *A Journal of the Captivity of Jean Lowery and Her Children* (Philadelphia: William Bradford, 1760), 9; Calloway, *North Country Captives*, 66.
16. Steele, *Setting All the Captives Free*, 219–20, 358, 361, 417, 446; Draper 23CC98–100.
17. Steele, *Setting All the Captives Free*, 232.
18. "Deposition of Patrick Burns," November 17, 1755, HSP, Penn Mss., vol. 2, Indian Affairs, 2: 44; Steele, *Setting All the Captives Free*, 87, 235, 378, 388, 510, 519.
19. "Journal of Charles Lewis, Oct. 10–Dec. 27, 1755," Draper 21U39–54, quote at 44.
20. Deposition of John Craig, March 30, 1756, HSP, Penn Mss., vol. 2, Indian Affairs, 2: 78; *Pennsylvania Gazette*, August 14, 1755.
21. "Examinations of Daniel McMullen and Thomas Moffitt," HSP, Penn Mss., vol. 2: Indian Affairs, 2: 101; *Col. Recs. Penn.* 7: 282–84.
22. Grace Toney Edwards, "Mary Draper Ingles: A Donegal Woman's Impact on Appalachian Virginia, 1747–2007," *Journal of Scotch-Irish Studies* 3, no. 1 (2009), 95–101; Joseph A. Waddell, *Annals of Augusta County, Virginia*, 2nd ed. (Staunton, VA: C. Russell Caldwell, 1902), 114–15; Steele, *Setting All the Captives Free*, 371. A 25-page memoir by John Inglis Jr. contains a detailed account of his mother's captivity and escape; Draper12U112.
23. Draper 21U136–37; Steele, *Setting All the Captives Free*, 194–95, 359, 460; Waddell, *Annals of Augusta County*, 169–70; Joseph Doddridge, *The Settlement and Indian Wars of the Western Parts of Virginia and Pennsylvania, 1763–1783* (Pittsburgh, 1912; reprint, Bowie, MD: Heritage Books, 1988), 169–70.
24. William Henry Egle, *Pennsylvania Genealogies, chiefly Scotch-Irish and German* (2nd ed., Harrisburg, 1896; reprint, Baltimore, MD: Genealogical Publishing, 1969), 64. Hanover, Pennsylvania, was founded about 1763 by Richard McAllister (McCalester; 1725–1795), a Scotch-Irish innkeeper and militia colonel.
25. *IILC* 156–78; alarms at 171; sons captured and quote at 172.
26. "A Narrative of the Captivity of John McCullough," in Loudon, *Selection of Some of the Most Interesting Narratives*, 1: 253–54, 257, 260, 276–77; Steele, *Setting All the Captives Free*, 211–12, 331–32, 421–22.
27. Steele, *Setting All the Captives Free*, 229.
28. James Axtell, "The White Indians of Colonial America," in *The European and the Indian: Essays in the Ethnohistory of Colonial North America*, ed. James Axtell (New York: Oxford University Press, 1981), 168–206; J. Hector St. John de Crèvecoeur, *Letters from an American Farmer* (London: J. M. Dent, 1971), 214–15.
29. *EAID* 3: 415.
30. James Axtell, *The Indian Peoples of Eastern America: A Documentary History of the Sexes* (New York: Oxford University Press, 1981), 41–43; John Heckewelder, *History, Manners, and Customs of the Indian Nations Who Once Inhabited Pennsylvania and the Neighboring States*

(Philadelphia: Historical Society of Pennsylvania, 1876; reprint, New York: Arno Press, 1971), 112–17, 163 ("sacred principle").
31. John Demos, *The Unredeemed Captive: A Family Story from Early America* (New York: Alfred A. Knopf, 1994).
32. Steele, *Setting All the Captives Free*, 199.
33. James Seaver, *A Narrative of the Life of Mary Jemison*, ed. June Namias (Norman: University of Oklahoma Press, 1992), 77–78.
34. Jerrold Casway, "Irish Women Overseas, 1500–1800," in *Women in Early Modern Ireland*, ed. Margaret MacCurtain and Mary O'Dowd (Dublin: Wolfhound Press, 1991), 129; James G. Leyburn, *The Scotch Irish: A Social History* (Chapel Hill: University of North Carolina Press, 1962), 263; David Hackett Fischer, *Albion's Seed: Four British Folkways in America* (New York: Oxford University Press, 1989), 676.
35. Susan Sleeper-Smith, *Indigenous Prosperity and American Conquest: Indian Women of the Ohio River Valley, 1690–1792* (Chapel Hill: University of North Carolina Press, 2018), ch. 1.
36. Seaver, *Narrative of the Life of Mary Jemison*, 83–84; cf. Heckewelder, *History, Manners, and Customs*, 154–57.
37. Seaver, *Narrative of the Life of Mary Jemison*, 119–20.
38. June Namias, *White Captives: Gender and Ethnicity on the American Frontier* (Chapel Hill: University of North Carolina Press, 1993), ch. 5 ("Irish emphasis" at 145; sequential families at 173).
39. Steele, *Setting All the Captives Free*, 495.
40. *The Diary of David McClure, 1748–1820*, ed. Franklin B. Dexter (New York: Knickerbocker Press, 1899), 86, 88.
41. "Renick Papers," Draper 4CC119–25; Draper 21U126–33 ("complete Indian" at 130); Steele, *Setting All the Captives Free*, 221, 357, 368, 523–24; Waddell, *Annals of Augusta County*, 49–50, 165, 201.
42. *Penn. Archives*, 1st ser., 4: 99.
43. *Penn. Archives*, 1st ser., 4: 100 (petition); Steele, *Setting All the Captives Free*, 255–56, 295–96.
44. *EAID* 3: 506–7, 509.
45. Julianna Barr, *Peace Came in the Form of a Woman: Indians and Spaniards in the Texas Borderlands* (Chapel Hill: University of North Carolina Press, 2007); *Penn. Archives*, 1st ser., 3: 461; Steele, *Setting All the Captives Free*, 272, 467.
46. Steele, *Setting All the Captives Free*, 286, 459–50; Elvert M. Davis, ed., "History of the Capture and Captivity of David Boyd from Cumberland County, Pennsylvania, 1756," *Western Pennsylvania Historical Magazine* 14 (1931), 28–42, esp. 38–39.
47. Steele, *Setting All the Captives Free*, 302.
48. *EAID* 3: 591 (Susannah Hudson Hatton Lightfoot as Irish at 662n).
49. *Col. Recs. Penn.* 8: 745; *EAID* 3: 363.
50. *Penn. Archives*, 4th ser., 3: 162.
51. *Col. Recs. Penn.* 8: 750; *Penn. Archives*, 1st ser., 4: 100–1; Steele, *Setting All the Captives Free*, 469, 548.
52. "Bouquet Papers," *Collections of the Michigan Pioneer Historical Society* 19 (1892), 280–81; Smith, *Historical Account of Bouquet's Expedition*, 53 (206 captives), 58; *Col. Recs. Penn.* 9: 207–8; *The Official Papers of Francis Fauquier, Lieutenant Governor of Virginia, 1758–1768*, ed. George Reese, 3 vols. (Charlottesville: University Press of Virginia, 1983), 3: 1161; *EAID* 3: 679, 689; *WJP* 4: 586; List of Captives delivered to Bouquet by Mingoes, Delawares, Shawnees, Wyandots and Mohicans at Tuskarawas and Muskingum, November 1764, *WJP* 11: 482–91.
53. Smith, *Historical Account of Bouquet's Expedition*, 62–64, 66–67.
54. June Lee Mefford Kinkead, *Our Kentucky Pioneer Ancestry: A History of the Kinkead and McDowell Families of Kentucky and Those Families Associated by Marriage* (Baltimore, MD: Gateway Press, 1992), 9.
55. Kinkead, *Our Kentucky Pioneer Ancestry*, 9, 19–24; Steele, *Setting All the Captives Free*, 331, 495; Waddell, *Annals of Augusta County*, 184–85.
56. Steele, *Setting All the Captives Free*, 332, 450; Davis, "History of the Capture and Captivity of David Boyd," 31.
57. *Col. Recs. Penn.* 9: 259–60; Smith, *Historical Account of Bouquet's Expedition*, 73–74; *WJP* 11: 727–28; Steele, *Setting All the Captives Free*, 356–57. The talks at Fort Pitt are in C.O. 5/66: 93–98. A list of prisoners delivered up by Shawnees at Fort Pitt, May 10, 1765, is in *WJP*

11: 720–21; a list of recovered captives in Sir William Johnson's treaty with the Delawares and Senecas in May 1765 is in *WJP* 4: 783–84. Most are children and unnamed.
58. Steele, *Setting All the Captives Free*, 230. William S. Ewing, "Indian Captives Released by Colonel Bouquet," *Western Pennsylvania Historical Magazine* 39 (1956), 187–203, provides lists of the names of the captives returned to Bouquet in 1764–1765.
59. South Caroliniana Library, University of South Carolina, Hobert W. Burns, *The Life of Anne Calhoun Mathews* (Palo Alto, CA: privately published, 1988), 21.
60. Lyman Chalkey, *Chronicles of the Scotch-Irish Settlement in Virginia, Extracted from the Original Court Records of Augusta County 1745–1800*, 3 vols. (1912; Baltimore, MD: Genealogical Publishing, 1965), 2: 453.
61. Steele, *Setting All the Captives Free*, 287, 363; *Pennsylvania Gazette*, September 9, 1762, p. 3; February 21, 1765, p. 3.
62. Steele, *Setting All the Captives Free*, 353, 368, 380 ("white Delaware"), 486; *Journals of Charles Beatty, 1762–1769*, ed. Guy Soulliard Klett (University Park: Pennsylvania State University Press, 1962), 49; "Bouquet Papers," *Collections of the Michigan Historical Society*, 19 (1892), 253–54, 258, 278, 689; *The Papers of Henry Bouquet*, ed. S. K. Stevens, Donald H. Kent, and Autumn L. Leonard, 6 vols. (Harrisburg: Pennsylvania Historical and Museum Commission, 1972–1994), 5: 381–82; 6: 514–16, 522–26, 540–41, 663.
63. Loudon, *Selection of Some of the Most Interesting Narratives*, 1: 119–251, esp. 205–7; *Scoouwa: James Smith's Indian Captivity Narrative* (Columbus: Ohio Historical Society, 1998), 121–27, 132–37.
64. Phillip W. Hoffman, *Simon Girty: Turncoat Hero* (Franklin, TN: Flying Camp Press, 2008), 2. Sarah Munger, Simon Girty, Jr.'s only surviving child in 1864, said she could give no information about Simon Girty, Sr., but her father used to say the family was a mix of English and Irish or Welsh; Draper 20S196.
65. Colin G. Calloway, "Simon Girty: Interpreter and Intermediary," in *Being and Becoming Indian: Biographical Studies of North American Frontier*, ed. James A. Clifton (Chicago: Dorsey Press, 1989), 38–43; "Depositions of Simon and Thomas Girty," 1777, *Calendar of Virginia State Papers*, 1: 280; Steele, *Setting All the Captives Free*, 222–23, 480–81; Hoffman, *Simon Girty*, 1–47; Consul Wilshire Butterfield, *History of the Girtys* (Cincinnati: Robert Clarke & Co., 1890), 1–16; "An Account Book of Baynton, Wharton, and Morgan at Fort Pitt, 1765–1767," *Western Pennsylvania Historical Magazine* 29 (1946), 144, lists the Girty brothers among the traders in the company's employ; Alexander McKee's Account, 1774, includes Simon Girty's pay as an interpreter; *WJP* 8: 1168.
66. *WJP* 11: 436–37, 723–24; Butterfield, *History of the Girtys*, 14; *Col. Recs. Penn.* 9: 256; *EAID* 3: 697, 705.
67. Steele, *Setting All the Captives Free*, 338, 350.
68. Steele, *Setting All the Captives Free*, 360–61, 491; Draper12U112; Waddell, *Annals of Augusta County*, 115 ("perfect savage"); *Documentary History of Dunmore's War, 1774*, ed. Reuben G. Thwaites and Louise Phelps Kellogg (Madison: Wisconsin Historical Society, 1905), 179–80n.
69. Elizabeth Hornor, "Intimate Enemies: Captivity and Colonial Fear of Indians in the Mid-Eighteenth Century Wars," *Pennsylvania History* 82 (2015), 162–85.

Chapter 8

1. Melissah J. Pawlikowski, "The Plight and the Bounty: Squatters, War Profiteers, and the Transforming Hand of Sovereignty in Indian Country, 1750–1774," Ph.D. diss., Ohio State University, 2014, 172; *Penn. Archives*, 1st ser. 4: 503; 4th ser. 3: 486–87; Clarence D. Stephenson, "The Wipey Affair: An Incident Illustrating Pennsylvania's Attitude during Dunmore's War," *Pennsylvania History* 23 (1956), 504–12. The Kittanning Path ran from Frankstown to Kittanning. Paul A. Wallace, *Indian Paths of Pennsylvania* (Harrisburg: Pennsylvania Historical and Museum Commission, 1993), front map and 79.
2. Gregory Evans Dowd, *War under Heaven: Pontiac, the Indian Nations, and the British Empire* (Baltimore, MD: Johns Hopkins University Press, 2002). For broader consideration of issues of status within the empire, see Samuel K. Fisher, *The Gaelic and Indian Origins of the American Revolution: Diversity and Empire in the British Atlantic, 1688–1783* (New York: Oxford University Press, 2022).
3. Peter C. Mancall, *Valley of Opportunity: Economic Culture along the Upper Susquehanna, 1700–1800* (Ithaca, NY: Cornell University Press, 1991), 72.

4. The Proclamation is in Adam Shortt and Arthur G. Doughty, eds., *Documents Relating to the Constitutional History of Canada, 1759–1791*, 2 vols. (Ottawa: Historical Documents Publication Board, 1918), 163–68, and *Col. Recs. Penn.* 9: 80–85. Colin G. Calloway, *The Scratch of a Pen: 1763 and the Transformation of North America* (New York: Oxford University Press, 2006); Woody Holton, *Forced Founders: Indians, Debtors, Slaves, and the Making of the American Revolution in Virginia* (Chapel Hill: University of North Carolina Press, 1999), 29–30; Woody Holton, "The History of the Stamp Act Shows How Indians Led to the American Revolution," *Humanities* 36, no. 4 (July–August 2015), https://www.neh.gov/humanities/2015/julyaugust/feature/the-history-the-stamp-act-shows-how-indians-led-the-american-revo; . Woody Holton develops the role of British attempts to pacify the frontier by keeping Indians and settlers apart as root causes of revolution in *Liberty Is Sweet: Hidden Histories of the American Revolution* (New York: Simon and Schuster, 2021)
5. Pawlikowski, "The Plight and the Bounty."
6. Patrick Griffin, *American Leviathan: Empire, Nation, and Revolutionary Frontier* (New York: Hill and Wang, 2007), 60, 77–78.
7. Judith Ridner, *A Town In-Between: Carlisle, Pennsylvania, and the Early Mid-Atlantic Frontier* (Philadelphia: University of Pennsylvania Press, 2010), 93–94, 109; Judith Ridner, "Relying on the 'Saucy' Men of the Backcountry: Middlemen and the Fur Trade in Pennsylvania," *PMHB* 129 (2005), 133–62; Richard K. MacMaster, "Searching for Community: Carlisle, Pennsylvania, 1750s–1780s," in *Ulster to America: The Scots-Irish Migration Experience, 1680–1830*, ed. Warren Hofstra (Knoxville: University of Tennessee Press, 2012), 95–97, 103–4; "Bouquet Papers," *Collections of the Michigan Pioneer and Historical Society* 19 (1892), 90 (quote).
8. *WJP* 4: 632 (Callender petition), 705–6, 710 (Wharton), 722 (Croghan losses), 732; 11: 643–45 (Gage); Captain Thomas Barnsley to Thomas Gage, March 11, 1765, and Depositions of James Maxwell and William Smith, April 3, 1765, Digital Paxton; Armand Francis Lucier, comp., *Pontiac's Conspiracy and Other Indian Affairs: Notices Abstracted from Colonial Newspapers, 1763–1765* (Bowie, MD: Heritage Books, 2000), 279–82.
9. John Armstrong to George Croghan, March 26, 1765, Digital Paxton.
10. *Scoouwa: James Smith's Indian Captivity Narrative* (Columbus: Ohio Historical Society, 1998), 121–27, 132–37; Col. James Smith, "An Account of his Captivity," in Archibald Loudon, *A Selection of Some of the Most Interesting Narratives, of Outrages, Committed by the Indians, in Their Wars with the White People*, 2 vols. (Carlisle: A. Loudon, 1808), 1: 208–11.
11. Quoted in Ridner, "Relying on the 'Saucy' Men of the Backcountry," 133–34.
12. Patrick Spero, *Frontier Rebels: The Fight for Independence in the American West, 1756–1776* (New York: W. W. Norton, 2018); Jay B. Donis, "The Black Boys and Blurred Lines: Reshaping Authority on the Pennsylvania Frontier," *Journal of Early American History* 6 (2016), 68–93.
13. John B. Franz and William Pencak, "Introduction: Pennsylvania and Its Three Revolutions," in *Beyond Philadelphia: The American Revolution in the Pennsylvania Hinterland*, ed. John B. Frantz and William Pencak (University Park: Pennsylvania State University Press, 1998), xx–xxi.
14. *WJP* 11: 664–65, quote at 665.
15. *WJP* 11: 759–61.
16. *Penn. Archives*, 4th ser. 3: 300–8, 310–11.
17. *Penn. Archives*, 1st ser. 4: 217.
18. George Henry Loskiel, *History of the Mission of the United Brethren among the Indians in North America* [1789], trans. Christian Ignatius Latrobe, 3 parts (London: The Brethren's Society for the Furtherance of the Gospel, 1794), 2: 170 ("snakes"); 3: 205.
19. *Collections of the Michigan Pioneer and Historical Society* 19 (1892), 294.
20. *WJP* 4: 771, 774 (quote); 5: 216; 11: 798–99 (quote); 12: 74–75. On the possibility of inherited prejudices, see Fintan O'Toole, *White Savage: William Johnson and the Invention of America* (New York: Farrar, Straus, and Giroux, 2005), 269–70.
21. *Penn. Archives*, 1st ser. 4: 260–61; *WJP* 12: 231–32, 240.
22. Spero, *Frontier Rebels*, xxvi, 154–55.
23. Albert H. Tillson, Jr., *Gentry and Commonfolk: Political Culture on a Virginia Frontier, 1740–1789* (Lexington: University of Kentucky, 1991), 48–49.
24. *EAID* 5: 309–18; *The Official Papers of Francis Fauquier, Lieutenant Governor of Virginia, 1758–1768*, ed. George Reese, 3 vols. (Charlottesville: University Press of Virginia, 1983), 3: 1234–42, 1248–49, 1253–62, 1265–69 (quotes at 1243, 1248, 1254, 1288); Thomas A. Lewis, *West from Shenandoah: A Scotch-Irish Family Fights for America, 1721–1781* (Hoboken, NJ: John Wiley and Sons, 2004), 187–89; Patricia Givens Johnson, *General Andrew Lewis of Roanoke and*

Greenbriar (privately published; printed by Southern Printing Co., Blacksburg, VA, 1980), 131–40; Jay Donis, "'No Man shall suffer for the murder of a Savage': The Augusta Boys and the Virginia and Pennsylvania Frontiers," *Pennsylvania History* 86 (2019), 38–66.
25. *SRNC* 7: 212; *Correspondence of General Thomas Gage*, 1: 134.
26. *Official Papers of Francis Fauquier*, 3: 1355–56, 1377–79, 1394; *Penn. Archives*, 1st ser. 4: 255; 4th ser. 3: 326–28.
27. *IILC* 112n (fortified Scotch-Irish settlement); *Penn. Archives*, 1st ser. 4: 251–52; *Official Papers of Francis Fauquier*, 3: 1407.
28. David L. Preston, *The Texture of Contact: European and Indian Settlers Communities on the Frontier of Iroquoia, 1667–1783* (Lincoln: University of Nebraska Press, 2009), 216–23, 253–55; *WJP* 5: 737.
29. *Penn. Archives*, 1st ser. 4: 283–85; 4th ser. 3: 347–49, 365–67, 383–86; *Correspondence of General Thomas Gage*, 1:157.
30. On the Annin and McKenzie murders, and Governor Franklin's motives for ensuring that justice was carried out in this case, see Robert M. Owens, *Killing over Land: Murder and Diplomacy on the Early American Frontier* (Norman: University of Oklahoma Press, 2024), ch. 1. Also Peter Silver, *Our Savage Neighbors: How Indian War Transformed Early America* (New York: W. W. Norton, 2008), 153–55.
31. *Col. Recs. Penn.* 9: 351–53; *Penn Archives*, 4th ser. 3: 329–32; *Correspondence of General Thomas Gage*, 1: 91; *Official Papers of Francis Fauquier*, 3: 1436–38, 1480–81.
32. Patrick Spero, *Frontier Country: The Politics of War in Early Pennsylvania* (Philadelphia: University of Pennsylvania Press, 2016), 187–93; *Penn. Archives*, 4th ser. 3: 350–65, 368–76, 387–89, 393–96; *Col. Recs. Penn.* 9: 414–21, 438, 441–52, 448, 450–52, 462–65, 484–87 (Armstrong quotes at 462–63; also in Armstrong to Penn, February 7, 1768, Digital Paxton); Armstrong to [?], January 24, 1768, HSP, Lamberton Collection on Scotch-Irish Settlements in Cumberland County, folder 80.
33. Samuel Cole Williams, ed., *Early Travels in the Tennessee Country, 1540–1800* (Johnson City, TN: Watauga Press, 1928), 509.
34. *Penn. Archives*, 1st ser. 4: 290.
35. *WJP* 6: 108, 111.
36. *DAR* 2: 248–50; *Correspondence of General Thomas Gage*, 1: 277–78.
37. *EAID* 5: 326–32; *Executive Journals*, 6: 279, 287, 306.
38. Colin G. Calloway, *Pen and Ink Witchcraft: Treaties and Treaty-Making in American Indian History* (New York: Oxford University Press, 2013), ch. 2; William J. Campbell, *Speculators in Empire: Iroquoia and the 1768 Treaty of Fort Stanwix* (Norman: University of Oklahoma Press, 2012).
39. Wayland F. Dunaway, *The Scotch-Irish of Colonial Pennsylvania* (Chapel Hill: University of North Carolina Press, 1944), 72–77; Guy S. Klett, "Scotch-Irish Presbyterian Pioneering along the Susquehanna River," *Pennsylvania History* 20 (1953), 170.
40. Pawlikowski, "The Plight and the Bounty," 176–77.
41. *IILC* 180.
42. "Deposition of Felix Donolly, keeper of Lancaster Jail," in Francis Parkman, *The Conspiracy of Pontiac and the Indian War after the Conquest of Canada*, 2 vols. (originally published 1851; reprint of revised 1870 edition, Lincoln: University of Nebraska Press, 1994), Appendix E, 2: 344.
43. Petition of Stewart in Julian P. Boyd et al., eds., *The Susquehannah Company Papers*, 11 vols. (Ithaca, NY: Cornell University Press for Wyoming Historical & Geological Society, Wilkes Barre, PA, 1930–1971), 3: 176–77; Paul B. Moyer, *Wild Yankees: The Struggle for Independence along Pennsylvania's Revolutionary Frontier* (Ithaca, NY: Cornell University Press, 2007), ch. 1; Kathryn Shively Meier, "'Devoted to Hardships, Danger, and Devastation': The Landscape of Indian and White Violence in Wyoming Valley, Pennsylvania, 1753–1800," in *Blood in the Hills: A History of Violence in Appalachia*, ed. Bruce E. Stewart (Lexington: University Press of Kentucky, 2012), ch. 2, esp. 60–63; *Penn. Archives*, 4th ser. 3: 430–31, 434–36 (proclamations for arrest); Frederick J. Stefon, "The Wyoming Valley," in *Beyond Philadelphia: The American Revolution in the Pennsylvania Hinterland*, ed. John B. Frantz and William Pencak (University Park: Pennsylvania State University Press, 1998), 139–40; James Kirby Martin, "The Return of the Paxton Boys and the Historical State of the Pennsylvania Frontier, 1764–1774," *Pennsylvania History* 38 (1971), 117–33.

44. Marcus Gallo, "'Fair Play Has Entirely Ceased, and Law Has Taken Its Place': The Rise and Fall of the Squatter Republic on the West Branch of the Susquehanna River, 1768–1800," *PMHB* 136 (2012), 405–34.
45. Karen Harvey, "'When I am at the farthest Frontiers of this Colony, & among the wild-natured Savages': Scotch-Irish and Native Americans on the Susquehanna Frontier of Colonial Pennsylvania," *Journal of Scotch-Irish Studies* 3, no. 1 (2009), 68–79 (esp. 73–74); Phillip Vickers Fithian, *Journal, 1775–1776; Written on the Virginia-Pennsylvania Frontier*, ed. Robert G. Albion and Leondias Dodson (Princeton, NJ: Princeton University Press, 1934), 81–82.
46. Pawlikowski, "The Plight and the Bounty."
47. *DAR* 2: 22 (leaving Susquehanna); William Patterson to Israel Pemberton, June 10, 1771, Digital Paxton.
48. *DAR* 2: 204.
49. Cameron B. Strang, "Michael Cresap and the Promulgation of Settler Land-Claiming Methods in the Backcountry, 1765–1774," *Virginia Magazine of History and Biography* 118 (2010), 106–35; Honor Sachs, *Home Rule: Households, Manhood, and National Expansion on the Eighteenth-Century Kentucky Frontier* (New Haven, CT: Yale University Press, 2015), 27–32.
50. Rob Harper, *Unsettling the West: Violence and State Building in the Ohio Valley* (Philadelphia: University of Pennsylvania Press, 2018), 28–29.
51. Stephen Aron, "Pigs and Hunters: 'Rights in the Woods' on the Trans-Appalachian Frontier," in *Contact Points: American Frontiers from the Mohawk Valley to the Mississippi, 1750–1830*, ed. Andrew R. L. Cayton and Fredricka J. Teute (Chapel Hill: University of North Carolina Press, 1998), 182.
52. Charles A. Hanna, *The Wilderness Trail, or The Ventures and Adventures of the Pennsylvania Traders on the Allegheny Path*, 2 vols. (New York: G. P. Putnam's Sons, 1911), 2: 212–36; John Mack Faragher, *Daniel Boone: The Life and Legend of an American Pioneer* (New York: Henry Holt, 1992), 70–79.
53. *George Croghan's Journal of His Trip to Detroit in 1767 with His Correspondence Relating Thereto*, ed. Howard H. Peckham (Ann Arbor: University of Michigan Press, 1939), 23; Andrea L. Smalley, "'They Steal Our Deer and Land': Contested Hunting Grounds in the Trans-Appalachian West," *Register of the Kentucky Historical Society* 114 (2016), 303–9; Aron, "Pigs and Hunters"; *The Diary of David McClure, 1748–1820*, ed. Franklin B. Dexter (New York: Knickerbocker Press, 1899), 85 (Killbuck); John Sugden, *Blue Jacket: Warrior of the Shawnees* (Lincoln: University of Nebraska Press, 2000), 460 ("crazy people" quote). See also Andrea L. Smalley, *Wild by Nature: North American Animals Confront Colonization* (Baltimore, MD: Johns Hopkins University Press, 2017).
54. Theodore Roosevelt, *The Winning of the West*, 6 vols. in 3 (New York: G. P. Putnam's Sons, 1899), 1, pt. 1: 196–97.
55. Harriette Simpson Arnow, *Seedtime on the Cumberland* (New York: Macmillan 1960), 167–68.
56. *Documentary History of Dunmore's War, 1774*, ed. Reuben G. Thwaites and Louise Phelps Kellogg (Madison: Wisconsin Historical Society, 1905), 111n, 239.
57. *Documentary History of Dunmore's War*, 225.
58. Michael Montgomery and Cherel Henderson, "Eighteenth-Century Emigrants from Ireland to Tennessee: A Report Using First Families of Tennessee Files," *Journal of East Tennessee History* 76 (2004), 88–99; Arnow, *Seedtime on the Cumberland*, 243, 349 (mixed); Arnow, *Flowering of the Cumberland* (East Lansing: Michigan State University Press, 2013), 70–71.
59. Thomas Perkins Abernethy, *From Frontier to Plantation in Tennessee: A Study in Frontier Democracy* (Chapel Hill: University of North Carolina Press, 1932), 3; John Buchanan, *Jackson's Way: Andrew Jackson and the People of the Western Waters* (New York: John Wiley and Sons, 2001), 25–26; A. W. Putnam, *History of Middle Tennessee or, Life and Times of Gen. James Robertson* (1859; reprint, Knoxville: University of Tennessee, 1971), ch. 1.
60. Philip M. Hamer, "The Wataugans and the Cherokee Indians in 1776," *East Tennessee Historical Publications* 3 (1931), 108–14; [Moses Fisk], "A Summary Notice of the First Settlements Made by White People within the Limits which Bound the State of Tennessee," *Collections of the Massachusetts Historical Society* 7 (1816), 58–62, quote at 60; Abernethy, *From Frontier to Plantation in Tennessee*, 2–10; Max Dixon, *The Wataugans* (Nashville: Tennessee American Revolution Bicentennial Commission, 1976), 4–21; J. M. Opal, *Avenging the People: Andrew Jackson, the Rule of Law, and the American Nation* (New York: Oxford University Press, 2017), 20–21; Natalie Inman, "Military Families: Kinship in the American Revolution," in *Before the Volunteer State: New Thoughts on Early Tennessee, 1540–1800*, ed. Kristofer Ray

456 NOTES

(Knoxville: University of Tennessee Press, 2014), 135; Draper 3QQ142 (Oconostota); *DAR* 8: 57 (Cameron).

61. Dartmouth to Dunmore, May 16, 1774, C.O. 5/1352: 141, quoted in Hamer, "The Wataugans and the Cherokee Indians in 1776," 113–14, and Dixon, *The Wataugans*, 20; Roosevelt, *Winning of the West*, 1, pt. 2: 227. It seems Dunmore misread the Watauga Association: the settlers were not separating themselves from England, but associating themselves with Virginia in an area that belonged to North Carolina. David Hackett Fischer and James C. Kelly, *Bound Away: Virginia and the Westward Movement* (Charlottesville: University of Virginia Press, 2000), 145–46.
62. *DAR* 6: 234.
63. *Penn. Archives*, 1st ser. 4: 411–12.
64. C.O. 5/90: 5 ("black clouds"), 78 ("exterminated"); also in *DAR* 3: 254–55; 5: 203 and *EAID* 3: 754.
65. "Letters of Colonel George Croghan," *PMHB* 15 (1891), 437–38.
66. Holton, *Liberty Is Sweet*, 116.
67. *Correspondence of General Thomas Gage*, 2: 601.
68. *Penn. Archives*, 4th ser. 3: 537–38. Penn recommended that the Assembly keep a small garrison there (538–39).
69. Spero, *Frontier Rebels*, 160, 162; Spero, *Frontier Country*, 207.
70. *WJP* 12: 1023–24.
71. *DAR* 5: 203; C.O. 5/90: 87; *Correspondence of General Thomas Gage*, 1: 336.
72. *Diary of David McClure*, 1–2, 36, 38, 41, 47, 93, 112, 123, 127, 129.
73. *Diary of David McClure*, 119.
74. Griffin, *American Leviathan*, 93.
75. "McAfee Papers," Draper 4CC69–71; "The Life and Times of Robert B. McAfee and His Family and Connections," *Register of the Kentucky State Historical Society* 25 (1927), 5–24 (origins at 7–9; Butler at 15; joined Lewis at 23–24); *Documentary History of Dunmore's War*, 207n.
76. *Documentary History of Dunmore's War*, 371, 376; *DAR* 8: 253–54.
77. Harper, *Unsettling the West*.
78. Reports that Cresap's men killed forty Indians appear to have been much exaggerated. Strang, "Michael Cresap and the Promulgation of Settler Land-Claiming Methods," 125–26; Robert G. Parkinson, *Heart of American Darkness: Bewilderment and Horror on the Early Frontier* (New York: W. W. Norton, 2024), 168–73. On Cresap's subsequent career and reputation, see Robert G. Parkinson, "From Indian Killer to Worthy Citizen: The Revolutionary Transformation of Michael Cresap," *William and Mary Quarterly* 63 (2006), 97–122.
79. In his careful reconstruction of the massacre, Robert Parkinson counts eight dead; other accounts say there were thirteen victims. *WJP* 12: 1097–98; *Documentary History of Dunmore's War*, 9–19, 246; Parkinson, *Heart of American Darkness*, xviii–xix, 176–82; Griffin, *American Leviathan*, 108–10; *The Washington-Crawford Letters: Being the Correspondence between George Washington and William Crawford, from 1767 to 1781, Concerning Western Lands*, ed. Consul W. Butterfield (Cincinnati: Robert Clarke and Co., 1877), 48–51; *The Papers of George Washington: Colonial Series*, ed. W. W. Abbot, Dorothy Twohig, et al., 10 vols. (Charlottesville: University Press of Virginia, 1983–1995), 10: 54, 93 For discussion of whether Logan was Soyechtowa (James Logan) or Tachnedorus (John Logan), see Parkinson, *Heart of American Darkness*, Appendix, 376–83.
80. *Penn. Archives*, 1st ser. 4: 512; *DRCHNY* 8: 464–65; *Documentary History of Dunmore's War*, 9–11 ("Kin to themselves" at 10), 15–17; *The Olden Time: A Monthly Publications devoted to the Preservation of Documents and other Authentic Information in relation to the Early Explorations and the Settlement and Improvement of the Country around the Head of the Ohio*, ed. Neville B. Craig, 2 vols. (1848; reprint, Cincinnati: Robert Clarke & Co., 1876), 2: 38–39.
81. *EAID* 3: 330n; Gary S. Wilson, *"No Man Knows the Country Better": The Frontier Life of John Gibson* (Akron, OH: University of Akron Press, 2022), 3–4.
82. C. Hale Sipe, *The Indian Wars of Pennsylvania* (Harrisburg, PA: Telegraph Press, 1929), 502; Charles W. Hanko, *The Life of John Gibson: Soldier, Patriot, Statesman* (Daytona Beach, FL: College Publishing Co., 1955), 10, 12–13, 15–16, 24; Wilson, *"No Man Knows the Country Better,"* 16–19, 29–32.
83. *Documentary History of Dunmore's War*, 29–32.
84. *Penn. Archives*, 1st ser. 4: 514, 518, 532.
85. *WJP* 8: 1182–83, 1185.

86. Colin G. Calloway, "Simon Girty: Interpreter and Intermediary," in *Being and Becoming Indian: Biographical Studies of North American Frontier*, ed. James A. Clifton (Chicago: Dorsey Press, 1989), 43–44; *WJP* 12: 107–99, 1100; see also *The Olden Time*, 2: 13–24 (negotiations with Connolly, Thomas McKee, White Eyes, Guyasuta, and others).
87. "Account of the Rise of the Indian War," *Penn. Archives*, 1st ser. 4: 568–70.
88. *Documentary History of Dunmore's War*, 66–67; *DAR*, 8:15; Barbara Rasmussen, "Anarchy and Enterprise on the Imperial Frontier: Washington, Dunmore, Logan, and Land in the Eighteenth-Century Ohio Valley," *Ohio Valley History* 6 (2006), 1–26; Strang, "Michael Cresap and the Promulgation of Settler Land-Claiming Methods," 125–29; Griffin, *American Leviathan*, 104–13; James Corbett David, *Dunmore's New World* (Charlottesville: University of Virginia Press, 2013), 76–93, offers a more generous interpretation of Dunmore's role.
89. *Penn. Archives*, 1st ser. 4: 540–42.
90. *Documentary History of Dunmore's War*, 37 (Ten Mile Creek), 396–425 (rosters).
91. Katherine L. Brown and Kenneth W. Keller, "Searching for Status: Virginia's Irish Tract, 1770s–1790s," in *Ulster to America: The Scots-Irish Migration Experience, 1680–1830*, ed. Warren Hofstra (Knoxville: University of Tennessee Press, 2012), 132.
92. *Documentary History of Dunmore's War*, xvii–xviii, 74–75.
93. Joseph A. Waddell, *Annals of Augusta County, Virginia*, 2nd ed. (Staunton, VA: C. Russell Caldwell, 1902), 120–21; *Documentary History of Dunmore's War*, 91–93, 430–31; Draper 21U58 (Londonderry, December 25); Draper 1QQ92 (Preston's company of rangers); Draper 1QQ96-123 (diary of Sandy Creek expedition).
94. *Documentary History of Dunmore's War*, 86.
95. James G. Leyburn, *The Scotch-Irish: A Social History* (Chapel Hill: University of North Carolina Press, 1962), 231n ("primarily of Scotch-Irish").
96. *Documentary History of Dunmore's War*, 422n; Draper 9BB63, 8ZZ71. In 1792, John Ward fought in a skirmish against Kentucky militia that included his brother; a year later he was killed in a fight where another brother was on the opposing side.
97. Lyman Chalkey, *Chronicles of the Scotch-Irish Settlement in Virginia, extracted from the Original Court Records of Augusta County 1745–1800*, 3 vols. (1912; Baltimore, MD: Genealogical Publishing, 1965), 1: 512.
98. Draper 3S11.
99. *Documentary History of Dunmore's War*, xxii–xxiii.
100. François Furstenberg, "The Significance of the Trans-Appalachian Frontier in Atlantic History," *American Historical Review* 113 (2008), 654; Holton, *Forced Founders*, 33.
101. "The Letters of Hon. James Habersham, 1756–1775," *Collections of the Georgia Historical Society* 6 (1904), 199; C.O. 5/74: 23; C.O. 5/75: 200.
102. "To Benjamin Franklin from Theodorus Swaine Drage, 2 March 1771," *Founders Online*, National Archives, https://founders.archives.gov/documents/Franklin/01-18-02-0028. [Original source: *The Papers of Benjamin Franklin*, vol. 18, *January 1 through December 31, 1771*, ed. William B. Willcox (New Haven, CT: Yale University Press, 1974), 38–50].
103. Richard J. Hooker, ed., *The Carolina Backcountry on the Eve of the Revolution: The Journal and Other Writings of Charles Woodmason, Anglican Itinerant* (Chapel Hill: University of North Carolina Press, 1953), 42.
104. Hooker, *Carolina Backcountry on the Eve of the Revolution*, 27.
105. Hooker, *Carolina Backcountry on the Eve of the Revolution*, 6–7.
106. Hooker, *Carolina Backcountry on the Eve of the Revolution*, 14–15.
107. Hooker, *Carolina Backcountry on the Eve of the Revolution*, 25, 33, 43, 50, 52, 56, 60–61, 82.
108. Lucier, *Pontiac's Conspiracy and Other Indian Affairs*, 75 ("in the middle of the Waxsaw settlement").
109. *EAID* 5: 305–6.
110. *NCCR* 5: 560.
111. *NCCR* 5: 561.
112. Hooker, *Carolina Backcountry on the Eve of the Revolution*, 20.
113. David Noel Doyle, *Ireland, Irishmen, and Revolutionary America, 1760–1820* (Dublin: Mercier Press, 1981), 135 (predominantly Scotch-Irish); Timothy J. Meagher, *Becoming Irish American: The Making and Remaking of a People from Roanoke to JFK* (New Haven, CT: Yale University Press, 2023), 44–45.
114. Rachel N. Klein, *Unification of a Slave State: The Rise of a Planter Class in the South Carolina Backcountry, 1760–1808* (Chapel Hill: University of North Carolina Press, 1990), 47–77.

115. Marjoline Kars, *Breaking Loose Together: The Regulator Rebellion in Pre-Revolutionary North Carolina* (Chapel Hill: University of North Carolina Press, 2002), 126, chs. 2–3; Wayne E. Lee, *Crowds and Soldiers in Revolutionary North Carolina: The Culture of Violence in Riot and War* (Gainesville: University Press of Florida, 2001), part 1; William S. Powell et al., eds., *The Regulators in North Carolina: A Documentary History, 1759–1776* (Raleigh, NC: Department of Archives and History, 1971); *DAR* 3: 97–99; *NCCR* 8 contains multiple Regulator documents.
116. C.O. 5/410: 38; *DAR* 8: 158; R. F. Foster, *Modern Ireland, 1600–1972* (New York: Penguin, 1989), 222–23.
117. Cynthia Cumfer, *Separate Peoples, One Land: The Minds of Cherokees, Blacks, and Whites on the Tennessee Frontier* (Chapel Hill: University of North Carolina Press, 2007), 44.
118. Quoted in Bryan C. Rindfleisch, *George Galphin's Intimate Empire: The Creek Indians, Family, and Colonialism in Early America* (Tuscaloosa: University of Alabama Press, 2019), 54.
119. Michael P. Morris, "Profits and Philanthropy: The Ulster Immigration Schemes of George Galphin and John Rae," *Journal of Scotch-Irish Studies* 1 (2002), 1–11; Richard K. MacMaster, "From Ulster to the Carolinas: John Torrans, John Greg, John Poaug, and Bounty Emigration, 1761–1768," in *The Irish in the Atlantic World*, ed. David T. Gleeson (Columbia: University of South Carolina Press, 2010), 251–74; Rindfleisch, *George Galphin's Intimate Empire*, 15, 35, 82–85; *IILC* 82–83; *Col. Recs. State of Georgia* 9: 269–70.
120. Morris, "Profits and Philanthropy"; *IILC* 82–84 (letter to brother). On Mathew Rae, see R. J. Dickson, *Ulster Emigration to Colonial America 1718–1775* (London: Routledge and Kegan Paul, 1966), 164–73.
121. *IILC* 85.
122. Minutes of Council discussing attack made by Creek Indians and the deposition of Martin Weatherford, as held in Savannah Council Chambers on the 9th of October, 1771, C.O. 5/661: 28.
123. Dickson, *Ulster Emigration to Colonial America*, 172; E. R. R. Green, "Queensborough Township: Scotch-Irish Emigration and the Expansion of Georgia, 1763–1776," *William and Mary Quarterly* 17 (1960), 183–99; Morris, "Profits and Philanthropy," 8–9; Rindfleisch, *George Galphin's Intimate Empire*, 150–64 (kill the first Indian at 158).
124. *DRCHNY* 8: 396.

Chapter 9

1. *IILC* 543–44.
2. *DAR* 9: 87 (Galloway); 9: 122 (Gage); C.O. 5/769: 51 (Gage); *IILC* 567; David Noel Doyle, *Ireland, Irishmen, and Revolutionary America, 1760–1820* (Dublin: Mercier Press, 1981), 110–11; James G. Leyburn, *The Scotch-Irish: A Social History* (Chapel Hill: University of North Carolina Press 1962), 305 (Scotch-Irish Presbyterian rebellion), 308; Michael O'Brien, *Irish Settlers in America: A Consolidation of Articles from "The Journal of the American Irish Historical Society,"* 2 vols. (Baltimore, MD: Genealogical Publishing, 1979, 1993), 1: 547–57 (Irish regiment at 548). Journalist Niall O'Dowd, *George Washington and the Irish: Incredible Stories of the Irish Spies, Soldiers, and Workers Who Helped Free America* (New York: Skyhorse, 2022), provides a popular treatment of the Irish role in the Revolution.
3. T. H. Breen, "Samuel Thompson's War: The Career of an American Insurgent," in *Revolutionary Founders: Rebels, Radicals, and Reformers in the Making of the Nation*, ed. Alfred F. Young, Gary B. Nash, and Ray Raphael (New York: Alfred A. Knopf, 2011), 58–59 ("It would not be a great exaggeration to claim that the American Revolution was also Ireland's revolution in America"); Patrick Griffin, *The Age of Atlantic Revolution: The Fall and Rise of a Connected World* (New Haven, CT: Yale University Press, 2023), 108, 130; S. J. Connolly, *Divided Kingdom: Ireland 1630–1800* (New York: Oxford University Press, 2008), 402; Timothy J. Meagher, *Becoming Irish American: The Making and Remaking of a People from Roanoke to JFK* (New Haven, CT: Yale University Press, 2023), ch. 3.
4. *Travels in North-America, in the years 1780, 1781, and 1782. By the Marquis De Chastellux. Translated from the French by an English Gentleman who resided in America at that period. With Notes by the Translator*, 2 vols. (London: G. G. J. and J. Robinson, 1787), 2: 36–37n.
5. Kerby A. Miller, *Emigrants and Exiles: Ireland and the Irish Exodus to North America* (New York: Oxford University Press, 1985), 163–65.
6. *IILC* 559–61; Meagher, *Becoming Irish American*, 49–53.
7. Natalie Inman, "Military Families: Kinship in the American Revolution," in *Before the Volunteer State: New Thoughts on Early Tennessee, 1540–1800* (Knoxville: University of

Tennessee Press, 2014), ch. 6; Natalie R. Inman, *Brothers and Friends: Kinship in Early America* (Athens: University of Georgia Press, 2017), chs. 2–3.

8. Henry J. Ford, *The Scotch-Irish in America* (Princeton, NJ: Princeton University Press, 1915), 497; Doyle, *Ireland, Irishmen, and Revolutionary America*, ch. 5; quote at 133; Kevin Phillips, *The Cousins' Wars: Religion, Politics, and the Triumph of Anglo-America* (New York: Basic Books, 1999), 177–90; *IILC* 561; Miller, *Emigrants and Exiles*, 165–66.

9. Matthew P. Dziennik, "Peasants, Soldiers, and Revolutionaries: Interpreting Irish Manpower in the Age of Revolutions," in *Ireland and America: Empire, Revolution, and Sovereignty*, ed. Patrick Griffin and Francis D. Cogliano (Charlottesville: University of Virginia Press, 2021), 110.

10. Samuel Swett Green, "The Scotch-Irish in America," *Proceedings of the American Antiquarian Society* 10 (1985), 44–45.

11. Paul L. Stevens, *A King's Colonel at Niagara, 1774–1776: Lt. Col. John Caldwell and the Beginnings of the American Revolution on the New York Frontier* (Youngstown, NY: Old Fort Niagara Association, 1987), 8.

12. Light Townsend Cummins, "Oliver Pollock and the Creation of an American Identity in Spanish Louisiana," in *Nexus of Empire: Negotiating Loyalty and Identity in the Revolutionary Borderlands, 1760s–1820s*, ed. Gene Allen Smith and Sylvia L. Hilton (Gainesville: University Press of Florida, 2010), 198–218. For this essay and more on Pollock, see also Cummins, *To the Vast and Beautiful Land: Anglo Migration into Spanish Louisiana and Texas, 1760s–1820s* (College Station: Texas A&M University Press, 2019, chs. 4, 6, and 8.

13. Patrick Griffin, *American Leviathan: Empire, Nation, and Revolutionary Frontier* (New York: Hill and Wang, 2007); Patrick Griffin, *The Age of Atlantic Revolution: The Fall and Rise of a Connected World* (New Haven, CT: Yale University Press, 2023), 124, 135; Daniel P. Barr, *A Colony Sprung from Hell: Pittsburgh and the Struggle for Authority on the Western Pennsylvania Frontier, 1744–1794* (Kent, OH: Kent State University Press, 2014), 175–93; Patrick Spero, *Frontier Rebels: The Fight for Independence in the American West, 1765–1776* (New York: W. W. Norton, 2018); Rob Harper, *Unsettling the West: Violence and State Building in the Ohio Valley* (Philadelphia: University of Pennsylvania Press, 2018).

14. Rachel N. Klein, "Frontier Planters and the American Revolution: The South Carolina Backcountry, 1775–1782," in *An Uncivil War: The Southern Backcountry during the American Revolution*, ed. Ronald Hoffman, Thad W. Tate, and Peter Albert (Charlottesville: University Press of Virginia, 1985), 51.

15. Leyburn, *Scotch-Irish*, 306.

16. Patrick Spero, *Frontier Country: The Politics of War in Early Pennsylvania* (Philadelphia: University of Pennsylvania Press, 2016), 228–30, 233–37.

17. Barr, *Colony Sprung from Hell*, 3–6, 227–28, 242–43.

18. Robert G. Crist, "Cumberland County" in *Beyond Philadelphia: The American Revolution in the Pennsylvania Hinterland*, ed. John B. Frantz and William Pencak (University Park: Pennsylvania State University Press, 1998), 125–126.

19. Barr, *Colony Sprung from Hell*, 9.

20. Jeffrey Ostler, *Surviving Genocide: Native Nations and the United States from the American Revolution to Bleeding Kansas* (New Haven, CT: Yale University Press, 2019), ch. 2.

21. Robert G. Parkinson, *Thirteen Clocks: How Race United the Colonies and Made the Declaration of Independence* (Chapel Hill: University of North Carolina Press, 2021).

22. Samuel K. Fisher, *The Gaelic and Indian Origins of the American Revolution: Diversity and Empire in the British Atlantic, 1688–1783* (New York: Oxford University Press, 2022), ch. 11.

23. *NCCR* 10: 764.

24. Max Dixon, *The Wataugans* (Nashville: Tennessee American Revolution Bicentennial Commission, 1976), 30, 32.

25. "The Life and Times of Robert B. McAfee and His Family and Connections," *Register of the Kentucky State Historical Society* 25 (1927), 25.

26. *NCSR* 22: 995.

27. *NCCR* 10: 246.

28. *DAR* 12: 131, 189 (John Stuart).

29. *DAR* 11: 176–77. The son of Presbyterian immigrants from Ireland, and a controversial figure, Richard Pearis held an officer's commission in Virginia, Maryland, and then Pennsylvania during the French and Indian War. After the war he had a successful career among the

460 NOTES

Cherokees in South Carolina as a land dealer and trader. He fought for the British during the Revolution and died in the Bahamas in 1794.

30. *DAR* 12: 131, 193, 203–04; *NCCR* 10: 777–80; Philip M. Hamer, "The Wataugans and the Cherokee Indians in 1776," *East Tennessee Historical Publications* 3 (1931), 108–26; Tyler Boulware discusses the generational divide in "'Our Mad Young Men': Authority and Violence in Cherokee Country," in *Blood in the Hills: A History of Violence in Appalachia*, ed. Bruce E. Stewart (Lexington: University Press of Kentucky, 2012), ch. 3.
31. William Moultrie, *Memoirs of the American Revolution, as far as it related to the States of North and South Carolina and Georgia*, 2 vols (New York: printed by D. Longworth, 1802), 1: 81; James H. Merrell, *The Indians' New World: Catawbas and Their Neighbors from European Contact through the Era of Removal* (New York: W. W. Norton, 1989), 215 (Stuart); Peter N. Moore, *World of Toil and Strife: Community Transformation in Backcountry South Carolina, 1750–1805* (Columbia: University of South Carolina Press, 2007), 68–69, 74–75; *DAR* 11: 118 (all 60 fighting men).
32. *EAID* 18: 211.
33. *DAR* 11: 164, 167, 211 ("usurped authority"); 12: 78, 240; 14: 49, 168–69, 193; 15: 122, 212, 214; 17: 181 (Taitt).
34. Reuben G. Thwaites and Louse P. Kellogg, eds., *The Revolution on the Upper Ohio, 1775–1777* (Madison: Wisconsin Historical Society, 1908), 53, 61–62; Robert L. Scribner, ed., *Revolutionary Virginia, The Road to Independence: A Documentary Record*, 7 vols. (Charlottesville: University Press of Virginia, 1973–1983), 3: 377–78 (determined upon War), 389–90; 7: 770 ("deprive us intirely").
35. Gregory Evans Dowd, *A Spirited Resistance: The North American Indian Struggle for Unity, 1745–1815* (Baltimore, MD: Johns Hopkins University Press, 1992), ch. 3.
36. *EAID* 18: 147.
37. *The Olden Time: A Monthly Publication devoted to the Preservation of Documents and other Authentic Information in relation to the Early Explorations and the Settlement and Improvement of the Country around the Head of the Ohio*, ed. Neville B. Craig, 2 vols. (1848; reprint, Cincinnati: Robert Clarke & Co., 1876), 2: 104.
38. *Penn. Archives*, 1st ser. 6: 445.
39. *Penn. Archives*, 4th ser. 3: 680–88.
40. Larry L. Nelson, *A Man of Distinction among Them: Alexander McKee and British-Indian Affairs along the Ohio Country Frontier, 1754–1799* (Kent, OH: Kent State University Press, 1999); Correspondence and Papers of Governor General Sir Frederick Haldimand, 1758–1791 (hereafter Haldimand Papers), British Museum, London, Additional Manuscripts, 21769: 26–27; 21770: 269 (salary); *DAR* 15: 107 (Hamilton quote to Sir Guy Carleton), 135.
41. Colin G. Calloway, "Simon Girty: Interpreter and Intermediary," in *Being and Becoming Indian: Biographical Studies of North American Frontier*, ed. James A. Clifton (Chicago: Dorsey Press, 1989), 44–47; Consul Wilshire Butterfield, *History of the Girtys* (Cincinnati: Robert Clarke & Co., 1890), 35–42; C. Hale Sipe, *The Indian Wars of Pennsylvania* (Harrisburg, PA: Telegraph Press, 1929), 529; *Collections of the Michigan Pioneer and Historical Society* 9 (1886), 442, 444; Haldimand Papers, 21782: 96; 21783: 294; 21769: 26–27 (Girty on Indian department pay lists as interpreter).
42. John H. Moore, "A Captive of the Shawnees, 1779–1784," *West Virginia History* 23 (1961–62), 290–91.
43. Reginald Horsman, *Matthew Elliott, British Indian Agent* (Detroit: Wayne State University Press, 1964), ch. 1.
44. *The Moravian Mission Diaries of David Zeisberger, 1772–1781*, ed. Hermann Wellenreuther and Carola Wessel; trans. Julie Tomberlin Weber (University Park: Pennsylvania State University Press, 2005), 35–36, 319–21, 608–10; Hermann Wellenreuther, "White Eyes and the Delawares' Vision of an Indian State," *Pennsylvania History* 68 (2001), 139–61.
45. *The Papers of George Washington: Revolutionary War Series*, ed. W. W. Abbot et al., 28 vols. to date (Charlottesville: University of Virginia Press, 1985–), 16: 273.
46. Born in Ireland: *EAID* 18: 575n.
47. *Moravian Mission Diaries of David Zeisberger*, 470 n.1289.
48. Amy C. Schutt, *Peoples of the River Valleys: The Odyssey of the Delaware Indians* (Philadelphia: University of Pennsylvania Press, 2007), 163–68. Colin G. Calloway, ed., *The World Turned Upside Down: Indian Voices from Early America* (Boston: Bedford Books, 1994), 156, 190–93.

49. David L. Preston, *The Texture of Contact: European and Indian Settler Communities on the Frontiers of Iroquoia, 1667–1783* (Lincoln: University of Nebraska Press, 2009).
50. Alan Taylor, *The Divided Ground: Indians, Settlers, and the Northern Borderland of the American Revolution* (New York: Alfred Knopf, 2006); Barbara Graymont, *The Iroquois in the American Revolution* (Syracuse: Syracuse University Press, 1972); Joseph T. Glatthaar and James Kirby Martin, *Forgotten Allies: The Oneida Indians and the American Revolution* (New York: Hill and Wang, 2006).
51. Harper, *Unsettling the West*, ch. 5.
52. Gregory T. Knouff, "Soldiers and Violence on the Pennsylvania Frontier," in *Beyond Philadelphia: The American Revolution in the Pennsylvania Hinterland*, ed. John B. Frantz and William Pencak (University Park: Pennsylvania State University Press, 1998), 171–93; Gregory T. Knouff, "'An Arduous Service': The Pennsylvania Backcountry Soldiers' Revolution," *Pennsylvania History* 61 (1994), 45–74.
53. Wayne E. Lee, *Crowds and Soldiers in Revolutionary North Carolina: The Culture of Violence in Riot and War* (Gainesville: University Press of Florida, 2001), ch. 7; cf. Christopher Duffy, *The Military Experience in the Age of Reason, 1715–1789* (New York: Barnes and Noble, 1987).
54. Paul Staiti, *The Killing of Jane McCrea: Love, Death, and the American Revolution* (forthcoming); Colin G. Calloway, *The American Revolution in Indian Country: Crisis and Diversity in Native American Communities* (Cambridge: Cambridge University Press, 1995), 295–98. There seems to be little evidence to support the story that colonial militia rallied to the American forces around Saratoga in response to McCrea's murder. Brian Burns, "Massacre or Muster: Burgoyne's Indians and the Militia at Bennington," *Vermont History* 45 (1977), 133–44.
55. *Penn. Archives*, 1st ser. 5: 344, 599, 741; 6: 3, 39–41, 68–69, 470, 516, 528–29, 535–36, 559, 576, 613–15, 657; Draper 1U13, 2U11.
56. Hector St. John de Crèvecoeur, *Letters from and American Farmer* (London: J. M. Dent, 1971), 200–1; Joseph Doddridge, *The Settlement and Indian Wars of the Western Parts of Virginia and Pennsylvania, 1763–1783* (Pittsburgh, 1912; reprint, Bowie, MD: Heritage Books, 1988), 95.
57. Barr, *Colony Sprung from Hell*, 194.
58. Tim H. Blessing, "The Upper Juniata Valley," in *Beyond Philadelphia: The American Revolution in the Pennsylvania Hinterland*, ed. John B. Frantz and William Pencak (University Park: Pennsylvania State University Press, 1998), 160–64.
59. Kevin M. Sweeney, "Revolutionary State Militias in the Backcountry and along the Frontiers," paper presented at the SAR Annual Conference on the American Revolution, Fort Pitt, June 3–5, 2022.
60. *Penn. Archives*, 1st ser. 6: 39–40.
61. Judith Ridner, *A Town In-Between: Carlisle, Pennsylvania, and the Early Mid-Atlantic Frontier* (Philadelphia: University of Pennsylvania Press, 2010), 143.
62. *Penn. Archives*, 1st ser. 4: 693–94; 6: 100.
63. *Penn. Archives*, 1st series, 6: 614; John Armstrong at Carlisle to Vice President, George Bryan, June 23 ("any Indian Town"), July 24 and 26, 1778, HSP, Lamberton Collection on Scots-Irish Settlements in Cumberland County, folders 33 and 35; Armstrong to James Wilson, n.d., folder 119 (day of humiliation and prayer).
64. *Papers of George Washington: Revolutionary War Series* 11: 238–39; 12: 179–80.
65. *Washington-Irvine Correspondence: The Official Letters which passed between Washington and Brig.-Gen. William Irvine and between Irvine and Others concerning Military Affairs in the West from 1781 to 1783*, ed. Consul W. Butterfield (Madison, WI: David Atwood, 1882), 15–16; Reuben G. Thwaites and Louise P. Kellogg, eds., *Frontier Defense on the Upper Ohio* (Madison: Wisconsin Historical Society, 1912), 215–23; *Papers of George Washington: Revolutionary War Series* 14: 182.
66. *Papers of George Washington: Revolutionary War Series* 15: 345, 373.
67. Rev. Horace Edwin Hayden, ed., *The Massacre of Wyoming: The Acts of Congress for the Defense of the Wyoming Valley, Pennsylvania, 1776–1778; with the Petitions of the Sufferers by the Massacre of July 3, 1778, for Congressional Aid* (Wilkes-Barre, PA: Wyoming Historical and Geological Society, 1895), 11.
68. Hubertis M. Cummings, *Scots Breed and Susquehanna* (Pittsburgh: University of Pittsburgh Press for the Presbyterian Historical Society, 1964), 259; Paul B. Moyer, *Wild Yankees: The Struggle for Independence along Pennsylvania's Revolutionary Frontier* (Ithaca, NY: Cornell University Press, 2007), 1–2. 32; Sipe, *Indian Wars*, 549–61.

69. *Penn. Archives*, 1st ser. 6: 634–35.
70. *Penn. Archives*, 1st ser. 7: 357.
71. Richard Smith, *A Tour of Four Great Rivers: The Hudson, Mohawk, Susquehanna and Delaware in 1769*, ed. Francis W. Halsey (Port Washington, NY: Ira J. Friedman, 1964), lviii, 30 ("mostly Scotch-Irish"); Peter C. Mancall, *Valley of Opportunity: Economic Culture along the Upper Susquehanna, 1700–1800* (Ithaca, NY: Cornell University Press, 1991), 112; Graymont, *The Iroquois in the American Revolution*, 187–89 (McClellan).
72. James Seaver, *A Narrative of the Life of Mary Jemison*, ed. June Namias (Norman: University of Oklahoma Press, 1992), 99–100.
73. *Penn. Archives*, 1st ser. 7: 586–97; Sipe, *Indian Wars of Pennsylvania*, 595–98; John H. Carter, "The Captivity of the Fort Freeland Prisoners of War," *Proceedings of the Northumberland County Historical Society* 28 (1980), 22–31.
74. *Penn. Archives*, 1st ser. 7: 362, 609–10, 616.
75. Elizabeth A. Perkins, *Border Life: Experience and Memory in the Revolutionary Ohio Valley* (Chapel Hill: University of North Carolina Press, 1998), 62–62 (stations), 155.
76. Billy Kennedy, *The Scots-Irish in the Carolinas* (Belfast and Greenville, SC: Causeway Press, 1997), 56.
77. Arthur Andrew Savery, "Forgotten Frontiersman: The Life and Times of Simon Kenton," MA thesis, University of Nebraska at Kearney, 2017.
78. Doug Drake, Jack Masters, and Bill Puryear, *Founding of the Cumberland Settlements: The First Atlas, 1779–1804* (Gallatin, TN: Warioto Press, 2009), 19, 68; "Voyage of the Donelson Party (1779–1780)," in *Early Travels in the Tennessee Country*, ed. Samuel Cole Williams (Johnson City, TN: The Watauga Press, 1928), 233–42; Paul Clements, *Chronicles of the Cumberland Settlements, 1779–1796* (self-published, 2012), 129–200; Thomas Perkins Abernethy, *From Frontier to Plantation in Tennessee: A Study in Frontier Democracy* (Chapel Hill: University of North Carolina Press, 1932), 27–31; Theodore Roosevelt, *The Winning of the West*, 6 vols. in 3 (New York: G. P. Putnam's Sons, 1899), 2, pt. 1, chs. 7–8; John Haywood, *The Civil and Political History of the State of Tennessee, from its Earliest Settlement up to the Year 1796; including the Boundaries of the State* (Knoxville, TN: Heiskell and Brown, 1823), 83–96.
79. Light Townsend Cummins, "'Her Weary Pilgrimage': The Remarkable Mississippi River Adventures of Anne McMeans, 1778–1882," in Cummins, *To the Vast and Beautiful Land*, ch. 5.
80. Clements, *Chronicles of the Cumberland Settlements*, 120, 132, 158–59, 178, 187, 197, 513; Rev. R. D. Miller, *Past and Present of Menard County, Illinois* (Chicago: S. J. Clarke, 1905), 269–83.
81. *Penn. Archives*, 1st ser. 6: 536.
82. *Penn. Archives*, 1st ser. 6: 528–29.
83. Honor Sachs, *Home Rule: Households, Manhood, and National Expansion on the Eighteenth-Century Kentucky Frontier* (New Haven, CT: Yale University Press, 2015), 29–30.
84. Colin G. Calloway, *The Indian World of George Washington: The First President, the First Americans, and the Birth of the Nation* (New York: Oxford University Press, 2018); *Penn. Archives*, 1st ser. 6: 211 (Harris), 524–25, 612–13 (Armstrong).
85. B. G. Moss, "The Roles of the Scots and Scotch-Irishmen in the Southern Campaigns in the War of the American War of Independence, 1780–1783," Ph.D. diss., University of St. Andrews, 1978; David C. Hsiung, *Two Worlds in the Tennessee Mountains: Exploring the Origins of Appalachian Stereotypes* (Lexington: University Press of Kentucky, 1997), ch. 1; Ronald Hoffman, Thad W. Tate, and Peter Albert, eds., *An Uncivil War: The Southern Backcountry during the American Revolution* (Charlottesville: University Press of Virginia, 1985)
86. Griffin, *American Leviathan*, 134.
87. Joseph A. Waddell, *Annals of Augusta County, Virginia*, 2nd ed. (Staunton, VA: C. Russell Caldwell, 1902), 124–25; *Documentary History of Dunmore's War, 1774*, ed. Reuben G. Thwaites and Louise Phelps Kellogg (Madison: Wisconsin Historical Society, 1905), 429–30.
88. Lee, *Crowds and Soldiers in Revolutionary North Carolina*, 128–29. A war of revenge "remained familiar to many colonists on the frontier from their experiences as Scottish colonists in a hostile Ireland and also correlated with the Cherokee manner of war that emphasized blood vengeance."
89. *NCCR* 10: 730–32.
90. On Rutherford, see J. M. Opal, *Avenging the People: Andrew Jackson, the Rule of Law, and the American Nation* (New York: Oxford University Press, 2017), 26, 37–38. Rutherford led his militia to South Carolina in the spring of 1780 to aid the defense of Charleston but returned to North Carolina when he learned that the city already had fallen. His troops defeated a Loyalist

force at the Battle of Ramseur's Mill, NC, in June 1780. He was wounded and taken prisoner at the Battle of Camden in August 1780. Exchanged in June 1781, he served as a militia brigadier for the remainder of the war. Elected to the North Carolina Council of State in 1782, Rutherford held his council post despite his strong anti-federalist views until he moved to the Tennessee territory in 1792. Washington appointed him to the territorial legislative council in June 1794.

91. *EAID* 18: 200; Calloway, *American Revolution in Indian Country*, 198; Draper 3VV164, 171-74.
92. Katharine L. Brown and Nancy T. Soreels, "Presbyterian Pathways to Power: Gentrification and the Scotch-Irish Heritage among Virginia Presbyterian Ministers, 1760-1860," in *Atlantic Crossroads: Historical Connections between Scotland, Ulster and North America*, ed. Patrick Fitzgerald and Steve Ickringill (Newtonards, N. Ireland: Colourpoint Books, 2001), 31-32.
93. *EAID* 18: 201; Draper 4QQ151-54.
94. *EAID* 18: 226, 240, 258.
95. Abernethy, *From Frontier to Plantation in Tennessee*, 15.
96. Dixon, *The Wataugans*, 52-53.
97. *NCSR* 11: 283.
98. Rev. Hall quoted in Lee, *Crowds and Soldiers in Revolutionary North Carolina*, 203-4.
99. Joseph A. Waddell, "Scotch-Irish of the Valley of Virginia," in *The Scotch-Irish in America: Proceedings of the Scotch-Irish Congress* 7 (1895), 94.
100. *Documentary History of Dunmore's War*, 39-40, 144-45; Waddell, *Annals of Augusta County*, 144-45; Ian K. Steele, *Setting All the Captives Free: Capture, Adjustment, and Recollection in Allegheny Country* (Montreal: McGill-Queens University Press, 2013), 376, 455.
101. Calloway, *American Revolution in Indian Country*, 50; Campbell's report to Jefferson, January 15, 1781, Draper 9DD24, and *Calendar of Virginia State Papers* 1: 434-37; C.O. 5/82: 287-88 (Raven's speech at 287).
102. *Calendar of Virginia State Papers* 2: 255, 264-65.
103. *Calendar of Virginia State Papers* 3: 138.
104. *Calendar of Virginia State Papers* 3: 188.
105. Draper 11S122; *Calendar of Virginia State Papers* 3: 398.
106. *EAID* 18: 431.
107. Rod Andrew, Jr., *The Life and Times of General Andrew Pickens* (Chapel Hill: University of North Carolina Press, 2017), ch. 3; Jeff W. Dennis, *Indians and Patriots: Shaping Identity in Eighteenth-Century South Carolina* (Columbia: University of South Carolina Press, 2017), ch. 5; David Andrew Nichols, *Red Gentlemen and White Savages: Indians, Federalists, and the Search for Order on the American Frontier* (Charlottesville: University of Virginia Press, 2008), 3-4, and citing Waring, *Fighting Elder*, 16-17.
108. Dennis, *Patriots and Indians*, 103.
109. *Papers of George Washington: Revolutionary War Series* 20: 717-18; *Letters and Papers of Major General John Sullivan*, ed. Otis G. Hammond, 3 vols. (Concord: New Hampshire Historical Society, 1939), 3: 48-53.
110. Frederick Cook, ed., *Journals of the Military Expedition of Major General John Sullivan against the Six Nations* (Auburn, NY: Knapp, Peck, and Thomson, 1887); Max M. Mintz, *Seeds of Empire: The American Revolutionary Conquest of the Iroquois* (New York: New York University Press, 1999); Joseph R. Fischer, *A Well-Executed Failure: The Sullivan Campaign against the Iroquois, July-September 1779* (Columbia: South Carolina University Press, 1997); *Papers of George Washington: Revolutionary War Series* 22: 533; *Letters and Papers of Major General John Sullivan*, 3: 134.
111. Seaver, *Narrative of the Life of Mary Jemison*, 105.
112. Calloway, *American Revolution in Indian Country*, ch. 5.
113. *Penn. Archives*, 1st ser. 8: 23.
114. Calloway, *American Revolution in Indian Country*, 141.
115. *Penn. Archives*, 1st ser. 7: 362.
116. *Penn. Archives*, 1st ser. 8: 217.
117. *Penn. Archives*, 1st ser. 9: 51-52, 79-80.
118. *Penn. Archives*, 1st ser. 9: 189, 238-39, 240-41, 246-47, 303-4, 369.
119. On Lochry: Sipe, *Indian Wars*, 635-38; *Col. Recs. Penn.* 13: 325, 473; *Penn. Archives*, 1st ser. 9: 333, 369, 458, 574, 733; *Washington-Irvine Correspondence*, 55, 77, 154, 229-31; Lieut. Isaac Anderson's journal in *Penn. Archives*, 2nd ser. vol. 14; on Clark: Patrick Griffin, "Searching for

Independence: Revolutionary Kentucky, Irish American Experience, and Scotch-Irish Myth," in *Ulster to America: The Scots-Irish Migration Experience, 1680–1830*, ed. Warren Hofstra (Knoxville: University of Tennessee Press, 2012), 220.
120. *Washington-Irvine Correspondence*, 233.
121. C. A. Weslager, *The Delaware Indians: A History* (New Brunswick, NJ: Rutgers University Press, 1972), 294; Richard S. Grimes, *The Western Delaware Indian Nation, 1730–1795* (Bethlehem, PA: Lehigh University Press, 2017), 172.
122. *Penn. Archives*, 1st ser. 8: 249–50.
123. Grimes, *Western Delaware Indian Nation*, 212; Louise P. Kellogg, ed., *Frontier Retreat on the Upper Ohio, 1779–1781* (Madison: Wisconsin State Historical Society, 1917), 290.
124. Crist, "Cumberland County," 125; Ridner, *A Town In-Between*, 119; Judith Ridner, "William Irvine and the Complexities of Manhood and Fatherhood in the Pennsylvania Backcountry," *PMHB* 125 (2001), 5–34; *Washington-Irvine Correspondence*, 65–67.
125. *Washington-Irvine Correspondence*, 75.
126. Spencer Records, "Pioneer Experiences in Pennsylvania, Kentucky, Ohio and Indiana, 1766–1836," *Indiana Magazine of History* 15 (1919), 209–10.
127. Eric Sterner, *Anatomy of a Massacre: The Destruction of Gnadenhutten, 1782* (Yardley, PA: Westholme, 2020); Harper, *Unsettling the West*, 136–42; Sipe, *Indian Wars of Pennsylvania*, 648–50; *Thirty Thousand Miles with John Heckewelder or Travels Amoung the Indians of Pennsylvania, New York & Ohio in the 18th Century* (original edition, Pittsburgh: University of Pittsburgh, 1958; reprint, Lewisburg, PA: Wennawoods, 1998), 189–200; *Penn. Archives*, 1st ser. 9: 511, 524–25; Papers of the Continental Congress, 1774–1789, National Archives, Washington, DC, Microfilm 247, reel 73, item 59, vol. 3: 49–51; *Calendar of Virginia State Papers* 3: 122–24; Haldimand Papers, 21762: 13–14 (Simon Girty's account); Doddridge, *The Settlement and Indian Wars of the Western Parts of Virginia and Pennsylvania*, 200 (Mary Wallace).
128. *Washington-Irvine Correspondence*, 100–3, 343–44; Lewis Clark Walkinshaw, *Annals of Southwestern Pennsylvania*, 2 vols. (New York: Lewis Historical Publishing, 1939), 2: 163.
129. The account was related to Moravian Frederick Linebach/k by two neighbors. Draper 11S146–49; *Calendar of Virginia State Papers* 3: 122–23; *Washington-Irvine Correspondence*, 237n–38n.
130. *Calendar of Virginia State Papers* 3: 124; *Penn. Archives*, 1st ser. 9: 524–25; *Washington-Irvine Correspondence*, 289.
131. *Penn. Archives*, 1st ser. 9: 629; also *Washington-Irvine Correspondence*, 345n.
132. Records, "Pioneer Experiences in Pennsylvania, Kentucky, Ohio and Indiana," 209.
133. Rob Harper, "Looking the Other Way: The Gnadenhutten Massacre and the Contextual Interpretation of Violence," *William and Mary Quarterly* 64 (2007), 621–44.
134. *Washington-Irvine Correspondence*, 343–45.
135. Sipe, *Indian Wars*, 653; *Penn Archives*, 1st ser. 9: 525, 540–41, 552; *Washington-Irvine Correspondence*, 236–42, 245–46.
136. Spero, *Frontier Country*, 240; *Penn. Archives*, 2nd ser. 14: 753 (list).
137. Quoted in Peter Silver, *Our Savage Neighbors: How Indian War Transformed Early America* (New York: W. W. Norton, 2008), 276.
138. *Washington-Irvine Correspondence*, 113, 118n.
139. Horsman, *Matthew Elliott*, 37, 50; L. L. Kulisek, "Caldwell, William (d. 1822)," in *Dictionary of Canadian Biography*, vol. 6 (University of Toronto/Université Laval, 2003–), accessed October 4, 2021, http://www.biographi.ca/en/bio/caldwell_william_1822_6E.html.
140. *Washington-Irvine Correspondence*, 126–27; Calloway, "Simon Girty," 49; Haldimand Papers, 21762: 80 (McKee's account).
141. Karin L. Huebner, "'Brother, after this conduct can you blame me?': The Echo of Native American Memory of the 1782 Massacre at Gnadenhutten," *Journal of the Early Republic* 42 (2022), 53–81.
142. *Penn. Archives*, 1st ser. 9: 522.
143. Calloway, *Indian World of George Washington*, 280–81; John Ferling, *The Ascent of George Washington: The Hidden Political Genius of an American Icon* (New York: Bloomsbury Press, 2009), 185–90, 222.
144. Sipe, *Indian Wars*, 665–71; *Penn. Archives*, 1st ser. 9: 595–96, 606; *Washington-Irvine Correspondence*, 176–77, 250–53, 381; *Olden Time*, 2: 354–59.

145. *IILC* 179–84; *Olden Time*, 2: 356–58; Peter Gilmore and Kerby A. Miller, "Searching for 'Irish' Freedom—Settling for 'Scotch-Irish' Respectability: Southwestern Pennsylvania, 1780–1810," in *Ulster to America: The Scots-Irish Migration Experience, 1680–1830*, ed. Warren Hofstra (Knoxville: University of Tennessee Press, 2012), 179.
146. Perkins, *Border Life*, 136 (McGary); John Mack Faragher, *Daniel Boone: The Life and Legend of an American Pioneer* (New York: Henry Holt, 1992), 16–25, 146–47; Haldimand Papers, 21762: 149–50; *DAR* 21: 114–15; *Calendar of Virginia State Papers* 3: 275–76, 280–83, 333–34.
147. *Calendar of Virginia State Papers* 3: 337. Of the officers in charge, Campbell said Todd and Trigg lacked experience; Boone, Harlin, and Lindsay had experience but were "defective in capacity"; Logan was "a dull, narrow body from whom nothing clever need be expected," and George Rogers Clarke "has lost the confidence of the people, and it is said become a Sot; perhaps something worse."
148. Sachs, *Home Rule*, 20–21.
149. "Journal of Daniel Boone," *Ohio Archaeological and Historical Publications* 13 (1904), 276; Draper 1AA 276–77.
150. *Calendar of Virginia State Papers* 3: 358–60, quote at 358.
151. Calloway, *American Revolution in Indian Country*, ch. 6.
152. Samuel Cole Williams, *Tennessee during the Revolutionary War* (Nashville: Tennessee Historical Commission, 1944), 165; "Lewis Brant's Memoranda of a Journey (1785)," in *Early Travels in the Tennessee Country*, 284.
153. Richard White, *The Middle Ground: Indians, Empires and Republics in the Great Lakes Region, 1650–1815* (Cambridge: Cambridge University Press, 1991) 410–11; Haldimand Papers, 21756: 91–92.
154. *Calendar of Virginia State Papers* 3: 445.
155. *Calendar of Virginia State Papers* 3: 495–96.
156. *Washington-Irvine Correspondence*, 149.
157. *Washington-Irvine Correspondence*, 406, 410–11.
158. *The Writings of George Washington from the Original Manuscript Sources, 1745–1799*, ed. John C. Fitzpatrick, 39 vols. (Washington, DC: Government Printing Office, 1931–1944), 25: 420; 26: 283, 305.
159. Griffin, *American Leviathan*, 154; White, *Middle Ground*, 378, 384, 395.
160. John F. D. Smyth, *A Tour in the United States of America: containing an account of the present situation of that country; the population, agriculture, commerce, customs, and manners of the inhabitants; with a description of the Indian nations . . .* , 2 vols. (London: Printed for G. Robinson, 1784), 1: 346.
161. Perkins, *Border Life*, 68.
162. Peter E. Gilmore, *Irish Presbyterians and the Shaping of Western Pennsylvania, 1770–1830* (Pittsburgh: University of Pittsburgh Press, 2018), 19–20.
163. Mary L. Briscoe, ed., *Thomas Mellon and His Times*, 2nd ed. (Pittsburgh: University of Pittsburgh Press, 1994), 42–43; Gilmore, *Irish Presbyterians and the Shaping of Western Pennsylvania*, 15, 20.
164. *Philip Vickers Fithian: Journal, 1775–1776. Written on the Virginia-Pennsylvania Frontier and in the Army around New York*, ed. Robert Greenhalgh Albion and Leonidas Dodson (Princeton, NJ: Princeton University Press, 1934), 54.
165. David Noel Doyle, "Scots Irish or Scotch-Irish," in *Making the Irish American: History and Heritage of the Irish in the United States*, ed. J. J. Lee and Marion R. Casey (New York: New York University Press, 2006), 168.
166. James Hall, *Sketches of History, Life, and Manners in the West*, 2 vols. (Philadelphia: Harrison Hall, 1835), 2: 76–77.
167. Benjamin Bankhurst, "Early Irish America and Its Enemies: Ethnic Identity Formation in the Era of the Revolution, 1760–1820," *Journal of Irish and Scottish Studies* 5 (Spring 2012), 17–37 (Lee quoted at 29).
168. Parkinson, *Thirteen Clocks*, 177–78.
169. Silver, *Our Savage Neighbors*, terms the uniting element in the 1760s an "anti-Indian sublime."
170. Robert G. Parkinson, *The Common Cause: Creating Race and Nation in the American Revolution* (Chapel Hill: University of North Carolina Press, 2017).

171. Joanna Brooks, "Held Captive by the Irish: Quaker Captivity Narratives in Frontier Pennsylvania," *New Hibernia Review/Iris Éireannach Nua* 8, no. 3 (Autumn 2004), 32–33.
172. Fisher, *Gaelic and Indian Origins of the American Revolution*, 211–15; Calloway, *American Revolution in Indian Country*, 292–301.
173. Miller, *Emigrants and Exiles*, 167; Leyburn, *Scotch-Irish*, 319.

Chapter 10

1. Charles H. Ambler, *George Washington and the West* (Chapel Hill: University of North Carolina Press, 1936), 173; *The Papers of George Washington: Confederation Series*, ed. W. W. Abbot et al., 6 vols. (Charlottesville: University Press of Virginia, 1992–1997), 1: 93n–95n.
2. Thomas P. Slaughter, *The Whiskey Rebellion: Frontier Epilogue to the American Revolution* (New York: Oxford University Press, 1986), 84–86; *The Diaries of George Washington*, ed. Donald Jackson and Dorothy Twohig, 6 vols. (Charlottesville: University Press of Virginia, 1976–1979), 4: 21–31; *Papers of George Washington: Confederation Series* 2: 338–56, 442–46; 3: 121–25, 245–46, 365–69, 438–39; 4: 172–73, 255–61, 339–43, 405–7; 5: 39–41, 327–28; 472; 6: 91–92.
3. Gregory Ablavsky, *Federal Ground: Governing Property and Violence in the First U.S. Territories* (New York: Oxford University Press, 2021), 40.
4. Michael A. Blaakman, *Speculation Nation: Land Mania in the Revolutionary American Republic* (Philadelphia: University of Pennsylvania Press, 2023); Paul B. Moyer, *Wild Yankees: The Struggle for Independence along Pennsylvania's Revolutionary Frontier* (Ithaca, NY: Cornell University Press, 2007); Alan Taylor, *Liberty Men and Great Proprietors: The Revolutionary Settlement on the Maine Frontier, 1760–1820* (Chapel Hill: University of North Carolina Press, 1990).
5. Judith Ridner, *The Scots Irish of Early Pennsylvania: A Varied People* (Philadelphia: Temple University Press, 2018), 76, 86.
6. *The Private Correspondence of Benjamin Franklin*, 2 vols. (London: Henry Colburn, 1817), 1: 171.
7. In the Post-Revolutionary Papers of the Pennsylvania Archives in Harrisburg, vol. 23: 16, cited in Hubertis M. Cummings, *Scots Breed and Susquehanna* (Pittsburgh: University of Pittsburgh Press for the Presbyterian Historical Society, 1964), 342–44.
8. Kevin L. Yeager, "The Power of Ethnicity: The Preservation of Scots-Irish Culture in the Eighteenth-Century American Backcountry," Ph.D. diss., Louisiana State University, 2000.
9. Ablavsky, *Federal Ground*.
10. Timothy J. Meagher, *Becoming Irish American: The Making and Remaking of a People from Roanoke to JFK* (New Haven, CT: Yale University Press, 2023), 59; Colin Woodward, *American Nations: A History of the Eleven Regional Cultures of North America* (New York: Viking, 2011), 158 "Many of them feel the same way today," notes Woodward.
11. *Documentary History of the First Federal Congress, 1789–1791*, ed. Linda Grant De Pauw et al., 22 vols. (Baltimore, MD: Johns Hopkins University Press, 1972–2017), 19: 1549–50.
12. IILC 169, 585; Meagher, *Becoming Irish American*, 57; Kerby A. Miller, *Emigrants and Exiles: Ireland and the Irish Exodus to North America* (New York: Oxford University Press, 1985), 169–70; James Kelly, "The Resumption of Emigration from Ireland after the American War of Independence: 1783–1787," *Studia Hibernica* 24 (1988), 61–88; Carlton Jackson, *A Social History of the Scotch-Irish* (Lanham, MD: Madison Books, 1993), 138.
13. David Noel Doyle, "The Irish in North America, 1776–1845," in *Making the Irish American: History and Heritage of the Irish in the United States*, ed. J. J. Lee and Marion R. Casey (New York: New York University Press, 2006), 178.
14. Extract of letter from Consul Miller to Lord Grenville, Charleston, December 28, 1791, C.O. 5/36, part 3, 13/1 (enclosed and referenced in Granville to John King, March 13, 1793, C.O. 5/36, part 3, 13/0).
15. Miller, *Emigrants and Exiles*, 170.
16. Elizabeth A. Perkins, *Border Life: Experience and Memory in the Revolutionary Ohio Valley* (Chapel Hill: University of North Carolina Press, 1998), 55.
17. IILC 568, 570–71n; Alun C. Davies, "'As Good a Country as any Man Needs to Dwell In': Letters from a Scotch-Irish Immigrant in Pennsylvania, 1766, 1767, and 1784," *Pennsylvania History* 50 (1983), 313–22.
18. Wayland Fuller Dunaway, "Pennsylvania as an Early Distributing Center of Population," *PMHB* 55 (1931), 160–61.

19. *Military Journal of Ebenezer Denny: An Officer in the Revolutionary and Indian Wars* (Philadelphia: J. B. Lippincott, 1859), 218; Patrick Griffin, *American Leviathan: Empire, Nation, and Revolutionary Frontier* (New York: Hill and Wang, 2007), 187.
20. H. Tyler Blethen and Curtis W. Wood, Jr., eds., *Ulster and North America: Transatlantic Perspectives on the Scotch-Irish* (Tuscaloosa: University of Alabama Press, 1997), 147, citing E. Estyn Evans, "Cultural Relics in the Old West of North America," *Ulster Folklife* 11 (1965), 33.
21. Stephen B. Weeks, "Tennessee: A Discussion of the Sources of Its Population and the Lines of Immigration," *Tennessee Historical Magazine* 2 (1916), 249 (11.2 percent); *IILC* 604 (106,000); Michael Montgomery and Cherel Henderson, "Eighteenth-Century Emigrants from Ireland to Tennessee: A Report Using First Families of Tennessee Files," *Journal of East Tennessee History* 76 (2004), 88–99.
22. Blethen and Wood, *Ulster and North America*, ch. 12; 213–26 (underrepresented at 216-17); David Hackett Fischer, *Albion's Seed: Four British Folkways in North America* (New York: Oxford University Press, 1993), 664 (Alexander).
23. Terry G. Jordan-Bychkov, *The Upland South: The Making of an American Folk Region and Landscape* (Santa Fe, NM: Center for American Places; Charlottesville: University of Virginia Press, 2003), 9, 15, 17, 23.
24. Thomas A. Lewis, *West from Shenandoah: A Scotch-Irish Family Fights for America, 1721–1781* (Hoboken, NJ: John Wiley and Sons, 2004), 237.
25. "Journal of Arthur Lee," in *The Olden Time: A Monthly Publication devoted to the Preservation of Documents and other Authentic Information in relation to the Early Explorations and the Settlement and Improvement of the Country around the Head of the Ohio*, ed. Neville B. Craig, 2 vols. (1848; reprint, Cincinnati: Robert Clarke & Co., 1876), 2: 334, 339, and John W. Harpster, ed., *Crossroads: Descriptions of Western Pennsylvania, 1720–1829* (Pittsburgh: University of Pittsburgh Press, 1938), 157.
26. John F. D. Smyth, *A Tour in the United States of America: containing an account of the present situation of that country; the population, agriculture, commerce, customs, and manners of the inhabitants; with a description of the Indian nations . . .* , 2 vols. (London: Printed for G. Robinson, 1784), 1: 161, 236 (directions and quote).
27. "Journal of Mrs. Mary Dewees," in Harpster, *Crossroads*, 179; "Journal from Philadelphia to Kentucky, 1787–1788," *PMHB* 28 (1904), 182–98.
28. "A Letter from a Citizen of Pennsylvania," in Harpster, *Crossroads*, 196; *Letters of Benjamin Rush*, ed. L. H. Butterfield, 2 vols. (Princeton, NJ: Princeton University Press, 1951), 1: 333, 400–1, 404–6; "Dr. Benjamin Rush's Journal of a Trip to Carlisle in 1784," *PMHB* 74 (1950), 443–56; Montgomery dinner at 452. Montgomery had emigrated from Ireland around 1740.
29. "Journal of Col. John May, of Boston, Relative to a Journey to the Ohio Country, 1789," *PMHB* 45 (1921), 101–79, quote at 159; Hendrik Booraem, *Young Hickory: The Making of Andrew Jackson* (Dallas, TX: Taylor Trade, 2001), 29 (scabies).
30. Harpster, *Crossroads*, 134.
31. "Lewis Brantz's Memoranda of a Journey (1785)," in *Early Travels in the Tennessee Country*, ed. Samuel Cole Williams (Johnson City, TN: Watauga Press, 1928), 285.
32. Louis Philippe, King of France, 1830–1848, *Diary of My Travels in America*, translated from the French by Stephen Becker (New York: Delaware Press, 1977), 115–16.
33. William Strickland, *Observations on the Agriculture of the United States of America* (London: W. Bulmer and Co., 1801), 71.
34. Ray Allen Billington, *Land of Savagery, Land of Promise: The European Image of the American Frontier* (New York: W. W. Norton, 1981), 162–69.
35. *EAID* 18: 517–20. See also Gregory Ablavsky and W. Tanner Allread, "We the (Native) People?: How Indigenous Peoples Debated the U.S. Constitution," *Columbia Law Review* 123 (March 2023), 243–318.
36. *The St. Clair Papers: The Life and Public Services of Arthur St. Clair . . . with his Correspondence and Other Papers*, ed. William Henry Smith, 2 vols. (Cincinnati: Robert Clarke and Co., 1881), 2: 124.
37. Daniel P. Barr, *A Colony Sprung from Hell: Pittsburgh and the Struggle for Authority on the Western Pennsylvania Frontier, 1744–1794* (Kent, OH: Kent State University Press, 2014), 255.
38. Ablavsky, *Federal Ground*, ch. 2; Andrew R. L. Cayton, *The Frontier Republic: Ideology and Politics in the Ohio Country, 1780–1825* (Kent, OH: Kent State University Press, 1986), ch. 1; John R. Van Atta, *Securing the West: Politics, Public Lands, and the Fate of the Old Republic,*

1785–1850 (Baltimore, MD: Johns Hopkins University Press, 2014), ch. 1; Peter S. Onuf, *Statehood and Union: A History of the Northwest Ordinance* (Bloomington: Indiana University Press, 1987), chs. 1–2; Timothy J. Shannon, "'This Unpleasant Business': The Transformation of Land Speculation in the Ohio Country, 1787–1820," in *The Pursuit of Public Power: Political Culture in Ohio, 1787–1861*, ed. Jeffery P. Brown and Andrew L. Cayton (Kent, OH: Kent State University Press, 1994), 20; Blaakman, *Speculation Nation*.

39. Alan Taylor, *American Republics: A Continental History of the United States, 1783–1850* (New York: W. W. Norton, 2021), 42.
40. François Furstenberg, "The Significance of the Trans-Appalachian Frontier in Atlantic History," *American Historical Review* 113 (2008), 659–65; Beth Saler, *The Settlers' Empire: Colonialism and State Formation in America's Old Northwest* (Philadelphia: University of Pennsylvania Press, 2015), ch. 1; Andro Linklater, *Measuring America: How the United States Was Shaped by the Greatest Land Sale in History* (New York: Penguin/Plume, 2002), 60; Carroll Smith-Rosenberg, *This Violent Empire: The Birth of an American National Identity* (Chapel Hill: University of North Carolina Press, 2010); Mark Rifkin, *Manifesting America: The Imperial Construction of U.S. National Space* (New York: Oxford University Press, 2009), 8–10, 38; Lisa Ford, *Settler Sovereignty: Jurisdiction and Indigenous People in America and Australia, 1788–1836* (Cambridge, MA: Harvard University Press, 2010); Paul Frymer, *Building an American Empire: The Era of Territorial and Political Expansion* (Princeton, NJ: Princeton University Press, 2017); Rachel St. John, "State Power in the West in the Early American Republic," *Journal of the Early Republic* 38 (2018), 87–94; Richard White, *The Middle Ground: Indians, Empires, and Republics in the Great Lakes Region, 1650–1815* (Cambridge: Cambridge University Press, 1991), 418–20.
41. Pickering to David Campbell, August 28, 1790, quoted in Ablavsky, *Federal Ground*, 120.
42. John Walton Caughey, *McGillivray of the Creeks* (Norman: University of Oklahoma Press, 1938), 66, 87.
43. David Andrew Nichols, *Red Gentlemen and White Savages: Indians, Federalists, and the Search for Order on the American Frontier* (Charlottesville: University of Virginia Press, 2008), 57–75; *The Papers of George Washington: Presidential Series*, ed. Dorothy Twohig et al., 21 vols. (Charlottesville: University of Virginia Press, 1987–2020), 8: 49–50.
44. *Journals of the Continental Congress*, ed. Washington C. Ford et al., 34 vols. (Washington, DC, 1904–37), 24: 503.
45. *Calendar of Virginia State Papers* 4: 2.
46. Ablavsky, *Federal Ground*, 45–46; *St. Clair Papers* 2: 3–5.
47. Simon Gratz, "Biography of General Richard Butler," *PMHB* 7 (1883), 7–10.
48. Randolph C. Downes, *Council Fires on the Upper Ohio* (Pittsburgh: Pittsburgh University Press, 1940), 294 (quote). The treaties and related documents are reprinted in *EAID* 18: ch. 4.
49. Barr, *Colony Sprung from Hell*, 256; citing Journal of Richard Butler, Draper 4U226; also Griffin, *American Leviathan*, 223–24.
50. *Calendar of Virginia State Papers* 4: 122.
51. *Documentary History of Dunmore's War, 1774*, ed. Reuben Gold Thwaites and Louise Phelps Kellogg (Madison: Wisconsin Historical Society, 1905), 82; Joseph A. Waddell, *Annals of Augusta County, Virginia*, 2nd ed. (Staunton, VA: C. Russell Caldwell, 1902), 318.
52. "Logan's Campaign—1786," *Ohio Archaeological and Historical Publications* 22 (1913), 520–21; *Military Journal of Major Ebenezer Denny*, 94.
53. Quoted in Robert Morgan, *Boone: A Biography* (Chapel Hill, NC: Algonquian Books, 2008), 238.
54. Robert M. Owens, *Killing over Land: Murder and Diplomacy on the Early American Frontier* (Norman: University of Oklahoma Press, 2024), ch. 6, examines McGary's murder of Moluntha.
55. *Calendar of Virginia State Papers* 3: 560–61.
56. "Bro. Martin Schneider's Report of His Journey to the Upper Cherokee Towns (1783–1784)," in *Early Travels in the Tennessee Country*, ed. Samuel Cole Williams (Johnson City, TN: Watauga Press, 1928), 253. Schneider spent the night at the home of Colonel James Smith who had moved to that country.
57. *Calendar of Virginia State Papers* 3: 601–2.
58. Nichols, *Red Gentlemen and White Savages*, 45.
59. *ASPIA* 1: 43.
60. *IILC* 336–37.
61. *NCSR* 22: 637–41.

62. Samuel Cole Williams, *History of the Lost State of Franklin*, rev. ed. (New York: Press of the Pioneers, 1933); Kevin Barksdale, *The Lost State of Franklin: America's First Secession* (Lexington: University Press of Kentucky, 2009); Kevin Barksdale, "Violence, Statecraft, and Statehood in the Early Republic: The State of Franklin, 1784–1788, in *Blood in the Hills: A History of Violence in Appalachia*, ed. Bruce E. Stewart (Lexington: University Press of Kentucky, 2012), ch. 1; Kevin Barksdale, "The State of Franklin: Separatism, Competition, and the Legacy of Tennessee's First State, 1783–1789," in *Before the Volunteer State: New Thoughts on Early Tennessee, 1540–1800*, ed. Kristofer Ray (Knoxville: University of Tennessee Press, 2014), 159; Kristofer Ray, "Leadership, Loyalty, and Sovereignty in the Revolutionary American Southwest: The State of Franklin as a Test Case," *North Carolina Historical Review* 92 (2015), 123–44; "The State of Franklin, 1785–1788," *NCSR* 22: 637–731; Jessica Chopin Roney, "The Strange Afterlife of the Declaration of Independence: The State of Franklin, 1784–c. 1789," in *Ireland and America: Empire, Revolution, and Sovereignty*, ed. Patrick Griffin and Francis D. Cogliano (Charlottesville: University of Virginia Press, 2021), 246–72.
63. *NCSR* 22: 705–14, quote at 706.
64. *Calendar of Virginia State Papers* 4: 4–5.
65. On Appalachian settler claims to Indigeneity more broadly, and its broader implications, see Stephen Pearson, "'The Last Bastion of Colonialism': Appalachian Settler Colonialism and Self-Indigenization," *American Indian Culture and Research Journal* 37 (2013), 165–84, and Roxanne Dunbar-Ortiz, *Not a "Nation of Immigrants": Settler Colonialism, White Supremacy, and a History of Erasure and Exclusion* (Boston: Beacon Press, 2021), 39–46.
66. *Calendar of Virginia State Papers* 4: 256.
67. *Calendar of Virginia State Papers* 4: 261.
68. Papers of the Continental Congress, 1774–1789, National Archives, Washington, DC, Microfilm 247, reel 69, item 56: 417–18; *Calendar of Virginia State Papers* 4: 261, 306–7.
69. Petition from the Inhabitants of Bluestone, on frontiers of Montgomery County, August 24, 1786, *Calendar of Virginia State Papers* 4: 166; Col. Walter Crockett to Governor, June 11, 1787, *Calendar of Virginia State Papers* 4: 295.
70. To Gov. Randolph, December 5, December 31, 1787, *Calendar of Virginia State Papers* 4: 363–64, 375.
71. "The Correspondence of General James Robertson," *American Historical Magazine* 1 (January 1896), 86–87.
72. John Carr, *Early Times in Middle Tennessee* (Nashville, TN: Stevenson and Owen, 1857), 38–47; Paul Clements, *Chronicles of the Cumberland Settlements, 1779–1796* (self-published, 2012), Appendix 4 (555–72) lists Cumberland settlers killed by Indians between 1780 and 1797; detailed accounts of the fighting and the names of "persons killed by Indians" comprise a substantial portion of John Haywood, *The Civil and Political History of the State of Tennessee, from its Earliest Settlement up to the Year 1796; including the Boundaries of the State* (Knoxville, TN: Heiskell and Brown, 1823).
73. Apparently, his brother-in-law showed him a letter purporting to have come from Ireland and informing Rogan that Nancy had remarried. The brother-in-law had taken a young wife and started a family in America, and evidently did not want Rogan spreading the news to the wife and child he had left back home in Ireland. Clements, *Chronicles of the Cumberland Settlements*, 163, 172, 190–91, 255; Harriette Simpson Arnow, *Seedtime on the Cumberland* (New York: Macmillan 1960), 234–35.
74. Clements, *Chronicles of the Cumberland Settlements*, 278–82, 296–97, 351; A. W. Putnam, *History of Middle Tennessee or, Life and Times of Gen. James Robertson* (1859; reprint, Knoxville: University of Tennessee, 1971), 304–8; J. G. M. Ramsey, *The Annals of Tennessee to the End of the Eighteenth Century: comprising its settlement, as the Watauga association, from 1769 to 1777; a part of North Carolina, from 1777 to 1784; the state of Franklin, from 1784–1788; a part of North-Carolina, from 1788–1790; the territory of the U. States, south of the Ohio, from 1790 to 1796; the state of Tennessee, from 1796 to 1800* (Charleston: J. Russell, 1853), 509–17 (Brown's account of his life in the Chickamauga towns).
75. Hubbard had angrily berated Brother Schneider regarding Joseph Martin's coddling of Indians three years earlier; "Schneider's Report of His Journey," 253.
76. Nichols, *Red Gentlemen*, 71; Cynthia Cumfer, *Separate Peoples, One Land: The Minds of Cherokees, Blacks, and Whites on the Tennessee Frontier* (Chapel Hill: University of North Carolina Press, 2007), 51; Ablavsky, *Federal Ground*, 142. See also *ASPIA* 1: 28–30;

(Charleston) *City Gazette and Daily Advertiser*, October 13, 1788 (letter from Andrew Pickens, Patrick Calhoun—who survived Long Canes in 1760—et al. expressing outrage).
77. *Calendar of Virginia State Papers* 4: 620.
78. *Territorial Papers* 4: 3–18 (quotes at 3, 9, 14).
79. Billy Kennedy, *The Scots-Irish in the Hills of Tennessee* (Londonderry/Belfast: Causeway Press/Ambassador Productions, 1995), ch. 9.
80. Taylor, *Liberty Men and Great Proprietors*, 37–47.
81. *Territorial Papers* 4: 76.
82. *ASPIA* 1: 113 ("Western waters"); *Territorial Papers* 2: 365–66.
83. "The Correspondence of General James Robertson," *American Historical Magazine* 1 (July 1896), 284; *Territorial Papers* 4: 117.
84. *Territorial Papers* 4: 131.
85. *ASPIA* 1: 321.
86. *Territorial Papers* 4: 282.
87. Clements, *Chronicles of the Cumberland Settlements*, 234–35, 275, 541.
88. Louis Chachere was sent to investigate conditions on the western American frontier in 1785. Lawrence Kinnaird, ed., *Spain in the Mississippi Valley, 1765–1794: Translations of Materials from the Spanish Archives in the Bancroft Library*, 3 parts, Annual Report of the American Historical Association for 1945, vols. 2–4 (Washington, DC: Government Printing Office, 1946), pt. 2: 152.
89. *Territorial Papers* 4: 169, 196.
90. *EAID* 18: 375; Wendy St. Jean, "How the Chickasaws Saved the Cumberland Settlement in the 1790s," *Tennessee Historical Quarterly* 68 (Spring 2009), 2–19.
91. Thomas Perkins Abernethy, *From Frontier to Plantation in Tennessee: A Study in Frontier Democracy* (Chapel Hill: University of North Carolina Press, 1932), 129; *ASPIA*, 1: 253.
92. Putnam, *History of Middle Tennessee*, 223, 381, 437–38, 508, 514; Clements, *Chronicles of the Cumberland Settlements*, 278, 347, 376–77, 396–98; Carr, *Early Times in Middle Tennessee*, 33; Thomas W. Cowger and Mitch Caver, *Piominko, Chickasaw Leader* (Ada, OK: Chickasaw Press, 2017), 34, 48, 71–72, 94–95.
93. *Territorial Papers* 4: 72–73; *Papers of George Washington, Presidential Series* 4: 481.
94. *Territorial Papers* 4: 149, 210 (clans quote), 356.
95. Ablavsky, *Federal Ground*, ch. 4.
96. Ablavsky, *Federal Ground*, 128–29.
97. Clements, *Chronicles of the Cumberland Settlements*, 397; *ASPIA*: 1: 363 ("disgraceful"); *Carlisle Gazette*, July 24, 1793.
98. *ASPIA* 1: 468, 2: 622; *Calendar of Virginia State Papers* 6: 575; Charles H. Faulkner, *Massacre at Cavett's Station: Frontier Tennessee during the Cherokee Wars* (Knoxville: University of Tennessee Press, 2013), family background at 65.
99. Matthew Kruer, *Time of Anarchy: Indigenous Power and the Crisis of Colonialism in Early America* (Cambridge, MA; Harvard University Press, 2021), 114, 144.
100. Kristofer Ray, "Land Speculation, Popular Democracy, and Political Transformation on the Tennessee Frontier, 1780–1800," *Tennessee Historical Quarterly* 61 (2002), 161–81.
101. *IILC* 681–82.
102. Stephen Aron, *How the West Was Lost: The Transformation of Kentucky from Daniel Boone to Henry Clay* (Baltimore, MD: Johns Hopkins University Press, 1996); Honor Sachs, *Home Rule: Households, Manhood, and National Expansion on the Eighteenth-Century Kentucky Frontier* (New Haven, CT: Yale University Press, 2015); Fischer, *Albion's Seed*, 751–58.
103. Patrick Griffin, "Searching for Independence: Revolutionary Kentucky, Irish American Experience, and Scotch-Irish Myth," in *Ulster to America: The Scots-Irish Migration Experience, 1680–1830*, ed. Warren Hofstra (Knoxville: University of Tennessee Press, 2012), 212.
104. Theodore Roosevelt, *The Winning of the West*, 6 vols. in 3 (New York: G. P. Putnam's Sons, 1899), 1, pt. 1: 27; 3, pt. 1: 43.
105. *Documentary History of the First Federal Congress*, 17: 1702–4; 19: 1421.
106. Waddell, *Annals of Augusta County*, 315–18.
107. Arthur Andrew Savery, "Forgotten Frontiersman: The Life and Times of Simon Kenton," MA thesis, University of Nebraska at Kearney, 2017, 62.
108. June Lee Mefford Kinkead, *Our Kentucky Pioneer Ancestry: A History of the Kinkead and McDowell Families of Kentucky and those Families Associated by Marriage* (Baltimore, MD: Gateway Press, 1992), 9.

109. Van Atta, *Securing the West*, 22–23.
110. *IILC* 106.
111. *Calendar of Virginia State Papers* 3: 605.
112. Sachs, *Home Rule*, 78–93, 100–1.
113. *Calendar of Virginia State Papers* 5: 7–8.
114. Knox to Gov of Virginia, December 10, 1789, *Calendar of Virginia State Papers* 5: 75.
115. Sachs, *Home Rule*, 32, 37–38, 43–45, 75–78; Ablavsky, *Federal Ground*, lawsuit quote at 20; Daniel Blake Smith, "'This Idea in Heaven': Image and Reality on the Kentucky Frontier," in *The Buzzel about Kentucke: Settling the Promised Land*, ed. Craig Thompson Friend (Lexington: University of Kentucky Press, 1999), 77–98; "Gen. Butler's Journal," in *The Olden Time*, 2: 507; Aron, *How the West Was Lost*, 79 (two-thirds and "not caring" quote).
116. *Calendar of Virginia State Papers* 4: 119–20.
117. Sachs, *Home Rule*, 46–60; Richard Lyman Bushman, *The American Farmer in the Eighteenth Century: A Social and Cultural History* (New Haven, CT: Yale University Press, 2018), 64; Matthew C. Ward, *Making the Frontier Man: Violence, White Manhood, and Authority in the Early Western Backcountry* (Pittsburgh: University of Pittsburgh Press, 2023).
118. Patrick Spero, *Frontier Rebels: The Fight for Independence in the American West, 1756–1776* (New York: W. W. Norton, 2018), 194–96.
119. Sachs, *Home Rule*, 145–46. See more broadly Samantha Seeley, *Race, Removal, and the Right to Remain: Migration and the Making of the United States* (Chapel Hill: University of North Carolina Press, 2021).
120. Griffin, "Searching for Independence," 222.
121. Van Atta, *Securing the West*, 22–23.
122. Aron, *How the West Was Lost*, 84.
123. Slaughter; *Whiskey Rebellion*; William Hogeland, *The Whiskey Rebellion: George Washington, Alexander Hamilton, and the Frontier Rebels Who Challenged America's Newfound Sovereignty* (New York: Scribner, 2006); Carol Berkin, *A Sovereign People: The Crises of the 1790s and the Birth of American Nationalism* (New York: Basic Books, 2017), 7–80; "Papers of the Whiskey Insurrection of Western Pennsylvania, 1794," *Penn. Archives*, 2nd ser. vol. 4.
124. Mary K. Bonstel Tachau, "The Whiskey Rebellion in Kentucky: A Forgotten Episode of Civil Disobedience," *Journal of the Early Republic* 2 (1982), 239–59.
125. Blaakman, *Speculation Nation*, 200.
126. Taylor, *Liberty Men and Great Proprietors*, 189; Paul A Gilje, *Rioting in America* (Bloomington: Indiana University Press, 1996), 35.
127. Woodward, *American Nations*, 158–59.
128. Slaughter, *Whiskey Rebellion*, 65–66, 93.
129. Hogeland, *Whiskey Rebellion*, 66; Steven Stoll, *Ramp Hollow: The Ordeal of Appalachia* (New York: Hill and Wang, 2017), ch. 3, "The Rye Rebellion"; Strickland, *Observations on the Agriculture of the United States of America*, 47; William Strickland, *Journal of a Tour in the United States of America 1794–1795*, ed. Rev. J. E. Strickland (New York: New-York Historical Society, 1971), 59n.
130. Slaughter, *Whiskey Rebellion*, 93–95.
131. Slaughter, *Whiskey Rebellion*, 109–10.
132. Patrick Spero, *Frontier Country: The Politics of War in Early Pennsylvania* (Philadelphia: University of Pennsylvania Press, 2016), 251–54.
133. *St. Clair Papers*, 2: 126; *Papers of George Washington: Presidential Series* 4: 141.
134. *The Proceedings of a Court of Inquiry, Held at the Special Request of Brigadier General Josiah Harmar, to Investigate his Conduct as Commanding Officer of the Expedition against the Miami Indians, 1790* (Philadelphia: John Fenno, 1791), 2; also in *American State Papers: Documents, Legislative and Executive, of the Congress of the United States. Class 5: Military Affairs*, ed. Walter Lowrie and Matthew St. Clair Clarke, Vol. 1 (Washington, DC: Gales and Seaton, 1832); Denny's report, January 1, 1791, Arthur St. Clair Papers, Ohio State Library, card 22.
135. *Papers of George Washington: Presidential Series* 7: 70–77; Draper 2W340–42; *Military Journal of Ebenezer Denny*, 146–49; Denny's report, January 1, 1791, Arthur St. Clair Papers, Ohio State Library, card 22; St. Clair to Knox, October 29 and November 6, 1790, Arthur St. Clair Papers, Ohio State Library, card 21, and *St. Clair Papers* 2: 188, 190; *Territorial Papers* 2: 309–10, 313; Leroy V. Eid, "'The Slaughter Was Reciprocal': Josiah Harmar's Two Defeats, 1790," *Northwest Ohio Quarterly* 65 (1993), 51–67.

136. *The Proceedings of a Court of Inquiry, Held at the Special Request of Brigadier General Josiah Harmar* in *American State Papers, Military Affairs*, 20–30; Draper 2W402–6, 419–26; 4U19–64.
137. *The Journal of William Maclay, United States Senator from Pennsylvania, 1789–1791* (New York: Albert and Charles Boni, 1927), 339–40, 384; *The Diary of William Maclay and Other Notes on Senate Debates*, in *Documentary History of the First Federal Congress* 9: 340, 342, 379, 385 ("Pretext").
138. Colin G. Calloway, *Victory with No Name: The Native American Defeat of the First American Army* (New York: Oxford University Press, 2015); Alan D. Gaff, *Field of Corpses: Arthur St. Clair and the Death of an American Army* (Nashville, TN: Knox Press/Permuted Press, 2023); Stephen P. Locke, *War along the Wabash: The Ohio Indian Confederacy's Destruction of the U.S. Army, 1791* (Philadelphia: Casemate, 2023); C. Hale Sipe, *The Indian Wars of Pennsylvania* (Harrisburg, PA: Telegraph Press, 1929), 514 (George Gibson).
139. *Calendar of Virginia State Papers* 6: 146–47, 149–50, 150–53.
140. *Calendar of Virginia State Papers* 6: 305–6, 588.
141. Colin G. Calloway, "Simon Girty: Interpreter and Intermediary," in *Being and Becoming Indian: Biographical Studies of North American Frontier*, ed. James A. Clifton (Chicago: Dorsey Press, 1989), 52–53; Reginald Horsman, *Matthew Elliott, British Indian Agent* (Detroit: Wayne State University Press, 1964), 102–4; *ASPIA* 1: 322 (Knox quote).
142. Savery, "Forgotten Frontiersman," 73.
143. "The Correspondence of General James Robertson," *American Historical Magazine* 4 (January 1899): 76; Draper 27CC17–18; 5XX52–56; *Territorial Papers* 4: 356–59; Clements, *Chronicles of the Cumberland Settlements*, 374, 435–45 (Ramsay at 442), 450; Haywood, *Civil and Political History of the State of Tennessee*, 392–98; John R. Finger, *Tennessee Frontiers: Three Regions in Transition* (Bloomington: Indiana University Press, 2001), 154.
144. Barr, *Colony Sprung from Hell*, 10, 269–70.
145. Ward, *Making the Frontier Man*, ch. 8; Slaughter, *Whiskey Rebellion*, 185–89.
146. *Washington-Irvine Correspondence: The Official Letters which passed between Washington and Brig.-Gen. William Irvine and between Irvine and Others concerning Military Affairs in the West from 1781 to 1783*, ed. Consul W. Butterfield (Madison, WI: David Atwood, 1882), 69.
147. Gaff, *Field of Corpses*, 85–88 (on Craig); Barr, *Colony Sprung from Hell*, 265.
148. December 2, 1794; *Founders Online*, National Archives, https://founders.archives.gov/documents/Adams/04-10-02-0180. Original source: *The Adams Papers, Adams Family Correspondence*, vol. 10, *January 1794–June 1795*, ed. Margaret A. Hogan, C. James Taylor, Sara Martin, Hobson Woodward, Sara B. Sikes, Gregg L. Lint, and Sara Georgini (Cambridge, MA: Harvard University Press, 2011), 284–85.
149. Peter Gilmore and Kerby A. Miller, "Searching for 'Irish' Freedom—Settling for 'Scotch-Irish' Respectability: Southwestern Pennsylvania, 1780–1810," in *Ulster to America: The Scots-Irish Migration Experience, 1680–1830*, ed. Warren Hofstra (Knoxville: University of Tennessee Press, 2012), 167; Kerby A. Miller, *Emigrants and Exiles: Ireland and the Irish Exodus to North America* (New York: Oxford University Press, 1985), 188; Jackson, *A Social History of the Scotch-Irish*, 138; Meagher, *Becoming Irish American*, 59–64.
150. Jane T. Merritt, *At the Crossroads: Indians and Empires on a Mid-Atlantic Frontier, 1700–1763* (Chapel Hill: University of North Carolina Press, 2003), 15.
151. *ASPIA* 2: 544.
152. *Papers of George Washington: Presidential Series* 18: 744.
153. Ablavsky, *Federal Ground*, 40–42 (Hawkins quote at 41). It would take forty years, and the intervention of the Supreme Court, in a case involving the Wabash & Illinois Company, before the persistent dream of private purchases from Natives finally died. Similarly, Anglo-American settlers waged, ultimately successfully, a forty-year campaign to overturn the federal government's hostility to preemption rights (Ablavsky, 50).
154. Cumfer, *Separate Peoples, One Land*, 64–65, 78–79, 234–35.
155. "Thomas Dillon's Account (1796)," in *Early Travels in the Tennessee Country*, 359–60.
156. Francis Baily, *Journal of a Tour in Unsettled Parts of North America in 1796 and 1797*, ed. Jack D. Holmes (Carbondale: University of Southern Illinois Press, 1969), 245, 262.
157. Jefferson to Washington, May 3, 1790, quoted in Paul Frymer, *Building an American Empire: The Era of Territorial and Political Expansion* (Princeton, NJ: Princeton University Press, 2017), 40; Taylor, *American Republics*, 66.
158. *Territorial Papers* 4: 300.

159. On Jefferson's Indian policy, see Anthony F. C. Wallace, *Jefferson and the Indians: The Tragic Fate of the First Americans* (Cambridge, MA: Harvard University Press, 1999), and Robert M. Owens, *Mr. Jefferson's Hammer: William Henry Harrison and the Origins of American Indian Policy* (Norman: University of Oklahoma Press, 2007).
160. Ablavsky, *Federal Ground*, 137.
161. White, *Middle Ground*, 413.
162. Harriette Simpson Arnow, *Flowering of the Cumberland* (East Lansing: Michigan State University Press, 2013), 71.
163. Nichols, *Red Gentlemen*, 68; Hofstra, ed., *Ulster to America*, xx ("became white").
164. Ablavsky, *Federal Ground*, 187–92 ("monthly" at 192).
165. In the anarchic times around Bacon's Rebellion, historian Matthew Kruer notes, "The power of politicized emotions to turn intimate tragedies into mass movements allowed even small groups of raiders and vigilantes to drag whole nations to war." In that sense, "[o]ften enough, it was the weakest and most precarious actors who shaped the future of North America." Kruer, *Time of Anarchy*, 244.

Chapter 11

1. Louis Philippe, King of France, 1830–1848, *Diary of My Travels in America*, translated from the French by Stephen Becker (New York: Delaware Press, 1977), 99.
2. David Hackett Fischer, *Albion's Seed: Four British Folkways in North America* (New York: Oxford University Press, 1989), 847–50, quote at 849.
3. Steve Inskeep, *Jacksonland: President Andrew Jackson, Cherokee Chief John Ross, and a Great American Land Grab* (New York: Penguin, 2015), 69 ("Jackson's famous life story probably went far to enshrine the stereotype"); John Buchanan, *Jackson's Way: Andrew Jackson and the People of the Western Waters* (New York: John Wiley and Sons, 2001), 6 ("a son of that people writ large"); John Buchanan, "Andrew Jackson, the Scotch-Irish, and the Conquest of the Old Southwest," *Journal of Scotch-Irish Studies* 1, no. 3 (2002), 86–102; Patrick Fitzgerald and Steve Ickringill, eds., *Atlantic Crossroads: Historical Connections between Scotland, Ulster and North America* (Newtonards, N. Ireland: Colourpoint Books, 2001), 8 ("that most Scotch-Irish of presidents").
4. Hendrik Booraem, *Young Hickory: The Making of Andrew Jackson* (Dallas, TX: Taylor Trade, 2001), 25, 54; Robert V. Remini, *Andrew Jackson and the Course of American Empire, 1767–1821* (New York: Harper and Row, 1977), 3.
5. John Henry Eaton, *The Life of Andrew Jackson, Major-General in the Service of the United States, comprising a History of the War in the South, from the Commencement of the Creek Campaign to the Termination of Hostilities before New Orleans* (Philadelphia: Samuel F. Bradford, 1824), 10. The original author, Jackson's aide de camp in the Creek War, John Reid, died before completing his biography of Jackson. Eaton, who served with Jackson during the War of 1812, took over and published the biography in 1817, with a revised edition in 1824. Eaton served as U.S. senator from Tennessee from 1818 to 1829 and then as Jackson's secretary of war.
6. Note on a letter from Andrew Jackson to Robert Hays, January 4, 1814, *PAJ* 3: 8n3.
7. D. J. McCartney, *The Ulster Jacksons: From Cumbria to the White House, Shenandoah and Australia* (Carrickfergus: Carrickfergus Borough Council, 1997).
8. *PAJ* 8: 374, 377, 407–8, 416–17, 439–40 (Jackson quote), 478.
9. *PAJ* 10: 727
10. Kevin Kenny, *The American Irish: A History* (Harlow, UK: Longman, 2000), 26–27. As Daniel Patterson notes, "We do not need to look to ancient miseries on the Atlantic rim or along bloody Scottish borders or in Ulster's towns and fields to explain Scotch Irish violence. They had their own 'Desert Places' so much nearer home." Daniel W. Patterson, *The True Image: Gravestone Art and the Culture of Scotch Irish Settlers in the Pennsylvania and Carolina Backcountry* (Chapel Hill: University of North Carolina Press, 2012), 400.
11. Peter N. Moore, *World of Toil and Strife: Community Transformation in Backcountry South Carolina, 1750–1805* (Columbia: University of South Carolina Press, 2007), 4.
12. Jon Meacham, *American Lion: Andrew Jackson in the White House* (New York: Random House, 2008), 10, 15.
13. Jefferson Davis to John Jenkins, July 5, 1845, in *The Papers of Jefferson Davis*, ed. Haskell M. Monroe, Jr., James T. McIntosh, and Lynda L. Crist (Baton Rouge: LSU Press, 1971), 2: 287, quoted in Grady McWhiney, *Cracker Culture: Celtic Ways in the Old South* (Tuscaloosa: University of Alabama Press, 1988), 35–36.

14. Robert V. Remini, *Andrew Jackson and His Indian Wars* (New York: Viking 2001), 1–14; Alfred A. Cave, *Sharp Knife: Andrew Jackson and the American Indians* (Santa Barbara, CA: Praeger, 2017), 3; Booraem, *Young Hickory*, 194, citing W. A. Graham, *General Joseph Graham and His Papers on North Carolina Revolutionary History* (Raleigh: Author, 1904). Booraem discusses the reliability of Susan Alexander's account in Appendix 2, 205–9.
15. Gregory Evans Dowd, *War under Heaven: Pontiac, the Indian Nations, and the British Empire* (Baltimore, MD: Johns Hopkins University Press, 2002), 203–4.
16. Cf. J. M. Opal, *Avenging the People: Andrew Jackson, the Rule of Law, and the American Nation* (New York: Oxford University Press, 2017), 2, 97–98; Samuel K. Fisher, *The Gaelic and Indian Origins of the American Revolution: Diversity and Empire in the British Atlantic, 1688-1783* (New York: Oxford University Press, 2022), 258–59.
17. A decade after John Donelson's death in 1786, at least 39 of Nashville's 250–300 inhabitants were relatives. On the Donelsons, see Natalie R. Inman, *Brothers and Friends: Kinship in Early America* (Athens: University of Georgia Press, 2017), ch. 4, quote at 83. Patterson, *True Image*, 401; Michael Paul Rogin, *Fathers and Children: Andrew Jackson and the Subjugation of the American Indian* (New York: Random House, 1975), 55.
18. Opal, *Avenging the People*, 74–75.
19. Rogin, *Fathers and Children*, 134, 136.
20. Colin G. Calloway, "Dragging Canoe and the Chickamauga Revolution," in *Forgotten Founders: Rebels, Radicals, and Reformers in the Making of the Nation*, ed. Alfred F. Young, Gary B. Nash, and Ray Raphael (New York: Knopf, 2011), 185–98.
21. *PAJ* 1: 48–49. John McKee was described as "a particular friend and acquaintance" of the Chickamauga chief John Watts, and who "stands also high in the esteem of the other chiefs of the Lower towns, and is a man from whom every thing may be expected by the Government that can be expected from any man in such a character." *ASPIA* 1: 435; *Territorial Papers* 4: 239.
22. Opal, *Avenging the People*, 97–98, 105, 133; Opal identifies Sevier as a warlord at 92.
23. "Jackson accused the Indians of designs actually his own." Rogin, *Fathers and Children*, 133.
24. Gregory Ablavsky, *Federal Ground: Governing Property and Violence in the First U.S. Territories* (New York: Oxford University Press, 2021), 194.
25. *PAJ* 1: 126.
26. Dinsmoor's account of his public service, Dinsmoor Papers, box 4, miscellaneous file, Rauner Library, Dartmouth College; James Dinsmoor, "Dinsmoor, or Dinsmore, Family," in Leonard A. Morrison, *The History of Windham in New Hampshire (Rockingham County), 1719-1833, a Scotch Settlement (commonly called Scotch-Irish) embracing nearly one third of the ancient settlement and historic township of Londonderry, N.H, with the History and Genealogy of its First Settlers and their Descendants* (Boston: Cupples, Upham and Co., 1883), 451–56.
27. *Indian Affairs: Laws and Treaties*, Vol. 2, *Treaties*, Charles J. Kappler, comp. (Washington, DC: Government Printing Office, 1904), 79, 87–88; *ASPIA* 1: 697, 749; William S. Coker and Thomas D. Watson, *Indian Traders of the Southeastern Spanish Borderlands: Panton, Leslie and Company and John Forbes and Company, 1783-1847* (Pensacola: University of West Florida Press, 1986), 255–55, 267–68; Arthur H. DeRosier, Jr., *The Removal of the Choctaw Indians* (Knoxville: University of Tennessee Press, 1970), 32.
28. "Genealogies: Col. Silas Dinsmoor," 452; Silas Dinsmoor Alumni file; Dinsmoor's account of his public service, Dinsmoor Papers, box 4, miscellaneous file; Dinsmoor, "Dinsmoor, or Dinsmore, Family," 461–63 (duel), 467 (Pushmataha).
29. *PAJ* 2: 277–79. See also the lengthy letter to George Washington Campbell, October 15, 1812, insisting that Dinsmore must be removed; *PAJ* 2: 334–35.
30. *PAJ* 2: 295.
31. Alan Taylor, *American Republics: A Continental History of the United States, 1783-1850* (New York: W. W. Norton, 2021), 252.
32. *PAJ* 2: 191–92; Cave, *Sharp Knife*, 26 (false rumors).
33. *PAJ* 2: 270.
34. *ASPIA* 2: 813–14; Peter Cozzens, *A Brutal Reckoning: Andrew Jackson, the Creek Indians, and the Epic War for the American South* (New York: Alfred Knopf, 2023), 81–83; Rogin, *Fathers and Children*, 147 ("gore"); Opal, *Avenging the People*, 143–45; *PAJ* 2: 300–1, 307–8.
35. *PAJ* 2: 310–11, 313–14; Cave, *Sharp Knife*, 27–28.
36. Albert Memmi, *The Colonizer and the Colonized* (Boston: Beacon Press, 1967), 87–88; *PAJ* 2: 464.

37. Tom Kanon, *Tennesseans at War: Andrew Jackson, the Creek War, and the Battle of New Orleans* (Tuscaloosa: University of Alabama Press, 2014), 198.
38. A Spanish census in 1793 listed 31 Upper Creek towns, 25 Lower Creek towns, and several smaller Seminole towns, and a total population of 15,160; Lawrence Kinnaird, ed., *Spain in the Mississippi Valley, 1765–1794: Translations of Materials from the Spanish Archives in the Bancroft Library*, in *Annual Report of the American Historical Association for 1945*, 4 vols., 3 parts (Washington, DC: Government Printing Office, 1946–1949), pt. 3: 231–32; John Walton Caughey, *McGillivray of the Creeks* (Norman: University of Oklahoma Press, 1938), 6.
39. Robbie Etheridge, "Creeks and Americans in the Age of Washington," in *George Washington's South*, ed. Tamara Harvey and Greg O'Brien (Gainesville: University Press of Florida, 2004), 278–79; Angela Pulley Hudson, *Creek Paths and Federal Roads: Indians, Settlers, and Slaves in the Making of the American South* (Chapel Hill: University of North Carolina Press, 2010), 3–4.
40. Colin G. Calloway, *The American Revolution in Indian Country: Crisis and Diversity in Native American Communities* (Cambridge: Cambridge University Press, 1995), ch. 9.
41. Claudio Saunt, *A New Order of Things: Property, Power, and the Transformation of the Creek Indians, 1733–1816* (Cambridge: Cambridge University Press, 1999).
42. Joel Martin, *Sacred Revolt: The Muskogees' Struggle for a New World* (Boston: Beacon Press, 1991).
43. Gregory A. Waselkov, *A Conquering Spirit: Fort Mims and the Redstick War of 1813–1814* (Tuscaloosa: University of Alabama Press, 2006), 3, 33, 159–60, 225–57 (Appendix 1: Participants); Cozzens, *Brutal Reckoning*, 146, 152, 300–1.
44. Cozzens, *Brutal Reckoning*, 155, 169.
45. Quoted in Kanon, *Tennesseans at War*, 68.
46. *PAJ* 2: 428–29; 3: 5.
47. Michael Wallis, *David Crockett: The Lion of the West* (New York: W. W. Norton, 2011), 16–20, 26, 105–7; Billy Kennedy, *The Scots-Irish in the Hills of Tennessee* (Londonderry/Belfast: Causeway Press/Ambassador Productions, 1995), 100–1.
48. Kathryn E. Holland Braund, ed., *Tohopeka: Rethinking the Creek War and the War of 1812* (Tuscaloosa: University of Alabama Press, 2012); Remini, *Andrew Jackson and the Course of American Empire*, 192–93.
49. Inman, *Brothers and Friends*, 88, 110.
50. Kennedy, *Scots-Irish in the Hills of Tennessee*, 79.
51. Kanon, *Tennesseans at War*, 75–76; John Brannan, *Official Letters of the Military and Naval Officers of the United States, During the War with Great Britain in the Years 1812, 13, 14 & 15* (Washington, DC: Way and Gidron, 1823), 255–56 (Coffee's report); David Crockett, *Narrative of the Life of David Crockett, Written by Himself* (Lincoln: University of Nebraska Press, 1987), 88–89; Eaton, *Life of Andrew Jackson*, 55.
52. Brannan, *Official Letters of the Military and Naval Officers of the United States*, 264–66; "Letters from Gen. Coffee," *American Historical Magazine* 6 (April 1901), 176–77; Eaton, *Life of Andrew Jackson*, 62.
53. Brannan, *Official Letters of the Military and Naval Officers of the United States*, 281–82; Eaton, *Life of Andrew Jackson*, 77, 165; Remini, *Andrew Jackson and His Indian Wars*, 67–69.
54. J. F. H. Claiborne, *Life and Times of Gen Sam. Dale, the Mississippi Partisan* (New York: Harper and Brothers, 1860), 15, 12–27.
55. Buchanan, *Jackson's Way*, 279.
56. Jackson's report, *PAJ* 3: 52–53; Jackson to Rachel, *PAJ* 3: 54–55; John Coffee's account, *PAJ* 3: 55–57 and "Letters from Gen. Coffee," 181–83. Eaton, *Life of Andrew Jackson*, 158–67; Thomas Kanon, "'A Slow Laborious Slaughter: The Battle of Horseshoe Bend," *Tennessee Historical Quarterly* 58 (1999), 2–15; Kanon, *Tennesseans at War*, 104; Braund, *Tohopeka*; Martin, *Sacred Revolt*, 2, 162–63; Remini, *Andrew Jackson and His Indian Wars*, 78; Sean Michael O'Brien, *In Bitterness and in Tears: Andrew Jackson's Destruction of the Creeks and Seminoles* (Westport, CT: Praeger, 2003), ch. 13; Cozzens, *Brutal Reckoning*, ch. 16; Brannan, *Official Letters of the Military and Naval Officers of the United States*, 319–23.
57. *PAJ* 3: 58–59; Brannan, *Official Letters of the Military and Naval Officers of the United States*, 320–21.
58. Kanon, *Tennesseans at War*, 101–2; Cozzens, *Brutal Reckoning*, 292.
59. Waselkov, *Conquering Spirit*, 171–73.

60. *PAJ* 3: 74.
61. *PAJ* 3: 103–4.
62. Big Warrior to Hawkins, August 6, and Jackson to Big Warrior, August 7, 1814, *PAJ* 3: 106–8, 109–11.
63. Remini, *Andrew Jackson and the Course of American Empire*, 225–26.
64. Kappler, *Indian Affairs: Laws and Treaties*, 2: 107.
65. Remini, *Andrew Jackson and the Course of American Empire*, 226–33; Remini, *Andrew Jackson and His Indian Wars*, 88 (Sharp Knife quote).
66. *PAJ* 3: 74.
67. Jackson's report of the battle to James Monroe, January 9, 1815, is in *PAJ* 3: 239–40.
68. Remini, *Andrew Jackson and the Course of American Empire*, 301–6; Colin G. Calloway, *Crown and Calumet: British-Indian Relations, 1783–1815* (Norman: University of Oklahoma Press, 1987), 240–48.
69. Remini, *Andrew Jackson and the Course of American Empire*, ch. 21.
70. *IILC* 682.
71. *PAJ* 4: 62.
72. *PAJ* 4: 93–96; Ronald N. Satz, *American Indian Policy in the Jacksonian Era* (Lincoln: University of Nebraska Press, 1975), 9–10, 13.
73. Quoted in Emilie Connolly, "Fiduciary Colonialism: Annuities and Dispossession in the Early United States," *American Historical Review* 127 (2022), 247.
74. Opal, *Avenging the People*, 207.
75. *PAJ* 10: 52; Remini, *Andrew Jackson and the Course of American Empire*, ch. 22; quote at 346; Cave, *Sharp Knife*, 81–102.
76. Sean Connolly, *On Every Tide: The Making and Remaking of the Irish World* (New York: Basic Books, 2022), 19; Timothy J. Meagher, *Becoming Irish American: The Making and Remaking of a People from Roanoke to JFK* (New Haven, CT: Yale University Press, 2023), 75–79.
77. Patrick Spero, *Frontier Rebels: The Fight for Independence in the American West, 1756–1776* (New York: W. W. Norton, 2018), 204.
78. Fisher, *Gaelic and Indian Origins of the American Revolution*, 259.
79. Robert M. Owens, *Mr. Jefferson's Hammer: William Henry Harrison and the Origins of American Indian Policy* (Norman: University of Oklahoma Press, 2007).
80. Gary Clayton Anderson, *The Conquest of Texas: Ethnic Cleansing in the Promised Land, 1820–1875* (Norman: University of Oklahoma Press, 2005), 41.
81. Cave, *Sharp Knife*, 134.
82. Remini, *Andrew Jackson and the Course of American Empire*, 398; Cave, *Sharp Knife*, ch. 3.
83. *PAJ* 6: 192.
84. Quoted in Cave, *Sharp Knife*, 133.
85. Ronald N. Satz, "Rhetoric Versus Reality: The Indian Policy of Andrew Jackson," in *Cherokee Removal: Before and After*, ed. William L. Anderson (Athens: University of Georgia Press, 1991), 29–32; Robert V. Remini, *Andrew Jackson and the Course of American Freedom, 1822–1832* (New York: Harper & Row, 1981), 264–65; Remini, *Andrew Jackson and the Course of American Democracy, 1833–1845* (New York: Harper & Row, 1984), 314.
86. Richard Slotkin, *Regeneration through Violence: The Mythology of the American Frontier, 1600–1860* (Middletown, CT: Wesleyan University Press, 1973), 414, Wallis, *David Crockett*, 221–26.
87. Nancy Isenberg, *White Trash: The 400-Year Untold History of Class in America* (New York: Viking, 2016), 117, 123.
88. Andrew Jackson, Second Annual Message Online by Gerhard Peters and John T. Woolley, The American Presidency Project, https://www.presidency.ucsb.edu/node/200833.
89. *PAJ* 7: 112–13, 494–95.
90. *PAJ* 8: 508.
91. DeRosier, *Removal of the Choctaw Indians*, 123–24; *PAJ* 8: 531n.
92. Remini, *Andrew Jackson and His Indian Wars*, 246.
93. *PAJ* 8: 114.
94. *PAJ* 8: 158–59.
95. Inskeep, *Jacksonland*, 215–16; *Cherokee Phoenix*, April 7, 1830.
96. Cave, *Sharp Knife*, 154–68.
97. Meacham, *American Lion*, 54.

98. Bryan Patrick McGovern, "Andrew Jackson and the Protestant Irish of Philadelphia: Early Nineteenth-Century Sectarianism," *Pennsylvania History* 87 (2020), 313–37.
99. Jefferson Cowie, *Freedom's Dominion: A Saga of White Resistance to Federal Power* (New York: Basic Books, 2022), 63–64
100. Isenberg, *White Trash*, ch. 5, esp. 106–7, 112–13; Paul Frymer, *Building an American Empire: The Era of Territorial and Political Expansion* (Princeton, NJ: Princeton University Press, 2017), 133; John Suval, Dangerous Ground: Squatters, Statesmen, and the Antebellum Rupture of American Democracy (New York: Oxford University Press, 2022), 2, 4, and ch. 1.
101. Noel Ignatiev, *How the Irish Became White* (New York: Routledge, 1995), 68.
102. Rogin, *Fathers and Children*, 167, 297, 312.
103. Cave, *Sharp Knife*, 112, 190.
104. Thomas Perkins Abernethy, *From Frontier to Plantation in Tennessee: A Study in Frontier Democracy* (Chapel Hill: University of North Carolina Press, 1932), 249.

Chapter 12

1. Russel L. Gerlach, *Settlement Patterns in Missouri: A Study of Population Origins* (Columbia: University of Missouri Press, 1986), 13–14; *Territorial Papers* 19: 7.
2. Terry G. Jordan, "Foreword," in Walter A. Schroeder, *Opening the Ozarks: A Historical Geography of Missouri's Ste. Genevieve District, 1760–1830* (Columbia: University of Missouri Press, 2002), xv.
3. Colin G. Calloway, *Crown and Calumet: British-Indian Relations, 1783–1815* (Norman: University of Oklahoma Press, 1987), 16–17, 188, 240–41; Robert F. Berkhofer, Jr., "Barrier to Settlement: British Indian Policy in the Old Northwest, 1783–1794," in *The Frontier in American Development: Essays in Honor of Paul Wallace Gates*, ed. David M. Ellis (Ithaca, NY: Cornell University Press, 1969), 249–76; C.O. 42/21: 283–87; C.O. 42/83: 134–42; C.O. 42/89: 47–50.
4. Jeremy Adelman and Stephen Aron, "From Borderlands to Borders: Empires, Nation-States, and the Peoples in between in North American History," *American Historical Review* 104 (1999), 827–28; Alan Taylor, "Remaking Americans: Louisiana, Upper Canada, and Texas," in *Contested Spaces of Early America*, ed. Julianna Barr and Edward Countryman (Philadelphia: University of Pennsylvania Press, 2014), 208–26; Stephen Aron, *American Confluence: The Missouri Frontier from Borderland to Border State* (Bloomington: Indiana University Press, 2006), ch. 3; Lawrence Kinnaird, ed., *Spain in the Mississippi Valley, 1765–1794: Translations of Materials from the Spanish Archives in the Bancroft Library*, 3 parts, Annual Report of the American Historical Association for 1945, vols. 2–4 (Washington, DC: Government Printing Office, 1946) pt. 1: 258–60; 2: 117–19, 269–91; 3: 61, 106, 141–43.
5. Alan Taylor, *American Republics: A Continental History of the United States, 1783–1850* (New York: W. W. Norton, 2021), 32.
6. Kinnaird, *Spain in the Mississippi Valley*, pt. 2: 117.
7. Quoted in Taylor, "Remaking Americans," 208.
8. John P. Bowes, *Land Too Good for Indians: Northern Indian Removal* (Norman: University of Oklahoma Press, 2016), ch. 3; C. A. Weslager, *The Delaware Indian Westward Migration: With the Texts of Two Manuscripts (1821–22) Responding to General Lewis Cass's Inquiries about Lenape Culture and Language* (Wallingford, PA: Middle Atlantic Press, 1978).
9. "Lewis Brantz's Memoranda of a Journey (1785)," in *Early Travels in the Tennessee Country*, ed. Samuel Cole Williams (Johnson City, TN: Watauga Press, 1928), 284.
10. Weslager, *Delaware Indian Westward Migration*, 57–58.
11. Weslager, *Delaware Indian Westward Migration*, 72, 209–13; Bowes, *Land Too Good for Indians*, 106–7; John Mack Faragher, "'More Motley than Mackinaw': From Ethnic Mixing to Ethnic Cleansing on the Frontier of the Lower Missouri, 1783–1833," in *Contact Points: American Frontiers from the Mohawk Valley to the Mississippi, 1750–1830*, ed. Andrew R. L. Cayton and Fredricka J. Teute (Chapel Hill: University of North Carolina Press, 1998), 306–7; Rodney Staab, "Settlements of the Missouri Shawnee, 1793–1825," *Papers of the Thirtieth Algonquian Conference* 30 (1999), 351–73; John P. Bowes, *Exiles and Pioneers: Eastern Indians in the Trans-Mississippi West* (Cambridge: Cambridge University Press, 2007), 24–29; Stephen Warren, *The Shawnees and Their Neighbors, 1795–1870* (Urbana: University of Illinois Press, 2005), ch. 3; Sami Lakomäki, *Gathering Together: The Shawnee People through Diaspora and Nationhood, 1600–1870* (New Haven, CT: Yale University Press,

2014), 165–75; Thomas Wildcat Alvord, *Civilization and the Story of the Absentee Shawnees* (Norman: University of Oklahoma Press, 1936), 200–2; Taylor, "Remaking Americans," 209–10; Schroeder, *Opening the Ozarks*, 94–96, 193, 371; Louis Houck, ed., *The Spanish Regime in Missouri*, 2 vols. (Chicago: R. R. Donnelly and Sons, 1909), 2: 11–12, 50; Louis Houck, *A History of Missouri from the Earliest Explorations and Settlements until the Admission of the State into the Union*, 3 vols. (Chicago: R. R. Donnelley and Sons, 1908; reprint, Arno Press, 1971), 1: 208–19; 2: 170–75; Aron, *American Confluence*, 81; Stephen Aron, *Peace and Friendship: An Alternative History of the American West* (New York: Oxford University Press, 2022), ch. 2; ****Major Amos Stoddard, *Sketches, Historical and Descriptive, of Louisiana* (Philadelphia: Mathew Carey, 1812), 210. On Lorimier, see Robert Englebert, "Colonial Encounters and the Changing Contours of Ethnicity: Pierre-Louis de Lorimier and Métissage at the Edges of Empire," *Ohio Valley History* 18 (Spring 2018), 45–69.

12. Nicolas de Finiels, *An Account of Upper Louisiana*, ed. Carl J. Ekberg and William E. Foley (Columbia: University of Missouri Press, 1989), 34–35. Francis Parkman, *The Oregon Trail* (Boston: Little, Brown, 1900), 15, reckoned the Shawnees had made more progress in agriculture than any other tribe on the Missouri frontier.
13. Schroeder, *Opening the Ozarks*, 374.
14. Stoddard, *Sketches, Historical and Descriptive, of Louisiana*, 215; *Territorial Papers* 14: 445–46. The secretary of war permitted the Shawnees to occupy a tract of land no more than three miles square and to work the lead mines in the area; *Territorial Papers* 14: 542.
15. Weslager, *Delaware Indian Westward Migration*, 72, 209–13; Bowes, *Land Too Good for Indians*, 107.
16. Jedidiah Morse, *A Report to the Secretary of War of the United States on Indian Affairs* (New Haven, CT: S. Converse, 1822), 366. A year later, the Indian agent for Arkansas Territory put the Delaware population at 3,000, the Shawnees at 2,500; *Territorial Papers* 19: 582.
17. Bowes, *Exiles and Pioneers*; Warren, *Shawnees and Their Neighbors*, 73–76. On the confluence of the Mississippi, Ohio, and Missouri rivers as a confluence of peoples, see Aron, *American Confluence*.
18. Spanish colonial officials were not, as some American historians have suggested, naïve and foolhardy; they understood the risks and adopted the policy out of strategic necessity. Silvia L. Hilton, "Being and Becoming Spanish in the Mississippi Valley, 1776–1803," in *Nexus of Empire: Negotiating Loyalty and Identity in the Revolutionary Borderlands, 1760s–1820s*, ed. Gene Allen Smith and Sylvia L. Hilton (Gainesville: University Press of Florida, 2010), 9–11.
19. *The Papers of George Washington: Presidential Series*, ed. Dorothy Twohig et al. (Charlottesville: University of Virginia Press, 1987–), 8:44; Adelman and Aron, "From Borderlands to Borders," 828.
20. Aron, *American Confluence*, 160, 168.
21. *IILC* 682.
22. Gerlach, *Settlement Patterns in Missouri*, 23, 28; Russel L. Gerlach, "The Ozark Scotch-Irish," in *Cultural Geography of Missouri*, ed. Michael O. Roark (Cape Girardeau: Southeast Missouri State University, 1983), 11–29; Milton D. Rafferty, *The Ozarks: Land and Life* (Norman: University of Oklahoma Press, 1980), 4, 47–48, 57–60; Brooks Blevins, *A History of the Ozarks*, 3 vols. (Urbana: University of Illinois Press, 2018–21), 1: 79.
23. *Territorial Papers* 21: 1158–59; Houck, *History of Missouri*, 1: 19–23; Schroeder, *Opening the Ozarks*, ch. 2.; "Description of the Missouri Territory," in John Bradbury, *Travels in the Interior of America in the Years 1809, 1810, and 1811* (Lincoln: University of Nebraska Press, 1986), 235–71.
24. George E. Lankford, "Shawnee Convergence: Immigrant Indians in the Ozarks," *Arkansas Historical Quarterly* 58 (1999), 390–413; Kent Blansett, "Intertribalism in the Ozarks," *American Indian Quarterly* 34 (2010), 475–97.
25. Kathleen DuVal, *The Native Ground: Indians and Colonists in the Heart of the Continent* (Philadelphia: University of Pennsylvania Press, 2006), chs. 1–2; Houck, *History of Missouri*, 1: ch. 2; *The De Soto Chronicles: The Expedition of Hernando de Soto to North America in 1539–1543*, ed. Lawrence A Clayton, Vernon James Knight, Jr., and Edward C. Moore, 2 vols. (Tuscaloosa: University of Alabama Press, 1993), 1: 127–30, 300–4; 2: 394–402. For Missouri's long Native history, see Greg Olson, *Indigenous Missourians: Ancient Societies to the Present* (Columbia: University of Missouri Press, 2023).

NOTES 479

26. Colin G. Calloway, *One Vast Winter Count: The Native American West before Lewis and Clark* (Lincoln: University of Nebraska Press, 2003), 60, 362–65, 375–76, 379–82; Willard H. Rollings, *The Osage: An Ethnohistorical Study of Hegemony on the Prairie-Plains* (Columbia: University of Missouri Press, 1992); DuVal, *Native Ground*, ch. 4; Kathleen DuVal, "Cross-Cultural Crime and Osage Justice in the Western Mississippi Valley, 1720–1826," *Ethnohistory* 54 (2007), 697–722; Kinnaird, *Spain in the Mississippi Valley*, pt. 1: 204–5; 2: 162–63; 3: 119–20, 201–2; Donald Jackson, ed., *The Letters of the Lewis and Clark Expedition with Related Documents, 1783–1854*, 2 vols. (Urbana: University of Illinois Press, 1978), 1: 200 (Jefferson quote).
27. Kinnaird, *Spain in the Mississippi Valley*, pt. 2: 369; 3: 56, 148–49, 155; DuVal, *Native Ground*, 160, 200–5 (1808 treaty); 216 (Quapaw alliance), 235 (Clark's figures); *Territorial Papers* 15: 304–5; 19: 5–7; Jacob F. Lee, *Masters of the Middle Waters: Indian Nations and Colonial Ambitions along the Mississippi* (Cambridge, MA: Harvard University Press, 2019), 214–21 (1808 treaty); Aron, *Peace and Friendship*, 114–17 (1808 treaty); Blansett, "Intertribalism in the Ozarks"; Blevins, *History of the Ozarks*, 1: ch. 2; *Territorial Papers* 14: 196–98, 209, 224–26 (Clark's account of the Treaty), 412–13, 587–88; John Joseph Mathews, *The Osages: Children of the Middle Waters* (Norman: University of Oklahoma Press, 1961), 292 ("brought their oxen"), 381–92 ("touched the feather").
28. DuVal, *Native Ground*, 196 (5,000 Cherokees); Dianna Everett, *The Texas Cherokees: A People between Two Fires, 1819–1840* (Norman: University of Oklahoma Press, 1990), ch. 1; Kinnaird, *Spain in the Mississippi Valley*, pt. 2: 255; 3: 106.
29. DuVal, *Native Ground*, 196, 208–11; Lynn Morrow, "Trader William Gilliss and Delaware Migration," *Missouri Historical Review* 75 (1981), 150; *Territorial Papers* 15: 304, 390–91 (Clark documents); 19: 191–94, 272–75 ("delightful country" at 273), 285, 299–300, 308–10, 337, 355, 460, 548–49.
30. Robert Flanders, "Caledonia: Ozarks Legacy of the High Scotch-Irish," *Gateway Heritage* 6 (1986), 38; Schroeder, *Opening the Ozarks*, 359–67; *"Bellevue—Beautiful View": The History of the Bellevue Valley, and Surrounding Area* (Caledonia, MO: Bellevue Historical Society, 1983), 7, 9–12, 25; Houck, *History of Missouri*, 1: 372n69.
31. Schroeder, *Opening the Ozarks*, 382–83; "Inhabitants of the Bois Brule Bottom in the 1790s," in Michael C. O'Laughlin, *Irish Settlers on the American Frontier* (Kansas City, MO: Irish Genealogical Foundation, 1984), 29.
32. Schroeder, *Opening the Ozarks*, 341–42.
33. Blevins, *History of the Ozarks*, 1: 90.
34. Schroeder, *Opening the Ozarks*, 396.
35. Blevins, *History of the Ozarks*, 1: 74–77, 79–80 (quotes), 87; Gerlach, "Ozark Scotch-Irish."
36. Paul Clements, *Chronicles of the Cumberland Settlements, 1779–1796* (self-published, 2012), 155, 178, 187, 481–82, 502, 505, 510.
37. Aron, *Peace and Friendship*, ch. 2; DuVal, *Native Ground*, 180; Lankford, "Shawnee Convergence," 391.
38. Morrow, "Trader William Gilliss and Delaware Migration," 147–67.
39. *Territorial Papers* 14: 786.
40. *Territorial Papers* 15: 52–53.
41. Aron, *American Confluence*, 69–70, 101, 105, 155; Faragher, "'More Motley than Mackinaw,'" 304–26; Du Val, *Native Ground*, 209, 229, 243–44; Thomas Nuttall, *A Journal of Travels into the Arkansas Territory during the Year 1819*, ed. Savoie Lottinville (Norman: University of Oklahoma Press, 1980), 193, 239 (preferred whites to Cherokees).
42. Aron, *Peace and Friendship*, 67–68.
43. Aron, *American Confluence*, 101; also 162.
44. *Forty Years of Frontier Life: Memoir of John Mason Peck D.D. edited from his Journals and Correspondence* by Rufus Babcock (Philadelphia: American Baptist Publication Society, 1864), 108, 112–13; Warren, *Shawnees and Their Neighbors*, 78; Christina Snyder, *Great Crossings: Indians, Settlers and Slaves in the Age of Jackson* (New York: Oxford University Press, 2017), 51, 75.
45. *The White River Chronicles of S. C. Turbo: Man and Wildlife on the Ozarks Frontier*, ed. James F. Keefe and Lynn Morrow (Fayetteville: University of Arkansas Press, 1994), 1, 16–19, 256–59.
46. Daniel W. Patterson, *The True Image: Gravestone Art and the Culture of Scotch Irish Settlers in the Pennsylvania and Carolina Backcountry* (Chapel Hill: University of North Carolina Press,

2012), 105–9, 371–74. Polly was a granddaughter of Samuel Watson's nephew, David, and daughter of James Houston Watson.
47. Tom Dunlay, *Kit Carson and the Indians* (Lincoln: University of Nebraska Press, 2000), 24–27.
48. *Territorial Papers* 19: 8.
49. Blansett, "Intertribalism in the Ozarks."
50. Stoddard, *Sketches, Historical and Descriptive, of Louisiana*, 215.
51. Faragher, "'More Motley than Mackinaw,'" 309–11; Blansett, "Intertribalism in the Ozarks," 475–97, esp. 476, 479, 482–87; evidence in stories, song, and dance in the appendix. Ozark Scotch-Irish were maligned by Kansans as Pukes and savages during Civil War. Blansett describes himself as a "Cherokee, Creek, Choctaw, Shawnee, and Potawatomi descendant from the Blanket, Panther, and Smith families."
52. Andrew J. Milson, *Arkansas Travelers: Geographies of Exploration and Perception, 1804–1834* (Fayetteville: University of Arkansas Press, 2019) discusses the observations of four early travelers—William Dunbar, Henry Schoolcraft, Thomas Nuttall, and George Featherstonhaugh—and the enduring images they helped to create of the land and the people.
53. Faragher, "'More Motley than Mackinaw,'" 312; Brackenridge, *Recollections*, 236–39.
54. Milton D. Rafferty, ed., *Rude Pursuits and Rugged Peaks: Schoolcraft's Ozark Journal 1818–1819* (Fayetteville: University of Arkansas Press, 1996), 55, 60, 63, 79.
55. For a critical review, see George E. Lankford, "'Beyond the Pale': Frontier Folk in the Southern Ozarks," in *The Folk: Identity, Landscapes and Lores*, ed. Robert J. Smith and Jerry Stannard; University of Kansas Publications in Anthropology 19 (1989), 53–70.
56. Nuttall, *Journal of Travels into the Arkansas Territory*, 136, 138.
57. Jack Gregory and Rennard Strickland, *Sam Houston with the Cherokees, 1829–1833* (1976; Norman: University of Oklahoma Press, 1996); *PAJ* 7: 240–41 (Carroll); *The Writings of Sam Houston, 1813–1863*, ed. Amelia W. Williams and Eugene C. Barker, 8 vols. (Austin: University of Texas Press, 1938–43), 1: 132–33, 141–43 (to Jackson), 185–86 (citizen). Carroll had just received a letter from Houston at Little Rock "stating that he was in good health and spirits—that he was about setting out for the Cherekees accompanied by Haroldson—a newly imported Irishman and four large dogs." Houston told Carroll he expected to be hunting buffalo by the summer and intended never to shave his beard again.
58. Schroeder, *Opening the Ozarks*, 347, 377.
59. *Territorial Papers* 14: 267–68.
60. Lee, *Masters of the Middle Waters*, 223; Faragher, "'More Motley than Mackinaw,'" 316; Peck, *Forty Years of Frontier Life*, 146.
61. DuVal, *Native Ground*, 228–29.
62. Russel L. Gerlach, *Immigrants in the Ozarks: A Study in Ethnic Geography* (Columbia: University of Missouri Press, 1976), 23, 26, 29–33; Aron, *American Confluence*, 198, 233; Hattie M. Anderson, "Missouri, 1804–1828: Peopling a Frontier State," *Missouri Historical Review* 31 (1937), 150–51, 174–80.
63. Aron, *American Confluence*, 158–59.
64. DuVal, *Native Ground*, ch. 8.
65. DuVal, *Native Ground*, 231–32; *Territorial Papers* 20: 135–42 (unjust at 139), 162–66, 604 ("victim"), 776–77.
66. *Territorial Papers* 15: 110–11, 113–14, 191–92; Aron, *Peace and Friendship*, 124.
67. Aron, *Peace and Friendship*, 126–28; Henry Egle, *Pennsylvania Genealogies, chiefly Scotch-Irish and German* (2nd ed., Harrisburg, PA, 1896; reprint, Baltimore, MD: Genealogical Publishing, 1969), 488–89.
68. William Clark assured the secretary of war in 1824 that their "friendly feelings . . . continue unimpaired"; *Territorial Papers* 19: 661; Lakomäki, *Gathering Together*, 183.
69. Faragher, "'More Motley than Mackinaw,'" 314–19, 321, 323; Warren, *Shawnees and Their Neighbors*, 84–95; Schroeder, *Opening the Ozarks*, 380–81, 450, 458.
70. *PAJ* 7: 64–65; Bowes, *Land Too Good for Indians*, 104–7; Weslager, *Delaware Indian Westward Migration*, 73 (bribe); John Johnston, *Recollections of Sixty Years on the Ohio Frontier*, ed. Charles Reeve Conover (1915; reprint, Van Buren, OH: Eastern Frontier/R. E. Davis, 2001), 9.
71. Aron, *Peace and Friendship*, 131–34; *Territorial Papers* 20: 42–43; 21: 411, 431 ("impatient to get them out").

72. *Territorial Papers* 19: 305 ("never to quit").
73. *Indian Affairs: Laws and Treaties*, Vol. 2: *Treaties*, Charles J. Kappler, comp. (Washington, DC: Government Printing Office, 1904), 288–92, quote at 290.
74. *Territorial Papers* 21: 804.
75. Lee, *Masters of the Middle Waters*, 228; DuVal, *Native Ground*, 242.
76. Blevins, *History of the Ozarks*, 1: 110.
77. DuVal, *Native Ground*, 247.
78. *IILC* 603–8.
79. William R. Nester, *From Mountain Man to Millionaire: The "Bold and Dashing Life" of Robert Campbell* (Columbia: University of Missouri Press, 1999); *A Narrative of Colonel Robert Campbell's Experiences in the Rocky Mountain Fur Trade from 1825 to 1835*, ed. Drew Alan Holloway (Fairfield, WA: Ye Galleon Press, 1991).
80. Leroy R. Hafen and W. J. Ghent, *Broken Hand: The Life Story of Thomas Fitzpatrick, Chief of the Mountain Men* (Denver, CO: Old West, 1931); Myles Dungan, *How the Irish Won the West* (Stillorgan, Dublin: New Island Books, 2006), ch. 4; Margaret Coel, *Chief Left Hand, Southern Arapaho* (Norman: University of Oklahoma Press, 1983), 4, 11, 24.

Chapter 13

1. Andrés Reséndez, *Changing National Identities at the Frontier: Texas and New Mexico, 1800–1850* (Cambridge: Cambridge University Press, 2005); Joaquín Rivaya-Martínez, "The Unsteady Comanchería: A Reexamination of Power in the Indigenous Borderlands of the Eighteenth-Century Greater Southwest," *William and Mary Quarterly* 80 (2023), esp. 252, 283. Although they were always viewed as "white," it took a long time for Catholic Irish, Germans, and Czechs to gain admittance into the "Anglo" category; Mary Jean Barber, "How the Irish, Germans, and Czechs Became Anglo: Race and Identity in the Texas-Mexico Borderlands," Ph.D. diss., University of Texas–Austin, 2010.
2. Reséndez, *Changing National Identities*, 27.
3. Gary Clayton Anderson, *The Conquest of Texas: Ethnic Cleansing in the Promised Land, 1820–1875* (Norman: University of Oklahoma Press, 2005), ch. 1; Russell Thornton, *American Indian Holocaust and Survival: A Population History* (Norman: University of Oklahoma Press, 1987), tables of Texas epidemics and population at 130–31; Pekka Hämäläinen, *The Comanche Empire* (New Haven, CT: Yale University Press, 2008); Paul Barba, *Country of the Cursed and the Driven: Slavery and the Texas Borderlands* (Lincoln: University of Nebraska Press, 2021), pt. 1, esp. 4–9; Rivaya-Martínez, "Unsteady Comanchería," 251–85.
4. Edward A. Bradley, *"We Never Retreat": Filibustering Expeditions into Spanish Texas, 1812–1822* (College Station: Texas A & M University Press, 2015), ch. 1; Maurine T. Wilson and Jack Jackson, *Philip Nolan and Texas: Expeditions to the Unknown Land, 1791–1801* (Waco, TX: Texian Press, 1987).
5. John L. Kessell, *Spain in the Southwest: A Narrative History of Colonial New Mexico, Arizona, Texas, and California* (Norman: University of Oklahoma Press, 2002), 362–65
6. David Hackett Fischer and James C. Kelly, *Bound Away: Virginia and the Westward Movement* (Charlottesville: University of Virginia Press, 2000), 181.
7. Alan Taylor, "Remaking Americans: Louisiana, Upper Canada, and Texas," in *Contested Spaces of Early America*, ed. Julianna Barr and Edward Countryman (Philadelphia: University of Pennsylvania Press, 2014), 220; Anderson, *The Conquest of Texas*, 52; Dianna Everett, *The Texas Cherokees: A People between Two Fires, 1819–1840* (Norman: University of Oklahoma Press, 1990), 22–25; Sami Lakomäki, *Gathering Together: The Shawnee People through Diaspora and Nationhood, 1600–1870* (New Haven, CT: Yale University Press, 2014), 186–89; *Territorial Papers* 20: 480 ("whirlpool"); José Maria Sánchez, "A Trip to Texas in 1828," translated by Carlos E. Castanada, *Southwestern Historical Quarterly* 29 (1926), 283, 286.
8. In Kent Blansett's view, "The Texas Cherokee were truly an intertribal nation comprised of Delaware, Shawnee, Kickapoo, Quapaw, and the adopted Scotch-Irish." Kent Blansett, "Intertribalism in the Ozarks," *American Indian Quarterly* 34 (2010), 480–81.
9. Everett, *Texas Cherokees*, 29–32.
10. Everett, *Texas Cherokees*, 22–25, 29–32; *Writings of Sam Houston, 1813–1863*, ed. Amelia W. Williams and Eugene C. Barker, 8 vols. (Austin: University of Texas Press, 1938–1943), 2: 345–46 (quote).

11. Reséndez, *Changing National Identities*, 28–29, 37–39; Anderson, *Conquest of Texas*, 5, 52 (Norton); Everett, *The Texas Cherokees*, 31.
12. Andrew J. Torget, *Seeds of Empire: Cotton, Slavery, and the Transformation of the Texas Borderlands, 1800–1850* (Chapel Hill: University of North Carolina Press, 2015), 61–66; Mary Austin Holley, *Texas: Observations, Historical, Geographical and Descriptive, in a series of Letters* (Baltimore, MD: Armstrong and Plaskitt, 1833), 113.
13. Reséndez, *Changing National Identities*, generally for Far North to Southwest; 40–45 for Fredonia.
14. First quote in Torget, *Seeds of Empire*, 69; second quote in Lakomäki, *Gathering Together*, 190.
15. Sánchez, "A Trip to Texas in 1828," 260, 271.
16. Taylor, "Remaking Americans," 224.
17. Anderson, *Conquest of Texas*, 3.
18. Torget, *Seeds of Empire*, 121–22.
19. Anne H. Sutherland, *The Robertsons, the Sutherlands, and the Making of Texas* (College Station: Texas A&M University Press, 2006); Malcolm D. McLean, ed., *Papers Concerning Robertson's Colony in Texas*, 19 vols. (Arlington: University of Texas at Arlington, 1974–93). McLean, a descendant of Robertson, evidently perpetuated anti-Austin bias in his editing; Gregg Cantrell, "A Matter of Character: Stephen F. Austin and the 'Papers concerning Robertson's Colony in Texas,'" *Southwestern Historical Quarterly* 104 (2000), 230–61.
20. Noah Smithwick, *The Evolution of a State, or Recollections of Old Texas Days* (Austin: University of Texas Press, 1983), 1, 4–5.
21. William H. Oberste, *Texas Irish Empresarios and Their Colonies: Power & Hewetson, McMullen & McGloin* (Austin, TX: Von Boeckmann-Jones, 1953), contract quote at 17; Holley, *Texas: Observations*, 70–71, 74.
22. Reséndez, *Changing National Identities*; Eric R. Schlereth, "Voluntary Mexicans: Allegiance and the Origins of the Texas Revolution," in *Contested Empire: Rethinking the Texas Revolution*, ed. Samuel W. Haynes and Gerald D. Saxon (College Station: Texas A&M University Press, 2015), 12–41.
23. Thomas W. Cutrer, *Ben McCulloch and the Frontier Military Tradition* (Chapel Hill: University of North Carolina Press, 1993); *Writings of Sam Houston*, 5: 502n–3n.
24. Sam W. Haynes, *Unsettled Land: From Revolution to Republic, The Struggle for Texas* (New York: Basic Books, 2022), 211.
25. Anderson, *Conquest*, 38, 41, and generally; Barba, *Country of the Cursed and the Driven*.
26. Brian DeLay, *War of a Thousand Deserts: Indian Raids and the U.S.-Mexican War* (New Haven, CT: Yale University Press, 2008), 5, citing Robert V. Remini, *Andrew Jackson and the Course of American Freedom, 1822–1832* (New York: Harper & Row, 1981), 202.
27. *PAJ* 7: 270; David S. Brown, *The First Populist: The Defiant Life of Andrew Jackson* (New York: Scribner, 2022), 330–33.
28. Michael Paul Rogin, *Fathers and Children: Andrew Jackson and the Subjugation of the American Indian* (New York: Random House, 1975), 304, 306–7.
29. DeLay, *War of a Thousand Deserts*, 231–32.
30. Calhoun to Wilson Shannon, September 10, 1844, quoted in DeLay, *War of a Thousand Deserts*, 232.
31. T. R. Fehrenbach, *Lone Star: A History of Texas and the Texans* (New York: Macmillan, 1968), 167; Fehrenbach, *The Comanches: The Destruction of a People* (London: Allen and Unwin, 1975), 240–41; Oberste, *Texas Irish Empresarios and Their Colonies*, 58. On patterns of Comanche raiding, see Joaquín Rivaya-Martínez, "Trespassers in the Land of Plenty: Comanche Raiding across the U.S.-Mexican Border, 1846–1853," in *These Ragged Edges: Histories of Violence along the U.S.-Mexico Border*, ed. Andrew J. Torget and Gerardo Gurza-Lavalle (Chapel Hill: North Carolina University Press, 2022), 48–73. Prior to Mexico's independence, Comanche raids tended to be confined to a one-hundred-mile corridor along the Rio Grande east of its confluence with Devil's River, in the areas of San Antonio and present-day Goliad. Between 1816 and 1822, however, Comanche alliance with Lipan Apaches opened a much larger extent of northern Mexico to their raids, and they extended their raiding reach into Chihuahua in 1825. As early as 1818–1819, Comanches reportedly stole upwards of ten thousand horses from settlements across the northern frontier of New Spain. Selling horses and mules north of the border became an important part of Comanche political economy, especially when the growth of the cotton kingdom in the U.S. South in the 1810s and the opening of the Santa Fe Trail in 1821 increased demand.

32. *PAJ* 8: 607.
33. *PAJ* 10: 124.
34. *PAJ* 11: 714.
35. DeLay, *War of a Thousand Deserts,* 74.
36. Barba, *Country of the Cursed and the Driven*, ch. 6.
37. Jack Gregory and Rennard Strickland, *Sam Houston with the Cherokees, 1829–1833* (1976; Norman: University of Oklahoma Press, 1996), 49–50.
38. DeLay, *War of a Thousand Deserts*, 64.
39. *Writings of Sam Houston,* 1: 342.
40. Everett, *Texas Cherokees,* ch. 4.
41. Quoted in Barba, *Country of the Cursed and the Driven*, 222.
42. Anderson, *Conquest of Texas*, 100.
43. John P. Bowes, *Land Too Good for Indians: Northern Indian Removal* (Norman: University of Oklahoma Press, 2014), 214; Dorman H. Winfrey et al., eds, *Texas Indian Papers*, 4 vols. (Austin: Texas State Library, 1959–1961), 1: 14–17; *Writings of Sam Houston,* 1: 356–60.
44. *Writings of Sam Houston,* 4: 60.
45. Everett, *Texas Cherokees,* 99–100; Lamar to John Linney (Shawnee letter), May 1839, *Texas Indian Papers* 1: 66–67.
46. *Texas Indian Papers* 1: 68–70, quote at 69.
47. *Texas Indian Papers* 1: 73–74.
48. Everett, *Texas,* 105 (Rusk quote), 108–10; *Writings of Sam Houston* 2: 277 (warning to Bowl).
49. *Writings of Sam Houston* 2: 317.
50. *Texas Indian Papers* 1: 24.
51. *Texas Indian Papers* 1: 80–81.
52. H. Allen Anderson, "The Delaware and Shawnee Indians and the Republic of Texas, 1820–1845," *Southwestern Historical Quarterly* 94 (1990), 231–60.
53. *Texas Indian Papers* 1: 115, 154, 246; 2: 282, 299–300 (refs to McCullouch).
54. Haynes, *Unsettled Land*, 258.
55. Smithwick, *Evolution of a State*, 143.
56. *Texas Indian Papers* 2: 155.
57. *Texas Indian Papers* 1: 105.
58. Everett, *Texas Indians,* 115; Barba, *Country of the Cursed and the Driven*, 280.
59. *Writings of Sam Houston* 5: 433–34 ("let them alone"), 466–503 (Kansas-Nebraska speech; "little sympathy" at 469).
60. *Texas Indian Papers* 2: 429.
61. *Texas Indian Papers* 3: 78.
62. *Texas Indian Papers* 3: 84–99; quotes at 87.
63. *Texas Indian Papers* 3: 270–71.
64. *Texas Indian Papers* 3: 297, 299.
65. *Texas Indian Papers* 3: 317–20.
66. Bowes, *Land Too Good for Indians*, 219; Barba, *Country of the Cursed and the Driven*, 291.
67. Fehrenbach, *Lone Star,* 282–83; John J. Linn, *Reminiscences of Fifty Years in Texas* (New York: D. and J. Sadler, 1883; reprint, Austin: State House Press, 1986), 333.
68. Anderson, *Conquest of Texas*, 74–75.
69. James Kimmins Greer, *Texas Ranger: Jack Hays in the Frontier Southwest* (College Station: Texas A&M University Press, 1993), 17–20, 217.
70. John R. Finger, *Tennessee Frontiers: Three Regions in Transition* (Bloomington: Indiana University Press, 2001), 274.
71. *Kit Carson's Own Story of His Life as Dictated to Col. and Mrs D. C. Peters about 1856–57*, ed. Blanche C. Grant (Taos: Santa Fe New Mexican Publishing Corporation, 1926), 122 (daily visits); Tom Dunlay, *Kit Carson and the Indians* (Lincoln: University of Nebraska Press, 2000), 57 (Delaware trappers), 190–91 (daily visits).
72. Marc Simmons, *Kit Carson and His Three Wives: A Family History* (Albuquerque: University of New Mexico Press, 2003); Dunlay, *Kit Carson and the Indians,* 33 (Indian children), 201–3 (adoptees); Anne E. Hyde, *Born of Lakes and Plains: Mixed-Descent and the Making of the American Wes*t (New York: W. W. Norton, 2022).
73. *Kit Carson's Own Story*, 69–70.
74. Richard S. Grimes, *The Western Delaware Indian Nation, 1730–1795* (Bethlehem, PA: Lehigh University Press, 2017), 278; John T. Irving, Jr., *Indian Sketches during an Expedition to the*

Pawnee Tribes, 1833, ed. John Francis McDermott (Norman: University of Oklahoma Press, 1955), 6, 130, 242, 244–47; George Catlin, *Letters and Notes on the Manners, Customs, and Conditions of North American Indians*, 2 vols. (New York: Dover Publications, 1973), 2: 101; Francis Parkman, *The Oregon Trail* (Boston: Little, Brown, and Co., 1900), 18–20.

75. Randolph Marcy, *Prairie Traveler: A Hand-book for Overland Expeditions* (New York: Harper and Brothers, 1859), ch. 6, quotes at 185; Percival G. Lowe, *Five Years a Dragoon ('49 to '54) and Other Adventures on the Great Plains* (Norman: University of Oklahoma Press, 1965), 185, 199, 223; Dee Brown, "Black Beaver," *American History Illustrated* 2 (May 1967), 32–40; Carolyn Thomas Foreman, "Black Beaver," *Chronicles of Oklahoma* 24 (1946), 269–92.
76. On Brady and McKnight, see Michael C. O'Laughlin, *Irish Settlers on the American Frontier* (Kansas City, MO: Irish Genealogical Foundation, 1984), 88–89.
77. Ralph Adam Smith, *Borderlander: The Life of James Kirker 1793-1852* (Norman: University of Oklahoma Press, 1999); "Don Santiago Kirker, The Indian Fighter," *Santa Fe Republican*, November 20, 1847: 2–3; DeLay, *War of a Thousand Deserts*, 160, 161 (photo), 243, 257, 277; William S. Kiser, "The Business of Killing Indians: Contract Warfare and Genocide in the U.S.-Mexico Borderlands," *Journal of American History* 110 (June 2023), 15–39.
78. DeLay, *War of a Thousand Deserts*, 395n35.
79. Myles Dungan, *How the Irish Won the West* (Stillorgan, Dublin: New Island Books, 2006), 344–45; Chip Colwell-Chanthaphonh, *Massacre at Camp Grant: Forgetting and Remembering Apache History* (Tucson: University of Arizona Press, 2007); Karl Jacoby, *Shadows at Dawn: A Borderlands Massacre and the Violence of History* (New York: Penguin, 2008), 75, 133, 230 (Lee's position); Ian W. Record, *Big Sycamore Stands Alone: The Western Apaches, Aravaipa, and the Struggle for Place* (Norman: University of Oklahoma Press, 2008), 269 (self-defense).
80. Benjamin Madley, *An American Genocide: The United States and the California Indian Catastrophe* (New Haven, CT: Yale University Press, 2016).
81. Sean Connolly, *On Every Tide: The Making and Remaking of the Irish World* (New York: Basic Books, 2022), 75, 105.
82. Connolly, *On Every Tide*, 75, 111.
83. John D. Unruh, Jr., *The Plains Across: The Overland Emigrants and the Trans-Mississippi West, 1840-60* (Urbana: University of Illinois Press, 1979), ch. 5; Michael L. Tate, *Indians and Emigrants: Encounters on the Overland Trails* (Norman: University of Oklahoma Press, 2006).
84. Virginia Reed Murphy, *Across the Plains in the Donner Party: A Personal Narrative of the Overland Trip to California, 1846-47* (Golden, CO: Outbooks, 1980), 11, 15–16, 18–19; Dungan, *How the Irish Won the West*, ch. 3.
85. Johnson quoted in Paul Frymer, *Building an American Empire: The Era of Territorial and Political Expansion* (Princeton, NJ: Princeton University Press, 2017), 149; Connolly, *On Every Tide*, 86.
86. Timothy J. Meagher, *Becoming Irish American: The Making and Remaking of a People from Roanoke to JFK* (New Haven, CT: Yale University Press, 2023), 92.
87. David M. Emmons, *Beyond the American Pale: The Irish in the West, 1845-1910* (Norman: University of Oklahoma Press, 2010), 9–10.
88. David M. Emmons, *The Butte Irish: Class and Ethnicity in an American Mining Town, 1875-1925* (Urbana: University of Illinois Press, 1989). On the experiences of predominantly Catholic Irish miners in the West, see Alan J. Noonan, *Mining Irish American Lives: Western Communities from 1849-1920* (Denver: University Press of Colorado, 2022).
89. Micheal MacGowan, *The Hard Road to Klondike*, translated from the Irish *Rotha Mór an tSaoil* by Valentin Iremonger (Boston: Routledge and Kegan Paul, 1973), quotes at 64, 122; Donal Déisach, "The Irish in the Arctic: A Perspective on the Irish in Canada," in *The Untold Story: The Irish in Canada*, ed. Robert O'Driscoll and Lorena Reynolds, 2 vols. (Toronto: Celtic Arts of Canada, 1988), 1: 383.
90. Robert M. Utley, *Frontiersmen in Blue: The United States Army and the Indian, 1818-1865* (New York: Macmillan, 1967), 40; John F. Finerty, *War-Path and Bivouac: The Big Horn and Yellowstone Expedition*, ed. Milo M. Quaife (Chicago: R. R. Donnelley and Sons, 1955), 115, 273; Douglas D. Scott, P. Willey, and Melissa A. Connor, *They Died with Custer: Soldiers' Bones from the Battle of the Little Bighorn* (Norman: University of Oklahoma Press, 1998), 90–93; Dungan, *How the Irish Won the West*, 3.
91. Emmons, *Beyond the American Pale*, 224.
92. Paul Andrew Hutton, *Phil Sheridan and His Army* (Lincoln: University of Nebraska Press, 1985).

Chapter 14

1. For example, Pat Speth Sherman, *American Tapestry: Portrait of a 'Middling' Family, 1746–1934* (Eugene, OR: Luminaire Press, 2021).
2. James G. Leyburn, *The Scotch-Irish: A Social History* (Chapel Hill: University of North Carolina Press, 1962), 270.
3. Kerby A. Miller, "'Scotch-Irish' Myths and 'Irish' Identities in Eighteenth- and Nineteenth-Century America," in *New Perspectives on the Irish Diaspora*, ed. Charles Fanning (Carbondale: Southern Illinois University Press, 2000), 80–81.
4. Henry Noble MacCracken, "Address to the Ulster Society of New York, 1939," in *Making the Irish American: History and Heritage of the Irish in the United States*, ed. J. J. Lee and Marion R. Casey (New York: New York University Press, 2006), 286.
5. Marianne S. Wokeck, *Trade in Strangers: The Beginnings of Mass Migration to North America* (University Park: Pennsylvania State University Press, 1999), 237–38.
6. Samantha Seeley, *Race, Removal, and the Right to Remain: Migration and the Making of the United States* (Chapel Hill: University of North Carolina Press, 2021). For "borders of belonging," see Barbara Young Welke, *Law and the Borders of Belonging in the Long Nineteenth Century United States* (Cambridge: Cambridge University Press, 2010); and Heide Castaneda, *Borders of Belonging: Struggle and Solidarity in Mixed-Status Immigrant Families* (Stanford, CA: Stanford University Press, 2019).
7. According to Theodore W. Allen, "This is the hallmark of racial oppression in its colonial origins, and as it has persisted in subsequent historical contexts." Theodore W. Allen, *The Invention of the White Race*, Vol. 1: *Racial Oppression and Social Control*, 2nd ed. (London: Verso, 2012), 32. Timothy J. Meagher, *Becoming Irish American: The Making and Remaking of a People from Roanoke to JFK* (New Haven, CT: Yale University Press, 2023).
8. William H. A. Williams, *"'Twas Only an Irishman's Dream": The Image of Ireland and the Irish in American Popular Song Lyrics, 1800–1920* (Urbana: University of Illinois Press, 1996), 1, quoted in *Making the Irish American: History and Heritage of the Irish in the United States*, ed. J. J. Lee and Marion R. Casey (New York: New York University Press, 2006), 16.
9. David M. Emmons, *Beyond the American Pale: The Irish in the West, 1845–1910* (Norman: University of Oklahoma Press, 2010).
10. Richard Slotkin, *The Fatal Environment: The Myth of the Frontier in the Age of Industrialization, 1800–1900* (1985; Norman: University of Oklahoma Press, 1998).
11. R. F. Foster, *Modern Ireland, 1600–1972* (New York: Penguin, 1988), 345.
12. Leyburn, *Scotch-Irish*, 331–32.
13. Donald Harman Akenson, *Being Had: Historians, Evidence, and the Irish in North America* (Port Credit, Ontario: P. D. Meany, 1985), ch. 3; Lawrence J. McCaffrey, *The Irish Diaspora in America* (Bloomington: Indiana University Press, 1976), 6 ("unwanted aliens" and "ghetto"); Kevin Kenny, "Race, Violence, and Anti-Irish Sentiment in the Nineteenth Century," in *Making the Irish American: History and Heritage of the Irish in the United States*, ed. J. J. Lee and Marion R. Casey (New York: New York University Press, 2006), 364–78; Bruce Nelson, *Irish Nationalists and the Making of the Irish Race* (Princeton, NJ: Princeton University Press, 2012), ch. 2; Meagher, *Becoming Irish American*.
14. Quoted in Sean Connolly, *On Every Tide: The Making and Remaking of the Irish World* (New York: Basic Books, 2022), 382.
15. Allen, *The Invention of the White Race*, Vol. 1, chs. 7–8; Noel Ignatiev, *How the Irish Became White* (New York: Routledge, 1995); David R. Roediger, *The Wages of Whiteness: Race and the Making of the American Working Class* (New York: Verso, 1991). For critical review and the limitations of such works, see Peter Kolchin, "Whiteness Studies: The New History of Race in America," *Journal of American History* 89 (2002), 157–73. Peter Quinn, "The Future of the Irish in America," in *Making the Irish American*, 682, dismisses *How the Irish Became White* as a "popular bedtime tale." The real story for Quinn is "how an immigrant group under already punishing cultural and economic pressures, reeling in the wake of the worst catastrophe to take place in Western Europe in the nineteenth century, a people not only devoid of urban experience but largely unacquainted with the town life prevalent throughout the British Isles, suddenly finding itself plunged into the fastest industrializing society in the world, regrouped as quickly as it did, built its own far-flung network of charitable and educational institutions, preserved its own identity, and had a profound influence on the future of both the country it left and the one it

came to." Nelson, *Irish Nationalists and the Making of the Irish Race*, chs. 3–4, examines how the Irish shaped their identity in the context of slavery and abolition.
16. Edward Said, "Reflections on Exile," *Granta* 13 (1984), 157–72, quote at 163.
17. Kevin Kenny, *The American Irish: A History* (Harlow, UK: Longman, 2000), 27.
18. Elizabeth A. Perkins, *Border Life: Experience and Memory in the Revolutionary Ohio Valley* (Chapel Hill: University of North Carolina Press, 1998), 175.
19. George Chambers, *A Tribute to the Principles, Virtues, Habits and Public Usefulness of the Irish and Scotch Early Settlers of Pennsylvania. By a Descendant* (1856; Chambersburg, PA: M. A. Foltz, printer, 1871).
20. Leyburn, *The Scotch-Irish*, ch. 16, esp. 296, 319.
21. Peter Gilmore and Kerby A. Miller, "Searching for 'Irish' Freedom—Settling for 'Scotch-Irish' Respectability: Southwestern Pennsylvania, 1780–1810," in *Ulster to America: The Scots-Irish Migration Experience, 1680–1830*, ed. Warren Hofstra (Knoxville: University of Tennessee Press, 2012), 169.
22. IILC 442–43, 448–49. John C. Linehan, *The Irish Scots and the "Scotch-Irish": An historical and ethnological monograph, with some reference to Scotia Major and Scotia Minor; to which is added a chapter on "How the Irish came as builders of the nation"* (Concord, NH: The American-Irish Historical Society, 1902), provided an exception to and a critique of the obsession with distancing the Scotch-Irish from the Irish.
23. Ralph Stuart Wallace, "The Scotch-Irish of Provincial New Hampshire," Ph.D. diss., University of New Hampshire, 1984, ch. 2.
24. Robert C. Mack, *Londonderry Celebration: June 10, 1869: Exercises on the 150th Anniversary of the Settlement of Old Nutfield, Comprising the Towns of Londonderry, Derry, Windham, and Parts of Manchester, Hudson, and Salem* (Manchester, NH: John B. Clarke, 1890), 39, 43.
25. William Henry Egle, *History of the Counties of Dauphin and Lebanon in the Commonwealth of Pennsylvania* (Philadelphia: Everts and Peck, 1883), 15.
26. Carlton Jackson, *A Social History of the Scotch-Irish* (Lanham, MD: Madison Books, 1993), 150–51.
27. *The Scotch-Irish in America: Proceedings of the Scotch-Irish Congress*, 10 vols., 1889–1901.
28. John Walker Dinsmore, *The Scotch-Irish in America: Their History, Traits, Institutions, and Influences: Especially as Illustrated in the Early Settlers of Pennsylvania and Their Descendants* (Chicago: Winona Publishing Co., 1906), 1–20; quotes at 3–4 (rest of mankind), 4 (no other race).
29. Dinsmore, *Scotch-Irish in America*, 7 (not one drop of Irish blood), 11 (Calvinists to a man).
30. Quoted in William F. Dunaway, *The Scotch-Irish of Colonial Pennsylvania* (Chapel Hill: University of North Carolina Press, 1944), 3.
31. Michael O'Brien, *Irish Settlers in America: A Consolidation of Articles from "The Journal of the American Irish Historical Society,"* 2 vols. (Baltimore, MD: Genealogical Publishing, 1979, 1993).
32. Connolly, *On Every Tide*, 372.
33. Matthew McKee, "'A Peculiar and Royal Race': Creating a Scotch-Irish Identity, 1889–1901," in *Atlantic Crossroads: Historical Connections between Scotland, Ulster and North America*, ed. Patrick Fitzgerald and Steve Ickringill (Newtonards, N. Ireland: Colourpoint Books, 2001), 67–83.
34. Quoted in McKee, "'A Peculiar and Royal Race,'" 68.
35. "An Irishman might be described as a lazy, ragged, dirty Celt when he landed in New York, but if his children settled in California they might well be praised as part of the vanguard of the energetic Anglo-Saxon people poised for the plunge into Asia." Reginald Horsman, *Race and Manifest Destiny: The Origins of American Anglo-Saxon Racism* (Cambridge, MA: Harvard University Press, 1981), 4 (quote), 250–54.
36. McKee, "'A Peculiar and Royal Race,'" 69, 76–77.
37. Alan Trachtenberg, *Shades of Hiawatha: Staging Indians, Making Americans, 1880–1930* (New York: Hill and Wang, 2004); Cécile R. Ganteaume, *Officially Indian: Symbols That Define the United States* (Washington, DC: National Museum of the American Indian, 2017).
38. Patrick Griffin, "Searching for Independence: Revolutionary Kentucky, Irish American Experience, and Scotch-Irish Myth," in *Ulster to America: The Scots-Irish Migration Experience, 1680–1830*, ed. Warren Hofstra (Knoxville: University of Tennessee Press, 2012), 223.

39. Samuel Swett Green, "The Scotch-Irish in America," *Proceedings of the American Antiquarian Society*, 10 (1895), 32–70, quotes at 64.
40. Theodore Roosevelt, *The Winning of the West*, 6 vols. in 3 (New York: G. P. Putnam's Sons, 1899), 1, pt. 1: 119–24.
41. Henry J. Ford, *The Scotch-Irish in America* (Princeton, NJ: Princeton University Press, 1915), 285.
42. Charles A. Hanna, *The Scotch-Irish, or the Scot in North Britain, North Ireland, and North America*, 2 vols (New York: G. P. Putnam's Sons, 1902), 2: 2.
43. Maude Glasgow, *The Scotch-Irish in Northern Ireland and in the American Colonies* (New York: Heritage, 1998), 266.
44. Kevin Bruyneel, *Settler Memory: The Disavowal of Indigeneity and the Politics of Race in the United States* (Chapel Hill: University of North Carolina Press, 2021); Jean M. O'Brien, *Firsting and Lasting: Writing Indians out of Existence in New England* (Minneapolis: University of Minnesota Press, 2010), xxii–xxiii; Razib Khan, "The Scots-Irish as Indigenous People," *Discover Magazine*, July 22, 2012; Roxanne Dunbar-Ortiz, *Not a "Nation of Immigrants": Settler Colonialism, White Supremacy, and a History of Erasure and Exclusion* (Boston: Beacon Press, 2021) (Appalachia, 39–46); Stephen Pearson, "'The Last Bastion of Colonialism': Appalachian Settler Colonialism and Self-Indigenization," *American Indian Culture and Research Journal* 37 (2013), 165–84; Roxanne Dunbar Ortiz, *Red Dirt: Growing Up Okie* (New York: Verso, 1997), 46; Mary L. Mullen, "How the Irish Became Settlers: Metaphors of Indigeneity and the Erasure of Indigenous Peoples," *New Hibernia Review* 3 (2016), 81–96.
45. Bruyneel, *Settler Memory*, ch. 5.
46. James Webb, *Born Fighting: How the Scots-Irish Shaped America* (New York: Broadway Books, 2004), 9 (quote), 12, 20, 139–40.
47. Colin Woodward, *American Nations: A History of the Eleven Regional Cultures of North America* (New York: Viking, 2011), 101.
48. Patrick R. Ireland, "Cracker Craic: The Politics and Economics of Scots-Irish Cultural Promotion in the USA," *International Journal of Cultural Policy* 20 (August 2014), 399–42. See, for example, the reactions to J. D. Vance's bestselling book, *Hillbilly Elegy: A Memoir of a Family and Culture in Crisis* (New York: Harper, 2016), and its reception in the media in Anthony Harkins and Meredith McCarroll, eds., *Appalachian Reckoning: A Region Responds to Hillbilly Elegy* (Morgantown: West Virginia University Press, 2019).

Index

For the benefit of digital users, indexed terms that span two pages (e.g., 52–53) may, on occasion, appear on only one of those pages.

Figures in this index are indicated by *f* following the page number

Abenaki peoples, 87–88, 161–63, 197–98
Abernethy, Thomas Perkins, 13, 351
Account of the European Settlements in America (Burke), 65, 74–75, 166–67
Act of Union (1707), 33
Adair, James, 106–7, 108, 120, 197–98
Adams-Onis Treaty (1819), 341–42, 384
Albion's Seed (Fischer), 324
Alexander, Archibald, 153–54
Allen, William, 63–64, 138
Allentown (Craig's Settlement), 63–64, 98–99
ambiguous loyalties during settlement, 352–55
American Indians. *See* Indian groups
American settlement. *See* borderlands; buffer zones; frontier myths; migration to America; Mississippi settlements; settlement of Scotch-Irish; settler colonialism; squatting
Amherst, Jeffery, 162–63, 169–70, 208
Anderson, James, 123
Anne (Queen), 35, 51–52
Annin, James, 226
Apache peoples, 376–77, 378–79, 396–99
Apology of the Paxton Volunteers, The (pamphlet), 187
Armstrong, John, 103, 119, 150–51, 157, 171–72, 179, 220–21, 264, 299
Armstrong, John, Jr., 339
Arnow, Harriette Simpson, 322
Ashley, William Henry, 373, 396–98
Atkin, Edmond, 108
atrocities. *See* Black Boys and White savages; borderlands; Indian-hating; Indian-killing; Indian removal; Paxton massacre (1763)
Attakullakulla (Cherokee chief), 224, 256
Augusta County, VA, 73–74, 127–28, 146
Augusta Boys, 224
Austin, Moses, 379–80
Austin, Stephen, 362–63, 381, 390–91

backcountry. *See* borderlands; buffer zones; frontier myths; relations between Scotch-Irish and Indians; settlement of Scotch-Irish
Bacon, Nathaniel, 177–78
Baily, Francis, 321
Bailyn, Bernard, 37–38, 82–84
Baker, John, 196
Baker's Bottom murders, 239–41
Barber, Rhoda, 67, 175–76
Barnett, Fanny, 199
Barton, Thomas, 152–53, 157–60, 170, 186
Bartram, John, 110, 248–49
Battle of Blue Licks (1782), 281–82
Battle of Fallen Timbers (1794), 317
Battle of King's Mountain (1780), 268
Battle of New Orleans (1815), 340
Battle of Pea Ridge (1862), 383
Battle of Pierre's Hole (1832), 374
Battle of Point Pleasant (1774), 242–43
Battle of the Monongahela (1755), 137–39
Battle of Three Rivers (1776), 275–77
Battle of Topoheka or Horseshoe Bend (1814), 336–37
Battle of Tallushatchee (1813), 335–36
Battle of Wyoming (1778), 264–65
Bean, William, 232
Beard, John, 309
Belcher, Jonathan, 54, 55, 58–59
Bellevue, MO, 360, 361
Beverley, William, 72–73
Big Warrior (Creek chief), 337
Black, Elizabeth, 44
Black, Robert, 44
Black Beaver (Sekttu Maquah), 394–96, 397*f*
Black Boys and White savages
  buffer zones and, 223
  Catawba peoples and, 245–47
  Cherokee peoples and, 224, 228, 232–35

Black Boys and White savages (*cont.*)
  clashes between settlers and, 228–29
  criticism of, 243–50
  Delaware peoples and, 235
  ethnic diversity of, 221
  exceptional case of punishment for Indian killings by, 226
  fair warnings and, 225
  French and Indian War and, 217–19
  general lack of punishment of, 223–24
  government policy toward, 217–18, 222–24, 225–27, 243
  hunting ground encroachment and, 229–32, 243
  incursions into Indian land by, 228–38
  Indian-hating and, 222–23
  Iroquois and, 227, 228–29
  leadership of, 221
  Lord Dunmore's War and, 238–43
  map of settlement areas and, 234*f*
  "New Purchase" lands and, 229–30
  origins of, 246–47
  overview of, 217–19
  Paxton Boys related to, 221, 247
  Proclamation of 1763 and, 218–19, 220–21, 225, 232–35, 237–38, 257
  pushing into Indian land by, 230–38
  Regulators and, 246–47
  Shawnee peoples and, 228, 240–43
  Sideling Hill attack of, 220–21
  Southern backcountry and, 243–50
  squatting and, 224–25
  Stamp Act and, 236
  Stump murders and, 227
  sympathetic portrait of families on the move and, 237
  as too lawless and licentious to be restrained, 223–30
  Treaty of Fort Stanwix and, 229–30, 237–38
  use of Indian dress and paint as disguises by, 220–21, 229, 246–47
  violence as pretext for moving frontier boundaries and, 227–28
  wagon attacked by, 220–21
  Wataugans and, 232–35
  "white Indians" and, 229
  Yellow Creek massacre and, 239–41
Black Stump (Shawnee chief), 353
Blaine, Alexander, 259–60
Blair, Robert, 44
Blount, Charles (Lord Mountjoy), 27
Blount, Willie, 331, 332
Blue Jacket (Shawnee war chief), 316–17

Blue Licks, 281–82, 300, 361–62
Boleyn, Ann, 27
Boone, Daniel, 230–31, 237–38, 256, 266, 281–82, 300, 353
Borden's Tract, 72–73, 128
borderlands. *See also* buffer zones; frontier myths; relations between Scotch-Irish and Indians
  Abenaki peoples and, 87–88
  bans on settlement in, 102
  buffer zones and, 85, 87, 89–90, 91, 95–104
  Catawba peoples and, 108–09
  Cherokee peoples and, 106–09
  coexistence between Indians and settlers on, 86, 87–88
  convoys and, 101
  definition of frontier and, 85–86
  Delaware peoples and, 91–92, 97–98, 105
  double-displacement of Indians in, 101
  escaping of the Susquehanna borderland, 104–6
  first contact between Indians and settlers on, 89, 90–91
  flight from by Indians, 104–6
  French colonialism and, 87–88
  government policy toward, 89–90, 102–4
  Great Warriors' Path and, 100
  holding the alliance and, 100–4
  Indian experience of, 86–95
  intertribal relations disrupted on, 86–87, 96–97
  Iroquois and, 88–89, 95–104
  King Philip's War and, 87–88
  lived experience of, 86–95
  map of settlements on, 93*f*
  military power of Indian groups on, 89–90
  motion as constituting, 86–95
  Ohio country as refuge for displaced peoples from, 105–6
  overview of, 85–87
  Pennsylvania's alliance with the Iroquois and, 95–104
  Piscataway peoples and, 89–91
  population growth as spurring settlement of, 94–95
  precarity of settlement on, 87–88
  responses of Indian groups to settlement of, 90–91, 101–2
  rival colonial power relations as strategy of survival for Indians in, 107
  Scotch-Irish settlement's impact in, 85–88, 96–97, 102–3, 109
  Shawnee peoples and, 92–95, 105
  Shenandoah Valley and, 100–1

sovereignty and space challenges in, 90
squatting and, 101–4
Susquehanna Valley and, 88–90, 94–95
Susquehannocks and, 89
Tuscarora peoples and, 95
Wabanaki peoples and, 87–88
waves of settlement and, 86–87
Boston-area settlements, 49–59
Bouquet, Henry, 171–72, 191, 219–20
Bow, Robert, 189
Boyd, David, 207–8
Boyd, John, 63–64
Boyd, Rhoda, 210
Braddock, Edward, 137
Brady, Thomas, 396–98
Brainerd, David, 112
Brant, Joseph, 260
Breckenridge, John, 291–92
Breen, Tim, 251–52
Brief View of the Conduct of Pennsylvania, A (Smith), 149, 194
Brown, James, 305–6
Brown, Joseph, 305–6
Brown, Patrick, 120–21
Brown, Thomas, 120
Brown, William, 280
Brownlee, William, 280–81
Brubaker, Jack, 180
Buchanan, Arthur, 68, 156–57
Buchanan, James, 410
Buchanan, John, 144, 146
Buckongahelas (Delaware war chief), 260, 316
Buffalo Fort, 363–64
buffer zones. *See also* borderlands; frontier myths
  Anglo-Scottish borders as, 28
  Black Boys and White savages and, 223
  borderlands and, 85, 87, 89–90, 91, 95–104
  Catawba peoples and, 108–09, 163
  Cherokee peoples and, 108
  controlling of, 100–4
  Delaware peoples and, 91
  French and Indian War and, 18, 151–52
  frontier myths and, 16, 19–21, 185
  Indian use of, 85
  Iroquois and, 91, 95–99
  Kentucky and, 310–12
  Mississippi settlements and, 352–55, 362, 368–69
  overview of, 18, 19–20
  Paxton massacre and, 172–73, 223
  Pennsylvania's use of, 95–99
  Pontiac's War and, 18

post-Revolutionary period and, 304, 308
Revolutionary War and, 18, 256, 263–65
Scotch-Irish used as, 16, 19–21, 51, 63, 85, 163, 185, 324
settlement of Scotch-Irish and, 51, 55, 67, 76, 79–81
settler colonialism and, 19–20
Texas and beyond and, 378–79
"wild Irish" and, 85
Bull, William, 247
Burke, Edmund, 65
Burnet, David, 390
Burns, Michael, 360–61
Burns, Patrick, 199–200
Butler, Richard, 240–41, 299–300, 312, 317
Byrd, William, 74–75, 380

Caldwell, James, 251
Caldwell, John, 75, 253
Caldwell, William, 281–82, 317–18
Calhoon, Thomas, 167
Calhoun, Ann, 211–12
Calhoun, John C., 326–27, 340–41, 359–60, 384–85
Calhoun, Patrick, 164
Calhoun, William, 164
Callender, Robert, 119, 219–21, 235
Cameron, Alexander, 232–35, 257
Cammerhoff, John Christopher Frederick, 119–20
Campbell, Arthur, 270, 281–82, 304
Campbell, David, 307
Campbell, John, 260
Campbell, Robert, 373–74
Campbell, William, 73–74, 241–42, 268
Camp Grant Massacre (1871), 399–400
Canasatego (Onondaga chief), 60, 97–98
Canrach Caghera (Conestoga chief), 175
Cape Giradeau, MO, Indian settlements near, 353, 354–55, 368–69
Captain Bull, 159–60, 228–29
captives
  adoption of, 201, 207, 211, 214–15
  agony over fate of, 206
  anguish on return of, 210
  bringing captives home and, 206–11
  British colonial approach to, 208
  challenges of returning to colonial society of, 211–12, 215–16
  child captives and, 201
  Creek peoples and, 305–6, 308, 309–10
  Delaware peoples and, 198, 201, 202, 207–8, 214–15

captives (cont.)
   early captivity narratives and, 194–95
   escape of, 199–201
   experience living with Indians of, 202–6
   French and Indian War and, 196–97, 214–15
   frequency of capture and, 196
   gauntlet runs forced on, 198
   going native and, 202–6
   horror stories and atrocities surrounding, 194–95, 197–98
   military use of knowledge gained by, 213–14
   narratives of, 194–95, 201–3
   new life and identity obtained through, 216
   overview of, 194–95
   peacemaking role of women and, 207–8
   Pontiac's War and, 209
   popularity of narratives surrounding, 194–95
   post-Revolutionary period and, 305–6
   reasons for capture and, 195, 196–97
   returned captives and, 211–16
   Revolutionary War and, 267
   savage image countered by, 196–97
   Seneca peoples and, 203–4
   Shawnee peoples and, 196, 199–201, 203, 209–11, 214–15
   sparing of life and, 196
   taking of captives and, 196–201
   toll of travel and conditions on, 198
   variation in fates and experiences of, 197
   "white Indians" and, 202–6, 211–12, 214–15
   women captives and their treatment, 197–99, 204
Cargill, James, 161
Carleton, Guy, 253
Carleton, James, 394
Carlisle, PA, 119, 160, 171–72, 219–20
Carolina-area settlements, 76–84
Carroll, William, 367
Carson, Alexander, 364
Carson, Kit, 392–94, 393*f*
Cass, Lewis, 372
Catawba peoples
   Black Boys and White savages and, 245–47
   borderlands and, 108–09
   buffer zones and, 108–09, 163
   food shortages and, 130
   French and Indian War and, 109, 146, 163, 165
   military strength of, 108
   relations with settlers of, 120, 128–32
   Revolutionary War and, 258
   Scotch-Irish compared to, 109
   smallpox outbreak among, 131–32

Cavett, Richard, 309–10
Cavett's Station, 309–10
Chambers, Benjamin, 159–60
Chambers, George, 406–7
Chambers, Joseph, 110
Charles II, 32–33, 183–84
Charleston, NH, 111
Charleston, SC, Scotch-Irish immigrants in, 80–81
Cherokee peoples
   Attakullakulla (Cherokee chief), 224, 256
   as attracted to rivers, 106–7
   Black Boys and White savages and, 224, 228, 232–35
   borderlands and, 106–09
   buffer zones and, 108
   Chickamauga Cherokees, 266, 308, 309–10, 329
   Franklinites and, 306
   French and Indian War and, 163–64, 165–66
   Hanging Maw (Cherokee chief), 303–4, 309
   Jackson and, 329, 340, 347–49
   migration and settlement of, 106–7
   Mississippi settlements and, 357, 359–60, 362, 371–72
   Old Tassel (Cherokee chief), 269–70, 271, 302, 303–4, 306
   post-Revolutionary period and, 302–4, 306, 308–10, 320–21
   relations with rival colonial powers as strategy of survival for, 107
   removal of, 347–49
   Revolutionary War and, 257–58, 268–73
   Scotch-Irish compared to, 106–7
   squatting and, 257, 306
   Texas and beyond and, 377–79, 385–88
Cherry Valley "massacre" (1778), 265
Chichester, Arthur, 28–29, 31
Chickamauga Cherokee peoples, 266, 308, 329
Chickasaw peoples, 266–67, 308, 340, 342–43, 347
Choctaw Academy, 362–63
Choctaw peoples, 330–31, 340, 342–43, 347
Christian, William, 268, 269–73, 312–13
Christie (Indian boy), 176
Civility (Conestoga chief), 64–65, 97
civilizing mission, 27–28, 153, 243–44, 322, 330, 346, 359–60
Clark, George Rogers, 266–67, 282, 299–300
Clark, William, 358, 359–60, 362, 370, 371
Clendinnen, Jennet (or Anne), 200–1
Clendinning, James, 224
Coahuila and Texas Colonization Law (1825), 379

coexistence between Indians and settlers, 2–4, 18–19, 86, 87–88, 125–26, 132, 140, 161–62, 176, 192, 302, 362, 368–69, 378
Coffee, John, 335–36, 347–48
Colhoun, James Patrick, 81
Collett, George, 242
Colley, Linda, 7–8
Colquhoun, Robert, 81
Comanche peoples, 376–77
Conduct of the Paxton Men, Impartially Represented, The (pamphlet), 186
Conestoga peoples, 1, 64–65, 100–1, 173–77, 180, 182–83, 189, 191
Cook, Edward, 278
Cookson, Thomas, 119
Cooper, James, 217
Cornstalk (Shawnee chief), 258–59
Cornwallis, Charles, 270, 280
Craig, Isaac, 283, 318–19
Craig, Jane, 63–64
Craig, John, 73–74, 127–28, 138–39, 152
Craig, Thomas, 63–64
Craighead, Thomas, 334–35
Craig's Settlement (Allentown), 63–64, 98–99
Crawford, William, 242–43, 260, 279–80
Crawford, William H., 340
Crawley, Martha, 332
Creek peoples
  aftermath of war against, 337
  attempts to diversify economy of, 334
  captives and, 305–6, 308, 309–10
  depiction of white people as innocent victims of, 335
  extermination as goal of war against, 336–39
  Jackson and, 332–42, 338f
  losses in war against, 337
  organization and diversity of, 333–34
  post-Revolutionary period and, 308, 309–10
  Red Stick towns and, 334
  Revolutionary War and, 258
  Scotch-Irish ancestry of later Creek people, 121
  Treaty of Augusta and, 248, 249
  Treaty of Fort Jackson and, 339–40
  war against, 332–51
  War of 1812 and, 334–35
Cresap, Michael, 96–97, 239
Cresap, Thomas, 4, 63
Crèvecoeur, Hector St. John de, 38, 116–17, 202
Crockett, David, 2–3, 335, 344, 345f, 383, 392
Crockett, Joseph, 282
Croghan, George, 102, 119, 147, 159, 197–98, 220–21, 226, 229–30, 235

Croghan, William, 279
Cromwell, Oliver, 183–84
culture of migration, 361
Cumberland, TN, settlements, 266, 295–96, 304–5, 308, 322, 329
Cumberland Valley, PA, settlements 68
Cummings, Charles, 269
cycles of vengeance, 306, 308–9

Dale, Samuel, 336
Daniel, Walker, 311–12
Davies, William, 271, 281–82
Davis, Jefferson, 327
Dearborn, Henry, 330
Decker, Sarah, 207–8
Declaration and Remonstrance (Smith and Gibson), 185–86, 190
Delaware peoples
  Black Beaver (Sekttu Maquah) 394–96, 397f
  Black Boys and White savages and, 235
  borderlands and, 91–92, 97–98, 105
  Buckongahelas (Delaware chief), 260, 316
  buffer zones and, 91
  captives and, 198, 201, 202, 207–8, 214–15
  complaints about settlement by, 68–69
  declaration of war against, 154–55
  diaspora of, 353–54
  French and Indian War and, 140, 141, 148–49, 154–55, 156–57
  as frontier people, 106
  Hopocan (Delaware chief), 260, 279–80
  identity and composition of, 25
  impact of disease on, 91
  Iroquois domination of, 97–99
  Killbuck (Delaware chief), 231–32
  Kithtuleland (William Anderson) (Delaware chief), 354–55
  languages of, 25
  migration and settlement of, 105
  missionary efforts and, 275
  Mississippi settlements and, 353–55, 357, 362–63, 370–71
  Moravian converts to, 275
  Neolin as prophet of, 170
  origin myth of, 25
  Paxton massacre and, 173–74
  relations with settlers of, 112, 128
  reputation of traders and, 117–18
  resettlement of, 353–54
  Revolutionary War and, 260–61, 275, 279–80, 353–54
  rumors and, 127
  Scotch-Irish compared to, 25–26, 91, 106

Buckongahelas (Delaware chief) (cont.)
  Shingas (Delaware chief), 148, 154–55, 156–57, 167, 196–97, 199–200, 206–7
  squatting and, 123
  Tamaqua (Delaware chief), 206–7
  Teedyuscung (Delaware chief), 99, 141–43, 159, 207–8, 228–29
  Tewea (Delaware chief), 156–58
  Texas and beyond and, 377–78, 385–89, 394–98
  unity and identity of, 25
  Walking Purchase and, 98–99
  White Eyes (Delaware chief), 240–41, 260, 275
Denny, William, 158
De Soto, Hernando, 108
dialogue between Andrew Truman and Thomas Zealot, A (pamphlet), 184–85
Dickinson, Jonathan, 39
Dillon, Thomas, 321
Dinsmoor, Silas, 330–31
Dinsmore, Walker, 409
Dinwiddie, Robert, 135–36, 146, 153
Dobbs, Arthur, 77–78, 108, 128–29, 163
Dodge, Richard, 394–96
Donegal, PA, 60–62, 64, 117, 126
Donelson, John, 266, 328
Donelson, Mary, 335
Donigan, Catherine, 396–98
Donnally, Felix, 178–79
Dougherty, Edward, 118
Dougherty, Peggy, 209
Dove, David James, 187–88
Drage, Theodorus Swaine, 243–44
Dragging Canoe (Chickamauga Cherokee chief), 256, 257, 268–69, 270
Draper, Lyman Copeland, 196–97, 230–31
Duffy, Nancy, 305
Duffy, Patrick, 224
Dunbar, David, 55
Dunbar-Ortiz, Roxanne, 2–3, 14
Dunlap, John, 54
Dunlap, Samuel, 54
Dunlop, Rev. Samuel, 58
Dunmore's War (1774), 215–16, 238–43, 259–60, 279
Duwali (the Bowl) (headman of Little Hiwasse town), 359, 377–78, 386, 388
Dysart, James, 231–32

Eaton, John Henry, 325–26, 335–36, 347
Edict of Nantes (1685), 75–76
Egle, William H, 182, 279
Elder, John, 139–40, 152, 175, 176

Elizabeth I, 27–28
Elliott, Matthew, 259–60, 279, 281–82
Enquiry into the Causes of the Alienation, An (Thomson), 141–42
Erskine, Margaret Handley, 259–60
Essay on the Trade and Improvement of Ireland, An (Dobbs), 77
Eustis, William, 331
Evans, Lewis, 85–86

Findley, William, 315–16
Finerty, John, 402–3
Finiels, Nicolas de, 354
Finley, John, 260
Finley, Joseph, 260
Fischer, David Hackett, 14–15, 29, 37, 326–27
Fisk, Moses, 232–35
Fithian, Philip Vickers, 229–30, 284
Fitzpatrick, Thomas, 374–75, 392–93
Fleming, Elizabeth, 197–98
Fleming, William, 197–98
"Flight of the Earls," 29
Forbes, John, 160–61
Ford, Henry Jones, 13–14, 16, 411–12
Fort Freeland, 265
Fort Granville, 156–57, 156f
Fort Mims, attack on, 334
Fort Pitt, 258; treaty at (1778), 254–55, 278; Franklin, Benjamin, 260, 264, 275–77
  Albany Congress and, 104
  on converting Pennsylvania into royal colony, 189–90
  French and Indian War and, 156
  on German population growth, 36
  Germantown negotiations of, 182
  pamphlet by, 182–83
  Paxton riots condemned by, 182–83, 186, 189–90
  Philadelphia march negotiations by, 182–83
  Revolutionary War and, 264
  on Scotch-Irish as true savages, 182–83
  on Scotch-Irish becoming majority post-Revolution, 290
  as troubled by immigrant, 36–37
  version of Paxton massacre critiqued and, 186
  on vulnerability of backcountry, 140
  war against the Delawares and, 154–55
Franklin, state of, 302–3
Franklin, William, 251
Fredonia Republic *(Republic of the Red and White People)* (1826), 380

INDEX   495

French and Indian War (1754-1763)
  Armstrong's expedition in, 157–58
  Augusta County, Virginia in, 146
  Battle of the Monongahela and, 137–39
  Black Boys and White savages and, 217–19
  Braddock's army in, 137–39, 150
  buffer zones and, 18, 151–52
  captives and, 196–97, 214–15
  Carlisle as center of, 219–20
  Catawba peoples and, 146, 163, 165
  Cherokee peoples and, 163–64, 165–66
  coexistence shattered by, 140, 161–62, 217
  context for, 135–41
  Delaware peoples and, 140, 141, 148–49, 154–55, 156–57
  depopulation in, 166–67
  early stages of, 135–37
  ending of, 169–70
  finding the path to peace in, 159–61
  Fort Dobbs in, 164–65
  Fort Duquesne in, 160–61
  Fort Granville in, 156–57, 156f
  forting up during, 150–51
  frontier rolled back during, 141–50
  Great Cove Valley and, 148
  guerilla tactics used during, 141, 162–63
  Indian-hating legacy resulting from, 17, 166–68
  Iroquois and, 135, 143, 148, 154, 159–60
  Kittanning raid during, 157–58
  lack of concern for settlers in, 149
  local defense organizations and, 139–40
  map of, 136f
  militia's role in, 165
  neutral Indians caught between fires in, 148–49
  Northern and Southern conflicts during, 161–68
  outcomes of, 169–70
  overview of, 135
  Peace of Paris and, 169–70
  Penn Creek in, 147–48
  petitions for protection and, 137–41, 157
  Quaker Assembly and, 139–40
  raids and refugees in, 140, 145–47
  Revolutionary War compared to, 263, 267, 284
  scalp bounties in, 155–56
  Scotch-Irish impacted by, 137–38, 149, 150–52, 157–58, 161, 164–67
  Shawnee peoples and, 144, 148–49
  smallpox during, 165
  soldiers and backcountry militia in, 150
  St. Francis attacked and burned in, 162–63
  striking back and striking out in, 150–58
  terror tactics and psychological warfare in, 144–47, 165
  tomahawk sent as petition in, 148
  Treaty of Easton and, 160–61
frontier myths. See also borderlands; buffer zones
  buffer zones and, 16, 19–21, 185
  definition of frontier and, 85–86
  ending of the frontier, 411
  French and Indian War and, 141–50
  frontiers of inclusion and, 362
  Indian-hating and, 16–17
  Indians and, 11–15, 85–86
  Jackson as archetype of frontiersman, 327
  Kentucky and, 310–13
  Mississippi settlements and, 361, 362, 366
  overview of, 11–15
  Paxton massacre and, 172–73, 185–86, 191
  post-Revolutionary period and, 310–13
  racial frontier and, 185–86
  Scotch-Irish self-identity as frontier people, 7, 11–15, 17–18, 106
  winning of the West and, 11, 400

Gage, Thomas, 179, 220–21, 222–23, 224, 225–27, 236, 240, 251
Gaines, Edmund P., 341
Galloway, James, 251
Galloway, William, 102–3, 154–55
Galphin, George, 82, 120–21, 249, 258
Gates, Horatio, 263
George III, 251, 255
Georgia, Worcester v. (1832), 348–49
German migration, 36
Germain, George, 257
Gibson, George, 317
Gibson, James, 182
Gibson, John, 239–40, 317
Gillespie, Jane, 305–6
Girty, George, 214–15
Girty, James, 214–15, 259
Girty, Simon, Sr. 214
Girty, Simon, 214–15, 240–41, 259, 279–80, 317–18
Girty, Thomas, 214–15
Glasgow, Maude, 412
Glorious Revolution (1688), 32–33
Gnadenhütten massacre (1782), 277–81
Gooch, William, 70–71, 72–73
Gordon, Patrick, 96–97, 105
Graham, Arthur, 260

Grahams (family), 28–29
Grant, James, 165
Great Awakening, 39
Great Cove, PA, 102; attack on, 68, 148
Great Famine (1845-1852), 45–46, 402
Greathouse, Daniel, 239
Great Migration (1629-1640), 37
Great Wagon Road, 2, 71, 75–76, 77, 82–84, 100, 271–73
Great Warriors' Path, 71, 100
Greeley, Horace, 408
Green, Samuel Swett, 411
Greenlee, James, 73, 278
Greenlees, Andrew, 401
Greg, John, 82
Grey, John, 159
grievances of the backcountry, 6–7, 140–41, 185–86, 240–41, 254–55, 302–3, 307–10, 314–16, 386, 413
Griffin, Patrick, 3–4, 5
Grover, Josiah, 55–56
Grubb, Nathaniel, 149
guerrilla tactics, 141, 162–63, 261
Guthrie, Elizabeth Brownlee, 280–81
Guthrie, William, 280–81
Gutiérrez, José Bernardo Maximiliano, 377
Guyasuta (Seneca chief), 170, 240–41, 280
Gyles, John, 56

Habersham, James, 82, 243
Hagler (King, Catwba chief), 129–31
Hall, James, 270, 284–85
Hamilton, Alexander, 313–14
Hamilton, Henry, 259–60
Hamilton, James, 68–69, 102, 137–38, 139–40, 172, 206–7
Hand, Edward, 264
Hanging Maw (Cherokee chief), 303–4, 309
Hanna, Charles, 180–81, 412
Hanna, Robert, 228, 254
Hanna's Town, PA, 228
 attack on, 280
Hardy, Hugh, 68
Harmar, Josiah, 292–93, 299, 316
Harris, John, 7, 117, 138, 145, 175
Harrison, Benjamin, 311–12
Harrison, Henry, 332
Harrod, James, 237–38
hatred of Indians. See Indian-hating
Haudenosaunee (League of the Iroquois). See Iroquois
Hawkins, Benjamin, 320, 330, 334
Hays, John Coffee (Captain Jack), 391–92

Hays, Robert, 391–92
Heckewelder, John, 25, 167, 202
Henderson, Patrick, 37–38
Henderson, Richard, 256
Henry, Patrick, 268, 299, 306
Henry II, 26–27
Henry VIII, 27
Hewetson, James, 381–83
Hicks, Barbara, 212–13
Hicks, Gershom, 212–13
Hinkston, John, 217
History of the American Indians (Adair), 120
Hite, Jost, 71
Hodge, Adam, 44
Holey, Mary Austin, 379–80
Hoops, Adam, 148
Hopocan (Delaware chief), 260, 279–80
Horner, Jane, 171
Horton, Albert C., 390
Houston, Samuel, 2–3, 367, 368f, 378–79, 386–87, 389
Hubbard, James, 306
Hunter, Daniel, 54
hunting ground encroachment, 101, 106–7, 124–25, 229–32, 236, 243, 311–12, 372–75

Indian groups. *See* captives; Catawba peoples; Cherokee peoples; Delaware peoples; Iroquois; relations between Scotch-Irish and Indians; Shawnee peoples
Indian-hating
 Black Boys and White savages and, 222–23
 federal denunciation of, 298
 French and Indian War as start of, 17, 166–68
 frontier myths and, 16–17
 Jackson and, 327, 329–30
 Mississippi settlements and, 361–62
 Paxton massacre and, 169–74
 post-Revolutionary period and, 322–23
 racialization and, 322
 repudiation of, 361–62
 Revolutionary War and, 283–86
 Scotch-Irish associated with, 16–17, 283, 406, 410–11
 spread of, 173–74
 Texas and beyond and, 383, 399
 white identity and, 322
Indian-killing, 17, 110, 125–26, 166–68, 283, 285–86, 399
Indian removal
 belief in necessity of, 342–43
 Indian Removal Act (1830), 344, 372
 Jackson and, 2–3, 342–51

INDEX 497

justifications provided for, 346–50
Mississippi settlements and, 370–72
opposition to, 344
post-Revolutionary period and, 319–20
shifting government policy on, 319–20, 342–51
Texas and beyond and, 378–79, 385, 388, 391–92
Ingles, Mary Draper, 200
Ingles, Thomas, 215–16
Ireland
backwardness associated with, 27
civilizing mission and, 30–32
colonization of, 26–35
domestic migration within, 31
emigration restriction legislation in, 77
English attempts to dominate, 26–35
Flight of the Earls and, 29
gallowglass in, 26–27
Indians compared to peasants of, 27, 31
Irish Catholic immigrants from, 349–50, 402, 405–6, 407–8, 409
Irish problem, 27
linen exports and, 38–39
Londonderry, siege of, 32–33
migrations from, estimates for, 37–38, 44–46, 291, 342, 402
Norman barons in, 26–27
Pale in, 26–27
Protestants planted in, 26–35
reasons for migration from, 41–42
religious division in, 27
resistance to colonization in, 27, 31–32
savagery associated with, 27
size of migrations to, 32
Ulster colonization scheme in, 27, 29–32, 34f, 39, 41–42
Ulster Presbyterianism in, 33–35
waves of migration from, 39–42
"wild Irish," 31, 85, 389
Irish Society, 29–30
Iroquois
Black Boys and White savages and, 227, 228–29
borderlands and, 88–89, 95–104
buffer zones and, 91, 95–99
Delaware peoples dominated by, 91, 97–99
French and Indian War and, 135, 143, 148, 154, 159–60
Great Warriors' Path and, 71
Kentucky and, 311–12
League of the Iroquois, 88–89
limits of federal power and, 296–97

Mohawk peoples' role in, 96
neutrality policy of, 95–96, 101
Paxton massacre and, 180
Pennsylvania's alliance with, 95–104
post-Revolutionary period and, 296–97
and "props," 88–89, 95–96
Revolutionary War and, 264–65, 273–74
Seneca peoples' role in, 96
squatting and, 148
Stump murders and, 227
Treaty of Lancaster and, 71–72, 100–1
Walking Purchase and, 98–99
Irvine, William, 275–77, 276f, 278, 283, 318–19

Jackson, Andrew
Adams-Onis Treaty of 1819 and, 384
as antithesis of Waxhaw community, 327
appointment as Tennessee representative of, 330
Battle of New Orleans and, 340
Battle of Topoheka and, 336–37
belief in necessity of Indian removals and, 342–43
as bringing border chieftain to White House, 349–50
Cherokee peoples and, 329, 340, 347–49
Chickasaw peoples and, 340, 342–43, 347
Choctaw peoples and, 330–31, 340, 342–43, 347
civilizing mission and, 330, 346
Creek war waged by, 332–42, 338f
early life of, 328–31
extermination as goal of Creek war and, 336–39
family and upbringing of, 325–27
frontiersman archetype associated with, 327
honor and masculine pride appealed to, 332
Indian-hating of, 327, 329–30
Indian Removal Act and, 344
Indian removals under, 2–3, 342–51
justification for Indian removals of, 346–50
legacy of, 349–51
making a name for himself, 328–31
mass retaliation advocated by, 329–30, 333
militia experience of, 330
negotiation tactics of, 340–41
overview of, 324–28
portrait of, 325f
presidential election of, 343
racialized beliefs about Indian incapacity of, 349
resistance to federal authority assertions by, 330
savages and, Indians as, 346, 349

Jackson, Andrew (*cont.*)
   Scotch-Irish as embodiment of Indian policies of, 324
   Scotch-Irish heritage and self-understanding of, 326–27, 349–51
   self-professed friendly feelings toward Indians by, 346–47
   Trade and Intercourse Act and, 331
   Tennessee experiences of, 328–31
   Tennessee Volunteers and, 334–35
   Texas policies of, 384–86
   Treaty of Cusseta and, 349–50
   Treaty of Dancing Rabbit Creek and, 347
   Treaty of Doaks Stand and, 342–43
   Treaty of Fort Jackson and, 339–40
   Treaty of Ghent and, 341–42
   Treaty of Holston and, 328–29
   Treaty of New Echota and, 348–49
   use of images of scalped wives and children by, 332
   War of 1812 and, 334–35
   white identity defended by, 341
   Worcester v. Georgia and, 348–49
Jacobite Rebellion (1746), 76–77
James I, 27–32, 236–38
James II, 32–33
James VI, 27–28
Jefferson, Thomas
   civilizing mission and, 322, 346
   frontier squatter as replacing yeoman farmer and, 350–51
   Indian removal policies of, 342, 359
   Indians as culturally inferior but capable of improvement, 346
   on lack of support for backcountry by government, 307
   Lewis and Clark expedition under, 357–58
   Louisiana Purchase initiated by, 359
   national expansion and, 321–22
   post-Revolutionary period and, 321–22
   republican principles of, 319
   Scotch-Irish as joining God's chosen people through civilizing project of, 322
Jemison, Mary (Dickewamis), 202–6, 205f, 273
Jennings, Edmund, 361–62
Jennings, Solomon, 98–99
Johnson, Gabriel, 76
Johnson, James, 111
Johnson, Job, 292
Johnson, Susanna, 197–98
Johnson, William, 18, 58, 154–55, 173, 179–80, 227–28, 249–50
Johnston, John, 370–71

Jones, David, 275
Juniata Valley settlements, 68, 69, 88–89, 101–2

Katherine of Aragon, 27
Kekionga, 316
Keightley, George, 311–12
Keith, William, 96
Kendal, Benjamin, 181
Kennedy, Billy, 14
Kenny, Kevin, 326–27
Kenton, Simon, 266, 311, 317–18
Kentucky
   buffer zones and, 310–12
   frontier myths and, 310–13
   as a good poor man's country, 310–11
   Indian raids in, 311–12
   Iroquois and, 311–12
   landless emigrants to, 312–13
   militia in, 311–12
   population growth in, 313
   post-Revolutionary period and, 310–13
   recognition of, 312
   Scotch-Irish as storm troopers of civilization in, 311
   self-government demands in, 313
   separatist calls in, 313
   Shawnee peoples and, 311–12
   Treaty of Fort Finney and, 312
   Treaty of Fort Stanwix and, 311–12
Kickapoo peoples, 370, 377–78, 385–89
Killbuck (Delaware chief), 230–31, 235
Kincaid, Eleanor, 205–6
Kincaid, William, 210
King, Thomas (Saghughsuniunt) (Oneida chief), 124–25, 208–9
King George's War (1744-1748), 197–98
King Philip's War (1675-1678), 51–52, 87–88, 194–95
Kinkead, William, 311
Kirk, John, 306
Kirker, James "Santiago," 396–98, 398f
Kishacoquillas (Shawnee chief), 68
Kithtuleland (William Anderson) (Delaware chief), 354–55
Kittanning, 156–58, 196
Know-Nothing Party, 349–50
Knox, Henry, 299, 306–7, 309, 319–20, 321–22
Knox, James, 231–32
Knox, John, 33–34

Lafferty, John, 360–61
Lamar, Mireau B., 387–88

INDEX 499

Lancaster, PA, 100
    massacre at, 177–79
Laurens, Henry, 42–43, 165
Lawoughqua (Shawnee chief), 211
Lechmere, Thomas, 51
Lee, Arthur, 294
Lee, James, 399
Le Roy, Marie, 198
Letters from an American Farmer (Crèvecoeur), 38, 116–17, 202
Lewis, Andrew, 153–54, 160, 224, 242, 258–59, 260, 268
Lewis, John, 72
Lewis, Thomas, 241–42, 260
lex talionis, 261, 308–9
Lindsey, John, 282
Linn, John, 391
Little Turtle (Miami war chief), 316–17
Lochry, Archibald, 274–75
Locke, John, 122–23
Lodge, Henry Cabot, 409
Logan (Mingo chief), 239, 241
Logan, Benjamin, 73–74, 300, 301*f*
Logan, James
    alliance with Iroquois sought by, 97
    birth of, 60
    buffer zones and, 151
    changed views on Scotch-Irish settlement of, 65
    Donegal settlement and, 126
    family and upbringing of, 60
    hard neighbors description used by, 110
    Indian policy of, 98–99
    oaths of loyalty and, 63
    Philadelphia settlement encouraged by, 60–62
    portrait of, 61*f*
    Scotch-Irish complaints of, 1–2, 62–63
    Shawnee interactions of, 94, 105
    Shikellamy's son named after, 110
    significance of, 60
    squatting and, 66, 114–15
    Walking Purchase and, 98–99
Londonderry Celebration, 408
Londonderry (NH) settlement, 52–53, 57–59
Long, Stephen, 365
Long Canes, SC, 81
    attack on 163–64
Looking-Glass for Presbyterians, A (Hunt), 183–84
Lord Dunmore's War (1774), 215–16, 238–43, 259–60, 279
Lorimier, Louis, 354

Louisiana Purchase (1803), 352, 355–57, 359, 360–61, 372–73
Louis-Philippe, king of France, 295–96, 324
Lowery, Jean, 117–18, 198
Lowry (Lowery), George, 348
loyalties, 63, 251, 253, 259, 298–99, 306–8, 352–55
Lycon, Andrew, 102–3
Lyttleton, Henry, 163

MacClay, William, 264–65, 316
MacCracken, Henry Noble, 404
MacFarlane, James, 299–300
MacGowan, Michael, 402
Mackay, Alexander, 225
Maclean, Allan, 282–83
MacSparran, James, 53, 57, 75
Magee, William Augustus, 377
Marquette, Jacques, 92–94
Marshall, Edward, 98–99
Martin, John, 206–7
Martin, Joseph, 300–2, 303–4
Maryland, Pennsylvania border dispute with, 63
massacres and violence. *See* Black Boys and White savages; borderlands; Indian-hating; Indian-killing; Indian removal; Paxton massacre (1763); relations between Scotch-Irish and Indians; savages
Mather, Cotton, 51
Matthews, John Joseph, 358
May, John, 294–95
McAden, Hugh, 138–39
McAfee brothers, 237–38, 242, 256, 311
McAlister, John, 118
McAllister, Alexander, 197
McCaffrey, J. E., 399–400
McClane, Jenny, 145
McClure, David, 53, 119, 157, 205–6, 236–37, 275
McCobb, Samuel, 57
McCoy, Isabella, 197–98
McCracken, Henry Noble, 25–26
McCrea, Jane, 261–63, 262*f*
McCulloch, Ben, 383
McCulloch, Henry, 383
McCullough, James, 201
McCullough, John, 106, 166–67
McCullough or McCullock, John, 317
McCutchen, Rachel, 284
McCutchen, Samuel, 318
McDonald, John, 265
McDowell, Ephraim, 73
McDowell, John, 73, 128

McFarland, Alexander, 362
McGary, Hugh, 281–82, 300
McGillivray, Alexander (Creek chief), 298, 305–6, 307–8, 333–34
McGinty, Ann Wilson Pogue Lindsey, 282
McGregor, James, 49–51, 52, 53, 54–55
McHenry, James, 321
McInnis, Robert, 127
McIntosh, William, 333–34, 341–42
McKee, Alexander, 240–41, 259
McKee, John, 329
McKee, Thomas, 101, 119–20, 147–48, 154, 159, 175, 222
McKendry, Daniel, 44
McKey, Catherine, 206
McKinley, William, 410
McKinney, John, 196–97
McKinsey or McKenzie, James, 226
McKnight, John, 396–98
McMeans, Andrew, 266–67
McMeans, Anne, 266–67
McMollin, Thomas, 44
McMullen, John, 381–83
McNair, Alexander, 370
McNeal, John, 360
McNutt, Alexander, 58–59
McSwaine, George (or Hugh), 199–200
Meachan, Jon, 349
Mellon, Thomas, 284
Mercer, Hugh, 208
Merrell, James, 192
Metacomet (Wampanoag chief), 87–88
migration to America. *See also* Ireland; settlement of Scotch-Irish
  changing composition and character of, 45–46
  dangers of, 42–43
  early stages in, 36
  English attempts to dominate Ireland and, 26–27
  estimating numbers of migrants and, 37–38
  experiences of, 35–47
  German immigration and, 36
  indentured servitude and, 43–44
  Jamestown settlement and, 31
  overview of, 25–26
  reception in New England and, 51
  Revolutionary War and, 40–41
  Ulster colonization scheme and, 31
Miller, Kerby, xv
Mississippi, settlements west of
  agricultural dimensions of, 357, 359–60, 361, 365

  ambiguous loyalties and, 352–55
  avalanche of non-Indian settlers to, 369
  Buffalo Fort and, 363–64
  buffer zones and, 352–55, 362, 368–69
  Cape Girardeau, Delaware and Shawnee villages near, 353, 354–55, 368–69
  Cherokee peoples and, 357, 359–60, 362, 371–72
  Choctaw Academy and, 362–63
  civilizing mission and, 359–60
  coexistence during early, 362, 368–69
  common and contested ground and, 355–67
  corridor used by Indians and, 355
  culture of migration and, 361
  Delaware peoples and, 353–55, 357, 362–63, 370–71
  exchange of culture and, 361–63, 365
  frontier myths and, 361, 362, 366
  fur trade and, 372–75
  gateway to the fur trade and, 372–75
  Indian-hating and, 361–62
  Indian removal and, 370–72
  intertribal relations in, 355–60
  Kickapoo peoples and, 370
  Louisiana Purchase and, 352, 355–57, 359, 360–61, 372–73
  map of Ozark, 356f
  migration and settlement in, 352–55
  motivations for, 369
  Osage peoples and, 353, 354, 357–60, 362, 366, 369, 370, 372, 378–79
  overview of, 352
  Ozarks, 355–67, 356f
  paths and patterns of early immigration and, 360–61
  racialization and, 370
  remaking a land without Indians and, 368–72
  Revolutionary War and, 352–53
  "savages" and, 359–60, 370
  Scotch-Irish role in, 355–57, 360–61, 372–75
  Shawnee peoples and, 353–55, 357, 362–63, 370
  Spanish colonialism and, 353–55
  squatting and, 368–69, 370
  trade and, 372–75
  Trail of Tears and, 372
  Treaty of Doaks Stand and, 369
  Treaty of St. Mary's and, 354–55
  War of 1812 and, 352–53, 363–64, 368–69
Mohawk peoples, 88–89, 96, 101, 194–95, 213–14, 257, 260–61, 352–53
Moluntha (Shawnee chief), murder of, 300
Montgomery, Archibald, 165

Montgomery, John, 231–32
Montgomery, Lamuel, 337
Montgomery, Richard, 253
Montour, Andrew, 68–69, 102
Moravians, 36, 173–74, 176, 179, 182, 222, 275, 278
Morgan, George, 258–59
Morris, Robert Hunter, 138, 139, 145–46, 175, 196
Moultrie, William, 258
Muhlenberg, Henry Melchior, 9, 182
myths of the frontier. *See* frontier myths

Nairne, Thomas, 106
Nancy (ship), 42–43
Narrative of the Late Massacres, A (Franklin), 182–83
Native Americans. *See* Indian groups
Neely, Mary, 267
Neolin (Delaware prophet), 170
Nevin, John, 373
New Orleans, Battle of (1815), 340
"New Purchase" lands, 229–30
Nickajack, attack on, 318
Nolan, Philip, 377
Norris, Isaac, 150
Northwest Ordinance (1787), 298–99
Norton, John, 379
Notes on the State of Virginia (Jefferson), 239

O'Brien, Michael, 409
Oconostota (Cherokee chief), 256
O'Donnell, Rory (Earl of Tyrconnell), 29
Ohio Valley, Indian migrations to, 105–6
  Scotch-Irish migrations to, 292–93
Old Tassel (Cherokee chief), 269–70, 271, 302, 303–4, 306
O'Neill of Tyrone, Hugh, 27, 29
Onondaga, 88–89, 94–95, 96
Opequon, VA, 72
O'Raw, John, 43
O'Reilly, Alejandro, 253
origin stories and Atlantic migrations. *See* Ireland; migration to America; Scotch-Irish; settlement of Scotch-Irish
O'Riley, Barney, 334
Orr, John, 400
Osage peoples, 353, 354, 357–60, 362, 366, 369, 370, 372, 378–79
Ostenaco (Cherokee chief), 153–54
O'Toole, Fintan, 10–11

Pardo, Juan, 108

Parsons, William, 139–40, 142–43, 145, 150
Patten, Matthew, 53
Patterson, James, 68, 173, 408
Patterson, William, 226–27
Patton, James, 144
Paug, John, 82
Paxinosa (Shawnee chief), 143–44
Paxton, PA, 62, 64, 66, 91–92, 117, 172–73, 223
Paxton massacre (1763)
  antipathy toward Moravian Indian converts and, 222
  Bacon's rebellion and, 177–78
  burial of dead from, 179
  carried out by front line of frontier defense, 172–73
  claims of popular support for, 186
  code of silence following, 189
  coexistence era killed off by, 169, 176, 192
  compared to other massacres, 169
  Conestoga peoples and, 173–77, 180
  Conestoga Town massacre and, 175–76
  context for, 183–84
  contrasted with other mob action, 192–93
  council culture repudiated by, 192
  Delaware peoples and, 173–74
  depiction of, 176–78, 178f
  frontier as racial frontier and, 185–86
  government policy and, 183, 222–24
  honor and, 191
  inability to identify perpetrators of, 180
  Indian atrocities equated with, 180
  Indian-hating and, 169–74
  Indian war redux and, 169–73
  Iroquois and, 180
  justification for, 177, 182
  justifications provided for, 1, 185–86, 191–92
  lack of arrest and punishment for, 180
  lynching law and, 180–81
  as message to legislature for failure to protect frontier, 191
  Moravians and, 173–74, 176, 182
  overview of, 1–4, 169, 172–73, 175–81
  pamphlets and publications on, 182–90
  patriarchal values as informing, 191
  Paxton Boys as now "Our Boys," 412
  Philadelphia march following, 181–82, 187
  political consequences of, 189–93
  Pontiac's Revolt and, 170
  Presbyterians criticized and stereotyped following, 183–85, 190
  Quakers and, 182, 186–90, 188f, 189f
  racialization and, 185–86
  ranger companies and, 172–73

Paxton massacre (1763) (*cont.*)
  reconstruction of, 180
  refugees from, 170–72
  responses to, 177–79, 182–83, 191
  Revolutionary War and, 265
  reward offered for perpetrators of, 179
  savages and, 181–89
  Scotch-Irish associated with, 110, 174–75, 177–78, 180–89, 191–92
  Shawnee peoples and, 173–74
  squatting and, 174–75
  storm explodes and, 173–81
  as threat to government, 177–79
  victim identity used to justify, 180, 191
Peace of Paris (1763), 169–70
Peace of Paris (1783), 299–300
Pea Ridge, Battle of (1862), 383
Pearis, Richard, 81, 153–54
Peck, John Mason, 368–69
Penal Laws (1690s), 35
Penn Creek, PA, 147–48
Penn, John, 65, 175, 189, 190, 191–92, 217, 229, 240
Penn, Richard, 236
Penn, Thomas, 97, 174–75
Penn, William
  buffer zone use by, 89–90
  coexistence promoted by, 169
  death of, 63–64
  manors and, 174–75
  Pennsylvania founded by, 25
  religious tolerance promoted by, 59
  reputation for fair dealings with Indians of, 91–92, 97–98
  settlers invited by, 36
  Susquehanna settlement and, 90
  Walking Purchase and, 99
Pennsylvania. *See also* settlement of Scotch-Irish
  buffer zones in, 95–99
  Iroquois's alliance with, 95–104
  map of, 142*f*
  Scotch-Irish as attracted to settlement in, 59–64
Penobscot peoples, 56, 57
Peters, Richard, 66, 68, 102, 103–4, 139–40, 145, 151, 157, 175
Philadelphia-area settlements, 59–69
Philadelphia, march on, 181–82
Philipps, Richard, 55
Pickens, Andrew, 75–76, 165, 271–73, 272*f*, 302, 308, 326–27
Pickering, Timothy, 298

Pierre's Hole, Battle of (1832), 374
Piscataway peoples, 89–91
Plain Dealer, A (Williamson), 187
Pollock, Oliver, 253
Pontiac's War (1763-1766), 17, 18, 170, 186, 192, 194, 209, 215–16, 220–21
Post, Christian Frederick, 117–18, 159–60, 202
post-Revolutionary period
  atrocities during, 323
  Blue Licks and, 300
  buffer zones and, 304, 308
  captives and, 305–6
  Cavett's Station and, 309–10
  Cherokee peoples and, 302–4, 306, 308–10, 320–21
  Chickamauga Cherokees and, 308, 309–10
  Chickasaw peoples and, 308
  civilizing mission and, 322
  conflict and coexistence hand in hand during, 302
  continuing migration during, 291–96
  Creek peoples and, 308, 309–10
  cycles of vengeance and, 306, 308–9
  federal attempts to curb violence and, 307–10
  frontier militia as part-time soldiers and, 304–5
  frontier myths and, 310–13
  government-Indian relations during, 319–23
  grievances of the backcountry and, 302–3, 307–10
  hearth areas and, 293–94
  improvements during, 290–91
  Indian-hating and, 322–23
  Iroquois and, 296–97
  Kentucky and, 310–13
  land speculation and, 313–14, 321
  lex talionis and, 261, 308–9
  limits of federal power and, 296–310
  loyalty to federal and state government and, 298–99, 306–8
  military warrants and, 292
  new immigrants during, 291–96
  Northwest Ordinance of 1787 and, 298–99
  overview of, 289–91
  Peace of Paris and, 299–300
  population of Scotch-Irish descent during, 291, 292–93
  prohibitions against settlement during, 298–99
  racialization during, 322–23
  Scotch-Irish as becoming American by opposing Indians in, 294–96, 322–23
  Scotch-Irish at forefront of, 297–99

separatist leaders in, 302–3
settler sovereignty during, 298
siege mentality during, 308
squatting and, 306, 320
Tennessee admitted into the Union and, 320–21
Treaty of Fort Finney and, 300
Treaty of Fort McIntosh and, 299–300
Treaty of Hopewell and, 302
triangular relationships and, 320–21
turn of the century government relations and, 319–23
Whiskey Rebellion and, 313–19
white identity and, 322–23
Power, James, 381–83
Preston, David, 111
Preston, William, 153–54, 232–35, 268, 282–83
Pringle, Henry, 162
Privy Council, 56–57
Proclamation of 1763, 218–19, 220–21, 225, 232–35, 237–38, 257

Quaker Assembly, 139–40
Quakers, 137–38, 149, 154–55, 182, 186–91, 188f, 189f, 218–19
Quaker unmask'd (Dove), 187–88
Queen Anne's War (1713), 51–52
Queensborough township, GA, 248–49

racial violence and racialization, 2, 8, 17, 19, 110, 185–86, 225, 261–65, 322–23, 370, 383. *See also* savages
Rae, John, 120–21, 248–49
Rae, Robert, 258
Ramsey, Jonathan, 318
Randolph, Edmund, 303–4
Randolph, John, 72–73
Randolph, Richard, 72–73
Rankin, William, 44
Raven of Chota (Cherokee chief), 256–57
Records, Spencer, 277–78
Red Dirt (Dunbar-Ortiz), 2–3, 14
Redstone Creek, PA. squatters at, 225
Redeemed Captive Returning to Zion, The (Williams), 194–95
Reed, James Frazier, 401
Regulators, 246–47, 256
relations between Scotch-Irish and Indians. *See also* borderlands; captives; Catawba peoples; Cherokee peoples; Delaware peoples; Iroquois; Shawnee peoples
agriculture and food preparation in, 113–16

alcohol in, 118, 126
ambivalence of, 111, 132
animal-human interactions in, 124–25
basis of, 111
Borden's Tract and, 128
clothing and, 115, 129–30
common land and, 122–23
competing and overlapping groups within, 123
contending the land and, 122–25
deterioration of, 128–29
distrust and suspicion in, 127
food shortages and, 130
gender roles and interaction in, 112–13, 120–21
government policy and, 116–17, 123, 126
hunting and, 124–25
Indians as "Canaanites" and, 112
individual relations and personal bonds in, 131–32
initial lack of warfare in, 127–28
intermediaries in, 119–20
killings leading to border conflict and, 126
kinship and, 115, 116
Kittanning Path and, 117
marrying of Indian women and, 120–21
merchants in cities and, 118
missionary efforts and, 112, 131
motion as basis of, 116, 123
occupation of cleared land and, 114–15
open field systems and, 122–23
overview of, 110
property rights and, 122–23, 126–27
racial violence and, 110
reputation of traders and, 117–18
roving Indian bands and, 127–28
rumors and, 127
Scotch-Irish living like Indians and, 113–17, 125
settler colonialism as requiring, 110
shared experience of displacement in, 113
simmering tensions and, 125–32
slash-and-burn farming and, 114–15
squatting and, 114–15, 123–24
trade and, 117–21
traveling traders and, 118
removal of Indians. *See* Indian removal
Renick, Robert, 206
Renick, William, 206
Renix, Joshua, 73–74
Renix, William, 73–74
Republic of Texas, 2–3, 386–89

Revolutionary War (1775-1783). *See also* post-Revolutionary period
  atrocity narratives and, 284–85
  attrition in, 261
  backcountry and, 261–68
  Back Water men and, 268
  Battle of Three Rivers and, 275–77
  Battle of Wyoming and, 264–65
  Blue Licks and, 281–82
  buffer zones and, 18, 256, 263–65
  captives and, 267
  Catawba peoples and, 258
  Cherokee peoples and, 257–58, 268–73
  Cherry Valley "massacre" and, 265
  Chickasaw peoples and, 266–67
  composition of militia units in, 251
  context for, 256–61
  Creek peoples and, 258
  Declaration of Independence and, 255
  Delaware peoples and, 260–61, 275, 279–80, 353–54
  French and Indian War compared to, 263, 267, 284
  Gnadenhütten massacre and, 277–81
  guerilla warfare tactics in, 261
  Indian fields and families in, 268–80
  Indian-hating and, 283–86
  Iroquois and, 264–65, 273–74
  Jane McCrea murder and, 261–63, 262f
  law of retaliation and, 261
  lead up to, 256–61
  loyalists in, 251, 253, 259, 268–70
  massacres condemned during, 278
  migration to America and, 40–41
  militia activity during, 263, 270–71, 274–75
  Mississippi settlements and, 352–53
  Mohawk peoples and, 260–61
  Moravians and, 275–78
  Ohio River and, 266
  Oneida peoples and, 260–61
  overview of, 251–55
  paths to war and, 256–61
  Paxton massacre and, 265
  peace process in, 282–83
  Pontiac's War compared to, 267, 284
  as pretext for settlement on Indian land, 255
  racial violence in, 261–65
  regional variation in participation in, 252–54
  as releasing backcountry violence, 255
  responses to massacres during, 278–79
  Sandusky expedition and, 279
  scorched-earth tactics used in background during, 273
  Scotch-Irish experience of, 259–60, 261–68, 271, 273, 280–86
  Scotch-Irish made into Americans through, 252, 284–86, 290–91
  Seneca peoples and, 273
  Shawnee peoples and, 281–82
  as shedding negative traits associated with Scotch-Irish, 285–86
  squatting and, 257
  Sullivan's expedition and, 274
  total war and, 261
  Treaty of DeWitt's Corner and, 269–70
  Treaty of Fort Pitt and, 260
  Westmoreland County experiences during, 274–75
Rhea, Joseph, 269
Richardson, William, 131
Rigby, Joseph, 221
Robertson, James, 232, 233f, 266, 269–70, 295–96, 307, 308, 329–30, 361–62
Robertson, Sterling Clark, 381
Robertson Colony, 381
Robinson, David, 310–11, 340, 355–57
Robinson, John, 72–73
Rocky Mountain Fur Company, 373
Rogan, Hugh, 305
Rogers, Robert, 161–63
Roosevelt, Theodore, 232–35, 311
Rowan, Matthew, 76–77
Royal Proclamation of 1763, 218–19, 220–21, 225, 232–35, 237–38, 257
Runnels, Hardin Richard, 390
Rush, Benjamin, 9, 294–95
Rusk, Thomas Jefferson, 388
Russell, William, 237–38
Rutherford, Griffith, 269
Rutherford, William, 329–30

Saghughsuniunt (Thomas King) (Oneida chief), 124–25, 208–9
Said, Edward, 406
Sánchez, José Maria, 380–81
Sandusky expedition, 279
Sandy Creek expedition, 153–54
savages. *See also* Black Boys and White savages; racial violence and racialization
  captives countering faceless portrayal of, 196–97
  civilizing mission against, 27–28, 153, 243–44, 322, 330, 346, 359–60
  Indians as culturally inferior but capable of improvement, 346
  Mississippi settlements and, 359–60, 370

Paxton massacre and, 181–89
racialized beliefs about Indian incapacity of, 349
Scotch-Irish as, 18, 125, 181–89, 218, 244–45, 247–48, 249–50, 365, 366
wild Irish as, 31
Scarouady (Oneida half king), 143, 147, 154, 196
Schermerhorn, John, 348–49
Schneider, Martin, 300–2
Schoepf, Johann David, 295–96
Schoolcraft, Henry Rowe, 366–67, 390
Scotch-Irish. *See also* borderlands; buffer zones; migration to America; relations between Scotch-Irish and Indians; settlement of Scotch-Irish
American identity as, 7–8, 168, 275–77, 383, 404–14
Anglo-Saxon relation to, 376, 409–10
Appalachian identity and, 9–10
becoming American of, 2–3, 5–6, 252, 284–86, 290–91, 294–96, 322–23, 404–14
as born fighting, 1–2, 7–8, 14, 238–39
celebratory accounts of, 14, 413
character and traits attributed to, 3, 5–6, 7–8, 9–10, 13–14, 46, 49, 290–91, 293–96, 404–5, 408, 410, 411
civilizing mission and, 27–28, 153, 243–44, 322, 330, 346, 359–60
as defined by conflict, 10–11, 13
as degenerated Europeans, 26–27, 116–17, 125, 245
as diasporic people, 87, 95
dissenting Protestantism of, 33–34
diversity of, 3, 8–10
as footsoldiers of empire, 2–3, 16, 31–32
frontier myths surrounding, 7, 10–15, 17–18, 106
as hard neighbors, 1–3, 15–21, 65, 110, 123–24, 132, 321–22, 368–69, 378–79
historical development of, 1–2, 25–35
identity of, 2–3, 4–11, 20–21, 33–34, 46–47, 285, 404–14
Indian-hating associated with, 16–17, 283, 406, 410–11
as Indian-killers, 17, 110, 125–26, 166–68
Indians compared with, 17, 25–26, 87, 91, 95, 106, 109, 110, 113, 123, 155, 238–39, 298
Irish Catholics contrasted with, 349–50, 402, 405–6, 407–8, 409
as lacking fixed identity, 10–11
legacy of, 404–14
main ports of arrival and departure of, 41–42

methodological approach of current volume on, 19–20
model of frontier development and, 12–13
motivation for current volume on, 19
myth of essentialized identity of, 5–6, 409
overview of, 1–21, 404–14
as rebellious by nature, 183–84, 221, 247
retention of identity by, 2–3, 6–7, 8, 294
role in American history of, 408–9
scholarship on, 2–12, 14
self-identity as frontier people of, 7, 10–15, 17–18, 106
settler-colonialism and, 16–18
surnames of, 4
terminological note on, xv–xvi
Ulster colonization scheme and, 6, 27, 29–33, 34f, 39, 41–42
Ulster Presbyterianism and, 33–35
victimhood identity and, 10–11, 15
violence associated with, 14–21
white identity and, 7–8, 322–23, 383, 406
Scotch-Irish Chronicles, The (Kennedy), 14
Scotch-Irish Congress, 410–11
Scotch-Irish Society, 408–9
Scottish Borders, 28
Seaflower (ship), 42–43
Seagrove, James, 307–8
Searchers, The (film), 206–7
Seaver, James, 202–3
Sekttu Maquah (Black Beaver), 394–96, 397f
Seneca peoples, 89–90, 96, 105–6, 170, 203–4, 240–41, 273, 280
settlement of Scotch-Irish. *See also* borderlands; buffer zones; frontier myths; migration to America; Mississippi settlements; Pennsylvania; settler colonialism; squatting; Texas and beyond
agricultural and industrial dimensions of, 54
Bordon's tract and, 73
Boston-area settlements and, 49–59
British borderland names and, 67
buffer zones and, 51, 55, 67, 76, 79–81
Carolina-area settlements and, 76–84
claims of illegal settlement and, 52–53
"cracker" designation and, 82
Cumberland, TN, settlements, 266, 295–96, 304–5, 308, 322, 329
Cumberland Valley, PA settlements, 67
distribution of settlements and, 83f
Dummer's war and, 54–55
Dunbar's colonists and, 55–57
early colonial settlements dominated by, 54
German migration and, 78–79

settlement of Scotch-Irish (cont.)
  Great Wagon Road and, 77
  Grover captured and, 55–56
  Indian resistance to, 54–55, 57, 64–65
  "Irish Paths" and, 73–74
  Juniata Valley settlements and, 68, 69, 88–89, 101–2
  Kittochtinny Hills and, 68–69
  land grants and, 70–73
  Londonderry (NH) settlement and, 52–53, 57–59
  map of, 50f
  mass migration's role in, 49–51
  Merrimack Valley settlements and, 53–54
  overview of, 48–49
  pattern of, 75, 79
  Pennsylvania as magnet for, 59–64
  Philadelphia-area settlements and, 59–69
  population growth and, 69, 82
  reactions to, 68–69, 74–75, 80–82
  settlement rights and, 69
  Shenandoah Valley settlements and, 70–75
  social relations and, 74
  squatting and, 63–64, 65–69
  St. George's River settlements and, 57
  Susquehanna Valley settlements and, 64–65
  treaties and, 71–72
  Virginia-area settlements and, 70–84
  Watauga Valley settlements, 232–35, 256–57
  Waxhaws settlements, 75–76, 79, 325–26, 327
  Yadkin Valley settlements, 78
settler colonialism, 3, 11, 16, 17–20, 48, 85, 110, 391–92
Seven Years' War (1756-1763), 104, 131–32, 135, 140–41, 151, 161, 225, 275–77
Sevier, John, 270
Shamokin, 88–89, 95
Shawnee peoples
  Black Boys and White savages and, 228, 240–43
  borderlands and, 92–95, 105
  captives and, 196, 199–201, 203, 209–11, 214–15
  complaints about settlement by, 68–69
  Dunmore's War and, 240–43
  French and Indian War and, 144, 148–49
  as frontier people, 17, 106
  Iroquois's attempt to control, 94–95
  Kentucky and, 311–12
  Kishacoquillas (Shawnee chief) and, 68
  map of settlements of, 93f
  migration and settlement of, 92–95, 105
  Mississippi settlements and, 353–55, 357, 362–63, 370
  Ohio Valley origins of, 92–94
  Paxton massacre and, 173–74
  relation to other groups of, 94–95
  resettlement of, 353–54
  Revolutionary War and, 281–82
  rumors and, 127
  Scotch-Irish compared to, 106
  Tecumseh (Shawnee war chief), 332, 334, 352–53, 362
  Texas and beyond and, 377–78, 385–89, 396–98
Shenandoah Valley settlements, 70–75, 100–1
Sheridan, Philip, 403
Shikellamy (Oneida chief), 94–95, 97, 102, 110, 127, 128, 159–60
Shikellamy, John, 154, 155
Shingas (Delaware chief), 148, 154–55, 156–57, 167, 196–97, 199–200, 206–7
Shippen, Edward, 138, 171–72, 176
Shirley, William, 147
Shute, Samuel, 52–53
Sideling Hill attack (1765), 220–21
Slim Tom, 306
Slotkin, Richard, 11–12
smallpox, 39, 41–42, 43, 51, 91, 109, 131–32, 165, 245–46, 376–77
Smilie, John, 42–43
Smith, Daniel, 307–8
Smith, James, 213–14, 213f, 313
Smith, John, 89
Smith, Katherine, 290
Smith, Matthew, 182, 265, 274
Smith, Thomas, 289
Smith, William, 210
Smithwick, Noah, 389
Smyth, John Ferdinand, 113–14
Sovereignty and Goodness of God, The (Rowlandson), 194–95
Spangenburg, August Gottlieb, 128–29
Spratt, Thomas, 131–32
squatting
  Black Boys and White savages and, 224–25
  borderlands and, 101–4
  Cherokee peoples and, 257, 306
  Iroquois and, 148
  Mississippi settlements and, 368–69, 370
  Paxton massacre and, 174–75
  post-Revolutionary period and, 306, 320
  as pretext for purchasing more land, 104
  relations between Scotch-Irish and Indians and, 114–15, 123–24

Revolutionary War and, 257
Scotch-Irish associated with, 2–3, 63–64, 65–69, 82–84
Stamp Act (1765), 218–19, 235–36
Stanhope, James, 95–96
St. Clair, Arthur, 217, 316–17, 352–53
Steele, Ian, 196
Stewart, Lazarus, 229, 264–65
St. Francis (Odanak), 162; attack on, 162–63
Stoddard, Amos, 294, 365
Strickland, William, 295–96
Stuart, Andrew, 29–30
Stuart, Charles, 197
Stuart, Henry, 256
Stuart, John, 111, 235, 257–58, 372
Stump, Frederick, 226–27
Sullivan, John, 273–74
Susquehanna Valley settlements, 64–65, 88–90, 94–95, 104–6
Susquehannock peoples, 1, 89–90, 91–92, 174–75
Swift, Jonathan, 85, 109

Taaffe, Michael, 119
Trade and Intercourse Act (1796), 331
Taitt, David, 258
Tamaqua (Delaware chief), 206–7
Taylor, Alan, 161
Tecumseh (Shawnee war chief), 332, 334, 352–53, 362
Teedyuscung (Delaware chief), 99, 141–43, 159, 207–8, 228–29
Tenskwatawa (Shawnee Prophet), 332
Terrell, John Dabney, 343
Tewea (Delaware chief), 156–58, 197–98
Texas and beyond
  Anglo-American migration to, 376
  Apache peoples and, 376–77, 378–79, 396–99
  as backcountry, 376–77
  buffer zones and, 378–79
  Californian mass invasion and, 400
  Camp Grant Massacre and, 399–400
  Cherokee peoples and, 377–79, 385–88
  coexistence patterns swept away in, 378
  colonization policies in, 378–81
  Comanches and, 376–77, 378–79, 384–85, 386, 390
  creation myth of, 384–85
  Delaware peoples and, 377–78, 385–89, 394–98
  emigrant Indian tribes and, 377–78, 386–89
  Fredonia and, 380
  government inability to maintain peace in, 390
  identity as fluid and ambiguous in, 376, 383
  Indian-killing as part of culture and, 383, 399
  Indian removal and, 378–79, 385, 388, 391–92
  intermixing of Indian tribes in, 378
  intertribal competition in, 378–79
  invasion imagery in, 380
  Irish participation in Indian-fighting U.S. army and, 402–3
  Kickapoo peoples and, 377–78, 385–89
  land grants and, 378–81, 384–85
  male honor code and, 383
  maps of settlement in, 382f, 395f
  mass Irish immigration and, 402
  Mexican independence and, 377–79
  Navajo peoples and, 394
  number of migrants to, 377–78
  overland trails and, 400
  overview of, 376–83
  Paxton Boys and, 390
  population loss of Indians in, 376–77
  property rights denied in, 391
  racialization and, 383
  reasons for settlement in, 381, 383
  reservations and, 390–92
  Scotch-Irish role in settlement of, 376–77, 380–83, 385, 391–92, 394, 399, 401
  securing Texas from Mexico and from Indians and, 384–92
  Shawnee peoples and, 377–78, 385–89, 396–98
  Spanish Texas, 376–77
  Texas Revolution, 386
  white identity and, 383
  winning of the West and, 392–403
  Wintu people and, 394
Thomas, George, 68–69, 100
Thompson, Samuel, 251–52
Thomson, Charles, 141–42
Three Rivers, Battle of (1776), 275–77
Tocqueville, Alexis De, 46
Tone, Theobold Wolfe, 319
Topoheka or Horseshoe Bend, Battle of (1814), 336–37
Tornel, José María, 385
Torrans, John, 82
Trade and intercourse Act (1796), 331
Trail of Tears, 320–21, 348–49, 372, 388. *See also* Indian removal
Treaty of Albany (1722), 100
Treaty of Augusta (1763), 248–49
Treaty of Camp Charlotte (1775), 258–59
Treaty of Cusseta (1832), 349–50

Treaty of Dancing Rabbit Creek (1830), 347
Treaty of DeWitt's Corner (1777), 269–70
Treaty of Doak's Stand (1820), 342–43, 369
Treaty of Easton (1758), 159–60
Treaty of Fort Finney (1786), 299–300, 312
Treaty of Fort Jackson (1814), 339–40
Treaty of Fort Laramie (1851), 374
Treaty of Fort McIntosh (1785), 299–300
Treaty of Fort Pitt (1778), 260
Treaty of Fort Stanwix (1768), 229–30, 237–38, 311–12
Treaty of Ghent (1814), 340
Treaty of Hard Labor (1768), 230, 232–35
Treaty of Holston (1791), 328–29
Treaty of Hopewell (1785), 302
Treaty of Lancaster (1744), 71–72, 100–1, 144
Treaty of New Echota (1835), 348–49
Treaty of St. Mary's (1818), 354–55
Treaty of Sycamore Shoals (1775), 256–57
Trent, William, 145
Trump, Donald, 413
Turnbo, Silas Claiborne, 362–63
Turner, Frederick Jackson, 12–13, 85–86, 116–17, 294–95, 323, 411
Turner, John, 156–57
Tuscarora peoples, 88–89, 95, 108, 222–23
Tuskegetchee (Long Fellow), 303–4

Van Buren, Martin, 343, 385
vengeance cycles, 306, 308–9
violence and massacres. *See* Black Boys and White savages; borderlands; Indian-hating; Indian-killing; Indian removal; Paxton massacre (1763); relations between Scotch-Irish and Indians; savages
Virginia-area settlements, 70–84
Voyages (Chastellux), 252

Wabanaki peoples, 54, 87–88
Waldo, Samuel, 57
Walking Purchase (1737), 98–99
Walpole, Robert, 54–55
Ward, John, 242
War of 1812, 291, 326–27, 334–35, 340, 352–53, 358, 362, 363–64, 368–69, 396–98
Washington, George
  French and Indian war role of, 135–36, 153
  frontier violence and, 146, 151, 283, 320
  great-grandfather of, 89–90
  local militia mobilized to burn Indian villages by, 261
  necessity of striking Indians in their homes and, 273
  post-Revolutionary period and, 321–22
  Revolutionary War experience of, 261, 267–68
  on Scotch-Irish, 267–68, 283
  surrender of, 135–36, 153
  trip to frontier of, 116–17
  western land tour of, 289
Watauga settlers, 232–35, 256–57, 269
Watson, David, 363
Watson, Samuel, 363
Watts, John (Cherokee chief), 309–10
Waxhaws settlements, 75–76, 79
  and Andrew Jackson, 325–26, 327
Wayne, Anthony, 317
Wayne, John, 206–7
Weatherford, William (Creek chief), 334
Webb, James, 7–8, 14, 413
Weiser, Conrad, 102, 110, 138
Well, Robert, 42–43
Wentworth, Benning, 56
Wharton, Samuel, 220–21
Whiskey Rebellion (1791-1794)
  American army's role in, 316–17
  collapse of, 318
  context of, 313–14
  defenses of, 315–16
  early stages of, 316–17
  excise tax on whiskey as test of eastern elites power and, 314
  grievances fueling, 314–15
  land encroachment and, 316–17
  land speculation and, 313–14
  Scotch-Irish as playing central role in, 313–15, 317–19
  tax perceived as targeting Scotch-Irish, 315–16
  Wayne's victory and, 318
White, James, 306–7
White Eyes (Delaware chief), 240–41, 260, 275
white identity and whiteness, 7–8, 322–23, 383, 406
"white Indians," 195, 202–6, 211–12, 214–15, 229. *See also* captives
white savages. *See* Black Boys and White savages; savages
Wilkins, Sally, 180
Wilkinson, James, 377
Willard, Susanna, 111
William III, 32–33, 183–84
Williams, Elizabeth, 209
Williamson, Andrew, 269

Williamson, David, 277–78
Wilson, Thomas, 171–72
Winning of the West, The (Roosevelt), 232–35, 311, 400, 411
Winthrop, John, 51
Wipey, Joseph, 217
Witherspoon, Robert, 79–80
Wolf, Patrick, 16
women and gendered experience, 207–8
Woodmason, Charles, 244–47

Woodward, Colin, 413
Worcester v. Georgia (1832), 348–49
Wyoming, Battle of (1778), 264–65
Wyoming Valley conflict, 228–29

Yadkin Valley settlements, 78
Yeates, James, 98–99
Yellow Creek massacre, 239–41
Yellow Hawk (Shawnee chief), 353
Young, Arthur, 41